Workbook to Accompany

3-2-1 Code It!

2020

Michelle A. Green, MPS, RHIA, FAHIMA, CPC

Technical Collaborators
Marsha Diamond, CCS, CPC, COC, CPMA
Lisa Riggs, CPC, CPC-I, AAS

CENGAGE

Australia • Brazil • Mexico • Singapore • United Kingdom • United States

CENGAGE

Workbook to Accompany 3-2-1 Code It! 2020
Michelle A. Green, MPS, RHIA, FAHIMA, CPC

SVP, Higher Education & Skills Product: Erin Joyner

Product Director: Matthew Seeley

Senior Product Manager: Stephen G. Smith

Product Assistant: Dallas Wilkes

Director, Learning Design: Rebecca von Gillern

Senior Manager, Learning Design: Leigh Hefferon

Learning Designer: Kaitlin Schlicht

Marketing Director: Sean H. Chamberland

Marketing Manager: Jonathan Sheehan

Director, Content Creation: Juliet Steiner

Content Creation Manager: Stacey Lamodi

Senior Content Manager: Kara A. DiCaterino

Digital Delivery Lead: Lisa Christopher

Art Director: Angela Sheehan

Text Designer: Angela Sheehan

Cover Designer: Angela Sheehan

Cover and Interior Design Images: © iStockPhoto.com/traffic_analyzer

The 2020 versions of CPT, HCPCS Level II, ICD-10-CM, and ICD-10-PCS were used in preparation of this product.

ISBN: 978-0-357-36266-2

Cengage
200 Pier 4 Boulevard
Boston, MA 02210
USA

Cengage is a leading provider of customized learning solutions with employees residing in nearly 40 different countries and sales in more than 125 countries around the world. Find your local representative at **www.cengage.com.**

Cengage products are represented in Canada by Nelson Education, Ltd.

To learn more about Cengage platforms and services, register or access your online learning solution, or purchase materials for your course, visit **www.cengage.com.**

Printed at CLDPC, USA, 12-19

CONTENTS

PREFACE

This workbook is designed to help students apply concepts learned from the textbook. Application-based assignments directly related to content in the textbook allow students to practice assigning codes to coding statements and case studies.

This workbook can be used by college and vocational school programs to train coding and reimbursement specialists, health insurance specialists, medical assistants, medical office administrators, and health information technicians. It can also be used as an in-service training tool for new medical office personnel and independent billing services or as an independent study by coding and reimbursement specialists who want to increase their skills and scope of knowledge.

OBJECTIVES

After completing assignments in each chapter, the student will be able to:

- Contact and interview a coding specialist and explore career opportunities.
- Identify situations in which a physician query for inpatient cases is appropriate.
- Assign codes using ICD-10-CM, ICD-10-PCS, HCPCS level II, and CPT coding manuals.
- Sequence inpatient and outpatient diagnoses and procedures.
- Interpret prospective payment system data (e.g., diagnosis-related groups).

ORGANIZATION OF THE WORKBOOK

- Chapter 1 contains assignments that assist students in conducting a comprehensive, professional job search. The chapter provides students with an opportunity to become acquainted with professional networking resources such as listservs. The chapter also provides students with the opportunity to assess computer-assisted coding (CAC) results.
- Chapters 2–5 contain introductory ICD-10-CM/PCS assignments about using the ICD-10-CM Index to Diseases and Injuries, ICD-9-CM as a Legacy Coding System, applying ICD-10-CM/PCS coding conventions to coding scenarios, applying ICD-10-CM official guidelines for coding and reporting, and assigning ICD-10-CM/PCS codes to diseases and procedures.
- Chapter 6 includes numerous ICD-10-CM/PCS hospital inpatient coding assignments about using the physician query process; selecting and coding principal diagnoses, other (additional) diagnoses, principal procedures, and other significant procedures; validating the accuracy of ICD-10-CM/PCS codes; performing face validity of data management reports; and assigning codes to hospital inpatient cases, skilled nursing facility cases, and hospice inpatient cases.
- Chapter 7 includes numerous ICD-10-CM outpatient and physician office coding assignments about using the physician query process; applying diagnostic coding and reporting guidelines for outpatient services; interpreting ICD-10-CM, coding guidelines for outpatient diagnostic tests; selecting the first-listed diagnosis and linking diagnoses with procedures/services for medical necessity; and assigning codes to outpatient cases.

- Chapter 8 includes HCPCS level II national coding system assignments about using the HCPCS level II index, assigning HCPCS level II modifiers, and assigning HCPCS level II codes.
- Chapter 9 includes introductory CPT coding assignments about using the CPT index, appendices, symbols, modifiers, and sections/subsections/categories/subcategories.
- Chapter 10 includes CPT Evaluation and Management (E/M) assignments to teach students how to interpret levels of E/M services and assign E/M codes.
- Chapter 11 includes CPT Anesthesia assignments about determining anesthesia service for patients, interpreting the use of anesthesia modifiers, and assigning anesthesia codes.
- Chapters 12 through 16 include CPT Surgery assignments to teach students how to assign surgery codes to cases and operative reports.
- Chapter 17 includes CPT Radiology assignments to teach students how to assign radiology codes to cases and reports.
- Chapter 18 includes CPT Pathology and Laboratory assignments to teach students how to assign pathology and laboratory codes to cases and reports.
- Chapter 19 includes CPT Medicine assignments to teach students how to assign codes to cases and reports.
- Chapter 20 includes insurance and reimbursement assignments about the chargemaster review process, interpretation of a remittance advice, interpretation of a Medicare fee-for-service payment error report, and assignment of ambulatory payment classifications. (This chapter might be excluded from your course if your academic program includes a separate insurance and reimbursement course.)
- Appendices A through D contain patient records to allow students additional coding practice.
- Appendix E contains a mock CPC coding exam to allow students practice taking the exam.
- Appendix F contains a mock CCS-P coding exam to allow students practice taking the exam.
- Appendix G contains a mock CCS coding exam to allow students to practice taking the exam.

CHAPTER 1

Overview of Coding

INTRODUCTION

This chapter familiarizes students with the coding profession by having them interview a coding professional and network with coding professionals by joining professional discussion forums. Students also complete application-based assignments.

ASSIGNMENT 1.1 – CAREER AS A CODER: INTERVIEW OF A CODING PROFESSIONAL

Objectives

At the conclusion of this assignment, the student should be able to:

- Delineate the responsibilities of a coding professional.
- Explain why the coding professional's position is one that the student would or would not be interested in pursuing.

Overview

This assignment will familiarize the student with specific job responsibilities of a coding professional. The student will contact a coding professional at a local health care facility or physician's office and schedule an on-site interview.

Instructions

1. Prepare ten questions that you would like to ask a coding professional.

NOTE:

Your instructor might devote classroom time to brainstorming sample questions or create a discussion board forum if you are an Internet-based student. This will allow you to share questions with other students in your course and to obtain additional questions to ask of the professional.

2. Locate a credentialed coding professional (e.g., CCS or CPC) and contact the professional to schedule an on-site interview. When you contact the professional, conduct yourself in a professional manner and explain that you are a student completing a required assignment.

NOTE:

If it is not possible to schedule an on-site interview, check with your instructor to determine whether a telephone or e-mail interview would be acceptable.

3. Prepare for the interview by reviewing and organizing the questions you will ask of the professional.
4. Dress appropriately (as if for a job interview), and arrive 10 minutes early for the interview.
5. Adopt a professional and respectful manner when asking interview questions, and be prepared to answer questions asked of you. Make sure you take notes as the coding professional responds to the interview questions. If you choose to tape-record the interview, ask the professional for permission to do so.
6. After the interview, thank the professional for his or her time. Follow up the interview by mailing a handwritten thank-you note within 10 days.
7. Prepare a three-page paper summarizing the interview as follows:
   a. Identify the coding professional's name, credential, position, and facility.
   b. Writing in the third person, summarize the professional's responses to interview questions. Make sure you organize the interview content in logical paragraphs. (A paragraph consists of at least three sentences.) *Do not prepare this paper in a question/answer format*. If you have questions about how to write this paper, ask your instructor for clarification.
   c. In the last paragraph of the paper, summarize your reaction to the interview and your interest in having this professional's position (along with an explanation of why or why not). Also predict your future by writing about where you will be in 10 years (in terms of employment, family, and so on).

ASSIGNMENT 1.2 – PROFESSIONAL DISCUSSION FORUMS

Objectives

At the conclusion of this assignment, the student should be able to:

- Explain the value of joining professional discussion forums.
- Join a professional discussion forum.
- Review discussion forum contents to identify topics relevant to coding.
- Demonstrate participation in a professional discussion forum.

Overview

Networking, or sharing information among professionals, is a valuable professional activity. The Internet has made it much easier to network with other professionals by using web-based professional forums. This assignment will familiarize the student with the value of Internet professional discussion forums.

Instructions

1. Select a professional discussion forum from Table 1-1 and follow its instructions to become a member.

NOTE:

Joining professional discussion forums is often free, and they allow you to network with other professionals.

TABLE 1-1 Discussion Forums and Internet Sites for Professionals

Name of Discussion Board	Website
AHIMA Engage communities	AHIMA members can go to engage.ahima.org and log in.
Billing-Coding forum	Go to www.billing-coding.com, scroll over More Resources, and select Forums from the drop-down menu.
Medicare Part B claims	Go to www.partbnews.com, scroll over the Communities link, and select Forum from the drop-down menu.

2. Access archived forum discussions and observe current discussions for the period designated by your instructor (e.g., one to three weeks), noting topics that are relevant to your field of study.
3. Post a discussion comment or question on the forum and observe responses from subscribers.
4. At the end of the period of observation and participation, determine whether the forum would be helpful to you on the job.

ASSIGNMENT 1.3 – CODING OVERVIEW: VALIDATING ACCURACY OF ICD-10-CM AND ICD-10-PCS CODES

(Adapted and reprinted with permission from the American Health Information Management Association.)

Overview

Coders and health information technicians routinely participate in department quality management activities by validating (confirming) the accuracy of codes submitted for inpatient, outpatient, and emergency department cases. The validation process involves reviewing and correcting codes submitted to payers. When erroneous codes are noted upon review, in-service education is provided to all coders to reeducate them about proper assignment and sequencing of codes for third-party billing purposes.

Objectives

At the conclusion of this assignment, the student should be able to:

- Explain the process involved in validating coding accuracy.
- Review codes to determine their validity and edit them as necessary.

Instructions

Use the appropriate coding manual to review and determine the accuracy of the following codes assigned to inpatient hospital diagnoses and procedures. Correct any inaccurate or incomplete codes.

Validating ICD-10-CM and ICD-10-PCS Coding Accuracy

1. Gastric carcinoma, no evidence of recurrence. Closure of gastrostomy performed. Z85.028, 0DQ67ZZ
2. Secondary carcinoma of bone. Chemotherapy administered percutaneously via peripheral vein. C40.80, Z08, 3E03305
3. Atherosclerotic heart disease of native coronary artery with congestive heart failure. I25.1, I50.9
4. Urinary tract infection due to *Escherichia coli*. N39.0
5. Single uterine pregnancy with spontaneous cephalic vaginal delivery of a full-term single live-born infant. O80, 10E0XZZ

ASSIGNMENT 1.4 – COMPUTER-ASSISTED CODING (CAC)

Objectives

At the conclusion of this assignment, the student should be able to:

- Explain the concept of computer-assisted coding (CAC).
- Interpret the data display on a CAC screen.

Overview

Computer-assisted coding (CAC) uses computer software to automatically generate medical codes by "reading" transcribed clinical documentation provided by health care practitioners. CAC uses "natural language processing" theories to generate codes that are reviewed and validated by coders for reporting on third-party payer claims. Similar to the medical editor's role ensuring accuracy of reports produced from speech recognition technology, the coder's role changes from data entry to validation/audit. The coder reviews and approves the CAC-assigned codes, improving efficiency and offering expanded career opportunities for enthusiastic coders.

Instructions

Refer to Figure 1-1, and answer the following questions to learn how to interpret the data display that results from the use of CAC software. The review and decision making associated with this assignment simulate the work flow process of a coder who works for a facility that has implemented CAC software.

1. Refer to the bottom half of the CAC demo application's computer screen in Figure 1-1 to complete the following:
   a. The date of procedure is ______________________________.
   b. The preoperative diagnosis is ______________________________.
   c. The postoperative diagnosis is ______________________________.
   d. The procedures performed include ______________________________
   ____
   ____
   ______________________________.
2. Refer to the top half of the CAC demo application's computer screen in Figure 1-1, and review data located on the left side of the screen (below the *Episode 0000002* heading) as well as on the right side of the screen (below the *Admitting Diagnosis* heading) to complete the following:
   a. The CAC software identified *admission diagnosis* code ______________ and *reason for admission* code ______________.
   b. The coder *set* code ______________ as the *admitting diagnosis*, abbreviated as (*A*).
3. Refer to the top half of the CAC demo application's computer screen in Figure 1-1, and review data located on the left side of the screen (below the *Episode 0000002* heading) to complete the following:
   a. The CAC software identified *diagnosis* codes ______________ and ______________.
   b. The CAC software identified *procedure* codes ______________ and ______________.
   c. *Procedure* code ______________ was captured as possible/deleted.

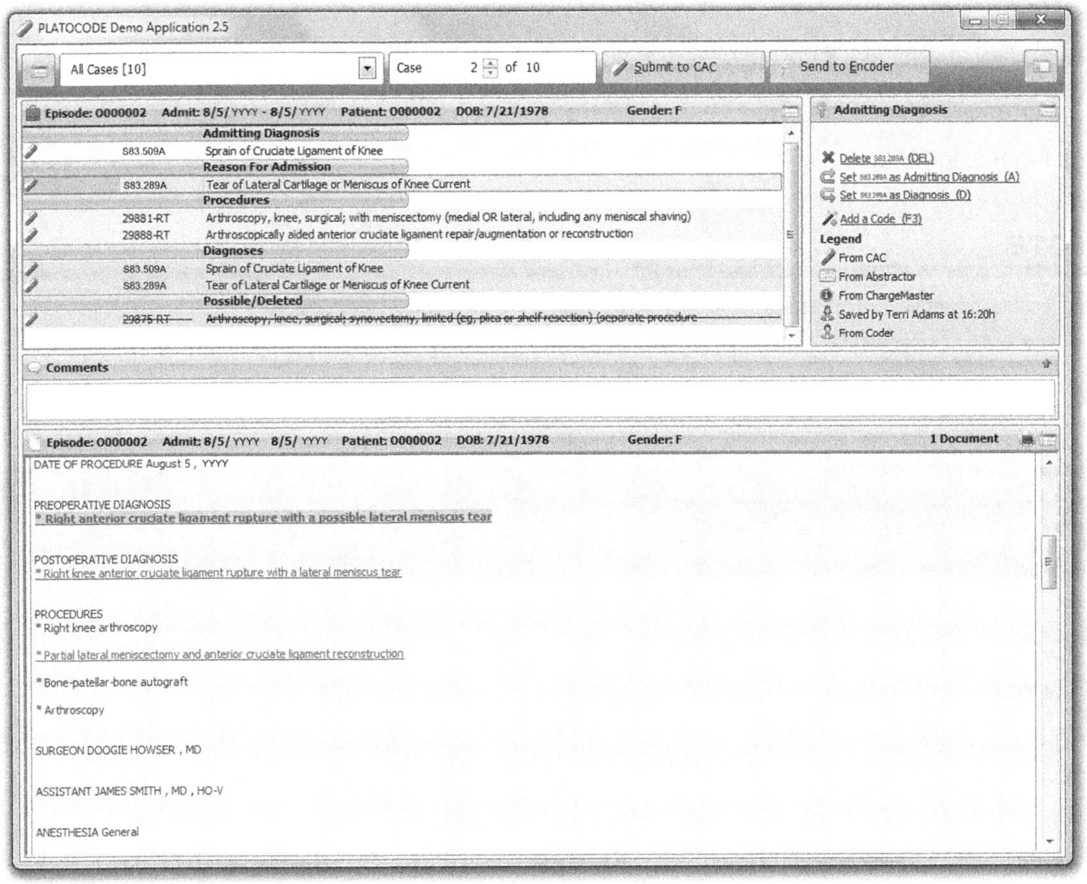

FIGURE 1-1 Sample screen from PLATOCODE computer-assisted coding (CAC) software

ASSIGNMENT 1.5 – HEALTH DATA COLLECTION: FACE VALIDITY OF DATA MANAGEMENT REPORTS

Objectives

At the conclusion of this assignment, the student should be able to:

- Interpret data contained on management reports.
- Review management reports for face validity to identify errors in data reporting.

Overview

Health care facilities (e.g., hospitals) generate data management reports to analyze data about services provided to patients. *Data management reports* contain statistical data in a table format that includes the number of patient discharges, deaths, and autopsies and the number of census days; the average length of stay; the number of consultations per specialty; third-party payer data; and patient discharge destination data. *Data analysis* is performed by health data analysts, health information managers, and executives to determine whether services should be added, expanded, and eliminated (e.g., discontinue offering services that result in consistent lost revenue). Prior to data analysis, the *face validity* of management reports is performed, which involves reviewing management reports to ensure that accurate data have been reported; errors identified during face validity are corrected.

Instructions

As the health data analyst at a local hospital, you are responsible for ensuring the accuracy of data reporting on the Analysis of Hospital Inpatient Services report. Carefully review each section of the statistical data included in Table 1-2 for face validity, and circle each data reporting error. The report contains five errors, as follows: 3 in Section A, 1 in Section B, and 1 in Section C.

NOTE:

All data located in subtotal and total rows in the Section A portion of the spreadsheet are correct.

TABLE 1-2 Analysis of Hospital Inpatient Services

Section A

Service	Discharges	Deaths	Autopsies[1]		Discharge Days	Average LOS[1]	Consults	Medicare Patients		Pediatric Patients	
			#	%				#	Days	#	Days
Medicine	725	40	8	25%	6,394	9	717	301	3,104	0	0
General Surgery	280	10	3	30%	2,374	8	184	80	916	0	0
Cardiac Surgery	64	1	1	100%	1,039	16	35	26	431	0	0
Hand Surgery	26	0	0	0%	81	3	2	3	10	0	0
Neurosurgery	94	0	0	0%	1,429	15	39	12	266	4	39
Plastic Surgery	46	0	0	0%	319	7	19	7	97	0	0
Dental Surgery	25	0	0	0%	81	3	46	2	11	1	3
Dermatology	20	0	0	0%	289	14	56	6	83	0	0
Neurology	83	0	0	0%	776	9	183	24	284	0	0
Ophthalmology	87	0	0	0%	352	4	98	51	183	0	0
Orthopedics	216	2	0	0%	1,920	9	64	39	563	1	2
Otolaryngology	139	2	0	0%	705	5	87	16	168	4	7
ICU[2]	8	1	1	50%	128	16	1	0	0	8	127
Psychiatry	126	0	0	0%	3,624	29	97	7	317	1	8
Urology	108	1	1	100%	810	8	74	36	318	0	0
Gynecology	184	2	1	50%	853	5	55	11	93	0	0
Obstetrics	451	2	2	0%	2,099	5	14	0	0	1	2
SUBTOTAL	2,682	62	17	27%	23,273	9	1,771	621	6,844	20	189
Newborn	310	0	0	0%	1,191	4	0	0	0	0	0
SCN[3]	38	4	1	25%	742	20	0	0	0	0	0
TOTAL	3,030	66	18	27%	25,206	8	1,771	621	6,844	20	189

(continues)

TABLE 1-2 Analysis of Hospital Inpatient Service (*continued*)

Section B		Section C		Section D			
Discharge Disposition	# of Patients	Results	# of Patients	Type of Death	Number of Deaths	Autopsies	
						#	%
Against medical advice	15	Discharged alive	2,964	Anesthesia	0	0	0%
Home	2,850	Not treated	0	Postoperative	8	2	25%
Home health care	10	Diagnosis only	0	Medical examiner	4	3	75%
Skilled nursing facility	37	Expired over 48 hours	54	Stillbirths	4	3	75%
Rehabilitation facility	39	Expired under 48 hours	12				
Other hospital	13						
Expired	65						
TOTAL	3,030	TOTAL	3,029	TOTAL	16	8	50%

[1]Round up mathematical calculations to the whole number (e.g., 8.82 is reported as 9).
[2]ICU is the abbreviation for intensive care unit, where patients who need constant monitoring receive care.
[3]SCN is the abbreviation for special care nursery, where premature infants, twins, triplets, and so on, receive care.

Source: American Health Information Management Association.

ASSIGNMENT 1.6 – PHYSICIAN QUERY PROCESS

Objectives

At the conclusion of this assignment, the student should be able to:

- Explain the *physician query process*.
- Complete a physician query to request clarification about documentation.

Overview

When coders have questions about documented diagnoses or procedures/services, they use a *physician query process* to contact the responsible physician to request clarification about documentation and the code(s) to be assigned. The electronic health record (EHR) allows for development of an automated physician query process, which is used by utilization managers (or case managers), clinical documentation improvement specialists, and coders to obtain clarification about patient record documentation. Integrating the automated physician query process with the EHR allows physicians to more easily receive and reply to queries, which results in better and timely responses from physicians.

Sample Physician Query

To:	Dr. Severens
From:	Sally Smith (Coder01)
Date:	January 7, YYYY
Subject:	Query about patient record number 123456

Patient Name	**Patient Record Number**
James Donolan	123456

Date of Encounter	**Location**
January 5, YYYY	Medical Center

Reason for Query

Inadequate documentation

Query or Comment

Documentation indicates patient received antibiotics. Would it be appropriate to document a diagnosis for coding purposes? If so, add an addendum to the patient record. Thank you. SS

Provider Reply

Instructions

Complete the blank physician query form in response to the following scenario.

Lisa Dubois, Coder04, at the Medical Center generates a physician query due to possible inadequate documentation in patient record number 987654 (Marian Reynolds), discharged May 5, YYYY. She notices that the patient received daily intravenous fluids for the nursing diagnosis of dehydration.

Physician Query	
To:	
From:	
Date:	May 8, YYYY
Subject:	
Patient Name	**Patient Record Number**
Date of Encounter	**Location**
	Medical Center
Reason for Query	
Query or Comment	
Provider Reply	

ASSIGNMENT 1.7 – DOCUMENTATION AS A BASIS FOR CODING: DETERMINING MEDICAL NECESSITY

Objectives

At the conclusion of this assignment, the student should be able to:

1. Define *medical necessity*.
2. Link diagnoses with procedures/services to justify medical necessity.

Overview

Documentation in the patient record serves as the basis for coding, which means information in the record must support codes submitted on claims for third-party payer reimbursement processing. The patient's diagnosis must also justify diagnostic and therapeutic procedures or services provided, which is called *medical necessity* and requires providers to document services or supplies that are:

- Proper and needed for the diagnosis or treatment of a medical condition.
- Provided for the diagnosis, direct care, and treatment of a medical condition.
- Consistent with standards of good medical practice in the local area.
- Not mainly for the convenience of the physician or health care facility.

Instructions

Match the diagnosis in column 2 with the procedure/service in column 1 to justify medical necessity.

______________	1. Allergy test	a. asthma
______________	2. EKG	b. chest pressure
______________	3. Inhalation treatment	c. cervical condyloma acuminata
______________	4. Pap smear	d. fractured ankle
______________	5. Removal of ear wax	e. hay fever
______________	6. Sigmoidoscopy	f. urinary tract infection
______________	7. Strep test	g. impacted cerumen
______________	8. Urinalysis	h. fibroid tumor, uterus
______________	9. Biopsy, uterus	i. rectal bleeding
______________	10. X-ray, tibia and fibula	j. sore throat

ASSIGNMENT 1.8 – OTHER CLASSIFICATIONS, DATABASES, AND NOMENCLATURES: SNOMED CT

Objectives

At the conclusion of this assignment, the student should be able to:

1. Explain how SNOMED CT supports computer-assisted coding.
2. Enter SNOMED CT concept identification numbers using a SNOMED CT Lookup Service.
3. Analyze SNOMED nomenclature data using the National Cancer Institute's SNOMED CT browser.

Overview

The *Systematized Nomenclature of Medicine Clinical Terms (SNOMED CT)* is the most comprehensive, multilingual clinical health care terminology in the world. SNOMED CT contributes to the improvement of patient care by underpinning the development of electronic health records (EHRs), which record (document) clinical information in ways that enable meaning-based retrieval. The result is effective access to information required for decision support and consistent reporting and analysis. Patients benefit from the use of SNOMED CT because it improves the recording (documentation) of EHR information and facilitates better communication, leading to improvements in the quality of care.

SNOMED CT is owned, maintained, and distributed by the International Health Terminology Standard Development Organisation (IHTSDO), which is a not-for-profit association owned and governed by its national members. According to the National Institutes of Health (NIH), SNOMED CT is an extensive clinical terminology that was formed by the merger, expansion, and restructuring of *SNOMED RT*® (Reference Terminology) and the United Kingdom National Health Service (NHS) *Clinical Terms* (also known as the *Read Codes*). It is the most comprehensive clinical vocabulary available in English (or any language). SNOMED CT is concept-oriented and has an advanced structure that meets most accepted criteria for well-formed, machine-readable terminology. It has been designated as a U.S. standard for electronic health information exchange in Interoperability Specifications produced by the Healthcare Information Technology Standards Panel and has also been adopted for use by the U.S. federal government, through the Consolidated Health Informatics (CHI) Initiative, for several clinical domains.

Instructions

Go to www.snomedbrowser.com to use the *Search by Name* feature. Enter Influenza in the Search Term box, leave [All types] in place as the Concept Type (so that all information about the condition displays), and click Search. When the results display, click on the Influenza (disorder) link, click on the "See more descriptions" link, and answer the following questions.

1. Which of the following is the Concept ID for Influenza?
   a. 6142004
   b. H27.. H271. H271z H27y. H27yz Hyu04 Hyu05 Hyu06 Hyu07
   c. J09X
   d. XE0YK
2. Which of the following are the ICD-10 code(s) that display for Influenza?
   a. 6142004
   b. H27.. H271. H271z H27y. H27yz Hyu04 Hyu05 Hyu06 Hyu07
   c. J09X J118 J108 J100 J110 J111 J101
   d. XE0YK

Go to www.snomedbrowser.com to use the *Search by Code* feature. Enter 22298006 in the Search Code box, and click Search. When the results display, click on the "See more descriptions" link, and answer the following questions. You will also need to click on the Myocardial necrosis (finding) link on the Concept ID 22298006 display page to answer one of the following questions.

3. Which of the following is the READ code?
   a. 22298006
   b. I211
   c. MI
   d. X200E
4. Which is listed as the Name: for SNOMED CT code 22298008?
   a. Ischemic heart disease
   b. Myocardial disease (disorder)
   c. Myocardial infarction
   d. Myocardial necrosis
5. Click on the Myocardial necrosis (finding) link. Which is its Concept ID?
   a. 251061000
   b. 414545008
   c. 57809008
   d. 609410002

REVIEW

Multiple Choice

Circle the most appropriate response.

1. Which is the relationship between nomenclatures and coding systems?
   a. A coding system defines a medical nomenclature according to similar conditions, diseases, procedures, and services.
   b. A coding system organizes a medical nomenclature according to similar conditions, diseases, procedures, and services.
   c. A medical nomenclature defines a coding system according to similar conditions, diseases, procedures, and services.
   d. A medical nomenclature organizes a coding system according to similar conditions, diseases, procedures, and services.

2. The *types* of code sets required by HIPAA for encoding are called:
   a. health-related and demographic.
   b. ICD-10-CM and CPT.
   c. large and small.
   d. local and national.
3. Continuity of care is defined as the:
   a. documentation of patient care services so that maximum reimbursement is obtained.
   b. documentation of patient care services so that other caregivers have a source of information on which to base additional care and treatment.
   c. evaluation of the patient care plan by the utilization review committee.
   d. verification that all documentation is in the correct order to implement easy retrieval.
4. "Medical necessity" requires patient record documentation to support the services and supplies provided to the patient:
   a. according to federal standards of good medical practice.
   b. for the convenience of the physician or health care facility.
   c. so they are billed according to the patient's ability to pay.
   d. to support diagnosis, care, and treatment of a medical condition.
5. A coder is responsible for coding all diagnoses, services, and procedures accurately so the facility can be properly paid. As a result, the __________ purpose of the patient record is being met.
   a. medicolegal
   b. reimbursement
   c. research
   d. statistical
6. Which of the following would be most helpful to a coder working from home?
   a. Application service provider
   b. Courier service
   c. Local area network
   d. Third-party administrator
7. Which of the following answers telephones, greets patients, updates and files patient medical records, and completes insurance claims?
   a. Coding intern
   b. Coding specialist
   c. Health insurance specialist
   d. Medical assistant
8. Which would determine the type of credential a coding professional should pursue?
   a. State regulations
   b. Number of credentialed employees at the facility
   c. Proximity of the credentialing testing center
   d. Type of health care setting in which employment is sought
9. A health insurance specialist would belong to which professional organization?
   a. AAMA
   b. AHIMA
   c. AMT
   d. MAB
10. A medical assistant would pursue a credential from:
    a. AAPC.
    b. AAMA.
    c. ACAP.
    d. AHIMA.
11. HIPAA named which as the national standard code set for physician services?
    a. CPT
    b. DSM
    c. ICD-10-PCS
    d. NDC
12. ICD-10-CM, ICD-10-PCS, CPT, HCPCS level II, CDT, and NDC are:
    a. code sets required by HIPAA for use by clearinghouses, health plans, and providers.
    b. code sets required by HIPAA for use by health care providers to document care.
    c. nomenclatures required by HIPAA for use by clearinghouses, health plans, and providers.
    d. nomenclatures required by HIPAA for use by health care providers to document care.

13. Which is completed by a physician's office to report procedures performed and/or services provided to obtain reimbursement from a third-party payer?
   a. CMS-1450
   b. UB-92
   c. CMS-1500
   d. UB-04
14. HCPCS level II is managed by the:
   a. American Medical Association (AMA).
   b. Centers for Medicare & Medicaid Services (CMS).
   c. National Archives and Records Administration (NARA).
   d. World Health Organization (WHO).
15. A student who is completing an internship at the Medical Center made arrangements with her supervisor to leave early for a scheduled appointment. As she made her way through the busy main entrance of the hospital, a coworker stopped and asked if she had finished the work she had been given. She responded, "I didn't have time to finish coding Jack Hardy's triple bypass and Alice Johnson's hernia repair. I'll do them tomorrow." The next day she was called into the office and terminated by her internship supervisor. What was the reason for her termination?
   a. Being rude to an employee
   b. Breaching patient confidentiality
   c. Leaving early without notifying her coworkers
   d. Not completing her assigned work
16. A patient is involved in a dispute regarding care he received at the Medical Center. The patient claims that a prescribed medication for a comorbid (coexisting) condition was not administered correctly during his inpatient encounter. What is the secondary purpose of the medical record in this situation?
   a. Education
   b. Medicolegal
   c. Research
   d. Statistics
17. Which is used to capture paper record images onto the storage media?
   a. Automated record
   b. Disk imaging
   c. Index
   d. Scanner
18. Coders are not allowed to perform ______________, which involve(s) assigning codes based on the belief, from a review of clinical evidence in the patient's record, that the patient has certain diagnoses or received certain procedures/services even though the provider did not specifically document those diagnoses or procedures/services.
   a. assumption coding
   b. encoding
   c. imaging
   d. physician queries
19. Which was developed by the National Center for Health Statistics (NCHS) to replace Volume 3 of ICD-9-CM and, when implemented, will be used to classify inpatient procedures and services?
   a. CPT
   b. ICD-10
   c. ICD-10-CM
   d ICD-10-PCS
20. Which is the process of standardizing data by assigning numeric values (codes or numbers) to text or other information?
   a. Downcoding
   b. Encoding
   c. Jamming
   d Upcoding

Introduction to ICD-10-CM and ICD-10-PCS Coding

CHAPTER 2

INTRODUCTION

This chapter includes application-based assignments about organization of ICD-10-CM and ICD-10-PCS and introduction of official coding guidelines.

ASSIGNMENT 2.1 – ICD-10-CM INDEX TO DISEASES AND INJURIES

Objectives

At the conclusion of this assignment, the student should be able to:

- Identify the main term in a diagnosis and locate it in the ICD-10-CM index.
- Locate main terms and codes in the ICD-10-CM index.

Overview

The ICD-10-CM index contains an alphabetical listing of main terms or conditions printed in boldface type that may be expressed as nouns, adjectives, or eponyms. The ICD-10-CM Index to Diseases and Injuries contains four sections: (1) Index to Diseases and Injuries, (2) Neoplasm Table, (3) Table of Drugs and Chemicals, and (4) Index to External Causes. Main terms in the ICD-10-CM Index to Diseases and Injuries (and the ICD-10-PCS Index to Procedures) are listed in alphabetical order, which means hyphens within main terms are ignored, but a single space within a main term is not ignored. When Arabic and Roman numerals and numerical words appear below a main term or subterm in the ICD-10-CM index, they are listed in numerical order, not in alphabetical order.

Instructions

Underline the main term in each of the following diagnostic statements, and enter the code listed in the ICD-10-CM index. (*For this assignment only*, do not verify codes in the ICD-10-CM Tabular List of Diseases and Injuries.)

1. Rheumatoid arthritis ____________________
2. Acute myocardial infarction ____________________
3. *Pseudomonas* pneumonia ____________________
4. Type 2 diabetes mellitus ____________________
5. Congestive heart failure ____________________

6. Crush injury of right index finger ________________
7. Sickle cell disease in crisis ________________
8. Comminuted fracture, traumatic, of lower end of tibia ________________
9. Congenital cleft lip, incomplete, unilateral ________________
10. Hypertensive heart disease ________________

ASSIGNMENT 2.2 – ICD-10-PCS INDEX

Objectives

At the conclusion of this assignment, the student should be able to:

- Identify the main term in a procedure and locate it in the ICD-10-PCS Index.
- Locate main terms and codes in the ICD-10-PCS Index.

Overview

The ICD-10-PCS index is an alphabetical listing of main terms or procedures printed in boldface type that may be expressed as nouns, adjectives, or eponyms. Letter-by-letter alphabetization is used, which means that single spaces and hyphens are ignored. When Arabic and Roman numerals and numerical words appear below a main term or subterm, they are listed in numerical order, not in alphabetical order. *Main terms* are printed in boldface type followed by the code number, and they may or may not be followed by a listing of parenthetical terms.

Instructions

Underline the main term in each of the following procedural statements, and enter the code listed in the ICD-10-PCS index. In the ICD-10-PCS index, usually just the first 3 or 4 characters of the 7-character code are listed. (*For this assignment only*, do not verify codes in the ICD-10-PCS tables.)

1. Incision and drainage of skin abscess, abdomen ________________
2. Low cervical Cesarean section ________________
3. Laparoscopic cholecystectomy, total ________________
4. Transurethral laser-induced total prostatectomy ________________
5. Extracorporeal shock wave lithotripsy of kidney pelvis, left ________________
6. Loop electrosurgical excision procedure, cervix ________________
7. Colostomy closure, descending colon ________________
8. Knee arthroscopy ________________
9. Extracapsular cataract (lens) extraction, right ________________
10. Abdominal total hysterectomy ________________

ASSIGNMENT 2.3 – ICD-10-PCS INDEX AND TABLES

Objectives

At the conclusion of this assignment, the student should be able to:

- Interpret ICD-10-PCS sections and axes.
- Explain ICD-10-PCS tables.

Overview

The *International Classification of Diseases, 10th Revision, Procedure Coding System (ICD-10-PCS)* is a procedure classification system developed by CMS for use in inpatient hospital settings *only*. ICD-10-PCS uses a multiaxial 7-character alphanumeric code structure (e.g., 047K04Z) that provides a unique code for all substantially different procedures. ICD-10-PCS allows new procedures to be easily incorporated as new codes, and the classification contains more than 87,000 seven-character alphanumeric procedure codes.

Instructions

Refer to Table 2-1, and complete each statement below.

1. Character 5 of *Radionuclide* is an axis that is associated with the ____________________ section.
2. The Physical Rehabilitation and Diagnostic Audiology section has a unique axis for character 2, which is entitled ____________________.
3. The character 7 axis classifies a(n) ____________________ for each section.
4. The character 5 axis of *Modality qualifier* is associated with the ____________________ section.
5. The character 3 axis for each section describes either operation or ____________________.

TABLE 2-1 Value Assigned to Each Character in a 7-Character ICD-10-PCS Code

Character 1	Character 2	Character 3	Character 4	Character 5	Character 6	Character 7
Medical and Surgical Section	Body system	Operation	Body part	Approach	Device	Qualifier
Obstetrics Section	Body system	Operation	Body part	Approach	Device	Qualifier
Placement Section	Body system	Operation	Body region	Approach	Device	Qualifier
Administration Section	Body system	Operation	Body system/ region	Approach	Substance	Qualifier
Measurement and Monitoring Section	Body system	Operation	Body system	Approach	Function/Device	Qualifier
Extracorporeal or Systemic Assistance and Performance Section	Body system	Operation	Body system	Duration	Function	Qualifier
Extracorporeal or Systemic Therapies Section	Body system	Operation	Body system	Duration	Qualifier	Qualifier
Osteopathic Section	Body system	Operation	Body region	Approach	Method	Qualifier
Other Procedures Section	Body system	Operation	Body region	Approach	Method	Qualifier
Chiropractic Section	Body system	Operation	Body region	Approach	Method	Qualifier
Imaging Section	Body system	Type	Body part	Contrast	Qualifier	Qualifier
Nuclear Medicine Section	Body system	Type	Body part	Radionuclide	Qualifier	Qualifier
Radiation Therapy Section	Body system	Modality	Treatment site	Modality qualifier	Isotope	Qualifier
Physical Rehabilitation and Diagnostic Audiology Section	Section qualifier	Type	Body system/ region	Type qualifier	Equipment	Qualifier
Mental Health Section	Body system	Type	Qualifier	Qualifier	Qualifier	Qualifier
Substance Abuse Treatment Section	Body system	Type	Qualifier	Qualifier	Qualifier	Qualifier
New Technology	Body system	Operation	Body part	Approach	Device/Substance/ Technology	Qualifier

Refer to Table 2-2, and complete each statement below.

6. The 5-character code associated with ICD-10-PCS index entry "spinal canal bypass" is ____________________.
7. The index entry for "bypass, cavity" has no associated ICD-10-PCS characters because ____________________.
8. The 7-character code for "open bypass of cerebral ventricle to atrium using synthetic substitute" is ____________________.
9. The 7-character code for "open bypass of spinal cord to urinary tract using autologous tissue substitute" is ____________________.
10. ICD-10-PCS code 0W110J is reported for a "bypass of the cranial cavity." (TRUE or FALSE. If false, why not?)

TABLE 2-2 **Portion of an ICD-10-PCS Index and Table**

ICD-10-PCS Index

Bypass
Canal, Spinal 001U0
Cavity
Cranial 0W110J
Pelvic 0W1J

ICD-10-PCS Table

0 Medical and Surgical
0 Central Nervous System
1 Bypass: Altering the route of passage of the contents of a tubular body part

Body Part	Approach	Device	Qualifier
6 Cerebral Ventricle	**0** Open	**7** Autologous Tissue Substitute **J** Synthetic Substitute **K** Nonautologous Tissue Substitute	**0** Nasopharynx **1** Mastoid Sinus **2** Atrium **3** Blood Vessel **4** Pleural Cavity **5** Intestine **6** Peritoneal Cavity **7** Urinary Tract **8** Bone Marrow **B** Cerebral Cisterns
6 Cerebral Ventricle	**0** Open **3** Percutaneous **4** Percutaneous Endoscopic	**Z** No Device	**B** Cerebral Cisterns
U Spinal Canal	**0** Open	**7** Autologous Tissue Substitute **J** Synthetic Substitute **K** Nonautologous Tissue Substitute	**4** Pleural Cavity **6** Peritoneal Cavity **7** Urinary Tract **9** Fallopian Tube

ASSIGNMENT 2.4 – GENERAL EQUIVALENCE MAPPINGS (GEMs)

Objectives

At the conclusion of this assignment, the student should be able to:

- Explain the purpose of general equivalence mappings (GEMs).
- Locate ICD-10-CM and ICD-10-PCS codes for their ICD-9-CM equivalents using the GEMs.

Overview

When the ICD-10-CM and ICD-10-PCS coding systems were implemented in 2015, the *International Classification of Diseases, Ninth Revision, Clinical Modification* (ICD-9-CM) became a *legacy coding system* (or *legacy classification system*), which means it will be used to archive data but will no longer be supported or updated by the ICD-9-CM Coordination and Maintenance Committee. For this reason, NCHS and CMS annually publish *general equivalence mappings (GEMs)*, which are translation dictionaries or crosswalks of codes that can be used to roughly identify ICD-10-CM and ICD-10-PCS codes for their ICD-9-CM equivalent codes (and vice versa). GEMs facilitate the location of corresponding diagnosis and procedure codes between two code sets.

Instructions

Refer to Table 2-3, and complete the following in the box below:

1. Review the ICD-9-CM codes in column 1, and enter each code *without a decimal* in column 2.
2. Locate the ICD-9-CM diagnosis code (without decimals), and enter each GEM ICD-10-CM diagnosis code (without decimals) in column 3, and then enter the equivalent ICD-10-CM code *with* decimals in column 4.
3. Locate the ICD-9-CM procedure code (without decimals). Enter the equivalent GEM ICD-10-PCS procedure code(s) in column 5. (ICD-10-PCS codes do not contain decimals.)

	Column 1 ICD-9-CM Code	Column 2 GEM ICD-9-CM Code	Column 3 GEM ICD-10-CM Diagnosis Code	Column 4 ICD-10-CM Diagnosis Code	Column 5 GEM ICD-10-PCS Procedure Code(s)
1.	003.24				n/a
2.	001.0				n/a
3.	002.1				n/a
4.	00.01		n/a	n/a	
5.	00.03		n/a	n/a	

TABLE 2-3 Portion of the GEM for (A) ICD-9-CM to ICD-10-CM Diagnoses and (B) ICD-9-CM to ICD-10-PCS Procedures

(A) General Equivalence Mapping for Diagnoses		(B) General Equivalence Mapping for Procedures	
ICD-9-CM Diagnosis Code	ICD-10-CM Diagnosis Code	ICD-9-CM Procedure Code	ICD-10-PCS Procedure Code
0010	A000	0001	6A750Z4
0019	A009	0001	6A751Z5
0021	A011	0002	6A750Z5
0023	A013	0002	6A751Z5
0030	A020	0003	6A750Z6
00321	A0221	0003	6A751Z6
00322	A0222	0009	6A750Z7
00324	A0224	0009	6A750ZZ

ASSIGNMENT 2.5 – ICD-10-CM OFFICIAL GUIDELINES FOR CODING AND REPORTING

Objectives

At the conclusion of this assignment, the student should be able to:

- List and explain general ICD-10-CM diagnosis coding guidelines.
- Assign codes by interpreting general ICD-10-CM diagnosis coding guidelines.
- Interpret abbreviations and lab values to appropriately assign ICD-10-CM codes.

Overview

The general ICD-10-CM diagnosis coding guidelines accompany and complement the official conventions and instructions provided within ICD-10-CM. HIPAA requires that official coding guidelines be used when assigning ICD-10-CM diagnosis codes. The ICD-10-CM diagnosis codes have been adopted under HIPAA for all health care settings. (ICD-10-PCS procedure codes are reported for inpatient hospital procedures.)

Instructions

Assign ICD-10-CM codes to the following diagnostic statements. Refer to the general ICD-10-CM diagnosis coding guidelines in your textbook when assigning codes (e.g., assigning codes to qualified diagnoses and coding signs/symptoms when a definitive diagnosis is documented).

________________ 1. Hearing loss, fever, swollen axillary lymph nodes, and infective otitis externa, left ear

________________ 2. Focal epilepsy

________________ 3. Type 2 diabetes mellitus without complication

________________ 4. Personal history of thyroid cancer

________________ 5. Shortness of breath

________________ 6. Foot pain (especially in the morning), plantar fasciitis

________________ 7. Peripheral neuropathy due to type 2 diabetes mellitus

________________ 8. Prostatitis

________________ 9. Acute and chronic salpingo-oophoritis

________________ 10. Chlamydial pneumonia

________________ 11. Hydronephrosis due to prostatic hyperplasia

________________ 12. Dysphasia due to previous cerebrovascular accident

________________ 13. Osteoarthritis of left hand due to previous crush injury

________________ 14. Impending myocardial infarction

________________ 15. Meningitis due to African trypanosomiasis

________________ 16. Right lower quadrant abdominal pain

________________ 17. Late effect of blood vessel injury, head

________________ 18. Streptococcal tonsillitis

________________ 19. Cystic fibrosis with pseudomonas infection

________________ 20. Acute glomerulonephritis due to systemic lupus erythematosus

REVIEW

Multiple Choice

Circle the most appropriate response.

ICD-10-CM Coding

1. Review the following ICD-10-CM index entry, and identify the main term.
   a. Spina
   b. Stenosis
   c. Stricture
   d. Sylvius

ICD-10-CM INDEX TO DISEASES AND INJURIES

```
Stricture (see also Stenosis)
   aqueduct of Sylvius (congenital) Q03.0
      with spina bifida – see Spina bifida, by site, with hydrocephalus
```

2. ICD-10-CM Index to Diseases and Injuries main terms are listed in alphabetical order, and hyphens within main terms are ignored; however, a single space within a main term is *not* ignored. Thus, main term:
   a. *Beer drinkers' heart (disease)* appears above main term *Bee sting*.
   b. *Carr-Barr-Plunkett syndrome* appears above main term *Carrier (suspected) of*.
   c. *Carrier (suspected) of* appears above main term *Carr-Barr-Plunkett syndrome*.
   d. *Débove's disease* appears above main term *Debility*.
3. *External Causes of Injury, Poisoning, or Other Adverse Reactions Affecting a Patient's Health* codes are:
   a. excluded from ICD-10-CM in their entirety.
   b. incorporated into ICD-10-CM as Chapter 19 (S00-T88).
   c. located in a supplementary classification of ICD-10-CM.
   d. processed as ICD-10-PCS codes for hospital cases.
4. The Centers for Medicare & Medicaid Services (CMS) abbreviates the classification systems of the *International Classification of Diseases, 10th Edition, Clinical Modification* and the *International Classification of Diseases, 10th Edition, Procedure Coding System* as ________________.
   a. ICD-10
   b. ICD-10-CM
   c. ICD-10-CM/PCS
   d. ICD-10-PCS
5. ICD-10-CM code T37.0x1A has an "x" as a placeholder in the fifth-character location, which means code T37.01A (without the "x" placeholder in the fifth-character location) creates a(n) ______________ code.
   a. authentic
   b. invalid
   c. optional
   d. supplemental
6. For the assignment of ICD-10-CM codes to complications of care, ______________.
   a. complications must have immediately followed a surgical procedure
   b. linking the condition to a procedure or service provided is unnecessary
   c. documentation must indicate that the condition is a complication
   d. generate a physician query in every case to confirm the complication
7. ICD-10-PCS is an entirely new procedure classification system developed by CMS for use in ______________ settings.
   a. ambulatory surgery center
   b. inpatient hospital
   c. outpatient office
   d. physician office

8. ICD-10-PCS uses a multiaxial ________________ alphanumeric code structure that provides a unique code for all substantially different procedures.
   a. 4-character
   b. 5-character
   c. 6-character
   d. 7-character
9. The multiaxial approach used by ICD-10-PCS means that:
   a. a build-a-code process is used in combination with verifying codes in a tabular list of codes.
   b. each individual axis retaining its meaning across broad ranges of codes to the extent possible.
   c. individual characters have different values, and each position has different meanings in different sections.
   d. digits 0–9 and all letters of the alphabet are used in each of the seven characters.
10. Review the Medical and Surgical Section table that follows, and assign the code for an *open procedure of the spinal canal to insert a subarachnoid-peritoneal shunt using an autologous tissue substitute*.
   a. 0016076
   b. 00160J6
   c. 001U076
   d. 001U0J6

0 Medical and Surgical
0 Central Nervous System
1 Bypass: Altering the route of passage of the contents of a tubular body part

Body Part	Approach	Device	Qualifier
6 Cerebral Ventricle	0 Open	7 Autologous Tissue Substitute J Synthetic Substitute K Nonautologous Tissue Substitute	0 Nasopharynx 1 Mastoid Sinus 2 Atrium 3 Blood Vessel 4 Pleural Cavity 5 Intestine 6 Peritoneal Cavity 7 Urinary Tract 8 Bone Marrow B Cerebral Cisterns
6 Cerebral Ventricle	0 Open 3 Percutaneous 4 Percutaneous Endoscopic	Z No Device	B Cerebral Cisterns
U Spinal Canal	0 Open	7 Autologous Tissue Substitute J Synthetic Substitute K Nonautologous Tissue Substitute	4 Pleural Cavity 6 Peritoneal Cavity 7 Urinary Tract 9 Fallopian Tube

ICD-10-CM and ICD-10-PCS Coding Conventions

CHAPTER 3

INTRODUCTION

This chapter includes application-based assignments about ICD-10-CM and ICD-10-PCS coding conventions, which are general rules used in classification, and they are independent of the coding guidelines. The conventions incorporated into ICD-10-CM and ICD-10-PCS include the following:

- Format and typeface
- Eponyms
- Abbreviations
- Punctuation
- Boxed notes
- Tables
- Includes and excludes notes and inclusion terms
- Other, other specified, and unspecified codes
- Etiology and manifestation rules
- And
- Due to
- In
- With
- Cross-references, including *see, see also, see* category, and *see* condition

ASSIGNMENT 3.1 – APPLYING ICD-10-CM AND ICD-10-PCS CODING CONVENTIONS

Objectives

At the conclusion of this assignment, the student should be able to:

- Interpret ICD-10-CM and ICD-10-PCS coding conventions.
- Assign ICD-10-CM and ICD-10-PCS codes to conditions and procedures after applying coding conventions.

Overview

ICD-10-CM and ICD-10-PCS *coding conventions* are general rules that are incorporated into the index and tabular list instructional notes. The conventions include format, abbreviations, punctuation and symbols, includes and excludes notes, inclusion terms, other and unspecified codes, etiology and manifestation rules, and, with, *see*, and *see also*.

Instructions

Use the appropriate ICD-10-CM and ICD-10-PCS index and tabular list to assign codes to each condition or procedure stated below. Make sure you review the applicable coding convention in the textbook chapter before assigning codes.

Format

NOTE:

Assign ICD-10-CM codes to 1–10 and ICD-10-PCS codes to 11–15.

_______________ 1. Kaposi's sarcoma of right lung

_______________ 2. Acute blood loss anemia

_______________ 3. Acute narrow angle glaucoma, left eye

_______________ 4. Subarachnoid hematoma of a newborn

_______________ 5. Acute cortical kidney necrosis

_______________ 6. Adult vertebral osteochondrosis, cervical region of spine

_______________ 7. Acute rheumatic fever with pancarditis

_______________ 8. Hysterical throat spasms

_______________ 9. Subjective tinnitus, right ear

_______________ 10. Meningitis due to Lyme disease

_______________ 11. Endoscopic excision of anal papilla (via natural opening) (HINT: In the ICD-10-PCS index, go to main term *Excision.*)

_______________ 12. Endoscopic fulguration of urethra (via natural opening) (HINT: In the ICD-10-PCS index, go to main term *Destruction*.)

_______________ 13. Incision of small intestine abscess (via percutaneous endoscopy) (HINT: In the ICD-10-PCS index, go to main term *Drainage*.)

_______________ 14. Dilation and irrigation of lacrimal punctum, left eye (HINT: In ICD-10-PCS, *lacrimal punctum* is called a *lacrimal duct*.)

_______________ 15. Open repair of lacerated extraocular muscle, left

Eponyms

NOTE:

Assign ICD-10-CM codes to 16–25.

_______________ 16. Niemann-Pick disease

_______________ 17. Erb palsy

_______________ 18. Horton's neuralgia

_______________ 19. Abramov-Fiedler myocarditis

_______________ 20. California disease

_______________ 21. Engman's disease

_______________ 22. Queensland seven-day fever

_______________ 23. Abderhalden-Kaufmann-Lignac syndrome

_______________ 24. Rust's disease

_______________ 25. Adams-Stokes disease

NEC and NOS Abbreviations

NOTE:

Assign ICD-10-CM codes to 26–35.

_______________ 26. Streptococcal pneumonia
_______________ 27. Lumbar radiculitis
_______________ 28. Serum sickness due to administration of whole blood (initial encounter)
_______________ 29. Chronic gonococcal infection
_______________ 30. Enteritis due to gram-negative bacteria
_______________ 31. Edema of right upper eyelid
_______________ 32. Pituitary insufficiency
_______________ 33. Mood disorder
_______________ 34. Hemorrhoids
_______________ 35. Chronic pulmonary edema

Punctuation

NOTE:

Assign ICD-10-CM codes to 36–45.

_______________ 36. Arterial hypotension
_______________ 37. Staphylococcal osteomyelitis
_______________ 38. Exophthalmic ophthalmoplegia
_______________ 39. Blackfan-Diamond syndrome
_______________ 40. Retinitis due to type 2 diabetes mellitus
_______________ 41. Type 2 diabetes mellitus due to Kimmelstiel-Wilson disease
_______________ 42. *Listeria monocytogenes*
_______________ 43. Acquired pancytopenia
_______________ 44. Insular pneumonia
_______________ 45. Obstructive rhinitis

Tables

NOTE:

Use the ICD-10-CM Neoplasm Table to assign codes to 46–50.

_______________ 46. Primary malignant neoplasm of lower lobe of right lung
_______________ 47. Carcinoma *in situ* of thyroid
_______________ 48. Metastatic (secondary) neoplasm of stomach

_______________ 49. Benign neoplasm of false vocal cords

_______________ 50. Neoplasm of optic nerve, uncertain behavior

NOTE:

Use the ICD-10-CM Table of Drugs and Chemicals to assign codes to 51–55.

_______________ 51. Chlorine bleach (accidental poisoning) (initial encounter)

_______________ 52. Adverse effect of therapeutic use of Tylenol (acetaminophen) (initial encounter)

_______________ 53. Librium, suicide attempt (initial encounter)

_______________ 54. Thyroxine, accidental overdose (initial encounter)

_______________ 55. Rash due to therapeutic use of penicillin (initial encounter)

Includes and Excludes Notes and Inclusion Terms

NOTE:

Assign ICD-10-CM codes to 56–65.

_______________ 56. Genetic amyloidosis

_______________ 57. Endophlebitis of right iliac vein

_______________ 58. Intracranial abscess due to tuberculosis

_______________ 59. Subacromial bursitis, left shoulder

_______________ 60. Gonococcal conjunctivitis

_______________ 61. Cystic lung, acquired

_______________ 62. Valgus foot deformity, acquired, right ankle

_______________ 63. Coma, hepatic

_______________ 64. Hereditary retinal dystrophy

_______________ 65. Spinocerebellar disease

Other, Other Specified, and Unspecified

NOTE:

Assign ICD-10-CM codes to 66–75.

_______________ 66. Polyalgia

_______________ 67. Bile duct adhesions

_______________ 68. Hypertrophic tongue

_______________ 69. Venofibrosis

_______________ 70. Gout

_______________ 71. Amebiasis

_______________ 72. Intellectual disability (mental retardation)

_______________ 73. Nontoxic thyroid goiter

_______________ 74. Ringworm

_______________ 75. Endocrine disorder

Etiology and Manifestation Rules

NOTE:

Assign ICD-10-CM codes to 76–90.

_______________ 76. Acute chest syndrome due to sickle cell disease in crisis

_______________ 77. Methicillin-susceptible *Staphylococcus aureus* infection of gastrostomy

_______________ 78. Chronic glomerulonephritis due to systemic lupus erythematosus (SLE)

_______________ 79. Acute pyelonephritis due to pneumococcus

_______________ 80. Subacute bacterial endocarditis (SBE) due to *Streptococcus*

_______________ 81. Cardiomyopathy due to Friedreich's ataxia

_______________ 82. Cystitis due to amebiasis

_______________ 83. Cryptococcal meningitis

_______________ 84. Seminal vesiculitis due to Group B *Streptococcus*

_______________ 85. Malignant reticulosis

_______________ 86. Pott's curvature of spine

_______________ 87. Reiter's disease, left shoulder

_______________ 88. Dermatitis due to penicillin (therapeutic use) (initial encounter)

_______________ 89. *Mycoplasma* empyema

_______________ 90. Arteriosclerotic (cerebral) dementia

And

NOTE:

Assign ICD-10-CM codes to 91–105.

_______________ 91. Hypertrophic tonsils

_______________ 92. Abscess of mediastinum

_______________ 93. Acute periodontitis

_______________ 94. Anorectal fistula

_______________ 95. Calculus of ureter

_______________ 96. Vulvovaginitis

_______________ 97. Postmenopausal bleeding

_______________ 98. Bilateral complete cleft palate with cleft lip

_______________ 99. Plethora of newborn

_______________ 100. Furuncle of trunk

_______________ 101. Abscess of right hand

_______________ 102. Chronic nasopharyngitis
_______________ 103. Ventricular flutter
_______________ 104. Cyst of conjunctiva, right eye
_______________ 105. C3 incomplete quadriparesis

Due to

NOTE:

Assign ICD-10-CM codes to 106–120.

_______________ 106. Corneal edema, right eye, due to wearing contact lenses
_______________ 107. Loss of teeth due to trauma
_______________ 108. Urticaria due to cold
_______________ 109. Torticollis due to birth injury
_______________ 110. Lymphadenitis due to diphtheria
_______________ 111. Pneumonia due to anaerobes
_______________ 112. Vitiligo due to pinta
_______________ 113. Duodenum obstruction due to torsion
_______________ 114. Urethra stricture due to trauma (male)
_______________ 115. Ethmoidal sinusitis due to fungus
_______________ 116. Pneumonia due to pulmonary actinomycosis
_______________ 117. Newborn jaundice due to maternal incompatibility
_______________ 118. Iridocyclitis due to allergy, right eye
_______________ 119. Cirrhosis due to hemochromatosis
_______________ 120. Uveitis due to toxoplasmosis

With

NOTE:

Assign ICD-10-CM codes to 121–135.

_______________ 121. Otitis with effusion, left ear
_______________ 122. Nephropathy with medullary necrosis
_______________ 123. Cirrhosis due to alcoholism
_______________ 124. Fever with chills
_______________ 125. Hypercapnia with mixed acid-base disorder
_______________ 126. Myocarditis with rheumatic fever
_______________ 127. Scleritis with corneal involvement, right eye
_______________ 128. Thrombocytopenia with absent radius (TAR) syndrome
_______________ 129. Ulcer of right lower extremity with muscle necrosis and gangrene
_______________ 130. Anemia with pentose phosphate pathway disorder

__________ 131. Closed displaced fracture of right clavicle shaft (initial encounter)

__________ 132. Bronchiolitis with bronchospasm

__________ 133. Histoplasmosis with pneumonia

__________ 134. Neurosyphilis with ataxia

__________ 135. Influenza with laryngitis

Cross-References: *See*, *See Also*, *See* Category, *See* Condition

NOTE:

Assign ICD-10-CM codes to 136–145 and ICD-10-PCS codes to 146–150.

__________ 136. Retinitis, left eye

__________ 137. Chronic valvulitis

__________ 138. Duplication of teeth

__________ 139. Acute osteitis of jaw

__________ 140. Injury of right thumb, crushing (initial encounter)

__________ 141. Fistula of multiple sites of right inner ear

__________ 142. Dissecting abdominal aneurysm

__________ 143. Corrosive burn of right hand (initial encounter)

__________ 144. Gastric atrophia

__________ 145. Type C cephalitis

__________ 146. Fascioplasty of scalp, percutaneous

__________ 147. Electromyogram (external)

__________ 148. Doppler flow imaging of urinary bladder

__________ 149. Yellow fever immunization, intramuscular

__________ 150. Transection of right ankle bursa and ligament, open

Code Assignment and Clinical Criteria

NOTE:

Assign ICD-10-CM codes to 151–155.

__________ 151. Patient admitted for severe pain, left hand. Physician discharge diagnosis is fracture, left hand.

__________ 152. Patient admitted for upper respiratory infection. Physician discharge diagnosis is acute sinusitis.

__________ 153. Patient admitted for enlarged cervical lymph nodes. Physician discharge diagnosis is Hodgkin lymphoma.

__________ 154. Patient admitted for chest pain. Physician discharge diagnosis is myocardial infarction.

__________ 155. Patient admitted for painful urination. Physician discharge diagnosis is urinary tract infection.

REVIEW

Multiple Choice

Circle the most appropriate response.

ICD-10-CM Disease Coding

1. Which code is reported for "secondary malignant neoplasm of the descending colon"?
   a. C18.0
   b. C18.6
   c. C78.4
   d. C78.5
2. The patient's final diagnosis is "malignant hydatidiform mole." The coder locates the main term *hydatidiform* in the ICD-10-CM index. This term directs the coder to ICD-10-CM code D39.2 in the tabular list. The next step is to assign code:
   a. D39.2 only.
   b. D39.2 and a code from category O01.
   c. O01.9 only.
   d. O01.9 and a code from category O08.
3. NEC and NOS are __________ used in ICD-10-CM.
   a. abbreviations
   b. eponyms
   c. essentials modifiers
   d. qualifiers
4. Fragilitas ossium, Osteogenesis imperfecta, and Osteopsathyrosis are all assigned to ICD-10-CM code __________.
   a. Q78
   b. Q78.0
   c. Q78.2
   d. Q78.9
5. Which code is assigned to menstrual migraine?
   a. G43.821
   b. G43.829
   c. G43.831
   d. G43.839

ICD-10-PCS Procedure Coding

6. It is not possible to construct an ICD-10-PCS procedure code from the alphabetic index. The purpose of the alphabetic index is to locate the appropriate __________ that contains all information necessary to construct a procedure code.
   a. axis
   b. character
   c. table
   d. tabular list
7. Each page of the ICD-10-PCS tables contains rows that specify the valid combinations of code __________.
   a. axes
   b. characters
   c. procedures
   d. values
8. An ICD-10-PCS code is derived by choosing a specific value for each of the __________ characters.
   a. 5
   b. 6
   c. 7
   d. 8
9. Each character of an ICD-10-PCS code is an axis of classification that specifies information about the procedure performed. Within a defined code range, a __________ specifies the same type of information in that axis of classification.
   a. character
   b. code
   c. procedure
   d. value
10. The purpose of the alphabetic index is to locate the appropriate table that contains all information necessary to construct a procedure __________.
    a. axis
    b. character
    c. code
    d. value

Chapter-Specific Coding Guidelines: ICD-10-CM Chapters 1–10

CHAPTER 4

INTRODUCTION

The *chapter-specific coding guidelines for ICD-10-CM chapters 1 through 10* are used as a companion document to the official version of the ICD-10-CM to accompany and complement official conventions and instructions provided within ICD-10-CM. They are based on coding and sequencing instructions in ICD-10-CM and provide additional instruction. This chapter includes application-based assignments that allow students to interpret the ICD-10-CM chapter-specific guidelines and coding conventions to assign codes to diagnosis statements.

NOTE:

ICD-10-PCS procedure coding assignments are located near the end of Chapter 6 in this workbook.

ASSIGNMENT 4.1 – ICD-10-CM DISEASE CODING

Objectives

At the conclusion of this assignment, the student should be able to:

- Interpret ICD-10-CM coding conventions and chapter-specific coding guidelines for ICD-10-CM chapters 1–10 to assign ICD-10-CM codes to diagnosis statements.
- Interpret abbreviations and lab values to assign ICD-10-CM codes appropriately.

Overview

To assign ICD-10-CM codes accurately to diagnoses, both the official guidelines and the conventions located in the classification must be followed.

Instructions

Assign ICD-10-CM code(s) to each diagnosis statement below.

Infectious and Parasitic Diseases

____________________ 1. Genital chancre
____________________ 2. Acute poliomyelitis, type II
____________________ 3. Gastroenteritis due to ECHO virus
____________________ 4. Food poisoning due to botulism
____________________ 5. Hansen's disease
____________________ 6. Scarlet fever
____________________ 7. Shingles
____________________ 8. Hepatitis E
____________________ 9. Mumps encephalitis
____________________ 10. Viral pharyngoconjunctivitis

Neoplasms

NOTE:

Make sure you use the Table of Neoplasms in the ICD-10-CM index to locate benign and malignant neoplasm codes.

____________________ 11. Benign neoplasm of cornea of right eye
____________________ 12. Benign neoplasm of colon
____________________ 13. Benign neoplasm of true vocal cords
____________________ 14. Benign neoplasm of left adrenal gland
____________________ 15. Hemangioma of peritoneum
____________________ 16. Malignant neoplasm of lower lip, inner aspect (or internal)
____________________ 17. Acute leukemia
____________________ 18. Letterer-Siwe disease
____________________ 19. Malignant neoplasm of brain, parietal lobe
____________________ 20. Malignant neoplasm of left ovary

Diseases of the Blood and Blood-Forming Organs

____________________ 21. Sideroblastic anemia
____________________ 22. Eosinophilia
____________________ 23. Nonautoimmune hemolytic anemia
____________________ 24. Mixed thalassemia
____________________ 25. Imerslund's syndrome
____________________ 26. HbSS disease with crisis of acute chest syndrome
____________________ 27. Pancytopenia, congenital
____________________ 28. Plasma thromboplastin antecedent (PTA) deficiency
____________________ 29. Fibrinolytic hemorrhage, acquired
____________________ 30. Big spleen syndrome

Endocrine, Nutritional, Metabolic, Immunity

_______________ 31. Atrophy of thyroid
_______________ 32. Lorain-Levi dwarfism
_______________ 33. Ascorbic acid deficiency
_______________ 34. DiGeorge's syndrome
_______________ 35. Phenylketonuria
_______________ 36. Premature menopause
_______________ 37. Postsurgical testicular hypofunction
_______________ 38. Postsurgical hypoinsulinemia
_______________ 39. Thymus abscess
_______________ 40. Conn's syndrome

Mental Disorders

_______________ 41. Acute alcoholic hallucinosis
_______________ 42. Senile dementia paranoid type
_______________ 43. Borderline schizophrenia
_______________ 44. Agoraphobia with panic disorder
_______________ 45. Heroin dependence
_______________ 46. Dissocial personality disorder
_______________ 47. Night terrors
_______________ 48. Tourette's disorder
_______________ 49. Acute nervous gastritis
_______________ 50. Pick's disease of the brain

Diseases of the Nervous System and Sense Organs

_______________ 51. Meningitis due to *Pseudomonas*
_______________ 52. Tension headache
_______________ 53. Hematomyelia
_______________ 54. Eales' disease, right eye
_______________ 55. Cluster headache
_______________ 56. Bullous retinoschisis, right eye
_______________ 57. Refsum's disease
_______________ 58. Tarsal tunnel syndrome, left side
_______________ 59. Congenital deafness
_______________ 60. Acute radial nerve palsy, left side

Diseases of the Circulatory System

_______________ 61. Tricuspid valve insufficiency
_______________ 62. External thrombosed hemorrhoids

__________ 63. Raynaud's syndrome with gangrene

__________ 64. Vena cava syndrome

__________ 65. Atrial fibrillation and flutter

__________ 66. Rupture of papillary muscle

__________ 67. Arteriosclerotic cardiovascular disease (ASCVD)

__________ 68. Right heart failure

__________ 69. Past myocardial infarction diagnosed by electrocardiogram, no current symptoms

__________ 70. Benign hypertension

Diseases of the Respiratory System

__________ 71. Hypertrophic adenoids and tonsils

__________ 72. Legionnaires' disease

__________ 73. Supraglottic edema

__________ 74. Acute exacerbation of bronchiectasis

__________ 75. Mediastinum abscess

__________ 76. Acute and chronic respiratory failure

__________ 77. Loffler's syndrome (also called Loffler's pneumonia)

__________ 78. Smokers' cough

__________ 79. Cyst of pharynx

__________ 80. Allergic rhinitis due to cat hair

REVIEW

Multiple Choice

Circle the most appropriate response.

1. Human immunodeficiency virus (HIV).
   a. B20
   b. O98.7S
   c. R75
   d. Z21
2. Streptococcal infection.
   a. A40.9
   b. A49.1
   c. B94.9
   d. B95.5
3. Malignant neoplasm, base of tongue.
   a. C01
   b. C02.0
   c. C02.1
   d. C02.9
4. Type 1 diabetes mellitus with diabetic cataract, right eye.
   a. E10.36
   b. E10.36, H26.491
   c. E11.36
   d. H26.491
5. Cocaine abuse with cocaine-induced anxiety disorder.
   a. F14.10
   b. F14.14
   c. F14.180
   d. F14.19

6. Mollaret meningitis
   a. G03.0
   b. G03.1
   c. G03.2
   d. G03.8
7. Chronic allergic otitis media, right ear.
   a. H65.191
   b. H65.21
   c. H65.31
   d. H65.411
8. Malignant hypertension.
   a. H35.039
   b. I10
   c. O10.92
   d. Z86.79
9. Ventilator-associated pneumonia.
   a. J95.851
   b. J95.851, J95.859
   c. P27.8
   d. P27.8, J18.9
10. Iron deficiency anemia secondary to blood loss (chronic)
   a. D50.0
   b. D62
   c. P61.3
   d. Z86.2

Chapter-Specific Coding Guidelines: ICD-10-CM Chapters 11–21

CHAPTER 5

INTRODUCTION

The *chapter-specific coding guidelines for ICD-10-CM chapters 11 through 21* are a companion document to the official version of the ICD-10-CM. They accompany and complement official conventions and instructions provided within ICD-10-CM. They are based on the coding and sequencing instructions in ICD-10-CM and provide additional instruction. This chapter includes application-based assignments that allow students to interpret the chapter-specific guidelines and coding conventions for ICD-10-CM chapters 11–21 to assign codes to diagnosis statements.

ASSIGNMENT 5.1 – ICD-10-CM DISEASE CODING

Objectives

At the conclusion of this assignment, the student should be able to:

- Interpret ICD-10-CM chapter-specific coding guidelines for ICD-10-CM chapters 11–21 to assign ICD-10-CM codes to diagnosis statements.
- Interpret abbreviations and lab values to assign ICD-10-CM codes appropriately.

Overview

To assign ICD-10-CM codes accurately to diagnoses, both the official guidelines and the conventions located in the classification must be followed.

Instructions

Assign ICD-10-CM code(s) to each diagnosis statement below.

Diseases of the Digestive System

_______________ 1. Chronic periodontitis

_______________ 2. Arthralgia of temporomandibular jaw, left side

_______________ 3. Corkscrew esophagus

_______________ 4. Furrowed tongue

_______________ 5. Infection of gastrostomy due to *Escherichia coli*

_______________ 6. Recurrent femoral hernia, with gangrene, unilateral
_______________ 7. Phlebitis of portal vein
_______________ 8. Tropical steatorrhea
_______________ 9. Gallstone ileus
_______________ 10. Exostosis of jaw

Diseases of the Genitourinary System

_______________ 11. Orthostatic proteinuria
_______________ 12. Benign prostatic hypertrophy
_______________ 13. Galactocele
_______________ 14. Prolapse of urethra
_______________ 15. Floating kidney
_______________ 16. Intrinsic urethral sphincter deficiency
_______________ 17. Renal osteodystrophy
_______________ 18. Nephrotic syndrome with lesion of focal glomerulonephritis
_______________ 19. Carbuncle of kidney
_______________ 20. Hunner's ulcer

Complications of Pregnancy, Childbirth, and the Puerperium

_______________ 21. Postpartum hemorrhage, third stage, due to placenta accreta in the third trimester
_______________ 22. Acute renal failure immediately following labor and delivery
_______________ 23. Vesicular mole
_______________ 24. Mural pregnancy
_______________ 25. Legally induced complete abortion complicated by shock
_______________ 26. Miscarriage, incomplete
_______________ 27. Postpartum fever
_______________ 28. Postpartum dehiscence of cesarean wound
_______________ 29. Delivery of twin boys, both alive (third trimester)
_______________ 30. Premature labor, second trimester, with preterm delivery of healthy female

Diseases of the Skin and Subcutaneous Tissue

_______________ 31. Cradle cap
_______________ 32. Decubitus ulcer, stage III, left heel
_______________ 33. Xerosis cutis
_______________ 34. Angioma serpiginosum
_______________ 35. Hypertrophic scar of the chest
_______________ 36. Koilonychia
_______________ 37. Heat rash
_______________ 38. Duhring disease

__________ 39. Third-degree sunburn

__________ 40. Rosacea

Diseases of the Musculoskeletal System and Connective Tissue

__________ 41. Panniculitis

__________ 42. Acquired wrist drop, right wrist

__________ 43. Lordosis, lumbar region

__________ 44. Sicca syndrome

__________ 45. Crystal arthropathy of the right hip

__________ 46. Caplan's syndrome

__________ 47. Ganglion of tendon sheath, right shoulder

__________ 48. Golfers' elbow, left

__________ 49. Tendinitis

__________ 50. Acute osteomyelitis of left tibia

Congenital Anomalies

__________ 51. Nuclear cataract, congenital

__________ 52. Incomplete atrioventricular block, congenital

__________ 53. Microtia

__________ 54. Choanal atresia

__________ 55. Bilateral incomplete cleft lip

__________ 56. Flat foot, right, congenital

__________ 57. Congenital absence of right foot

__________ 58. Six toes on left foot

__________ 59. Edward's syndrome

__________ 60. Strawberry nevus

Certain Conditions Originating in the Perinatal Period

__________ 61. Fetal alcohol syndrome

__________ 62. Perinatal alveolar hemorrhage

__________ 63. Fracture of right clavicle of newborn at delivery

__________ 64. Hematemesis and melena due to swallowed maternal blood

__________ 65. Neonatal tachycardia

__________ 66. Birth weight of 650 grams, 25 weeks

__________ 67. Neonatal jaundice due to Gilbert syndrome

__________ 68. Neonatal hyperthyroidism

__________ 69. Vomiting, baby is 2 days old

__________ 70. Drug withdrawal syndrome, newborn, mother addicted to cocaine

Symptoms, Signs, and Ill-Defined Conditions

_______________ 71. Shadow of lung found on chest x-ray

_______________ 72. Elevated lactic acid dehydrogenase (LDH)

_______________ 73. Ascites

_______________ 74. Elevated blood pressure reading

_______________ 75. Abnormal kidney function test

_______________ 76. Sudden infant death syndrome (SIDS)

_______________ 77. Senility

_______________ 78. Periumbilical abdominal pain

_______________ 79. Elevated prostate specific antigen (PSA)

_______________ 80. Elevated sedimentation rate

Injury and Poisoning

_______________ 81. Injury to auditory nerve, left ear (initial encounter)

_______________ 82. Flail chest, bilaterally (initial encounter)

_______________ 83. Fracture of C2 (second cervical vertebra) with central cord syndrome at the C2 level (initial encounter)

_______________ 84. Fracture of coracoid process of right scapula, closed (initial encounter)

Coding Tip

According to ICD-10-CM, a fracture that is not specified as displaced or nondisplaced should be coded as displaced. In addition, a fracture that is not specified as open or closed should be coded as closed.

_______________ 85. Dislocation of left wrist, carpal bone (initial encounter)

_______________ 86. Poisoning by barbiturates (initial encounter)

_______________ 87. Bimalleolar fracture of right ankle, closed (initial encounter)

_______________ 88. Open fracture of lesser toes, distal and medial phalanges of right foot (initial encounter)

_______________ 89. Bucket handle tear of medial meniscus, right knee (initial encounter)

_______________ 90. Closed skull fracture, three hours of unconsciousness (initial encounter)

Factors Influencing Health Status and Contact with Health Services

_______________ 91. Personal history of leukemia

_______________ 92. Family history of Huntington's chorea

_______________ 93. History of heart valve replacement

_______________ 94. Encounter for reprogramming of cardiac defibrillator

_______________ 95. Long-term use of NSAIDs

_______________ 96. Encounter for speech therapy due to childhood-onset stuttering

_______________ 97. Nutrition counseling, patient recently diagnosed with type 2 diabetes mellitus

_______________ 98. Sleep deprivation

_______________ 99. Blood alcohol test

_______________ 100. Screening examination for cystic fibrosis

External Causes of Injury

NOTE:

Refer to the ICD-10-CM Index to External Causes to locate just the V through Y codes for statements in this assignment.

_______________ 101. Fire aboard a cruise ship, injured person is a passenger (initial encounter)

_______________ 102. Accidental perforation during heart catheterization (misadventure)

_______________ 103. Newborn abandoned in park (confirmed) (initial encounter)

_______________ 104. Assault by human biting (initial encounter)

_______________ 105. Injury due to (unarmed) fight (initial encounter)

_______________ 106. Stung by bee while gardening (accidental) (initial encounter) (Refer to the ICD-10-CM Table of Drugs and Chemicals)

_______________ 107. Injury caused by dust storm (initial encounter)

_______________ 108. Mismatched blood in transfusion (misadventure)

_______________ 109. Accidental poisoning with diazepam while on an airplane (initial encounter) (Refer to the ICD-10-CM Table of Drugs and Chemicals)

_______________ 110. Fall from chair (initial encounter)

REVIEW

Multiple Choice

Circle the most appropriate response.

1. Encephalocele.
   a. Q01.0
   b. Q01.2
   c. Q01.8
   d. Q01.9
2. Nondisplaced fracture, second cervical vertebra.
   a. S12.100A
   b. S12.101A
   c. S12.9xxA
   d. T14.8xxA
3. Accident involving driver of car. Select the external cause code for the accident.
   a. V40.5xxA
   b. V43.52xA
   c. V46.5xxA
   d. V48.9xxA
4. Accident occurred on an interstate highway. Select the place of occurrence external cause code.
   a. Y92.411
   b. Y92.488
   c. Y92.89
   d. Y92.9
5. Facial contusions, nose and bilateral cheeks.
   a. S00.03xA, S00.31xA
   b. S00.33xA, S00.83xA
   c. S00.90xA, T18.9
   d. S05.1xA, S00.03xA

6. Congenital short leg syndrome, right.
   a. D82.2
   b. M21.721
   c. Q68.8
   d. Q72.811
7. Shortness of breath.
   a. R06.00
   b. R06.01
   c. R06.02
   d. R06.09
8. Which ICD-10-CM code is reported for "now-healed multiple perforations of the tympanic membrane?"
   a. H72.811
   b. Z83.52
   c. Z86.69
   d. Z87.720
9. Acute ruptured appendix.
   a. K35.2
   b. K35.32
   c. K35.80
   d. K35.89
10. Congenital transposition of appendix.
   a. Q40.9
   b. Q43.8
   c. Q45.9
   d. Q89.9
11. Eczema.
   a. L30.2
   b. L30.3
   c. L30.8
   d. L30.9
12. Severe back pain.
   a. M54.00
   b. M54.5
   c. M54.9
   d. R52
13. Gynecomastia.
   a. N62
   b. N64.59
   c. N64.89
   d. N64.9
14. Spontaneous delivery of full-term pregnancy (single liveborn).
   a. O80, Z37.0
   b. O82, Z37.0
   c. Z34.00, Z37.0
   d. Z34.90, Z38.00
15. Transient tachnypnea of newborn.
   a. P22.1
   b. P22.8
   c. P28.5
   d. P28.81

ICD-10-CM and ICD-10-PCS Hospital Inpatient Coding

CHAPTER 6

INTRODUCTION

This chapter includes application-based assignments that allow students to apply ICD-10-CM and ICD-10-PCS general and inpatient coding guidelines to the assignment of codes for inpatient case scenarios. Coding scenarios incorporate abbreviations and lab values, which students are expected to interpret. Students are also presented with situations that allow for practice of the physician query process and the assignment of DRGs.

ASSIGNMENT 6.1 – PHYSICIAN QUERY PROCESS

Objectives

At the conclusion of this assignment, the student should be able to:

- Explain the concept of *physician query* regarding the ICD-10-CM and ICD-10-PCS hospital inpatient coding of diagnoses and procedures statements.
- Identify situations in which *physician query* for inpatient cases is appropriate.

NOTE:

Chapter 1 of your textbook contains information about the physician query process.

Overview

Coders are prohibited from performing *assumption coding*, which is the assignment of codes based on assuming, from a review of clinical evidence in the patient's record, that the patient has certain diagnoses or has received certain procedures/services even though the provider did not specifically document those diagnoses or procedures/services. Assumption coding is considered fraud because the coder assumes certain facts about a patient's condition or procedures/services, although the physician has not specifically documented the level of detail to which the coder assigns codes. Coders can avoid fraudulent *assumption coding* by implementing the *physician query process*, which involves contacting the responsible physician to request clarification. The process is activated when the coder notices a problem with documentation quality (e.g., incomplete diagnostic statement when clinical documentation indicates that a more specific ICD-10-CM code should be assigned).

NOTE:

Remember! You *are* allowed to assign an ICD-10-CM code to a diagnosis, a sign, a symptom, or an ill-defined condition if the physician does not list it as final diagnosis *as long as the physician's documentation is clear and consistent and the condition was medically managed during the stay.* If the coder is uncertain about whether to code a diagnosis because documentation is contradictory, incomplete, or vague, the coder should query the physician to determine if the diagnosis should be a part of the final diagnosis.

Instructions

Read each case scenario carefully, and select the statement below the case that best represents the action the coder should take when reporting inpatient diagnosis and procedure codes. As you review each case, make sure you look up any unfamiliar abbreviations and lab values. Be prepared to defend your selected statement.

1. A 65-year-old man presents with pain in his midabdominal region. The patient has a history of hypertension and benign colon polyps. It is noted that the patient's blood pressure upon admission is 205/100. The patient is admitted as an inpatient for further workup and treatment. Diagnostic testing includes abdominal ultrasound, barium enema, and lab work. Abdominal ultrasound is positive for enlarged pancreas and enlarged gallbladder. Barium enema is negative. Lab work reveals elevated serum amylase. The patient is asked about his use of alcohol, and he denies use. The patient receives intravenous antihypertensive and antibiotic medications. Discharge diagnosis is acute pancreatitis and cholecystitis. The patient is discharged in satisfactory condition to be evaluated on an outpatient basis for cholelithiasis. Upon review of this case, the coder should:
   a. assign an ICD-10-CM code for acute pancreatitis and cholecystitis only.
   b. assign ICD-10-CM codes for acute pancreatitis and hypertension.
   c. assign an ICD-10-CM code for acute pancreatitis, cholecystitis, and hypertension.
   d. query the physician to ask whether hypertension and cholelithiasis should be documented as final diagnoses.
2. Mr. James Forrest is a male patient seen in the emergency department (ED) with a chief complaint of severe fatigue. The patient has a past medical history of gastroesophageal reflux disease (GERD) and renal insufficiency. After a short time in the ED, the patient complains of shortness of breath and chest pain. The patient is admitted for further workup and treatment. Diagnostic testing includes laboratory testing and an EKG, and the patient is determined to have congestive heart failure (CHF). On the second day of admission, a chest x-ray reveals an abnormality noted by the radiologist as pleural effusion. The patient is administered intravenous (IV) antibiotics and IV diuretics to treat the CHF and pleural effusion. Discharge diagnosis is CHF. The coder should:
   a. report the ICD-10-CM code for CHF only.
   b. query the physician to ask whether the shortness of breath and chest pain should be listed as final diagnoses.
   c. query the physician to ask whether GERD instead of CHF should be listed as the final diagnosis.
   d. query the physician to ask whether the patient has pneumonia, based on the radiology report and the antibiotic treatment.
3. A female patient is admitted to the emergency department from a nursing facility. The patient has senile dementia and is unable to provide any verbal medical history. Based on a copy of the patient's record that accompanied her, she has a history of breast cancer, hypertension, diabetes mellitus, and chronic renal insufficiency. The patient had a right mastectomy five years prior. The patient is seen due to abnormal lab work, specifically high blood glucose levels. She is admitted for further workup and treatment. After testing, the patient is found to need insulin to control her diabetes. The patient's creatinine level is elevated at 2.6. (Normal range is 1–2.) Discharge diagnoses include senile dementia, diabetes mellitus, and chronic renal

insufficiency. The patient is transferred to the nursing facility with orders for the administration of insulin to control her diabetes mellitus. The coder should:
a. assign a code for type 2 diabetes mellitus.
b. assign a code for type 1 diabetes mellitus.
c. query the physician to ask whether breast cancer should be listed as a final diagnosis.
d. query the physician to ask whether type 1 or type 2 diabetes mellitus should be coded.

4. A 75-year-old male patient was seen with a complaint of itching, especially at night. The patient has a past medical history of crushing injury to the left hand due to an industrial accident. The patient also underwent cholecystectomy five years ago. Upon examination, the patient was noted to have a rash on all four extremities. Laboratory work revealed elevated blood urea nitrogen (BUN) and creatinine levels. The patient was admitted for further workup and treatment. The patient received intravenous medication and after two days was discharged in improved condition. Discharge diagnosis was pruritus. The coder should:
   a. assign a code to pruritus only.
   b. assign codes to pruritus and the crushing injury.
   c. query the physician to ask whether the patient has a renal disorder, based on the clinical findings of elevated BUN and creatinine levels.
   d. query the physician to ask whether the patient has current gallbladder disease.

5. A 25-year-old female patient was admitted with complaints of pelvic tenderness and vaginal bleeding. The patient was admitted for further workup and treatment. Her human chorionic gonadotropin (HCG) level was elevated. An abdominal ultrasound report stated that the patient has an "interstitial ectopic pregnancy." The patient underwent surgical removal of the ectopic pregnancy and was discharged on the third day. Discharge diagnosis was ectopic pregnancy. The coder should:
   a. assign a code to the symptom of pelvic tenderness.
   b. assign an unspecified code to the ectopic pregnancy.
   c. query the physician to request documentation of the type of ectopic pregnancy (e.g., interstitial).
   d. query the physician to ask if a code for vaginal bleeding should be reported.

Instructions

Read each case scenario carefully and respond to the question located below the case. Make sure you include statement(s) justifying your answer.

6. A 40-year-old male was admitted with a diagnosis of severe back and knee pain. Laboratory workup and urinalysis determined that the patient has kidney stones. He was administered intravenous (IV) pain medication. The orthopedic service was consulted for the patient's knee pain. X-rays of his knee showed joint effusion. The patient's knee pain was reduced due to the IV pain medication administered for his back pain. He was referred to the orthopedic physician for follow-up of his knee joint effusion, possible magnetic resonance imaging (MRI), and possible knee arthroscopy. Final diagnosis is nephrolithiasis. Upon review of this case, the coder should ______________________________
   because ______________________________.

7. A 35-year-old female presents with the complaint of neck swelling and feeling very tired, duration one month. The patient is being treated as an outpatient in the HIV clinic, and she was diagnosed and treated for *Pneumocystis jiroveci* pneumonia in the past. The patient denies fever, weight loss, or night sweats during the duration of the neck swelling and fatigue. Upon physical examination, swelling of lymph nodes of the neck is noted. The patient is admitted for further workup and treatment. Diagnostic testing is scheduled, and a lymph node excisional biopsy is performed. Biopsy results are negative for malignancy or other findings. Diagnostic workup reveals elevated white blood cell count. Final diagnosis is human immunodeficiency virus (HIV) and HIV-related lymphadenopathy. Upon review of this case, the coder should ______________________________
   because ______________________________.

8. The patient is a 41-year-old female who presents with complaints of headache and blurred vision. The patient undergoes MRI of the brain. MRI report reveals a pituitary lesion, possible tumor. Various options are presented to the patient, and she elects to undergo hormonal or drug therapy before surgical treatment. The discharge diagnosis is not completed by the physician. Upon review of this case, the coder should ____________________
because ____________________.

9. A 90-year-old man is admitted with complaints of difficulty urinating and painful urination. An indwelling catheter is inserted to assist the patient with urination. A urinalysis is obtained from urine from his Foley catheter. After examination and testing, it is determined that the patient has benign prostatic hypertrophy. Surgical treatment with transurethral resection of the prostate is recommended. The patient decides to wait until family members can come to town before having the surgery. The patient is discharged with a prescription for oral antibiotics. The discharge diagnosis is benign prostatic hypertrophy. Upon review of this case, the coder should ____________________
because ____________________.

10. An 80-year-old female is admitted due to severe back pain. The patient has a history of cataracts, osteoarthritis, and mitral valve prolapse (MVP). The pain is so severe that the patient cannot walk and has difficulty sleeping. The patient is admitted to undergo x-rays and intravenous medication. X-rays reveal microscopic fractures at T1 and L5. A bone density test done during admission will be followed on an outpatient basis when results are available. Discharge diagnosis is reported as compression fractures of the spine. Upon review of this case, the coder should ____________________
because ____________________.

ASSIGNMENT 6.2 – ICD-10-PCS PROCEDURE CODING

(Adapted from the ICD-10-PCS *Reference Manual*. Courtesy of the Centers for Medicare & Medicaid Services, www.cms.gov)

The first section of ICD-10-PCS tables is entitled the *Medical and Surgical Section*, and it contains the majority of procedures typically reported in an inpatient setting. *All procedure codes in the Medical and Surgical Section of ICD-10-PCS begin with a section value of 0.* Subsequent sections of the ICD-10-PCS tables are related to the *Medical and Surgical Section*, and they are individually named.

Section: Medical and Surgical

The *Medical and Surgical Section* includes operations, which are subdivided into groups that share similar attributes. The groups and their operations are listed below.

- *Takes out some or all of a body part*: destruction, detachment, excision, extraction, resection
- *Takes out solids, fluids, and gases from a body part*: drainage, extirpation, fragmentation
- *Involves cutting or separation only*: division, release
- *Puts in, puts back, or moves some or all of a body part*: reattachment, reposition, transfer, transplantation
- *Alters the diameter/route of a tubular body part*: bypass, dilation, occlusion, restriction
- *Always involves a device*: change, insertion, removal, replacement, revision, supplement
- *Involves examination only*: inspection, map

Section Value (First Character)	Section Title
0	Medical and Surgical
1	Obstetrics
2	Placement
3	Administration
4	Measurement and Monitoring
5	Extracorporeal or Systemic Assistance and Performance
6	Extracorporeal or Systemic Therapies
7	Osteopathic
8	Other Procedures
9	Chiropractic
B	Imaging
C	Nuclear Medicine
D	Radiation Therapy
F	Physical Rehabilitation and Diagnostic Audiology
G	Mental Health
H	Substance Abuse
X	New Technology

- *Includes other repairs*: control, repair
- *Includes other objectives*: alteration, creation, fusion

Procedures That Take Out Some or All of a Body Part

Operation	Objective of Procedure	Site of Procedure	Example
Destruction	Eradicating without replacement	Some/all of a body part	Fulguration of endometrium
Detachment	Cutting out/off without replacement	Extremity only, any level	Amputation above elbow
Excision	Cutting out/off without replacement	Some of a body part	Breast lumpectomy
Extraction	Pulling out/off without replacement	Some/all of a body part	Suction dilation and curettage
Resection	Cutting out/off without replacement	All of a body part	Total mastectomy

Operation: Destruction

____________________ 1. Cryotherapy of wart, left hand

____________________ 2. Percutaneous radiofrequency ablation, right vocal cord lesion

____________________ 3. Left heart catheterization with laser destruction of arrhythmogenic focus, AV node

_______________ 4. Cautery of nosebleed

_______________ 5. Transurethral endoscopic laser ablation of prostate

_______________ 6. Cautery of oozing varicose vein, left calf

Coding Tip

The location of an oozing varicose vein has likely eroded, which means the approach is classified as percutaneous. (Percutaneous is the normal route to a vein.) If an open or percutaneous endoscopic approach was performed, it would be documented as such in the operative report.

_______________ 7. Laparoscopy with destruction of endometriosis, bilateral ovaries

_______________ 8. Laser coagulation of right retinal vessel hemorrhage, percutaneous

Coding Tip

Retinal vessels are associated with the *Eye* body system.

_______________ 9. Percutaneous injection of sterile talc powder for pleurodesis of left pleura

Coding Tip

Injecting sterile talc powder into the pleural cavity causes adherence of visceral and parietal pleurae to prevent accumulation of air or excess fluid in the space between the pleural and visceral membranes. Pleurodesis with talc powder is meant to correct the problem of too much space, which can cause lung collapse. The pleural space is not destroyed. There will always be a space between the thoracic and pleural membranes in which a small amount of fluid allows the two membranes to slide smoothly against each other as the lungs expand and contract. Assign one code for this pleurodesis procedure.

- Pleurodesis (chemical): Introduction (injection) of a therapeutic agent; in this case, the left pleural cavity

_______________ 10. Sclerotherapy of brachial plexus lesion via alcohol injection

Coding Tip

The *brachial plexus* is a network of nerves that exit the cervical (neck) and upper thoracic (chest) regions of the spinal column to provide control to the arms and hands. *Brachial* refers to the arm, and *plexus* means network.

Sclerotherapy is performed to destroy a lesion when local excision is not a suitable option. Assign two codes for a sclerotherapy procedure.

- Sclerotherapy (mechanical): Destruction of blood vessel malformations, lesions, varicose veins, and so on; in this case, the brachial plexus
- Introduction (injection): Destructive agent into a body part; in this case, the nerve plexus

Operation: Detachment

_______________ 11. Amputation at right elbow level

_______________ 12. Below-knee amputation of proximal tibia and fibula, right

Coding Tip

In the procedure statement, proximal refers to that portion of the tibia and fibula located closest to the knee, which means the qualifier value for *high* is selected from the ICD-10-PCS table.

_______________ 13. Fifth ray carpometacarpal joint amputation, left hand

Coding Tip

- A *complete* amputation is performed through the *carpometacarpal joint* of the hand, or through the *tarsal-metatarsal joint* of the foot.
- A *partial* amputation is performed anywhere along the *shaft or head of a metacarpal bone* of the hand, or the *shaft or head of a metatarsal bone* of the foot.

_______________ 14. Right leg and hip amputation through ischium

Coding Tip

An amputation along any part of the hip bone (ischium) is performed on the *hindquarter* body part.

_______________ 15. Distal interphalangeal (DIP) joint amputation, right thumb

Coding Tip

For an amputation through the DIP joint, select the qualifier value for *low* from the ICD-10-PCS table.

_______________ 16. Right wrist joint amputation

Coding Tip

An amputation at the wrist joint is a *complete* amputation of the hand, which means qualifier values for *hand* and *complete* are selected from the ICD-10-PCS table.

_______________ 17. Transmetatarsal amputation of foot at left big toe

Coding Tip

An amputation through the shaft of a metatarsal bone (transmetatarsal) in the foot (or shaft of a metacarpal bone in the hand) is classified as *partial* amputation.

_______________ 18. Mid-shaft amputation, right humerus

_______________ 19. Left fourth toe amputation, mid-proximal phalanx

Coding Tip

Mid-proximal phalanx is considered proximal, which means the qualifier value for *high* is selected from the ICD-10-PCS table. The ICD-10-PCS qualifier *high* refers to *anywhere along the proximal phalanx.*

_______________ 20. Right above-knee amputation, distal femur

Operation: Excision

_______________ 21. Excision of malignant melanoma from skin of right ear

_______________ 22. Laparoscopy with excision of endometrial implant from left ovary

_______________ 23. Percutaneous needle core biopsy of right kidney

_______________ 24. Esophagogastroduodenoscopy with gastric biopsy

_______________ 25. Open endarterectomy of left common carotid artery

_______________ 26. Excision of basal cell carcinoma of lower lip

_______________ 27. Open excision of tail of pancreas

_______________ 28. Percutaneous biopsy of right gastrocnemius muscle

_______________ 29. Sigmoidoscopy with sigmoid polypectomy

_______________ 30. Open excision of lesion from right Achilles tendon

Operation: Extraction

_______________ 31. Total mouth extraction, upper and lower teeth, using forceps

_______________ 32. Removal of left thumbnail

Coding Tip

There is no separate *body part* value for thumbnail; therefore, assign the fingernail value.

_______________ 33. Extraction of right intraocular lens without replacement, percutaneous

_______________ 34. Laparoscopy with needle aspiration of ova for *in vitro* fertilization

_______________ 35. Nonexcisional debridement of skin ulcer, right foot

Operation: Resection

_______________ 36. Open resection of cecum

_______________ 37. Total excision of pituitary gland, open

_______________ 38. Explantation of left failed kidney, open

_______________ 39. Open left axillary total lymphadenectomy

Coding Tip

Resection is the operation, *not Excision*, when an *entire chain of lymph nodes* is cut out from a region of the body. If *less than an entire chain of lymph nodes* is cut out, *Excision* is the operation.

_______________ 40. Laparoscopic-assisted total vaginal hysterectomy

_______________ 41. Right total mastectomy, open

_______________ 42. Open resection of papillary muscle

Coding Tip

Papillary muscles are associated with atrioventricular valves; they contract during systole to tighten *chordae tendinae* to prevent regurgitation of blood into the atria. Thus, papillary muscles are located in the *heart and great vessels* body system.

_______________ 43. Radical retropubic prostatectomy, open

_______________ 44. Laparoscopic cholecystectomy

_______________ 45. Endoscopic bilateral total maxillary sinusectomy

Procedures That Take Out Solids, Fluids, and Gases from a Body Part

Operation	Objective of Procedure	Site of Procedure	Example
Drainage	Taking/letting out fluids/gases	Within a body part	Incision and drainage
Extirpation	Taking/cutting out solid matter	Within a body part	Thrombectomy
Fragmentation	Breaking solid matter into pieces	Within a body part	Lithotripsy

Operation: Drainage

_______________ 46. Routine Foley catheter placement

_______________ 47. Incision and drainage of external perianal abscess

_______________ 48. Percutaneous drainage of ascites

Coding Tip

Drainage of the peritoneal cavity is performed during percutaneous drainage of ascites.

_______________ 49. Laparoscopy with left ovarian cystotomy and drainage

_______________ 50. Laparotomy with hepatotomy and drain placement for liver abscess, right lobe

_______________ 51. Right knee arthrotomy with drain placement

_______________ 52. Thoracentesis of left pleural effusion

Coding Tip

Drainage of the pleural cavity is performed during thoracentesis of left pleural effusion.

_____________________ 53. Phlebotomy of left median cubital vein for polycythemia vera

Coding Tip

The median cubital vein is a branch of the cephalic vein.

_____________________ 54. Percutaneous chest tube placement to treat right pneumothorax

_____________________ 55. Endoscopic drainage, left ethmoid sinus

Operation: Extirpation

_____________________ 56. Removal of foreign body, right cornea

_____________________ 57. Percutaneous mechanical thrombectomy, left brachial artery

_____________________ 58. Esophagogastroscopy with removal of bezoar from stomach

_____________________ 59. Foreign body removal, skin of left thumb

Coding Tip

There is no specific ICD-10-PCS value for skin of the thumb; thus, the value for the hand is selected.

_____________________ 60. Transurethral cystoscopy with removal of bladder stone

_____________________ 61. Forceps removal of foreign body in right nostril

Coding Tip

Nostril is assigned a value for the *Nose* body part.

_____________________ 62. Laparoscopy with excision of old suture from mesentery

_____________________ 63. Incision and removal of right lacrimal duct stone

_____________________ 64. Nonincisional removal of intraluminal foreign body from vagina

Coding Tip

Do *not* select *External* as the approach. *External* procedures are performed directly on the skin or mucous membrane or indirectly by the application of external force through the skin or mucous membrane.

_____________________ 65. Open excision of retained sliver, subcutaneous tissue of left foot

Operation: Fragmentation

_____________________ 66. Extracorporeal shock wave lithotripsy (ESWL), bilateral ureters

Coding Tip

Assign two separate codes for *ESWL of bilateral ureters* because a value for bilateral ureters as a body part is not available for operation *Fragmentation*.

_______________ 67. Endoscopic retrograde cholangiopancreatography (ERCP) with lithotripsy of common bile duct stone

Coding Tip

An ERCP is performed through the mouth to the biliary system via the duodenum; thus, the approach value is *via natural or artificial opening endoscopic.*

_______________ 68. Thoracotomy with crushing of pericardial calcifications

_______________ 69. Transurethral cystoscopy with fragmentation of bladder calculus

_______________ 70. Hysteroscopy with intraluminal lithotripsy of left fallopian tube calcification

Procedures That Involve Cutting or Separation Only

Operation	Objective of Procedure	Site of Procedure	Example
Division	Cutting into/separating a body part	Within a body part	Neurotomy
Release	Freeing a body part from constraint	Around a body part	Adhesiolysis

Operation: Division

_______________ 71. Division of right foot tendon, percutaneous

_______________ 72. Left heart catheterization with division of bundle of His

_______________ 73. Open osteotomy of capitate, left hand

Coding Tip

The capitate is one of the carpal bones of the hand.

_______________ 74. EGD with esophagotomy of esophagogastric junction

_______________ 75. Sacral rhizotomy for pain control, percutaneous

Operation: Release

_______________ 76. Laparotomy with exploration and adhesiolysis of right ureter

_______________ 77. Incision of scar contracture, right elbow

Coding Tip

Skin of the elbow region is classified to the body part value for *Lower arm.*

_______________ 78. Frenulotomy for treatment of tongue-tie syndrome

Coding Tip

Frenulum is classified to the body part value for *Tongue.*

_______________ 79. Right shoulder arthroscopy with coracoacromial ligament release

_______________ 80. Mitral valvulotomy for release of fused leaflets, open approach

_______________ 81. Percutaneous left Achilles tendon release

_______________ 82. Laparoscopy with lysis of peritoneal adhesions

_______________ 83. Manual rupture of right shoulder joint adhesions under general anesthesia

_______________ 84. Open posterior tarsal tunnel release

Coding Tip

For open posterior tarsal tunnel release, the nerve released is the tibial nerve.

_______________ 85. Laparoscopy with freeing of left ovary and left fallopian tube

Procedures That Put In, Put Back, or Move Some or All of a Body Part

Operation	Objective of Procedure	Site of Procedure	Example
Reattachment	Putting back a detached body part	Some/all of a body part	Reattach finger
Reposition	Moving a body part to normal or other suitable location	Some/all of a body part	Move undescended testicle
Transfer	Moving a body part to function for a similar body part	Some/all of a body part	Skin transfer flap
Transplantation	Putting in a living body part from a person/animal	Some/all of a body part	Kidney transplant

Operation: Reattachment

_______________ 86. Replantation of avulsed scalp

_______________ 87. Reattachment of severed right ear

_______________ 88. Reattachment of traumatic left gastrocnemius avulsion, open

_______________ 89. Closed replantation of three avulsed teeth, lower jaw

_______________ 90. Reattachment of severed left hand

Operation: Reposition

_______________ 91. Open fracture reduction, right tibia

_______________ 92. Laparoscopy with gastropexy for malrotation

_______________ 93. Left knee arthroscopy with reposition of anterior cruciate ligament

_______________ 94. Open transposition of ulnar nerve

_______________ 95. Closed reduction with percutaneous internal fixation of right femoral neck fracture

Operation: Transfer

_______________ 96. Right hand open palmaris longus tendon transfer

_______________ 97. Endoscopic radial to median nerve transfer

_______________ 98. Fasciocutaneous flap closure of left thigh, open

Coding Tip

Assigning a value to the qualifier that identifies *skin, subcutaneous tissue,* and *fascia* is permitted because to get to the fascia, the skin and subcutaneous tissue layers are also accessed.

______ 99. Transfer left index finger to left thumb position, open

______ 100. Percutaneous fascia transfer to fill defect, anterior neck

______ 101. Trigeminal to facial nerve transfer, percutaneous endoscopic

______ 102. Endoscopic left leg flexor hallucis longus tendon transfer

______ 103. Right scalp advancement flap to right temple

______ 104. Bilateral transverse rectus abdominus muscle (TRAM) pedicle flap reconstruction, status post mastectomy, muscle only, open

Coding Tip

Assign a separate code to each TRAM flap developed because the procedure is performed bilaterally.

______ 105. Skin transfer flap closure of complex open wound, left lower back

Operation: Transplantation

______ 106. Liver transplant with donor-matched liver

______ 107. Orthotopic heart transplant using porcine heart

Coding Tip

The donor heart came from an animal (pig); thus, assign a value for qualifier *Zooplastic*.

______ 108. Right lung transplant, open, using organ donor match

______ 109. Transplant of large intestine, organ donor match

______ 110. Left kidney and pancreas transplant with organ bank donor

Procedures That Alter the Diameter or Route of a Tubular Body Part

Operation	Objective of Procedure	Site of Procedure	Example
Bypass	Altering route of passage	Tubular body part	Coronary artery bypass graft (CABG)
Dilation	Expanding orifice or lumen	Tubular body part	Percutaneous transluminal coronary angioplasty (PTCA)
Occlusion	Completely closing orifice or lumen	Tubular body part	Fallopian tube ligation
Restriction	Partially closing orifice or lumen	Tubular body part	Gastroesophageal fundoplication

Operation: Bypass

______ 111. Open gastric bypass with Roux-en-Y limb to jejunum

______ 112. Right temporal artery to intracranial artery bypass using Gore-Tex graft, open

______ 113. Tracheostomy formation with tracheostomy tube placement, percutaneous

_______________ 114. Percutaneous *in situ* coronary venous arterialization (PICVA) of single coronary artery

_______________ 115. Open left femoral-popliteal artery bypass using cadaver vein graft

_______________ 116. Shunting of intrathecal cerebrospinal fluid to peritoneal cavity using synthetic shunt

_______________ 117. Colostomy formation, open, transverse colon to abdominal wall

_______________ 118. Open urinary diversion, left ureter, using ileal conduit to skin

_______________ 119. CABG of LAD using left internal mammary artery, open off-bypass

_______________ 120. Open pleuroperitoneal shunt, right pleural cavity, using synthetic device

Operation: Dilation

_______________ 121. Endoscopic retrograde cholangiopancreatography (ERCP) with balloon dilation of common bile duct

_______________ 122. Percutaneous transluminal coronary angioplasty (PTCA) of two coronary arteries, left anterior descending with stent placement, right coronary artery with no stent

Coding Tip

Assign a separate code to each artery dilated because the *Device value* differs for each artery.

_______________ 123. Cystoscopy with intraluminal dilation of bladder neck stricture

_______________ 124. Open dilation of old anastomosis, left femoral artery

_______________ 125. Dilation of upper esophageal stricture, direct visualization, with Bougie sound

_______________ 126. PTA of right brachial artery stenosis

_______________ 127. Transnasal dilation and stent placement in right lacrimal duct

_______________ 128. Hysteroscopy with balloon dilation of bilateral fallopian tubes

_______________ 129. Tracheoscopy with intraluminal dilation of tracheal stenosis

_______________ 130. Cystoscopy with dilation of left ureteral stricture, with stent placement

Operation: Occlusion

_______________ 131. Percutaneous ligation of esophageal vein

_______________ 132. Percutaneous embolization of left internal carotid-cavernous fistula

_______________ 133. Laparoscopy with bilateral occlusion of fallopian tubes using Hulka extraluminal clips

_______________ 134. Open suture ligation of failed AV graft, left brachial artery

_______________ 135. Percutaneous embolization of vascular supply, intracranial meningioma

Operation: Restriction

_______________ 136. Cervical cerclage using Shirodkar technique

_______________ 137. Thoracotomy with banding of left pulmonary artery using extraluminal device

_______________ 138. Restriction of thoracic duct with intraluminal stent, percutaneous

_______________ 139. Craniotomy with clipping of cerebral aneurysm

Coding Tip

During clipping of a cerebral aneurysm, the clip is placed lengthwise on the outside wall of the widened portion of the vessel.

_______________ 140. Nonincisional, transnasal placement of restrictive stent in right lacrimal duct

Procedures That Always Involve a Device

Operation	Objective of Procedure	Site of Procedure	Example Operation
Change	Exchanging device without cutting or puncturing	In/on a body part	Drainage tube change
Insertion	Putting in nonbiological device	In/on a body part	Central line insertion
Removal	Taking out device	In/on a body part	Central line removal
Replacement	Putting in device that replaces a body part	Some/all of a body part	Total hip replacement
Revision	Correcting a malfunctioning or displaced device	In/on a body part	Revision of pacemaker insertion
Supplement	Putting in device that reinforces or augments a body part	In/on a body part	Abdominal wall herniorrhaphy using mesh

Operation: Change

_______________ 141. Exchange of drainage tube from right hip joint

_______________ 142. Tracheostomy tube exchange

_______________ 143. Change chest tube for left pneumothorax

_______________ 144. Exchange of cerebral ventriculostomy drainage tube

_______________ 145. Foley urinary catheter exchange

Coding Tip

Because urine is being drained, a Foley urinary catheter exchange is classified as a drainage device.

Operation: Insertion

_______________ 146. End-of-life replacement of spinal neurostimulator generator, dual array, in lower abdomen, open

Coding Tip

Assign two separate codes for this procedure.

- Insertion of dual array stimulator generator into lower abdomen
- Removal of old spinal neurostimulator generator from lower abdomen (trunk)

______________________ 147. Percutaneous replacement of broken pacemaker lead in left atrium

Coding Tip

A pacemaker lead is also called a cardiac lead. Assign two separate codes for this procedure.

- Insertion of pacemaker lead into left atrium
- Removal of broken pacemaker lead from left atrium

______________________ 148. Open placement of dual chamber pacemaker generator in chest wall

______________________ 149. Percutaneous placement of venous central line in right internal jugular

______________________ 150. Open insertion of multiple channel cochlear implant, left ear

______________________ 151. Percutaneous placement of Swan-Ganz catheter in superior vena cava

Coding Tip

A Swan-Ganz catheter is assigned a device value for *monitoring device* because it monitors pulmonary artery output.

______________________ 152. Bronchoscopy with insertion of brachytherapy seeds, right main bronchus

______________________ 153. Placement of intrathecal infusion pump into fascia of the back for pain management, percutaneous

______________________ 154. Open placement of bone growth stimulator, left femoral shaft

______________________ 155. Cystoscopy with placement of brachytherapy seeds in prostate gland

Operation: Removal

______________________ 156. Open removal of lumbar sympathetic neurostimulator

______________________ 157. Nonincisional removal of Swan-Ganz catheter from right pulmonary artery

______________________ 158. Laparotomy with removal of pancreatic drain

______________________ 159. Extubation of endotracheal tube

______________________ 160. Nonincisional percutaneous endoscopic gastrostomy (PEG) tube removal

______________________ 161. Transvaginal removal of brachytherapy seeds

______________________ 162. Incision with removal of K-wire fixation, right first metatarsal

______________________ 163. Cystoscopy with retrieval of left ureteral stent

______________________ 164. Removal of nasogastric drainage tube for decompression

______________________ 165. Removal of external fixator, left radial fracture

Coding Tip

Assign just the replacement procedure code to each procedure statement. Per ICD-10-PCS coding guidelines, an additional code is not necessary for any Excision, Resection, or Destruction procedure performed on the body part at the same time the Replacement procedure is performed to replace that body part.

Operation: Replacement

_______________ 166. Full-thickness skin graft to right lower arm from left thigh autograft

_______________ 167. Excision of necrosed left femoral head and replacement with bone bank bone graft to fill the defect, open

_______________ 168. Penetrating keratoplasty of right cornea with donor matched cornea, percutaneous approach

_______________ 169. Bilateral mastectomy with concomitant saline breast implants, open

_______________ 170. Excision of abdominal aorta with Gore-Tex graft replacement, open

Coding Tip

Do not assign a separate code for excision of the abdominal aorta; the excision was performed as part of the replacement procedure.

_______________ 171. Total right knee arthroplasty with insertion of total knee prosthesis

_______________ 172. Bilateral mastectomy with free transverse rectus abdominis myocutaneous (TRAM) flap reconstruction, open

_______________ 173. Partial tenonectomy of right ankle with replacement graft to right ankle using cadaver graft, open

_______________ 174. Mitral valve replacement using porcine valve, open

_______________ 175. Percutaneous phacoemulsification of right eye cataract with insertion of prosthetic lens

Operation: Revision

_______________ 176. Reposition of Swan-Ganz catheter in superior vena cava

_______________ 177. Open revision of right hip replacement, with recementing of the prosthesis

_______________ 178. Adjustment of position, pacemaker lead in left ventricle, percutaneous

_______________ 179. Taking out loose screw and putting larger screw in fracture repair plate, left tibia

_______________ 180. Revision of ventricular access device (VAD) reservoir placement in chest wall, which was causing patient discomfort, open

Operation: Supplement

_______________ 181. Aortic valve annuloplasty using ring, open

_______________ 182. Laparoscopic repair of left inguinal hernia with Marlex plug

_______________ 183. Autograft nerve graft to right median nerve, percutaneous endoscopic (do not code *graft harvest* for this exercise)

______________________ 184. Exchange of liner in femoral component of previous left hip replacement, open approach

Coding Tip

Assign two separate codes for this procedure.

- Supplement left hip joint replacement with liner
- Removal of the old liner from the left hip joint

______________________ 185. Anterior colporrhaphy with polypropylene mesh reinforcement, open approach

______________________ 186. Implantation of CorCap cardiac support device, open approach

______________________ 187. Abdominal wall herniorrhaphy, open, using synthetic mesh

______________________ 188. Tendon graft procedure performed to strengthen injured left shoulder using autograft tendon that was removed from right thigh, open

Coding Tip

Assign two separate codes for this procedure.

- Replacement, left shoulder with tendon autograft
- Removal, hamstring tendon (right thigh) to create autograft

______________________ 189. Onlay lamellar keratoplasty of left cornea using synthetic substitute, external approach

______________________ 190. Resurfacing procedure on right femoral head, open approach

Procedures That Involve Examination Only

Operation	Objective of Procedure	Site of Procedure	Example
Inspection	Visual or manual exploration	Some or all of a body part	Diagnostic cystoscopy
Map	Location electrical impulses or functional areas	Brain or cardiac conduction mechanism	Cardiac electrophysiological study

Operation: Inspection

______________________ 191. Thoracotomy with exploration of right pleural cavity

______________________ 192. Diagnostic laryngoscopy

______________________ 193. Exploratory arthrotomy of left knee

______________________ 194. Colposcopy with diagnostic hysteroscopy

______________________ 195. Digital rectal exam

______________________ 196. Diagnostic arthroscopy of right shoulder

______________________ 197. Endoscopy of maxillary sinus

______________________ 198. Laparotomy with palpation of liver

______________________ 199. Transurethral diagnostic cystoscopy

______________________ 200. Colonoscopy, discontinued at sigmoid colon

Operation: Map

_______________ 201. Percutaneous mapping of basal ganglia

_______________ 202. Heart catheterization with cardiac mapping

_______________ 203. Intraoperative whole brain mapping via craniotomy

_______________ 204. Mapping of left cerebral hemisphere, percutaneous endoscopic

_______________ 205. Intraoperative cardiac mapping during open heart surgery

Procedures That Include Other Repairs

Operation	Objective of Procedure	Site of Procedure	Example
Control	Stopping or attempting to stop postprocedural bleed	Anatomical region	Control of postprostatectomy bleeding
Repair	Restoring body part to its normal structure	Some/all of a body part	Suture laceration

Operation: Control

_______________ 206. Hysteroscopy with cautery of posthysterectomy oozing and evacuation of clot

_______________ 207. Open exploration and ligation of postoperative arterial bleeder, left forearm

_______________ 208. Control of postoperative retroperitoneal bleeding via laparotomy

_______________ 209. Reopening of thoracotomy site with drainage and control of postoperative hemopericardium

_______________ 210. Arthroscopy with drainage of hemarthrosis at previous operative site, right knee

Operation: Repair

_______________ 211. Suture repair of left radial nerve laceration, open

_______________ 212. Laparotomy with suture repair of blunt force duodenal laceration

_______________ 213. Perineoplasty with repair of old obstetric laceration, open

_______________ 214. Suture repair of right biceps tendon laceration, open

_______________ 215. Closure of abdominal wall stab wound

Procedures That Include Other Objectives

Operation	Objective of Procedure	Site of Procedure	Example
Fusion	Rendering joint immobile	Joint	Spinal fusion
Alteration	Modifying body part for cosmetic purposes without affecting function	Some/all of a body part	Face lift
Creation	Making new structure for sex change operation	Perineum	Artificial vagina

Operation: Alteration

_______________ 216. Cosmetic face lift, open, no other information available

_______________ 217. Bilateral breast augmentation with silicone implants, open

_______________ 218. Cosmetic rhinoplasty with septal reduction and tip elevation using local tissue graft, open

_______________ 219. Abdominoplasty (tummy tuck), open

_______________ 220. Liposuction of bilateral thighs

Operation: Creation

_______________ 221. Creation of penis in female patient using tissue bank donor graft

> **Coding Tip**
>
> Tissue bank donor graft is a nonautologous tissue substitute.

_______________ 222. Creation of vagina in male patient using synthetic material

_______________ 223. Creation of penis in female patient using autologous tissue substitute

_______________ 224. Creation of vagina in male patient using autologous tissue substitute

_______________ 225. Creation of penis in female patient using synthetic material

Operation: Fusion

_______________ 226. Radiocarpal fusion of left hand with internal fixation, open

_______________ 227. Spinal fusion at L1–L3 level with BAK cage interbody fusion device, open, posterior approach anterior column

_______________ 228. Intercarpal fusion of right hand with bone bank bone graft, open

_______________ 229. Sacrococcygeal fusion with bone graft from same operative site, open

_______________ 230. Interphalangeal fusion of left great toe, percutaneous pin fixation

Section: Obstetrics

_______________ 231. Abortion by dilation and evacuation following laminaria insertion

_______________ 232. Manually assisted spontaneous delivery

_______________ 233. Abortion by abortifacient insertion

_______________ 234. Bimanual pregnancy examination

_______________ 235. Extraperitoneal C-section, low transverse incision

_______________ 236. Fetal spinal tap, percutaneous

_______________ 237. Fetal kidney transplant, laparoscopic

_______________ 238. Open *in utero* repair of congenital diaphragmatic hernia

> **Coding Tip**
>
> The complete name for *diaphragm* is *thoracic diaphragm* because it extends along the bottom of the rib cage, separates the thorax from the abdomen, and contracts and relaxes during respiration to draw air in and expel air from the lungs. Thus, the diaphragm is associated with the *Respiratory* body system in the *Medical and Surgical Section.*

_______________ 239. Laparoscopy with total excision of tubal pregnancy

_______________ 240. Transvaginal removal of fetal monitoring electrode

Section: Placement

_______________ 241. Placement of packing material, right ear

_______________ 242. Mechanical traction of entire left leg

_______________ 243. Removal of splint, right shoulder

_______________ 244. Placement of neck brace

_______________ 245. Change of vaginal packing

_______________ 246. Packing of wound, chest wall

_______________ 247. Sterile dressing placement to left groin region

_______________ 248. Removal of packing material from pharynx

_______________ 249. Placement of intermittent pneumatic compression device, covering entire right arm

_______________ 250. Exchange of pressure dressing to left thigh

Section: Administration

_______________ 251. Peritoneal dialysis via indwelling catheter

_______________ 252. Transvaginal artificial insemination

_______________ 253. Infusion of total parenteral nutrition via central venous catheter

_______________ 254. Esophagogastroscopy performed after injection of Botox into esophageal sphincter as temporary paralyzing agent

_______________ 255. Percutaneous irrigation of knee joint

_______________ 256. Epidural injection of mixed steroid

_______________ 257. Chemical pleurodesis using injection of tetracycline

_______________ 258. Transfusion of antihemophilic factor (nonautologous), via arterial central line

_______________ 259. Transabdominal *in vitro* fertilization, implantation of donor ovum

_______________ 260. Autologous bone marrow transplant via central venous line

Section: Measurement and Monitoring

_______________ 261. Cardiac stress test, single measurement

_______________ 262. EGD with biliary flow measurement

_______________ 263. Temperature monitoring, rectal

_______________ 264. Peripheral venous pulse, external, single measurement

_______________ 265. Holter monitoring

_______________ 266. Respiratory rate, external, single measurement

_______________ 267. Fetal heart rate monitoring, transvaginal

_______________ 268. Visual mobility test, single measurement

_______________ 269. Pulmonary artery wedge pressure monitoring from Swan-Ganz catheter

_______________ 270. Olfactory acuity test, single measurement

Section: Extracorporeal or Systemic Assistance and Performance

_______________ 271. Intermittent mechanical ventilation, 16 hours

_______________ 272. Liver dialysis, single encounter

_______________ 273. Cardiac countershock with successful conversion to sinus rhythm

_______________ 274. Intermittent positive pressure breathing for mobilization of secretions, 22 hours

_______________ 275. Hemodialysis, 6 hours per day

Section: Extracorporeal or Systemic Therapies

_______________ 276. Donor thrombocytapheresis, single encounter

_______________ 277. Bili-lite UV phototherapy, series treatment

_______________ 278. Whole body hypothermia, single treatment

_______________ 279. Circulatory phototherapy, single encounter

_______________ 280. Shock wave therapy of plantar fascia, single treatment

_______________ 281. Antigen-free air conditioning, series treatment

_______________ 282. Transcranial magnetic stimulation, series treatment

_______________ 283. Therapeutic ultrasound of peripheral vessels, single treatment

_______________ 284. Plasmapheresis, series treatment

_______________ 285. Extracorporeal electromagnetic stimulation for urinary incontinence, single treatment

Section: Osteopathic

_______________ 286. Isotonic muscle energy treatment, right leg

_______________ 287. Low velocity-high amplitude osteopathic treatment, head

_______________ 288. Lymphatic pump osteopathic treatment, left axilla

_______________ 289. Indirect osteopathic treatment, sacrum

_______________ 290. Articulatory osteopathic treatment, cervical region

Section: Other Procedures

_______________ 291. Near infrared spectroscopy, leg vessels

_______________ 292. Computerized tomography computer-assisted partial ethmoid sinusectomy, right

_______________ 293. Suture removal, abdominal wall

_______________ 294. Isolation after infectious disease exposure

_______________ 295. Robotic-assisted open prostatectomy

Section: Chiropractic

_______________ 296. Chiropractic treatment of lumbar region using long lever specific contact

_______________ 297. Chiropractic manipulation of abdominal region, indirect visceral

_______________ 298. Chiropractic extra-articular treatment, hip region

_______________ 299. Chiropractic treatment of sacrum using long and short lever specific contact

_______________ 300. Mechanically assisted chiropractic manipulation of head

Section: Imaging

_______________ 301. Noncontrast CT of abdomen and pelvis

_______________ 302. Intravascular ultrasound, left subclavian artery

_______________ 303. Chest x-ray, AP/PA and lateral views

_______________ 304. Endoluminal ultrasound of gallbladder and bile ducts

_______________ 305. MRI of thyroid gland, contrast unspecified

_______________ 306. Esophageal videofluoroscopy study with oral barium contrast

_______________ 307. Portable x-ray study of right radius/ulna shaft, standard series

_______________ 308. Routine fetal ultrasound, second trimester twin gestation

_______________ 309. CT scan of bilateral lungs, high osmolar contrast with densitometry

_______________ 310. Fluoroscopic guidance for percutaneous transluminal angioplasty, left common femoral artery, low osmolar contrast

Section: Nuclear Medicine

_______________ 311. Planar nuclear medicine imaging scan of right and left heart, with radiopharmaceutical, qualitative gated rest

_______________ 312. Technetium pentetate assay of kidneys, ureters, and bladder

_______________ 313. Uniplanar scan of spine using technetium oxidronate, with first pass study

_______________ 314. Thallous chloride tomographic scan of bilateral breasts

_______________ 315. PET scan of myocardium using rubidium

_______________ 316. Gallium citrate scan of head and neck, single plane imaging

_______________ 317. Xenon gas nonimaging probe of brain

_______________ 318. Upper GI scan, radiopharmaceutical unspecified, for gastric emptying

_______________ 319. Carbon 11 PET scan of brain with quantification

_______________ 320. Iodinated albumin nuclear medicine assay, blood plasma volume study

Section: Radiation Therapy

_______________ 321. Plaque radiation of left eye, single port

_______________ 322. 8 MeV photon beam radiation to brain

_______________ 323. IORT of colon, 3 ports

_______________ 324. HDR brachytherapy of prostate using palladium 103

_______________ 325. Electron radiation treatment of right breast, custom device

_______________ 326. Hyperthermia oncology treatment of pelvic region

_______________ 327. Contact radiation of tongue

_______________ 328. Heavy particle radiation treatment of pancreas, four risk sites

_______________ 329. LDR brachytherapy to spinal cord using iodine

_______________ 330. Whole body phosphorus 32 administration with risk to hematopoietic system

Section: Physical Rehabilitation and Diagnostic Audiology

_______________ 331. Bekesy assessment using audiometer

_______________ 332. Individual fitting of left eye prosthesis

_______________ 333. Physical therapy for range of motion and mobility, patient right hip, no special equipment

_______________ 334. Bedside swallow assessment using assessment kit

_______________ 335. Caregiver training in airway clearance techniques

Section: Mental Health

_______________ 336. Cognitive-behavioral psychotherapy, individual

_______________ 337. Narcosynthesis

_______________ 338. Light therapy

_______________ 339. ECT (electroconvulsive therapy), unilateral, multiple seizure

_______________ 340. Crisis intervention

_______________ 341. Neuropsychological testing

_______________ 342. Hypnosis

_______________ 343. Developmental testing

_______________ 344. Vocational counseling

_______________ 345. Family psychotherapy

Section: Substance Abuse Treatment

_______________ 346. Naltrexone treatment for drug dependency

_______________ 347. Substance abuse treatment family counseling

_______________ 348. Medication monitoring of patient on methadone maintenance

_______________ 349. Individual interpersonal psychotherapy for drug abuse

_______________ 350. Patient in for alcohol detoxification treatment

_______________ 351. Group motivational counseling

_______________ 352. Individual 12-step psychotherapy for substance abuse

_______________ 353. Post-test infectious disease counseling for IV drug abuser

_______________ 354. Psychodynamic psychotherapy for drug-dependent patient

_______________ 355. Group cognitive-behavioral counseling for substance abuse

Section: New Technology

_______________ 356. Percutaneous extirpation of one coronary artery site using orbital atherectomy technology, new technology group 1

_______________ 357. Percutaneous extirpation of five coronary artery sites using orbital atherectomy technology, new technology group 1

______________________ 358. Right knee joint monitoring using an intraoperative knee replacement sensor that was placed via open approach, new technology group 1

______________________ 359. Introduction of Ceftazidime-Avibactam anti-infective into central vein, percutaneous approach, new technology group 1

______________________ 360. Introduction of Isavuconazole anti-infective into peripheral vein, percutaneous approach, new technology group 1

ASSIGNMENT 6.3 – SELECTING AND CODING PRINCIPAL DIAGNOSIS, OTHER (ADDITIONAL) DIAGNOSES, PRINCIPAL PROCEDURE, AND OTHER SIGNIFICANT PROCEDURES

Objectives

At the conclusion of this assignment, the student should be able to:

- Define principal diagnosis, other (additional) diagnosis, comorbidity, complication, principal procedure, and other significant (or secondary) procedure.
- Review case scenarios and select the principal diagnosis, other (additional) diagnosis(es), principal procedure, and other significant (or secondary) procedure(s).
- Assign and properly sequence ICD-10-CM and ICD-10-PCS codes to all diagnoses and procedures identified in case scenarios.

Overview

The *principal diagnosis* is the condition established after study that is chiefly responsible for occasioning the admission of the patient to the hospital for care. The phrase *after study* directs the coder to review all patient record documentation associated with the inpatient hospitalization to determine the clinical reason for the admission. The circumstances of admission that impact selection of the principal diagnosis include the patient's chief complaint; the signs and symptoms on admission; and the entire patient record, which helps the coder determine the clinical reason for the admission (e.g., ancillary test results, operative report, and/or pathology report). *Other (additional) diagnoses* include all conditions that coexist at the time of admission, that develop subsequently, or that affect the treatment received and/or the length of stay. A *comorbidity* is a condition that coexists at the time of admission, and a *complication* is a condition that occurs during the course of the inpatient hospital episode. The *principal procedure* is performed for definitive treatment rather than for diagnostic or exploratory purposes, is necessary to treat a complication, or is most closely related to the principal diagnosis. *Other significant procedures* (or *secondary procedures*) carry an operative or anesthetic risk, require highly trained personnel, or require special facilities or equipment.

NOTE:

The Centers for Medicare & Medicaid Services (CMS) does not require identification of the principal procedure or other significant procedures (or secondary procedures) for MS-DRG purposes. However, other third-party payers may require their identification.

Instructions

Review each case scenario to identify, code, and sequence the principal diagnosis, other (additional) diagnosis(es), principal procedure, and other significant (or secondary) procedure(s).

1. A 61-year-old male patient is admitted with the chief complaint of shortness of breath on minimal exertion and chest discomfort. The patient has a personal history of lung infections and smoking for a long period of time. The patient has a family history of diabetes and hypertension. Physical examination reveals rhonchi. Blood pressure is 110/75. During hospitalization, the patient undergoes lab workup, chest x-ray, and chest CT scan. A right upper lobe lesion is noted on chest CT scan. A bronchoscopy with biopsy is performed, and the pathology report identified non-small cell lung carcinoma. Diagnosis and treatment options are discussed with the patient. The patient is discharged and scheduled for chemotherapy.

   FINAL DIAGNOSIS: Non-small cell carcinoma of the right upper lobe, primary site.

   PROCEDURE: Bronchoscopy of right lung, via natural opening, with biopsy of upper lobe of the right lung.

	ICD Code(s)
Principal Diagnosis:	
Other (Additional) Diagnosis(es): (e.g., comorbidities, complications, and secondary diagnoses)	
Principal Procedure:	
Other Significant Procedure(s):	

2. Full-term female born via vaginal delivery on 05/04/YYYY to a 27-year-old in the hospital. Estimated gestational age, 40 weeks. Mother had two prenatal visits. Rupture of membranes was clear fluids. Delivery was uncomplicated, and Apgar scores were 9/9. Examination of single liveborn revealed birth weight of 3,535 grams, head circumference 35 centimeters, length 53.5 centimeters, and extra digits on all four extremities. Infant admitted to nursery for routine care and feeding. X-rays of both hands and feet and surgical consultation ordered. X-rays of all extremities revealed that this newborn has no bony involvement in the extra digits. Surgical consultation was requested for evaluation of the infant's hands and feet. The mother consented to the procedure of having the extra digits of the newborn's hands and feet tied off. This was done on 05/05/YYYY. The baby was discharged with her mother on 05/06/YYYY with a follow-up appointment for postsurgical evaluation of the feet.

	ICD Code(s)
Principal Diagnosis:	
Other (Additional) Diagnosis(es): (e.g., comorbidities, complications, and secondary diagnoses)	
Principal Procedure:	
Other Significant Procedure(s):	

   FINAL DIAGNOSIS: Stable full-term female infant. Polydactyly of fingers and toes, both hands and feet.

   PROCEDURE: Ligation of extra digits, both hands and both feet.

3. A 78-year-old female was admitted on 01/27/YYYY for progressive exertional shortness of breath and leg edema. The patient has a history of hypertension and nonobstructive hypertrophic cardiomyopathy. On admission, she was in mild respiratory distress. She had distended neck veins. Her heart was irregular with systolic murmur at the apex. Her lungs were clear; however, she had 3 plus hepatomegaly, which was tender. She had 3 plus leg edema. Her chest x-ray showed cardiomegaly with pulmonary vascular congestion. Her laboratory studies were essentially unremarkable. An echocardiogram was done that showed biatrial enlargement and significant left ventricular hypertrophy. The patient was initially treated with bed rest, fluid and sodium restrictions, and intravenous Lasix. She was also started on Norpace to convert to normal sinus rhythm, which was unsuccessful. Eventually, the patient underwent cardioversion, which readily converted the patient to normal sinus rhythm; after cardioversion, she was started on Rythmol 150 milligrams three times a day. She remained in normal sinus rhythm throughout her hospital stay. She is to be followed closely as an outpatient.

   FINAL DIAGNOSES: Congestive heart failure. Hypertrophic cardiomyopathy. Systemic hypertension.

   PROCEDURE: Cardioversion.

	ICD Code(s)
Principal Diagnosis:	
Other (Additional) Diagnosis(es): (e.g., comorbidities, complications, and secondary diagnoses)	
Principal Procedure:	
Other Significant Procedure(s):	

4. A 25-year-old HIV-positive female patient was admitted for tubal ligation. Her last menstrual period started last month (June 11). Physical exam revealed blood pressure of 132/74 and no breast masses. Cardiovascular exam revealed regular rate and rhythm. Lungs were clear to auscultation. Abdomen revealed positive bowel sounds and was soft and nontender. Pelvic exam revealed vulva without lesions, white discharge, and closed cervix. Uterus was normal, and adnexa was without masses. The patient underwent elective sterilization procedure bilaterally with the use of Falope ring extraluminal device. Postoperatively, the patient was noted to have a run of bradycardia in the recovery room. She was administered intravenous medications for this and was sent to the medical floor for continued care. After one additional day of treatment, the patient was discharged.

   FINAL DIAGNOSES: HIV positive. Elective sterilization. Postoperative bradycardia.

   PROCEDURE: Female sterilization procedure with Falope ring, percutaneous endoscopic approach.

	ICD Code(s)
Principal Diagnosis:	
Other (Additional) Diagnosis(es): (e.g., comorbidities, complications, and secondary diagnoses)	
Principal Procedure:	
Other Significant Procedure(s):	

5. A 25-year-old female presented to the hospital for thyroidectomy. Past medical history revealed that on routine examination in the physician's office, the patient was found to have a lump in her neck. The patient was referred for ultrasound and a thyroid biopsy. Ultrasound of the neck confirmed a 3-centimeter solitary thyroid nodule of the right lobe and a 4-centimeter nodule of the left lobe. Fine-needle aspiration demonstrated classic findings for papilloma thyroid neoplasm. Thyroid function tests were normal. The patient underwent complete thyroidectomy. Postoperatively, the patient did well with normal calcium levels. The patient was discharged two days after surgery with a follow-up appointment in 10 days.

   FINAL DIAGNOSIS: Papilloma, thyroid.

   PROCEDURE: Complete thyroidectomy, open approach.

	ICD Code(s)
Principal Diagnosis:	
Other (Additional) Diagnosis(es): (e.g., comorbidities, complications, and secondary diagnoses)	
Principal Procedure:	
Other Significant Procedure(s):	

6. Matthew Saunders was brought to the emergency department by his parents, who stated that the 12-week-old child had been vomiting for three days. Physical exam revealed a listless child with sunken eyes. His abdomen was soft with normal bowel sounds. Lab workup was done, and the child was admitted as an inpatient. Intravenous fluids were immediately started because the child was severely dehydrated. Upper gastrointestinal series showed pyloric mass and narrow pyloric channel. The child was transferred to the local children's hospital for surgical treatment.

   FINAL DIAGNOSES: Infantile hypertrophic pyloric stenosis. Severe dehydration.

	ICD Code(s)
Principal Diagnosis:	
Other (Additional) Diagnosis(es): (e.g., comorbidities, complications, and secondary diagnoses)	
Principal Procedure:	
Other Significant Procedure(s):	

7. An 84-year-old male patient was admitted with a chief complaint of tarry and red-colored stools. The patient has a history of colon polyps, although he underwent colonoscopy about two years ago that showed he was free of disease. His additional past medical history includes a history of hypertension, for which he is on Lopressor 50 milligrams twice daily and Prinzide 10/12.5 milligrams once daily. He is also on Lipitor 10 milligrams daily for hyperlipidemia. Physical exam revealed normal color and blood pressure of 130/60 supine, dropping to about 116 systolic upon sitting up, associated with mild dizziness. He was afebrile. Regular rhythm was normal. Neck: carotid pulsations two plus bilaterally without bruits. Lung fields were clear. Abdomen was not distended. Bowel sounds were normal. Rectal exam showed melanotic stool that was strongly positive for occult blood. The patient was admitted for intravenous fluids. He was typed for 2 units of blood. Frequent hematocrit and hemoglobin lab tests were obtained, and frequent vital signs were taken. The patient underwent upper endoscopic study. Lab results revealed white blood cell count of 7,000. Hemoglobin 12.1 with hematocrit of 33.6 and a normal platelet count. Blood urea nitrogen was 38 and creatinine 1.1, probably reflective of blood in the gut. During hospital course, the patient's hemoglobin gradually dropped to the range of 9.9 to 10.4. Oral medications for hypertension and hyperlipidemia were continued. An esophagogastroduodenoscopy was done, which revealed a prepyloric ulcer. There was some bleeding noted in the area surrounding this ulcer. The patient was stable after the procedure. Discharge medications: Prilosec 20 milligrams once a day, Feosol 325 milligrams three times each day after meals, Prinzide 10/12.5 milligrams daily, and Lipitor 10 milligrams once a day.

   FINAL DIAGNOSES: Prepyloric peptic ulcer with acute hemorrhage. Hypertension. Hyperlipidemia.

   PROCEDURE: Esophagogastroduodenoscopy.

	ICD Code(s)
Principal Diagnosis:	
Other (Additional) Diagnosis(es): (e.g., comorbidities, complications, and secondary diagnoses)	
Principal Procedure:	
Other Significant Procedure(s):	

8. A 68-year-old male was admitted for elective cystectomy due to bladder carcinoma. The patient has a medical history of hypertension and glaucoma. While hospitalized, oral antihypertensive and ocular medications were continued. The patient underwent partial cystectomy via open approach with enterocystoplasty, using part of the sigmoid colon. (Sigmoid colon was excised using open approach.) Postoperative diagnosis was malignant neoplasm of trigone of the bladder. Postoperatively, the patient did well until the third postoperative day, when his creatinine and blood urea nitrogen (BUN) were 2.4 and 35 milligrams, respectively. The patient was in acute renal failure. Medications were administered, which brought his creatinine down to 1.7 and his BUN down to 29 milligrams. The patient was discharged on the seventh day after surgery with home health care ordered. He will be monitored closely.

   FINAL DIAGNOSES: Carcinoma, bladder. Hypertension. Glaucoma. Postoperative acute renal failure.

   PROCEDURE: Partial cystectomy with enterocystoplasty, using part of the sigmoid colon.

	ICD Code(s)
Principal Diagnosis:	
Other (Additional) Diagnosis(es): (e.g., comorbidities, complications, and secondary diagnoses)	
Principal Procedure:	
Other Significant Procedure(s):	

9. A 30-year-old male is admitted with right lower quadrant (RLQ) abdominal pain. The patient also complains of loss of appetite and nausea. Pain is noted by patient to be 7 out of 10. Exam reveals hypoactive bowel sounds, tenderness, and guarding in RLQ. The patient is admitted with the diagnosis of rule out appendicitis. Lab work shows white blood cell count of 12,000, and complete blood count is within normal limits. The patient consents to an exploratory laparotomy, which revealed a normal appendix and Meckel's diverticulum. Laparotomy incision was extended, and appendix and a segment of the patient's ileum are resected during the procedure.

   FINAL DIAGNOSIS: Meckel's diverticulum.

   PROCEDURE: Exploratory laparotomy with open resection of appendix and excision of a segment of ileum.

	ICD Code(s)
Principal Diagnosis:	
Other (Additional) Diagnosis(es): (e.g., comorbidities, complications, and secondary diagnoses)	
Principal Procedure:	
Other Significant Procedure(s):	

10. A 2-day-old male infant is admitted to the local Children's Hospital for cleft lip repair. Baby boy Mitchell was born the previous day at a local community hospital. He has a complete cleft lip on the left side. On the third day of admission to Children's Hospital, preoperative lab results reveal a blood glucose level of less than 40 after a feeding. The baby is observed, and scheduled surgery for repair of the cleft lip is rescheduled. A fasting blood glucose done after 12 hours reveals a level of 30. The baby receives subcutaneous injections of glucagon for hypoglycemia and is evaluated for possible insulinoma. After diagnostic testing, insulinoma is ruled out. The baby is monitored for 72 hours in the neonatal intensive care unit. After blood glucose is normal per lab results, the cleft lip repair is done. The infant is discharged home for close follow-up with his pediatrician to monitor the hypoglycemia.

    FINAL DIAGNOSES: Complete cleft lip, left side. Neonatal hypoglycemia.

    PROCEDURE: Repair, cleft lip (upper lip).

	ICD Code(s)
Principal Diagnosis:	
Other (Additional) Diagnosis(es): (e.g., comorbidities, complications, and secondary diagnoses)	
Principal Procedure:	
Other Significant Procedure(s):	

ASSIGNMENT 6.4 – CODING PRACTICE: HOSPITAL INPATIENT CASES

Instructions

Review each case and underline the diagnoses and procedures to which ICD-10-CM and ICD-10-PCS codes are to be assigned. Then assign appropriate ICD-10-CM and ICD-10-PCS codes for each diagnosis and procedure in correct sequence.

Textbook Chapter 6 contains guidelines for sequencing inpatient diagnoses, and textbook Chapters 4 and 5 contain ICD-10-CM chapter-specific official coding guidelines that you should refer to when assigning codes. When assigning ICD-10-CM and ICD-10-PCS codes, carefully review each case to verify conditions, diseases, procedures, and services to which codes are assigned. *Do not assign codes to untreated diagnoses.*

Infectious and Parasitic Diseases

1. Patient admitted because of pain in his back and low-grade fever with chills. He gave a history of having had malaria while overseas several years ago. Physical examination was essentially negative except for a slightly elevated temperature. Chest x-ray was normal. Urinalysis was essentially normal, as was the complete blood count. Throat culture revealed hemolytic *Streptococcus* in spite of normal appearance of throat. Urine culture negative. Reports have not been received on agglutination tests.

   Patient was treated initially with Pyrilgin, Darvon, and Loridine injections. He was later given a course of Aralen and primaquine. He was also put on Terramycin because the throat culture showed presence of *Streptococcus*. He felt better the second day but then felt worse with fever and pain on the third day. This was when it was decided to give him the Aralen and primaquine. He has been afebrile and feeling much better for the past two days.

   Patient is discharged to continue 11 more days with primaquine, which will be equivalent to 14 full days of therapy. He is also to take Mycebrin-T once daily.

   FINAL DIAGNOSES: Probable exacerbation of malaria. Strep throat.

   ____

2. Patient admitted with night sweats, fever, headache, poor appetite, dizziness, and weakness. Height 5 feet 6 inches and weight 164 pounds. Past medical history reveals obesity, hyperopia, astigmatism, presbyopia with decrease in field of vision of left eye inferiorally, visual and hearing deficiencies, and benign prostatic hypertrophy. Physical exam reveals membrana tympanica slightly scarred and dull. Teeth in poor repair. Tonsils tiny. Atrophic right teste. Crepitation on motion with pain and restriction of motion in knees.

   Lab results showed increased antibody titer of tularemia; dilutions of 1:160 up to 1:1280 in a period of about one week. Erythrocyte sedimentation rate elevated to 31 millimeters per one hour. Alkaline phosphatase 7.4 (normal is 7.0). All other laboratory tests were normal. Chest x-rays, PA and lateral views, were negative except for a small amount of arteriosclerotic changes in the aorta.

   Patient received intravenous fluids with intravenous Terramycin, Sumycin, and Fiorinal with codeine. Patient's condition has shown satisfactory improvement during hospitalization. Discharged home.

   FINAL DIAGNOSIS: Tularemia.

   ____

Neoplasms

3. This 93-year-old white female was admitted to the hospital with the chief complaint of a mass in her left breast in the upper outer quadrant. Breast examination revealed a large hard nodule with skin thickening and had the appearance of being a carcinoma. All blood work and electrolytes were within normal limits, except she did have cholesterol of 304. Urinalysis was negative, and EKG was normal. Chest x-ray showed some calcification of the mitral valve and dilation of the aorta, otherwise negative.

   The patient was admitted to the hospital, prepared for surgery, and taken to the operating room where, under satisfactory general endotracheal anesthesia, a mass was removed from her left breast and sent for frozen section. The frozen section was positive for carcinoma; therefore, a modified radical mastectomy was done of the left side. Following the operation, she had an uncomplicated postoperative recovery. The wound is clean and healing satisfactorily, and she is afebrile and ambulatory. She is discharged home in an asymptomatic condition.

   FINAL DIAGNOSIS: Carcinoma of the upper outer quadrant of the left breast with metastasis of 2 out of 14 axillary lymph nodes.

   PROCEDURES: Removal of breast tumor. Modified radical mastectomy, left (which includes resection of axillary lymph nodes, left side).

   ____

4. This 62-year-old male who has undergone preoperative chemotherapy and radiation treatment for distal rectal adenocarcinoma is now admitted for surgical treatment. The patient was taken to the operating room, where he underwent lower abdominal resection, sigmoid coloanal anastomosis, and diverting ileostomy. Patient tolerated the procedure well. He was transferred to the surgical floor postoperatively. He continued to progress, and his ileostomy began to produce stool. His labs remained stable throughout his stay. He was tolerating a regular diet very well with good ostomy output. The incision remained clean, dry, and intact throughout his stay. Staples were left intact at discharge. Patient was discharged home with home health nursing for ileostomy care.

   FINAL DIAGNOSES: Rectal carcinoma. Coronary artery disease. Gastroesophageal reflux disease.

   PROCEDURES: Abdominoperineal resection of rectum with sigmoid coloanal anastomosis and diverting ileostomy.

   ____

Endocrine, Nutritional, and Metabolic Diseases and Immunity Disorders

5. Female patient admitted with uncontrolled type 2 diabetes mellitus and pain of the hands, which is of questionable etiology. Rule out vasculitis. The patient is a 64-year-old white female with history of diabetes mellitus for several years and is now type 2. For the last several weeks, her glucose levels have been very high at 290 to 350. We increased her insulin, but she was still running quite high. She has been complaining of pain in her right hand and, to a lesser degree, her left hand. They get red, tingly, and painful; it looks as though she may have vasculitis. Blood pressure 120/64, weight 139 pounds. Patient has some funduscopic arteriosclerotic changes and has been treated for diabetic retinopathy. Lungs are clear. She has some clubbing of the fingers. No cyanosis. Tips of her fingers and thumbs on both hands look red. She is quite tender over the first metacarpal phalangeal joint of the right hand. Doesn't appear to be particularly swollen or feel hot to the touch.

   She is admitted for vigorous treatment and further evaluation. Urinalysis normal. Complete blood count normal. Sedimentation rate was 77. Fasting sugar on the day after admission was 230; later that day, 166. Glucose levels remained high for the next few days. Chest x-ray was normal. Hand x-rays revealed demineralization of bones but no significant arthritic changes.

The patient's hospital course was one of gradual improvement. We started her on prednisone 20 milligrams twice daily, maintained her usual medications, and had to increase her insulin somewhat. The redness in her hands went away. Of course, her glucose levels remained high on the prednisone until we got the insulin increased enough. She had a percutaneous temporal artery biopsy, which revealed no diagnostic changes. I still believe she has both collagen vascular disease and vasculitis. She has responded to treatment. She is being discharged home. We will see her in the office in one week for follow-up; sooner if any difficulty.

FINAL DIAGNOSES: Type 2 diabetes mellitus, uncontrolled. Probable collagen vascular disease. Probable vasculitis of both hands.

PROCEDURE: Left percutaneous temporal artery biopsy.

____

6. Patient admitted with hypokalemia, diuretically induced due to medication for hypertensive vascular disease. Suspect streptococcal pharyngitis. The patient is a 34-year-old white female seen in the emergency room for fevers, chills, and severe pharyngitis. The patient was on Moduretic 5/50 for hypertension and Micro-K tablets 6 milliequivalents, one tablet twice daily, for low potassium levels. The patient has been sick with fever, very sore throat, and difficulty swallowing. Potassium in the emergency room was only 2.5.

   She was admitted for intravenous potassium therapy and treatment of her severe sore throat. She was maintained on her hypertensive vascular disease medications. Her temperature was 102.4, pulse 118, respirations 20, blood pressure 122/82. The patient had hyperemia of the pharynx, had difficulty swallowing, and felt very tired and run down. Potassium was 2.5. Complete blood count was normal. Electrolytes levels were repeated the next day and were normal with potassium of 4.3. Throat culture was negative for beta strep Group A.

   The patient's course in the hospital was one of rapid improvement. She had intravenous fluids and potassium, and she was administered NSAIDs for her severe pharyngitis. By the next day, the patient was feeling quite a bit better. By the afternoon, she was feeling a lot better and did not feel so tired. She still had a sore throat but was able to swallow better, and her potassium was normal. She's being discharged home on no medications.

   FINAL DIAGNOSES: Hypopotassemia, diuretic induced. Acute pharyngitis. Hypertension. Long-term use of therapeutic diuretics. (Initial encounter.)

____

Diseases of the Blood and Blood-Forming Organs

7. The patient was admitted through the emergency room following an acute hemorrhage in an area of oral surgery and multiple extractions. The patient presented with profuse bleeding, stating that the area suddenly started bleeding approximately two to three hours prior. She had all sutures removed two days ago from an area of multiple extractions in the mandible and had no incidence until now. Patient has a history of idiopathic thrombocytopenic purpura, and it is likely that the bleeding was a result of this syndrome; however, her prothrombin times were normal. Complete blood count was normal. The patient's mouth was resutured in the emergency room, and she was admitted to the hospital for overnight observation. She did very well and did not rebleed at all. She was discharged home with a follow-up appointment.

   FINAL DIAGNOSES: Acute hemorrhage. Idiopathic thrombocytopenic purpura.

   PROCEDURE: Suture repair, external buccal mucosa (mouth).

____

Mental Disorders

8. Patient admitted to the hospital from the emergency room with history of having taken several tranquilizer or nerve-type tablets. She was groggy and sleepy upon arrival. Patient states that she was not trying to hurt herself but that she just "wanted to calm down." Examination revealed a well-developed 43-year-old white woman who appeared to be very groggy, but she was aroused with very little difficulty. Complete blood count was normal. Potassium was a little low at 3.7. Other electrolytes were normal. Fasting blood sugar and blood urea nitrogen were normal. Patient had nasogastric tube passed and was given intravenous lactated Ringer's. Later, after she became more alert, Valium 5 milligrams three times per day. The nasogastric tube was removed after a few hours. The patient was allowed to be up. She has been sleeping most of the time on the sedatives given. Patient was discharged home. She will be followed as an outpatient.

   FINAL DIAGNOSES: Accidental overdose of tranquilizer. Acute anxiety state. (Initial encounter.)

   ____

Diseases of the Nervous System and Sense Organs

9. Patient admitted with probable cerebrovascular accident and probable seizure secondary to arteriosclerotic cerebrovascular disease. The patient is a 79-year-old white male with a history of transient ischemic attacks in the past. His wife woke up this morning and found him shaking all over and thought maybe he had a chill or fever, but he did this for about five minutes and was unresponsive. After he stopped shaking, he remained unresponsive for another 10 minutes or so. He drooled at the mouth a little bit, but he did not lose control of his bowels or bladder. When he finally came to, he didn't seem to know where he was and did not remember what happened. By this time, the ambulance had arrived. No history of previous seizure disorder. Patient was worked up in the last year and was found to have arteriosclerotic cerebrovascular disease, for which he was started on medication.

   Upon admission, his blood pressure was 119/76, pulse 64, respirations 18, and temperature 97.6. Carotid pulses about one to two plus bilaterally with a slight bruit heard in the right carotid. Grade 1 out of 6 systolic murmur heard best along the left sternal border in the third or fourth intercostal space. Neurological exam within physiologic limits. No localizing signs. Urinalysis and complete blood count were normal. Chest x-ray revealed an area of infiltrate or fibrosis in the right upper lung field involving the lateral portion of the apical segment. Bilateral apical pleural thickening is present as well, slightly more severe on the right side. Two nodules are present in the left lung; one near the anterior border of the first rib measures about 15 millimeters in size, and the other measures slightly under 1 centimeter and is just lateral to the left hilum. Two other very vague nodules are present lateral to the hilum, but these are only a few millimeters in size. The radiologist was concerned about the possibility of metastatic disease as well as possible primary lung tumor in the right upper lobe, but there are no x-ray films for comparison. EKG on admission was normal. CT scans of the brain were normal. Electroencephalogram (EEG) revealed an abnormal focus; however, his brain CT was negative.

   The patient's hospital course was benign. He felt good after he was admitted, and he did not have any further dizziness or seizures whatsoever. He was continued on medications for arteriosclerotic cerebrovascular disease. Because of the abnormal EEG, he was started on Dilantin 100 milligrams four times each day for seizures, and he is being discharged on that.

   FINAL DIAGNOSES: Seizures. Arteriosclerotic cerebrovascular disease.

   ____

Diseases of the Circulatory System

10. Patient admitted for recent memory loss of questionable etiology, rule out cerebrovascular accident and rule out brain tumor. Patient has hypertension and suffered an acute hypertensive episode during admission to the emergency room. The patient is a 65-year-old female who had been feeling quite well until the day of admission. She went to a church meeting and suddenly got up and told everybody that something was terribly wrong and that she could not remember anything, and she seemed quite confused. She was rushed to the emergency room.

At the time of admission, her blood pressure was 190/120. Neurological examination was negative, so the patient was admitted to my service for further evaluation and treatment. Blood pressure on admission to the floor was 170/96. Neurological exam was within normal limits. The patient was oriented; however, she has a problem with her recent memory, and she does not remember leaving the house this morning, driving to church, and going to the meeting or who she was sitting with or anything. The first thing she remembers is being in the emergency room. She seemed to have a retrograde amnesia but seemed to be intact neurologically otherwise. Urinalysis was negative. Glucose fasting was 165, which is somewhat elevated. Electroencephalogram (EEG) was normal. Cerebral flow study and brain scan were normal. CT scan of the brain was normal.

The patient's course in the hospital was one of rapid improvement. Blood pressure came down after the administration of intravenous antihypertensive medications. She acted perfectly normal except for the retrograde amnesia, and this persisted. By the day of discharge, she did not remember any more about the day of her admission than she did in the beginning. She was seen in neurological consultation, and it was determined that her problem was one of transient global amnesia that is most commonly not a recurrent thing, and is believed to be due to some sort of a vascular spasm. She is being discharged home, taking Dyazide once daily for her hypertension.

FINAL DIAGNOSES: Transient global amnesia. Hypertension.

____

11. Patient is a 76-year-old female with prior history of cerebrovascular accident, suffered on the left side without any residual initially. The patient was treated for this four weeks ago and discharged. She has previous subendocardial infarction and type 2 diabetes mellitus controlled with diet. Patient also has mild Parkinson's disease, which is controlled with Sinemet.

    Patient is readmitted with dense nondominant side right hemiplegia with aphasia. (Patient identified as left-handed.) While hospitalized, her medications for atherosclerotic cardiovascular disease and Parkinson's were continued, and she was placed on a diabetic diet. Flaccid paralysis continued, but she did start to develop some finger and arm motion and minimal leg motion before discharge. She also showed further improvement regarding use of the right arm and foot. We considered the need for rehabilitation, and she is being transferred to the rehabilitation hospital for further treatment.

    FINAL DIAGNOSES: Status post–left hemisphere cerebrovascular accident. Dense right nondominant side hemiplegia with aphasia. Atherosclerotic cardiovascular disease of native coronary arteries. Previous subendocardial myocardial infarction. Type 2 diabetes mellitus. Parkinson's disease.

    ____

12. Patient is admitted with acute ST elevation (STEMI) anteroseptal myocardial infarction. This 62-year-old man stopped his Procardia one month ago and had an onset of precardial pressure going up his neck and down the inside of both arms at 10:30 this evening. This lasted for approximately one hour. He was brought to the emergency room where, upon EKG, he was found to be having an acute ST elevation (STEMI) anteroseptal myocardial infarction. Chest x-ray showed chronic obstructive pulmonary disease.

    Upon admission, creatine kinase (CK) isoenzymes were 89; later that evening total CK was 1680. The following day, CK was 1170. Urinalysis was normal. Electrolytes and complete blood count were normal. Arterial blood gas on 4 liters revealed PO_2 of 73, PCO_2 of 40, pH of 7.43. On the day of discharge, PO_2 on room air was 67. In the intensive care unit, his Procardia was restarted, and lidocaine drip was begun. Lasix was also added to his IV. He had no further angina. His lungs remained clear, and telemetry showed normal sinus rhythm. After 48 hours, the lidocaine was weaned, the patient suffered no arrhythmias, and he was moved to the floor. He was able to walk in his room without angina. He remained out of failure and free of angina or arrhythmia.

    FINAL DIAGNOSES: Acute ST elevation (STEMI) anteroseptal myocardial infarction. Chronic obstructive airway disease. Arteriosclerotic cardiovascular disease. Status post myocardial infarction in 1977.

    ____

Diseases of the Respiratory System

13. An 85-year-old woman has been coughing up some sputum, has not been eating well, sounds congested, and was admitted for a probable bronchitis. EKG showed atrial fibrillation with a controlled ventricular response, left bundle branch block. On examination, a sacral decubitus was noted on the left side. Admission chest x-ray showed cardiomegaly without any infiltrates. Repeat chest x-ray the following day revealed a right lower lobe bronchopneumonia. Cultures revealed Group A *Streptococcus*. Three days after admission, a chest x-ray revealed that the pneumonia was beginning to clear, but there was mild congestive heart failure with small bilateral pleural effusions.

    The patient was admitted and started on chest physical therapy (PT) and later intermittent positive pressure breathing (IPPB). Ancef was begun as well as intravenous fluids. Betadine and sugar compound were begun for the sacral decubitus. While she was on Ancef, her Macrodantin was held. Her cough was very poor. The chest physical therapy seemed to help bring it up. We had to add IPPB to help bring up the sputum. Initially, her second chest x-ray showed progression. Later there was improvement; but then the patient went into congestive heart failure, and Lasix was begun. The patient did improve after several days, and she was able to sit on the side of the bed prior to discharge. She looked much better and was discharged home on bed rest, low-salt diet.

    FINAL DIAGNOSES: Right lower pneumonia due to Group A *Streptococcus*. Congestive heart failure. Sacral decubitus.

    ____

14. Patient admitted to the hospital for cough, shortness of breath, difficulty breathing, and inability to sleep. Upon admission, she was treated with intravenous aminophylline, steroids, and Lasix. She also received oxygen. The second and third day after admission, she was still wheezing throughout lung fields. By the fourth day, her symptoms markedly improved. By the fifth day after admission, the patient was doing well on room oxygen. She was able to ambulate in the hallway without any return of bronchospasms. Patient was discharged with a strict set of instructions.

    FINAL DIAGNOSES: Asthma with acute exacerbation, resolving. Chronic obstructive pulmonary disease.

    ____

15. A severely dehydrated 91-year-old woman was admitted to the hospital with respiratory rate of 40. She complained of shortness of breath, and peripheral cyanosis and hypotension were noted. Medications included Lasix and potassium supplementation. In the emergency room, she had an orthostatic fall in her blood pressure. EKG was normal. Chest x-ray showed normal heart size with atelectasis at the left base. Lung scan was normal. Arterial blood gases on room air showed a PO_2 of 43, PCO_2 of 25, and a pH of 7.57. (Normal range: PO_2 75 to 100; PCO_2 35 to 42; and pH 7.38 to 7.42.) On 6 liters of oxygen, her PO_2 rose to 73.

    The patient was admitted to the intensive care unit, and routine orders were followed. Her Lasix was held, as well as her potassium supplementation. Intravenous fluids were given for hypotension and dehydration. Medications for coronary atherosclerosis were administered. After several days of treatment, she was discharged to a skilled nursing facility with portable oxygen. Her PO_2 at discharge was 85.

    FINAL DIAGNOSES: Acute respiratory failure, questionable etiology, with hypoxia. Dehydration. Coronary atherosclerosis of native arteries.

    ____

Diseases of the Digestive System

16. An 84-year-old white female admitted with dehydration, malnutrition, and late-stage Alzheimer disease. The patient is not on medication for Alzheimer disease. She has had poor to no oral intake over the last several days, and her urine output within the last 15 hours prior to admission was 200 cubic centimeters. She is completely confused and disoriented. Her past history is remarkable for occasional transient ischemic attacks.

    EKG on the day of admission was essentially normal. Chest x-ray showed a small area of infiltrate in the left upper lung field near the hilum consistent with acute pneumonia, approximately 2 centimeters in diameter. Repeat chest x-ray five days after admission showed clearing of the infiltrate. Electrolytes returned to normal range four days after admission with potassium 4 and sodium 140. Blood cultures were negative. Urine culture showed greater than 100,000 cfu/ml of *Streptococcus*.

    Her fever came down 24 hours after admission, and she remained afebrile throughout the hospital course. Other vitals were within acceptable ranges. Appetite was very poor initially but then progressed to 50%–95% intake with all meals. Intravenous antibiotics were administered for pneumonia and urinary tract infection. The patient's intake and outputs were followed; approximately 4,000 cubic centimeters were noted during the first three days, and then this began to stabilize. The patient's mental status improved quite significantly over the course of the hospitalization, with increased alertness and responsiveness, although she remained confused and disoriented. She was able to sit in a chair without great difficulty and was eating quite well. She was discharged to the skilled nursing facility.

    FINAL DIAGNOSES: Dehydration. Severe malnutrition. Acute left upper lobe pneumonia, improved. Alzheimer disease. Urinary tract infection due to *Streptococcus*.

    ____

17. Patient admitted for chronic diarrhea. Small bowel series showed prominent jejunal diverticulitis near gastric anastomosis. Patient has history of gastric bypass surgery 10 years ago for obesity. Colonoscopy revealed a normal colon. Biopsies taken of the sigmoid colon were also normal. She was initially started on Tequin and Flagyl; however, her diarrhea did not improve. All stool studies were negative for *Clostridium difficile*. Her antibiotic regimen was changed to triple therapy, which included Cipro, doxycycline, and Flagyl. She should be on this antibiotic regimen for one month.

    General surgery was consulted regarding evaluation of the patient as candidate for surgery to repair her jejunal diverticulum. She will first be tried on a prolonged course of triple antibiotic therapy and follow-up in general surgery as an outpatient for reevaluation. Regarding her chronic diarrhea, as mentioned, by negative stool studies, she was ruled out for any infectious cause. Her thyroid blood tests were within normal range. In addition, patient underwent a colonoscopy specifically looking for microscopic colitis; however, the colon appeared normal, and biopsies were normal. The patient is discharged home on triple antibiotic therapy and will follow up in the gastrointestinal clinic and with general surgery.

    FINAL DIAGNOSIS: Jejunal diverticulitis.

    PROCEDURE: Colonoscopy with biopsy of the sigmoid colon.

    ____

Diseases of the Genitourinary System

18. Patient admitted with history of left ureterolithiasis status post–left ureteroscopy, laser lithotripsy, and stent placement two years prior. Her stent was removed approximately one month following the procedure; she had no issues until a year later, when she presented to an outside physician complaining of left-sided flank pain. CT scan was performed and revealed left hydronephrosis. She then underwent cystoscopy and retrograde pyelography, which revealed complete obstruction of the mid ureter. Left percutaneous nephrostomy tube was placed, and antegrade pyelogram was completed, which also revealed a complete obstruction. Renal scan was performed, which revealed a nonfunctioning left kidney with 12% function. She was then referred here for evaluation regarding left nephrectomy.

    Patient was admitted and underwent left nephrectomy without complication. She underwent preoperative bowel prep and was medicated with Kefzol 1 gram intravenous prophalactically. On postoperative day one, the patient was tolerating clear liquids and was out of bed to chair. On postoperative day two, her oxygen was weaned off and she was advanced to a regular diet, which she was tolerating well. On postoperative day three, her Foley catheter was discontinued and she was urinating without difficulty. On postoperative day four, she was afebrile with stable vital signs and good urine output. She had adequate oral intake and was ambulating without difficulty. Patient was discharged home on postoperative day four, doing extremely well after procedure.

    FINAL DIAGNOSIS: Nonfunctioning left kidney due to hydronephrosis.

    PROCEDURE: Left nephrectomy (open approach).

    ____

Complications of Pregnancy, Childbirth, and the Puerperium

19. Patient admitted for 34-week intrauterine pregnancy. This 34-year-old para 0-2-4-1 agrees with the 15-week sonogram, giving her a 34-week intrauterine pregnancy with estimated date of confinement for five weeks from now. She was recently hospitalized for elevated blood pressures and proteinuria. She received two doses of betamethasone. The patient left against medical advice.

    She is admitted today for increase in blood pressures to 180s over 100s and a headache. The unborn fetus had previously been transverse and today on ultrasound is vertex. Patient is crying and appears to be very upset about early delivery. She denies rupture of membranes or vaginal bleeding. Her prenatal labs include blood type B+, antibody negative, Pap within normal limits, positive PPD, rubella immune, hepatitis B surface antigen negative, VDRL nonreactive, HIV negative. Cystic fibrosis screen negative. Toxo IgG and IgM negative. Patient has an obstetric history of spontaneous vaginal delivery with preterm labor times two at 35 and 36 weeks. Elective abortion times two. Spontaneous abortion times two. She has a history of preeclampsia in both of her vaginal deliveries.

    The patient was admitted to labor and delivery unit, and she was thoroughly informed about having early delivery. She was started on magnesium sulfate as seizure prophylaxis. Intravenous antibiotics were also started. It was decided that since she had severe preeclampsia, cesarean section was warranted. In addition, the patient also requested a bilateral tubal interruption. She stated that she understands the permanence of the procedure and the fact that there is a failure rate and an increased risk of ectopic pregnancy. A low cesarean section was performed, which resulted in a single healthy male child weighing 6 pounds. Postoperatively, the patient was transferred to the mother/baby unit where she has remained without complaints. Her pain has been well controlled initially by IV medication and then by oral medication.

Currently, she is ambulating and voiding without difficulty. She is tolerating a regular diet, and her lochia has been less than menses. On postoperative day three, patient was discharged home.

FINAL DIAGNOSIS: 34-week intrauterine pregnancy with severe preeclampsia.

PROCEDURES: Low transverse cesarean delivery. Pomeroy bilateral tubal ligation.

____

20. Patient admitted with intrauterine pregnancy, 39 weeks' gestation with spontaneous rupture of membranes. The patient is an 18-year-old white female, gravida 1, para 0, abortions 0. The patient had an essentially benign pregnancy until the last several weeks, when her blood pressure went up. She had a spontaneous rupture of membranes (ROM) about 27 hours ago; however, she did not start contractions.

    She was started on a Pitocin drip to induce labor and then progressed into spontaneous labor. She had very little pain tolerance and was crying out with the pains and not cooperating by doing the breathing exercises. She was given Nubain 10 milligrams intramuscularly; after that, she calmed down. She did much better with her breathing through complete dilatation and then pushed fairly well. She delivered a live female infant from a vertex presentation over a midline episiotomy over local anesthesia. The patient had a first-degree tear of the anterior fourchette area. She had a normal 3-vessel cord, although it was quite fat. The baby's weight was 7 pounds 4 ounces. Apgar was 8 at 1 minute and 10 at 5 minutes. The patient did well postpartum. She remained afebrile. Her blood type was noted to be A+. The patient had a normal urinalysis on admission. She is not breastfeeding; she is bottlefeeding. Her breasts are not too uncomfortable. She is being discharged on ferrous sulfate three times a day with meals. She is to see me in six weeks for checkup. Anterior perineum fourchette area healed, and the episiotomy is healing nicely. Her flow is appropriate.

    FINAL DIAGNOSES: Intrauterine pregnancy, 39 weeks' gestation, delivered after Pitocin induction because of ruptured membranes. First-degree fourchette tear. Single liveborn female.

    PROCEDURES: Induction of labor. Midline episiotomy with repair of first-degree fourchette tear.

    ____

Diseases of the Skin and Subcutaneous Tissue

21. A 41-year-old white female admitted for cellulitis of the left lower leg and obesity. Patient was experiencing pain in her left leg. Patient's weight upon admission was 337 pounds, which is a contributing factor in the development of her cellulitis. The patient is exactly 5 feet tall. The Sunday prior to admission, the patient's son found her lying on the floor with some kind of binding wrapped around her ankle. She does not remember the entire incident exactly, but she may have fallen out of bed. Around the area where her leg was bound, there are abrasions, erythema, and obvious infection.

    During inpatient admission, the patient was treated with Cephalosporin antibiotics and tolerated this well. She was also placed on a special diet, and the dietician met with the patient daily to discuss a diet and exercise regimen for the patient upon discharge. The patient kept her leg elevated during her hospitalization and went for whirlpool treatments of her leg for debridement of the infected area. The patient was discharged to the care of a local health care center. She will be seen for a dressing change and further debridement if necessary. Whirlpool debridement was done on the day of discharge, and there was no pustular material underneath the two rather large blisters on her lower left leg. Results are pending for culture and sensitivity done at the time of debridement. The patient was discharged on Velosef 500 milligrams three times a day.

    FINAL DIAGNOSES: Cellulitis, left lower leg. Severe obesity due to excess calories.

    PROCEDURE: Whirlpool debridement.

    ____

22. Patient is a 3-year-old white male who was involved in a motor vehicle accident as a passenger. He was riding in his car seat up front with one of his parents when the accident occurred. The glass broke on his side of the vehicle, and he sustained lacerations of the right cheek area. Physical exam at the time of admission revealed a stellate laceration with a small piece of tissue missing in the right midcheek area. There was another linear laceration somewhat below that and posteriorly with approximately a small piece of tissue missing, and there was also glass in it. He would not let us touch it at the time; the rest of the physical exam was consistent with age and body habitus and was within normal limits.

    We elected to repair this under general anesthesia; he was taken to the operating room where he was given intramuscular Ketamine with no adverse reaction. There were only one or two pieces of glass; they were cleaned out and discarded. The wound was cleaned, prepped, and draped appropriately; we went ahead and repaired this without too much difficulty. We applied an appropriate dressing and decided to keep him overnight because of the Ketamine anesthesia. He did fine overnight and did not have any problems. This morning the wound was clean and dry. His current immunizations were up to date, so there was no reason to give him tetanus toxoid. The wound appeared to be clean, dry, and healing nicely. We gave his father appropriate instructions for how to care for his son's wound. I will see the patient in the office in five days, at which time the sutures will be removed and Steri-Strips will be applied.

    FINAL DIAGNOSES: Lacerations, right cheek, as the result of automobile accident. Glass embedded in skin, right cheek. (Initial encounter.)

    PROCEDURES: Suture of lacerations, right cheek. Removal (extirpation) of glass from skin, right cheek.

    ____

Diseases of the Musculoskeletal System and Connective Tissue

23. The patient is an 81-year-old female who presented to the hospital with severe left upper quadrant pain and vomiting. There was a question of nephrolithiasis as she has had stones in the past.

    The patient was admitted to the hospital and started on intravenous therapy. The patient continued to have pain in the left upper quadrant and underwent an abdominal series, which was unremarkable. Chest x-ray was within normal limits except for the possibility of abnormality associated with two ribs on the left side. Chest and abdominal CT scans revealed fractures of the lower two ribs on the left side, no injury to the liver or spleen, and marked left hydronephrosis. The rib fractures were treated with pain management. The patient was seen in consultation for hydronephrosis; the consultant thought that since this was a chronic condition and was unrelated to the patient's pain, no further workup was indicated. By day seven of hospitalization, the patient was able to eat and was no longer vomiting, and was thought to be stable for discharge. The patient left in improved condition. She will be seen in the office for follow-up in one month.

    FINAL DIAGNOSES: Right upper quadrant abdominal pain due to pathological fracture of the lower two ribs on the left side. Hydronephrosis, left kidney.

    ____

24. This 48-year-old male is readmitted because of current excruciating back pain due to herniated L4 disc. Complete blood count and urinalysis were normal. Glucose and electrolytes were normal. The patient was continued on his usual medication. He was started on Dolobid for pain and Flexeril as a muscle relaxant,

used bed boards, and was administered parenteral Demerol for pain. Physical therapy was started, from which the patient derived benefits. He had noted that his back was worse after he got up and went to the bathroom. But the physical therapy exercises have helped with this.

During hospitalization, reflexes were increased in the right lower extremity. The patient was discharged to family members at home, and he promised that he would stay at bed rest while he was home. The patient was discharged with bed rest, regular diet, and a follow-up appointment in one week.

FINAL DIAGNOSIS: Herniated L4 disc and lumbosacral strain.

PROCEDURE: Physical therapy therapeutic exercise, musculoskeletal system (lower back).

____

Congenital Anomalies

25. A 5-year-old male diagnosed with polycystic disease of the kidneys, autosomal recessive type at age 3, is admitted at this time to undergo reevaluation. Examination reveals normal blood pressure and average height for his age. Kidneys are slightly enlarged. The patient's mother stated that he had been complaining of painful urination, and she had noticed a bit of blood when he urinated.

    Urine culture was positive for *Escherichia coli*, which was treated during inpatient hospitalization. Lab results revealed normal blood cell counts. CT scan of the kidneys revealed multiple cysts. Treatment options were discussed with the patient's parents, including the consideration of kidney transplant since there is no cure for polycystic kidney disease and the condition does not appear to recur in transplanted kidneys.

    FINAL DIAGNOSES: Polycystic kidney disease, autosomal recessive type. Urinary tract infection due to *Escherichia coli*.

    ____

Certain Conditions Originating in the Perinatal Period

26. Patient is a 2-week-old baby who was admitted because of bloody diarrhea and impending dehydration. Lab data showed stool cultures to be negative. A urine culture grew 100,000 colonies of *Proteus mirabilis*, which might be a contaminant and will be repeated. Hemoglobin 14.7. White count 13,700 with 20 segs, 66 lymphs, and 14 monos. Urinalysis was normal. Electrolytes were normal.

    During the hospital course, the baby was placed on Lytren, and her neonatal bradycardia was also treated. Questran was added, which firmed up the baby's stools; however, as soon as Questran was discontinued, the child had seven very loose, watery stools. At that time, because of impending dehydration, an IV was started and IV fluids were administered for 24 hours. The baby was again started on Lytren and on half-strength Nutramigen, which was brought up to full strength. The baby did very well on this; tolerated it well; and had no more diarrhea, vomiting, or blood in her stool. Repeat urine culture was done just prior to discharge, which showed no growth. This proved the first culture to be contaminant. The baby was sent home on Nutramigen to be followed as an outpatient in three days.

    FINAL DIAGNOSES: Gastroenteritis. Neonatal bradycardia.

    ____

Symptoms, Signs, and Ill-Defined Conditions

27. Patient admitted for a fever of undetermined origin, morbid obesity, and seizures. A 46-year-old white female, a resident of a local nursing home with a known history of morbid obesity and seizures. She had been hospitalized recently for control of seizures, returned to the nursing home, and developed high fever and delirium. Temperature on admission was 103 degrees Fahrenheit. Chest x-ray revealed cardiomegaly probably more related to technique rather than actual. Initial complete blood count was essentially normal; her white blood count was 3,600, which is low (normal 4,500 to 10,500).

    Upon admission, she was treated with bed rest and IV fluids. She was started on Tylenol every 4 hours for the fever and continued on her Theo-Dur SR 300 milligrams every 12 hours, and on Phenobarbital 2 grains at bedtime for her seizures. Her temperature continued to go up and down until she was ultimately started on Bactrim DS 1 tablet twice daily; with this, her temperature returned to normal. Then there was a problem with ambulation because of her morbid obesity, and she was started on physical therapy. Now she is up and ambulating, looking better, feeling better, and mentally alert. Temperature is down, and she is transferred to continue her convalescence at the nursing home.

    FINAL DIAGNOSES: Fever of unknown etiology. Morbid obesity due to excess calories. Seizures under good control.

    PROCEDURE: Functional ambulation physical therapy.

    ____

Injury and Poisoning

28. Patient is a 2-year-old white female who ingested approximately three-quarters of a Fleet enema at home and was brought to the emergency department. Ipecac was administered immediately, and the patient admitted for observation. During hospital course, the patient did not develop any shakiness, and there were no side effects of low calcium and potassium. The child was doing well. No diarrhea developed. No neurological deficit developed. On the third hospital day, patient's vital signs were normal. No evidence of diarrhea noted. Father was instructed to call if any shakiness or diarrhea symptoms develop. Patient discharged home to the care of her father.

    FINAL DIAGNOSIS: Sodium (basic) phosphate poisoning due to ingestion of Fleet enema, resolved without significant side effects. (Initial encounter.)

    ____

29. A 29-month-old male child with a chief complaint of vomiting for three hours duration was admitted due to iron ingestion. The patient was well until three hours prior to admission, when he began vomiting. Approximately one hour prior to the vomiting episode while at home, the mother discovered the child with her iron tablets, which she is taking because she is pregnant. She states that he had eaten the green coating off 23 of the pills and that there were approximately 30 in the bottle. Approximately one hour later, he began vomiting. He vomited approximately four times during the interval between the onset of vomiting and his arrival at the emergency room. Vomitus is described as dark brown with green flecks (enteric coating). He also vomited twice after arrival here in the emergency room and had a very dark, loose, watery bowel movement. Except for the vomiting episodes, the patient has been alert, active, and playful and without any apparent distress.

    The patient was admitted to Pediatrics and given gastric lavage with phosphate. He was also given a phosphate enema. IV fluids of 1-2-7-maintenance solution were started, and vital signs were obtained frequently to watch for any signs of shock. After 24 hours, the patient was alert and active and without any distress. He has had no vomiting since admission and had only one small tarry stool. He ate breakfast eagerly and was placed on a soft diet. His course in the hospital was completely benign and uneventful. His IV fluids were discontinued after 24 hours. He had been completely asymptomatic since admission. He was tolerating a regular diet well and was alert, active, and playful. He was discharged home with parents to be followed in the pediatric outpatient department.

FINAL DIAGNOSIS: Iron intoxication secondary to iron ingestion. Vomiting. Diarrhea. (Initial encounter.)

PROCEDURES: Gastric lavage with phosphate. Phosphate enema.

____

30. The patient is a 54-year-old white male who was a passenger in a car his son was driving. Apparently, the boy fell asleep at the wheel; the car was totaled. Patient was brought to the emergency room by ambulance. He is not sure whether he had any head trauma but complains primarily of pain in his left anterior chest and left shoulder. He was seen in the emergency room, which revealed that he had displaced fracture of his left fourth anterior rib. The physician did not see any fracture of the left shoulder but thought that there might be an acromioclavicular separation.

    The patient was admitted for observation and treatment of his pain. He had tenderness over the left third and fourth anterior ribs and very little use of his left shoulder. He also had tenderness to palpation over the acromioclavicular joint. The patient was admitted and started on analgesics. He did not have much movement of his left shoulder, although this gradually improved during his hospital stay. On the second hospital day, it was noted that he had very little movement of air in the left upper lobe; repeat chest x-ray was obtained, which showed a small pleural effusion on the left and possible pneumonia in the left lower lobe. He was started on Velosef, and the chest x-ray was repeated. The pleural effusion gradually resolved, and the area of pneumonia improved. The patient was continued on the Velosef. He was subsequently discharged.

    FINAL DIAGNOSES: Automobile accident. Closed fracture, left fourth anterior rib. Possible acromioclavicular joint dislocation, left. Pneumonia. Pleural effusion. (Initial encounter.)

    ____

REVIEW

Multiple Choice

Circle the most appropriate response.

1. Which data set is used to collect information about patients and also provides definitions of *principal diagnosis* and *significant procedure*?
   a. Minimum data set
   b. National data set
   c. UACDS
   d. UHDDS
2. A patient, Solomon Johnson, has a central line inserted by Dr. Long at the bedside while the patient is in the intensive care unit under local anesthesia. This procedure is done 12 hours before the patient undergoes a coronary artery bypass graft for his coronary artery disease. The central line insertion is coded and reported as a(n):
   a. ancillary test.
   b. principal diagnosis.
   c. principal procedure.
   d. significant procedure.
3. Lisa Wilcox is admitted with a severe headache via the emergency department (ED). She is seen and evaluated by the ED physician. The ED physician decides to admit her for further workup. She undergoes a computed tomography scan and has blood work done. Final diagnosis for the inpatient admission is "headache, migraine vs. cerebral aneurysm." The coder should:
   a. assign a code to the headache only.
   b. assign codes to both headache and migraine.
   c. assign codes to headache, migraine, and cerebral aneurysm and report the headache code as the principal diagnosis.
   d. query the physician to ask which documented diagnosis should be coded and reported.

4. Mr. Andrew Scofield is admitted to the hospital with the chief complaint of severe back pain. Mr. Scofield has a medical history that includes hiatal hernia and Crohn's disease. Currently, he is undergoing treatment for diverticulitis and epilepsy. After study, it is determined that his main problem during this admission is a herniated lumbar disc at L3. The medications for his diverticulitis and epilepsy are continued while he is in the hospital. The diagnosis of herniated lumbar disc would be considered the:
   a. comorbidity.
   b. complication.
   c. principal diagnosis.
   d. secondary diagnosis.
5. For the case described in #4 above, Mr. Scofield's diagnoses of diverticulitis and epilepsy would be considered:
   a. comorbidities.
   b. complications.
   c. principal diagnoses.
   d. secondary procedures.
6. A patient is admitted to Mingo River Hospital with the complaint of headaches and nosebleeds. The 67-year-old patient takes daily medication for arthritis. He is admitted with an elevated blood pressure of 185/100. While in the hospital, the patient falls on a wet hallway and fractures his left wrist, which is treated and casted. His daily medications for arthritis are continued while he is in the hospital. He is also given intravenous antihypertensive medications. Discharge diagnoses are hypertension, degenerative joint disease, and left wrist fracture. Which is the principal diagnosis?
   a. Fracture of the wrist
   b. Headache
   c. Hypertension
   d. Nosebleed
7. A patient is admitted to the acute care facility with a chief complaint of chest pain. Further examination and history determine that the patient also has joint pain, swelling of the extremities, and hair loss. Laboratory testing confirms that the patient is slightly anemic. After two days in the hospital, the patient is discharged to follow up as an outpatient. Discharge diagnoses include myocardial infarction ruled out and possible systemic lupus erythematosus. Which is the principal diagnosis?
   a. Anemia
   b. Chest pain
   c. Myocardial infarction
   d. Systemic lupus erythematosus
8. A patient is admitted to the acute care facility with the chief complaint of shortness of breath. Per the patient's history, he has been diagnosed and treated for congestive heart failure (CHF) in the past. The patient is treated during this admission with intravenous Lasix and oxygen therapy. A chest x-ray reveals minor atelectasis, which was not treated during the admission. Discharge diagnosis is CHF. Which action should the coder take regarding the documented atelectasis on the chest x-ray report?
   a. Assign a code for the atelectasis (along with congestive heart failure).
   b. Do not code it because the patient did not receive treatment for it.
   c. Query the attending physician to ask if the condition should be reported.
   d. Query the radiologist to ask if the condition should be coded and reported.
9. A 55-year-old male patient is admitted with the chief complaints of dizziness, shortness of breath, and chest pain. The patient undergoes an electrocardiogram to determine heart functioning and serum enzymes to rule out myocardial infarction. Digoxin is administered for suspected dilated cardiomyopathy, and the patient is placed on oxygen via nasal cannula to treat both conditions. The patient also undergoes an echocardiogram and a cardiac catheterization. The echocardiogram confirms that the patient has dilated cardiomyopathy, and the cardiac catheterization confirms a myocardial infarction. After five days in the cardiac care unit, the patient is discharged to an intermediate care facility. Discharge diagnoses include myocardial infarction and dilated cardiomyopathy. The coder should:
   a. assign a code for the chest pain only.
   b. assign a code for the dilated cardiomyopathy only.
   c. query the physician to ask which condition is principal.
   d. report either dilated cardiomyopathy or myocardial infarction as principal.

ICD-10-CM and ICD-10-PCS Coding

10. Use your coding manual to review the following codes assigned to these diagnoses and determine the accuracy of each code reported for the infant's hospital stay. Then select the most appropriate response. Term birth, single living infant. Congenital talipes valgus, left foot. O80, Z37.0, Z38.00, Q66.42
    a. Assign Z38.00 (term, single living infant) as principal diagnosis, then O80, Q66.42.
    b. Delete O80, report Z38.00 as principal diagnosis, and report Q66.42 and O80 as secondary diagnoses.
    c. Remove O80 and Z37.0, report Z38.00 as principal diagnosis, and report Q66.42 as secondary diagnosis.
    d. Resequence the codes and report Z37.0 as principal diagnosis, then O80, Q66.42, and Z38.00.
11. A 45-year-old male patient is admitted with the complaints of fever, headache, fatigue, and a sore throat. This patient is also seen frequently in the HIV clinic. The patient is admitted for further evaluation. Laboratory testing reveals that the patient has toxoplasmosis. The patient's CD4 cell count is 125, which is below the normal of 200. The patient is treated for several days with intravenous pyrimethamine and clindamycin. After 15 days, the patient is in slightly improved condition and will be followed at the clinic. Medications administrated intravenously will be continued by mouth after hospital discharge. Discharge diagnosis is disseminated toxoplasmosis due to AIDS. Which code(s) are reported?
    a. B20
    b. B20, B58.89
    c. B58.9, B20
    d. R50.9, R51, R53.83, J02.9, B58.89
12. A 35-year-old female is seen in the emergency department (ED) with the main complaint of musculoskeletal pain. The patient has had this "all over" pain for over a year and has never seen a physician about it. Examination in the ED reveals that the patient has pain in her shoulders and low back. She also reports difficulty sleeping due to the pain. The patient also has some mild edema of the extremities. She is admitted to rule out congestive heart failure and kidney failure, both of which could be a cause of the edema. Laboratory tests are all within normal range. Chest x-ray and shoulder x-ray are all normal per radiology reports. The patient is discharged after two days in the hospital with medications to alleviate pain and to help her sleep. Discharge diagnosis is musculoskeletal pain, likely fibromyalgia. Which code(s) are reported?
    a. M54.2, M25.519, M54.5
    b. M79.0, M79.7
    c. M79.7
    d. M79.18, M54.2, M25.519, M54.5
13. Admission diagnoses include weight loss, hypotension, and weakness. Final diagnosis is adrenal hypofunction. Which code is reported?
    a. E27.0
    b. E27.1
    c. E27.2
    d. E27.3
14. A 25-year-old male patient is seen in the emergency department (ED) with the symptom of epigastric pain. The patient reports that he has had this pain for four weeks. In the ED, the patient vomits, but the pain is not relieved. The patient is admitted, and the following diagnostic tests are performed: complete blood count, urinalysis, and gastrointestinal x-ray series. Testing determines that the patient has acute pancreatitis. The patient is discharged in improved condition. Which code is reported?
    a. K85.90
    b. K85.80
    c. K85.30
    d. K85.00
15. A 16-year-old female patient is seen in the urgent care center of a hospital with the complaint of shortness of breath. Upon examination, the patient is found to be using accessory muscles to breath. Pulse oximetry is placed on the patient, and arterial blood gases are monitored. The patient is given several nebulizer treatments. However, her breathing does not improve. She is admitted with the diagnosis of asthma. Upon admission, the patient receives intravenous corticosteroids, nebulizer treatments, and subcutaneous epinephrine. Her breathing does improve after this treatment. The patient is monitored for 24 hours and discharged. Discharge diagnosis is "asthma, status asthmaticus." Which code(s) are reported?
    a. J45.21
    b. J45.32
    c. J45.902
    d. J45.20, J45.22

16. Which code is reported for mastoidectomy, right, open approach?
    a. 09BB3ZZ
    b. 09BB0ZX
    c. 09BC0ZZ
    d. 09BB0ZZ
17. Which codes are reported for laparoscopic cholecystectomy with intraoperative cholangiogram, plain radiography with low osmolar contrast?
    a. 0FT44ZZ, BF031ZZ
    b. 0FT44ZZ, BF030ZZ
    c. 0FT44ZZ, BF03YZZ
    d. 0FT40ZZ, BF031ZZ
18. Which code is reported for open reduction and internal fixation of left radius fracture?
    a. 0PSJ06Z
    b. 0PSH06Z
    c. 0PSH04Z
    d. 0PSJ04Z
19. Which code is reported for open insertion of vascular port into chest?
    a. 0JH63XZ
    b. 0JH60VZ
    c. 0JH60XZ
    d. 0JH80XZ
20. Which code is reported for esophagogastroduodenoscopy with biopsy of duodenal polyp?
    a. 0DB98ZZ
    b. 0DB94ZX
    c. 0DB98ZX
    d. 0DB97ZX
21. Which codes are reported for open aortocoronary artery bypass and open right internal mammary coronary artery bypass using synthetic substitute for each bypass?
    a. 02110JW, 02100J8
    b. 02100ZF, 02100J8
    c. 02100JW, 02100J8
    d. 02100JW, 02100J9
22. A 14-day-old infant is admitted to the hospital to receive intravenous fluids. The discharge diagnosis is dehydration. Which code(s) are reported?
    a. E86.0
    b. E87.1
    c. P74.1
    d. P74.1, E87.1
23. A patient undergoes aortic valve replacement surgery with synthetic substitute due to aortic valve stenosis. The surgery is successful, and the patient is discharged. Which codes are reported?
    a. I08.0, 02RF4KZ
    b. I34.2, 02RF4KZ
    c. I06.2, 02RF0JZ
    d. I35.0, 02RF0JZ
24. A patient is admitted for an open reduction with internal fixation of a closed distal fibula fracture, left. (Initial encounter.) Which codes are reported?
    a. S82.92xA, 0QSK05Z
    b. S82.302A, 0QSK05Z
    c. S82.832A, 0QSK04Z
    d. S82.92xA, 0QSK04Z
25. A patient undergoes a carpal tunnel release procedure on the right wrist. Postoperatively, she experienced bradycardia. Medication for the bradycardia is administered, and the patient is monitored in the cardiac care unit for 36 hours before release. Which codes are reported?
    a. G56.00, R00.1, Y83.8, 01N50ZZ
    b. G56.01, I97.89, R00.1, Y83.8, 01N50ZZ
    c. G56.02, R00.1, Y83.8, 01N50ZZ
    d. G56.11, I97.88, R00.1, 01N50ZZ
26. A patient is admitted for open resection of the lining of the maxillary sinus membrane, bilaterally, due to chronic maxillary sinusitis. Which codes are reported?
    a. J32.0, 09TK0ZZ
    b. J32.0, 09TN0ZZ
    c. J32.0, 09TQ0ZZ, 09TR0ZZ
    d. J32.9, 09TK0ZZ

ICD-10-CM Outpatient and Physician Office Coding

CHAPTER 7

INTRODUCTION

This chapter includes application-based assignments that allow students to apply ICD-10-CM general and outpatient coding guidelines to the assignment of diagnosis codes to outpatient case scenarios, which incorporate abbreviations and lab values that students are expected to interpret. Students also complete assignments to practice the physician query process for outpatient cases, interpret diagnostic and reporting guidelines for outpatient services and ICD-10-CM coding guidelines for outpatient diagnostic tests, and assign APCs and RBRVs.

NOTE:

ICD-10-PCS codes are assigned to inpatient procedures only. Chapter 5 of this workbook provided ICD-10-PCS coding practice.

ASSIGNMENT 7.1 – PHYSICIAN QUERY PROCESS

Objectives

At the conclusion of this assignment, the student should be able to:

- Explain the concept of *physician query* regarding the ICD-10-CM coding of outpatient diagnosis statements.
- Identify situations in which *physician query* for outpatient cases is appropriate.

Overview

Coders are prohibited from performing *assumption coding*, which is the assignment of codes based on assuming, from a review of clinical evidence in the patient's record, that the patient has certain diagnoses or has received certain procedures/services even though the provider did not specifically document those diagnoses or procedures/services. Assumption coding is considered fraud because the coder assumes certain facts about a patient's condition or procedures/services, although the physician has not specifically documented the level of detail to which the coder assigns codes. Coders can avoid fraudulent *assumption coding* by implementing the *physician query process*, which involves contacting the responsible physician to request clarification. The process is activated when the coder notices a problem with documentation quality (e.g., incomplete diagnostic statement when clinical documentation indicates that a more specific ICD-10-CM code should be assigned).

NOTE:

- Remember! You are allowed to assign an ICD-10-CM code to a diagnosis, a sign, a symptom, or an ill-defined condition if the physician does not list it as final diagnosis as long as the physician's documentation is clear and consistent. If the coder is uncertain about whether to code a diagnosis because documentation is contradictory, incomplete, or vague, the coder should query the physician to determine if the diagnosis should be a part of the final diagnosis.
- Chapter 1 of your textbook contains information about the physician query process.

Instructions

Read each case scenario carefully and select the statement below the case that best represents the action the coder should take when reporting outpatient diagnosis and procedure codes. As you review each case, make sure you look up any unfamiliar abbreviations and lab values. Be prepared to defend your selected statement.

1. A patient presents to the hospital ED complaining of "severe facial pain" and "headache." After radiographic studies, the radiologist determines that the patient has "frontal sinusitis." The patient is discharged with a prescription for antibiotics and directed to follow up with his family doctor in two days. On the ED record, the physician documents the diagnoses for this patient as headache, facial pain, and sinusitis. The coder should:
   a. assign a code for "sinusitis, unspecified" alone.
   b. assign a code for "sinusitis, unspecified," "headache," and "facial pain."
   c. assign a code for "frontal sinusitis."
   d. query the physician to ask if "frontal sinusitis" should be documented as a final diagnosis.
2. Mary Caulfield presents to her primary physician's office with a complaint of abdominal pain. Mary is seen and examined by her physician, Dr. Stone. In his examination note, Dr. Stone documents that Mary has epigastric abdominal pain and abdominal tenderness as well as history of type 2 diabetes mellitus and hypertension. Dr. Stone refers Mary to the local outpatient radiology center for diagnostic studies to further evaluate her abdominal pain. Dr. Stone also orders blood glucose testing for Mary and writes a refill prescription for her hypertensive medication, Verelan. He documents the diagnosis as epigastric abdominal pain and abdominal tenderness. The coder should:
   a. assign codes for abdominal pain, abdominal tenderness, type 2 diabetes mellitus, and hypertension.
   b. assign codes for abdominal pain and abdominal tenderness and report them on the CMS-1500 claim.
   c. query the physician to ask whether abdominal pain or abdominal tenderness should be documented.
   d. query the physician to ask whether type 2 diabetes mellitus and hypertension should be included in the final diagnosis.
3. A 10-year-old female patient presents to the hospital ED following a fall from a jungle gym. The patient is complaining of arm pain. The ED physician examines the patient and orders radiographic films of the child's right arm, wrist, and hand. The radiologist's report indicates a normal forearm and hand x-ray. However, the wrist x-ray reveals that the child has a Colles' fracture. The patient's wrist is placed in a cast, and she is discharged from the ED. On her ED record, the physician documents "Colles' fracture." The ED coder locates the code for Colles' fracture. The coder should:
   a. assign and report a code for the Colles' fracture.
   b. assign codes for the Colles' fracture, forearm fracture, and hand fracture.
   c. query the physician to ask that the wrist x-ray be properly documented.
   d. query the physician to ask whether "arm pain" should also be coded.

4. John Novell presents to his physician's office with the complaint of a rash. Mr. Novell is examined, and his record contains the following documentation:

   S: Patient presents with a one-day history of itching, which appeared about three days after he had been bitten by a spider.

   O: Patient has multiple swollen raised areas of the skin of his left forearm.

   A: Rash due to spider bite.

   P: The patient received Benadryl in the office. He was directed to take another dosage of Benadryl in 12 hours if the itching does not subside. The patient is to follow up in two days if there is no resolution of his symptoms.

   The coder should:
   a. assign and report a code for rash first and then a code for spider bite.
   b. assign and report a code for spider bite first and then a code for rash.
   c. query the physician to ask whether "itching" should be coded.
   d. query the physician to ask whether "swelling" should be coded.

5. A patient is admitted for a laparoscopic cholecystectomy. The preoperative diagnosis is "cholecystitis with cholelithiasis." On the operative report, the postoperative diagnoses are documented as "obstructive cholecystitis" and "chronic cholecystitis with cholelithiasis." The postoperative diagnoses are confirmed by the pathology report. The face sheet has "cholecystitis" documented as the final diagnosis. The coder should:
   a. assign a code to "chronic cholecystitis" because it is documented on the face sheet of the record.
   b. assign codes to the postoperative diagnoses "obstructive cholecystitis" and "chronic cholecystitis with cholelithiasis" from the operative report.
   c. query the surgeon to ask whether the postoperative diagnoses should be documented on the face sheet.
   d. query the pathologist to request the results of the pathology report before assigning any diagnosis codes.

Instructions

Read each case scenario carefully and respond to the question located below the case. Make sure you include statement(s) justifying your answer.

6. Kevin Maxwell presents to a dermatologist's office with the complaint of a lesion on his nose. The patient is examined, and the lesion is removed and sent to pathology for analysis. The patient is scheduled for a follow-up appointment in two weeks. Discharge diagnosis documented by the physician is "lesion of the nose." The pathology report is present and located in the patient's record when the office visit is coded for insurance purposes. The pathologist documents "actinic keratosis" on the pathology report.

   Upon review of this case, the coder should ______________________________
   because ____.

7. During the follow-up visit with Mr. Maxwell, the physician reviews the pathology report with him. During that visit, the patient reports that he has a lesion under his arm that is bothering him. The dermatologist examines the patient, determines that he has a skin tag, and removes that lesion. The dermatologist does not document a diagnosis.

   Upon review of this case, the coder should ______________________________
   because ____.

8. Mrs. Scott presents to her physician's office for a six-month checkup. Mrs. Scott has a history of "hypertension" and "osteoarthritis of the hip," and she is a seven-year breast cancer survivor. Upon questioning, Mrs. Scott reports a decrease in her activity level due to "fatigue" and "blurred vision." Her weight during this encounter is documented as 175 pounds, which is an increase of 25 pounds since her last visit six months ago. On Mrs. Scott's encounter form, the physician orders a "fasting blood glucose." Diagnoses documented on the record include "hypertension" and "osteoarthritis."

   Upon review of this case, the coder should ______________________________
   because ______________________________.

9. A patient presents to the hospital ED with complaints of flank pain, abdominal pain, and dysuria. The patient is examined by the ED physician and submits a urine sample; the UA reveals WBCs too numerous to count. The patient is discharged from the ED with a prescription for antibiotics to be taken for 10 days. No final diagnosis is listed on the ED record.

   Upon review of this case, the coder should ______________________________
   because ______________________________.

10. A 23-year-old female presents to her local clinic on a Monday morning. She states that she was cooking outside on Sunday using a portable grill, which tipped over. Hot coals fell on her lower leg and foot. She is experiencing pain of this area with noticeable blistering. The discharge diagnosis is "burn, leg and foot."

   Upon review of this case, the coder should ______________________________
   because ______________________________.

ASSIGNMENT 7.2 – DIAGNOSTIC CODING AND REPORTING GUIDELINES FOR OUTPATIENT SERVICES: HOSPITAL-BASED AND PHYSICIAN OFFICE

Objectives

At the conclusion of this assignment, the student should be able to:

- List and explain the diagnostic coding and reporting guidelines for outpatient services.
- Assign ICD-10-CM codes to diagnostic statements by interpreting the diagnostic coding and reporting guidelines for outpatient services.
- Interpret abbreviations and lab values to assign ICD-10-CM diagnosis codes appropriately.

Overview

The diagnostic coding and reporting guidelines for outpatient services were developed by the federal government and have been approved for use by hospitals and providers for coding and reporting hospital-based outpatient services and provider-based office visits. When reviewing the coding guidelines, remember that the terms *encounter* and *visit* are used interchangeably when describing outpatient and physician office services. In addition, you will notice that some outpatient coding guidelines were previously discussed in the general coding guidelines.

Instructions

Assign ICD-10-CM codes to the following diagnostic statements. When multiple codes are assigned, make sure you sequence them properly according to coding conventions and guidelines, including the definition of first-listed diagnosis. Refer to the diagnostic coding and reporting guidelines for outpatient services in your textbook when assigning codes.

______________________ 1. Fever, difficulty swallowing, acute tonsillitis

______________________ 2. Chest pain, rule out arteriosclerotic heart disease

______________________ 3. Hypertension, acute bronchitis, family history of lung cancer

_______________ 4. Lipoma, subcutaneous tissue of left thigh

_______________ 5. Audible wheezing, acute exacerbation of asthma

_______________ 6. Routine annual gynecological visit and exam with Pap smear

_______________ 7. Laceration of right forearm, severe pain of the left ankle and left wrist, possible left ankle fracture, possible left wrist fracture

_______________ 8. Pregnancy visit (normal female at 16 weeks, first pregnancy)

_______________ 9. Renal calculi with hematuria

_______________ 10. Encounter for occupational therapy, aphasia due to previous cerebrovascular accident

_______________ 11. Fever, throat pain, acute otitis media, rule out thrush, hemangioma of skin of the face

_______________ 12. Epstein-Barr mononucleosis

_______________ 13. Severe nausea and vomiting, gastroenteritis due to salmonella food poisoning

_______________ 14. Congestive heart failure with bilateral leg edema

_______________ 15. Elevated fasting blood glucose level of 145 mg/dL

_______________ 16. Gastroesophageal reflux disease

_______________ 17. Severe headache, stuffy nose, allergic sinusitis

_______________ 18. Epigastric abdominal pain, fever, vomiting, tachycardia, acute pancreatitis, cellulitis of right finger

_______________ 19. Pyogenic arthritis of right knee due to *Haemophilus influenzae*

_______________ 20. Acute pericarditis due to tuberculosis

ASSIGNMENT 7.3 – SELECTING THE FIRST-LISTED DIAGNOSIS AND LINKING DIAGNOSES WITH PROCEDURES/SERVICES FOR MEDICAL NECESSITY

Objectives

At the conclusion of this assignment, the student should be able to:

- Identify the first-listed diagnosis upon review of conditions, diagnoses, and signs/symptoms.
- Link diagnoses with procedures/services to justify medical necessity.
- Interpret general ICD-10-CM coding guidelines, diagnostic coding and reporting guidelines for outpatient services, and coding guidelines for outpatient diagnostic tests.
- Review case studies and patient records and appropriately assign ICD-10-CM codes to diagnostic statements.
- Interpret abbreviations and lab values in patient records to assign ICD-10-CM diagnosis codes appropriately.

Overview

In the outpatient setting, the *first-listed diagnosis is reported* (instead of the inpatient setting's *principal diagnosis*), and it is the condition chiefly responsible for the outpatient services provided during the encounter/visit. It is determined in accordance with ICD-10-CM *coding conventions* (or rules) as well as general and disease-specific coding guidelines. Because diagnoses are often not established at the time of the patient's initial encounter or visit, two or more visits may be required before the diagnosis is confirmed.

When outpatient records are reviewed for the selection of ICD-10-CM codes to report to third-party payers, documentation in the patient record serves as the basis for coding. This means that information in the record supports the codes submitted on claims for third-party payer reimbursement processing. The patient's diagnosis must justify diagnostic and/or therapeutic procedures or services provided, which is called *medical necessity*. Claims are also denied if the *medical necessity* of procedures or services is not established—every procedure or service reported on the health insurance claim must be linked to a condition that justifies the necessity for performing that procedure or providing that service. If the procedures or services delivered are determined to be unreasonable and unnecessary, the claim is denied.

Assigning ICD-10-CM codes to diagnostic statements in previous exercises allowed you to develop skills in interpreting and applying coding conventions and guidelines. Reviewing patient records to locate diagnostic statements and assigning ICD-10-CM codes will further develop your coding skills.

Selecting the First-Listed Diagnosis

Review each case and underline the first-listed diagnosis.

> **EXAMPLE:** Patient was seen in the office to rule out cervical radiculopathy. Patient has a recent history of pain in both scapular regions along with spasms of the left upper trapezius muscle. Patient has limited range of motion, neck and left arm. X-rays reveal significant *cervical osteoarthritis.*
>
> Do not select differential diagnoses such as "rule out cervical radiculopathy" as the answer because such diagnoses are not coded and reported on the CMS-1500 claim for outpatient cases. "Spasms of the left upper trapezius muscle" and "limited range of motion, neck and left arm" are symptoms of *cervical osteoarthritis,* which is reported as the first-listed diagnosis in block 21, line 1, of the CMS-1500 claim.

1. Pain, left knee. History of injury to left knee 20 years ago. Patient underwent arthroscopic surgery and medial meniscectomy, right knee (10 years ago). Probable arthritis, left knee.
2. Patient admitted to the emergency department with complaints of severe chest pain. Possible myocardial infarction. EKG and cardiac enzymes revealed normal findings. Diagnosis upon discharge was gastroesophageal reflux disease.
3. Female patient seen in the office for follow-up of hypertension. The nurse noticed upper arm bruising on the patient and asked how she sustained the bruising. The physician renewed the patient's hypertension prescription of hydrochlorothiazide.
4. A 10-year-old male was seen in the office for sore throat. Nurse swabbed patient's throat and sent swabs to the hospital lab for strep test. Physician documented "likely strep throat" on the patient's record.
5. Patient was seen in the outpatient department to have a lump in his abdomen evaluated and removed. Surgeon removed the lump, and pathology report revealed that the lump was a lipoma.

Linking Diagnoses with Procedures/Services for Medical Necessity

Match the diagnosis in Column 2 with the procedure in Column 1 that justifies medical necessity for the procedure.

	Procedure	**Diagnosis**
___	6. Allergy test	a. Bronchial asthma
___	7. EKG	b. Chest pain
___	8. Inhalation treatment	c. Family history, cervical cancer
___	9. Pap smear	d. Fractured wrist
___	10. Removal of ear wax	e. Hay fever
___	11. Sigmoidoscopy	f. Hematuria
___	12. Strep test	g. Impacted cerumen
___	13. Urinalysis	h. Jaundice
___	14. Venipuncture	i. Rectal bleeding
___	15. X-ray, radius and ulna	j. Sore throat

ASSIGNMENT 7.4 – CODING PRACTICE

Instructions

Carefully review each case study below, determine the diagnoses to be coded, and assign ICD-10-CM codes to each. Make sure you sequence codes properly according to coding conventions and guidelines, including the definition of first-listed diagnosis. Refer to the coding guidelines for outpatient diagnostic tests in your textbook when assigning codes.

Ambulatory Surgery Center (ASC)

1. A 16-year-old patient developed a nodule in the left lobe of the thyroid. The clinical working diagnosis was autoimmune thyroiditis. Ultrasound of the thyroid revealed a hypoechoic nodule, and thyroid function tests were within normal limits. Fine-needle aspiration was nondiagnostic, left thyroid lobectomy was performed, and pathology report revealed a diagnosis of dyshormonogenic goiter.

   DIAGNOSIS: Dyshormonogenic goiter.

   ____

2. Patient is a 5-year-old white male with history of a right undescended testicle since birth. He is scheduled at this time for right orchiopexy.

   PHYSICAL EXAMINATION: Lungs clear. Heart regular; 3/6 systolic murmur heard best at the right sternal border. Abdomen soft. No CVA tenderness. Genital examination showed a circumcised penis. Testis was down on the left side, and the right testis was in the area of the external ring.

   LABORATORY VALUES: Hemoglobin 13.5. Normal differential. Urinalysis unremarkable. Chest x-ray normal. Patient was admitted to the short stay unit and on the day of admission underwent right inguinal herniorrhaphy and right orchiopexy. Postoperatively, the patient did well. There were no apparent anesthesia complications, and he was discharged to home the afternoon after surgery.

   DIAGNOSES: Right inguinal hernia and right abdominal cryptorchidism.

   ____

3. This 63-year-old white male was seen with chief complaint of large right indirect inguinal hernia, which is easily reduced but has been painful and is getting larger.

   PHYSICAL EXAMINATION: Large right indirect inguinal hernia easily reduced. Also noted 1+ benign prostatic hypertrophy. The patient was prepared for surgery; under satisfactory general anesthesia, a right indirect inguinal hernia was repaired and a lipoma of the spermatic cord removed. Following the operation, he had an uncomplicated postoperative recovery. He was awake and alert, and he had no anesthetic complications. He is released to see Dr. Smith in one week and me in two weeks or immediately if there is any evidence of wound infection.

   DIAGNOSIS: Right indirect inguinal hernia.

   ____

4. Patient is a 40-year-old white female who in June had a sudden exacerbation of right upper quadrant and midepigastric pain radiating around both subcostal margins to the back. She saw Dr. Cosby, who ordered the appropriate studies; the patient was found to have acute cholecystitis. Within a very short period of time, she proceeded to get right lower quadrant pain. Just before she was due to see me in the office about her gallbladder, I saw her in the emergency room with right lower quadrant pain. She had acute appendicitis. She had an appendectomy at that time, and she has done fairly well during the three months or so since then. But recently she began to have abdominal pain intermittently; on five occasions within a week prior to admission, she began having severe pain and could hardly eat anything at all. She had no evidence of jaundice or hepatitis. The pain would last several hours at

times, and she had not been able to eat anything well. I saw her, and we proceeded to make arrangements for cholecystectomy and operative cholangiography. She did not take any medication regularly at the time of admission. Past medical history reveals that she had an appendectomy, no other surgery, no known medical illnesses or drug allergies. She did have wisdom teeth removed in the past. At the time of surgery, she's a well-developed, well-nourished white female in no apparent distress. Vital signs are stable; she was afebrile and in no pain at that time. Physical examination revealed, other than an obese abdominal wall, that the abdominal exam was unremarkable. The rest of the physical exam was consistent with age, and body habitus was generally within normal limits. Chest x-ray was normal. EKG showed no acute changes. CBC was normal. She was taken to the operating room, where she was under antibiotic prophylaxis. Cholecystectomy and operative cholangiography were done.

DIAGNOSES: Chronic cholecystitis, quite symptomatic, with acute cholecystitis.

____

5. The patient is a 46-year-old white male who was seen in the office on December 19. At that time, he was complaining of a nodule on both testicles, which he had seen for two months. He stated they were initially felt to be a cyst of the tunica albuginea of the testicle. He was reassured at that time and instructed to return in six weeks. When he returned for a follow-up visit, it was thought that this area had increased in size and was nontender. But in view of the fact that it had changed in size, I thought that we should explore him to biopsy and remove this area. The possibility of a testicular tumor was also considered. Physical examination was remarkable only for a 0.5-cm nodule, which extended off the surface of the testicle near the lateral aspect of the head of the epididymis on the right side. The left testicle felt normal.

   LABORATORY VALUES: Chest x-ray was normal. Urinalysis showed 0–1 white cells. The patient was admitted the morning of surgery, and under general endotracheal anesthesia had a right inguinal exploration with removal of what then became apparent as a multicystic epididymis with a small spermatocele. The upper third of the epididymis was removed along with the spermatocele. Postoperatively, the patient did well, tolerated adequate diet, and was discharged in good condition.

   DIAGNOSIS: Right spermatocele, multiple cysts.

   ____

Chiropractic Office

6. Mr. Davis, a 52-year-old CPA, presents with a complaint of neck and right shoulder pain accompanied with frequent right arm numbness of three weeks' duration following a busy tax season. Physical examination procedures lead to a diagnosis of thoracic outlet syndrome. Treatment consists of chiropractic manipulative treatment and therapeutic stretching of the cervical and thoracic region.

   ____

7. Mr. Clark, a 61-year-old farmer, presents with a complaint of right gluteal pain with pain radiating down his right leg posteriorly of one-day duration following prolonged operation of a tractor. Physical examination procedures confirm a diagnosis of sciatica. Treatment consisted of chiropractic manipulative treatment of the sacral region and electrical stimulation application.

   DIAGNOSIS: Sciatica, right.

   ____

8. Cheryl Miller, a 12-year-old female, presents with a complaint of low back pain following a gymnastic recital one day prior. Physical examination procedures lead to a diagnosis of lumbar radiculitis. Treatment consists of chiropractic manipulative treatment and traction of the lumbar spine.

____

9. Ms. Greeley, a 45-year-old author, presents with a complaint of generalized neck pain of one week's duration after several days of long hours at her computer. Physical examination procedures lead to a diagnosis of myalgia, neck. Treatment consists of chiropractic manipulative treatment and massage of the cervical region.

____

10. Ms. Thomas, a 27-year-old receptionist, presents with a complaint of neck pain with muscle spasms after sneezing two hours prior. Physical examination procedures confirm a diagnosis of cervical (neck) strain. Treatment consists of chiropractic manipulative treatment and application of ultrasound to the cervical region. (Initial encounter.)

____

Hospital Emergency Department

11. Patient referred to me by Dr. Brown on 9/19. Dr. Brown had seen the patient twice as an outpatient for problems with swallowing and pain and discomfort in his throat. She believed there was a problem in the throat, possibly a strep pharyngitis. The patient came to the hospital ED, arriving at 1600 on 9/19. Shortly thereafter, I interviewed the patient. During the course of the interview, it became apparent that his symptoms were those of esophageal obstruction; I quickly arranged for him to go to the radiology department for a barium swallow, which was perplexing in that there appeared to be an obstruction of an unusual type. The radiologist was called in and evaluated the obstruction, and then we talked with Dr. Ardell concerning the apparent lesion. Dr. Ardell thought the lesion was too high for him to do gastroscopy safely. For this reason, they suggested (and I concurred) that we refer him to an ear, nose, and throat specialist at the county clinic. The patient was in full agreement with this. No laboratory studies were done at this time. His respirations were 20, blood pressure 120/66, weight 178, all recorded by the nurses.

    DIAGNOSIS: Esophageal obstruction.

____

12. The patient was examined in the ED and found to have a large fungating, pigmented lesion 2 cm in diameter over the left temporal area near the ear. With the patient in a supine position and his head rotated to the right, the left side of his face and head were prepared with pHisoHex and draped with sterile drapes. Marcaine anesthesia 0.5% solution was infiltrated in the skin and subcutaneous tissues about the lesion, and about 5 cc of solution was used. Then the lesion was excised by elliptical incision, trying to stay in normal skin and taking the subcutaneous tissues with it. Bleeding points were ligated with 4-0 Vicryl ligatures. The wound was prepared with pHisoHex and then closed with interrupted 4-0 Prolene suture in a vertical mattress type of suture. The wound was prepared with pHisoHex. Following this, the patient withstood the procedure well and returned home awake and in good condition. He has been instructed to return immediately if there is any evidence of infection such as excessive pain, tenderness, redness, swelling, bleeding, discharge, red streaks, or fever. Otherwise, he should see me in about 9 or 10 days for removal of the sutures.

    DIAGNOSIS: Pigmented lesion, skin of left temporal area near the ear (2 cm).

____

13. A 31-year-old male was seen in the ED for pain and swelling of his right middle finger. He had been working with some PVC pipe and had a fragment of it enter his finger just over the PIP joint. He was seen in the ED at that time and had the fragment extracted under local anesthesia. The wound pulled was approximately 3/8 inches long. Overnight the finger became very swollen and sore, and the patient returns to the ED this evening for subsequent care. X-rays reveal no apparent injury to the bony structures. There is no apparent abscess present. The wound is not draining, although the finger is red and very tender.

    ASSESSMENT: Infection of puncture wound, right middle finger.

    PLAN: Keflex 500 milligrams 4 times daily, warm soaks to the finger (if possible 4 × daily), and rechecked in 24 hours. (Subsequent encounter.)

    ____

14. This 81-year-old female presented to the ED with a complaint of right foot pain. The patient stated that she bumped the foot one month ago, and ever since then she has had intermittent pain in the right great toe. Physical exam of the right foot reveals that the patient has a significant bunion over the first metatarsal head. The patient is tender minimally in this area. There is some redness, but no significant warmth to touch. The patient has full range of motion of the toe, with moderate pain. X-ray of the first great toe of the right foot reveals no fractures.

    DIAGNOSIS: Right foot pain. Sprain of the right great toe versus early gout.

    TREATMENT: Uric acid level was drawn; this was 6.6, which was within the normal range. Because of the patient's physical findings, I did not think that it would be appropriate to tap her joint at this time. I will start her on Motrin 600 milligrams 3 times daily, and she will see Dr. Thomas in five days. The patient was instructed that if the pain worsens or does not show some improvement before she can see Dr. Thomas, she should return to the emergency department, at which time further evaluation and possible tapping of the joint will be undertaken.

    ____

15. This 39-year-old male states that ever since he can remember he has had episodes where he blacked out. Patient states that over the last few days, this seems to have increased in frequency. Today, the patient had a near syncopal episode and one episode where he did completely lose consciousness. Patient states he will occasionally get a pain in his left arm before he has a syncopal episode. He also feels somewhat lightheaded.

    PHYSICAL EXAMINATION: This 39-year-old male is alert, well nourished, and appears in no distress. HEENT is unremarkable. Neck is supple, lungs are clear, heart is regular rate and rhythm (RRR), and abdomen is soft and nontender. Neurological exam is completely within normal limits. EKG shows sinus rhythm with no myocardial changes. CBC shows a white count of 8,000 with a normal differential. Electrolytes, BUN, and glucose are all normal.

    DIAGNOSIS: Periodic syncopal episodes of questionable etiology.

    TREATMENT: I reassured the patient at this time that nothing significant could be found. He was told to contact Dr. Morrow (his family physician) for further evaluation of this problem. If it recurs or becomes worse in the meantime, he is to return to the emergency department for further evaluation.

    ____

Hospital Outpatient Department

16. A 31-year-old male patient previously diagnosed with end-stage renal disease (ESRD) and diabetic nephropathy due to type 1 diabetes mellitus and aggravated by chronic alcoholism undergoes scheduled dialysis. The dialysis technician starts dialysis. It soon becomes apparent that the patient is drunk because after just 20 minutes of dialysis treatment, the patient becomes belligerent, yanks out the needles, and leaves the hospital.

    DIAGNOSES: End-stage renal disease. Diabetic nephropathy due to type 1 diabetes mellitus. Chronic alcoholism.

    ____

17. A 59-year-old woman who presents to the outpatient pain clinic has suffered from the occurrence of severe headaches each week for the past 35 years. Upon assessment, it is determined that the headaches are cervicogenic in origin. Cephalic cervical nerve block was administered, and the patient was scheduled to return for a follow-up visit in 30 days. She was also instructed to call if the headaches recurred before her scheduled visit.

    DIAGNOSIS: Recurrent headaches.

    ____

18. Patient seen in the outpatient clinic for suspected cholecystitis. The patient reports right upper quadrant (RUQ) abdominal pain. Family history is positive for cholecystitis with cholelithiasis and cholecystectomy. Laboratory work reveals mild hyperglycemia, which apparently has been under control with oral antidiabetic agents. Chest x-ray is negative. Blood tests revealed that bilirubin is essentially negative, but there is slightly elevated alkaline phosphatase. Blood chemistry tests indicate that sodium, CO_2, and chloride results are somewhat depressed. Potassium is normal. Ultrasound of gallbladder reveals significant hypertrophy.

    DIAGNOSES: Hypertrophy of gallbladder. Right upper quadrant abdominal pain. Mild hyperglycemia. Abnormal blood chemistry levels. Probable cholecystitis.

    ____

19. This 18-month-old male with a past history of having undergone elective repair of right inguinal hernia and right hydrocele presents for evaluation of possible left-sided strabismus. Surgical wound is healing nicely, and the patient is experiencing no complaints related to the surgery. The patient was cleared by the surgeon last week in his office. The patient's medical history reveals an uncomplicated medical history and surgical history. He has no known allergies or illnesses. He has had an appropriate development. It is noted today that he does have strabismus, which has not been previously evaluated by an ophthalmologist. All immunizations by history have been up-to-date. There is no appreciable family or social history that is contributory. Physical exam reveals appropriate growth and development for this 18-month-old male. His left-sided strabismus is noted. Ears were clear bilaterally with some cerumen retained, but tympanic membranes were observed. Nasal septum midline. Posterior pharynx is noninjected. Neck is supple without lymphadenopathy. Lungs auscultated clear to base. Cardiac was RRR without S3, S4, or murmurs auscultated. The abdomen was soft without organomegaly or masses. Patient was circumcised. Patient is referred to Dr. Allen, Ophthalmologist, for evaluation of strabismus.

    DIAGNOSIS: Strabismus, left eye.

    ____

20. This 5-year-old child is seen for evaluation of temperature of 103°F, which has lasted three days and has not been controlled by Tylenol or Motrin. The lungs are clear. The neck is no longer rigid. The pharynx is slightly injected. Strep test performed, and results are pending lab evaluation. Spinal tap L3 and L4 performed without difficulty. The fluid is crystal clear and is sent to the laboratory. Lab results were negative.

    DIAGNOSES: Elevated temperature. Sore throat. Possible strep throat.

    ____

Hospital Same Day Surgery

21. This is a 75-year-old white female presenting with a recent increase in size of her thyroid gland on the right side. It gives her trouble swallowing but is otherwise asymptomatic for thyroid disease. She has had a thyroid mass for many years. There is no family history of thyroid disease. Thyroid scan shows a large nodule, and ultrasound reveals that the mass is mostly solid but with some cystic component. She is euthyroid. Past medical history is positive for coronary artery disease with angina, recent cataract surgery on the left eye, congestive heart failure, hypertension, and adult-onset diabetes mellitus. Medications: Isordil 20 mg by mouth every 6 hours, propranolol 80 mg by mouth every 6 hours, hydrochlorothiazide 100 mg by mouth 4 times daily, Nitro-Bid paste 1½ inch every evening, nitroglycerin 0.4 milligrams sublingual as needed, Valium 10 mg by mouth 3 times daily. No allergies. No smoking. No ethanol use.

    REVIEW OF SYSTEMS: Positive for two-pillow orthopnea, nocturia times 2; occasionally paroxysmal nocturnal dyspnea and edema, none recently, however. Dipstick reveals 1 to 2+ sugar in urine. The patient has lost about 25 pounds on the recent diet. Physical: HEENT: Left cataract removed, right eye with cataract, thyroid not inflamed. Neck: Supple, thyroid enlarged on right side extending to isthmus. Left side feels normal. Lungs: Clear. Breasts: Benign. Heart: Regular rate with positive S4, no murmur heard. Abdomen: Protruberant umbilical hernias, soft, nontender, no masses. Extremities: No edema, pulses 2+ and symmetrical and no focal motor or neurological deficits. Impression: Thyroid nodule. On 4/13, the patient was taken to the operating room where she underwent subtotal thyroidectomy for her enlarged thyroid. Frozen section diagnosis was nodular thyroid tissue consistent with follicular adenomas. She underwent the surgery well and did well in her postoperative course. Blood pressure was 130/80. She will be discharged today on her preadmission medications. She will be seen by Dr. Numann by appointment.

    DIAGNOSES: Thyroid follicular adenoma. Hypertension.

    ____

22. The patient was admitted with gross hematuria following a long duration of prostatic symptoms and intermittent hematuria for several days. After the insertion of the Foley catheter and drainage of 400 cc of grossly bloody urine, chemistry tests revealed that he was in chronic renal insufficiency with a BUN of 66. His urinary output was very adequate. IVP showed poorly functioning kidneys but enough also to show an elevation of the bladder floor consistent with enlarged prostate (benign). Cystoscopy was carried out to rule out other causes of hematuria and the bladder found to be heavily trabeculated with many diverticuli and again a large prostatic gland.

    DIAGNOSES: Chronic renal insufficiency. Bladder diverticula. Benign prostatic hypertrophy.

    ____

23. This 17-year-old white female was admitted to the hospital with the chief complaint of a past history of recurrent bouts of tonsillitis, having missed three days of school this year because of a severe bout and having another sore throat that started as soon as the penicillin stopped. She also has had earaches. She has had streptococcal sore throats. She consulted Dr. Port, who advised her to have a T&A. Physical examination revealed the tonsils to be large, but they appeared benign at the time of admission. She had an anterior lymphadenopathy. Laboratory studies on admission revealed hemoglobin 13.3 grams,

hematocrit 39.6, and white blood count 6700 with 42 polys. Urinalysis was negative. The bleeding time was 1 minute 30 seconds. Partial prothrombin time was 24 seconds. Chest x-ray normal. The patient was admitted to the hospital, prepared for surgery, and taken to the operating room where, under satisfactory general endotracheal anesthesia, a T&A was performed. Following the operation, she had an uncomplicated postoperative recovery. That afternoon she was awake, alert, and afebrile; had no bleeding; no anesthetic complications. The tonsillar fossa were clean; she is accordingly discharged on April 13 to see Dr. Port in one week and me in two weeks.

DIAGNOSES: Diseased and hypertrophied tonsils and adenoids. Past history of recurrent bouts of streptococcal sore throats and tonsillitis.

____

24. This is a 15-year-old who was involved in a truck and bicycle accident in August. He continued to have problems with his right knee. He was referred to Dr. Jones, who diagnosed him as having torn medial meniscus of right knee as the sequela of previous fracture right patella and knee soft tissue injuries. Patient was admitted to the hospital on August 17 and underwent surgery that consisted of arthrotomy and medial meniscectomy of right knee. Patient did well on a postoperative period and was sent home in good condition.

    DIAGNOSIS: Bucket-handle tear of medial meniscus, right knee. (Sequela.)

____

25. Two weeks ago on a routine examination, Dr. Woughter detected a firm ridge in the right lobe of the prostate, became suspicious, and suggested to the patient that he have this biopsied at an early date. Patient presents now for biopsy procedure. A needle biopsy of the prostate reveals adenocarcinoma of prostate. Pathology results report adenocarcinoma of prostate. I have advised a radical prostatectomy.

    DIAGNOSIS: Carcinoma of prostate.

____

Physician Office

26. This 27-year-old white male was working at home in his workshop, making a toy for his daughter, when he accidentally punctured his left fourth finger with a drift pin. The patient states that the pin entered from the radial aspect and exited through the ulnar aspect of the finger. Physical exam reveals a puncture wound through and through on the pad of the left ring finger. X-rays of the finger show no evidence of involvement of the bone. The patient was given a tetanus-diphtheria booster. The wound was debrided and cleaned with Betadine, and Betadine ointment was placed over the wound.

    DIAGNOSIS: Puncture wound, left ring finger.

    PLAN: The patient was instructed to soak the finger with half hydrogen peroxide and half water three or four times a day for four to five days; he is to return immediately if any signs of infection appear. (Initial encounter.)

____

27. This man was participating in a softball tournament this weekend. He has had brief episodes of dizziness off and on for about a week, which last for 20 minutes and occur once a day. He is dizzy at this time; at other times, his left ear feels plugged up. No history of any injury or trauma. His vitals are all stable. Neurological exam is completely unremarkable. No evidence of any other symptomatology, such as chest pain. He has no carotid bruits. ENT okay. Neck: Supple, no nodes or thyroid abnormalities. Chest: Peripheral lung fields are clear. Heart sounds are good. Eyes: Disc margins are sharp. No evidence of any increased pressure. His BP was 120/80. Romberg is negative. He is steady on his feet. His left ear is slightly dull, and I suspect that he has a low-grade serous otitis media. I started him on Pen-Vee K 500 mg

4 times daily along with 1 Actifed tablet 4 times daily with the understanding that if he has any increase in symptoms or any persistence of symptoms beyond two or three days, he is to be rechecked by his family physician at home. If that were to be the case, he would need a central nervous system workup.

DIAGNOSIS: Low-grade serous otitis media, left.

____

28. This young man walked into a tree limb while setting traps last week, and he lacerated the left cornea. I could see no hyphema when he came in for an office visit at that time, but the anterior chamber may have been affected. He returns for an office visit three weeks later because he has blurred vision, and I could not see well into the eye when he was treated during his last visit. He is now being referred to Dr. Andrews for further and more definitive evaluation and treatment.

DIAGNOSIS: Laceration, left cornea. Blurred vision. (Subsequent encounter.)

____

29. This young lady came to the office due to laryngitis and quite a cough. Chest x-ray did not show any specific consolidation, but I suspect bronchitis. She had a white count of 10,300. Hgb was 13.5 gm %; she had 71 segs, 18 lymphs, 7 monos, 1 eosinophil, and 3 band cells. She is being started on 500 mg of V-Cillin-K four times daily for one day and then 250 mg 4 times daily for eight days along with Phenergan expectorant. She is to return to her family physician in four to six days for follow-up care.

DIAGNOSIS: Bronchitis.

____

30. This young lady apparently did something to injure her right hip approximately two weeks prior to her arrival in the office. When she arrived here, she was ambulatory but had some soreness in the lateral surface of the hip. Range of motion of the leg and hip was perfectly okay. She has no neurological deficits of either leg. Deep tendon reflexes were equal and active, no sensory loss; no low back pain as such. X-rays were taken of the lumbar spine and hip and reported as normal. She is being treated symptomatically with warm soaks, Equagesic 2 every 6 hours, and recheck in the office in three or four days.

DIAGNOSIS: Sprain, right hip and ligaments of lumbar spine. (Initial encounter.)

____

Stand-Alone Radiology Center

31. A patient is referred to the radiology center for magnetic resonance imaging (MRI) due to complaints of severe back pain. MRI revealed a bulging disc between C5–C6, which was slightly pressing against the nerve root on the right. MRI also revealed that disc material had not broken away as a loose fragment, and there was no evidence of a ruptured disc.

DIAGNOSIS: Displaced intervertebral disc, C5–C6 (midcervical region).

____

32. A patient was referred to the radiology center for neck x-ray due to complaints of neck pain. Neck x-ray, which included a view that allowed for examination of the bony openings where the spinal nerves exit the spinal joint, revealed a normal foramen and negative x-ray results.

DIAGNOSIS: Neck pain.

____

33. A patient was referred to the radiology center for x-ray of the neck due to aching and stiffness of both sides of his neck. The patient has been diagnosed in the past as having arthritis in his neck. Neck x-ray confirms findings of degenerative osteoarthritis of the cervical spine and evidence of thinning of the discs between the vertebrae.

DIAGNOSIS: Degenerative osteoarthritis, cervical spine.

____

34. A patient was referred to the radiology center for ankle x-ray due to a sore and tender left ankle. Patient had injured left ankle playing baseball. Left ankle x-ray reveals no evidence of fracture or dislocation.

    DIAGNOSIS: Negative ankle x-ray. Pain, left ankle.

____

35. A patient was referred to the radiology center for chest x-ray due to complaints of difficulty breathing. Chest x-ray reveals the heart and mediastinum to be normal. There is generalized increase of the interstitial lung markings, suggesting some type of chronic lung disease. In addition, there are irregular patchy densities at the left lung base posteriorly. A follow-up study might be warranted.

    DIAGNOSIS: Chronic obstructive lung disease. Possible acute pneumonia.

____

Stand-Alone Urgent Care Center

36. This 26-year-old female was driving her car today when she noticed sudden loss of vision in her right eye and numbness of her right arm. Patient pulled over to the side of the road, both of her symptoms resolved, and she then developed a right frontal headache and presented to the urgent care center for evaluation. Patient stated this happened to her approximately seven years ago in just about the same manner.

    PHYSICAL EXAMINATION: Patient is alert, and she appears in moderate distress with complaints of right frontal headache. HEENT is unremarkable. PERRL. EOMs are intact. Funduscopic exam is unremarkable. Patient's vision was tested, and this was normal.

    NEUROLOGICAL EXAMINATION: Cranial nerves are intact. Patient has good motor strength bilaterally; sensation is completely within normal limits. Reflexes are two plus bilaterally. Plantar reflex is downgoing bilaterally. Finger-to-nose and Romberg were also normal.

    DIAGNOSIS: Migraine headache.

    TREATMENT: The patient was given an injection of Demerol 50 mg and Phenergan 50 mg and allowed to rest for approximately one hour. She felt improved and was discharged. She was told to make an appointment with her family physician for further evaluation of this problem. She was also given a home pack of Tylenol 3 for pain.

____

37. This is a college student who has a history of injuring his knee. He injured it again last week while participating in sports, and today there is a lot of fluid in his knee. He says this happens quite frequently. Physical exam reveals the left knee to have a moderate effusion present. There is limitation of motion. He has only about 45 degrees of flexion. He is able to walk on it, but he limps on that left leg. The drawer test is positive, and the cruciate ligaments are lax. The medial collateral ligament is a little bit loose and tender. X-ray of the left knee showed no bony abnormalities. The patient related that Tylenol 3 does not help him very much, so he was given a shot of Demerol and Phenergan. He was given a prescription for Percodan to have filled in the morning. An Ace wrap or mobilizer was to be used until the effusion clears. Crutches were given for ambulation, and he was to keep weight off the left leg as much as possible. If this injury continued more than several days, he was to see an orthopedic physician.

    DIAGNOSIS: Internal derangement, left knee. (Initial encounter.)

____

38. This is a 47-year-old man, who is a patient of mine, who has a history of Prinzmetal angina and supraventricular tachycardia. This exacerbated this afternoon, and he obtained intermittent relief with some nitroglycerin. However, the pain in his arm and left chest continued. The pain was a type of aching tenderness, but there was no associated shortness of breath or diaphoresis. The patient is quite an anxious man and tends to make more of his symptoms than necessary. He has a history of three cardiac catheterizations, all of which were normal. He is taking Procardia 20 mgs t.i.d., which he stopped on his own when he increased his Inderal to 40 mgs. q.i.d. Physical exam reveals an anxious white middle-aged male in no apparent distress. The neck is supple; carotids are two plus, without bruits. The chest has symmetrical expansion; the lungs are clear to auscultation and percussion. Heart is regular rate and rhythm; S1 and S2 are 2/4; no murmurs, clicks, heaves, gallops, or rubs were appreciable. The abdomen is obese, soft, and nontender. An EKG showed no change from a tracing in February. The monitor showed a normal sinus rhythm. The patient was given 100 mg of Demerol, 50 mg of Phenergan, IM.

DIAGNOSIS: Prinzmetal angina.

---

39. SUBJECTIVE: Patient is a 42-year-old white male who was struck on the head by a pipe today. The patient was not knocked unconscious and has no visual or ambulatory difficulties.

OBJECTIVE: Patient is an alert white male in no apparent distress. Pupils are equal, round, and reactive to light; extraocular muscles are intact; the patient is fully oriented in all three spheres. He has a 5-cm laceration on the posterior scalp. There is no evidence of any foreign debris within the wound. The wound was cleansed well with Betadine; the adjacent hair was shaved; and the wound was closed with #4-0 silk sutures, requiring a total of five skin sutures to close.

ASSESSMENT: 5-cm laceration of scalp.

PLAN: He is to keep the area clean and dry and return for any sign of infection; he will have the sutures removed in nine days, and he was given a DT booster. (Initial encounter.)

---

40. DIAGNOSIS: Pancytopenia with splenomegaly. The patient is a 5-year-old white male who presents at the request of a private medical doctor for reevaluation of persistent febrile illness associated with coughing. Patient has been on Amoxil for approximately three weeks with no response. At the time, physical exam in the office was essentially unremarkable. A palpable spleen tip was appreciated. The child was sent for a CBC, quantitative immunoglobulins, at which time it was apparent that he had pancytopenia and was advised to undergo further evaluation. Liver-spleen scan revealed the presence of splenomegaly without increased bone marrow uptake. He spiked a temperature to 101. Blood cultures, throat cultures, urine, and chest x-ray were obtained, and he was placed on Claforan 100 mg per kg per day in divided doses. All cultures were subsequently negative. Quantitative immunoglobins and an iron TIBC and ferritin were obtained. Quantitative immunoglobins were all within normal range. Ferritin was 104, which is within normal range; iron of 22, which is low; and TIBC of 255, which is marginally elevated with 9% saturation, which is low. PT and PTT were within normal limits. SCG-II profile was within normal limits with the exception of an LDH, which was marginally elevated to 232. CBC on admission was white count of 2.9 with hemoglobin of 12.1, hematocrit 36, platelets of 110, 19 segs, 66 lymphs, 5 monos, 2 eos, 1 baso, 7 bands. Sed rate 18. Urinalysis was within normal limits. Chest x-ray was read as essentially normal. The patient was transferred to Dr. Kelly's service for bone marrow aspiration to attempt to ascertain the etiology of his pancytopenia.

REVIEW

Multiple Choice

Circle the most appropriate response.

ICD-10-CM Coding

1. Patient's discharge statement is CVA with hemiplegia resolved.
   a. G81.90, I63.9
   b. I63.9
   c. I63.9, G81.90
   d. Query physician to ask if hemiplegia is clinically significant.
2. Acute salpingitis due to gonococcal infection.
   a. A54.24
   b. N70.01
   c. N70.91
   d. N70.91, A54.24
3. A 16-month-old infant was treated at the ambulatory surgery unit (ASU) for correction of a congenital cleft lip, complete, unilateral. Shortly after the start of surgery, the patient started running a fever; it became apparent that she had acute otitis media, left. She was placed on antibiotics and discharged. Surgery is to be rescheduled at a later date.
   a. H66.92
   b. H66.92, Z53.09
   c. Q36.9, H66.92, Z53.09
   d. Z53.09
4. A patient presents to his local clinic with complaints of dysuria and abdominal pain. He is examined, and a urine sample is submitted for culture. The urine culture is positive for 100,000 colony forming units per milliliter of *Escherichia coli*. The results of the urine culture are on the chart when it is coded. The physician documents urinary tract infection due to *E. coli* on the patient's record.
   a. N39.0
   b. N39.0, B96.20
   c. R10.9, R30.0, N39.0
   d. R10.84, R30.0, N39.0
5. Acute osteomyelitis of left distal femur; type 1 diabetes mellitus.
   a. E10.9, M86.152
   b. E10.610, M86.152, M86.9
   c. M86.152, E11.9
   d. M86.152, E10.9
6. Suzie Johnson is seen in the clinic with right upper quadrant (RUQ) abdominal pain. She has a history of pneumonia treated six months prior and a history of asthma. The clinic physician performs a complete examination of the patient and documents clear lungs and no abdominal tenderness. She is referred to the radiology department for further testing. The clinic physician also refills her prescription for her asthma medication, Singulair. Diagnoses listed on the clinic record include rule out cholelithiasis and RUQ abdominal pain.
   a. K82.A1, J45.909
   b. K82.A1, R10.11, J45.909
   c. R10.11, J45.909
   d. R10.11, J45.909, J18.9, K82.A1
7. Patient admitted to a local clinic with increasing shortness of breath, weakness, and ineffective cough. The patient is treated and discharged. Diagnosis is acute exacerbation of chronic obstructive pulmonary disease (COPD).
   a. J44.1
   b. J44.1, J80
   c. J96.90, J44.1
   d. J80, J44.1
8. A 26-year-old patient presents to her physician's office complaining of headache, runny nose, and teeth pain. Her history includes chronic sinusitis, ear infections, and repeated episodes of thrush. The patient is examined. The diagnosis is acute and chronic maxillary sinusitis.
   a. J01.00, J32.0
   b. J01.00, J32.0, R51, J31.0, K08.9
   c. J01.00, R51
   d. J32.0, K08.9

9. A 25-year-old patient presents to the radiology department for a diagnostic test. The diagnostic statement for the test is rule out hiatal hernia. The diagnostic test is negative. No signs or symptoms are documented in the referral information that accompanied the patient. Which action should the coder take?
   a. Assign a V code for screening examination from ICD-10-CM.
   b. Contact the chief radiologist to obtain the patient's diagnosis.
   c. Request that the patient provide his signs and/or symptoms.
   d. Submit the insurance claim without an ICD-10-CM code.

10. A 20-year-old patient has just returned to the United States after working abroad. The patient is seeking medical evaluation due to an exposure to dengue fever while working abroad. The patient responds negatively when questioned if he has any symptoms of a severe headache or severe myalgia. The patient requests an evaluation and radiographic films of his left index finger because he suffered a fracture of his right index finger five months ago and now reports swelling of his left index finger. He does not report any pain associated with the swelling of his left index finger. An x-ray of his left hand, including fingers, is negative. Laboratory blood testing is pending at the time of coding.
    a. A90, M79.89, Z47.89
    b. M79.89, Z11.59
    c. R50.9, M79.89, Z11.59
    d. Z11.59, Z20.828, M79.89

HCPCS Level II Coding System

CHAPTER 8

INTRODUCTION

This chapter includes application-based assignments that familiarize students with coding procedures, services, and supplies according to HCPCS level II. Students code procedural statements and case studies by applying HCPCS level II coding conventions, principles, and rules.

ASSIGNMENT 8.1 – HCPCS LEVEL II INDEX

Objectives

At the conclusion of this assignment, the student should be able to:

- Explain the organization of the HCPCS level II index.
- Identify the word in a service or procedural statement that would be considered the main term in the HCPCS level II index.
- Locate main terms in the HCPCS level II index.

Overview

Because of the wide variety of services and procedures described in HCPCS level II, the alphabetical index is very helpful in finding the correct code. It is important never to code directly from the index and always to verify the code in the appropriate code section of the coding manual. Make sure you read code descriptions very carefully before selecting a code.

Instructions

Underline the word in each of the following statements that would be considered the main term in the HCPCS level II index.

1. Breast pump
2. Chemotherapy administration
3. Dialysate solution
4. External defibrillator electrode
5. Fracture orthosis
6. Liquid gas system

7. Oral antiemetic
8. Pneumatic nebulizer administration set
9. Pneumococcal vaccination administration
10. Wheelchair shock absorber

ASSIGNMENT 8.2 – HCPCS LEVEL II MODIFIERS

Objectives

At the conclusion of this assignment, the student should be able to:

- Locate HCPCS level II national modifiers in the coding manual.
- Assign HCPCS level II national modifiers to special circumstances associated with procedures, services, and supplies.

Overview

HCPCS level II modifiers are attached to HCPCS level II codes to provide additional information regarding the product or service reported. Modifiers supplement the information provided by a HCPCS code descriptor to identify specific circumstances that may apply to an item or a service. HCPCS level II modifiers contain alpha or alphanumeric characters.

NOTE:

HCPCS level II alpha and alphanumeric modifiers may also be added to CPT codes to further define the procedure or service reported (e.g., 69436-RT, tympanostomy, right ear).

Instructions

Match the modifier in the left column to its appropriate description in the right column.

________	1. AH	a. Clinical psychologist
________	2. E4	b. Four patients served
________	3. FA	c. Left foot, great toe
________	4. NU	d. Left hand, thumb
________	5. RC	e. Lower right eyelid
________	6. SB	f. New equipment
________	7. TA	g. Nurse midwife
________	8. TC	h. Registered nurse (RN)
________	9. TD	i. Right coronary artery
________	10. UQ	j. Technical component

ASSIGNMENT 8.3 – ASSIGNING HCPCS LEVEL II CODES

Objectives

At the conclusion of this assignment, the student should be able to:

- Locate main terms in the HCPCS level II index.
- Locate codes in the HCPCS level II index and verify them in the tabular section.

Overview

HCPCS level II code sections are identified by an alphabetical first character (e.g., *B* for enteral and parenteral therapy, *C* for outpatient PPS). Some code sections are logical, such as *R* for radiology, whereas others, such as *J* for drugs, appear to be arbitrarily assigned.

Instructions

Assign HCPCS level II national codes to each procedure or service.

Transport Services Including Ambulance (A0000–A0999)

_______________ 1. Taxi, nonemergency transportation

_______________ 2. Basic Life Support (BLS) nonemergency ambulance transport

_______________ 3. Neonatal emergency ambulance transport, one way

_______________ 4. Caseworker nonemergency transportation, one mile

_______________ 5. Level 2 Advanced Life Support (ALS)

Medical and Surgical Supplies (A4000–A8999)

_______________ 6. Male external catheter with adhesive coating

_______________ 7. Two-way latex (with silicone coating) indwelling Foley catheter

_______________ 8. Ostomy belt

_______________ 9. Reusable enema bag with tubing

_______________ 10. One pair of apnea monitor electrodes

_______________ 11. Supply of radiopharmaceutical imaging agent, techneticum Tc-99m, medronate

_______________ 12. Imaging agent sodium iodide I-131 capsule for therapeutic imaging

_______________ 13. Nonprescription drug

_______________ 14. Exercise equipment

_______________ 15. Injectable contrast material for echocardiography

Enteral and Parenteral Therapy (B4000–B9999)

_______________ 16. Portable parenteral nutrition infusion pump

_______________ 17. Nasogastric (NG) tubing without stylet

_______________ 18. Pediatric enteral formula to replace fluids and electrolytes

_______________ 19. 7% amino acid parenteral nutrition solution

_______________ 20. Adult enteral formula for fluid and electrolytes

CMS Hospital Outpatient Payment System (C1000–C9999)

_______________ 21. Single-chamber implantable cardioverter-defibrillator

_______________ 22. Vena cava filter

_______________ 23. Dual-chamber pacemaker, rate-responsive

_______________ 24. Long-term hemodialysis (HD) catheter

_______________ 25. Integra meshed bilayer wound matrix skin substitute, 1 cm^2

Durable Medical Equipment (E0100–E9999)

_______________ 26. Four-lead transcutaneous electrical nerve stimulation (TENS) unit

_______________ 27. Freestanding cervical traction stand

_______________ 28. Heavy-duty, extra-wide hospital bed with mattress to accommodate patient who weighs 460 lbs

_______________ 29. Heparin infusion pump for hemodialysis

_______________ 30. Jug urinal (male)

Temporary Procedures/Professional Services (G0000–G9999)

_______________ 31. Screening colonoscopy on patient with personal history of colon cancer and resection

_______________ 32. Glaucoma screening on patient with hypertension and family history of glaucoma, done by ophthalmologist

_______________ 33. Bilateral removal of impacted cerumen by physician, patient also had hearing test done after the removal of cerumen

_______________ 34. Routine electrocardiogram (ECG) 12-lead with interpretation and report, done as a screening as part of an initial preventive physical examination on a 40-year-old

_______________ 35. Home health aide assistance with bathing and dressing at the client's home, 60 minutes

Behavioral Health and/or Substance Abuse Treatment Services (H0001–H9999)

_______________ 36. Rehab program, ½ day

_______________ 37. Outpatient detoxification for alcohol

_______________ 38. Hotline for Behavioral Health

_______________ 39. Training and development in job skills, 30 minutes

_______________ 40. Hospital inpatient acute drug detoxification

Drugs Administered Other Than Oral Method (J0100–J8999)

NOTE:

HCPCS level II includes a table of drugs that lists the J codes assigned to medications. The HCPCS level II table of drugs lists drugs by generic and chemical name. (Drugs are listed by trade name only if no generic or chemical name is available.) When searching the table for a drug according to its trade name, you are instructed to "see" the generic or chemical name. (Some publishers print brand names beneath the generic description, and other publishers provide a special expanded index of the drug codes.) For assistance with identifying generic or chemical drug names, go to http://www.rxlist.com.

_______________ 41. Ancef 500 mg injection

_______________ 42. Botulinum toxin type B, 100 units

_______________ 43. Clonidine HCl, 1 mg

_______________ 44. Duramorph 10 mg SC

_______________ 45. Kenalog-40 20 mg

Temporary Codes Assigned to DME Regional Carriers (K0000–K9999)

_______________ 46. Wheelchair accessory

_______________ 47. Wheelchair, heavy-duty

_______________ 48. Defibrillator, external and automatic with integrated electrocardiogram analysis, garment type

_______________ 49. IV (intravenous) hanger

_______________ 50. Temporary standard wheelchair, patient-owned wheelchair is being repaired

Orthotics (L0000–L4999)

_______________ 51. Spenco left foot insert

_______________ 52. Knee immobilizer orthotic, canvas longitudinal, prefabricated

_______________ 53. Shoe addition, insole, rubber

_______________ 54. Scott-Craig type reinforced solid stirrup, addition

_______________ 55. Newington-type Legg Perthes orthotic, custom fabricated

Prosthetics (L5000–L9999)

_______________ 56. Breast prosthesis (mastectomy bra) with integrated breast prosthesis form (for patient's left breast)

_______________ 57. Cochlear device

_______________ 58. Complete prosthesis shoulder disarticulation, passive restoration

_______________ 59. Mechanical terminal hand device, voluntary opening

_______________ 60. Synthetic vascular graft implant

Other Medical Services (M0000–M0301)

_______________ 61. Abdominal aneurysm, fabric wrapping

_______________ 62. Prolotherapy

_______________ 63. Chemical endarterectomy

_______________ 64. Cellular therapy

_______________ 65. Intragastric hypothermia using gastric freezing

Laboratory Services (P0000–P9999)

_______________ 66. One unit of frozen irradiated RBCs (red blood cells), leukocytes reduced

_______________ 67. One unit whole blood for transfusion

_______________ 68. One unit of washed RBCs

_______________ 69. Infusion of plasma protein fraction 5%; 50 milliliters

_______________ 70. Pap (Papanicolaou) smear, cervical done by technician under physician supervision

Temporary Codes Assigned by CMS (Q0000–Q9999)

_______________ 71. Pinworm examination

_______________ 72. 20-year-old patient was provided with long leg cylinder cast (plaster)

________________ 73. Static finger splint

________________ 74. Chemotherapy infusion and push technique

________________ 75. 500 milliliters of Renacidin (irrigation solution) for treatment of bladder calculi

Diagnostic Radiology Services (R0000–R9999)

________________ 76. Portable EKG transport to patient's home

________________ 77. Portable chest x-ray transport to nursing home, one x-ray done

________________ 78. Portable chest x-ray transport to nursing home, 25 patients underwent x-rays

________________ 79. Transportation of portable x-ray equipment to nursing facility; five patients underwent x-ray

________________ 80. Transportation of portable x-ray equipment and x-ray technician to patient's home; husband and wife underwent x-ray

Temporary National Codes Established by Private Payers (S0000–S9999)

________________ 81. Vaginal birth after cesarean (VBAC) classes

________________ 82. Transplantation of small intestine and liver allografts

________________ 83. Annual gynecologic examination on an established patient

________________ 84. Genetic testing for sickle cell anemia

________________ 85. Coma stimulation, 1 day

Temporary National Codes Established by Medicaid (T1000–T9999)

________________ 86. Sign language service, 15 minutes

________________ 87. Family training for child development, 30 minutes

________________ 88. Waiver for one month of assisted living

________________ 89. Intramuscular medication administration by home health LPN

________________ 90. Patient received 30 minutes of private duty nursing from an RN

Vision Services (V0000–V2999)

________________ 91. Eyeglass case

________________ 92. Low-vision aid, hand-held

________________ 93. Purchase of frames

________________ 94. Transporting, processing, and preserving corneal tissue

________________ 95. Antireflective coating, both lenses

Hearing Services (V5000–V5999)

________________ 96. Speech screening

________________ 97. Television amplifier

________________ 98. Hearing screening

________________ 99. Digital hearing aid, completely in the ear canal, analog and monaural

________________ 100. Digital hearing aid, completely in the ear canal, monaural

ASSIGNMENT 8.4 – CODING PRACTICE

Objectives

At the conclusion of this assignment, the student should be able to:

- Use the HCPCS level II index to locate procedure and service codes.
- Verify codes in the appropriate section of HCPCS level II.
- Assign modifier(s) when special circumstances are documented in a case study.

Overview

In practice, the assignment of HCPCS level II codes is not done according to individual code sections. Instead, you will review a coding case (e.g., patient record) and determine the codes to assign for all appropriate code sections of HCPCS level II. (In practice, ICD-10-CM and CPT codes are also assigned.)

Instructions

Code the following case studies using the HCPCS level II index. Make sure you verify each code in the appropriate HCPCS level II code section. Do not forget to add appropriate HCPCS level II modifiers where appropriate. (Assign just the HCPCS level II code for each case study. Do not assign ICD-10-CM or CPT codes.)

1. S: The established patient presented today for annual physical exam with Pap. She is now 34, has two healthy children, and is doing well except for some complaints of fatigue and recent weight gain.

   O: VITAL SIGNS: Blood pressure is 124/72. Pulse is 64 and regular. Respiratory rate is 20. Temperature is 98.8. Weight is 156, which is up 12 lbs since her last visit.

   HEENT: Within normal limits. The patient wears glasses.

   NECK: No thyromegaly or lymphadenopathy.

   HEART: Regular sinus rhythm.

   CHEST: Clear breath sounds throughout all lung fields.

   ABDOMEN: No tenderness. No organomegaly.

   PELVIC: Normal external genitalia. Vagina is pink and contains rugae. Pap specimen was obtained without difficulty.

   RECTAL: Exam was deferred.

   EXTREMITIES: Pulses were full and equal.

   NEUROLOGIC: No complaints; exam within normal limits.

   LABORATORY: Lab performed in the office today included a CBC with differential, thyroid panel, and complete metabolic panel.

   A: Fatigue and weight gain in an otherwise healthy 34-year-old female.

   P: Will await the results of the blood work and call the patient to discuss them. Instructed the patient to take a daily multivitamin and drink at least two glasses of milk daily. Discussed dietary modifications to help stop weight gain. If the patient's blood work indicates abnormal thyroid function, will refer to endocrinology service.

   ____

2. PROSTHESIS CLINIC NOTE: The patient presented today because of complaints of discomfort from his right ocular prosthesis. The prosthesis is relatively new and may need some modification. Upon examination, the patient appeared otherwise generally well. The right eye prosthesis was removed and given to the technician for evaluation. The right eye socket had a very small patch of irritated tissue in the upper medial wall. The technician resurfaced and polished the prosthesis, and after refitting, the patient reported a noticeable improvement in his level of comfort. The patient and I then discussed the psychological struggles he has had with the loss of his eye, but overall he feels more optimistic and states that he believes he will be able to fully resume his normal level of activity.

____

3. GENETIC CLINIC NOTE: The patients are a 30-year-old female and a 32-year-old male who present for genetic testing. The couple have two children aged 2 and 3. One of the children was diagnosed with retinoblastoma at the age of 1 month. The child's eye was removed, and she had two rounds of radiation therapy. The couple wishes to have one more child but would like genetic testing and counseling. Blood specimens were drawn, and the couple is scheduled for a second appointment when the results should be back from the laboratory.

____

4. ORTHOTIC CLINIC NOTE: Patient underwent a halo procedure during which the cervical halo was incorporated into a jacket vest. Patient also received a magnetic resonance image compatible system during the same encounter.

____

REVIEW

Multiple Choice

Circle the most appropriate response.

1. A patient was transported via helicopter from the scene of a motor vehicle crash (MVC) to a level 1 trauma hospital.
   a. A0426-SH
   b. A0430-SH
   c. A0431-SH
   d. A0436-SH
2. Jason Anderson, a 7-year-old asthma patient, was prescribed an intermittent positive pressure breathing (IPPB) machine that has a supplemental humidification device.
   a. E0500
   b. E0550
   c. E0560
   d. E0500, E0560
3. Court-ordered sex offender treatment services, per day.
   a. H2028
   b. H2029-H9
   c. H2018
   d. H2018-H9
4. Karen Towne was recently diagnosed with type 2 diabetes mellitus. Her primary care physician prescribed attendance at self-management training for the disease, with a registered dietician. Karen attends one 30-minute meeting where there are three other newly diagnosed patients besides herself. Two weeks after this group meeting, Karen attends an additional 30-minute training session that includes just the dietician and herself.
   a. G0109
   b. G0109-AE, G0108-AE
   c. G0108, S9141
   d. S9141
5. Injection, amphotericin B lipid complex, 10 mg.
   a. J0287
   b. J0288
   c. J0289
   d. J0290

6. To obtain reimbursement for biologicals and other items associated with implantable devices, the coder should:
   a. report ICD-10-CM diagnosis codes.
   b. report level I and level II HCPCS codes.
   c. report HCPCS C code(s) only.
   d. report level I code(s) only.
7. Chemotherapy intravenous infusion of cyclophosphamide, 100 mg, 50 minutes.
   a. J9045, J9045
   b. J9050
   c. J9070
   d. J8098 × 10
8. Mr. William Hansberry attended a local clinic's administration of influenza vaccine at a local shopping mall. Mr. Hansberry asks that the clinic bill Medicare for the shot.
   a. G8483
   b. G0008
   c. G0009
   d. G0010
9. A bedridden patient with Alzheimer disease and congestive heart failure resides at a nursing home facility. The attending physician is concerned about the patient developing pressure ulcers, and he contacts the local Medicare administrative contractor (MAC) for approval of a water pressure mattress for use by the patient. The MAC approves the request.
   a. E0184
   b. E0186
   c. E0187
   d. E0189
10. A brachytherapy needle was used during the patient's cancer treatment.
   a. C1715
   b. C1716
   c. C1717
   d. C1719
11. A 10-year-old female patient presents to the medical clinic for an evaluation of possible head lice infestation, where several children also have been diagnosed with head lice. The nursing assistant performs the evaluation and determines that the child does have head lice. The mother is given lice shampoo and instructions for its application.
   a. A9150
   b. A9180
   c. A9270
   d. A9999
12. The local HIV clinic distributes free condoms, and a 45-year-old male patient receives a supply.
   a. A4267
   b. A4268
   c. A4269
   d. A4270
13. Mrs. Grace Payne presents to the local medical clinic for podiatry services to have her toenails trimmed. She has type 2 diabetes mellitus and also complains of a painful corn on her right foot.
   a. G0127
   b. S0390
   c. G0247
   d. S9141
14. A female patient presents with complaint of recurring headaches. While being examined by the physician, the patient reports an aura that indicates she is starting to have a migraine. The physician injects 6 mg of Imitrex before the patient leaves the office. The patient is scheduled for a one-week follow-up visit.
   a. J1380
   b. J1410
   c. J2505
   d. J3030
15. Foley catheter insertion tray that contains Foley with Teflon coating, two-way.
   a. A4300
   b. A4310
   c. A4311
   d. A4312
16. HCPCS is the abbreviation for the:
   a. HCFA Common Procedural Coding System.
   b. HCFA Common Procedure Coding System.
   c. Healthcare Common Procedural Coding System.
   d. Healthcare Common Procedure Coding System.

17. Which HCPCS level is used to report the drug injected into a patient?
    a. Level I
    b. Level II
    c. Level III
    d. Level IV
18. A 75-year-old terminal lung cancer patient is admitted to hospice care for general inpatient care.
    a. T2042
    b. T2043
    c. T2044
    d. T2045
19. Louise Matthews presents to the outpatient radiology clinic today and undergoes cervical PET imaging for initial diagnosis of breast cancer.
    a. G0219
    b. G0235
    c. G0252
    d. S8085
20. Mr. Howard Burrows undergoes a prostate-specific antigen (PSA) screening test and a screening colonoscopy. Mr. Burrows is a 50-year-old male with a medical history of hypertension and gout.
    a. G0102, G0104
    b. G0102, G0105
    c. G0103, G0121
    d. G0103, G0105

CHAPTER 9

Introduction to CPT Coding

INTRODUCTION

This chapter includes application-based assignments that introduce students to the following CPT coding conventions:

- Index
- Appendices
- Symbols
- Sections, subsections, categories, and subcategories
- Modifiers

ASSIGNMENT 9.1 – CPT INDEX

Objectives

At the conclusion of this assignment, the student should be able to:

- Explain the organization of the CPT index.
- Identify the word in a service or procedural statement that would be considered the main term in the CPT index.
- Locate main terms in the CPT index.

Overview

The CPT index is organized by alphabetical main terms printed in boldface. The main terms represent procedures or services, organs, anatomical sites, conditions, eponyms, or abbreviations. The main term may be followed by indented terms that modify the main term; these are called subterms. The CPT index organizes procedures and services according to procedure or service (e.g., arthroscopy), organ or other anatomical site (e.g., ankle), condition (e.g., wound), synonyms (e.g., finger joint or intercarpal joint), eponyms (e.g., Billroth I or II), and abbreviations (e.g., EKG). To locate a CPT code, review patient record documentation to locate the service and/or procedure performed and locate the main term in the index (located in the back of the coding manual).

Instructions

Refer to the CPT index and underline the word in each statement that is considered the main term.

Identification of Main Term in CPT Index

1. Laparoscopic jejunostomy
2. Removal of a foreign body embedded in the conjunctiva of the eye
3. Suture of a wound of the kidney
4. Kasai procedure
5. Repair of an inguinal hernia

Identification of Procedure or Service as Main Term in CPT Index

6. Postpartum dilation and curettage
7. Ileum endoscopy via stoma
8. Clamp circumcision of newborn
9. Arthrotomy of toe, interphalangeal joint
10. Gastrostomy with vagotomy

Identification of Organ or Other Anatomical Site as Main Term in CPT Index

11. Repair of diaphragm laceration
12. Excision of heel spur
13. Excision of cyst of pericardium
14. Pulmonary valve replacement
15. Excision of epiphyseal bar of radius

Identification of Condition as Main Term in CPT Index

16. Toe polydactyly reconstruction
17. Repair of sliding inguinal hernia; patient is a 35-year-old male
18. Drainage of cyst of liver
19. Drainage of hip hematoma
20. Destruction of kidney calculus

Identification of Synonym as Main Term in CPT Index

21. Albarran test
22. Binding globulin, testosterone-estradiol
23. Digital slit-beam radiograph
24. Energies, electromagnetic
25. Urine test for epinephrine

Identification of Eponym as Main Term in CPT Index

26. Blom-Singer prosthesis
27. Waldius procedure
28. Dupuytren's contracture
29. Lee and White test
30. Ober-Yount procedure

Identification of Abbreviation as Main Term in CPT Index

31. Manual sedimentation rate of RBCs
32. MRA of the leg
33. Urine pH
34. Standard EEG
35. Complete MRI of the heart

CPT Index Code Ranges

Refer to the CPT index and underline the word in each statement that is considered the main term. Then enter the code range from the CPT index.

____________________ 36. Adrenal venography

____________________ 37. Intracranial artery aneurysm repair

____________________ 38. Chorionic gonadotropin

____________________ 39. Bone autograft

____________________ 40. Mitral valve valvotomy

Use of the Directional Term *See* in the CPT Index

Refer to the CPT index and locate each procedure or service. Enter the directional phrase provided in the index.

____________________ 41. AcG

____________________ 42. Nissen operation

____________________ 43. Heller operation

____________________ 44. *Miyagawanella*

____________________ 45. *Clostridium tetani* anaerobic bacillus

ASSIGNMENT 9.2 – CPT APPENDICES

Objectives

At the conclusion of this assignment, the student should be able to:

- Explain the contents of CPT appendices.
- Use the appropriate CPT appendix when assigning codes.

Overview

CPT contains appendices that are located between the Medicine section and the index. Insurance specialists should carefully review these appendices to become familiar with coding changes that affect the practice annually.

- Appendix A (modifiers)
- Appendix B (summary of deletions, additions, and revisions)
- Appendix C (clinical examples)
- Appendix D (summary of CPT add-on codes)
- Appendix E (summary of CPT codes exempt from modifier -51)
- Appendix F (summary of CPT codes exempt from modifier -63)

- Appendix H (alphabetical clinical topics listing)
- Appendix J (electrodiagnostic medicine listing of sensory, motor, and mixed nerves)
- Appendix K (product pending FDA approval)
- Appendix L (vascular families)
- Appendix M (renumbered CPT codes–citations crosswalk)
- Appendix N (summary of resequenced CPT codes)
- Appendix O (multianalyte assays with algorithmic analyses)
- Appendix P (CPT codes that may be used for synchronous telemedicine services)

Instructions

Circle the most appropriate response.

Appendix A

1. Modifiers -25, -27, and -50 are all considered ______________.
   a. anesthesia physical status modifiers
   b. approved for ambulatory surgery center use
   c. approved for inpatient hospital use
   d. HCPCS modifiers
2. Dr. Wilson provided an evaluation and management service on a new patient, Wendy Criswell, in his office. Wendy hit her head on a shelf in her kitchen. She was also complaining of a rash on her left forearm that had not resolved with over-the-counter medication. Dr. Wilson examined Wendy's forehead wound and the rash on her arm. He prescribed medication for the rash. The wound of her forehead required two stitches, which Dr. Wilson placed after cleaning the wound. The coder assigned CPT codes 99202-25 and 12011. Modifier -25 was added to code 99202 because this case:
   a. consists of surgery that was performed bilaterally.
   b. includes an E/M service on the same day as a procedure.
   c. is an example of unusual procedural service.
   d. reflects professional services provided.
3. A patient underwent a laparoscopic cholecystectomy 20 days ago, which was performed by Dr. Rosa. The postoperative period for the laparoscopic cholecystectomy is 90 days. Today the patient presents with severe abdominal pain. Abdominal ultrasound reveals that the patient has an ectopic pregnancy, which requires surgery. Dr. Rosa performed laparoscopic removal of the ectopic pregnancy. The coder assigned code 59150-79 for treatment of the ectopic pregnancy. Modifier -79 was added to code 59150 because the laparoscopic removal of the ectopic pregnancy is a(n):
   a. related procedure during the postoperative period.
   b. repeat procedure performed by Dr. Rosa.
   c. staged procedure performed by Dr. Rosa.
   d. unrelated procedure performed during the postoperative period.
4. A patient with end-stage renal disease undergoes surgery on his left ankle to repair a fracture. The coder assigns anesthesia code 01462-AA-P4-LT for the anesthesiologist. Physical status modifier -P4 was added to code 01462 because the patient is a:
   a. normal healthy patient.
   b. patient with a mild systemic disease.
   c. patient with a severe systemic disease that is a constant threat to life.
   d. patient with severe systemic disease.

5. While on vacation, Jill Smith sustained a tibial shaft fracture of her right leg and underwent closed treatment by Dr. Jones. Upon return to her hometown, Jill received follow-up care from a local orthopedist, Dr. Collins. Code 27750-55-LT is reported for services provided by Dr. Collins, and modifier -55 was added to the code because:
   a. Dr. Collins provided postoperative care services only to the patient.
   b. repeat services had to be provided by a different physician.
   c. requirements specified in the medical policy and procedure were not met.
   d. services were provided by a substitute physician under a reciprocal agreement.

Appendix B

6. What is used in Appendix B to identify deleted wording in a specific code descriptor?
   a. Star
   b. Strikethrough
   c. Bullet
   d. Triangle
7. In Appendix B, which describes the purpose of the bullet symbol?
   a. Changed code
   b. New code
   c. Revised code
   d. Deleted code
8. Which of the below is *not* part of Appendix B?
   a. Revised codes
   b. Deleted language
   c. Heading revisions
   d. New codes
9. In Appendix B, how is a new narrative for an existing code identified?
   a. By the use of the bullet symbol
   b. By the use of the triangle symbol
   c. By the use of strikethrough
   d. By the use of underlining
10. What CPT symbol is used to identify a revised code?
    a. Bullet
    b. Star
    c. Triangle
    d. Flash

Appendix C

11. Review the examples for codes 99211 to 99214 and then answer the following scenario: A 3-year-old presents to the pediatrician's office for follow up of a superficial bite of the cheek from the family's 4-month-old husky puppy. The puppy is current on all shots including rabies. The bite did not penetrate the skin. What code, based on your review of the clinical examples in CPT Appendix C, would you assign to this case?
    a. 99211
    b. 99212
    c. 99213
    d. 99214
12. Codes 99222 and 99223 are both reported for ______________.
    a. office consultations
    b. subsequent hospital care, new patient
    c. emergency department services
    d. initial hospital care
13. The clinical examples for codes 99281 to 99285 cover ______________.
    a. established patients seen in consultation
    b. new or established patients seen in consultation
    c. new or established patients seen in the emergency department
    d. new patients only, seen in the emergency department
14. The clinical examples for code 99291 apply to ______________.
    a. elderly patients only, in critical medical situations
    b. only very young patients in critical medical situations
    c. services determined by the amount of time spent, such as one hour of critical care service rendered to a patient
    d. system arrest (respiratory or cardiac), as documented in the patient's record

15. Review the examples for codes 99241 to 99245 and then select the code for the following scenario: A 30-year-old female new patient was referred by an ED physician to an endocrinologist for diagnosis of possible Graves' disease and possible thyrotoxicosis. During the history taken by the endocrinologist, the patient reports recent onset of rapid weight loss, loss of hair, and severe fatigue. The endocrinologist performed a comprehensive examination and ordered a battery of laboratory tests to determine the cause of the patient's symptoms. Review the clinical examples in CPT Appendix C and locate a similar case. Identify the code that would be assigned.
    a. 99242
    b. 99243
    c. 99244
    d. 99245

Appendix D

16. Which CPT symbol identifies an add-on code?
    a. Bullet
    b. Pair of triangles facing each other
    c. Plus sign
    d. Triangle
17. Which code is *not* an add-on code?
    a. 15002
    b. 15003
    c. 15101
    d. 15121
18. Which code is an add-on code?
    a. 47531
    b. 47550
    c. 47552
    d. 47555
19. Which code is an add-on Category III code?
    a. 0076T
    b. 1000F
    c. 2000F
    d. 4011F
20. Which code is an add-on code from the Medicine section of CPT?
    a. 01953
    b. 64623
    c. 93621
    d. 99355

Appendix E

21. Which code is exempt from modifier -51 and is located in the Musculoskeletal subsection of CPT Surgery?
    a. 17004
    b. 20975
    c. 61107
    d. 93620
22. Which CPT medicine code is exempt from modifier -51?
    a. 17004
    b. 20974
    c. 61107
    d. 99152
23. An emergency department patient presented who was having severe difficulty breathing. Based on the patient's history of asthma, immediate medical attention was given. The patient's O_2 saturation was at 70%, and the patient was tachycardic. The decision was made to intubate the patient. In addition to the intubation, the patient also received repair of a scalp laceration that he had received in a minor car accident in the parking lot of the hospital. The CPT code for the laceration is 12002. The CPT code for the intubation is 31500. The coder should:
    a. add modifier -51 to code 12002 because two procedures were performed on this patient during the same operative session.
    b. not add modifier -51 to code 31500 because it is exempt from that modifier.
    c. not report code 12002 because that procedure is included in the description of the evaluation and management code.
    d. report code 12002 on the claim with the date of service and report code 31500 on a different claim with the next date of service.

24. Which code is exempt from modifier -51?
    a. 93454
    b. 93531
    c. 93610
    d. 93619
25. A patient presents to the physician's office for the removal of multiple lesions. The lesions are actinic keratoses and skin tags. The keratoses are removed in the office using a laser, and the skin tags are removed using scissors. There are 17 keratoses removed and 3 skin tags removed on this visit. The coder assigned 11200 and 17004-51 for the removal procedures. Using Appendix E and the main section of the CPT coding manual, review the codes assigned. Based on information from these two parts of the manual, which statement below is true?
    a. Both codes are assigned correctly.
    b. 11200 needs a -25 modifier.
    c. 11201 should be used instead of code 17004.
    d. 11200 is exempt from modifier -51.

Appendix F

26. Modifier -63 applies to CPT codes that are commonly reported for ________.
    a. adults
    b. adults with systemic disease
    c. infants
    d. people over the age of 70
27. Which code is exempt from modifier -63?
    a. 46700
    b. 46706
    c. 46730
    d. 46751
28. Which code is located in the Digestive subsection of CPT Surgery and is exempt from modifier -63?
    a. 44055
    b. 36420
    c. 63702
    d. 54000
29. Which code is located in the eye and ocular adnexa subsection of CPT Surgery and is exempt from modifier -63?
    a. 36460
    b. 46716
    c. 53025
    d. 65820
30. Dr. Bellows performs a Kasai procedure on a 2-month-old patient. The code assigned for this procedure is 47701, and it contains a plus symbol in front of it. This means that the code is ________.
    a. a code with revised text
    b. an add-on code
    c. exempt from modifier -51
    d. exempt from modifier -63

Appendix J

31. The medial brachial cutaneous sensory nerve is a nerve of the ________.
    a. cranium
    b. head and trunk
    c. lower extremity
    d. upper extremity
32. Which is a sensory nerve of the lower extremities?
    a. Median nerve
    b. Saphenous nerve
    c. Suprascapular nerve
    d. Radial nerve
33. Code 95909 is reported for a sensory nerve conduction study totaling ________.
    a. 1–2 studies
    b. 3–4 studies
    c. 5–6 studies
    d. 7–8 studies
34. The lateral femoral cutaneous sensory nerve is located in the ________.
    a. head
    b. ilioinguinal
    c. lower extremity
    d. upper extremity

35. Mary Marshall presents to the physician with a complaint of pain and numbness in her left leg. She does not report any symptoms in her right leg. The physician orders nerve conduction studies. Based on information in CPT Appendix J, what is the maximum number of sensory nerve conduction studies (NCS) this patient should undergo for the physician to arrive at a diagnosis?
    a. 6
    b. 7
    c. 8
    d. 9

Appendix K

36. What symbol is CPT using to identify pending FDA approval of vaccine products?
    a. Bullet
    b. Star
    c. Flash
    d. Plus sign
37. What federal government agency approves vaccines?
    a. AMA
    b. CMS
    c. FDA
    d. OIG
38. A 35-year-old woman receives a vaccine at her physician's office. The coder recognizes that per information in the CPT coding book, this vaccine is pending FDA approval. What resource can the coder use to check the status of this vaccine with the FDA?
    a. Internet site of AMA
    b. Physician who ordered vaccine
    c. Nurse who administered vaccine
    d. Insurance carrier for patient
39. Appendix K provides information on what type of medical product?
    a. Globulins
    b. Vaccines
    c. Nerve studies
    d. Intravenous drugs
40. If the CPT code for a vaccine product is not listed in Appendix K, that would mean:
    a. that the vaccine product will not be paid for by Medicare.
    b. that the vaccine product will not be paid for by a managed care insurance carrier.
    c. that the vaccine product is FDA approved.
    d. that the vaccine product is only administered via an intramuscular (IM) route.

Appendix L

41. Which is the second-order branch of the celiac trunk?
    a. Brachial
    b. Costocervical trunk
    c. Splenic
    d. Superior mesenteric
42. Which is a third-order branch of the common iliac artery?
    a. Peroneal of the superficial femoral
    b. Right internal carotid
    c. Sigmoid inferior mesenteric
    d. Transverse lateral circumflex femoral
43. Which is the most commonly reported artery for arteriographic procedures of the innominate third-order branch of the right subclavian and axillary?
    a. Axillary
    b. Brachial
    c. Subscapular
    d. Subclavian
44. Which artery is located beyond the third order for the celiac trunk?
    a. Gastric
    b. Dorsal pancreatic
    c. Supraduodenal
    d. Transverse cerebral

45. What are the second-order branches of the common iliac artery?
    a. Common femoral, external iliac, and internal iliac
    b. Common hepatic and splenic
    c. Iliolumbar, internal iliac, and cremasteric
    d. Profunda femoris, transverse lateral circumflex, and popliteal

Appendix M

NOTE:

Appendix M is a crosswalk of deleted CPT codes from previous year of publication to current year of publication. The codes listed on this crosswalk will change each year. The multiple-choice questions below are on the concept and usage of this appendix and do not list or require answers based on any specific year of CPT manual publication.

46. What is the purpose of Appendix M?
    a. To provide a summary of code additions and deletions
    b. To provide a crosswalk of deleted codes from the previous year
    c. To provide a listing of add-on codes
    d. To provide a listing of newly created level I modifiers
47. Review the below. In which situation would Appendix M be useful?
    a. To make revisions to the CPT index
    b. To make assignment of CPT modifiers
    c. To update a physician office encounter form
    d. To make a list to view updates on vaccines at FDA website
48. What is identified in column 1 of Appendix M?
    a. Current codes
    b. Deleted codes
    c. Former codes
    d. Revised codes
49. What is identified in column 2 of Appendix M?
    a. Deleted/former codes
    b. Code descriptors for deleted codes
    c. Deleted codes from last year
    d. Code descriptors for current CPT codes
50. What is identified in column 3 of Appendix M?
    a. Current CPT codes
    b. Year a code was deleted
    c. Deleted codes from last year
    d. Code descriptors for current CPT codes

Appendix N

51. CPT codes that do not appear in numeric sequence in the listing of CPT codes are identified with a(n) __________ symbol.
    a. asterisk
    b. caret
    c. number
    d. plus

Appendix O

52. Multianalyte assays with algorithmic analyses (MAAAs) are __________ that utilize multiple results derived from assays of various types.
    a. assessments
    b. modifiers
    c. procedures
    d. supplies
53. MAAAs are typically unique to a single __________.
    a. clinical laboratory or manufacturer
    b. health care organization
    c. physician or other provider
    d. third-party payer
54. The results of individual component procedure(s) that are inputs to the MAAAs may be provided on the associated __________; however, these assays are not reported separately using additional codes.
    a. health care claim
    b. explanation of benefits
    c. laboratory report
    d. remittance advice

Appendix P

55. CPT codes that may be used for synchronous telemedicine services include codes for electronic communication using interactive telecommunications equipment. In the CPT manual, these codes are preceded by the star symbol. Which modifier is reported with Appendix P codes?
    a. -25
    b. -50
    c. -95
    d. -99

ASSIGNMENT 9.3 – CPT SYMBOLS

Objectives

At the conclusion of this assignment, the student should be able to:

- Explain the purpose of each CPT symbol.
- Interpret CPT symbols.

Overview

The following symbols are located throughout the CPT coding manual:

● A **bullet** located to the left of a code number identifies new procedures and services added to CPT.

▲ A **triangle** located to the left of a code number identifies a code description that has been revised.

►◄ **Horizontal triangles** surround revised guidelines and notes. This symbol is *not* used for revised code descriptions.

; To save space in CPT, some code descriptions are not printed in their entirety next to a code number. Instead, the entry is indented and the coder must refer back to the common portion of the code description that is located before the **semicolon**. The common portion begins with a capital letter, and the abbreviated (or subordinate) descriptions are indented and begin with lowercase letters.

✚ The **plus** symbol identifies add-on codes (Appendix D of CPT) for procedures that are commonly, but not always, performed at the same time and by the same surgeon as the primary procedure. Parenthetical notes, located below add-on codes, often identify the primary procedure to which add-on codes apply.

⊘ This **forbidden** (or **prohibitory**) symbol identifies codes that are exempt from modifier -51. These codes are reported in addition to other codes, but they are not classified as add-on codes.

⚡ The **flash symbol** indicates codes that classify products pending FDA approval but that have been assigned a CPT code.

The **number symbol** indicates out-of-numeric sequence codes. Resequencing allows existing codes to be relocated to a more appropriate location (rather than deleting and renumbering codes).

➲ The **blue reference symbol** located below a code description indicates that the coder should refer to the *CPT Assistant* monthly newsletter.

➲ The **green reference symbol** located below a code description indicates that the coder should refer to the *CPT Changes: An Insider's View* annual publication that contains all coding changes for the current year.

➲ The **red reference symbol** located below a code description indicates that the coder should refer to the *Clinical Examples in Radiology* quarterly newsletter.

★ The **star symbol** indicates codes that may be used for synchronous telemedicine services.

♓ The **duplicate PLA symbol** identifies duplicate proprietary laboratory analyses (PLA) tests. PLA codes are included in Appendix O, and they contain the proprietary name of the procedure. Descriptor language of some PLA codes are identical, and codes are differentiated only by listed proprietary names in Appendix O. Such codes are denoted by the symbol.

⇅ The **Category I PLA symbol** is used to identify CPT category I codes

Instructions

Circle the most appropriate response.

1. Suzie New is coding a chart on a patient that had 20 skin tags removed. Suzie assigns CPT codes 11200 and 11201 to this case. What symbol is next to 11201?
   a. The symbol is a star, which means that 11201 has modifier -95 added to it.
   b. The symbol is a bullet, which means that 11201 is a new code for the current year.
   c. The symbol is a plus sign, which stands for an add-on code that does not require modifier -51.
   d. There is no symbol next to 11201.
2. The star symbol associated with code 90791 (Psychiatric diagnostic evaluation) means that ______.
   a. evaluations of motor threshold are performed
   b. hypnotherapy is provided as part of the evaluation
   c. interactive telecommunication equipment is used
   d. therapeutic repetitive transcranial magnetic stimulation treatments are included
3. What symbol is used in the CPT coding manual to identify a new code for the current year of publication?
   a. Plus sign
   b. Triangle
   c. Star
   d. Bullet
4. How many symbols are used in the CPT coding manual?
   a. Six
   b. Seven
   c. Ten
   d. Twelve
5. A patient has a bundle of His recording and intra-atrial pacing done by Dr. Henry on 07/01/YY. When coding these procedures, the coder should:
   a. assign CPT level I codes with no modifier.
   b. assign CPT level II codes with the -51 modifier on the 2nd code.

c. assign CPT level II codes and assign the -51 modifier to the CPT level I codes.
d. assign CPT level I codes with modifier -51 on both codes.

6. The number sign in front of code 21552 indicates __________.
a. codes that are exempt from modifier -51
b. out-of-numeric sequence codes
c. products pending FDA approval
d. reinstated or recycled codes

7. Code 93571 is __________.
a. a code that is out of sequence
b. an add-on code
c. approved for telemedicine services
d. exempt from modifier -51

8. What symbol is used to denote revised guidelines?
a. Triangle
b. Bullet
c. Star
d. Horizontal triangles

9. Mary Joseph is a patient at a local hospital. She underwent surgery and had severe postoperative complications that included respiratory arrest and acute blood loss. She received critical care service for 85 minutes. Codes 99291 and 99292 are reported. Code 99292 is considered a(n) __________ code.
a. add-on
b. conscious sedation
c. reinstated
d. revised

10. A patient had two breast cysts aspirated. One was located in the left breast, and the other was located in the right breast. Which coder reported the codes correctly and why?
- Coder A assigned 19000-50.
- Coder B assigned 19000 and 19001.
- Coder C assigned 19000 and 19001-51.
- Coder D assigned 19000.

a. Coder A is correct; the patient had bilateral cysts removed, so modifier -50 is added to code 19000.
b. Coder B is correct; no modifier is added to code 19001 because it is an add-on code.
c. Coder C is correct; two separate procedures (cyst aspirations) via separate incisions were performed.
d. Coder D is correct; no modifier is added to code 19000.

ASSIGNMENT 9.4 – CPT SECTIONS, SUBSECTIONS, CATEGORIES, AND SUBCATEGORIES

Objectives

At the conclusion of this assignment, the student should be able to:

- Explain the content of CPT sections, subsections, categories, and subcategories.
- Given a case scenario, locate the appropriate CPT section, subsection, category, or subcategory.

Overview

CPT Category I codes are organized according to six sections that are subdivided into subsections, categories, and subcategories. (CPT is inconsistent in its use of "categories" and "subcategories." Some sections use that terminology; others refer to "headings" and "subheadings.")

Instructions

Circle the most appropriate response.

1. A patient presents to the emergency department with multiple lacerations of the face and upper arm due to a motor vehicle crash. The patient requires repairs of the lacerations, both simple and intermediate level. In which section of CPT would you find the code for repair of this patient's lacerations?
   a. Anesthesia
   b. Evaluation and Management
   c. Medicine
   d. Surgery
2. A 12-month-old infant presents to a physician's office for a DTP vaccine. In which section of CPT would you find the correct code for this vaccine?
   a. Anesthesia
   b. Evaluation and Management
   c. Medicine
   d. Surgery
3. A patient is seen and evaluated in the emergency department (ED) of a local hospital. Which CPT E/M category contains a code for ED services provided to the patient?
   a. Critical Care Services
   b. Emergency Department Services
   c. Hospital Inpatient Services
   d. Hospital Observation Services
4. In which subcategory of the E/M section would you find a code for prolonged patient services with direct face-to-face contact?
   a. 99354–99357
   b. 99358–99359
   c. 99366–99368
   d. 99450–99456
5. Review the codes listed below. Which is associated with the ethmoid region?
   a. 31290
   b. 31390
   c. 31515
   d. 31584
6. Which is the title of the subsection for CPT codes 17000–17250?
   a. Burns, Local Treatment
   b. Destruction, Benign or Premalignant Lesions
   c. Destruction, Malignant Lesions, Any Method
   d. Mohs Micrographic Surgery
7. Allergy and clinical immunology codes are found in what section of CPT?
   a. Evaluation and Management
   b. Medicine
   c. Surgery
   d. Vaccines, Toxoids
8. The code for physiological support for harvesting of organ(s) from brain-dead patient is located in the __________ section of CPT.
   a. Evaluation and Management
   b. Anesthesia
   c. Surgery
   d. Medicine
9. Codes for PET scans, SPECT scans, and MRI scans are found in which CPT section?
   a. Evaluation and Management
   b. Medicine
   c. Pathology and Laboratory
   d. Radiology
10. Codes for clinical pathology consultations are found in the __________ section of CPT.
    a. Evaluation and Management
    b. Medicine
    c. Pathology and Laboratory
    d. Radiology

ASSIGNMENT 9.5 – CPT MODIFIERS

Objectives

At the conclusion of this assignment, the student should be able to:

- State the purpose of CPT modifiers.
- Assign CPT modifiers to case scenarios.

Overview

CPT modifiers clarify services and procedures performed by providers. Although the CPT code and description remain unchanged, modifiers indicate that the description of the service or procedure performed has been altered. CPT modifiers are reported as two-digit numeric codes added to the five-digit CPT code. (HCPCS level II national modifiers are reported as two-character alphabetical and alphanumeric codes added to the five-digit CPT or HCPCS level II code.)

Instructions

Circle the most appropriate response.

1. Dr. Marshall is scheduled to perform an adrenalectomy on a patient. However, after the initial incision, the patient has a run of tachycardia and a falling pulse oximetry rate. The surgery is discontinued before the adrenal gland is removed. What modifier is added to the CPT code for the adrenalectomy?
   a. -25
   b. -52
   c. -53
   d. -54
2. A patient underwent a bronchoscopy with biopsy on November 1. On November 15, the patient underwent a repeat bronchoscopy with biopsy because the biopsy sample from the procedure on November 1 was too small for pathologic analysis. Both procedures were performed by Dr. Campbell. Which modifier would be added to the bronchoscopy performed on November 15?
   a. -76
   b. -77
   c. -78
   d. -79
3. Karen Miller received the following services on May 15: annual OB/GYN examination and Pap smear, annual eye examination and eyeglass prescription check by an ophthalmologist, and cast removal from the orthopedics clinic due to a healed wrist fracture. These services were provided at a hospital outpatient department. Which modifier would be added to the codes reported?
   a. -25
   b. -27
   c. -51
   d. -59
4. Repair of a severed tendon on the index finger of the left hand would require what informational modifier?
   a. -FA
   b. -F1
   c. -F2
   d. -LT
5. A patient underwent an appendectomy on June 7. The global period for this operation is 90 days. On postoperative day 5, during the patient's follow-up visit to the surgeon's office, the surgeon finds an inguinal hernia that will require surgical reduction. Which modifier is added to the E/M code reported for the follow-up visit?
   a. -22
   b. -24
   c. -25
   d. -59
6. A patient presents to the emergency department after having fallen off his bicycle. The patient sustained multiple contaminated wounds of his hands. All of the wounds require extensive cleaning before suture closure. The wounds vary in length. The coder assigned codes 12037 and 12044. Which modifier is added to codes 12037 and 12044?
   a. No modifier is assigned
   b. -22
   c. -54
   d. -58
7. Dr. Huston sees a patient in her office, during which time the patient has many questions about her newly diagnosed hyperthyroidism. Dr. Huston provided the patient with disease information and discussed lab tests with the patient and her spouse. The E/M visit resulted in the patient being scheduled for thyroid surgery next week. The coder assigns E/M code 99215 to this encounter. What modifier is added to code 99215?
   c. -25
   d. -26
   c. -57
   d. -59

8. On the morning of July 7, a patient presents to the hospital ED vomiting blood. The GI service recommends an EGD to evaluate the patient for a possible gastric or esophageal source of the bleed. This procedure is performed at 10:30 AM. However, no bleeding source is found. At 1 PM, while in recovery from the EGD, the patient is noted to have melena. The same physician who performed the EGD procedure at 10:30 AM then performs a colonoscopy at 2:00 PM to locate the source of the melena. Which modifier should be added to the colonoscopy code?
   a. -51
   b. -58
   c. -59
   d. -76
9. A patient had a hairy nevus removed from his left forearm. During that surgery, only part of the arm was skin grafted. The patient now returns for a scheduled second graft of a different portion of the skin of the forearm. The patient will also require one more grafting procedure to complete the entire area of the nevus removal. The original procedure for the removal of the nevus was performed one month previously. The second surgery was performed on day 45 of the 90-day global period for the original removal and grafting operation. Which modifier is added to the code for the second grafting operation?
   a. -51
   b. -58
   c. -76
   d. -78
10. A patient suffers bilateral wrist factures in a motorcycle accident. What modifier is added to the CPT surgical code?
    a. -50
    b. -51
    c. -76
    d. -77
11. A patient with uncontrolled diabetes mellitus undergoes gastric bypass surgery. The patient also has hypertension. Which physical status modifier is added to the anesthesia code reported for this procedure?
    a. -P1
    b. -P2
    c. -P3
    d. -P4
12. In an ambulatory surgery center, modifier __________ is not approved for use.
    a. -25
    b. -27
    c. -50
    d. -51
13. A patient presents to an ambulatory surgery center (ASC) for diagnostic arthroscopy of his knee. The patient is waiting in the preop room for the administration of anesthesia. Before the anesthesiologist can examine the patient, the nurse documents a blood pressure reading of 200/125. The attending surgeon examines the patient and performs a blood pressure reading on the patient's opposite arm, which is 195/100. The surgeon orders intravenous antihypertensive medication, which is administered. After medication, the patient's blood pressure is 165/80 on the right and 160/80 on the left. The patient has no history of hypertension, and after consultation with internal medicine, the attending surgeon decides not to perform the arthroscopy. The patient is discharged from the ASC with medication, and an appointment is scheduled with an internist. Which modifier is added to the arthroscopy code?
    a. -53
    b. -59
    c. -73
    d. -74
14. Patient undergoes repair of a laceration of the right upper eyelid, which is performed during the same operative session as a repair of the fourth finger of the right hand. Which modifiers are added to the surgery codes?
    a. -E3 and -F8
    b. -E3 and -RT
    c. -E3 and -RT × 2
    d. -E3, -F8, and -RT

15. Mr. Harrell underwent an open reduction with internal fixation of a left femoral fracture, which was performed by Dr. Jacobs. The patient's leg was placed in a cast, and he was told to return for cast removal in eight weeks. Mr. Harrell's job moved him to another state, and he received postoperative care and cast removal by Dr. Cameron. Which modifier should Dr. Cameron assign for services provided to Mr. Harrell?
    a. -26
    b. -52
    c. -54
    d. -55
16. A patient is diagnosed with breech presentation of two fetuses, and she is pregnant with triplets. The third fetus has the cord wrapped around its neck three times. A cesarean section was performed by Dr. Sutton with assistance from Dr. Lincoln. Both physicians are fully qualified surgeons who have privileges at the teaching hospital where this procedure was performed. No resident or intern was available or present in the operating room for this surgical procedure. Which modifier is added to the CPT code available for this case?
    a. -59
    b. -62
    c. -80
    d. -82
17. A 5-year-old presents to a pediatrician's office for evaluation of a fever and cough. Upon examination, the physician notes that the child has impacted cerumen in his ear canals bilaterally and performs an irrigation of the patient's ear canals requiring instrumentation. After irrigation, the physician notes inflammation in the patient's left ear. The diagnosis for the patient is acute bronchitis, impacted cerumen, and otitis media of the left ear. Upon review of the E/M documentation, the coder assigns codes 99213 and 69210. To ensure correct payment, code 69210 should have modifier:
    a. -22 added because this is an unusual situation (E/M and ear canal irrigation performed on the same day of service).
    b. -50 added because a bilateral procedure was performed (in addition to the E/M service).
    c. -51 added because two services were performed, an E/M and an irrigation.
    d. -57 added because the decision to perform the irrigation was made during the E/M service.
18. A patient undergoes ureterolithotomy of the right ureter. After ureterogram, the physician performed ureterolithotomy on the left ureter. Which of the below is correct for this case?
    a. Modifier -22
    b. Modifier -50
    c. Modifiers -LT and -RT
    d. Report surgical code twice to reflect right and left sides
19. A patient presents to a radiology clinic for a CT scan of the brain with contrast to rule out a pituitary tumor. Dr. Hartz is covering the radiology service for that day and dictates the report for this scan. To report the service for interpretation and reporting of the scan, Dr. Hartz should add modifier __________ to the CT scan code.
    a. -22
    b. -25
    c. -26
    d. -52
20. A patient underwent a colonoscopy on July 29. During the procedure, the surgeon removed a polyp from the transverse colon via snare technique and a polyp of the sigmoid colon via ablation. All colonoscopy instruments were removed, and the patient was prepped and draped for esophagoduodenoscopy (EGD). EGD procedure was performed without incident. Which modifier is added to the EGD code?
    a. -51
    b. -59
    c. -76
    d. -77

REVIEW

Multiple Choice

Circle the most appropriate response.

1. How many sections are contained in CPT?
   a. 1
   b. 2
   c. 4
   d. 6
2. Instructions provided at the beginning of each section that define terms particular to that section and provide explanation for codes and services that apply to that section are called __________.
   a. guidelines
   b. instructional notes
   c. qualifiers
   d. special reports
3. Rather than using unlisted procedure or service CPT codes, Medicare and other third-party payers require providers to:
   a. assign ICD-10-PCS procedure codes.
   b. attach a special report.
   c. perform a known procedure.
   d. report HCPCS level II codes.
4. CPT modifiers are used to indicate that:
   a. a special report does not need to be attached to the claim.
   b. the description of the procedure performed has been altered.
   c. the provider should receive a higher reimbursement rate.
   d. the technique of the procedure was performed differently.
5. Which component is included in the surgical package?
   a. Assistant surgeon services
   b. Epidural or spinal anesthesia
   c. Prescription pain medications
   d. Uncomplicated postoperative care
6. Which modifier is reported if a third-party payer requires a second opinion for a surgical procedure?
   a. -26 (professional component)
   b. -32 (mandated services)
   c. -59 (distinct procedural service)
   d. -62 (two surgeons)
7. The time frame during which all postoperative services are included in the surgical package is the global __________.
   a. billing
   b. package
   c. period
   d. surgery
8. What organization or agency implemented the NCCI?
   a. AMA
   b. AHIMA
   c. AMBA
   d. CMS
9. What is the term used when a service is divided and coded into separate components?
   a. Unbundling
   b. Global package
   c. Unlisted procedure
   d. Add-on code
10. What federal act requires the use of CPT and HCPCS level II codes for physician services?
    a. ACA
    b. HIPAA
    c. MMA
    d. *Federal Register*
11. CPT codes that are optional and are used for tracking performance measurements are called __________ codes.
    a. Category I
    b. Category II
    c. Category III
    d. Category IV

12. A bullet located to the left of a code number identifies:
    a. a revised code description.
    b. codes exempt from modifier -51.
    c. new procedures and services.
    d. revised guidelines and notes.

13. A patient undergoes an "office toenail avulsion procedure." Which main term do you locate in the index to identify the CPT code?
    a. Avulsion
    b. Evacuation
    c. Excision
    d. Repair

14. CPT supports:
    a. the goals of the American Medical Association.
    b. requirements of electronic data interchange.
    c. requirements of the National Correct Coding Initiative.
    d. requirements of the Office of Inspector General for coding compliance.

15. Which code of those listed below is part of Category I in CPT?
    a. A0433
    b. 99215
    c. 4060F
    d. 0159T

16. In which section of CPT is code 77295?
    a. Anesthesia
    b. Pathology and Laboratory
    c. Radiology
    d. Surgery

17. Which of the below is in the correct format for a CPT level I code?
    a. 585.48
    b. 58.548
    c. 58548
    d. A5854

18. How is the CPT index organized?
    a. Alphabetically by site of service (physician office, clinic, hospital, etc.)
    b. Numerically by site of service (physician office, clinic, hospital, etc.)
    c. Alphabetically by main term
    d. Numerically by main term

19. In CPT, which of the below would be in italicized type?
    a. Main terms
    b. Cross-reference terms
    c. Code ranges
    d. Eponyms

20. Which CPT appendix contains annual coding changes (added, deleted, revised codes)?
    a. A
    b. B
    c. C
    d. D

CPT Evaluation and Management

CHAPTER 10

INTRODUCTION

This chapter introduces students to CPT evaluation and management (E/M) coding. Students determine levels of E/M services and assign codes to case studies by applying CPT coding guidelines and notes.

ASSIGNMENT 10.1 – EVALUATION AND MANAGEMENT LEVELS OF SERVICES

Objectives

At the conclusion of this assignment, the student should be able to:

- Determine whether a patient is new or established.
- Identify evaluation and management categories and subcategories.
- Determine levels of history and examination and complexity of medical decision making.

Overview

To assign evaluation and management codes, a coder must determine the

- Patient's new or established status
- Category/subcategory from which a code is to be assigned
- Levels of history and examination performed
- Complexity of medical decision making for the case

A new patient has *not* received any professional services within the past three years from the physician or from another physician of the same specialty who belongs to the same group practice. An established patient *has* received professional services within the past three years from the physician or from another physician of the same specialty who belongs to the same group practice. Evaluation and management (E/M) categories are listed in the guidelines located at the beginning of the E/M section. Levels of history and examination are determined by comparing documentation in the patient record with E/M documentation guidelines (or by using a tool such as the E/M CodeBuilder located in Appendix I of your textbook). Complexity of medical decision making is determined by comparing documentation in the patient record with the corresponding table in the E/M guidelines (or by using a tool such as the E/M CodeBuilder).

Instructions

Read each case to determine new or established status of the patient and the category and subcategory of service provided.

1. A patient was seen in the hospital as an inpatient by Dr. Maxwell. This patient was admitted two days ago and has been seen each day by the physician. Today on his third visit, Dr. Maxwell documents an expanded problem focused exam, a problem focused history, and medical decision making of moderate complexity.

   Is this an initial or subsequent visit? ________________

   Identify the CPT category and subcategory. ________________

2. Carrie Barron was seen at the medical office of Perkiomen Valley Practice. This practice is a family practice that sees general medical care patients. Carrie is new to the area, and this is her first visit to this practice. Carrie has a history of asthma and needs refills on her asthma medication. She also has questions about beginning to take an antioxidant since she has a family history of ovarian cancer. Carrie is seen by Dr. Lennox. The physician documents a detailed history, a comprehensive examination, and medical decision making of moderate complexity.

   Is the patient new or established? ________________

   Identify the CPT category and subcategory. ________________

3. A patient was treated in the emergency department (ED) following a fall from a ladder. The patient was cleaning the gutters at his home when he fell approximately 40 feet. He presents to the hospital ED with complaints of right leg and ankle pain. The patient also has multiple contusions, abrasions, and avulsions of his trunk, legs, and forearms. He is sent to x-ray to rule out fractures of his leg and ankle. The ED physician documents a detailed examination, medical decision making of moderate complexity, and a detailed history.

   Is the patient new or established? ________________

   Identify the CPT category and subcategory. ________________

4. Millie Lawton is a 45-year-old female seen for her annual physical. She has been seeing the same physician for this physical for the past five years. Millie has a history of hypertension, currently controlled by diet and exercise, and osteoarthritis, for which she takes Advil. She has been compliant with her diet and exercise program, and she has no new medical complaints. Routine blood work was ordered, and she was instructed to call for an appointment if she has any problems or questions. The physician will call her to report the blood work results.

   Is the patient new or established? ________________

   Identify the CPT category and subcategory. ________________

5. Seventy-five-year-old Milton Gray was admitted to the Alzheimer Unit at the Shady Hills Nursing Facility. The facility's medical director examined Mr. Gray upon his admission to the facility and documented a detailed examination and medical decision making of moderate complexity. Mr. Gray was unable to provide a history; therefore, the medical director, Dr. Perez, used medical records from Mr. Gray's private physician and spoke with the patient's wife and son. He learned that the patient was previously diagnosed with type 2 diabetes mellitus, hyperlipidemia, and gout. Dr. Perez documented the review of the medical record and his conversation with the family in the patient's record (detailed history).

   Is the patient new or established? ________________

   Identify the CPT category and subcategory. ________________

6. The following history information was documented in the office record of Ms. Sally Wells. Use the E/M CodeBuilder (Appendix I of your textbook) to determine the level of history performed.

   HISTORY: Patient complains of blurring vision, eye redness, and tearing. This has been happening on and off for the past three weeks. The patient's boyfriend gave her a kitten for a birthday present. The kitten sleeps with the patient in her bed. The patient has tried over-the-counter eye drops and cool compresses. The patient is on no medications. The patient has no history of eye problems or allergies to outdoor environment. The patient reports no skin problems or respiratory problems in the past. Normal childhood diseases, including chickenpox and measles. The patient does have a family history of allergies and asthma. The patient does not smoke or take any recreational drugs.

   Level of history performed: ____________

7. The following examination findings were documented on a patient seen in Dr. Blake's office. Use the E/M CodeBuilder (Appendix I of your textbook) to determine the level of examination performed.

General:	Appears in good health, no complaints.
EENT:	No abnormalities seen.
Abdomen:	Soft and nontender.
Heart:	Regular rate and rhythm.
Respiratory:	No abnormalities.
Genitalia:	Deferred.
Skin:	Area of redness on left and right elbows, with scaling.
Neurological:	Deferred.
Rectal Exam:	Deferred.

   Level of examination performed: ____________

8. The following information was documented in the office record of Ms. Sandy Thomas. Use the E/M CodeBuilder (Appendix I of your textbook) to determine the level of history and level of examination performed.

   S: The patient presents to the clinic today as a walk-in patient. The patient complains of falling over the curb while jogging last evening. The patient took Advil last night due to her ankle pain. This morning her ankle was "throbbing" and appeared swollen.

   O: Exam shows a swollen left ankle, tender on palpation.

   A: Impression: Possible ankle fracture, sprain left ankle.

   P: Patient will be scheduled for an x-ray today here at the clinic. Ace wrap will be applied until x-ray is done. If no fracture is seen, patient will be placed in a soft cast and given sprain/strain instruction sheet.

   Level of history performed: ____________

   Level of examination performed: ____________

9. The following consult note was documented on hospital inpatient Don Wentworth. Use the E/M CodeBuilder (Appendix I of your textbook) to determine the level of history and level of examination performed and complexity of medical decision making.

    Patient seen today at the request of Dr. Stone. Patient complains of chest pain, which is present at the moment and rates a 5 on a scale of 1 to 10 (with 10 being the worst). The patient has a past medical history of hypertension treated with medication for 10 years. Recently diagnosed with diabetes, uncontrolled with diet and oral medications. Current blood sugar at admission was 378. Patient is on sliding scale of insulin per Dr. Stone.

    Physical exam shows a well-appearing 65-year-old male who appears stated age. Patient is in mild discomfort.

    HEENT: Normal.

    Skin: Normal.

    Heart: Rate slightly tachycardic; no murmurs heard.

    Respiratory: Normal.

    GU:Deferred.

    EKG has slight elevations. Repeat EKG will be done. Cardiac enzymes done in emergency department on October 1 were normal. Chest x-ray results were essentially normal, also done on October 1. My plan for this patient is a repeat chest x-ray and repeat cardiac enzymes. Based on these findings, possible cardiac catheterization will be required to rule out blockage of heart vessels or arteries.

    IMPRESSION: Possible angina pectoris or atherosclerosis.

    Level of history performed: ______________

    Level of examination performed: ______________

    Complexity of medical decision making: ______________

10. The following consult note was documented on hospital inpatient Hagit Bashour. Use the E/M CodeBuilder (Appendix I of your textbook) to determine the level of history and level of examination performed and complexity of medical decision making.

    S: The patient presents with a three-day history of fever, chills, and nausea. The patient has been taking Tylenol for muscle pain. The patient's boyfriend has been encouraging liquid intake, juice, water, hot tea, and chicken soup.

    O: Vital Signs: Normal-appearing 25-year-old female looking stated age, temp 100.1, BP 120/75. Heart: RRR, no murmurs or bruits. Respiratory: Clear. EENT: Slight redness of throat. No lymphadenopathy felt. Abdomen: Nontender, normal bowel sounds. Musculoskeletal: ROM normal.

    A: Impression: Influenza.

    P: Recommendation: Continue with rest and fluids, note given for work excuse for the rest of the week. Return to the office if not better by Monday.

    Level of history performed: ______________

    Level of examination performed: ______________

    Complexity of medical decision making: ______________

ASSIGNMENT 10.2 – ASSIGNING EVALUATION AND MANAGEMENT CODES

Objectives

At the conclusion of this assignment, the student should be able to:

- Interpret the use of key components when locating evaluation and management codes.
- Assign CPT evaluation and management codes.

Overview

The levels of evaluation and management (E/M) services code descriptions include seven components.

- History
- Examination
- Medical decision making
- Counseling
- Coordination of care
- Nature of presenting problem
- Time

The *key components* of history, examination, and medical decision making are required when an E/M level of service code is selected. For new patients, all three key components must be considered when codes are assigned. For established patients, two of the three key components must be considered when codes are assigned. This means that documentation in the patient's chart must support the key components used to determine the E/M code selected.

Contributory components include counseling, coordination of care, nature of presenting problem, and time; they are used to select the appropriate E/M service code when patient record documentation indicates that they were the focus of the visit. Counseling and/or coordination of care components drive CPT code selection only when they dominate the encounter (e.g., office visit), requiring that more than 50 percent of the provider's time be spent on such components. In such circumstances, the provider must be sure to document these elements carefully so as to support the higher-level code selected. (Some E/M code descriptions include notes about time and nature of the presenting problem to assist in determining the appropriate code number to report.)

Instructions

Assign the ICD-10-CM code(s) according to outpatient coding guidelines (e.g., assign codes to signs and symptoms when a diagnosis has not been established), and assign the CPT evaluation and management code(s) and appropriate modifier(s). Do not assign ICD-10-CM external cause codes.

1. Jim Davis (age 28) was admitted to the hospital by his primary care provider, Dr. Jackson. During the hospitalization, Dr. Jackson asked Dr. Morales to provide consultation services for the patient to rule out a rash due to an allergy. (Dr. Morales is an ENT doctor who specializes in allergies and sinus problems.) Dr. Morales provided inpatient consultation services to Mr. Davis during his inpatient admission for a total body rash. Dr. Morales documented a comprehensive history, a comprehensive examination, and medical decision making of moderate complexity. Dr. Morales ordered allergy blood tests, which were negative.

   ____

2. Gerry Smith was seen in the emergency department (ED) following a house fire. The patient sustained third-degree burns over 20 percent of his body and second-degree burns over 10 percent of his body, resulting in a total of 30 percent of his body being burned. Based on information obtained from the patient's Medic Alert bracelet, the patient has type 2 diabetes mellitus and a heart condition. The ED physician documented a detailed examination and medical decision making of high complexity. The patient was unable to provide any history due to severe pain, which made it impossible for him to speak. Therefore, the ED physician obtained a detailed history from the patient's spouse. The ED physician documented a total of 80 minutes spent with this patient before the patient was transferred to the hospital's inpatient burn unit. During the 80 minutes, the patient had an episode of ventricular tachycardia, which converted with medication. The patient's blood sugar was closely monitored in the ED.

____

3. Kate Martin is a long-time patient of Dr. Hardy's office, and she presents to the office today with the complaint of "feeling very tired all of the time even after sleeping for eight hours." The patient reports that she has been feeling this way for the past three weeks. The physician documented a detailed history, an expanded problem focused exam, and medical decision making of low complexity.

____

4. New patient Daniel Cook presented to Dr. Lowell's office today because he is new to the area and needs to establish himself with a physician. He explained that he has asthma for which he takes a prescription medication and that he is almost out of his medication. No medical history other than asthma is reported, and old health records from his previous primary care physician are unavailable. The review of systems is positive for asthma. During today's visit, the patient complained of a sore throat and loss of appetite. These symptoms have been present for four days, per the patient. The patient describes the sore throat pain as on and off with worsening in the morning and late at night. The patient has taken only his prescribed asthma medication. He has not taken any over-the-counter medications in an attempt to relieve the sore throat. The patient stated that he needs a refill of his asthma medications, which the physician provided. The physician also instructed the patient to take Tylenol to relieve his sore throat symptoms and to eat foods that will not irritate his throat, such as soup. The patient was further instructed that if the sore throat and loss of appetite did not abate in five to seven days, the patient should contact the office to obtain a follow-up appointment. The physician documented a detailed examination and medical decision making of moderate complexity. (NOTE: Use the E/M CodeBuilder in Appendix I of your textbook to determine the level of history performed.)

____

5. The patient is a 52-year-old female presenting to the emergency department (ED) after falling down an embankment while hiking on her single-family private residential 25-acre property with her dog. (The patient reminded me that her residential 25-acre property is considered her yard for the purpose of assigning an external cause "place of occurrence" code.) The patient complains of left wrist pain. The ED physician diagnosed left wrist sprain and wrapped the wrist with an Ace bandage. The physician documented an expanded problem focused history, a detailed examination, and medical decision making of moderate complexity.

____

6. Mrs. Austin has been a resident of a nursing facility for the past year due to Alzheimer's disease. Today during this month's follow-up visit by her primary care physician, she was seen for a chief complaint of difficulty sleeping. The patient states that she is sleeping only a few hours each night and often awakens around 3 AM and is unable to go back to sleep. The primary care physician prescribed medication to treat the patient's inability to sleep, and he reviewed the patient's Alzheimer's disease prescription medications to ensure that no adverse reaction would result from her taking the prescribed sleep medication. He documented a problem-focused history, a detailed examination, and medical decision making of low complexity.

____

7. A patient was seen by her primary care physician for an initial inpatient visit. She was admitted to the hospital for an intestinal obstruction. The patient was previously diagnosed with bone cancer, which was treated last year. The attending physician documented a detailed history, comprehensive examination, and medical decision making of high complexity.

____

8. Ms. Hardy was seen in Dr. Stockwell's office. This patient was referred by her primary care physician due to complaints of muscle weakness and diplopia. The consulting physician, Dr. Stockwell, documented a comprehensive history, a detailed examination, and medical decision making of moderate complexity. (Ms. Hardy's health plan permits the reporting of CPT E/M consultation codes.)

____

9. A patient presented to her family physician's office with the chief complaint of aching muscles. The patient has fibromyalgia and was last seen two months ago for exacerbation of her symptoms. The physician documented a detailed history, a comprehensive examination, and medical decision making of moderate complexity.

____

10. The attending physician was preparing to discharge a patient for an inpatient hospital stay, during which time the patient's acute bronchitis was treated. The physician examined the patient and reviewed discharge instructions with the patient and the family. The physician also contacted home health services for the patient's continued care. The total time spent discharging the patient was 45 minutes.

____

ASSIGNMENT 10.3 – CODING PRACTICE

Instructions

Assign the ICD-10-CM code(s) according to outpatient coding guidelines and assign the CPT evaluation and management code(s) and appropriate modifier(s) to each case. Do not assign ICD-10-CM external cause codes.

1. An established patient was diagnosed with hypertension six months ago and visited the office today for a routine blood pressure check. The nurse recorded the reading in the patient's chart.

____

2. An 80-year-old female was admitted for 24-hour observation after falling down a short staircase in the kitchen of her single-family home and hitting her head. Her daughter reported that she was confused and disoriented. A comprehensive history and examination were done. Medical decision making was of moderate complexity.

____

3. A patient was admitted as a hospital inpatient last evening by her physician for a suspected bilateral deep venous thrombosis after noticing edema in both ankles and calves. The physician performed a comprehensive history and examination; medical decision making was of moderate complexity. A bilateral complete duplex scan of her lower extremity veins was performed.

____

4. A patient was referred to a cardiologist by her physician after an abnormal electrocardiogram. The cardiologist performed a comprehensive history and examination. Medical decision making was of moderate complexity. The diagnosis was ventricular arrhythmia. The cardiologist ordered a microvolt T-wave alternans to further assess the condition.

____

5. A patient was admitted to the emergency department (ED) with a closed fracture, left femur shaft, after falling from the jungle gym at a community playground. The ED physician performed a level 3 evaluation and management service. He then contacted the on-call orthopedic surgeon, who stated that he would perform surgery to treat the fracture.

____

6. The respiratory care physician hospitalist was called to the inpatient respiratory care unit to provide care for a patient in acute respiratory failure. The patient was admitted through the emergency department three days ago with shortness of breath. Admitting diagnosis was chronic obstructive pulmonary disease with acute exacerbation, which is being treated by her attending physician. It took the physician one hour to stabilize the patient. Two hours later the physician hospitalist was called back to assist the patient again and spent 45 minutes with the patient until she was stabilized.

____

7. A premature infant of 32 weeks' gestation, weighing 1,900 grams, was born in Community Hospital at 11:35 PM on April 30. The mother is a heroin addict, and the infant was found to have withdrawal syndrome. The infant was immediately transferred to Children's Hospital where a neonatal specialist provided initial inpatient neonatal care services on May 1. (Assign codes for the Children's Hospital admission only.)

____

8. An 85-year-old patient with acute osteoarthritis of both knees moved into the Daybreak Rest Home because she and her family believe this facility will be best suited to her physical needs. The rest home's medical director performed an expanded problem focused history and detailed examination. Medical decision making was of low complexity.

____

9. A morbidly obese patient who is bedridden was seen at home by her primary care physician. She was last seen by the physician two months ago. During this home visit, the physician performed a detailed interval history and detailed examination. Medical decision making was of moderate complexity. The physician referred the patient to a dietician and made arrangements for a visiting nurse.

____

10. A 78-year-old established patient with a history of type 1 diabetes mellitus and hypertension was seen for her annual physical. Her blood pressure was 180/120, and the physician immediately administered clonidine and had the patient rest in the examination room. He had intermittent face-to-face contact with the patient during a 45-minute period of time. Her blood pressure returned to normal, and the physician proceeded with the physical examination.

____

11. Mrs. Johnson underwent a cervical biopsy two weeks ago after a Pap smear tested positive. Dr. Smith called Mrs. Johnson today to inform her that her test results were positive for genital warts due to human papillomavirus and that she should come to the office for follow-up within 90 days. Medical discussion on the telephone was 10 minutes in duration.

____

12. A patient with native coronary artery disease was discharged last month after undergoing coronary artery bypass graft surgery with two coronary venous grafts. The patient has had a visiting nurse come in twice a week for four weeks. After each visit, the nurse reported her findings to the cardiologist. The physician spent 45 minutes reviewing the home health care plan, which included reviewing reports of the patient's status, communicating with the home health care nurse and the patient's family to assess the patient, and adjusting prescribed medical therapy.

____

13. A 1-year-old established patient visited the pediatrician for her well-baby exam, which included discussion with the mother about the need for administration of routine vaccines.

____

14. An infant was born in the hospital by cesarean section. A staff pediatrician was in attendance during delivery to provide newborn care services for initial stabilization of newborn.

____

15. Mr. O'Reilley applied for life insurance with MetLife. An insurance examination was conducted by the insurance company's physician, and a whole life insurance policy was issued.

____

REVIEW

Multiple Choice

Circle the most appropriate response.

1. A physician documented that a patient's "brother died at 65 of heart attack, mother alive with osteoporosis, father deceased at 45 with possible cancer." This documentation is part of the:
   a. family history.
   b. history of present illness.
   c. past history.
   d. social history.
2. Which of the following categories/subcategories of E/M service requires only two out of three key components for a level to be assigned?
   a. Emergency Department Service
   b. Home New Patient
   c. Initial Nursing Facility Care
   d. Subsequent Hospital Care
3. A patient presents to his physician's office after having twisted his ankle while playing football with a group of friends. The patient complains of pain of his left ankle. The physician examines the patient's ankle, notes swelling and tenderness, and sends the patient to a local hospital for an x-ray to rule out any fracture. The nursing staff at the practice places the patient's ankle in a soft cast before the patient leaves. This type of examination would be:
   a. comprehensive.
   b. detailed.
   c. expanded problem focused.
   d. problem focused.
4. What is the correct code range for the subcategory of inpatient Critical Care Services for a pediatric patient?
   a. 99281–99288
   b. 99466–99467
   c. 99468–99469
   d. 99471–99476

5. A patient presents to the emergency department (ED) following a motor vehicle crash. The patient is in and out of consciousness. When the patient is conscious, he complains of abdominal pain, head pain, and right arm pain. Upon examination, an open fracture of the ulna is noted. Also, upon abdominal exam, pain and tenderness are found. The patient is catheterized for urine, which returns blood. An abdominal ultrasound done soon after admission to the ED confirms intra-abdominal bleed possible from the patient's spleen. What is the level of presenting problem in this patient?
   a. Self-limited
   b. Low severity
   c. Moderate severity
   d. High severity
6. A new patient is seen in the office of Dr. Baldwin. She is being seen because she has recurrent heartburn that is getting worse and is not responding to over-the-counter medication such as Tums and Pepcid. She is asked to answer the following questions before undergoing an examination:
   - Any eye problems, such as blurred or double vision?
   - Any nose or throat problems, such as a stuffy nose or sore throat?
   - Any heart problems, such as rapid heartbeat?
   - Any respiratory problems, such as difficulty breathing?
   - Any gastrointestinal problems, such as heartburn, abdominal pain, or bloating?

   Answers to these questions are considered part of this patient's:
   a. history of present illness.
   b. past family history.
   c. past medical history.
   d. review of systems.
7. Questions about a patient's marital status and occupation are considered part of the:
   a. family history.
   b. history of present illness.
   c. past history.
   d. social history.
8. Dr. Merriweather treated a new patient, Nina Cartwright, in her office on 10/16/YY. She documented the following progress note:

   This 35-year-old single female has just recently moved to area. S: Patient needs refill on medication for hypertension. Patient also complains of "soreness" of her right elbow. No recent physical trauma. O: Limited range of motion, right elbow. Tenderness upon palpation. BP 140/80. A: Possible tennis elbow. Send for radiographs of elbow this week. Scripts given for atenolol for BP. P: Schedule appointment in one week to review x-ray results and check BP.

   Which part of this note is used to determine medical decision making?
   a. Limited range of motion, right elbow.
   b. Patient complains of "soreness" of her right elbow.
   c. Possible tennis elbow. Send for radiographs of elbow this week.
   d. Schedule appointment in one week to review x-ray results and check BP.
9. Which category/subcategory of evaluation and management would be reviewed to select an appropriate code for Nina Cartwright's office visit?
   a. Office Consultations
   b. Office or Other Outpatient Services, Established Patient
   c. Office or Other Outpatient Services, New Patient
   d. Preventive Medicine Service, New Patient
10. What are the three key components of an E/M service?
    a. History, examination, and medical decision making
    b. Medical decision making, examination, and time
    c. Nature of presenting problem, time, and medical decision making
    d. Time, examination, and counseling

11. Dr. Smith saw Maria Santos for a subsequent hospital visit. Ms. Santos is post-tonsillectomy × 2 days. Patient is still unable to speak in a clear voice. Bleeding has increased in the surgical area. Patient will have to be taken back to the operating room for hemorrhage control. Which level of MDM is documented?
    a. High
    b. Low
    c. Moderate
    d. Straightforward

12. The patient presents to the office with the chief complaint of difficulty swallowing. All types of food are a problem. Liquids are not. The patient does not report any chest pain or pain when lying down. The patient has pain only when swallowing; the pain is a severe burning-type pain. He has been eating soft foods and soups for the past two weeks. This problem started two weeks ago and slowly has gotten worse over time. The patient is on no medications. The patient has a family history of breast and colon cancer. The patient is a former one-pack-per-week smoker. He quit smoking 10 years ago. The ROS is positive for joint pain in the right knee on and off. No medication or treatment for this. The patient did injure his knee as a child in a skiing accident, but that was 30 years ago. Remainder of ROS is negative. Which level of history is documented?
    a. Comprehensive
    b. Detailed
    c. Expanded problem focused
    d. Problem focused

13. The following was documented on the initial visit note for Mrs. Jones, a new patient at a skilled nursing facility (SNF). Mrs. Jones is a 55-year-old female who suffered a stroke on December 14. The patient was found on that date by her daughter, unconscious on the kitchen floor. It was not known how long the patient was there. Her family reports having spoken to her the previous night at around 9 PM. The patient was taken to Valley Road Hospital and was admitted for treatment. Severe left-sided hemiplegia and dysphasia were present at admission to hospital. The patient also has a history of type 2 diabetes mellitus and GERD. The patient's diabetes has been out of control since the stroke. Current orders from hospital attending are for sliding scale of insulin injections. The patient also has a feeding tube present. The left-sided hemiplegia is still present and is of a moderate nature, and the patient will require physical and speech therapy. Reminder of review of systems is negative. Social history: The patient has been a widow for the past two years. The patient is a nonsmoker. Husband died in a car accident at the age of 55. The patient has three children, ages 25, 23, and 22, all of whom are healthy. The patient has a family history of heart disease, asthma, and Parkinson's. Mother lived to be 70 years of age and died of acute myocardial infarction. Father died at a young age of an industrial accident. The patient is admitted for physical and speech therapy. Her blood sugars will be closely monitored, and her tube feedings will continue. Which level of history is documented?
    a. Comprehensive
    b. Detailed
    c. Expanded problem focused
    d. Problem focused

14. The following is documented on the observation note of a patient: The patient was admitted yesterday to the observation unit with the r/o diagnosis of severe back pain. The patient was in an automobile accident prior to admission to the unit. Physical exam at the time was negative for any fractures. Radiology reports were also negative for any fractures. However, due to the patient's severe discomfort, he was admitted for observation. Examination on day 2 in the unit shows a 45-year-old man in moderate distress despite analgesics. Vital signs: BP 135/90, temp 98.0. MS: Pain over the lower lumbar region, ROM is limited especially on the left side. No visible swelling but tenderness on palpation. Muscle strength and tone normal on right. Decreased on left. Gait abnormal with leaning at midsection. Lungs: Clear to auscultation, no rales or wheezing. EENT: Normal, no difficulty breathing or swallowing. Abdomen: Normal bowel sounds, no palpation of spleen, liver not enlarged. No masses felt or hernias present upon examination. CV: Heart RRR, carotid arteries, no bruit, lower extremities no edema. Plan: Reexamine radiograph reports and films. Possible MRI of lumbar spine to rule out herniation of disc. Which level of exam is documented?
    a. Comprehensive
    b. Detailed
    c. Expanded problem focused
    d. Problem focused

15. The following information was documented on a patient seen in the physician's office. Review of lab tests and uroflowmetry suggests benign prostatic hypertrophy. The patient's urine flow was 8 mm. PSA test was slightly elevated. Repeat PSA today. TURP was discussed with patient. Risks and benefits of procedure discussed in detail. Patient has agreed to surgery. Surgery will be scheduled for next week. Which level of medical decision making is documented?
    a. High
    b. Low
    c. Moderate
    d. Straightforward
16. Fifty-five-year-old Nella Warner is seen by her primary care physician in his office. Mrs. Warner complains of having hand pain and stiffness. She is finding it difficult to grasp items and to hold utensils while cooking or eating. Mrs. Warner has been a patient of Dr. Manning's for the past seven years. Dr. Manning documents an expanded problem focused examination and a problem focused history and decides to send Mrs. Warner to the local hospital for blood testing and x-rays of her hand. The physician differential diagnoses are osteoarthritis, pinched nerve, or nerve compression. This is a moderate level of medical decision making. Which CPT code is reported?
    a. 99212
    b. 99213
    c. 99214
    d. 99204
17. A patient presents to the emergency department (ED) of a local hospital complaining of nausea, vomiting, and abdominal pain. The patient is a 55-year-old female with no significant medical history. The patient is seen and examined in the ED by the attending ED physician. A 12-lead EKG reveals some abnormalities. The patient also has abnormal lab tests. Because of these clinical findings, the ED physician requests a cardiology consultation. The ED physician documents a comprehensive history, a detailed exam, and medical decision making of a moderate level. Which CPT code is reported?
    a. 99221
    b. 99222
    c. 99284
    d. 99285
18. Dr. Henry is asked to consult on a patient of another physician. Dr. Henry is a neurologist. The patient is seen by Dr. Henry during her inpatient hospital stay, where her admitting diagnosis was foot pain. The patient has a history of uncontrolled diabetes mellitus and pancreatitis. Dr. Henry documents a detailed history, a comprehensive exam, and medical decision making of a moderate level. The differential diagnosis for this patient is diabetic neuropathy. Which code is reported by Dr. Henry?
    a. 99253
    b. 99243
    c. 99233
    d. 99223
19. A nurse practitioner provides home services to several patients in a rural area. Today she is visiting a patient with end-stage renal disease that does peritoneal dialysis at home. This is the fourth visit the nurse practitioner has made to this patient in the past eight months. The patient also has a moderate cardiac murmur that requires monitoring. The nurse documents a detailed interval history, an expanded problem focused examination, and medical decision making of a low complexity level. Which CPT code is reported?
    a. 99212
    b. 99308
    c. 99335
    d. 99348
20. A patient was admitted overnight to the local hospital due to complaints of abdominal and chest pain. Today the patient is seen by his primary care physician, who will also be his attending physician during this hospital admission. On this initial visit, the physician documents a comprehensive history and examination. The medical decision making documented is of a moderate level. Which code is reported?
    a. 99221
    b. 99222
    c. 99223
    d. 99233

CPT Anesthesia

CHAPTER 11

INTRODUCTION

This chapter introduces students to CPT anesthesia coding. Students assign codes to coding cases by applying CPT coding guidelines and notes.

ASSIGNMENT 11.1 – DETERMINING ANESTHESIA SERVICE PAYMENTS

Objectives

At the conclusion of this assignment, the student should be able to:

- Calculate anesthesia time units.
- Differentiate between monitored anesthesia time and nonmonitored anesthesia time.
- Determine anesthesia service payments.

Overview

Anesthesia services are reported based on time, which begins when the anesthesiologist or qualified nonphysician anesthetist (e.g., anesthesiologist's assistant, CRNA) starts preparing the patient to receive anesthesia and ends when the anesthesiologist or qualified nonphysician anesthetist is no longer in personal attendance. Anesthesia time units are reported for the amount of time the anesthesiologist or qualified nonphysician anesthetist spends administering anesthesia, and reimbursement for anesthesia services varies according to increments of time. (Nonmonitored time is not considered when calculating time units.) Payment for anesthesia services is based on the sum of an anesthesia code-specific base unit value adding in anesthesia time units and modifying units multiplied by the locality-specific anesthesia conversion factor. The formula for calculating the anesthesia fee is as follows:

```
[code-specific base unit value + anesthesia time unit(s) + modifying unit(s)] ×
locality-specific anesthesia conversion factor = anesthesia fee
For example, [5 + 3 + 0] × $17.04 = $136.32
```

- The code-specific base unit value for anesthesia codes (00100–01999) represents the degree of difficulty associated with providing anesthesia for a surgical procedure (Table 11-1).
- Anesthesia time units are based on the total anesthesia time, and they are reported as one unit for each 15 minutes (or fraction thereof) of anesthesia time. (Anesthesia time begins when the anesthesiologist or

qualified nonphysician anesthetist begins to prepare the patient for anesthesia care and ends when the anesthesiologist or CRNA is no longer in personal attendance.)

- Modifying units recognize added complexities associated with the administration of anesthesia, including physical factors and difficult circumstances.
- Physical factors indicating the patient's condition at the time anesthesia was administered are reported by adding the appropriate physical status modifier (P1–P6) to the anesthesia code. Difficult circumstances are reported with qualifying circumstances codes located in the CPT Medicine section.
- The relative values for physical status modifiers and qualifying circumstances codes are located in the current year's American Society of Anesthesiologists (ASA) *Relative Value Guide* publication (Table 11-2).
- The locality-specific anesthesia conversion factor is the dollar amount assigned to a geographic location (Table 11-3).

TABLE 11-1 Sample Portion of Anesthesia Base Unit Values

CPT Code	Base Unit Value
00210	10
01968	6
01967	5

TABLE 11-2 Sample Portion of Modifying Units and Relative Values

CPT Physical Status Modifier	Relative Value
-P1	0
-P2	0
-P3	1
-P4	2
-P5	3
-P6	0
CPT Qualifying Circumstances Code	**Relative Value**
99100	1
99116	5
99135	5
99140	2

TABLE 11-3 Sample Portion of Locality-Specific Anesthesia Conversion Factors

Payer Number	Locality Number	Locality Name	Conversion Factor
00510	00	Alabama	$17.04
00831	01	Alaska	$29.66
00832	00	Arizona	$17.83
00520	13	Arkansas	$16.52

Courtesy of the Centers for Medicare & Medicaid Services. http://www.cms.gov

When an anesthesiologist or a qualified nonphysician anesthetist provides multiple anesthesia services for the same patient during the same operative session, the anesthesia fee is based on the *highest* code base unit value when multiple stand-alone anesthesia codes are reported (which is added to the total anesthesia time for all services provided). When an anesthesia code and its add-on codes are reported, reimbursement for multiple anesthesia services is based on the sum of the base unit values.

Instructions

Calculate anesthesia service payments by

- Assigning the appropriate anesthesia code and modifier
- Determining the base unit values for the code assigned (Table 11-1)
- Determining the relative values for the modifier (and, if applicable, qualifying circumstances code) (Table 11-2)
- Selecting the state anesthesia conversion factor (Table 11-3)
- Calculating the anesthesia time units

1. A 34-year-old female patient who has controlled diabetes mellitus underwent a planned vaginal delivery at the Arkansas Medical Center on August 5, during which 45 minutes of neuraxial labor anesthesia was administered by an anesthesiologist.

   CPT anesthesia code: __________

   Base unit value (anesthesia code): __________

   Anesthesia time units: __________

   Relative value (modifier + qualifying circumstances code, if applicable): __________

   Conversion factor: __________

   Anesthesia service payment: __________

2. A 42-year-old female patient who has chronic emphysema was prepared for a planned vaginal delivery at the Arizona Women's Center on December 10, during which 75 minutes of neuraxial labor anesthesia was administered by an anesthesiologist. Complications required that an emergency cesarean delivery be performed instead of the planned vaginal delivery.

   CPT anesthesia codes: __________

   Base unit value (anesthesia code): __________

   Anesthesia time units: __________

   Relative value (modifier + qualifying circumstances code, if applicable): __________

   Conversion factor: __________

   Anesthesia service payment: __________

3. A 54-year-old otherwise healthy male patient sustained multiple trauma in an automobile accident. He was administered 60 minutes of general anesthesia at the Alabama Trauma Center by an anesthesiologist during emergency cranial surgery.

   CPT anesthesia codes: __________

   Base unit value (anesthesia code): __________

   Anesthesia time units: __________

   Relative value (modifier + qualifying circumstances code, if applicable): __________

   Conversion factor: __________

   Anesthesia service payment: __________

ASSIGNMENT 11.2 – ANESTHESIA MODIFIERS

Objectives

At the conclusion of this assignment, the student should be able to:

- Differentiate among HCPCS level II, physical status, and standard modifiers.
- Assign HCPCS level II, physical status, and standard modifiers to anesthesia codes.

Overview

All anesthesia services require the following types of modifiers be reviewed for assignment with reported anesthesia codes:

- HCPCS level II modifiers
- Physical status modifiers
- Standard modifiers

The following HCPCS level II anesthesia modifiers are added to reported anesthesia codes when applicable.

HCPCS Level II Anesthesia Modifier	Description
-AA	Anesthesia services performed personally by anesthesiologist
-AD	Medically supervised by a physician for more than four concurrent procedures
-G8	Monitored anesthesia care for deep complex, complicated, or markedly invasive surgical procedure

NOTE:

- Report modifier -G8 with CPT codes 00100, 00400, 00160, 00300, 00532, and 00920 only.
- Do not report modifier -G8 with modifier -QS.

HCPCS Level II Anesthesia Modifier	Description
-G9	Monitored anesthesia care for patient who has history of severe cardiopulmonary condition
-QK	Medical direction of two, three, or four concurrent procedures involving qualified individuals
-QS	Monitored anesthesia care

NOTE:

Monitored anesthesia care involves the intraoperative monitoring of the patient's vital physiologic signs in anticipation of the need for administration of general anesthesia or of the development of adverse physiologic patient reaction to the surgical procedures.

HCPCS Level II Anesthesia Modifier	Description
-QX	Qualified nonphysician anesthetist service, with medical direction by physician
-QY	Medical direction of one qualified nonphysician anesthetist by an anesthesiologist
-QZ	CRNA service, without medical direction by physician

A *physical status modifier* is added to each reported anesthesia code to indicate the patient's condition at the time anesthesia was administered, and it serves to identify the complexity of services provided. Physical status modifiers are represented by the letter *P* followed by a single digit from 1 to 6.

Physical Status Modifier	Description
-P1	Normal healthy patient (e.g., no biochemical, organic, physiologic, psychiatric disturbance)
-P2	Patient with mild systemic disease (e.g., anemia, chronic asthma, chronic bronchitis, diabetes mellitus, essential hypertension, heart disease that only slightly limits physical activity, obesity)
-P3	Patient with severe systemic disease (e.g., angina pectoris, chronic pulmonary disease that limits activity, history of prior myocardial infarction, heart disease that limits activity, poorly controlled essential hypertension, morbid obesity, type 1 diabetes mellitus with vascular complications)
-P4	Patient with severe systemic disease that is a constant threat to life (e.g., advanced pulmonary/renal/hepatic dysfunction, congestive heart failure, persistent angina pectoris, unstable/rest angina)
-P5	Moribund patient who is not expected to survive without the operation (e.g., abdominal aortic aneurysm)
-P6	Declared brain-dead patient whose organs are being removed for donor purposes

CPT modifiers should be reviewed to determine whether they should be added to the reported anesthesia codes.

CPT Modifier	Description
-23	Unusual anesthesia

NOTE:

When a patient's circumstances warrant the administration of general or regional anesthesia (instead of the usual local anesthesia), add modifier -23 to the anesthesia code. The following may require general or regional anesthesia services (when local anesthesia services are usually provided):

- Extremely apprehensive patients
- Individuals with an intellectual disability
- Patients who have a physical condition (e.g., spasticity or tremors)

-59	Distinct procedural service

NOTE:

An anesthesiologist or a qualified nonphysician anesthetist reports the anesthesia code with the highest base unit value first. Modifier -59 is added to each separately reported anesthesia code.

-74	Discontinued outpatient hospital/ambulatory surgery center procedure after anesthesia administration
-99	Multiple modifiers

HCPCS Level II Anesthesia Modifiers

Instructions: Assign the appropriate HCPCS level II anesthesia modifier to each case.

________________ 1. A patient received monitored general anesthesia care for a complicated surgical procedure.

________________ 2. A patient was administered general anesthesia by a CRNA, who did not receive medical direction by a physician or an anesthesiologist.

______________________ 3. A patient was administered general anesthesia by the anesthesiologist.

______________________ 4. The patient was one of five surgical patients who was concurrently medically supervised by an anesthesiologist.

Physical Status Modifiers

Instructions: Assign the appropriate CPT physical status modifier to each case.

______________________ 5. A patient who sustained trauma during an automobile accident was diagnosed with a ruptured spleen and was administered general anesthesia during the splenectomy procedure.

______________________ 6. A patient previously diagnosed with end-stage renal disease was administered general anesthesia during an open reduction internal fixation procedure, left femur.

______________________ 7. A patient with chronic asthma was administered general anesthesia during an open cholecystectomy procedure.

CPT Modifiers

Instructions: Assign the appropriate CPT modifier to each case.

______________________ 8. An outpatient ambulatory surgery center procedure was discontinued after general anesthesia was administered due to hypotension.

______________________ 9. Due to severe anxiety during a procedure, a patient was administered regional anesthesia instead of the usually indicated local anesthesia.

______________________ 10. The anesthesiologist performed a Swan-Ganz catheterization at the conclusion of the operative procedure.

ASSIGNMENT 11.3 – CODING PRACTICE

Instructions

Assign the ICD-10-CM code(s) to diagnoses and conditions and assign the CPT anesthesia code(s) and appropriate HCPCS level II, physical status, and CPT modifier(s). Do not assign ICD-10-CM external cause codes.

Head

1. A 54-year-old female with chronic hypertension was admitted as an acute care hospital inpatient for vertigo and headaches. After testing, her cerebrospinal fluid pressure was high due to a subdural hematoma with no loss of consciousness. General anesthesia was administered by an anesthesiologist. The surgeon drilled burr holes to evacuate the hematoma and relieve the pressure. The anesthesiologist inserted a percutaneous arterial line (catheter) to monitor the patient while providing the anesthesia services during the surgical procedure. Following surgery, the anesthesiologist inserted a Swan-Ganz (flow-directed) cardiac catheter.

   ____

2. A hypertensive 64-year-old male received general anesthesia from a CRNA who received medical direction from an anesthesiologist (who was not in the same operating room but provided direction from an adjacent operating room). Excision of a salivary parotid malignancy, lateral lobe, was performed.

   ____

Nook

3. An 11-month-old male was brought to the emergency room after trapping his head between two fence posts. He was having severe breathing problems and was cold and sweaty. Pulse rate was low. General anesthesia was administered by the anesthesiologist prior to emergency surgical repair of the crushed larynx and trachea. The anesthesiologist inserted a percutaneous arterial line (catheter) to monitor the patient while providing the anesthesia services during the surgical procedure.

____

4. A 12-year-old male with metastatic cancer was administered general anesthesia by the CRNA, who did not receive medical direction from a physician or an anesthesiologist. A malignant lesion was removed from the muscles of the patient's neck. (HINT: Muscles are classified as *connective tissue* in the ICD-10-CM Table of Neoplasms.)

____

Thorax (Chest Wall and Shoulder Girdle)

5. An otherwise healthy 15-year-old female skateboarder fell while riding, which resulted in a right clavicular fracture. The fracture was repaired with internal fixation under general anesthesia, which was administered by the anesthesiologist.

____

6. An 85-year-old female was admitted to the hospital for metastatic bone cancer. The primary site of cancer is unknown. A malignant lesion was discovered on her right third rib. She underwent a partial rib resection under general anesthesia, which was administered by the anesthesiologist.

____

Intrathoracic

7. A 74-year-old male with symptomatic atrioventricular blockage and a permanent pacemaker implantation developed Twiddler syndrome two weeks after implantation of the pacemaker. The pacemaker was replaced under general anesthesia, which was administered by the anesthesiologist.

____

8. An 82-year-old female with type 1 diabetes and a history of tobacco abuse was diagnosed with a malignancy on her esophagus. She underwent a total esophagectomy under general anesthesia, which was administered by the anesthesiologist.

____

Spine and Spinal Cord

9. An otherwise healthy 43-year-old male was diagnosed with a benign thoracic spinal tumor. He underwent a neurological resection under regional anesthesia, which was administered by a CRNA who received medical direction from the physician.

____

10. An obese 57-year-old male with type 2 diabetes was diagnosed with recurring upper back pain due to displacement of cervical intervertebral disc. He underwent posterior extradural laminotomy for decompression of the cervical spine, under regional anesthesia, which was administered by the anesthesiologist.

____

Upper Abdomen

11. A 59-year-old male alcoholic with a long history of cirrhosis underwent liver transplant surgery under general anesthesia, which was administered by the anesthesiologist. The patient is the recipient of the liver. Following surgery, the anesthesiologist inserted a Swan-Ganz (flow-directed) cardiac catheter.

____

12. A morbidly obese 37-year-old hypertensive female with type 2 diabetes and high cholesterol was admitted to a private hospital for bariatric surgery, which was administered by the anesthesiologist. A gastric ring procedure was performed under general anesthesia.

____

Lower Abdomen

13. A 55-year-old male otherwise healthy patient presents with a lump in the lower abdominal area, which was due to an abdominal hernia. An abdominal hernia repair was performed under general anesthesia, which was administered by the CRNA without medical direction by the physician.

____

14. A renal transplant was performed on a 61-year-old female with type 1 diabetes and related end-stage renal disease. General anesthesia was administered by the anesthesiologist. (The patient is the recipient of the kidney.) The anesthesiologist inserted a percutaneous arterial line (catheter) to monitor the patient while providing the anesthesia services during the surgical procedure. Following surgery, the anesthesiologist inserted a Swan-Ganz (flow-directed) cardiac catheter.

____

Perineum

15. A two-month-old healthy male underwent a procedure for exploration of a bilateral undescended testis. The patient was administered general anesthesia, which was administered by the CRNA without medical direction by the physician.

____

16. An HIV-infected 24-year-old male is post amputation of penis (partial) due to a malignant lesion with resultant impotence. Patient underwent insertion of a penile prosthesis (perineal approach) under regional anesthesia, which was administered by the anesthesiologist.

____

Pelvis

17. An otherwise healthy 18-year-old male was driving his motorcycle and had an accident. He was brought to the emergency department and after radiologic exam was diagnosed with a fractured pelvis. He underwent emergency surgery during which closed treatment of a pelvic rim fracture was performed under general anesthesia, which was administered by the anesthesiologist.

____

18. An otherwise healthy 27-year-old female was hit by a car while crossing the street. She sustained closed fractures of right humerus and left femur. She underwent emergency surgery for fracture treatment and was placed in a body cast, including both thighs. She was administered general anesthesia, which was administered by the anesthesiologist. (Initial encounter)

____

Upper Leg

19. A 68-year-old female with severe varicose veins of both lower extremities and ulcers of both thighs underwent surgical repair. General anesthesia was administered by the anesthesiologist.

____

20. An otherwise healthy 85-year-old male tripped on a curb, fell, and fractured his upper femur, left. Surgery to treat the closed femur fracture was performed under general anesthesia, which was administered by the CRNA without medical direction by the physician. (Initial encounter)

____

Knee and Popliteal Area

21. A 59-year-old hypertensive female runner underwent surgery due to recurring left knee pain. A diagnostic arthroscopy, left knee, was performed under regional anesthesia that was administered by the anesthesiologist.

____

22. A 74-year-old female with type 2 diabetes was hit in a parking lot by a slow-moving car. A right proximal fibula fracture was discovered via radiologic exam. The patient underwent an open fracture treatment under general anesthesia, which was administered by the anesthesiologist. (Initial encounter)

____

Lower Leg

23. A 38-year-old male with a history of right foot problems was diagnosed with a cocked-up fifth toe, which was surgically corrected under regional anesthesia that was administered by the anesthesiologist.

____

24. A 69-year-old male was diagnosed with metastatic cancer of his proximal right great toe (bone). Resection of the toe was performed under general anesthesia, which was administered by the anesthesiologist.

____

Shoulder and Axilla

25. An otherwise healthy 16-year-old high school baseball pitcher with right recurring shoulder pain underwent radiologic exam, which revealed osteochondritis dissecans. A surgical arthroscopic procedure of the humeral head was performed under regional anesthesia, which was administered by the anesthesiologist.

____

26. An otherwise healthy four-year-old female slipped and fell at a shopping mall and fractured her upper humerus, left. A shoulder cast was applied, and general anesthesia was administered by the anesthesiologist. (Initial encounter)

____

Upper Arm and Elbow

27. An HIV-infected 41-year-old male fell off a roof while working and landed on his right side. Upon radiologic exam, it was noted that the right elbow was crushed. Arthroplasty of the right elbow with prosthetic replacement was performed under general anesthesia, which was administered by the CRNA under medical direction by an anesthesiologist. (Initial encounter)

____

28. A 55-year-old male with celiac disease and high cholesterol developed a lump on his upper arm, left. A bone cyst of the left humerus was diagnosed, and the patient underwent surgery for excision of the cyst. Regional anesthesia was administered by the anesthesiologist.

____

Forearm, Wrist, and Hand

29. An otherwise healthy four-year-old female was brought to the emergency department with pain in her right forearm. Radiologic exam revealed a closed fracture, right radius. A closed procedure was performed to reduce the fracture, and general anesthesia was administered by the anesthesiologist. (Initial encounter)

____

30. An otherwise healthy 18-year-old male arrived in the emergency department complaining of pain in the left hand. He stated that he was jacking up a car to fix a flat tire when the jack handle struck his hand. Radiologic exam revealed a fractured left wrist, which required closed surgical repair under general anesthesia. The CRNA administered the anesthesia under medical direction by a physician. (Initial encounter)

____

Radiological Procedures

31. Diagnostic venography was performed on an otherwise healthy 31-year-old female because of severe left leg pain. Regional anesthesia was administered by the anesthesiologist.

____

32. A 35-year-old male with type 2 diabetes and back pain underwent therapeutic percutaneous image-guided spine and spinal cord discography under general anesthesia, which was administered by the CRNA under medical direction by an anesthesiologist.

____

Burn Excisions or Debridement

33. A 45-year-old tobacco-abusing (cigarettes) male started a fire while smoking in bed. He sustained third-degree burns of his chest, which included 3 percent of his body. After the patient was stabilized, surgical debridement was performed under regional anesthesia which was administered by the anesthesiologist. (Initial encounter)

____

34. An otherwise healthy 45-year-old chef spilled boiling water on his left leg and sustained second-degree burns of the left thigh, left knee, and left calf (5 percent of his body). After the patient was stabilized, he underwent surgical debridement for which regional anesthesia was administered by the CRNA without medical direction by a physician or an anesthesiologist. (Initial encounter)

____

Obstetric

35. An HIV-infected 19-year-old female underwent an emergency cesarean hysterectomy under general anesthesia, which was administered by the anesthesiologist. A single liveborn infant was delivered.

____

36. A healthy 25-year-old female underwent a normal vaginal delivery during her third trimester, for which an epidural was administered by the CRNA with medical direction by an anesthesiologist. Liveborn twins were delivered.

____

37. An anesthesiologist provided neuraxial labor anesthesia for a planned vaginal delivery. She also performed repeat subarachnoid needle placement and drug injection of the epidural catheter during labor. The patient was a 34-year-old healthy female in her third trimester. Liveborn triplets were delivered.

____

Other Procedures

38. An anesthesiologist provided physiologic support during the harvesting of a kidney from a 34-year-old brain-dead patient.

____

39. An anesthesiologist provided nerve block, upper arm, left, of a 29-year-old patient with parkinsonism. The patient was placed in prone position for procedure.

____

40. An anesthesiologist provided daily hospital management of subarachnoid continuous drug administration to a 34-year-old female patient who had undergone emergency surgery to correct an atrial septal defect. (Without the surgery, the patient would have died.)

____

REVIEW

Multiple Choice

Circle the most appropriate response.

1. For anesthesia code 00866-AA-P2-23, the physical status modifier is ___________.
   a. 00866
   b. -23
   c. -AA
   d. -P2
2. A 25-year-old patient undergoes a cesarean section procedure performed by her surgeon. Anesthetic agents were injected into the spinal fluid to block the nerve supply to the pelvic and lower regions of the patient's body. The patient could not feel pain in those areas during the procedure, and she remained awake but sedated. Which type of anesthesia was administered to this patient?
   a. General anesthesia
   b. Local anesthesia
   c. Moderate (conscious) sedation
   d. Regional anesthesia
3. Which anesthesia code is reported for a patient who undergoes a C-section?
   a. 01961
   b. 00800
   c. 00940
   d. 00944
4. A patient undergoes a heart transplant procedure. During surgery, the anesthesiologist monitored the patient's capnography, electrocardiogram (EKG), and oximetry; he also placed a central venous line. Which service is reported as a separate code?
   a. Capnography
   b. Central venous line placement
   c. EKG monitoring
   d. Oximetry monitoring

5. Central venous access device (CVAD) is a type of ___________.
   a. anesthesia
   b. catheter
   c. radiograph
   d. pulse oximetry

6. An anesthesiologist provided general anesthesia services for a 25-year-old patient who underwent partial thyroidectomy. The patient has mild rheumatoid arthritis in his hands and feet, which is a chronic condition.
   a. 00320-AA-P1
   b. 00320-AA-P2
   c. 00320-AA-P3
   d. 00320-AA-P4

7. A 12-year-old patient sustained a carpal bone fracture that was treated by open reduction with internal fixation. The anesthesiologist administered a Bier block, which is considered ___________ anesthesia.
   a. general
   b. local
   c. regional
   d. topical

8. An anesthesiologist administered general anesthesia services to a 75-year-old male who underwent removal of femoral artery emboli. This patient has a history of uncontrolled type 1 diabetes mellitus, gastroesophageal reflux disease, and chronic pancreatitis.
   a. 01430-AA-P2, 99100
   b. 01440-AA-P2, 99100
   c. 01274-AA-P3, 99100
   d. 01500-AA-P3, 99100

9. A Hickman catheter is a(n) ___________ catheter.
   a. internal
   b. nontunneled
   c. port
   d. tube

10. A patient sustained second- and third-degree burns to 30 percent of his body during a house fire. The patient underwent debridement of his burns. The anesthesiologist performed intraoperative monitoring of the surgical patient's vital physiologic signs, which is a service abbreviated as ___________.
    a. electroconvulsive therapy (ECT)
    b. electromyogram (EMG)
    c. lumbar puncture (LP)
    d. monitored anesthesia care (MAC)

11. Code 00754 is reported for anesthesia services administered during a hernia repair procedure performed on the ___________.
    a. lower abdomen
    b. lumbar and ventral regions
    c. omphalocele
    d. transabdominal region

12. An otherwise healthy six-month-old child underwent repair of a cleft palate. Which codes are reported by the anesthesiologist?
    a. 00172-AA-P1, 99100
    b. 00190-AA-P1, 99100
    c. 00192-AA-P1, 99100
    d. 00210-AA-P1, 99100

13. Martin Stevens is a 40-year-old man who is donating his left kidney to his younger brother Tom, who has polycystic kidney disease. Martin is a healthy man who has three children and no evidence of any chronic conditions or medical issues. Report CPT code(s) ___________.
    a. 00862-AA
    b. 00862-AA-P1
    c. 00868-AA-P1, 99100
    d. 01990-AA-P2, 99100

14. Code 00950 is reported for anesthesia services provided during a vaginal ___________ procedure.
    a. cerclage
    b. culdoscopy
    c. hysterectomy
    d. hysteroscopy

15. Max Walker underwent coronary artery bypass graft surgery due to blockage of his anterior coronary artery, which caused angina pectoris. The patient has chronic type 2 diabetes mellitus, which is controlled with oral medications, a diabetic diet, and exercise. At the start of surgery, the anesthesiologist inserted an endotracheal tube (ET) to maintain the patient's respiratory function. During surgery, the anesthesiologist monitored the patient's arterial blood gas levels. At the conclusion of the procedure, before sending the patient to the recovery room, the anesthesiologist inserted a nasogastric tube. Before the patient was transferred from the recovery room to the cardiac care unit (CCU), the anesthesiologist removed the patient's ET tube. That night the CCU staff noted that the patient was experiencing respiratory insufficiency. The anesthesiologist assessed the patient and placed another ET tube to assist the patient with his breathing. Report CPT code(s) ___________.
   a. 00566, 31500-AA-P2
   b. 00566-AA-P2, 31500-59, 31500-59, 43752-59
   c. 00566-AA-P3, 43752-59
   d. 00566-AA-P3, 31500-59
16. A registered nurse licensed to administer anesthesia is called a(n) ___________.
   a. CVAD
   b. CRNA
   c. ECT
   d. LP
17. When anesthesia services are provided to a patient who is under one year of age or over 70 years of age, the coder should report ___________.
   a. a qualifying circumstance code
   b. modifier -23 with the anesthesia code and a qualifying circumstance code
   c. modifier -23 with the anesthesia code
   d. physical status modifier -P3 with the anesthesia code
18. A 50-year-old female patient with a recent history of fainting underwent an interventional radiologic procedure, left carotid artery. All diagnostic tests were normal. The patient is not on any medications and has no other medical problems. Report code(s) _________.
   a. 00216-AA-P1
   b. 00350-AA-P1
   c. 01925-AA-P1
   d. 01933-AA-P1
19. An otherwise healthy patient received a steroid injection, which was performed by his surgeon, in his lumbar vertebrae for chronic back pain. The patient was placed in the prone position, and the anesthesiologist administered regional anesthesia. Report code(s) _________.
   a. 00630-AA-P1
   b. 00635-AA-P1
   c. 00640-AA-P1
   d. 01992-AA-P1
20. Which component of the anesthesia fee is based on degree of difficulty?
   a. Base unit value
   b. Conversion factor
   c. Modifying unit
   d. Time unit

CHAPTER 12

CPT Surgery I

INTRODUCTION

This chapter introduces students to CPT surgery coding (General subsection and Integumentary System subsection). Students assign codes to coding cases by applying CPT coding guidelines and notes.

Objectives

At the conclusion of this chapter, the student should be able to:

- Assign CPT Surgery codes from the General and Integumentary System subsections.
- Add CPT and/or HCPCS level II modifiers to codes as appropriate.

ASSIGNMENT 12.1 – CODING PRACTICE

Instructions

Assign the ICD-10-CM code(s) to diagnoses and conditions and assign the CPT surgery code(s) and the appropriate HCPCS level II and CPT modifier(s). Do not assign ICD-10-CM external cause codes.

1. Under local anesthesia, the patient's lacerated nail bed, left thumb, was repaired by removing the damaged nail from the nail bed. A small foreign object that appeared to be a piece of metal was removed. The nail bed wound was irrigated and sutured closed. Bleeding was controlled through electrocautery, and the wound was dressed. (Initial encounter)

   ____

2. Patient presented with a mole on her back. The 2.0-cm lesion was removed by Dr. Jones via shaving technique.

   ____

3. Patient had a malignant melanoma on her right cheek, which was confirmed by biopsy last week. Patient underwent excision of the 3.5-cm diameter lesion (including margins) today.

   ____

4. Patient presented to the emergency department with two lacerations, one on her right wrist and another on her right forearm, as the result of breaking a glass window by accident. Simple repair of the 2.0-cm laceration on her right wrist and simple repair of the 4.0-cm laceration on her right forearm were performed by the emergency department. (Initial encounter)

   ____

5. With the patient under local anesthesia, a small incision of a carbuncle of the left thigh was made to allow the contents to drain. After the contents of the carbuncle were drained, the carbuncle sac was curetted and irrigated.

____

ASSIGNMENT 12.2 – CODING OPERATIVE REPORTS

Instructions

Assign the ICD-10-CM code(s) to diagnoses and conditions and assign the CPT surgery code(s) and the appropriate HCPCS level II and CPT modifier(s). Do not assign ICD-10-CM external cause codes.

1. PREOPERATIVE DIAGNOSIS: 1.5-cm perianal cyst.

   POSTOPERATIVE DIAGNOSIS: 1.5-cm perianal cyst.

   OPERATION PERFORMED: Excision of perianal cyst.

   The patient was placed on the operating table in the prone position. In the left perianal region, a 1.5-cm perianal cyst was noted. The area was sterilely prepped and draped and infiltrated with local anesthetic. The 1.5-cm perianal cyst was excised with a radial elliptical incision. The specimen was sent to pathology for examination. Hemostasis was obtained. The incision was closed with a running simple suture of 3-0 catgut. There was no bleeding. The wound was cleaned and dressed. The patient was sent to the recovery room in stable condition.

   ____

2. PREOPERATIVE DIAGNOSIS: Pyogenic granuloma, right index finger.

   POSTOPERATIVE DIAGNOSIS: Pyogenic granuloma, right index finger.

   OPERATION PERFORMED: Excision of pyogenic granuloma, right index finger.

   This is a 35-year-old female who presents to the office with the complaint of a painful growth on the ulnar side of her right index finger. On physical exam, the patient has a red raised granular lesion on the ulnar portion of her fingernail. The decision was made after discussion with the patient to take her to the operating room for excision of this lesion. The patient was brought to the operating room, identified, and placed on the operating table in the supine position. Lidocaine plain 1% was used for a digital block. Once the block had taken, the patient was prepped and draped in a sterile fashion. A scalpel was used to excise the 0.8-cm granuloma. Once it was excised, cautery was used to cauterize the vessels. Bacitracin was placed over the wound, followed by a bandage. The patient tolerated the procedure and was discharged home in a stable condition.

   ____

3. PREOPERATIVE DIAGNOSIS: Lesion, skin of forehead.

   POSTOPERATIVE DIAGNOSIS: Basal cell carcinoma, skin of forehead.

   OPERATION PERFORMED: Excision of lesion and advancement flap.

   The patient is a 45-year-old male who presented to the office with a mole of the forehead that had grown in size and shape over the last few months. After examining the patient, it was thought that he should have the lesion excised and biopsied to determine what type of lesion it was. The circular mole was 4.0 cm in diameter and was located on the right side of upper forehead just at the patient's hairline. The patient was brought into the operating room and, after the administration of adequate anesthesia, was prepped and draped in the usual sterile fashion. The patient's hair was shaved above the site of the lesion. The lesion was excised with a 1.0-cm margin, and a specimen was sent to pathology for frozen section analysis. The section was returned as basal cell carcinoma. The resulting defect after removal of the lesion was too deep for suture closure, so an advancement flap from the patient's scalp was used to close the surgical wound.

The size of the flap was approximately 4 cm × 4 cm. The patient experienced minimal blood loss, and after the wound was dressed, he was discharged in a stable condition.

____

4. PREOPERATIVE DIAGNOSIS: Decubitus ulcer, stage IV, left hip.

   POSTOPERATIVE DIAGNOSIS: Decubitus ulcer, stage IV, left hip.

   OPERATION PERFORMED: Excision of stage IV decubitus ulcer, left hip.

   The patient is a 30-year-old autistic male who also has multiple sclerosis. The patient is bed-bound and totally nonambulatory at this point, and he has developed a decubitus ulcer of the left hip. The patient was brought to the operating suite, and after administration of a regional block, the patient was prepped and draped in a sterile fashion. The area of the ulcer over the patient's left hip was probed and examined. The ulcer had moved down through the fascia and muscle level to the greater trochanteric process. The size of the ulcer was 6.0 × 7.0 × 8.0 cm. The ulcer was removed, and the defect created from this excision required a myocutaneous flap. This was done after a section of the trochanteric process was removed. The area was bandaged. The patient was in stable condition when he was moved to the recovery room.

   ____

5. PREOPERATIVE DIAGNOSIS: Inverted breast nipples.

   POSTOPERATIVE DIAGNOSIS: Inverted breast nipples.

   OPERATION PERFORMED: Correction of inverted breast nipples.

   The patient is a 25-year-old female who was unable to breast-feed her infant due to an inversion of her breast nipples bilaterally. The patient presented to the office for a correction procedure. After administration of local anesthetic, a small incision was made in the areola of the right nipple and the nipple was elevated to a correct everted position. The same technique was used on the left breast. The left breast ductal tissue was slightly denser, and a small amount of ductal tissue was removed to allow for the correction. The tissue was sent for analysis. After the surgical incision was sutured closed, an antibiotic ointment was applied followed by a sterile dressing.

   ____

REVIEW

Multiple Choice

Circle the most appropriate response.

1. Dr. Summers removed a 2.5 cm in diameter basal cell carcinoma (BCC), using a shaving technique, from the nose of a patient. A BCC lesion of the cheek, 1.5 cm in diameter, was also excised. Report CPT code(s) ___________.
   a. 17283, 11642-51
   b. 11313, 11642-51
   c. 11644
   d. 11643, 11642-51
2. Patient underwent fine needle aspiration without imaging guidance, solid mass of right breast.
   a. 10021
   b. 19120
   c. 19281
   d. 19499
3. A patient presented to the urgent care center with an open wound of her left hand. The patient had fallen and cut her hand on a goal post while playing soccer. The 4.5 cm in length wound was full of debris, grass, dirt, and paint from the goal post. The physician carefully cleaned the wound with 1.5 liters of saline before performing a single-layer closure with 3.0 Vicryl. Report CPT code ___________.
   a. 12002
   b. 12013
   c. 12032
   d. 12042

4. Henry Cain was a victim of a house fire that occurred three months ago. Today, he is undergoing surgery to graft skin tissue from his left thigh to his entire left forearm and the left side of his upper chest. This type of grafting is called a(n)
   a. allograft.
   b. autograft.
   c. pinch graft.
   d. xenograft.
5. Code 19105 is located in the ____________ subsection of CPT Surgery.
   a. Integumentary
   b. Musculoskeletal
   c. Respiratory
   d. Urinary
6. Code 19120, which is located in the Integumentary subsection of CPT Surgery, represents a(n)
   a. endoscopy.
   b. excision.
   c. incision.
   d. repair.
7. A patient underwent cryosurgery of papillomata. Cryosurgery is categorized as a(n) ____________ in CPT.
   a. destruction
   b. excision
   c. incision
   d. reconstruction
8. Which CPT symbol designates telemedicine services?
   a. Bullet
   b. Star
   c. Lightning bolt
   d. Plus sign
9. When a lesion is excised and the resultant surgical defect requires closure with a V-Y plasty, the coder should:
   a. assign a code for the V-Y plasty procedure only.
   b. code excision of the lesion as well as the V-Y plasty procedure.
   c. query the physician to determine whether the excision of lesion or V-Y plasty procedure is coded.
   d. report separate codes for excision of the lesion, the closure procedure, and the V-Y plasty procedure.
10. A patient presented to the hospital emergency department (ED) with four wounds sustained in a motorcycle accident: 3.0-cm wound of the scalp, 1.0-cm wound of the neck, 3.0-cm wound of the right hand, and 2.0-cm wound of the right foot. The ED physician performed wound debridement and then repaired the hand and foot wounds with a layered closure due to their depth. The scalp and neck wounds involved epidermal and dermal layers only, and they were repaired with a one-layer suture closure technique. Report CPT code(s) ____________.
    a. 12004
    b. 12032, 12002-51
    c. 12042, 12002-51
    d. 13121, 12002-51
11. A 30-year-old patient underwent tonsillectomy and adenoidectomy (T&A) on May 1 and was discharged from the hospital on May 3. The T&A procedure has a 90-day global period as established by the patient's third-party payer. On May 20, the patient was seen in his surgeon's office for a surgical follow-up visit. The patient reported no medical complaints during this visit and was experiencing no bleeding, pain, or difficulty swallowing. The physician performed a problem focused examination and history. A code is not reported for the follow-up office visit with the surgeon because the
    a. follow-up visit is considered part of the surgical package.
    b. patient did not have any complaints to report at this visit.
    c. patient had no bleeding or pain documented by the physician.
    d. physician did not document medical decision making for this visit.
12. A patient had 35 fibrocutaneous skin tags removed from various places on his body. After the skin tags were removed, the dermatologist also performed excision of a pilonidal cyst. After reviewing the health record, the coder assigned codes 11770, 11200, and 11201. Which CPT modifier is added to code 11200?
    a. -27
    b. -50
    c. -51
    d. -58

13. A 15-year-old male underwent bilateral mastectomy for moderate gynecomastia. Report CPT code ____________.
    a. 19300
    b. 19300-50
    c. 19300-51
    d. 19303-50

14. A patient required excision of a trochanteric pressure ulcer, which was done via skin flap closure and ostectomy. Report CPT code ____________.
    a. 15934
    b. 15945
    c. 15953
    d. 15958

15. CPT code 17313 is reported for a ____________ procedure.
    a. curettement
    b. debridement
    c. graft
    d. staged

16. A patient underwent removal of an inflammatory cystic lesion on the left side of neck, which measured 4.5 cm in diameter. The removal was done via excision. Report CPT code ____________.
    a. 11406
    b. 11426
    c. 11606
    d. 11626

17. A patient underwent nail bed reconstruction of the left index finger, which was done using a graft. Report CPT code(s) ____________.
    a. 11760
    b. 11762
    c. 11762-F1
    d. 11760-F1, 15050-F1-51

18. The code descriptor for CPT code 15272 classifies a(n) ____________ graft procedure.
    a. acellular dermal allograft
    b. allograft
    c. skin substitute
    d. xenograft

19. A patient underwent excision of a benign lesion of the trunk. After performing the excision, the surgeon performed an intermediate skin closure using sutures. How many CPT codes are reported for this procedure?
    a. 1
    b. 2
    c. 3
    d. 3, with modifier -51 added to the second and third codes

20. What is the term for bioengineered artificial skin?
    a. Autograft
    b. Acellular dermal replacement
    c. Allograft
    d. Xenograft

CHAPTER 13

CPT Surgery II

INTRODUCTION

This chapter introduces students to CPT surgery coding (Musculoskeletal System subsection and Respiratory System subsection). Students assign codes to coding cases by applying CPT coding guidelines and notes.

Objectives

At the conclusion of this chapter, the student should be able to:

- Assign CPT surgery codes from the Musculoskeletal and Respiratory System subsections.
- Add CPT and/or HCPCS level II modifiers to codes as appropriate.

ASSIGNMENT 13.1 – CODING PRACTICE

Instructions

Assign the ICD-10-CM code(s) to diagnoses and conditions and assign the CPT surgery code(s) and the appropriate HCPCS level II and CPT modifier(s). Do not assign ICD-10-CM external cause codes.

1. Under anesthesia, open treatment of a traumatic right closed posterior hip dislocation was performed by an incision made along the posterior aspect of the right hip. After the gluteus maximus muscle was identified, the muscle was split and retracted. The right hip joint was exposed, and the dislocation was reduced. The incision was closed in multiple layers with sutures. (Initial encounter)

   ____

2. The patient presented with the complaint of chronic bronchitis. After the procedure was discussed and all consents signed, the patient was taken to the ambulatory surgical unit. With the patient under adequate anesthesia, a needle was inserted into the cricoid cartilage of the neck. The needle allowed for the catheter placement, which facilitated the collection of a bronchial brush biopsy. The needle and catheter were withdrawn, with the sample being sent to pathology for analysis.

   ____

3. With the patient under general anesthesia, gradual pressure was applied in the desired direction after manual manipulation was performed to increase motion. A small number of adhesions were released by gradual pressure. Manipulation of right hip joint was a closed procedure; no surgical incision was made. This was done due to the patient having congenital dislocation of the right hip.

   ____

4. Patient presented with a nondisplaced left ulnar styloid fracture, which was treated with closed reduction and application of a cast. (Initial encounter)

____

5. A patient with pleural effusion underwent thoracentesis, which allowed the placement of an aspirating needle into the pleural space, and drainage of .10 cc of fluid from the space.

____

6. With the patient under general anesthesia, the tracheal laceration wound was closed via cervical approach after the edges were debrided and sutures were used in layers. No foreign objects or materials were found in the wound. (Initial encounter)

____

7. A topical anesthetic was administered to the oral cavity of the patient. A flexible fiberoptic laryngoscope was inserted. The interior of the larynx was examined. Moderate inflammation was noted; the size of the larynx was normal.

____

8. Patient presented with a broken nose from a fall. Dr. Marcus treated a displaced nasal fracture by manipulating the fractured bones. He placed forceps in the nose and realigned the nasal bones. The bones were stable, and no nasal splint was needed. (Initial encounter)

____

9. The patient presented with nontraumatic compartment syndrome of the upper extremity, right, and consented to a decompression fasciotomy. Dr. Jameson decompressed the hand fascia and incised the skin overlying the affected fascia. The fascia and the underlying tissues were also incised, and the surgical wound area was thoroughly irrigated. The incision was closed in sutured layers.

____

10. The patient presented to the ambulatory surgical suite for a diagnostic endoscopy to rule out lung carcinoma. The biopsy was done with the aid of an endobronchial ultrasound. The bronchial biopsy specimens were sent to pathology. Diagnosis: Rule out lung carcinoma; hematemesis.

____

ASSIGNMENT 13.2 – CODING OPERATIVE REPORTS

Instructions

Assign the ICD-10-CM code(s) to diagnoses and conditions and assign the CPT surgery code(s) and the appropriate HCPCS level II and CPT modifier(s). Do not assign ICD-10-CM external cause codes.

1. PREOPERATIVE DIAGNOSIS: Left middle trigger finger.

   POSTOPERATIVE DIAGNOSIS: Left middle trigger finger.

   OPERATION PERFORMED: Tenolysis.

   Under satisfactory IV block anesthesia, the patient was prepped and draped in the usual fashion. A transverse incision was made parallel to the distal palmar crease area overlying the middle finger, and the wound was then deepened and sharply dissected. All blood vessels were carefully preserved. The flexor tendon sheath was identified and divided longitudinally for a distance of approximately 1.4 cm. There was no bow-stringing of the flexor tendon following this, and there was good gliding motion of the flexor tendon passively without any obstruction. The patient then had closure of the subcutaneous tissue with interrupted

4-0 plain catgut suture, and the skin was approximated with three interrupted 4-0 nylon vertical mattress sutures. Betadine ointment and dry sterile dressing were applied. Bulky hand dressing was applied. The patient, having tolerated the procedure well, had the tourniquet released without any untoward effects and was discharged from the surgical suite in a stable condition.

---

2. PREOPERATIVE DIAGNOSIS: Hemoptysis.

   POSTOPERATIVE DIAGNOSIS: Mucosal lesion of bronchus.

   OPERATION PERFORMED: Bronchoscopy.

   The bronchoscope was passed through the nose. The vocal cords were identified and appeared normal. No lesions were seen in this area. The larynx and trachea were then identified and also appeared normal with no lesions or bleeding. The main carina was sharp. All bronchial segments were visualized. There was an endobronchial mucosal lesion. This was located on the right lower bronchus. No other lesions were seen. Transbronchial biopsies were taken of the area of the lesion. The patient tolerated the procedure well and was sent to the recovery area in stable condition.

---

3. PREOPERATIVE DIAGNOSIS: Retained hardware, left hip, status post closed reduction and subcutaneous pinning of the subcapital fracture of her left hip.

   POSTOPERATIVE DIAGNOSIS: Same.

   OPERATION PERFORMED: Subcutaneous removal of hardware.

   The patient was taken to the operating room and placed in the supine position. After adequate general anesthesia was administered, the left hip was prepped and draped in usual sterile fashion. The previous incision was used to make a 2.0-cm incision. A guidewire was used to get into the screws easily. All of the screws were then removed. The wound was irrigated out and closed in layers, and the skin was closed with 3-0 Prolene. Xeroform and dry sterile dressing were placed over the wound and covered with foam tape. The patient was extubated and taken to the recovery room in stable condition.

---

4. PREOPERATIVE DIAGNOSIS: Displaced medial epicondyle fracture, left elbow.

   POSTOPERATIVE DIAGNOSIS: Displaced medial epicondyle fracture, left elbow.

   OPERATION PERFORMED: ORIF, left medial epicondyle fracture. (Initial encounter)

   After IV sedation was started, the patient was brought into the operating room and placed supine on the table. Once an adequate level of anesthesia was obtained, the patient was taken out of the splint. He was noted to have significant swelling and instability with valgus stress to the elbow. The tourniquet was placed about the left proximal arm. The arm was sterilely prepped and draped from the tips of the fingers to the tourniquet. The arm was exsanguinated. The tourniquet was inflated to 300 mmHg. A curved incision was done down to the medial aspect of the elbow and through the fascia. The elbow joint was entered. The medial epicondyle was completely avulsed and pulled distally. The fracture's edges were debrided of hematoma. The medial epicondyle was grasped with a towel clip, and the elbow was flexed. Another guidewire was placed to control rotation. A 4.5 cannulated screw was placed across the fracture site plane, obtaining anatomical reduction. X-rays showed excellent position of both AP and lateral views. The guide pin was removed. The fracture was very stable. The wound was irrigated and closed with 2-0 Vicryl and skin staples. Sterile dressings were applied. The patient was placed in a long-arm posterior splint, well-padded, with the elbow at 90 degrees. The patient tolerated the procedure well and was taken to the recovery room in good condition.

---

5. PREOPERATIVE DIAGNOSIS: Mass of lung.

   POSTOPERATIVE DIAGNOSIS: Carcinoma of the right lung.

   OPERATION PERFORMED: Bronchoscopy and right upper lobectomy.

   The patient was brought into the operating room, and after the administration of anesthesia, the patient was prepped and draped in the usual sterile fashion. The patient was placed in the left lateral decubitus position. A thoracotomy incision was made. This exposed the chest muscles, which were incised and retracted. The fourth and fifth ribs were visualized and transected to allow entrance to the chest. A tumor mass was noted. This mass measured 7.0 cm in diameter, involving the right lung upper lobe. The mass was excised in its entirety, and a biopsy of the mass was taken and sent for frozen section. The frozen section revealed squamous cell carcinoma. Nodes were then dissected around the pulmonary artery and the trachea. The nodes were sent for frozen section. The nodes were identified as negative per pathology. Saline was irrigated into the chest. It was noted that the liver and diaphragm appeared to be normal with no lesions seen. After verification that the sponge count was correct, chest tubes were placed for drainage. The surgical wound was closed in layers with chromic catgut and nylon. The patient tolerated this portion of the procedure well.

   The patient was then placed in the supine position for the bronchoscopy. The patient was still under anesthesia. A flexible fiberoptic bronchoscope was inserted. Patent bronchi were noted bilaterally. The scope was withdrawn. The patient was awakened and sent to the recovery area in stable condition.

   ____

6. PREOPERATIVE DIAGNOSIS: Hallux valgus, right great toe. Bone spur, right second toe.

   POSTOPERATIVE DIAGNOSIS: Same.

   OPERATION PERFORMED: Austin bunionectomy. Exostectomy, right second toe.

   The patient was brought into the operating room. After adequate sedation was obtained, lidocaine was infiltrated for local anesthesia. The right foot and ankle were prepped and draped in the usual sterile fashion. A linear incision was made overlying the first metatarsophalangeal joint and was deepened below the extensor capsule. Bleeders were clamped and bovied. The vital structures were reflected. A full lateral release was noted. The first metatarsal head was transected utilizing a sagittal saw. A V-shaped osteotomy was performed. The capital fragment was shifted laterally, thus correcting the elevated metatarsal angles with the hallux valgus deformity. Once this was achieved, it was stabilized utilizing a K-wire. The overledge of bone was transected utilizing a sagittal saw. The deep structures were closed utilizing 3-0 Vicryl; the skin, utilizing staples.

   Attention was then directed to the second toe. At the medial aspect of the distal interphalangeal joint, a prominent bone spur was noted. A linear incision was made overlying this bone spur. It was identified, transected, and rasped smooth. The skin was then closed utilizing 3-0 Vicryl. Dry sterile dressing was applied after Marcaine was infiltrated for an extended anesthesia. The tourniquet was deflated. Normal vascular flow was noted to return. The patient left the operating room in satisfactory condition. Minimal blood loss. No complications.

   ____

7. PREOPERATIVE DIAGNOSIS: Recurrent obstructive polyposis.

   POSTOPERATIVE DIAGNOSIS: Recurrent obstructive polyposis.

   OPERATION PERFORMED: Revision of maxillary sinus.

   The patient was placed in the supine position and anesthesia was given, and the patient was prepped and draped in the usual sterile fashion. The patient's oropharynx and nasal fossa were packed. A rigid video endoscope was introduced for the nasal endoscopy. Polyposis of the right ethmoid bed was visualized. These recurrent polyps were obstructive. The left ethmoid and maxillary appeared unremarkable. A Caldwell-Luc operation was done to remove the antrochoanal polyps from the right maxillary sinus and right ethmoid sinus. The area was packed with gauze soaked in Bacitracin ointment. The area was suctioned clear of any secretions, and the patient was sent to the recovery area in stable condition.

8. PREOPERATIVE DIAGNOSIS: Lesion of vocal cords.

POSTOPERATIVE DIAGNOSIS: Tumor of left vocal cord.

OPERATION PERFORMED: Laryngoscopy.

The patient was a 25-year-old student of opera who presented with a lesion of her left vocal cord seen on office laryngoscopy. Today she was seen in the ambulatory suite for further examination of this lesion, using the operating microscope. After the administration of local anesthesia, a direct endoscope was introduced. The operating microscope was brought into the field, and the pharynx and larynx were visualized. The pharynx appeared normal. There was a mass noted of the left vocal cord. The mass was approximately 2.0 cm in size and was removed in total and sent to pathology for analysis. All secretions were suctioned, and the area was irrigated with saline. The patient had minimal blood loss. It should be noted that the pathology report stated benign tumor of the vocal cord.

9. PREOPERATIVE DIAGNOSIS: Nosebleed.

POSTOPERATIVE DIAGNOSIS: Nosebleed.

OPERATION PERFORMED: Nasal packing.

The patient's nasal cavity was examined and noted to be bleeding posteriorly on the right and anteriorly on the left. There was extensive bleeding. First, the patient's right nasopharynx was cauterized in an attempt to stop the bleeding. After four minutes, this side of the patient's nose was still bleeding; therefore, a more extensive posterior packing was done. The patient's left nasopharynx was bleeding posteriorly; this was cauterized and also packed since the cautery did not arrest the bleeding totally. After packing and one hour of observation in the waiting room, the patient's bleeding had resolved considerably. He was discharged to follow up with his primary care physician in 24 hours.

10. PREOPERATIVE DIAGNOSIS: Respiratory insufficiency due to amyotrophic lateral sclerosis (ALS).

POSTOPERATIVE DIAGNOSIS: Severe respiratory insufficiency due to ALS.

OPERATION PERFORMED: Tracheostomy.

The patient, a 45-year-old male with ALS, has been experiencing severe shortness of breath of a progressive nature over the last several weeks. After discussion of all risks, the decision has been made to perform a tracheostomy on this patient. The patient was brought into the operating suite for this procedure and placed supine on the table. General anesthesia was given, and the patient was prepped and draped in the usual sterile fashion. A 2.5-cm incision was made of the neck over the trachea. The trachea was carefully isolated from the surrounding structures after the tracheal rings were identified. The second ring was identified, and a tube was advanced after incision. The patient's breath sounds were checked and were adequate. The tracheostoma was packed with gauze, and the ties were secured. A chest x-ray will be done postoperatively to check for tube placement, but breath sounds were good when the patient went to recovery room.

REVIEW

Multiple Choice

Circle the most appropriate response.

1. The patient, an 85-year-old female, presents with the complaint of foreign body being stuck in her throat. After application of a local anesthetic, the patient is examined by use of a direct laryngoscope with use of an operating microscope. Upon examination, a small bone is seen and removed. Report CPT code ___________.
   a. 31511
   b. 31530
   c. 31531
   d. 31536
2. Mr. Williams, a 70-year-old man with the diagnosis of emphysema, presents for lung volume reduction (LVR) surgery. The physician removes a portion of the patient's right upper lung via a transthoracic approach. Report CPT code(s) ___________.
   a. 32440
   b. 32484
   c. 32491
   d. 32501, 32491-51
3. The patient, a 15-year-old female, presents to the ED after falling off a skateboard. The patient is examined and determined to have a Colles fracture of the left wrist. The fracture is reduced with closed manipulation by the orthopedic attending of the hospital. After the orthopedic physician reduces the fracture, x-rays are taken to check for alignment and the patient is placed in a short-arm cast. Report CPT code(s) ___________.
   a. 25600-LT
   b. 25605-LT
   c. 25600-LT, 29075-LT
   d. 25605-LT, 29075-LT
4. The patient presented to the ambulatory surgical center for an arthroscopy of the shoulder due to severe pain. The diagnostic procedure revealed only slight inflammation. Report CPT code ___________.
   a. 29805
   b. 29806
   c. 29819
   d. 29820
5. The patient presented for a procedure. The physician punctured the patient's pleural space with a needle and drained fluid. The fluid was sent to pathology for analysis. This procedure is known as a
   a. bronchoscopy.
   b. pleurectomy.
   c. pneumocentesis.
   d. pneumonectomy.
6. A patient with the diagnosis of lung carcinoma presents for a surgical procedure. The physician, after accessing the patient's lungs, removes a portion of the right upper lobe that measures approximately 7.0 × 6.0 cm in size. On the left side, the physician removes a portion of the left upper lobe that is 1.5 × 1.0 cm in size. The portion of the lung that was removed on the right side is classified as a:
   a. lobe.
   b. pneumonectomy.
   c. segment.
   d. wedge.
7. A patient presents with a dislocated right shoulder. The physician uses a bed sheet and the assistance of a member of the nursing staff to realign this patient's dislocation. This is done after the patient is sedated. Which term does CPT use to describe this type of realignment of a dislocation?
   a. Arthrodesis
   b. Internal fixation
   c. Manipulation
   d. Reduction
8. Percutaneous needle biopsy of the lung. Report CPT code ___________.
   a. 32098
   b. 32400
   c. 32554
   d. 32405

9. A patient presents with the diagnosis of plantar fasciitis of the right foot. The patient has an extracorporeal shock wave therapy (ESWT) done on this foot to break up the spur and reduce the inflammation. Report CPT code ___________.
   a. 28100
   b. 28108
   c. 28118
   d. 28890
10. A patient presented for a bone grafting procedure. The patient had a portion of cervical spinal bone, which was obtained from a bone bank, grafted at C6. This type of grafting would be known as a(n):
   a. allograft.
   b. autograft.
   c. osteogenesis.
   d. xenograft.
11. Knee arthroscopy with removal of osteochondritis fragment. Report CPT code ___________.
   a. 29866
   b. 29870
   c. 29874
   d. 29877
12. The patient presented for a diagnostic laryngoscopy. The flexible fiberoptic scope was advanced, and a biopsy of the larynx was done due to redness and inflammation that was found. Report CPT code(s) ___________.
   a. 31535
   b. 31576
   c. 31575, 31576-51
   d. 31578, 31535-51
13. Dr. Watson performed a pneumonectomy from a donor whose lung was to be transplanted into a patient in Florida. The donor was an 18-year-old male killed in a traffic accident. Dr. Watson did this procedure in Texas, and the organ was flown to the patient at a Florida hospital. Report CPT code(s) ___________.
   a. 32850
   b. 32850, 32852-51
   c. 32850, 32852-51, 32855-51
   d. 32850, 32855-51
14. Excision of a Morton neuroma between the second and third toes of the right foot. Report CPT code(s) ___________.
   a. 28043-RT
   b. 28045-RT
   c. 28080-RT
   d. 28080-RT, 28080-51-RT
15. LeFort I operation done via an open approach. Report CPT code ___________.
   a. 21422
   b. 21423
   c. 21432
   d. 21433
16. Fascia biopsy of upper arm. Report CPT code ___________.
   a. 20206
   b. 24066
   c. 24075
   d. 24076
17. Excision of a nasal cyst found underneath the juncture of the patient's nasal bone and nasal cartilage. Report CPT code ___________.
   a. 30115
   b. 30117
   c. 30124
   d. 30125
18. Diagnostic thoracoscopy with biopsy of pericardial sac. Report CPT code(s) ___________.
   a. 32604
   b. 32659
   c. 32601, 32604-51
   d. 32601, 32606
19. Wedge resection via thoracotomy of right upper lobe of lung and left upper lobe of lung. Report CPT code(s) ___________.
   a. 32440
   b. 32482
   c. 32505, 32505-51
   d. 32505, 32506
20. Treatment of malunion of distal femur, left. Report CPT code ___________.
   a. 27470-LT
   b. 27508-LT
   c. 27510-LT
   d. 27514-LT

CHAPTER 14

CPT Surgery III

INTRODUCTION

This chapter introduces students to CPT surgery coding (Cardiovascular System subsection and Hemic and Lymphatic Systems subsection). Students assign codes to coding cases by applying CPT coding guidelines and notes.

Objectives

At the conclusion of this chapter, the student should be able to:

- Assign CPT surgery codes from the Cardiovascular System and Hemic and Lymphatic Systems subsections.
- Add CPT and/or HCPCS level II modifiers to codes as appropriate.

ASSIGNMENT 14.1 – CODING PRACTICE

Instructions

Assign the ICD-10-CM code(s) to diagnoses and conditions and assign the CPT surgery code(s) and the appropriate HCPCS level II and CPT modifier(s). Do not assign ICD-10-CM external cause codes.

1. With the patient under general anesthesia with intubation, multiple fairly large varicosities of the left leg were ligated using four separate incisions due to the tortuosity of the veins. Incision was made for a distance below the pubic bone through the skin and superficial fascia and fat to expose the long saphenous vein at its entrance into the femoral artery. Two fairly large tributaries of the saphenous vein were isolated and ligated. Multiple incisions were made to strip the long saphenous and tributary veins. All bleeding points were ligated. Suture closure, dressing, and bandage were applied.

   ____

2. The patient presented for an excision of enlarged lymph node. Under IV sedation, an incision of the palpable cervical node was made transversely through the skin. The node was in the fascia; it was excised.

   ____

3. The patient has a third-degree heart block. She presents for the insertion of a temporary transvenous pacemaker. This was done in the fluoroscopy suite. After the administration of adequate anesthesia, a 5-French introducer was placed and introduced into the right subclavian vein. The fluoroscope was used to guide the wire into the right atrium. The pacemaker lead wire was threaded through the introducer and placed in the apex of the right ventricle. We had good capture and the pacemaker wire was sewed in place and a sterile dressing was applied.

____

4. A patient presented with the diagnosis of enlarged retroperitoneal lymph nodes bilaterally. After discussion of the procedure and its risks, the patient consented to the lymph node biopsy. After the administration of adequate anesthesia, laparoscopic retroperitoneal lymph node biopsies were performed. The biopsy samples were sent to pathology for analysis.

____

5. The patient is on a respirator and needs a percutaneous arterial line for repeated blood sampling. For this reason, under sterile technique, an arterial line was inserted at the patient's bedside. The left wrist was prepped and dressed. With the surgeon using an arterial line catheter, the left radial artery was accessed without difficulty, and it was fixed to the skin with two 3-0 nylon sutures.

____

6. Preoperative diagnosis was cervical lymphadenopathy. With the patient under general anesthesia, a large curved incision was made starting at the ear, going down and continuing to the chin. The skin flaps were folded back out of the field with retractors. The tissue of the lymph nodes was dissected. These were sent in total to pathology for analysis.

____

7. A patient presented with a diagnosis of tricuspid valve regurgitation. With the patient under general anesthesia, cardiopulmonary bypass was initiated, the right atrium was incised, and the tricuspid valve was identified. An annuloplasty ring was placed. The right atrium was closed with sutures. The patient was removed from cardiopulmonary bypass.

____

8. The patient, a 25-year-old female with a diagnosis of portal hypertension, presented to the surgical suite for a splenectomy. After informed consent was obtained, the patient was given a preoperative anesthesia injection. Then the patient was prepped and draped in the usual sterile fashion. With the patient under general anesthesia, a midline incision was made. After the spleen was identified, surrounding tissue was dissected free. The splenic artery and vein were visualized, divided, and ligated. The spleen was removed. A Penrose drain was placed, and the wound was irrigated. The incision was closed with sutures.

____

9. Due to a mechanical complication of a cardiac pulse generator (battery), the patient presented for the removal and replacement of the battery. This was done after adequate anesthesia was administered. The generator pocket was opened, and the electrode wires were disconnected. The old chest incision was opened, the electrodes were dissected out, and the old cardiac pulse generator (battery) was removed. The permanent implantable defibrillator system was replaced along with dual chamber transvenous leads. The chest incision was closed. (Initial encounter.)

____

10. With the patient under general anesthesia, an upper midline incision was made and dissected around the spleen. The ruptured segment of the spleen was identified at the distal portion, and this was resected. The

wound was irrigated, and the incision was closed using sutures and a sterile dressing. Three-fourths of the spleen was left intact. DIAGNOSIS: Ruptured spleen due to *Plasmodium vivax malaria*.

ASSIGNMENT 14.2 – CODING OPERATIVE REPORTS

Instructions

Assign the ICD-10-CM code(s) to diagnoses and conditions and assign the CPT surgery code(s) and the appropriate HCPCS level II and CPT modifier(s). Do not assign ICD-10-CM external cause codes.

1. PREOPERATIVE DIAGNOSIS: Third-degree heart block with bradycardia and recent inferior myocardial infarction.

   POSTOPERATIVE DIAGNOSIS: Same.

   OPERATION PERFORMED: Insertion of a transvenous temporary pacemaker.

   The patient was brought to the fluoroscopy suite in the radiology department. He was placed prone on the fluoroscopy table. The right subclavicular area was prepped with Betadine and then infiltrated with Carbocaine. A 5-French introducer was inserted and easily located the right subclavian vein. The pacemaker wire was easily passed through the 5-French introducer and was placed in the tip of the right ventricular apex. The ventricles were captured very easily with 5 milliamps down to 1 milliamp. Fluoroscopy was again performed to verify the location, the pacemaker wire was sewn into place, and a sterile dressing was applied. The patient was then returned to the intensive care unit.

   ---

2. PREOPERATIVE DIAGNOSIS: Carcinoma of the left breast.

   POSTOPERATIVE DIAGNOSIS: Carcinoma of the left breast.

   PROCEDURE: Insertion of Groshong catheter.

   ANESTHESIA: Local MAC.

   ESTIMATED BLOOD LOSS: Minimal.

   OPERATIVE INDICATIONS: The patient is a 55-year-old female diagnosed with carcinoma of the breast. She requires a catheter for chemotherapy.

   The patient was prepped and draped with the right neck and chest in the operative field, in deep Trendelenburg, with a rolled sheet between the shoulder blades. One percent lidocaine was used for the skin incisions. Percutaneous access to the right subclavian was obtained with a needle, and a wire was introduced. The needle was removed, and an introducer and sheath were passed over the wire. The wire and introducer were removed. Then a Groshong 8-French catheter was introduced through the peel-away sheath and allowed to lie at the junction of the right atrium and superior vena cava. The sheath was then peeled away. A tunnel was developed in the anterior chest down to about the level of the midbreast to allow the Vitacuff and 5-0 cuff to lie subcutaneously. All of the above was done under fluoroscopic guidance with the Siemens unit. The catheter was irrigated with heparinized saline, and it had been soaked in Chloromycetin solution prior to the event. It was sutured in place with 4-0 nylon. The patient tolerated the procedure well.

   ---

3. PREOPERATIVE DIAGNOSIS: Status post–hyperemesis gravidarum, post–Hickman catheter.

   POSTOPERATIVE DIAGNOSIS: Same.

   PROCEDURE: Removal of Hickman catheter.

   ANESTHESIA: Local.

   ESTIMATED BLOOD LOSS: Minimal.

   The patient was placed on the operating table in the supine position and monitored appropriately. The right neck and chest were sterilely prepped and draped. The suture securing her Hickman catheter exit site was removed. The area was infiltrated with local anesthetic of 1% Xylocaine with bicarbonate. The catheter was manipulated with a clamp, was freed up, and was extruded and removed completely without the need to open the subclavian site. The catheter and its Teflon cuff were removed intact without difficulty. The wound was clean and dry and closed with one suture of 4-0 nylon. Sterile dressings were applied. She was taken to recovery in stable condition, tolerating the procedure well. Blood loss was minimal.

   ____

4. PREOPERATIVE DIAGNOSIS: Arteriosclerotic heart disease.

   POSTOPERATIVE DIAGNOSIS: Arteriosclerotic heart disease.

   PROCEDURE: Coronary artery bypass graft × 5.

   The patient was brought into the operating suite and placed in the supine position. Anesthesia was administered, and monitoring lines were placed. The patient was prepped and draped in the usual sterile fashion. The sternum was opened through a midline incision. The saphenous vein was harvested from the left ankle. After the sternum was opened, the pericardium was incised and the coronary field was carefully examined. The mammary artery was taken down with cautery, and a drain was placed in the pleural space. Cardiopulmonary bypass was started. The patient's core temperature was dropped to 30 degrees. The aorta was cross-clamped, and cardioplegia was administered. The acute marginal branch was grafted with continuous 6-0 Prolene and the saphenous vein. The graft was brought up to the ascending aorta. The heart was turned over; significant disease was seen in the proximal PDA. A segment of saphenous vein was sewn in with 7-0 Prolene. The mid OM was opened; an anastomosis was created. The graft was brought up to the aorta. Then the diagonal branch of the artery was grafted side-to-side with the left mammary. The distal LAD was opened and grafted to the tip of the left mammary. The patient was rewarmed, and the heart pinked up. The vein graft clamps were released and filled well. There was no distal or proximal bleeding. The patient was paced into normal sinus rhythm. The patient was disconnected from bypass. Two chest tubes and a drain were placed. The aortic site was closed with oversewn sutures. The area was irrigated with antibiotic solution. The entrance incisions were closed with Vicryl, and the leg was wrapped. The sternum was closed with wire and layered suture closures. The patient tolerated the procedure well and was transferred to CICU.

   ____

5. PREOPERATIVE DIAGNOSIS: Acute pericarditis.

   POSTOPERATIVE DIAGNOSIS: Acute pericarditis.

   OPERATION PERFORMED: Drainage of fluid from pericardial space.

   Under fluoroscopic guidance with the patient in a prone position, an incision was made below the sternum and a needle was inserted and directed into the pericardial space. A guidewire was introduced through the needle and used to introduce a drainage catheter. Approximately 400 mL of fluid was removed. A sample of fluid was sent to pathology for analysis. The catheter was removed. The incision site was closed with sutures.

   ____

6. PREOPERATIVE DIAGNOSIS: Rule out lymphoma. Enlarged lymph node of axillary area on the left.

POSTOPERATIVE DIAGNOSIS: Same.

PROCEDURE: Excisional biopsy left axillary lymph node.

ANESTHESIA: Local, using 0.5% Marcaine without epinephrine.

The patient was brought to the operating room, and after adequate prepping and draping of the left axillary area, a large several-centimeters-in-diameter lymph node was palpated medially and superiorly. The skin overlying this node was infiltrated with 0.5% Marcaine without epinephrine, and the skin was incised over it. We then went down through the subcutaneous fat; bleeders were coagulated with the electrocautery unit or clamped and tied off with 4-0 Vicryl ties. The node was exposed through sharp and blunt dissection while we tried to keep the node intact since these nodes are generally quite friable. Using blunt dissection around the node, we clamped the blood supply in this area and tied it off with 2-0 Vicryl ties. The node was finally freed up and dissected out, passed off the table in a saline sponge, and sent to pathology quickly for definite diagnosis by permanent section. The bleeding was minimal, and after the node was excised, we irrigated the wound area with diluted Betadine saline solution several times and sponged it off. There was no problem with hemostasis, and the axillary areolar tissue was reapproximated with inverting interrupted simple sutures of 2-0 Vicryl. When these were closed, the subcutaneous tissue was reapproximated with inverting simple interrupted sutures of 4-0 PDS and the skin was closed with 4-0 PDS subcuticular-style suture, continuous with the knots buried at both ends. The wound was dressed. The patient seemed to tolerate the procedure well and left the operating room for his room in satisfactory condition.

____

7. PREOPERATIVE DIAGNOSIS: Splenic cysts.

POSTOPERATIVE DIAGNOSIS: Same.

PROCEDURE: Laparoscopic splenectomy.

After the administration of general anesthesia, the patient was prepped and draped in the usual fashion. A small incision was made in the epigastric region; the first trocar was placed. The area was inspected, and the pancreas was visualized. The remaining three trocars were placed through small incisions in the low epigastric area, suprapubic region, and left upper quadrant. No accessory spleen was identified, but the spleen did have multiple cysts. The spleen was lifted superiorly, with careful attention paid to the pancreas. Dissection was continued laterally. Short gastric vessels and all spleen vessels were addressed and tied off. The spleen was removed in total after it was broken up into pieces and removed through the trocar. The patient's abdomen was deflated. A drain was left in place through the subcutaneous tissue. The patient tolerated the procedure well and was sent to the recovery room in a stable condition.

____

8. PREOPERATIVE DIAGNOSIS: Cervical lymph node abscess.

POSTOPERATIVE DIAGNOSIS: Same.

PROCEDURE: Lymph node drainage.

ANESTHESIA: Local.

After the administration of adequate local anesthesia, the patient was prepped and draped in the usual sterile fashion. The enlarged left cervical lymph node was palpated. An incision was made over the node, and a whitish gray fluid was drained. A sample of the fluid from the abscess was sent to the pathology department for culture. Approximately 15 cc of fluid was drained from the abscess. After the drainage, the abscess cavity was not easily palpated. The incision was closed with sutures.

____

9. PREOPERATIVE DIAGNOSIS: Rule out lymphoma.

   POSTOPERATIVE DIAGNOSIS: Non-Hodgkin's lymphoma.

   PROCEDURE: Laparoscopic biopsy of retroperitoneal lymph nodes.

   The patient was brought into the surgical suite. After the administration of general anesthesia, the procedure was begun. The patient was prepped and draped in a sterile fashion. An incision was made at the patient's umbilicus, and the first trocar was introduced. Gas was introduced into the patient's retroperitoneal cavity. After the insertion of additional trocars, the patient's retroperitoneal lymph nodes were directly visualized. Multiple biopsy samples were taken and sent to pathology for diagnosis. After the biopsies, the trocars were removed and the surgical incisions were closed with sutures. The patient tolerated the procedure well. Pathologist reported samples as mediastinal (thymic) large B-cell non-Hodgkin's lymphoma.

   ____

10. PREOPERATIVE DIAGNOSIS: Bone marrow donor.

    POSTOPERATIVE DIAGNOSIS: Bone marrow donor.

    PROCEDURE: Bone marrow harvest.

    The patient is an unrelated donor found in a bone marrow registry who is a match to patient with aplastic anemia. After the administration of general anesthesia, the patient is prepped and draped. An incision is made, and a large bore needle is inserted through the site into the iliac crest. A large hollow syringe is used to extract the marrow. The marrow is placed in a container and sent for storage. The surgical wound is closed with sutures and a pressure dressing. The patient tolerates the procedure well and is awakened and taken to the recovery room.

    ____

REVIEW

Multiple Choice

Circle the most appropriate response.

1. A 15-day-old infant presents for surgery to correct his condition of tetralogy of Fallot. The surgeon repairs the congenital heart defects using a transannular patch that came from the patient's pericardium. The patient is put on a cardiac bypass machine for this procedure. Report CPT code(s) ____________.
   a. 33694-63
   b. 33692
   c. 33694
   d. 33697, 33692-51-63
2. Removal of a patient's spleen in total using a laparoscope and three small incisions. Report CPT code(s) ____________.
   a. 38100
   b. 38100, 38102
   c. 38102
   d. 38120
3. Transvenous intrahepatic portosystemic shunt (TIPS) revision under radiology guidance using a portography. Report CPT code(s) ____________.
   a. 37182
   b. 37183
   c. 37182, 75885
   d. 37183, 75887
4. A healthy human being has ______________ heart valves.
   a. two
   b. three
   c. four
   d. five

5. Repair of a pulmonary artery via the construction of a tunnel within the artery. Report CPT code ____________.
   a. 33502
   b. 33503
   c. 33504
   d. 33505

6. Today, patient May Farrell is undergoing transplant of stem cells. The cells were harvested from the patient six months ago. Report CPT code ____________.
   a. 38210
   b. 38220
   c. 38240
   d. 38241

7. Partial splenectomy via an open abdominal incision. Report CPT code ____________.
   a. 38100
   b. 38101
   c. 38120
   d. 38129

8. The patient has an embolism of his pulmonary artery. After anesthesia is administered, the patient is put on a heart and lung bypass machine and the embolism is removed. Report CPT code ____________.
   a. 33910
   b. 33915
   c. 33916
   d. 33920

9. The patient was placed on a cardiopulmonary bypass machine, and a repair of patient's fistula located in sinus of Valsalva was done. Report CPT code ____________.
   a. 33702
   b. 33710
   c. 33720
   d. 33722

10. Bilateral diagnostic laparoscopy of retroperitoneal lymph system performed. Enlarged lymph nodes were seen. Report CPT code ____________.
    a. 38570
    b. 38571
    c. 49320
    d. 49321

11. Which is not considered a peripheral vascular vessel?
    a. artery
    b. capillary
    c. valve
    d. vein

12. Ligation and stripping of short saphenous vein of the right leg and ligation of long saphenous vein from knee of left leg. Report CPT code(s) ____________.
    a. 37718-RT, 37722-LT
    b. 37780-RT, 37722-LT
    c. 37735
    d. 37765

13. Needle biopsy of right inguinal lymph node. Report CPT code ____________.
    a. 38500-RT
    b. 38505-RT
    c. 38510-RT
    d. 38525-RT

14. The two types of stem cells contained in bone marrow are:
    a. cartilage and bone.
    b. hemopoietic and stromal.
    c. RBCs and platelets.
    d. RBCs and WBCs.

15. Complete removal of axillary lymph nodes. Report CPT code ____________.
    a. 38720
    b. 38724
    c. 38740
    d. 38745

16. Arteriovenous cannula insertion for hemodialysis access. Report CPT code ____________.
    a. 36800
    b. 36810
    c. 36815
    d. 36818

17. How many regions of a human body contain lymph nodes?
    a. Four
    b. Six
    c. Eight
    d. Ten

18. Transfusion of platelets; patient is a 45-year-old male. Report CPT code ____________.
    a. 36430
    b. 36450
    c. 36455
    d. 36460

19. Cerebral thrombolysis via intravenous infusion. Report CPT code ____________.
    a. 37195
    b. 37211
    c. 37242
    d. 61645

20. Which is not part of the lymphatic system?
    a. Adenoids
    b. Spleen
    c. Thyroid
    d. Tonsils

CHAPTER 15

CPT Surgery IV

INTRODUCTION

This chapter introduces students to CPT surgery coding (Mediastinum and Diaphragm System subsection, Digestive System subsection, and Urinary System subsection). Students assign codes to coding cases by applying CPT coding guidelines and notes.

Objectives

At the conclusion of this chapter, the student should be able to:

- Assign CPT surgery codes from the Mediastinum and Diaphragm, Digestive System, and Urinary System subsections.
- Add CPT and/or HCPCS level II modifiers to codes as appropriate.

ASSIGNMENT 15.1 – CODING PRACTICE

Instructions

Assign the ICD-10-CM code(s) to diagnoses and conditions and assign the CPT surgery code(s) and the appropriate HCPCS level II and CPT modifier(s). Do not assign ICD-10-CM external cause codes.

1. With the patient under anesthesia, an incision was made in the base of the right neck just above the clavicle in the supraclavicular fossa; this was carried down through the platysma with electrocautery. Dissection was continued between the heads of the sternocleidomastoid muscle; the omohyoid was transected with electrocautery exposing an obvious mass of the mediastinum. Several pieces were removed; one was sent for frozen and several for permanent histoanalysis. Hemostasis was obtained. The platysma was closed with sutures.

   ____

2. The patient presented for colonoscopy due to colon polyps. After the Olympus colonoscope was inserted through the anus, it was advanced past the splenic flexure. The lumen of the colon and rectum was visualized. Through use of snare technique, several small polyps of the transverse colon were identified and removed. The polyps were taken for analysis. The colonoscope was withdrawn at the completion of the procedure.

   ____

3. The patient presented for liver biopsy due to a palpable mass. After an incision was made and ultrasound guidance was used, the hollow bore needle was placed between the third and fourth ribs on patient's right side. Tissue from the liver mass was taken for examination and sent to pathology for analysis.

___

4. The patient presented for a diagnostic cystourethroscopy due to hematuria. After the cystourethroscope was inserted, all urinary structures were examined. No abnormalities were visualized. All anatomical structures appeared normal in appearance. No masses or lesions were seen. The urethra and bladder were carefully examined as the scope was withdrawn; again, no abnormalities were seen.

___

5. The patient's previous cholecystectomy incisional scar was excised, and the incisional hernia sac was identified. An elliptical incision was made in the rectus sheath surrounding the hernia sac. The excess of the sac was excised, and the peritoneum was closed. The rectus sheaths were brought together by sutures. The wound was closed in layers.

___

6. With the patient under local anesthesia, a small incision was made above the sternum. The mediastinoscope was inserted, and the trachea was examined. The mediastinal lymph nodes, thymus, and thyroid were also visualized. A thymus mass of approximately 2.0 in diameter was visualized; a biopsy sample was taken through the mediastinoscope. The scope was removed, and the incision was closed with sutures. The thymus gland mass was identified as a benign tumor.

___

7. With the patient under IV anesthesia, scope was passed. There was considerable bleeding from the passage of the scope. A large mass of the trigone rendered any visualization of the bladder impossible. No catheterization of ureters. A small portion of the bladder that was visible does not show any pathology. This mass was biopsied.

___

8. PREOPERATIVE DIAGNOSIS: Abdominal adhesions. With the patient under general anesthesia, a midline incision was made through the abdominal wall. Ascites was present, and liver metastasis was noted. The small intestine was quite dilated and had multiple areas of adhesion bands wrapped on it. One loop was tightly adherent in the pelvis, causing obstruction. These adhesions were dissected free, and the small intestine was then followed from the ligament of the Treitz down to ileocolic valve. No obstruction was noted in both the colon and the small intestine. The small intestine was completely free of any obstruction at this point. The colon was also free of any obstruction. The abdominal wall was then closed with sutures.

   POSTOPERATIVE DIAGNOSIS: Small intestinal obstruction due to adhesions. Status post–sigmoid resection due to adenocarcinoma of the colon. Liver metastasis from adenocarcinoma of the colon.

___

9. After the administration of anesthesia, a surgical incision was made from the axilla to the tip of the shoulder blade. After access to the thoracic cavity was achieved, the mediastinum was identified. A tumor approximately 4.0×5.0 cm was visualized. This mass was dissected free from the surrounding tissue. The tumor in total was sent to pathology for analysis. All instrument and sponge counts were correct. The rib spreader was released. The thoracic muscles were closed with staples. The skin was closed with sutures. The patient had minimal blood loss. Pathologic analysis returned a diagnosis of benign thymoma.

___

10. The patient, a 45-year-old male, presented with a diagnosis of acute anal fissure. The patient was brought into the surgical suite. Prepped and draped in the usual fashion and under adequate anesthesia, the patient was placed in the prone position. In this position, the opening to a large fistula in ano could be seen on the right anal border over the rectal fascia. The skin was excised in elliptical fashion around the opening, and the tract was dissected sharply through the anal sphincter to the subserosa of the rectum; the tract was excised and removed completely. The wound was left open to allow drainage but was packed with gauze. The wound should heal by granulation rather than primary intention.

____

11. The patient presented for the repair of a paraesophageal hiatus hernia. After the administration of adequate general anesthesia, a thoracotomy incision was made. Tissues of the area were identified and exposed. A portion of the esophagus was used to create a fold, and the repair was made. The surgical incision was closed with sutures.

____

12. A patient presents after having a cystoscopy for the relief of a urethral stricture. This was done three weeks ago, and the patient has experienced postoperative urethral hemorrhage. Today the patient will have a transurethral cystourethroscopy with fulguration to control this postoperative bleeding. After prep and drape in the usual fashion, an endoscope was inserted into the urethra. Several small areas of bleeding in the urethra were noted, and these were fulgurated. The area was irrigated, and no bleeding in the urethra was noted.

____

13. Under anesthesia, tissue from the urethra was biopsied by using sharp dissection. The incision was closed in layers with absorbable sutures. Per the pathologist, the biopsy sample was noted to be moderate inflammation caused by gonococcal bacteria.

    DIAGNOSIS: Gonococcal urethritis.

____

14. The patient is a 7-month-old infant with febrile illness of unknown origin. A sterile urine sample is required for diagnostic purposes. Therefore, the patient is having a bladder aspiration to obtain the urine sample. Under anesthesia, a needle was used for insertion through the skin into the bladder to withdraw urine. The urine sample was sent to pathology for analysis.

____

15. Patient was taken to the operating room, the chest was surgically opened, and the operation was performed. Part of the diaphragm was removed. The wound was closed in layers. The specimen was sent for analysis and was returned as metastatic cancer of the diaphragm.

____

ASSIGNMENT 15.2 – CODING OPERATIVE REPORTS

Instructions

Assign the ICD-10-CM code(s) to diagnoses and conditions and assign the CPT surgery code(s) and the appropriate HCPCS level II and CPT modifier(s). Do not assign ICD-10-CM external cause codes.

1. PREOPERATIVE DIAGNOSIS: Umbilical and ventral hernia.

   POSTOPERATIVE DIAGNOSIS: Obstructed ventral hernia. Umbilical hernia.

   PROCEDURE: Repair of umbilical and ventral hernia.

   ANESTHESIA: Local.

   The patient, a 35-year-old male, was brought to the operating suite. The patient was placed in a supine position, and his abdomen was prepped and draped with Betadine. Anesthesia of 1% Xylocaine with dilute epinephrine was achieved, using a total of 44 cc. An incision was made under the umbilicus with bleeders cauterized. The dissection was continued down to the fascia. There were two defects, one above the umbilicus and another small umbilical hernia. There was incarcerated omentum in the ventral hernia. This was carefully dissected free. Bleeders were cauterized, and the hernia sac was dissected off the umbilicus and also off the fascia above the umbilicus. Both defects were approximated together, and the hernia repair was with #1 Ethibond suture using figure-of-eight Tom Jones-type technique. There was no evidence of bleeding at the end of the procedure. The repair felt very strong, and with coughing, there was no evidence of any weakness. The fascia under the umbilicus was sutured to the abdominal wall fascia with interrupted 3-0 Vicryl, 3-0 Vicryl to subcutaneous tissue, and staples to skin. He tolerated the procedure well and returned to the recovery room in satisfactory condition. Sponge and instrument counts were correct. Blood loss was minimal.

   ____

2. PREOPERATIVE DIAGNOSIS: Acute appendicitis.

   POSTOPERATIVE DIAGNOSIS: Acute suppurative appendicitis.

   PROCEDURE: Appendectomy.

   OPERATIVE FINDINGS: The patient was found to have an acute appendicitis, very high, going up under the cecum. No adenopathy was noted, and because we did run into infecting material, we did not look for a Meckel's diverticulum or do any other exploring.

   With the patient under satisfactory general endotracheal anesthesia in a supine position, the abdomen was prepared with pHisoHex and draped with sterile drapes. A linear incision about 5 or 6 cm long was made in a transverse manner in the right lower quadrant over McBurney's point. The subcutaneous tissues were divided; bleeding points were picked up with hemostats and ligated with 4-0 Vicryl ligatures. The external oblique aponeurosis was divided down in the direction of its fibers, the internal oblique muscle and transversalis fascia were divided in the direction of their fibers, and the peritoneum was opened. We had trouble getting the omentum away from the appendix and a little trouble finding the appendix since it was retrocecal. However, we were able to find it and deliver it through the wound. The mesoappendix was clamped with Kelly clamps down the base of the appendix and divided and doubly ligated with 2-0 Vicryl ligatures. The base of the appendix was doubly ligated with 2-0 Vicryl ligatures, the appendix was removed between Kelly clamps, and the base of the appendix was cauterized with phenol and alcohol and inverted with a purse-string suture. A search for bleeding then failed to reveal any. Sponge counts and instrument counts were verified. The peritoneum was closed with a continuous suture of 0 PDS; the internal oblique muscle and transversalis fascia were washed with a Hibiclens solution and closed with interrupted 0 PDS suture in a figure-of-eight manner. The external oblique aponeurosis was closed with a continuous 0 PDS. The wound was again washed with a Betadine solution. Scarpa's fascia was closed with continuous 3-0 PDS; skin and subcutaneous tissue were closed with a continuous 4-0 PDS in the subcuticular position. The wound was covered with sterile dressing. The patient withstood the procedure well and returned to the recovery room in good condition.

---

3. POSTOPERATIVE DIAGNOSIS: Diffuse small and large intestinal gangrene, including necrosis of proximal stomach. Pneumatosis, small bowel and colon.

   OPERATION PERFORMED: Exploratory laparotomy. Abdominal irrigation.

   INDICATIONS FOR SURGERY: This is a teenage boy with neurologic impairment and gastroesophageal reflux. Due to worsening pulmonary status and aspiration, an antireflux operation was performed approximately one week ago. He had been recovering fine from this and was undergoing advancing feedings. He developed a fever today, and fluid resuscitation and antibiotics were started. Radiographs showed evidence of abdominal catastrophe with extensive pneumatosis throughout a large portion of the intestine with evidence of free air. He was brought urgently to the operating room; he had been transferred to the pediatric intensive care unit earlier in the evening. Upon arrival in the operating room, the patient was in extremis. The abdomen was distended and firm. Upon opening the abdomen, foul-smelling air emanated from the abdomen. There was extensive pneumatosis involving the small bowel and the colon. There was fluid in the abdomen, which was whitish in color. This measured approximately 500 cc. The intestine was necrotic in many areas and pale and poorly perfused. The distal stomach was viable, but the proximal stomach, especially the fundus, appeared necrotic. Again, the fundus was dark, hemorrhagic, and appeared to be necrotic. This was different from the lower stomach.

   The patient was placed supine on the operating table and after satisfactory induction of general anesthesia was prepped and draped in a sterile fashion. The abdomen was opened through the previous upper midline incision, which was extended down through the umbilicus and slightly around the umbilicus. Upon opening the abdomen, a moderate amount of foul-smelling gas emanated from the abdomen. The abdomen was suctioned, and approximately 500 cc of whitish material was suctioned. This was sent for culture.

---

4. PREOPERATIVE DIAGNOSIS: Polyp of hepatic flexure, status post–multiple endoscopic polypectomies.

   POSTOPERATIVE DIAGNOSIS: Polyp of hepatic flexure, status post–multiple endoscopic polypectomies.

   OPERATION PERFORMED: Right hemicolectomy.

   INDICATIONS FOR PROCEDURE: The patient is a 67-year-old white female with a history of a sessile polyp in the hepatic flexure. Despite multiple prior polypectomies, the polyp could not be eradicated. Biopsies demonstrated that there was moderate to severe dysplasia within the lesion. Subsequently, the patient was taken to the operating room suite for hemicolectomy.

   INTRAOPERATIVE FINDINGS: Included a 2-cm margin distal to the polyp.

   Informed consent was obtained prior to surgical intervention. The patient was taken to the major operating suite and placed in the supine position, where general endotracheal anesthesia was successfully administered. The patient's abdomen was prepped and draped in a typical sterile manner. The patient's prior right paramedian incision was excised using a knife. Subcutaneous tissues were transected using a Bovie electrocautery, and the midline fascia was incised. Great care was taken upon entering the abdomen not to injure underlying bowel. A modest number of thin adhesions were then taken down sharply, using the Metzenbaum scissors. Following adequate adhesiolysis, the Bookwalter retractor was placed in position. The right colon was mobilized by incising the lateral peritoneal attachments. Following elevation of the right colon, the hepatic flexure was taken down using a combination of sharp and blunt dissection. The right branch of the middle colic artery was identified, and this was thought to be a good site for division of the transverse colon. This will allow the left branch of the middle colic to maintain flow to the distal segment of colon. The mesentery of the right colon was then sequentially clamped, divided, and ligated using 0 silk ties. Stick ties were used as larger vessels were encountered. The terminal ileum was then positioned in a side-to-side manner with the transverse colon just distal to the right branch of middle colic artery. Entrotomies were made in the transverse colon and terminal ileum, and a side-to-side anastomosis was performed using a GIA 80 stapler. The anastomosis was completed by firing a second load of the GIA stapler. The specimen was then placed on the back table and was inspected. A 2-cm margin from the polyp was identified. The polyp was marked with a stitch, and the specimen was sent to pathology for histologic evaluation. The lumen of the anastomosis was palpated and found to be widely patent. The mesenteric defect was then closed using a series of 3-0 silk simple interrupted sutures. The abdomen was copiously irrigated using warm normal saline solution. Hemostasis was confirmed, and the midline fascia was reapproximated using a running #2 Prolene suture. Subcutaneous tissues were copiously irrigated, and the skin was closed with staples. Sterile dressing was applied, and the patient was awakened from general endotracheal anesthesia and escorted to the recovery room, having tolerated the procedure without apparent incident.

   ____

5. PREOPERATIVE DIAGNOSIS: Incarcerated right inguinal hernia.

   POSTOPERATIVE DIAGNOSIS: Incarcerated right inguinal hernia.

   OPERATION: Right inguinal herniorrhaphy with reduction of incarcerated small bowel.

   INDICATION FOR PROCEDURE: This patient, who is 3 months of age, was a full-term birth. He now presents with an inguinal hernia that is possibly incarcerated. After a discussion of the procedural and anesthetic risks, the parents of this child consented to surgical intervention to reduce the hernia.

   The patient was prepped and draped under a general inhalation anesthetic. An incision was made in the inguinal fold and carried through the external oblique fascia overlying the incarcerated inguinal mass. Upon opening the external oblique fascia and the indirect hernial sac, a fairly large amount of small bowel was found. The color of the bowel upon first opening the sac was quite dusky in appearance. The mesentery at this point was somewhat congested and edematous. The internal ring was cut, and the color of the bowel and mesentery immediately improved. With some difficulty, the small bowel was replaced in the abdominal cavity, and the hernial sac was dissected off the cord. The hernial sac was closed with two fine cotton sutures, and the internal ring was closed with interrupted cotton sutures. The external oblique fascia was closed with interrupted cotton. The subcutaneous tissue was closed with interrupted 000 plain gut, and the skin was closed with a continuous subcuticular suture of 000 plain gut. The baby tolerated the procedure well and left the operating room in good condition.

---

6. PREOPERATIVE DIAGNOSIS: Bladder tumor.

   POSTOPERATIVE DIAGNOSIS: Papillary tumor, right side lateral to right orifice of urinary bladder. Tumor, urinary bladder, going up to the right orifice.

   PROCEDURES: Cystoscopy. Bilateral retrograde pyelograms. Right stent placement. TURB fulguration.

   ANESTHESIA: General.

   INDICATIONS: This man had a gross total painless hematuria. He had a previous history of prostatectomy a year ago. He had a papillary tumor along the right side lateral to the right orifice but also a smaller velvety tumor going right up to the right orifice. Informed consent was obtained for risks and benefits and for possible risks of stricture and stenosis of the right ureter.

   The patient was brought to the operating room. Under satisfactory general anesthesia, he was placed in the lithotomy position. He was prepped and draped in the usual sterile fashion. The anterior urethra was normal. The sphincter mechanism looked very good. There was no contraction. There was a papillary tumor measuring 2.5 to 3.0 cm on the right lateral wall. It also extended in a more papillary fashion around the right orifice and behind the right orifice. Bilateral retrograde pyelograms were taken, first on the left and then on the right. These revealed normal upper tracks and good drainage. I placed a wire up to the right renal pelvis under fluoroscopic guidance; then I placed a #6-French 26-cm double-J stent in order to protect the right ureter. Then the resectoscope was placed easily. The tumor was resected down in the muscle, and remaining parts of the tumor were fulgurated. From about three o'clock to nine o'clock around the orifice did not appear to be involved. The entire tumor was completely resected. There was no visible tumor at the end of the case. There was good hemostasis. All chips were evacuated. A Foley catheter was placed, the urine was clear, and the procedure was brought to an end. The patient tolerated it well.

---

7. PREOPERATIVE DIAGNOSIS: Bladder stone with hydronephrosis.

   POSTOPERATIVE DIAGNOSIS: Bladder stone with hydronephrosis.

   PROCEDURES: Cystoscopy with laser lithotripsy of bladder calculus and placement of stent.

   ANESTHESIA: Local.

   The patient was placed in the relaxed dorsal lithotomy position, Betadine prepped, and sterilely draped. With use of a #21-French panendoscope, a bladder stone measuring approximately 3 cm in diameter was visualized. Under video control using the 500-micron fiber at 8 watts of energy, fragmentation of the calculus was performed. The entire stone was fragmented. On injection of contrast, there was considerable hydronephrosis to the system. Prior to placement of the stent, the bladder was all clear. It was necessary to laser some marginal bladder stone fragments from the specimen. Following this, a #6-French 22-cm double-pigtail stent was placed. The patient tolerated the procedure well and left the operating room in satisfactory condition.

---

8. PREOPERATIVE DIAGNOSIS: Right ureteral calculus.

   POSTOPERATIVE DIAGNOSIS: Right ureteral calculus.

   OPERATION PERFORMED: Attempted ureteroscopic stone manipulation.

   With the patient under satisfactory general endotracheal anesthesia in the low lithotomy position, penis was prepped and draped in the usual sterile manner. Initially, a #24-French cystourethroscope was introduced under direct vision. Initial attempts at inserting a #028 guidewire into the ureteral orifice were unsuccessful. The orifice could be negotiated, but the guidewire would not pass past 2 cm, this being the location of the stone. Multiple attempts at passing this were unsuccessful. Attempts at forcing the stone back with a #6-French olive tip ureteral catheter were also unsuccessful. A retrograde ureterogram was obtained with a #8-French cone tip ureteral catheter. Attempts at passing the stone with a #5-French flexi-tip ureteral catheter were also unsuccessful. A balloon dilator was inserted in the ureteral orifice and inflated. With attempts at inserting the ureteroscope, the ureteroscope could be advanced about 1 to 1½ cm into the intramural ureter but could not be advanced past this. It was thought that with inadequate dilation, the procedure should not continue; therefore, the instrument was removed. Again, attempts at passing the ureteral catheter back up past the stone were unsuccessful. Patient was discharged to the recovery room with no catheters in place.

   ____

9. PREOPERATIVE DIAGNOSIS: Gross hematuria.

   POSTOPERATIVE DIAGNOSIS: Carcinoma of the bladder.

   OPERATION PERFORMED: Cystoscopic examination and biopsy and fulguration of bladder mass.

   With the patient in dorsolithotomy position, the perineum was prepped and draped in the usual sterile manner. A #21-French cystourethroscope was introduced under direct vision. There was a moderate amount of bloody urine in the bladder, which was cleaned from the bladder. Examination with the 25° and 70° lens showed a mass originating in the high posterior wall, more toward the right side. A large clot was adherent to the area. The clot was evacuated free with an Ellick evacuator. Tauber biopsy forceps were used to remove a few pieces of the tumor, which were sent for pathologic interpretation. The biopsy sites were lightly fulgurated. There were other bleeding sites of the tumor itself, which were also fulgurated with the biopsy forceps. Postoperatively, the patient did well, with the bladder being irrigated clear. The patient was discharged in good condition.

   ____

10. PREOPERATIVE DIAGNOSIS: Obstructed left kidney.

    POSTOPERATIVE DIAGNOSIS: Left ureteral stone, passed into the bladder.

    PROCEDURE: Cystourethroscopy with manipulation of calculus.

    INDICATION FOR PROCEDURE: This 32-year-old man was admitted through the emergency room where he presented with marked left renal colic. IVP showed obstructed left kidney.

    The patient was prepped and draped in the sterile manner in lithotomy position. Ten milligrams of Valium was slowly given IV, and the urethra was anesthetized with Anestacon. A #24 cystourethroscope entered the bladder with ease. Bladder was inspected. No tumor, calculi, or diverticuli were found. There was marked edema of the left ureteral orifice, and the right orifice was normal and effluxing clear urine.

    A #5 ureteral catheter was inserted with slight difficulty into the left orifice and advanced to the lower third of the left ureter. Left ureteral fluoroscopy confirmed the catheter's position. Contrast material was injected into the catheter, and the entire left ureter and renal collecting system were outlined. Ureteral dilation was performed under fluoroscopic guidance, and there appeared to be a round density in the lower left ureter to the ureteral orifice.

The ureteral catheter was then removed, and the stone passed into the bladder from the left orifice. It was impossible to irrigate the stone out of the bladder, but the patient will pass this stone easily himself. Procedure was terminated, bladder was emptied, and cystoscope was withdrawn. Patient was returned to his room in good condition after he tolerated the procedure well. He was placed on Macrodantin 50 mg q.i.d.

---

11. PREOPERATIVE DIAGNOSIS: Hiatal hernia.

    POSTOPERATIVE DIAGNOSIS: Hiatal hernia.

    PROCEDURE: Repair of paraesophageal hiatal hernia.

    This 45-year-old male patient was brought to the operating suite. After the administration of general anesthesia, the patient was prepped in the usual sterile fashion. After laparotomy incision was made and abdominal muscles were retracted, a rather large paraesophageal hernia was directly visualized. No strangulation or obstruction was noted. The hernia measured approximately 6 cm in diameter. The hernia sac was dissected from the diaphragm. The resulting defect in the diaphragm was closed with 4-0 Prolene. Penrose drains were placed. The incision site was closed in layers with staples and sutures. The patient tolerated the procedure well.

---

12. PREOPERATIVE DIAGNOSIS: Rule out sarcoidosis.

    POSTOPERATIVE DIAGNOSIS: Rule out sarcoidosis.

    PROCEDURE: Endoscopic view of mediastinum.

    INDICATION FOR PROCEDURE: The patient is a 35-year-old female with the complaints of several years of numbness in extremities and ongoing pain in joints. The patient has a paternal family history of sarcoidosis; therefore, this outpatient procedure was done for diagnostic purposes.

    With the patient under adequate anesthesia, a small incision was made above the sternum. The endoscope was inserted. The thymus and thyroid were visualized and appeared normal. The mediastinum was seen, and several biopsies were taken of the surrounding lymph nodes. The scope was withdrawn. The surgical incision site was closed with one suture and sterile dressing.

---

13. PREOPERATIVE DIAGNOSIS: Rule out injury to diaphragm.

    POSTOPERATIVE DIAGNOSIS: Tear of diaphragm. (Initial encounter)

    PROCEDURE: Repair of diaphragm.

    INDICATION FOR PROCEDURE: The patient, a 20-year-old female, suffered a motor vehicle crash (MVC) and complained of pulmonary symptoms. She also had a liver laceration that was repaired by Dr. Wilcox last week on 04/04/YY. Today she presents for exploration and possible repair.

    After the administration of anesthesia, an abdominal incision was made. The muscles were retracted, and the diaphragm was visualized. A 3.0-cm long laceration was seen in the midsection of the diaphragm. The laceration of the diaphragm was repaired with sutures. Sponge and instrument counts were correct. The patient's incision was closed in layers with sutures. The patient was awakened and taken to the recovery room. Blood loss was minimal.

---

14. PREOPERATIVE DIAGNOSIS: Cyst of mediastinum.

    POSTOPERATIVE DIAGNOSIS: Congenital cyst of mediastinum.

    INDICATION FOR PROCEDURE: This 16-year-old male patient has been complaining of respiratory symptoms for the past three months. MRI of the chest demonstrated a large mediastinal cyst. The patient presents for removal of this cyst.

    After the patient was brought into the operating room, anesthesia was administered. A chest incision was made. Muscles were retracted, and a rib spreader was used to gain access to the mediastinum. A cyst measuring approximately 7.5 cm in diameter was visualized. The cyst appeared fluid-filled. The cyst in its capsule was totally removed and placed in a specimen jar. This was sent to pathology. After all sponge and instrument counts were verified as correct, the patient's incision was closed and a sterile dressing was applied. The patient was moved into the recovery room in a stable condition.

    ____

15. PREOPERATIVE DIAGNOSIS: Rule out metastatic lung carcinoma.

    POSTOPERATIVE DIAGNOSIS: Rule out metastatic lung carcinoma.

    PROCEDURE: Chamberlain procedure.

    INDICATION FOR PROCEDURE: The patient is a 45-year-old female, nonsmoker, who has had an abnormal chest x-ray and MRI. She now presents for a mediastinotomy with biopsy to rule out lung carcinoma. The patient originally presented with the chief complaint of a cough for the past eight months.

    After all consents had been signed, the patient was brought into the surgical suite. The patient was given anesthesia. Under fluoroscopic guidance, an incision was made to the left anterior parasternal space slightly below the third intercostal space. The muscles of the sternal area were exposed and retracted out of the way. The mediastinum was seen, and multiple biopsies were taken of the lymph nodes in the area. These samples were sent in sterile containers to pathology for analysis. A drain was placed, and the incision site was closed with sutures and a sterile dressing. Biopsy results are expected in a few hours.

    ____

16. PREOPERATIVE DIAGNOSIS: Mass and inflammation of the right parotid gland.

    POSTOPERATIVE DIAGNOSIS: Acute sialoadenitis.

    An incision was made in the skin anterior to the right ear down to the angle of the mandible and anteriorly along the lower quarter of the mandible approximately 6 cm. This was carried down to the capsule of the parotid, and the anterior skin flap was developed anteriorly to the zygomatic arch and the anterior border of the parotid gland. An incision was then begun next to the cartilage of the external ear canal, transecting the fascia between the cartilage and the parotid gland. The facial nerve was identified deeply.

    The gland was separated from the right sternocleidomastoid muscle. The branches of the facial nerve were all identified and left intact; the superficial portion of the parotid gland was dissected off the facial nerve, leaving the facial nerve completely intact. The temporal zygomatic buccal mandibular and cervical branches were identified. Hemostasis was obtained by electrocautery and by clamping and ligating with 00 black silk suture. A drain was left in the subcutaneous area, brought out through the lower end of the incision, and attached to the skin with a silk suture; a safety pin was placed through the drain. The skin edges were then approximated with interrupted stitches of 0000 black silk sutures. A combination of plastic spray dressing and sterile dressing was applied. The patient tolerated the procedure well.

    ____

REVIEW

Multiple Choice

Circle the most appropriate response.

1. Repair of anterior urethra on a male patient in one operation. Which CPT code is assigned?
   a. 53400
   b. 53410
   c. 53415
   d. 53420
2. Resection of portion of diaphragm. Defect created by resection required closure with reinforced mesh. Which CPT code is assigned?
   a. 39540
   b. 39545
   c. 39560
   d. 39561
3. Vermilion thickness repair one-half vertical height. Which CPT code is assigned?
   a. 40650
   b. 40652
   c. 40654
   d. 40700
4. Endoscopic retrograde cholangiopancreatography (ERCP) with biopsy of ampulla of Vater. Which CPT code(s) are assigned?
   a. 43260
   b. 43261
   c. 43262
   d. 43260, 43261-51
5. Esophagogastroduodenoscopy (EGD) with biopsy of stomach and esophagus. Which CPT code(s) are assigned?
   a. 43200
   b. 43235, 43202-51
   c. 43235, 43239-51
   d. 43239
6. Colonoscopy with removal of a polyp of the splenic flexure using snare technique and the removal of a polyp of the descending colon using ablation. Which CPT code(s) are assigned?
   a. 45385
   b. 45388
   c. 45388, 45385-59
   d. 45378, 45385-51, 45388-59
7. Bladder voiding pressure study. Which CPT code is assigned?
   a. 51728
   b. 51797
   c. 51798
   d. 51999
8. A 70-year-old male patient presented with the diagnosis of benign prostatic hypertrophy (BPH). After discussion and an understanding of the risks, the patient consented to a transurethral resection of the prostate (TURP). During this procedure, the physician also performed a cystourethroscopy, a vasectomy, and an internal urethrotomy. Which CPT code(s) are assigned?
   a. 52601
   b. 52601, 52000-51, 55250-51
   c. 52601, 52000-51, 55250-51, 53000-51
   d. 52601, 55250-51
9. Percutaneous drainage of pseudocyst of pancreas. Which CPT code is assigned?
   a. 48000
   b. 48120
   c. 48510
   d. 49405
10. Internal and external hemorrhoidectomy, single column/group. Which CPT code is assigned?
    a. 46250
    b. 46255
    c. 46257
    d. 46260

11. Total excision of parotid tumor with dissection and preservation of facial nerve. Which CPT code is assigned?
    a. 42410
    b. 42420
    c. 42425
    d. 42426
12. Removal of adenoids of 20-year-old female patient. She had adenoids first excised during a tonsillectomy when she was five years of age. Which CPT code(s) are assigned?
    a. 42825, 42830-51
    b. 42831
    c. 42835, 42826-51
    d. 42836
13. Open drainage of liver abscess via incision. Which CPT code is assigned?
    a. 47010
    b. 47015
    c. 47300
    d. 49405
14. Wedge biopsy of pancreas. Which CPT code is assigned?
    a. 48000
    b. 48100
    c. 48102
    d. 48120
15. ESWL for kidney stones. Which CPT code is assigned?
    a. 50561
    b. 50580
    c. 50590
    d. 50592
16. Diagnostic cystoscopy due to diagnosis of hematuria. Which CPT code is assigned?
    a. 52000
    b. 52001
    c. 52204
    d. 52320
17. Removal of diseased gallbladder via laparoscope. Which CPT code is assigned?
    a. 47550
    b. 47562
    c. 47600
    d. 47720
18. Right upper quadrant resection of gum. Which CPT code is assigned?
    a. 41820
    b. 41821
    c. 41825
    d. 41872
19. Repair of recurrent inguinal hernia via laparoscope. Which CPT code is assigned?
    a. 49520
    b. 49525
    c. 49650
    d. 49651
20. Repair of sphincter on a four-year-old child. Which CPT code is assigned?
    a. 46700
    b. 46705
    c. 46750
    d. 46751

CPT Surgery V

CHAPTER 16

INTRODUCTION

This chapter introduces students to CPT surgery coding (Male Genital System subsection, Intersex Surgery subsection, Female Genital System subsection, Maternity Care and Delivery subsection, Endocrine System subsection, Nervous System subsection, Eye and Ocular Adnexa subsection, Auditory System subsection, and Operating Microscope subsection). Students assign codes to coding cases by applying CPT coding guidelines and notes.

Objectives

At the conclusion of this chapter, the student should be able to:

- Assign CPT surgery codes from the Male Genital System, Intersex Surgery, Female Genital System, Maternity Care and Delivery, Endocrine System, Nervous System, Eye and Ocular Adnexa, Auditory System, and Operating Microscope subsections.
- Add CPT and/or HCPCS level II modifiers to codes as appropriate.

ASSIGNMENT 16.1 – CODING PRACTICE

Instructions

Assign the ICD-10-CM code(s) to diagnoses and conditions and assign the CPT surgery code(s) and the appropriate HCPCS level II and CPT modifier(s). Do not assign ICD-10-CM external cause codes.

1. With the patient under general anesthesia, a vertical midline scrotal incision was made, carried down through the skin and subcutaneous tissues. With use of the cautery, the hemiscrotum was entered. The left testicle was delivered into the wound. There was no active bleeding, and the testicle was sent for analysis. The operative wounds were closed in multiple layers. Blood loss was minimal. The pathology report was positive for testicular cancer, left testicle. Thus, patient also underwent placement of needles into pelvic organs for subsequent interstitial radioelement application.

   ____

2. Patient's neck was palpated, and a thyroid cyst was identified on the right. Local anesthesia was administered; the cyst was confirmed. A needle was inserted through the skin into the cyst. The needle was withdrawn with the sample of tissue and sent for analysis.

   ____

3. The patient presented with a laceration of the common sensory nerve of the right foot. After the operating microscope was brought into the operating field, the nerve was repaired with sutures. (Initial encounter.)

____

4. Patient was a 25-year-old female who went into active labor spontaneously and delivered full-term vaginally. The attending obstetrician was also responsible for normal antepartum care. At the hospital, the patient's lab results were within normal limits. She had an uncomplicated postpartum course. The patient was discharged to home, and the pregnancy delivered full-term via occipitoanterior presentation. The physician will continue to follow during the postpartum period.

____

5. After adequate general anesthesia was given, a transverse cervical incision was made. Skin, fascia, and muscle were retracted to expose the thyroid gland. The entire thyroid, including substernal thyroid, was removed and sent to pathology for analysis. Parathyroid glands were carefully inspected and found to be normal. These were not removed, but left intact. The skin and muscle were closed in layers. Pathology report stated Hashimoto's disease.

____

6. The patient presented with the complaint of severe photophobia. The patient stated that this was present in the left eye only. After the surface of the corneal defect was scraped with a spatula, it was taken for culture to determine the diagnosis.

____

7. Dr. Smith removed a portion of a skin lesion on the penis by punch biopsy. The incision required simple repair with sutures. The analysis was returned as Bowen's disease of the penis.

____

8. With the patient under general anesthesia, an incision was made directly into the vaginal cyst; 0 Dexon was used to marsupialize the vaginal cyst by suturing the vaginal mucosa to the cyst wall. This left a stoma present. The vaginal cyst was excised and the area packed with a small amount of ¼-inch iodoform gauze. The blood loss was negligible. The cyst did not appear to be a Bartholin cyst.

____

9. A neurostimulator electrode device is placed through the skin to the peripheral nerve of the patient's right lower leg. This was done to alleviate the patient's peripheral neuropathy.

____

10. The greater occipital nerve of the scalp was identified. A nerve block injection was done. This was done for the patient's complaint of chronic migraine headaches without aura.

____

11. A nonpregnant woman presented with a nontraumatic ruptured (herniated) uterus. Dr. Malloy repaired the ruptured uterus by suturing. An incision was made in the abdomen, and the uterus was sutured in multiple layers. Then the abdominal incision was closed.

____

12. The patient presents with a traumatic subperiosteal hematoma of the left eyeball. With the aid of a fluoroscope, a fine needle was inserted directly into the eyeball area and aspirated blood. No incision was made, and no repair was required. (Initial encounter.)

____

13. Patient presents for removal of ventilating tubes (myringotomy devices) due to resolution of right and left middle and inner ear problems. With the patient under general mask anesthesia, the left ear was examined

and the tube was removed. No abnormalities in the ear structure were visualized. The same procedure was repeated on the right ear. Estimated blood loss was nil. No complications.

____

14. After adequate local anesthesia, an incision was made over the abscess of the scrotal wall. A purulent puslike material was expressed. The abscess cavity was thoroughly irrigated and dressed with a sterile bandage.

____

15. A 35-year-old male who presented with phimosis due to infection and recurrent balanitis is admitted to the surgical suite for a circumcision. The physician removed the foreskin of the penis by excision of the skin. Bleeding was controlled by chemical cautery. The skin edges were sutured together with absorbable suture material.

____

16. The patient presented with the diagnosis of uncontrolled primary hyperparathyroidism. With the patient under general anesthesia, a transverse cervical incision was made. The skin and muscle were retracted to expose the thyroid gland. Parathyroid glands were identified and removed. The tissue was excised and sent to pathology for analysis. After a drain was placed, the muscle and skin were closed in layers.

____

17. The patient presented for a bilateral vasogram. After adequate anesthesia, an incision was made in the upper outer scrotum overlying the spermatic cord and the tissues dissected to expose the vas deferens. The vas deferens was entered to test the patency of the spermatozoa-collecting system.

    POSTOPERATIVE DIAGNOSIS: Infertility due to oligospermia.

____

18. After adequate general anesthesia, a cervical incision was made. The muscles were retracted back to expose the thyroid gland. A left upper lobe thyroid mass was visualized. A partial left lobectomy was done to remove the thyroid mass. The mass was sent in total to pathology for analysis. The edges of the remaining thyroid lobe were closed with electrocautery. The surgical wound was closed with clips after a drain was placed.

____

19. After adequate general anesthesia, an incision was made anterior to the sternocleidomastoid to expose the carotid body. After dissection down to the carotid sheath, the tumor was identified and removed. The incision was closed. The tissue mass was sent to pathology for examination, where it was identified as benign.

____

20. Patient underwent the last in a series of intersex male-to-female staged procedures due to congenital absence of penis. All staged procedures were performed by the same surgeon.

____

21. The patient presented with the complaint of corneal ulcer, left eye. Cryotherapy was performed to destroy the corneal ulcer, left eye.

____

22. A 35-year-old female presents in her third trimester with placenta previa. Dr. Jones delivered the baby via cesarean section through vertical incision in the abdomen and the uterus. After the incisions were made, the baby was delivered and the placenta was separated and removed. The uterine and abdominal incisions were closed with sutures. The child had Apgar scores of 6 and 6 and was transferred to the neonatal intensive care unit (NICU). Postpartum care will be transferred back to the patient's obstetrician, Dr. Williams, who also provided her antepartum care.

____

23. Preoperative diagnosis was carpal tunnel syndrome on the left. Postoperative diagnosis was the same. The patient presented for a release of the transverse carpal ligament on the left through a transverse incision. Under axillary block anesthesia, a transverse incision was made at the level of the wrist creases between two major creases and carried down through the skin and subcutaneous tissue. The palmaris longus was noted going ulnar to this. The transverse ligament was divided; a hemostat was passed distally between the nerve and the ligament that transected the transverse ligament distally and proximally. Good release was obtained by palpation with instrument and finger. Nerve was in good shape before and after. No definite constriction was noted in the nerve. The skin was closed with sutures, and a bandage and wrap were applied.

___

24. The patient presented for a biopsy due to an external ear mass on the left. A small biopsy forceps was used to excise a portion of a lesion on the left external ear for diagnostic purposes. Ear canal packing was done. The biopsy report showed squamous cell carcinoma. The patient will be notified and advised of treatment options.

___

25. A woman presented with vaginal hemorrhage. Dr. Jones pushed gauze packing into the vagina to stop the bleeding. After 20 minutes of the packing being in place, it was removed; minimal bleeding was observed at this point. The patient was discharged after observation of another hour, during which time the bleeding stopped.

    DIAGNOSIS: Dysfunctional uterine bleeding. It is important to note that the pregnancy test was negative for this patient.

___

26. A 27-year-old male presented with the diagnosis of neuritis of the left supraorbital nerve. With the patient under local anesthesia, a transverse incision was made through the skin above the left eyebrow. This was carried down through the frontal musculature and the periosteum identified. The supraorbital nerve was identified, and it emerged through the supraorbital foramen. It was transected and cauterized. Hemostasis was good. The muscular layers were approximated with sutures, and the subcuticular area was closed with sutures. The patient tolerated the procedure well.

___

27. A 50-year-old patient with a diagnosis of acute primary angle-closure glaucoma, right eye, presented to the ambulatory surgical suite for an iridoplasty, right eye. After the patient was prepped and draped in the usual sterile fashion, an argon laser was used. The patient left the surgical suite in a satisfactory condition.

___

28. The patient presented to the ambulatory surgical suite for treatment of her incomplete miscarriage. Demerol IV and local anesthesia were administered and the contents of the uterine cavity were evacuated. There appeared to be endometrial and placental tissue. There were some areas of dark clot associated with it, and there was no evidence of fluid. The total quantity was approximately 10 cc. The uterine cavity was explored with forceps and appeared empty. The walls were curetted gently without evidence of residual debris, and the procedure was concluded.

___

29. A local anesthetic was administered. The face and left eyelid were draped and prepped for surgery. An electrocautery tool was used to destroy the small 0.5-cm lesion of the eyelid, upper left. Pathologic analysis confirmed this to be a benign lesion of the left eyelid.

____

30. The female patient presented with a pelvic abscess. With the patient under conscious sedation, Dr. Sutton used a transvaginal approach and image guidance of the catheter to drain an abscess in the pelvis percutaneously. After the abscess was drained, the cavity was cleaned out and irrigated with antibiotics. Temporary catheter was left in place to help drainage.

____

31. Through the right external ear canal opening, the aural polyp was removed with an ear snare. Bleeding was controlled with cotton ball packing. Antibiotic drops were instilled.

____

32. The patient presented at 11 weeks pregnant with the complaint of heavy vaginal bleeding. This was her fourth office visit. After examination, it was confirmed that the patient had suffered a miscarriage. No complications were noted on the examination of this patient. Discharge instructions were thoroughly explained to the patient.

____

33. With the patient under local anesthesia, an incision in the skin was made. The abscess of the left external auditory canal was identified and drained. Gauze packing was inserted to absorb the drainage and to facilitate healing. The small stab incision did not require suture closure.

____

34. After a local anesthetic was injected into the vaginal mucosa, a sample of the vaginal mucosa was obtained for examination. The biopsy was large, and the resulting surgical wound from the biopsy was closed with sutures. Pathologic analysis showed vaginitis due to *Trichomonas*.

____

35. After the administration of Versed and Demerol, an incision in the skin behind the left ear was made. Skin was lifted off the auricle cartilage. Several sutures were needed to create a new skin fold to allow the ear to appear more normal and not protrude as severely. The size of the auricle was not changed. The skin was closed in layers with sutures. A sterile dressing was applied.

    DIAGNOSIS: Bat ear.

____

ASSIGNMENT 16.2 – CODING OPERATIVE REPORTS

Instructions

Assign the ICD-10-CM code(s) to diagnoses and conditions and assign the CPT surgery code(s) and the appropriate HCPCS level II and CPT modifier(s). Do not assign ICD-10-CM external cause codes.

1. PREOPERATIVE DIAGNOSIS: Carcinoma of the prostate.

   POSTOPERATIVE DIAGNOSIS: Carcinoma of the prostate.

   PROCEDURES: Cystoscopy. Transurethral electrosurgical resection of prostate.

   ANESTHESIA: General.

   INDICATIONS: This is a 77-year-old gentleman who has been diagnosed with extensive carcinoma of the prostate. He had a previous transurethral resection of the prostate (TURP) done. On cystoscopy, he had a lobe of somewhat necrotic-appearing tissue right at 10 o'clock, which I thought would be prudent to resect for diagnostic purposes.

   The patient was brought to the operating room. After satisfactory induction of anesthesia, he was placed in the lithotomy position and prepped and draped in the usual sterile fashion. A cystoscope was introduced into the bladder under direct vision. The anterior urethra was normal. The prostate had some residual apical tissue and also had a lobe of tissue on the right wall from about 10 o'clock to 8 o'clock with some yellowish necrotic-appearing tissue on it. The bladder was scoped and found without lesion. It was trabeculated. The orifices were normal. The bladder was otherwise fairly open. The resectoscope was placed, and about 5 g of tissue was electrosurgically resected from the right wall, all of the suspicious tissue having been resected. All of the chips were evacuated. Hemostasis meticulously attended to a good effect with use of the cautery device. Reinspection showed no chips in the bladder. Orifices were intact. The sphincter and verumontanum were intact. A #20-French Foley catheter was placed and irrigated easily, and the procedure was brought to an end. The patient tolerated the procedure well.

   ____

2. PREOPERATIVE DIAGNOSIS: Elevated prostate-specific antigen (PSA).

   POSTOPERATIVE DIAGNOSIS: Benign prostatic hypertrophy (BPH).

   PROCEDURE: Transrectal ultrasound and biopsy.

   ANESTHESIA: Local.

   The patient was brought to the procedure room and placed on the procedure table in the dorsal lithotomy position. A transrectal ultrasound probe was placed in the rectum after digital rectal exam was performed. Local anesthesia was achieved by injecting 2.5 cc of 1% Xylocaine solution into the apex of the prostate subcapsularly using ultrasound guidance. This was performed on the right and left sides. An ultrasound examination of the prostate was then performed. The ultrasound imaging revealed the prostate size of 31 cc. This combined with the previously measured PSA of 3.8 yields a PSA density of 0.12. The prostate length was 4.6 cm, the height was 2.7 cm, and the width was 4.7 cm. The central gland had a well-defined central adenoma consistent with BPH. The peripheral zone was homogeneous, and no dispute hypoechoic area was seen. The capsule appeared intact, and the seminal vesicles were symmetrical without alteration. Ultrasound guidance and a biopsy gun were used to take a total of 10 biopsies. Each biopsy was sent separately to pathology for examination, pending at the time of this dictation.

   ____

3. PREOPERATIVE DIAGNOSIS: Elective sterilization.

POSTOPERATIVE DIAGNOSIS: Elective sterilization.

PROCEDURE: Bilateral vasectomy.

ANESTHESIA: Local.

The patient was brought to the operating room and placed on the operating table in the supine position. He was prepped and draped in the usual sterile fashion. Local anesthesia was achieved by injecting 1% Xylocaine solution into the skin of the median raphe of the scrotum. Skin opening was made with a sharpened hemostat, and local anesthesia was carried down to the left vas deferens with 1% Xylocaine. The left vas deferens was grasped with a vas clamp, brought through the skin surface, and dissected at 360 degrees. It was divided between two hemostats, and a 1-cm segment was excised. Each end was cauterized and tied with a 3-0 chromic tie, and the distal end was sharpened into the vas sheath. The vas sheath was oversewn with the 3-0 chromic, separating the two ends. The left vas deferens was dropped down to the left hemiscrotum, and attention was focused to the right side. Again, anesthesia was achieved by injecting the right vas deferens with local anesthesia. It was then grasped and brought to the skin surface with the vas clamp. The vas deferens was then dissected free at 360 degrees and divided between two hemostats. A 1-cm segment was excised. Each end was cauterized and tied with a 3-0 chromic suture. The distal end of the vas deferens was brought back into the vas sheath. The vas sheath was oversewn with a 3-0 chromic, thus separating the two ends. The right vas deferens was then dropped into the right hemiscrotum. The skin edges were pinched together for hemostasis. Bacitracin and sterile dry dressing were applied, and the patient was awakened and returned to the recovery room in stable condition.

---

4. PREOPERATIVE DIAGNOSIS: Third-degree enterocele.

POSTOPERATIVE DIAGNOSIS: Same.

OPERATION PERFORMED: Repair of enterocele.

OPERATIVE FINDINGS: The patient was found to have a vagina that was completely turned inside out. There was nothing in the way of any good tissue of any kind to repair with or anything in the abdomen that I could suture anything to. The first incision took us right into the peritoneal cavity.

Under satisfactory general endotracheal anesthesia with the patient in a lithotomy position, the perineum, vagina, and abdomen were prepared with pHisoHex and draped with sterile drapes and the drapes were sutured in place. A pelvic examination was done, and nothing could be felt in the pelvis. The catheter was inserted and the bladder emptied of about 700 cc of clear urine, and she had just urinated not more than five minutes before that. The apex of the vagina was grasped with Allis forceps. An incision about 3–4 cm long was made in a transverse manner, and this took us right into the peritoneal cavity. Then searching for anything in the way of uterosacral ligaments or anything was completely futile. There was nothing inside that could be used. Therefore, the bladder and rectum were dissected free from the anterior and posterior vagina mucous membrane. These mucous membranes were divided in the midline up to a point where we could feel where the defect was in the peritoneum, and then we just closed the peritoneum with a continuous suture of 2-0 Vicryl. Then we inverted all of the excess tissue that was hanging down into the vagina and inverted it into the pelvis and sutured it with interrupted 0 PDS suture in a horizontal mattress-type suture. This seemed to give her some support, but there was just no good tissue at all to repair with. The mucous membrane was edematous and thickened but very friable. Then when these tissues were inverted and seemed to be holding pretty well, the large amount of vagina mucous membrane was trimmed both anteriorly and posteriorly and then closed in the midline using interrupted 0 PDS sutures in a figure-of-eight manner. Following this, a catheter was inserted and clear urine obtained. A vaginal pack was placed in the vaginal vault. This was dipped in Hibiclens solution. A rectal examination failed to reveal any sutures or anything in the rectum. The patient withstood the procedure well and returned to the recovery room in good condition.

---

5. PREOPERATIVE DIAGNOSIS: Uterine fibroids.

   POSTOPERATIVE DIAGNOSIS: Same, with possible adenomyosis of endometriosis.

   PROCEDURE: Total abdominal hysterectomy, bilateral salpingo-oophorectomy, and incidental appendectomy.

   Under general anesthesia, a bimanual examination was performed. The uterus was definitely enlarged and seemed to be irregular. A lower abdominal midline incision was made through the skin, subcutaneous tissue, and anterior rectus fascia. The recti muscles were retracted laterally, and the peritoneum was entered. Upon exploration, both lobes of the liver were normal. The gallbladder had many adhesions around it but no palpable stones within it. The kidneys were normal, and the aorta was normal. The appendix was in place; and at the end of the procedure, a routine appendectomy was performed. A panhysterectomy was performed by incising the perineal reflection of the bladder, dissecting the bladder downward anteriorly and onto the anterior wall of the vagina. Bilaterally the infundibulopelvic ligament, broad ligament, and cardinal ligament were clamped, transected, and ligated. The vagina was entered, and the uterus along with the tubes and ovaries were removed. The vaginal cuff was then closed with a continuous stitch of a chromic catgut suture. The round ligaments were then attached to the vaginal cuff with a chromic suture. Hemostasis was good. Routine appendectomy was performed, and the abdominal wall was closed in layers.

   ____

6. PREOPERATIVE DIAGNOSIS: Multiple miscarriages and hemorrhaging.

   POSTOPERATIVE DIAGNOSIS: Metrorrhagia. Acute salpingitis, bilaterally. History of multiple miscarriages.

   PROCEDURE: Dilation and curettage. Laparoscopic salpingectomy, bilateral.

   GROSS FINDINGS: Cervix dilated easily with dilator. The internal measurement of the uterus was 3 inches, and no adnexal masses were noted. Moderate amount of endometrial tissue was present. Inspection of the abdomen revealed no injuries noted of the bowel or mesentery, and both tubes and ovaries appeared normal, as did the uterus. Liver edge was sharp, and no unusual masses were noted.

   After adequate anesthesia, the patient was placed in the lithotomy position; the vaginal area was prepped and draped in the usual manner. The cervix was grasped with a single-tooth tenaculum and dilated without difficulty. The endometrium was curettaged with a sharp curette, and the curette was removed. A uterine cannula was put in place. The abdomen was then prepped and draped in the usual manner, and a needle was placed through an infraumbilical incision in the pelvis. The abdomen was then insufflated with 3 liters of CO_2 and the needle removed. An 8-mm trocar was placed through an enlarged infraumbilical incision and a laparoscope put in place with findings as noted above. A 6-mm trocar was placed through the suprapubic incision in the pelvis and the abdomen then viewed. The right tube was identified, grasped 2 cm from the cornea, and electrically cauterized and a portion excised. The left tube was identified, grasped, and cauterized and a portion excised in a similar manner. The view was excellent. No injury was noted, and the gas was allowed to escape from the abdomen. All instruments were removed, and the infraumbilic incision was closed with an interrupted 00 subcutaneous chromic suture. The single-tooth tenaculum and uterine cannula were removed, and the patient was taken to the recovery room in satisfactory condition.

   ____

7. PREOPERATIVE DIAGNOSIS: Repeat elective cesarean section.

POSTOPERATIVE DIAGNOSIS: Same.

OPERATION PERFORMED: Repeat elective cesarean section via low transverse cervical incision with delivery of living white male child.

ANESTHESIA: General endotracheal at patient's request.

Patient was placed in supine position on the operating table; after adequate prepping and draping of the abdomen for repeat C-section, she was immediately placed under general endotracheal anesthesia. Immediately, an incision was made in the old low transverse cervical incisional scar down through the midline from below the umbilicus to near the suprapubic region through several inches of subcutaneous fat and scar tissue to the midline fascia and scar tissue, which was opened along with the peritoneum. The abdominal cavity was entered. There were some adhesions of the omentum on the anterior wall here, but I managed to get them out of the way without too much difficulty and without cutting them for the present time. Peritoneum was incised in the midline and continued out transversely on both sides, and bladder was reflected by blunt and sharp dissection inferiorly and cut behind the retractor for the rest of the case and kept out of harm's way. I then made a low transverse midline incision in the cervix beginning in the midline, continuing laterally with my fingers. As the incision went through the uterine wall and we hit the chorioamniotic fluid, there were some very large vessels here. I do not believe the placenta was right here, but the vessels were certainly in the uterine wall here, trapped in scar tissue and very large. The chorioamniotic fluid was of normal color, odor, consistency, and volume. Child's head was delivered without problems; baby was suctioned, and the rest of the baby was delivered without problem. It turned out to be a living white male child. The cord was doubly clamped and cut, and the child was passed off the table to Dr. Clark, who was acting as the baby doctor. Then 2 g of Mefoxin and IV Pitocin were given, the uterus contracted nicely, and the placenta was delivered without problem and passed off the table as specimen. The intrauterine cavity and cervical regions were cleaned with dry sponges on several occasions to clean out any retained membranes that might be present, but there were none. When we were finished, the uterine incision was closed beginning at the left lateral side and continued over to the right lateral side using a 0 chromic continuous interlocking suture. A second suture was applied, 0 chromic continuous interlocking, for added hemostasis. When this was complete, there was no bleeding anywhere and hemostasis was achieved without problems. We went ahead and reapproximated the peritoneal edges over the uterine incision, thereby reperitonealizing the incision, and placed the bladder back in anatomical position by using 2-0 chromic catgut continuous suture. The clots and blood from behind the bladder were extracted laterally behind the uterus. All of these were taken out, and the adhesions of the omentum on the intra-abdominal wall were incised. Everything fell back into normal anatomical position without problem. Hemostasis was achieved without problem. The abdominal incision was reapproximated using 0 PDS continuous suture to reapproximate the peritoneum; 0 PDS continuous sutures, two in number, to reapproximate the midline fascia; 3-0 PDS continuous suture to reapproximate the subcutaneous tissue; and 4-0 PDS continuous sutures, subcuticular style, with the knots buried at approximately the skin edges. As each layer of the abdominal incision was reapproximated, the wound was irrigated with Betadine saline solution and suctioned and sponged off. Blood clots were removed manually from the vaginal vault. The uterus was contracting nicely. The patient seemed to tolerate the procedure well and left the operating room for the recovery room in satisfactory condition with a clear adequate urine output throughout the case.

8. PREOPERATIVE DIAGNOSIS: Full-term baby with preeclampsia in the mother (third trimester).

   POSTOPERATIVE DIAGNOSIS: Same.

   PROCEDURE: Cesarean section.

   Patient was placed under general anesthesia quickly, and a lower abdominal midline incision was made from the umbilicus to the pubis. This was carried through the skin, subcutaneous tissue, fascia, and peritoneum. Upon exploration of the lower abdomen, the uterus was lying in a normal position with only slight rotation. The peritoneal reflection of the bladder was incised, and the bladder was dissected downward off the anterior part of the lower part of the uterus. A midline incision was then made through the anterior wall of the uterus, the placenta was presenting, the incision in the uterus was vertical, the placenta and baby were delivered, and the cord was clamped and transected. The baby cried immediately and was not sedated. After the placental fragments were removed from the uterine cavity, the uterine wall was closed in three layers using a running stitch of 0 chromic catgut suture on each layer. Hemostasis was good. Pitocin and Ergotrate had been given, and there was minimal bleeding. Upon exploration, the gallbladder was normal. The blood and fluid were cleaned out of the colic gutters and out of the cul-de-sac. The abdominal wall was then closed in layers. Patient tolerated the procedure well.

   ____

9. PREOPERATIVE DIAGNOSIS: Term pregnancy in active labor.

   POSTOPERATIVE DIAGNOSIS: Same, with midline episiotomy repaired.

   OPERATION: Full-term vaginal delivery of a term male, with midline episiotomy repaired and artificial rupture of membranes.

   This very pleasant 23-year-old gravida 1, para 0 female presented to the obstetrical suite in active labor with an uncomplicated past medical and obstetrical history. Her obstetrician is currently out of town, and our practice is covering for him. Her LMP was 2/22/YY, with an EDC of 11/30/YY. She presented to the obstetrical suite with a course of labor that was 11 hours for first stage, 1 hour for second stage, and 9 minutes for third stage. She had analgesia of Nubain X1 with Carbocaine 1%; she did have mild bradycardia in the second stage, which was secondary to vasovagal effect of the second stage. Delivery was of midline episiotomy with spontaneous delivery, vertex presentation; no lacerations were noted. Both mother and infant went to the recovery room in good condition. Placenta was delivered with three vessels intact and was expressed. Infant weighed 6 lbs. 14 oz., with Apgar scores of 8 and 9. The bradycardia that was noted in the second stage as only minimal had good recovery and responded and dissipated by the time crowning had occurred. Only brief episodes when heart rate went down into the 110 range. Mother's postpartum course was uncomplicated. She bonded well, breast-fed well, and had an uncomplicated course. She is nursing well. Upon discharge, the patient will receive postpartum care from her obstetrician, who provided prenatal care.

   ____

10. PREOPERATIVE DIAGNOSIS: Thyroid nodules.

POSTOPERATIVE DIAGNOSIS: Same. Adenoma of lobe of thyroid.

PROCEDURE: Right total lobectomy, thyroid.

GROSS FINDINGS: Only after the thyroid gland was exposed was a well-defined solitary nodule measuring approximately 2 cm in diameter encountered in the right lobe of the thyroid. There was no lesion on the left lobe.

A collar incision was made. The skin flap, including the platysma muscles, was adequately developed. A midline incision was then made; the thyroid muscles were retracted laterally. Thorough exploration of the thyroid gland was then carried out. Decision was then made to remove the entire right lobe of the thyroid. The middle thyroid vein was small. It was ligated and divided. The superior thyroid vessels were doubly ligated and divided. The inferior thyroid vein was then likewise dealt with. The recurrent laryngeal nerve was identified and carefully preserved. The inferior thyroid artery was then ligated and divided. The parathyroid glands were carefully preserved. The thyroid gland was then transected left to the midline, and the right lobe was completely removed. Oozing was minimal, and a Penrose drain was let out through the right angle of the wound. The thyroid muscles were approximated with interrupted chromic catgut sutures and the skin with 0000 black silk.

____

11. PREOPERATIVE DIAGNOSIS: Neuritis of the left supraorbital nerve.

POSTOPERATIVE DIAGNOSIS: Same.

PROCEDURE: Transection, supraorbital nerve.

With the patient under local anesthesia, a transverse incision was made through the skin just above the left eyebrow. This was carried down through the frontal musculature, and the periosteum was identified. The supraorbital nerve was identified, and it emerged through the supraorbital foramen. It was transected and cauterized. Hemostasis was good. The muscular layers were approximated with 000 chromic catgut suture, and the subcuticular area was approximated with interrupted 000 chromatic catgut suture. Patient tolerated the procedure well.

____

12. PREOPERATIVE DIAGNOSIS: Neuroma, left foot.

POSTOPERATIVE DIAGNOSIS: Neuroma, left foot.

PROCEDURE: Excision of neuroma and decompression.

ANESTHESIA: General.

The patient was brought to the operating room. She was given general anesthesia. The left extremity was prepped and draped in the usual fashion. The incision was infiltrated with 0.5% lidocaine with epinephrine. An incision between the third and fourth metatarsals was placed carefully. Care was taken to score down to subcutaneous tissue, and a reamer was used to resect the third and fourth metatarsal heads. The intermetatarsal ligament was dissected carefully with a Freer elevator to protect the neurovascular bundle. The digital nerve was then finally visualized to be decompressed and found to be extremely bulbous and fibrotic. It was excised very proximally; the stump was inverted into the intrinsics and distally was traced to the bifurcation and released carefully. Hemostasis was controlled. The subcutaneous tissue was closed with 2-0 Vicryl and 3-0 Prolene for the skin. A sterile dressing was placed.

____

13. PREOPERATIVE DIAGNOSIS: Postoperative complication due to failed craniotomy performed elsewhere (17 weeks ago). Right-sided rhinorrhea of cerebrospinal fluid.

POSTOPERATIVE DIAGNOSIS: Same.

OPERATION PERFORMED: Craniotomy and repair, including use of operating microscope.

INDICATIONS FOR PROCEDURE: This patient presented status post failed craniotomy elsewhere 17 weeks earlier for right-sided rhinorrhea of cerebrospinal fluid. After a discussion of the options and risks, he elected to proceed with repeat surgery. Because this was a reoperation and a status post failed procedure, the procedure was judged unusually complex.

The patient was taken to the operating room. After the induction of satisfactory general anesthesia, he was placed on his left side, his back was prepped and draped, a needle was inserted without difficulty into the lumbar interspinous space, and a lumbar drain was inserted and sutured in place. The patient was then positioned supine for a right frontal craniotomy. His head was shaved, prepped, and draped. His old skin incision was reopened. Raney clips were applied to control skin bleeding, and the scalp flap was elevated. The old bone flap was removed. The dura was opened and tacked back. The operating microscope was draped and introduced. The frontal lobe was gently retracted. A large hole immediately posterior to the olfactory plate in the ethmoid sinuses was easily identified through which a piece of brain had herniated. This brain was amputated and removed. A piece of temporalis muscle was inserted into this hole, and a large piece of temporalis fascia was used to cover the entire area, which was bolstered in place with Gelfoam. Bleeding was controlled. The wound was irrigated. Dura was reapproximated with 3-0 silk sutures and covered with Gelfoam. The bone flap was replaced with the CranioFix system. The wound was irrigated and closed in layers with 0 Polysorb and staples. The wound was dressed. The patient was returned to the recovery room with the intact lumbar drain taking pressure off the repair site.

____

14. PREOPERATIVE DIAGNOSIS: Cataract, left eye.

POSTOPERATIVE DIAGNOSIS: Foreign body, left eye.

OPERATION PERFORMED: Removal of foreign body, left eye

INDICATIONS FOR PROCEDURE: The 65-year-old patient was seeking cataract surgery on her left eye. Under examination, it was noted that she actually has a foreign body in her left eye, which is greenish in color. The patient was informed about this finding and consent was obtained to perform removal of the foreign body.

OPERATIVE PROCEDURE: The patient was prepared for the procedure with appropriate prepping and draping. Upon removal, it was determined that the foreign body consisted of many greenish contact lenses. The patient acknowledged that she does wear green-tinted contact lenses. She said that she must have forgotten to remove one of them when she inserted a new contact lens last month. In total, 34 contact lenses were successfully removed from the patient's eye. The patient tolerated the procedure well, and a follow-up appointment was scheduled. Postoperatively, the patient commented that she "probably should go back to wearing eyeglasses instead of contact lenses." The surgical team unanimously agreed.

____

15. PREOPERATIVE DIAGNOSIS: Chronic otitis media, left ear.

POSTOPERATIVE DIAGNOSIS: Same.

OPERATION PERFORMED: Myringotomy with aspiration and Eustachian tube inflation, left ear.

OPERATIVE PROCEDURE: The patient was appropriately prepped and draped, and placed in supine position. General anesthesia was administered. Operating microscope was draped and positioned, and the left ear canal was well visualized. A 4-mm operating speculum was introduced, and anteroinferior quadrant radial myringotomy was performed. Mucoid middle ear effusion was aspirated, and Reuter bobbin tube was inserted. Floxin otic drops and a cotton ball were placed in the external meatus. The patient was transported to the recovery room in stable condition, having tolerated the procedure well.

REVIEW

Multiple Choice

Circle the most appropriate response.

1. Postpartum vaginal hematoma that was incised and drained. Which code is assigned?
   a. 10140
   b. 57022
   c. 57023
   d. 57061
2. Epidural injection, blood patch. Which code is assigned?
   a. 62263
   b. 62272
   c. 62273
   d. 62281
3. Laser surgery correction of ingrown eyelash of the right eye. Which code is assigned?
   a. 67820-RT
   b. 67825-RT
   c. 67830-RT
   d. 67840-RT
4. Complete removal of right adrenal gland using a laparoscope. Which code is assigned?
   a. 60540-RT
   b. 60545-RT
   c. 60650-RT
   d. 60659-RT
5. Vaginal delivery with episiotomy, normal antepartum care, and normal postpartum care. Which code(s) are assigned?
   a. 59400
   b. 59409
   c. 59409, 59300-51, 59426-51, 59430-51
   d. 59426, 59430-51, 59409-51
6. Biopsy of both testicles after making a small incision to gain access and remove tissue sample. Which code is assigned?
   a. 54500-50
   b. 54505-50
   c. 54500
   d. 54505
7. Decompression internal auditory canal, left ear.
   a. 61591-LT
   b. 69420-LT
   c. 69440-LT
   d. 69960-LT
8. A patient with Bell's palsy undergoes total facial nerve decompression. Which code is assigned?
   a. 64742
   b. 64771
   c. 64864
   d. 69955
9. A patient suffers from strabismus. Resection of the right lateral rectus horizontal muscle was done with absorbable sutures. Which code(s) are assigned?
   a. 67311-RT
   b. 67311-RT, 67335-51-RT
   c. 67311-RT, 67335-RT
   d. 67314-RT, 67335-RT

10. Total abdominal hysterectomy with bilateral salpingo-oophorectomy and removal of the omentum due to the patient's diagnosis of ovarian cancer. Catheters were placed into pelvic organs for subsequent interstitial radioelement application. Which code is assigned?
    a. 58200, 55920
    b. 58210
    c. 58953, 55920
    d. 58956
11. Patient underwent removal of left thyroid lobe on October 13. Patient had right thyroid lobe removed five years ago. Which code is assigned?
    a. 60220
    b. 60240
    c. 60260
    d. 60270
12. A 25-year-old male patient underwent circumcision by surgical excision. Which code is assigned?
    a. 54120
    b. 54150
    c. 54160
    d. 54161
13. Surgical excision of tumor mass of left aural glomus using the operating microscope and a transmastoid approach. Which code(s) are assigned?
    a. 69550-LT
    b. 69550-LT, 69552-51-LT
    c. 69552-LT, 69990
    d. 69552-LT, 69990-51
14. The patient is a 25-year-old female diagnosed with an ovarian pregnancy. After making an abdominal incision, the physician removed the patient's right ovary, which was the site of the pregnancy. Which CPT code is assigned?
    a. 59120
    b. 59121
    c. 59130
    d. 59150
15. Successful VBAC delivery of a healthy female infant weighing 7 pounds 3 ounces. The mother had a normal prenatal and postpartum course. Which CPT code is assigned?
    a. 59400
    b. 59610
    c. 59612
    d. 59618
16. Nerve block of suprascapular nerve. Which CPT code is assigned?
    a. 64418
    b. 64445
    c. 64450
    d. 64490
17. Removal of a benign penile lesion using cryosurgery; the lesion was 1.0 cm in diameter. Which CPT code is assigned?
    a. 11421
    b. 54050
    c. 54056
    d. 54057
18. Upper right eyelid total reconstruction due to removal of malignant melanoma, first of two surgeries that will be required. The operating microscope was used throughout this procedure. Which CPT code(s) are assigned?
    a. 67973-E3
    b. 67973-E3, 69990
    c. 67974-E3
    d. 67974-E3, 69990
19. Staged intersex surgery, female to male.
    a. 55970
    b. 55970-58
    c. 55980
    d. 55980-58
20. Surgical repair of myelomeningocele that was 2.0 cm in diameter on a patient who is 3 days old. Which CPT code is assigned?
    a. 63700
    b. 63700-63
    c. 63704
    d. 63704-63

CHAPTER 17

CPT Radiology

INTRODUCTION

This chapter introduces students to CPT radiology coding. Students assign codes to coding cases by applying CPT coding guidelines and notes.

Objectives

At the conclusion of this chapter, the student should be able to:

- Assign CPT radiology codes.
- Add CPT and/or HCPCS level II modifiers to codes as appropriate.

ASSIGNMENT 17.1 – CODING PRACTICE

Instructions

Assign the ICD-10-CM code(s) to diagnoses and conditions and assign the CPT radiology code(s) and the appropriate HCPCS level II and CPT modifier(s). Do not assign ICD-10-CM external cause codes.

1. GALLBLADDER ULTRASOUND

   REASON FOR EXAM: Right upper quadrant abdominal pain.

   Multiple B-mode scans of right upper quadrant reveals good visualization of the gallbladder. There are several small, dense echoes in the dependent portion of the gallbladder with acoustic shadowing defects distally. The findings are suggestive of cholelithiasis. The rest of the abdominal cavity organs appear normal in size and appearance; this includes the liver, pancreas, spleen, and kidneys.

   ____

2. X-RAY OF CERVICAL SPINE, ANTEROPOSTERIOR AND ODONTOID VIEWS; X-RAY OF LUMBOSACRAL SPINE, ANTEROPOSTERIOR, ODONTOID, AND OBLIQUE VIEWS

   REASON FOR EXAM: Rule out lumbar fracture. Lumbar back pain.

   No fractures or dislocations are evident. A total of four views are obtained of the lumbar spine, which show the lumbar vertebrae to be normal. The alignment is anatomical. The disc spaces and intervertebral foramina are well maintained.

   IMPRESSION: Normal lumbar and cervical spine.

   ____

3. X-RAY, RIGHT RIBS

REASON FOR EXAM: Rib pain.

Two views reveal no evidence of any rib fracture. The underlying lung is normal. The heart is moderately enlarged, and there is evidence of coronary artery surgery. Incidentally demonstrated is a 4-cm laminated gallstone in the right upper abdomen.

---

4. X-RAY, LEFT WRIST; X-RAY, LEFT SHOULDER

REASON FOR EXAM: Pain, left shoulder. Check left wrist closed (upper end) fracture healing and left humerus (upper end) closed fracture healing.

LEFT WRIST: Anteroposterior and lateral views taken through plaster show that the fracture of the distal radius remains in excellent alignment.

LEFT SHOULDER: Multiple views of the left shoulder show that the fracture of the upper end of left humerus is in excellent alignment.

---

5. X-RAY, CHEST, TWO VIEWS

REASON FOR EXAM: Shortness of breath.

The lungs are clear. No pleural effusion. The heart is normal. Pneumothoracic scoliosis is noted. In comparison with the previous examination of 10/10/YY, there is no essential interval change.

The patient has known pneumothoracic scoliosis and has long experienced shortness of breath. The patient's primary care provider monitors increased shortness of breath via chest x-ray to determine if it has become lung-related. For this encounter, the shortness of breath remains related to pneumothoracic scoliosis. Reason for chest x-ray is shortness of breath.

SUMMARY: Negative.

---

6. X-RAY, LEFT MANDIBLE

REASON FOR EXAM: Pain in jaw.

Three views of the left mandible show no definite evidence of a fracture. However, the mandible is not optimally visualized on this study.

---

7. LIVER AND SPLEEN SCAN, WITH VASCULAR FLOW

REASON FOR EXAM: Abnormal liver function studies per laboratory report.

The liver and spleen were imaged under vascular flow. The liver is slightly enlarged, but good flow was seen. The spleen appears normal.

---

8. CT SCAN OF LUMBAR SPINE

REASON FOR EXAM: Lumbar back pain.

Axial images were obtained throughout L3, L4, and L5 levels using magnification technique. There is disc material protruding from the posterior aspect of L4 level on the right side. This is causing almost complete obliteration of the nerve canal and measures roughly 6 mm in size. The remainder of this disc as well as L3 and L5 disc levels appear normal.

CONCLUSION: Findings consistent with a herniated disc at L4 level on the right side.

DIAGNOSIS: Herniated disc, L4, right.

____

9. X-RAY, LEFT ELBOW

REASON FOR EXAM: Elbow pain, left.

Anteroposterior and lateral views are normal.

____

10. X-RAY, LEFT SHOULDER

REASON FOR EXAM: Pain, left shoulder. Rule out fracture.

Anteroposterior and lateral views reveal a comminuted, slightly angulated closed fracture of the neck of the humerus. I do not see any other acute abnormality. There is an old healed fracture of the left clavicle.

DIAGNOSIS: Comminuted nondisplaced closed fracture, neck of left humerus. (Initial encounter for closed fracture.)

____

11. X-RAY, LEFT WRIST

REASON FOR EXAM: Pain in left wrist. Rule out fracture.

Three views reveal a transverse fracture of the distal radius with about 30 degrees of dorsal angulation of the distal fragment. The radius and ulna bones otherwise appear intact.

DIAGNOSIS: Transverse nondisplaced closed fracture, left distal radius. (Initial encounter for closed fracture.)

____

12. CHEST X-RAY

REASON FOR EXAM: Chest pain.

A single view reveals the heart and lungs to be grossly normal with no major change from the study done on August 5.

____

13. X-RAY, PELVIS

REASON FOR EXAM: Pain in hip.

There is an old healed fracture of the left hip held by a compression lag screw. The right hip is normal except for narrowing of the joint space compatible with degenerative arthritis.

DIAGNOSIS: Pain, right hip.

____

14. MODIFIED BARIUM SWALLOW

REASON FOR EXAM: Dysphagia.

The patient had some difficulty initiating the swallowing mechanism. There is no evidence of any direct esophageal or pharyngeal invasion due to the mass in the left side of the neck. The cervical and thoracic portions of the esophagus were also within normal limits. Videos of swallowing ability were done.

CONCLUSION: There is no evidence of any invasion of the pharynx or cervical esophagus by tumor.

____

15. ABDOMINAL SERIES

REASON FOR EXAM: Abdominal pain, generalized.

Complete acute abdomen series show no evidence of any obstruction. The bowel gas pattern is normal. There is considerable amount of fecal material in the right colon. There is no radiographic evidence of free air. The single view film of the chest taken with the abdominal series shows no significant abnormalities.

____

16. MAXILLOFACIAL CT SCAN

REASON FOR EXAM: Rule out sinus mass.

The patient is seen in the ambulatory radiology suite for a CT scan to rule out a tumor. After the injection of contrast agent, the patient's maxillofacial area was scanned. A mass was observed in the right sagittal sinus area. This should be biopsied to confirm behavior.

IMPRESSION: Mass, right sagittal sinus.

____

17. CHEST X-RAY

REASON FOR EXAM: Shortness of breath. Chest pain.

Three views of the chest are compared to the prior examination done on November 15. The heart is normal in size, and the lungs are somewhat hyperaerated. A calcified granuloma is seen within the right lower lobe. The left lung appears clear. There are no pleural effusions. The hilar and mediastinal contours are normal. There is no evidence of congestive failure. Mild degenerative changes are seen within the spine.

____

18. PELVIC ULTRASOUND

REASON FOR EXAM: Pelvic pain, right side.

A patient presents for an initial pelvic ultrasound. Real-time imaging is done to visualize the structures of the pelvic area. A small ovarian cyst is noted on the right side. The left ovary is normal in size and appearance. The fallopian tube on the right is twisted. The left fallopian tube is normal. The uterus appears normal with no abnormalities.

DIAGNOSES: Ovarian cyst, right. Torsion, fallopian tube, right.

____

19. BRACHYTHERAPY

REASON FOR TREATMENT: Prostate carcinoma.

Intermediate brachytherapy isodose plan was prepared using multiplane dosage calculations with seven temporary ribbons and nine sources for remote afterloading brachytherapy. The plan was determined by isodose mapping.

____

20. RADIOPHARMACEUTICAL THERAPY

REASON FOR TREATMENT: Thyroid carcinoma.

Using radiolabeled monoclonal antibodies, the patient was infused for radiopharmaceutical therapy. The patient was observed for a total of 2.0 hours after the intravenous infusion.

____

ASSIGNMENT 17.2 – CODING RADIOLOGY REPORTS

Instructions

Assign the ICD-10-CM code(s) to diagnoses and conditions and assign the CPT radiology code(s) and the appropriate HCPCS level II and CPT modifier(s). Do not assign ICD-10-CM external cause codes.

1. HISTORY: Patient states that she has been experiencing pain in her neck for the past six weeks.

   CERVICAL SPINE X-RAY: Two views reveal the vertebral body heights to be normal. There is narrowing of C4, C5, and C6 (mid-cervical region) disc spaces with spurring at the margins, indicating degenerative disease. There is also some facet joint disease at several levels. I do not see any acute abnormality.

   CHEST X-RAY: Posteroanterior and lateral views reveal the heart to be of normal size, although the left ventricle and ascending aorta are prominent, suggesting possible hypertension. The lungs are clear except for a 12-mm oval nodule at the cardiac apex. This is not visible on any of the patient's previous microfilms. It might represent a nipple shadow, but I would recommend a repeat film with nipple markers for confirmation. There is prominence in the right upper mediastinal area that I believe is due to dilatation of the great vessels.

   STERNUM X-RAY: Posteroanterior and lateral views reveal a very slightly depressed fracture through the lower portion of the manubrium. This is depressed about 5 mm. I do not see any other abnormality.

   DIAGNOSES: Degeneration, cervical intervertebral disc. Closed fracture, sternum. (Initial encounter for closed fracture.)

   ____

2. BRAIN CT SCAN: Axial images were made at 1-cm increments throughout the brain, both with and without intravenous contrast enhancement. There is a well-circumscribed low-density area involving the right temporal region that extends slightly superior into the posterior parietal area. This measures about 7 cm in size and does not show any peripheral enhancement on the contrast images. This is consistent with a temporoparietal ischemic infarct. There is no midline shift or any other mass lesions. The ventricles are not dilated. Also demonstrated is a cluster of small calcifications in the left occipital region involving an area about 4 cm in size. I do not see any definite dilated vessels associated with these. This most likely represents an old arteriovenous malformation that has calcified, although conceivably an old abscess might give this appearance as well.

   DIAGNOSES: Right temporoparietal ischemic infarct. Aphasia following cerebral infarction.

   ____

3. DIAGNOSES: Rule out aortic dissection. Chest pain.

   CHEST CT SCAN: Routine axial views have been performed with administration of intravenous contrast media. The study was performed to rule out aortic dissection. Aortic dissection protocol was followed with scans through the aortic root and arch with a total dose of 100 cc of nonionic contrast. The study does not reveal any evidence for aortic dissection. Heart size is within normal limits. There is no mediastinal or hilar adenopathy or evidence suggestive of endobronchial lesion. There are no parenchymal opacities or pleural changes. No significant chest wall abnormalities are seen. The upper abdomen included in the study does not include any significant abnormalities.

   IMPRESSION: CT scan of the chest is within normal limits. There is no evidence of aortic dissection. Follow-up as indicated clinically is suggested.

   ____

4. DIAGNOSIS: Abnormal kidney function test.

   INTRAVENOUS PYELOGRAM (IVP): No calculi are seen on the preliminary film. Prompt concentration is noted at five minutes in the kidneys. Collecting systems appear intact; the renal outlines are obscured somewhat by patient's thickness and overlying gas. There appears to be a soft tissue mass adjacent to both the left and the right kidneys, which might represent bilateral cyst disease or tumor formation. A retrograde exam is recommended (and possibly tomography or kidney scans with radioactive material) to delineate the outlines more completely. Ureters and bladder are normal. Both kidneys drain well on the erect exam.

   CONCLUSIONS: The IVP has revealed prompt function with no calyceal abnormalities. Attention is drawn to the kidney outlines, which are obscured by patient's size and gas. There appear to be bilateral soft tissue masses attached or adjacent to the kidneys. Cystic disease or neoplasm is a possibility.

---

5. PREOPERATIVE DIAGNOSIS: Cerebral arteriovenous malformation.

   POSTOPERATIVE DIAGNOSIS: Same.

   OPERATION PERFORMED: Radiosurgery.

   INDICATIONS FOR PROCEDURE: This patient presented with a known cerebral arteriovenous malformation. After discussion of the options and risks, she elected to proceed with stereotactic radiosurgery.

   DESCRIPTION OF PROCEDURE: The patient underwent application of a stereotactic head ring under local anesthesia. She then underwent a sterotactic CT scan. The stereotactic CT scan and a previously acquired MRI were transferred to the dosimetry planning computer, where an optimal treatment plan was derived. The patient was transported to the radiation oncology department, where the radiosurgery machine was assembled and tested in the usual fashion. She received a dose of 2,000 cGy to the enhancing margin of her lesion using 5 isocenter. The head ring was removed, the patient was observed for a short period, and the patient was discharged home.

---

6. UPPER GASTROINTESTINAL SERIES (DOUBLE-CONTRAST STUDY): Patient appears to be in severe epigastric abdominal pain. There is no delay in the passage of the barium through the esophagus. There is a hiatus hernia present, about the size of a small plum, of the sliding variety. The stomach shows no evidence of an ulcer crater or organic defect. The duodenal bulb is not deformed, and an ulcer crater is not noted. There is no gross abnormality of the duodenal curve. At the end of one hour, there is no significant gastric residue. The portions of the small bowel that are opacified show no significant abnormality; there is some functional hypermotility through loops of distal jejunum.

   IMPRESSION: Note that his examination had to be done with the patient completely in the recumbent position because of the condition of the patient. No organic abnormality of the upper gastrointestinal system is noted except for the presence of a hiatus hernia as described.

---

7. Patient underwent x-ray examination of chest, kidneys/ureters/bladder (KUB), and sinuses due to chest pain, back pain, and facial pain as the result of a motor vehicle collision.

   CHEST: Single view of the chest reveals the heart, mediastinum, diaphragm, and lungs are within normal limits.

   IMPRESSION: Negative chest x-ray.

   PARANASAL SINUSES, TWO VIEWS: There is a marked increase in density of left maxillary antrum and similar involvement of frontal sinus predominating on the left side. Upright films show no fluid accumulation, nor is disruption of bony margins identified. Lateral view of sphenoid sinuses reveals a normal-appearing pituitary fossa.

IMPRESSION: Maxillary and frontal sinusitis, left.

INTRAVENOUS PYELOGRAM: Preliminary film is unremarkable except for splenic enlargement of moderate degree. After injection of dye, there is prompt and symmetrical function demonstrating no abnormality of calices, pelvis, ureters, or urinary bladder.

IMPRESSION: Splenomegaly of unknown etiology.

DIAGNOSES: Chest pain. Back pain. Chronic maxillary and frontal sinusitis, left. Splenomegaly of unknown etiology.

____

8. DIAGNOSIS: Chest pain.

STRESS THALLIUM MYOCARDIAL SCAN: At peak exercise, 3 mCi of thallium chloride was injected intravenously. The immediate and redistribution images were obtained utilizing tomographic technique. Reconstructions were performed in the horizontal and vertical long axis and short axis. The study reveals normal distribution of the radioisotope in the myocardium in both the immediate and delayed redistribution images. There is no significant ventricular cavity dilatation noted on the immediate stress images. The level of stress achieved by the patient is submaximal.

IMPRESSION: Negative submaximal stress thallium myocardial scans. Follow-up as indicated clinically is suggested.

____

9. ABDOMINAL ULTRASOUND: The examination was done in longitudinal, transverse, and oblique projections. There is mild hepatomegaly. The spleen is prominent. There is no ascites. The gallbladder is visualized. No gallstone is noted. The pancreas and bile ducts are within normal limits. There is no hydronephrosis.

IMPRESSION: Mild hepatomegaly. Prominent spleen.

____

10. REASON FOR EXAM: Residual aphasia due to previous cerebrovascular accident.

CT BRAIN SCAN WITH CONTRAST MEDIA: The examination was compared with the scan done on May 6. There are small foci of ischemic infarct seen at the left caudate nucleus. This has remained unchanged and appears to be old ischemic infarct. The ventricles are normal in size. There is no evidence of midline shift. The remaining parenchyma of both hemispheres of the brain, posterior fossa, and midbrain reveals no abnormality.

There are no interval changes noted when compared with the previous examination. Old small foci of ischemic infarct at the left basal ganglia are noted.

____

11. DIAGNOSIS: Asthma.

CHEST X-RAY: Four views reveal equal perfusion to both lungs. There are multiple tiny areas of diminished activity scattered throughout the lungs; however, none of these is segmental to indicate an embolus. The changes would be consistent with some type of diffuse lung disease, either acute or chronic. Asthma, bronchitis, and chronic obstructive lung disease can give this type of pattern.

CONCLUSION: There is no evidence of any emboli; however, there does appear to be some type of diffuse lung disease.

____

12. REASON FOR EXAM: Pain in hand. Rule out fracture.

X-RAY OF LEFT HAND IN FRONTAL AND OBLIQUE PROJECTIONS WITH ATTENTION TO THE FOURTH DIGIT: No osseous or articular abnormalities are demonstrated other than tiny chip fracture involving the lateral and flexor side of the articulating surface of the proximal end of the middle phalanx.

DIAGNOSIS: Chip fracture of finger, proximal end of middle phalanx, fourth digit of left hand. (Initial encounter for closed fracture.)

---

13. REASON FOR EXAM: Numbness of fingers and pain in neck.

CERVICAL MYELOGRAMS: Nine cubic centimeters of Pantopaque was introduced into the lumbar spinal canal, and the patient was tilted head-down close to 90 degrees. There was free flow of the contrast medium down to the cervical spine at the level of the foramen magnum, with a small amount of the contrast medium into the cistern. There is no evidence of any filling defect or deformity of the column of the contrast medium. The spinal cord shows no deformity. There is visualization of the distal portion of the vertebral arteries on both sides, and these arteries appear to be normal. Most of the contrast medium was removed after completion of this study.

CONCLUSION: Normal cervical myelograms.

---

14. REASON FOR EXAM: Pain in hip, chest, and left trunk.

PELVIS X-RAY IN FRONTAL PROJECTION: There is some osteoporosis of the pelvis and proximal femurs, but no fracture or dislocation is demonstrated.

LEFT HIP X-RAY IN LATERAL PROJECTION: No fracture or dislocation is identified.

CHEST X-RAY: Single view chest x-ray reveals that no pulmonary lesions are demonstrated. There is no pneumothorax or hemothorax. The heart and mediastinal structures are within normal limits. There are calcific arteriosclerotic changes involving the thoracic and abdominal aorta and iliac and femoral arteries.

X-RAY, LEFT RIBS: Two views of ribs show fractures in the left seventh and eighth ribs at the posterior axillary line. There is generalized osteoporosis of the thoracic bony structures.

IMPRESSION: Left hip negative for fracture or dislocation. Pelvis negative for fracture or dislocation. Chest free of acute lesions.

DIAGNOSES: Fracture in the left seventh and eighth ribs, left side. (Initial encounter for closed fracture.) Generalized osteoporosis. Chest pain. Left hip pain.

---

15. REASON FOR EXAM: Thyroid goiter.

X-RAY, SOFT TISSUES OF NECK: Frontal and lateral radiographs were taken using soft tissue technique. There is displacement of the trachea to the left at the thoracic inlet. There is also some mild compression on the anterior margin of the trachea in this area that is producing some mild narrowing of the trachea. These findings are consistent with the patient's clinical diagnosis of thyroid goiter.

---

16. REASON FOR EXAM: Abnormal renal function studies.

RETROGRADE PYELOGRAPHY: Catheters have been inserted to the levels of the collecting systems, bilaterally. Following the retrograde injection of the opaque substance, neither collecting system shows gross dilatation or deformity. Segments of the ureters outlined are not dilated. The bladder is not opacified for diagnostic purposes. The renal shadows appear normal in size, shape, and position. The psoas margins are identified bilaterally. There is no evidence of opaque urinary or biliary concretions.

IMPRESSION: No significant abnormality of either urinary tract is demonstrated.

---

17. UPPER GASTROINTESTINAL SERIES (SINGLE-CONTRAST STUDY): There is neuromuscular incoordination of the tubular esophagus, and there is slight, intermittent, and hard-to-elicit reflux. It is difficult to imagine that this patient's hiatus hernia should be of great clinical significance. The stomach is of normal appearance but empties relatively slowly due to intermittent spasticity in the region of the duodenal bulb. The patient is placed in a prone position for small intestine views. There is a typical ulcer niche at the upper aspect of the base of the bulb, and it is surrounded by a zone of radiolucency due to edema. Three diverticuli are noted off the duodenal loop, which is otherwise unremarkable. The small bowel distal to the loop is normal as seen. The remainder of the small bowel is normal.

    IMPRESSION: Small, direct hiatus hernia with slight intermittent reflux. Active duodenal ulcer associated with edema and spasticity. Diverticula of the duodenal loop viewed through serial films.

---

18. REASON FOR EXAM: Chronic migraines.

    CT SCAN OF BRAIN: The patient was scanned without contrast enhancement. Multiple attempts at venipuncture for dye administration were unsuccessful. The study demonstrates a fairly well-demarcated low-density area in the left occipital lobe in the distribution of the left posterior cerebral artery. The unenhanced scan is otherwise normal. The apparent low-density area is strongly indicative of an ischemic infarction in the left posterior cerebral artery distribution. Although it would have been helpful to have obtained an enhanced scan, it is quite unlikely that this represents a tumor.

---

19. DIAGNOSIS: Rule out hypothyroidism.

    THYROID SCAN: Following the oral administration of radioactive I-131, an anterior scan of the neck shows mild diffuse thyroid enlargement with inhomogeneous uptake. There is no evidence of any focal significant nodularity. The radiographic findings are compatible with a multinodular goiter. The thyroid uptake was measured at 27 percent, which is in the euthyroid range.

    IMPRESSION: Nontoxic multinodular goiter.

---

20. X-RAY, LEFT KNEE: Three views of the left knee show that the bones forming the knee exhibit a considerable degree of spotty osteoporosis. The articular surfaces of these bones are smooth and regular. The joint space is of normal width. There is some increase in soft tissue density in the suprapatellar region. No other abnormality of significance is seen.

    SUMMARY AND COMMENT: Marked spotty osteoporosis is visible in the bones forming the knee joint and appears to extend a considerable distance from the epiphysis into the shafts of these bones. The significance of this osteoporosis is not clearly apparent on the films obtained. The possibility that it relates to an inflammatory soft tissue process such as synovitis has to be considered and further evaluated in view of the increased soft tissue density noted in the suprapatellar region. However, the clinical background suggests that the osteoporosis might simply be related to disuse.

REVIEW

Multiple Choice

Circle the most appropriate response.

1. Static liver and spleen imaging. Which code is assigned?
   a. 78201
   b. 78202
   c. 78215
   d. 78216
2. CT scan of lumbar spine after the injection of contrast medium. Which code is assigned?
   a. 72128
   b. 72131
   c. 72132
   d. 72133
3. Imaging for gastrointestinal protein loss. Which code is assigned?
   a. 78278
   b. 78282
   c. 78290
   d. 78299
4. Chest x-ray, two views. Which code is assigned?
   a. 71045
   b. 71046
   c. 71047
   d. 71048
5. X-ray of cervical spine, two views. Which code is assigned?
   a. 72040
   b. 72050
   c. 72070
   d. 72100
6. Cardiac magnetic resonance imaging for morphology and function, with stress imaging. Which code is assigned?
   a. 75557
   b. 75559
   c. 75561
   d. 75563
7. Patient is a 45-year-old female and presents for her first mammography. The patient has no family history of cancer, and personal medical history includes only hypertension. The bilateral screening mammography is negative for the presence of any carcinoma and shows only mild fibrocystic disease in the left breast. Which code is assigned?
   a. 77066
   b. 77067
   c. 77062
   d. 77063
8. Thyroid ultrasound. Which code is assigned?
   a. 70360
   b. 70490
   c. 70498
   d. 76536
9. Computed tomography of the heart, with contrast material, for evaluation of cardiac structure and morphology. Which code is assigned?
   a. 75571
   b. 75572
   c. 75573
   d. 75574
10. Complex radiation treatment delivery for prostate cancer, 12 MeV. Which code is assigned?
    a. 77401
    b. 77402
    c. 77407
    d. 77412
11. Nuclear medicine imaging of lymph nodes. Which code is assigned?
    a. 75801
    b. 75803
    c. 75805
    d. 78195
12. MRI of the brain after administration of contrast dye. Which code is assigned?
    a. 70551
    b. 70552
    c. 70553
    d. 70557

13. Intraoperative left hip x-ray. Which code is assigned?
    a. 73501-LT
    b. 73502-LT
    c. 73503-LT
    d. 73551-LT
14. Placement of six ribbons of cobalt isotope into patient's abdominal cavity for metastatic breast cancer. Which code is assigned?
    a. 77761
    b. 77762
    c. 77771
    d. 77799
15. Total body bone scan to r/o metastatic carcinoma. Which code is assigned?
    a. 78305
    b. 78306
    c. 78816
    d. 78999
16. Complete pelvic ultrasound on a 15-year-old female patient. Urine pregnancy test was negative. Which code is assigned?
    a. 76801
    b. 76856
    c. 76857
    d. 78605
17. Posteroanterior and lateral sinus x-ray. Which code is assigned?
    a. 70210
    b. 70220
    c. 70250
    d. 70486
18. MRI of the chest to rule out mediastinum lymph tumor. Which code is assigned?
    a. 71550
    b. 71551
    c. 71552
    d. 71555
19. Dr. Gusman provided the interpretation and report for a patient's lateral and anteroposterior views of right wrist. (The x-ray was performed at another facility.) Which code is assigned?
    a. 73100
    b. 73100-26
    c. 73110
    d. 73110-26
20. Chest x-ray, 5 views. Which code is assigned?
    a. 71046
    b. 71047
    c. 71048
    d. 76000

CPT Pathology and Laboratory

CHAPTER 18

INTRODUCTION

This chapter introduces students to CPT pathology and laboratory coding. Students assign codes to coding cases by applying CPT coding guidelines and notes.

Objectives

At the conclusion of this chapter, the student should be able to:

- Assign CPT pathology and laboratory codes.
- Add CPT and/or HCPCS level II modifiers to codes, as appropriate.

ASSIGNMENT 18.1 – CODING PRACTICE

Instructions

Assign the ICD-10-CM code(s) to diagnoses and conditions and assign the CPT pathology and laboratory code(s) and the appropriate HCPCS level II and CPT modifier(s). Do not assign ICD-10-CM external cause codes.

1. The following laboratory tests were ordered on a patient's blood sample of two vials due to complaint of weight loss: albumin, automated complete blood count (CBC), total bilirubin, direct bilirubin, phosphatase, total protein, alanine aminotransferase (ALT), and aspartate aminotransferase (AST).

   ____

2. Platelet antibody identification for immunology.

   DIAGNOSIS: Kidney donor transplant workup.

   ____

3. Western blot with analysis of protein with physician interpretation and report. (Outpatient test.)

   DIAGNOSES: Fatigue. Rule out Lyme disease.

   ____

4. DNA probe used for fluorescent *in situ* hybridization (FISH).

   DIAGNOSIS: Advanced maternal age (first trimester); patient is age 46, gravida 1, para 0.

   ____

5. Microscopic and gross pathologic analysis of tonsils and adenoids.

   DIAGNOSIS: Hypertrophied tonsils and adenoids.

   ____

6. Antinuclear antibody titer of blood sample for possible anti-immune disease.

   DIAGNOSES: Skin rashes and anemia. Rule out lupus erythematosus.

   ____

7. Stool culture to test for presence of *Shigella*.

   DIAGNOSIS: Bloody diarrhea.

   ____

8. Tissue culture of blood cell sample and bone marrow sample to rule out acute myelogenous leukemia.

   DIAGNOSES: Shortness of breath. Fatigue.

   ____

9. Pathologic analysis of sample taken from patient's right kidney during a biopsy.

   DIAGNOSIS: Hematuria.

   ____

10. Qualitative chromatographic drug screening for cocaine and opiates.

    DIAGNOSIS: Preemployment examination (drug screening).

    ____

11. A 45-year-old male patient had the following blood tests done on three vials of blood taken during a venipuncture: total serum cholesterol, quantitative glucose, high-density lipoprotein (HDL) cholesterol, and triglycerides.

    DIAGNOSIS: Preoperative blood panel.

    ____

12. Urine culture to rule out bacterial urinary tract infection.

    DIAGNOSIS: Urinary frequency.

    ____

13. Gross and microscopic autopsy of human brain.

    DIAGNOSIS: Benign neoplasm of cerebrum.

    ____

14. Surgical pathology analysis of specimen taken during liver wedge biopsy.

    DIAGNOSIS: Metastatic liver carcinoma.

    ____

15. Testing for presence of rubella antibodies.

    DIAGNOSIS: Screening for rubella antibodies.

    ____

16. Creatinine level in blood sample.

    DIAGNOSIS: Rule out renal insufficiency.

    ____

17. Cervical specimen, thin prep, under pathologist supervision.
    DIAGNOSIS: Routine yearly gynecological examination. Negative results.

    ____

18. Testing for level of growth hormone antibodies.
    DIAGNOSIS: Short stature.

    ____

19. Semen analysis to determine motility.
    DIAGNOSIS: Male infertility.

    ____

20. Analysis of hair for fungi infestation.
    DIAGNOSIS: Hair loss.

    ____

ASSIGNMENT 18.2 – CODING PATHOLOGY AND LABORATORY REPORTS

Instructions

Assign the ICD-10-CM code(s) to diagnoses and conditions, and assign the CPT pathology and laboratory code(s) and the appropriate HCPCS level II and CPT modifier(s). Do not assign ICD-10-CM external cause codes.

1. CODE(S): ______________________________

LABORATORY TEST

DIAGNOSIS: Chest pain
PATIENT DATA: Male Age 64

CARDIAC ISOENZYMES

TEST	RESULT	FLAG	REFERENCE
Total CPK	88.0		35-232 IU/L (Male) 21-215 IU/L (Female)
LDH Isoenzymes	134.0		100-190 IU/L

End Results

2. CODE(S): ____________________

LABORATORY TEST

DIAGNOSIS: Fatigue and rule out anemia

PATIENT DATA: Male Age 64

Complete Blood Count

TEST	RESULT	FLAG	REFERENCE
WBC	14.0	**H**	4-10
RBC	3.88	**L**	4.5-6.5
Hgb	10.1	**L**	13.0-18.0
Hct	31.4	**L**	37-54
MCV	80.9		79-104
MCH	25.9		27.5-33.5
MCHC	32.0		32-36
RDW	15.4	**H**	11.5-14.5
Platelet count	1,207,000	**H**	140,000-500,000

End Results

3. CODE(S): ____________________

LABORATORY TEST

DIAGNOSIS: HIV positive

PATIENT DATA: Male 32

Cerebral Spinal Fluid Culture (Anaerobic)

TEST	RESULT
Gram stain	No organisms observed
Cerebral spinal fluid	No growth observed

End Results

4. CODE(S): ____________________

LABORATORY TEST

DIAGNOSIS: Painful urination

PATIENT DATA: Female Age 47

Urinalysis

TEST	RESULT	FLAG	REFERENCE
Color	Yellow		
Character	Clear		
Specific Gravity	1.016	**L**	1.005-1.020 Units
Leukocytes	Negative		
Protein (Qualitative)	Negative		
Glucose	Trace		
pH	6.0		5.0-9.0 Units
Bilirubin	< 0.5 Negative		
Nitrite	Negative		

End Results

5. CODE(S): ______________________

LABORATORY TEST

DIAGNOSIS: Acute respiratory insufficiency
PATIENT DATA: Male Age 64

Chemistry: Blood Gases (Arterial)

TEST	RESULT 9/18/YYYY	FLAG	RESULT 9/19/YYYY	FLAG	REFERENCE
pH	7.49	**H**	7.53	**H**	7.35-7.45
pCO_2	32	**L**	32	**L**	34-40
pO_2	64	**L**	115	**H**	65-75
HCO_3	24	**H**	27	**H**	18-22
BE	3.2	**H**	5.6	**H**	-3-3
Total CO_s	25	**H**	28	**H**	20-24
O_2 Saturation	87	**L**	89	**L**	90-100

End Results

6. CODE(S): ______________________

LABORATORY TEST

DIAGNOSIS: Skin rash
PATIENT DATA: Female Age 18

Syphilis Serology (Qualitative)

TEST	RESULT
Blood	Specimen non-reactive

End Results

7. CODE(S): ______________________

LABORATORY TEST

DIAGNOSIS: Ruptured (perforated) duodenal ulcer
PATIENT DATA: Female Age 54

Culture - Peritoneal Fluid

TEST	RESULT
1st Preliminary	2+ gram negative rods
2nd Preliminary	3+ E. coli and 3+ Diphtheroids
Final Report	2+ E. coli, 3+ Diphtheroids, and 3+ Bacteroides (anaerobe)

End Results

8. CODE(S): ______________________

LABORATORY TEST

DIAGNOSIS: Dysuria and hematuria
PATIENT DATA: Male Age 31

Urine Culture and Sensitivity

TEST	RESULT
Urine	No growth at 48 hours

End Results

9. CODE(S): ______________________

LABORATORY TEST

DIAGNOSIS:	Chronic Obstructive Pulmonary Disease
PATIENT DATA:	Male Age 72

Arterial Blood Gases (Puncture Site: Right Radial Artery)

TEST	RESULT	FLAG	REFERENCE
% O_s Concentration: Mask O_2 at 4 L/min			
pH	7.46	**H**	7.35-7.45
pCO_2	28	**L**	35-45 mmHg
pO_2	142	**H**	80-100 mmHg
HCO_3	19	**L**	24-27 mEq/L
Final Report: Uncompensated Respiratory Alkalosis			

End Results

10. PATHOLOGY REPORT

PREOPERATIVE DIAGNOSIS: Possible bladder tumor.

SPECIMEN: Biopsy of bladder.

DESCRIPTION: The specimen consists of a small fragment of gray tissue that measures 0.5 cm in diameter.

MICROSCOPIC DESCRIPTION: One section of submitted specimen shows considerable edema, congestion, and areas of infiltration with leukocytes and few plasma cells. Another segment of the biopsy tissue consists of completely necrotic material and numerous leukocytes.

DIAGNOSES: Inflamed bladder wall tissue and fragment of necrotic material with leukocytic exudate.

____

11. PATHOLOGY REPORT

OPERATION: Excision of pilonidal cyst and abscess.

SPECIMEN: Pilonidal cyst and sinus.

GROSS DESCRIPTION: The specimen consists of an ellipse of skin containing a longitudinal crease with the skin surface measuring 10 × 2.4 cm in greatest dimension. There is underlying fibrofatty tissue measuring up to 3.8 cm in depth with one end being enlarged and ovoid measuring 7 × 5 × 3 cm in greatest dimension. Section through the specimen reveals the enlarged subcutaneous region to contain an apparent abscess cavity measuring up to 3 cm in greatest dimension that contains purulent material. Sections through the remainder of the specimen reveal a subcutaneous sinus tract measuring 1–2 cm in diameter. Representative sections are submitted.

MICROSCOPIC DESCRIPTION: Sections consist of portions of skin and underlying subcutaneous tissue containing a sinus tract that is partially lined with squamous epithelium and that leads to a large abscess cavity containing acute and chronic inflammation and granulation tissue. There is surrounding fibrosis.

DIAGNOSIS: Portion of skin is pilonidal sinus and associated abscess cavity as a result of removal of pilonidal cyst and abscess.

____

12. PATHOLOGY REPORT

OPERATION: Vaginal tubal excision for sterilization.

SPECIMEN: Right tube portion and left tube portion.

GROSS DESCRIPTION: The specimen is submitted in two portions: number one is a portion of clinically right fallopian tube measuring 1.8 cm in length by up to 0.6 cm in diameter. The specimen is sectioned and entirely submitted as "A." Number two is a portion of clinically left fallopian tube measuring 1.4 cm in length by 0.6 cm in diameter. The specimen is sectioned and entirely submitted as "B."

MICROSCOPIC DESCRIPTION: Sections labeled as "A" and "B" both consist of portions of fallopian tubes containing no diagnostic alterations.

DIAGNOSIS: Portion of clinically right fallopian tube, no diagnostic alterations are recognized. Portion of clinically left fallopian tube, no diagnostic alterations are recognized.

---

13. PATHOLOGY REPORT

OPERATION: Cataract extraction of right eye with implant.

SPECIMEN: Cataract O.D.

GROSS DESCRIPTION: The specimen submitted as "cataract right eye" consists of a discoid lens measuring 0.9 cm in greatest dimension.

GROSS DIAGNOSIS ONLY: Lens, clinically right eye.

---

14. CODE(S): ____________________

LABORATORY TEST

DIAGNOSIS: Menopausal night sweats

PATIENT DATA: Female Age 54

Blood Chemistry

TEST	RESULT	FLAG	REFERENCE
BUN	26	**H**	7-22 mg/dl
Sodium	139		136-147 mEq/l
Potassium	5.0		3.7-5.1 mEq/l
CO_2	19	**L**	24-32 mEq/l
Chloride	102		98-108 mEq/l
Total Cholesterol	317	**H**	120-280 mg/dl
SGOT	38	**H**	22-37 (Female) 27-47 (Male)
Creatinine	1.1		0.6-1.3 mg/dl
Calcium	9.4		8.7-10.2 mg/dl
Phosphatase alkaline	4.1		2.5-4.9 mg/dl
Total Bilirubin	0.6		Less than 1.5 mg/dl
Total Protein	7.9		6.4-8.2 g/dl
Albumin	4.2		3.4-5.0 g/dl
Uric Acid	8.6	**H**	2.6-7.1 mg/dl
Glucose	242	**H**	70-110
SGPT	25		22-47

End Results

15. CODE(S): ______________________________

LABORATORY TEST

DIAGNOSIS: Joint stiffness

PATIENT DATA: Male Age 82

Complete Blood Count With Differential

TEST	RESULT	FLAG	REFERENCE
WBC	13.2		4-10
RBC	4.65		4.5-6.5
Hgb	14.2		13.0-18.0
Hct	42.4		37-54
MCV	91.1		79-104
MCH	30.5		27.5-33.5
MCHC	33.5		32-36
Sed Rate	55		
Segs	84%		
Lymph	12%		
Mono	4%		

End Results

16. CODE(S): ______________________________

LABORATORY TEST

DIAGNOSIS: Preoperative clearance

PATIENT DATA: Female Age 38

Urinalysis

TEST	RESULT	FLAG	REFERENCE
Color	Yellow		
Character	Clear		
Specific Gravity	1.019		1.005-1.020 Units
Leukocytes	Negative		
Protein (Qualitative)	Negative		
Glucose	Negative		
pH	5.0		5.0-9.0 Units
Bilirubin	Negative		
Nitrite	Negative		
Albumin	1+		
Acetone	Negative		
Blood	Negative		
Epithelials	Rare		
WBC	8-12		
RBC	Rare		
Bacteria	4+		
Casts	Negative		
Crystals	Negative		

End Results

17. PATHOLOGY REPORT

GROSS DESCRIPTION: A roughly rectangular thyroid tissue segment 4 × 3 cm with a well-delineated nodule occurring at one point; the size of the latter is 18 mm × 12 mm, and it is ovoid in shape and gray to gray-white centrally with some ill-delineated areas of redness. The thyroid tissue proper varies from red to gray-red and is devoid of additional bosselations.

MICROSCOPIC DESCRIPTION: The nodule shows benign acini of various sizes with single epithelial cell layers and absence of enfoldings. The colloid content is fair to good with minimal scalloping. The margin of the mass is fairly well delineated at some places by rather dense connective tissue that in places is permeated by occasional round cells. The surrounding thyroid tissue shows benign acini with fairly good colloid content.

IMPRESSION: Segment of thyroid lobe with benign colloid adenoma.

---

18. PATHOLOGY REPORT

SPECIMEN: Uterine curettings.

DIAGNOSIS: Incomplete spontaneous abortion.

GROSS DESCRIPTION: Shaggy gray-red friable bits of soft tissue and mixed blood clot totaling 1.5 mL. Entire specimen for histologic study.

MICROSCOPIC DESCRIPTION: Straight glandular elements occur in compact cellular stroma. Here and there disrupted segments of blood clot occur. Further present is a segment of compact fibrous tissue with scattered varying in size cystically dilated glands. This is consistent with proliferative phase endometrium.

DIAGNOSIS: Incomplete spontaneous abortion.

---

19. PATHOLOGY REPORT

SPECIMEN: Scar from left lower leg. Debridement tissue and rod from left hip.

GROSS DESCRIPTION: The specimen is submitted in two portions: number one, submitted as "scar from left lower leg and debridement tissue," consists of an elongated portion of skin measuring 5.5 × 1.2 cm in surface dimension by up to 0.8 cm in thickness. Also present are four portions of bone varying from 2.8 to 1.5 cm in greatest dimension. Representative portions of skin are submitted. Also present in the container are several small portions of pink-tan fibrous-like tissue, one measuring 1.4 cm and the other measuring 1 cm in greatest dimension. The soft tissue is entirely submitted. Number two, submitted as "rod from left tibia," consists of a slightly curved metal rod that is 28 cm in length.

MICROSCOPIC DESCRIPTION: Sections consist of portions of dense fibrous tissue and a small amount of skin. There is slight chronic inflammation in the fibrous tissue. Fragments of bone are also present on the section.

DIAGNOSIS: Portion of skin and underlying fibrous tissue containing slight chronic inflammation and portions of bone, which are consistent with scar clinically from left lower leg and associated debridement tissue. Silver-colored metal rod consistent with orthopedic prosthetic device clinically from region of left tibia.

---

20. PATHOLOGY REPORT

SPECIMEN: Bladder stones.

GROSS DESCRIPTION: The specimen consists of innumerable calculi that vary in size from 1 to 6 millimeters. No sections cut.

DIAGNOSIS: Bladder stones seen for gross inspection.

REVIEW

Multiple Choice

Circle the most appropriate response.

1. Acute hepatitis panel including hepatitis A antibody, hepatitis B core antibody, hepatitis B surface antigen, and hepatitis C antibody. Which code(s) are assigned?
   a. 80074
   b. 80074, 80076
   c. 80074, 86709, 86705, 87340, 86603
   d. 86709, 86705, 87340, 86603

2. Testing of specimen from digital rectal exam for blood. Which code is assigned?
   a. 82270
   b. 82271
   c. 82272
   d. 82274
3. Testing of blood for lead. Which code(s) are assigned?
   a. 83015
   b. 83655
   c. 83735
   d. 83655, 83015
4. Coombs test direct. Which code is assigned?
   a. 86880
   b. 86885
   c. 86886
   d. 86900
5. Testing of stool for *H. pylori*. Which code is assigned?
   a. 83013
   b. 86677
   c. 87338
   d. 87339
6. Total necropsy of infant, including gross and microscopic analysis. Which code is assigned?
   a. 88012
   b. 88028
   c. 88029
   d. 88036
7. Thawing of ovarian tissue. Which code is assigned?
   a. 89344
   b. 89352
   c. 89354
   d. 89356
8. Bethesda analysis of vaginal specimens, manual method under direction of pathologist. Which code is assigned?
   a. 88142
   b. 88147
   c. 88164
   d. 88165
9. Basic metabolic blood panel for Dr. Wolfe's office includes calcium, glucose, and sodium. Which code(s) are assigned?
   a. 80048
   b. 80048-52
   c. 80048-52, 82310, 82947, 84295
   d. 82310, 82947, 84295
10. Blood testing for presence of Epstein-Barr virus nuclear antigens. Which code is assigned?
    a. 86663
    b. 86664
    c. 86665
    d. 86666
11. Pathology analysis of organ specimen taken from patient during laparoscopic cholecystectomy. Which code is assigned?
    a. 88300
    b. 88302
    c. 88304
    d. 88305
12. Cell count of fluid taken from knee joint effusion. Which code is assigned?
    a. 87070
    b. 87075
    c. 89050
    d. 89051
13. Report of breast tissue submitted for frozen section during mastectomy procedure. Which code is assigned?
    a. 88307
    b. 88309
    c. 88329
    d. 88331
14. Testing of blood for LDL and HDL cholesterol. Which code(s) are assigned?
    a. 83718
    b. 83721
    c. 83718, 83721
    d. 83718, 83719
15. Blood testing for presence of antigen to varicella zoster (chickenpox). Which code is assigned?
    a. 86635
    b. 86644
    c. 86757
    d. 86787

16. Test of blood for clotting factor VIII. Which code is assigned?
    a. 85230
    b. 85240
    c. 85250
    d. 82590
17. Sedimentation rate using automated method. Which code is assigned?
    a. 85651
    b. 85652
    c. 85660
    d. 85810
18. Analysis of chromosomes from amniotic fluid. Which code is assigned?
    a. 88267
    b. 88280
    c. 88271
    d. 88285
19. Gross examination of tonsils. Which code is assigned?
    a. 88300
    b. 88302
    c. 88305
    d. 88309
20. Specimen from the peripheral nerve of the patient's left ankle submitted for morphometric analysis. Which code is assigned?
    a. 88300
    b. 88309
    c. 88321
    d. 88356

CPT Medicine

CHAPTER 19

INTRODUCTION

This chapter introduces students to CPT medicine coding. Students assign codes to coding cases by applying CPT coding guidelines and notes.

Objectives

At the conclusion of this chapter, the student should be able to:

- Assign CPT medicine codes.
- Add CPT and/or HCPCS level II modifiers to codes, as appropriate.

ASSIGNMENT 19.1 – CODING PRACTICE

Instructions

Assign the ICD-10-CM code(s) to diagnoses and conditions and assign the CPT medicine code(s) and the appropriate HCPCS level II and CPT modifier(s). Do not assign ICD-10-CM external cause codes.

1. Stress testing for pulmonary function with CO_2 production and O_2 uptake. The patient also had electrocardiographic recordings of this test.

   DIAGNOSIS: Emphysema.

   ____

2. The patient is being evaluated to rule out diabetic retinopathy. The blood vessels of the eye are examined using an ophthalmoscope with fluorescein angiograph. Films of both eyes are done, and the physician provides a written interpretative report.

   DIAGNOSES: Blurred vision and type 2 diabetes mellitus.

   ____

3. A patient is on hemodialysis at a local unit due to chronic renal failure. The patient is evaluated by the physician at the start of the dialysis treatment on April 5. The patient is on dialysis for 90 minutes. The patient is taken off the dialysis machine, and the physician reevaluates the patient before he is discharged from the unit.

   ____

4. Intravenous infusion of chemotherapy agents for two hours due to diagnosis of right breast cancer.

____

5. Psychotherapy with the patient's family for a period of 45 minutes. Patient was also present for this therapy session.

   DIAGNOSIS: Depression.

____

6. Auditory assessment for complaint of tinnitus in both ears. This testing included pitch, loudness, and masking.

____

7. Electrical cardioversion for heart arrhythmia done with external paddles.

____

8. Fitting of trifocal eyeglasses by physician due to presbyopia.

____

9. A 20-year-old hospital worker stepped on an empty hypodermic needle at work. The needle went through his shoe and punctured the skin of the bottom of his right foot. The patient removed the needle and has it with him. He has a small amount of bleeding at puncture site. The patient presents to the employee clinic for a tetanus (and diphtheria) vaccine, which is administered IM into his upper left arm.

____

10. Three-year-old patient underwent quantitative screening test of visual acuity, bilateral. At the conclusion of the exam, the patient loudly announced that he was all ready to go to McDonald's for his Happy Meal.

____

ASSIGNMENT 19.2 – CODING MEDICINE REPORTS

Instructions

Assign the ICD-10-CM code(s) to diagnoses and conditions and assign the CPT medicine code(s) and the appropriate HCPCS level II and CPT modifier(s). Do not assign ICD-10-CM external cause codes.

1. CAROTID ULTRASOUND

   DIAGNOSIS: Screening exam, risk factors for cardiovascular disease.

   Multiple real-time images were made of both carotid arteries from the supraclavicular area to the bifurcation. The common carotid arteries are of normal caliber bilaterally with no evidence of any plaque formation or stenosis. The bifurcations are well demonstrated bilaterally and are normal. There is a very tiny calcified plaque involving the posterior wall of the left carotid artery just proximal to the bifurcation. This is only about 2 mm in size, and I do not think it is significant.

   CONCLUSION: Normal carotid ultrasound.

____

2. ELECTROENCEPHALOGRAM (EEG)

   COMPLAINT: Seizure.

   CURRENT MEDICATIONS: Phenobarbital, Theo-Dur, Peri-Colace.

   STATE OF PATIENT DURING RECORDING: Awake.

DESCRIPTION OF EEG: The background is not well developed. Much muscle tension artifact is superimposed; electrode artifact also present at times. No spike-wave discharges, paroxysmal slowing, or focal abnormality present. Hyperventilation procedure was not done. Sleep did not occur. Total recording time was 35 minutes.

EEG INTERPRETATION: Normal EEG.

---

3. SPEECH LANGUAGE EVALUATION

Patient was administered a complete Boston Diagnostic Aphasia Examination test for aphasia and was placed in the 41st percentile of all aphasics. Individual test scores were characterized with a severe involvement in graphic abilities, a marked involvement in gestural abilities, a moderate involvement in verbal abilities, and a mild to moderate involvement in auditory and visual receptive abilities. During the testing, many responses were repeated and cued. Patient showed a moderate involvement in reading abilities. Patient also demonstrated a severe involvement in graphic abilities. However, this is misleading because patient refused to do any graphic tests. I am uncertain at this point as to how well this patient can do graphically. The test results on the graphic tests also dropped her overall score a great deal.

However, a positive high/low gap was noted between the scores. This suggests that speech therapy will benefit this patient. Patient was given an oral exam, and no abnormalities were noted. Patient refused a hearing test. Patient was very, very nervous during the whole testing, and it was very hard to relax her. This may also have affected her test scores and helped in the refusing of the graphic part. Speech therapy is recommended daily for the patient.

---

4. STRESS TEST (OUTPATIENT)

FINDINGS: The patient is a 62-year-old female who has paroxysmal atrial tachycardia and takes Inderal 40 mg four times a day and Lanoxin 0.25 mg daily for this. She has also complained of some chest discomfort and has had some mild hypertension for which she takes Dyazide once a day. She is referred to take an outpatient stress test to rule out coronary artery disease.

The patient was prepared in the usual fashion. Electrodes were applied to the chest. She was taken at 1.6 metabolic equivalents (METs), 3 METs, 6 METs, and 9 METs during her exercise on the treadmill. During that time, her pulse rate increased linearly from 60 up to 150. The systolic blood pressure increased from 140 to 160. The blood pressure at the final MET level apparently was not recorded. During the course of the test, the patient did not really complain of chest pain, but she did become quite noticeably tired and short of breath, complaining of some tightness in her chest and feelings of weakness and dizziness. The rhythm strips at 1.6, 3, and 6 METs did not show any real ST segment depression. However, at the 6-MET level, there was noted about a 1/2-mm horizontal ST segment depression. At 9 METs, the changes were somewhat more pronounced with about a 1–2 mm. ST segment depression was actually horizontal to downward sloping. With these changes at 9 METs, I would think that this is sort of a borderline test with indeed some signs of positive at 9 METs. At this point, I would think this lady probably could be watched. She is essentially asymptomatic at rest and at low levels of exercise. I will continue her medications and see her frequently in the office if her symptoms increase. It may be that she should be restressed or at any rate that she should have yearly stress tests to keep tabs on the status of her coronary arteries. If the symptoms worsen and so forth, it might be worth referral for further studies.

DIAGNOSES: Paroxysmal atrial tachycardia. Chest pain. Hypertension. Rule out coronary artery disease.

---

5. RESPIRATORY THERAPY

SUBJECT: Patient was seen in the office with complaints of shortness of breath.

OBJECTIVE: Patient received one hour of continuous inhalation treatment with 0.3 cc Alupent/2 cc NS via mask at 6 LPM aerosol medication for acute airway obstruction. Bilateral sounds very coarse with fair aeration and severe upper airway congestion with audible stridor. Good respiratory effort with severe suprasternal and substernal and intercostal retractions. CPAP initiated during this encounter to improve breathing.

ASSESSMENT: Slight changes with nebulizer.

PLAN: Copious amounts of thick beige secretions from patient. Fair aeration on CPAP with moist rales and rhonchi at right base. Ambulance was called and patient is being transported to the hospital for direct admission to the ICU.

____

6. PHYSICAL THERAPY

INITIAL EVALUATION AND BEHAVIOR/MAIN COMPLAINT: Patient has history of back pain off and on for five years. Recently, patient had severe back pain radiating down right lower extremity (RLE). Pain is worse when rising after lying; it is also severe upon sitting for more than a few minutes and when bending while sitting. Patient has no personal factors and/or comorbidities that impact the plan of care. Clinical presentation is stable.

JOINT EVALUATION: Examination used standardized testing and measures to address range of motion limitation, right leg and hip. Pain upon straight leg raising right leg at 45 degrees. Pain is in right buttock and down posterior right thigh and leg. Pain also when flexing trunk on hips in same areas.

MUSCLE/MOTOR EVALUATION: Not evaluated for muscle power. Patient has muscle spasms of moderate degree in the right lower quadrant (RLQ) of the back.

FUNCTIONAL EVALUATION: Moves about easily in no apparent discomfort. When ambulating, no limp; but patient states pain is immediate upon coming to sitting or standing position.

SENSATION: Burning pain, sometimes numbness down RLE from buttock to ankle. Pain is present unless patient lies reclined.

OTHER COMMENTS: Patient had myelogram on 09/11/YY. This has not definitely concluded that she has a ruptured disc. Moist heat applied to back provides no relief according to patient. Twenty minutes was spent evaluating this patient using the standardized patient assessment instrument.

PLAN: Modalities to be used; whirlpool and hot packs for six weeks, twice per week for 30 minutes.

DIAGNOSES: Severe back pain. Muscle spasms, RLQ of back. Burning pain with numbness, RLE.

____

7. HAIR ANALYSIS

DIAGNOSIS: Rule out alopecia or hair shaft abnormality.

The patient is a 45-year-old female who has been diagnosed with hypothyroidism. She is seen in the office today with complaints of hair loss. Hair was removed from the patient's scalp and examined under the microscope. Extracted hairs show that 20 percent are in telogen. This level is within the expected normal range.

DIAGNOSIS: Alopecia (unrelated to hypothyroidism).

____

8. Lisa Morales is a type 1 diabetic patient who presents for the refilling of her insulin pump. The pump is identified as a Paradigm model number 515/715, and 250 units per milliliter of insulin was placed in the pump. The patient is discharged.

____

9. TRANSESOPHAGEAL ECHOCARDIOGRAM (TEE)

DIAGNOSIS: Rule out Ebstein's anomaly.

DESCRIPTION OF TEE: Patient is a 5-day-old infant in NICU with low saturation of oxygen and heart murmur. A TEE is ordered to evaluation the patient's heart for a possible Ebstein's anomaly. After the transducer and endoscope were placed at the patient's esophagus, a recording with imaging was done.

TEE INTERPRETATION: Congenital aortic stenosis, no other abnormalities seen.

____

10. COLONIC MOTILITY

DIAGNOSES: Nausea and vomiting.

The patient, a 50-year-old male, presents for electrogastrography study for his complaint of a six-year history of frequent nausea and vomiting. Ultrasound films were inconclusive; therefore, the patient's primary care physician referred the patient for this study. Electrodes are placed on the patient over the stomach region. Gastric activity is recorded by computer. Analysis shows two cycles per minute with dysrhythmia.

FINDINGS: Abnormal electrogastrography with two cycles per minute gastric electrical activity.

____

REVIEW

Multiple Choice

Circle the most appropriate response.

1. Intramuscular injection of varicella-zoster immune human globulin. Which code(s) are assigned?
   a. 90716
   b. 90396, 90471
   c. 90396, 96372
   d. 90716, 96372
2. Which term is used to identify a physician who specializes in physical medicine and rehabilitation services?
   a. Gerontologist
   b. Physiatrist
   c. Physical therapist
   d. Psychotherapist
3. A 70-year-old female patient received an influenza virus vaccine via intramuscular (IM) route. Which codes are assigned?
   a. 90471, 90655
   b. 90471, 90658
   c. 90471, 90658-51
   d. 90473, 90658
4. A 45-year-old male patient underwent 80-minute EEG test. Which code(s) are assigned?
   a. 95812
   b. 95813
   c. 95812, 99172
   d. 95812, 99199
5. A patient received a total of five manipulations of her cervical, thoracic, and lumbar spine during a chiropractic session. Which code is assigned?
   a. 98940
   b. 98941
   c. 98942
   d. 98943
6. A patient had a complete transcranial Doppler of intracranial arteries and ultrasound of right and left anterior territories and an ultrasound of the posterior circulation territory. Which code(s) are assigned?
   a. 93880
   b. 93882, 93886
   c. 93886
   d. 93886, 93890

7. A 25-year-old male patient received end-stage renal disease (ESRD) monthly outpatient services during April, which included two face-to-face physician visits. Which code is assigned?
   a. 90952
   b. 90955
   c. 90958
   d. 90961
8. Bekesy audiometry for diagnostic purpose. Which code is assigned?
   a. 92551
   b. 92559
   c. 92560
   d. 92561
9. Dr. Stevens interpreted and prepared the report for a signal-averaged electrocardiography (SAECG) with electrocardiography ECG. (The SAECG with ECG was performed at another facility.) Which code is assigned?
   a. 93227-26
   b. 93278-26
   c. 93660-26
   d. 93799-26
10. A patient presents to her cardiologist's office so that tests could be conducted to determine whether her dual lead pacemaker system was functioning properly. The device was reprogrammed by the cardiologist after he analyzed, reviewed, and reported on the test results. Which code is assigned?
   a. 93280
   b. 93283
   c. 93286
   d. 93289
11. Application of infrared modality. Which code is assigned?
   a. 97022
   b. 97024
   c. 97026
   d. 97028
12. Home visit with Robinson family to check on adjustment and well care of their 2-day-old infant. Which code is assigned?
   a. 99502
   b. 99509
   c. 99510
   d. 99600
13. Nystagmus test with recording of results. The patient was put in six different positions in an attempt to duplicate rapid eye movements. Which code is assigned?
   a. 92532
   b. 92534
   c. 92541
   d. 92542
14. Dr. Wilcox was present for a treadmill cardiac stress test on his patient Mr. Lander. After the test was completed, Dr. Wilcox analyzed the results and prepared a report for the patient's record. Which code(s) are assigned?
   a. 93015
   b. 93015, 93016
   c. 93224
   d. 93225, 93227
15. Suzie Matthews, a 22-year-old nursing student, received a HepA and HepB vaccine via IM route prior to starting her clinical rotations. Which codes are assigned?
   a. 90471, 90634-51
   b. 90471, 90636
   c. 96372, 90634
   d. 96372, 90633
16. Testing to rule out gastroesophageal reflux disease. The test took 1 hour 14 minutes. Which code is assigned?
   a. 91030
   b. 91034
   c. 91037
   d. 91038
17. Ophthalmological examination of a 10-year-old patient who is complaining of not being able to see the board from her seat in the third row of her classroom. The physician obtained a history from the patient and her mother, performed an exam using the ophthalmoscope, and provided a prescription for eyeglasses. Which code(s) are assigned?
   a. 92002
   b. 92012
   c. 99213
   d. 92002, 92340

18. Balloon valvuloplasty of the pulmonary heart valve done percutaneously. Which code is assigned?
    a. 92943
    b. 92986
    c. 92987
    d. 92990
19. Patient underwent intracardiac catheter ablation of arrhythmogenic focus procedure for treatment of ventricular tachycardia. Catheter manipulation was also performed with intraventricular mapping of tachycardia site to identify origin of tachycardia. Which code(s) are assigned?
    a. 93650
    b. 93653
    c. 93654, 93609
    d. 93655, 93609
20. Acupuncture using 10 needles. Provider spent 30 minutes of personal contact with the patient. Which code(s) are assigned?
    a. 97810
    b. 97810, 97811
    c. 97810, 97811-51
    d. 97810, 97813

CHAPTER 20

Insurance and Reimbursement

INTRODUCTION

This chapter familiarizes students with issues related to reimbursement methodologies by having them complete the following application-based assignments:

- Chargemaster review process
- Interpretation of a remittance advice
- Interpretation of Medicare fee-for-service payment errors report

ASSIGNMENT 20.1 – CHARGEMASTER REVIEW PROCESS

Objectives

At the conclusion of this assignment, the student should be able to:

- Explain the purpose of a chargemaster.
- Review and edit a chargemaster to update it.

Overview

Hospitals use a chargemaster to record encounter data about ambulatory care provided to patients. The *chargemaster* (or *charge description master, CDM*) (Figure 20-1) is a document that contains a computer-generated list of procedures, services, and supplies and corresponding revenue codes along with charges for each. Chargemaster data are entered in the facility's patient accounting system, and charges are automatically posted to the patient's bill (UB-04). The bill is submitted to the payer to generate payment for ancillary and other services (e.g., emergency department, laboratory, and radiology). The chargemaster allows the facility to accurately and efficiently bill the patient for services rendered, and it usually contains the following:

- Department code (refers to the specific ancillary department where the service is performed)
- Service code (internal identification of specific service rendered)
- Service description (narrative description of the service, procedure, or supply)
- Revenue code (four-digit UB-04 code assigned to each procedure, service, or supply that indicates the location or type of service provided to a patient)
- Charge amount (dollar amount facility charges for each procedure, service, or supply)

- Relative Value Units (RVUs) (numeric values assigned to procedures that are based on difficulty and time consumed)

A *chargemaster review process* is routinely conducted by designated hospital personnel (e.g., coding specialists) to ensure accurate reimbursement by updating CPT and HCPCS codes and linking each to appropriate UB-04 revenue codes. These designated individuals must have knowledge of proper revenue and expense matching to the Medicare cost center report (e.g., revenue codes) and be willing to spend the time necessary on an extremely detailed and time-consuming task. Because the chargemaster results in generation of gross revenue for the health care facility, all who use it must be educated about its proper use and its impact on the facility's financial status.

Goodmedicine Hospital, Anywhere US 12345					
Dept:	Radiology	Date Printed: 04/05/YYYY			
Service Code	Service Description	CPT Code	Revenue Code	Charge	RVU
81500098	Chest x-ray, single view	71045	320	73.95	.72
81500099	Chest x-ray, two views	71046	320	94.65	0.93
81500100	Chest x-ray, two views w/ apical lordotic	71047	320	114.25	1.11
81500101	Chest x-ray, four or more views	71048	320	212.85	2.09
81500103	Upper GI x-ray, with single-contrast study	74240	324	250.55	2.42
81500104	Upper GI x-ray, with double-contrast study	74214	324	353.50	2.44
81500107	Small bowel x-ray (separate procedure)	74250	324	200.15	1.95

FIGURE 20-1 **Portion of hospital chargemaster (Some codes in the "CPT Code" column are intentionally incorrect.)**

Instructions

Review the partial chargemaster document in Figure 20-1 to familiarize yourself with its organization and contents. Locate, circle (or highlight), and correct the errors on the chargemaster document.

1. Is the hospital's address complete? (If not, explain.)

____

NOTE:

The address should include the hospital's name, street address, city, state, and ZIP code.

2. Is the date printed accurate? (If not, explain.)

____

NOTE:

Today is June 15, YYYY.

3. Is the name of the department correct? (If not, explain.)

____

NOTE:

Compare the service descriptions listed in Column 2 to the name of the department, abbreviated as *Dept:* on the chargemaster, to make this determination.

4. Are the CPT codes listed in Column 3 correct? (If not, explain.)

____

NOTE:

Use your CPT coding manual to look up each code and its description to verify the accuracy of codes and descriptions on the chargemaster.

5. Are the revenue codes in Column 4 correct? (If not, explain.)

____

NOTE:

Chest x-rays are assigned to revenue code 320, and gastrointestinal x-rays are assigned to revenue code 324.

ASSIGNMENT 20.2 – INTERPRETING A REMITTANCE ADVICE

Objectives

At the conclusion of this assignment, the student should be able to:

- Explain the purpose of a remittance advice.
- Interpret data contained on a remittance advice.

Overview

Once the claims adjudication process has been finalized, the claim is either denied or approved for payment. The provider receives a remittance advice, which contains information used to process payments and adjustments to patients' accounts. Payers often include multiple patients on the same remittance advice (remit), which means that the remit must be reviewed carefully for payments and adjustments to be processed properly. The remittance advice is also reviewed to make sure that there are no processing errors, which would result in the office resubmitting a corrected claim (e.g., coding errors).

Instructions

Review the remittance advice in Figure 20-2 to familiarize yourself with its organization and legend (explanation of abbreviated terms). Use the remittance advice to answer the following questions.

1. What is the check number and amount paid to the provider as recorded on the remittance advice? (HINT: This information is recorded in two different places on the remittance advice.)

____

```
ABC INSURANCE COMPANY
100 MAIN STREET
ALFRED  NY 14802
1-800-555-1234                                                   REMITTANCE ADVICE

DANIEL SPRING, M.D.                                              PROVIDER #:    987654
101 MAIN STREET                    PAGE #: 1 OF 1                DATE:          05/05/YY
ANYWHERE, US 12345                                               CHECK#:        9568547

            SERV DATES     POS     PROC   BILLED  ALLOWED        COINSURANCE    PROVIDER PAID
---------------------------------------------------------------------------------------------
FISCHER, JENNY  HIC 235962541    ACNT  FISC1234567-01    ICN 1235626589651  ASG Y  MOA MA01
236592ABC       0405 0405YY   11      99213  75.00  60.00          15.00            60.00
PT RESP: 15.00        CLAIM TOTAL: 75.00
                                                                                NET: 60.00
---------------------------------------------------------------------------------------------
GREER, JAMES    HIC 569856217    ACNT  GREE2326254-01    ICN 23562145898547 ASG Y  MOA MA01
326526ABC       0406 0406YY   11      99214  100.00 80.00          20.00            80.00
PT RESP: 20.00        CLAIM TOTAL: 100.00
                                                                                NET: 80.00
---------------------------------------------------------------------------------------------
HENDY, FRAN     HIC 562659452    ACNT  HEND2369214-01    ICN 6265975312562  ASG Y  MOA MA01
123652ABC       0410 0410YY   11      99212  50.00  40.00          10.00            40.00
PT RESP: 10.00        CLAIM TOTAL: 50.00
                                                                                NET: 40.00
---------------------------------------------------------------------------------------------
LYNCH, JOSEPH   HIC 626594594    ACNT  LYNC2365214-01    ICN 5695321453259  ASG Y  MOA MA01
126954ABC       0415 0415YY   11      99385  125.00 125.00          0.00            125.00
PT RESP: 0.00         CLAIM TOTAL: 125.00
                                                                                NET: 125.00
---------------------------------------------------------------------------------------------
MONROE, PETER     HIC 365956214    ACNT  MONR1236521-01   ICN 9652154125632  ASG Y  MOA MA01
695214ABC       0420 0420YY   11      17000  750.00 600.00         150.00           600.00
PT RESP: 150.00       CLAIM TOTAL: 750.00
                                                                                NET: 600.00
---------------------------------------------------------------------------------------------
TOTALS:
# BILLED      ALLOWED       COINSURANCE    TOTAL         PROV PAID     CHECK
CLAIMS        AMOUNT        AMOUNT         AMOUNT        AMOUNT        AMOUNT

   5          905.00        195.00         1100.00       905.00        905.00
```

LEGEND

SERV DATES (dates of service)
POS (place of service code)
PROC (CPT procedure/service code)
BILLED (amount provider billed payer)
ALLOWED (amount authorized by payer)
COINSURANCE (amount patient paid)
PROVIDER PAID (amount provider was reimbursed by payer)
NET: (amount provider billed payer)
PT RESP: (amount patient paid)

FIGURE 20-2 Remittance advice (multiple claims)

2. What was the date of service for patient Jenny Fischer? ______
3. What was patient James Greer's coinsurance amount for his visit on 04-06-YY? ______
4. Patient Joseph Lynch was not charged a coinsurance amount for his 04-15-YY visit. What are the possible explanations for this? ______
5. What is patient Jenny Fischer's account number? ______
6. Identify the place of service code for each patient. ______
7. What procedure code is listed for patient Fran Hendy? ______
8. According to the remittance advice, how much was Dr. Spring reimbursed by the payer? ______
9. What is the allowed amount for procedure code 99213? ______
10. How much did the provider bill the insurance company for the care of patient Peter Monroe?

______

ASSIGNMENT 20.3 – INTERPRETING A MEDICARE FEE-FOR-SERVICE PAYMENT ERROR REPORT

Objectives

At the conclusion of this assignment, the student should be able to:

- Interpret data from a table.
- Analyze data and draw conclusions.

Overview

The Centers for Medicare & Medicaid Services (CMS) publishes an annual error rate report that highlights improper fee-for-service (FFS) payments made to providers. Figure 20-3 summarizes net errors identified for fiscal year (FY) Year 1 through Year 5. CMS calculates the *net error rate* after subtracting overpayments from underpayments. For FY Year 5, the goal was to reduce the payment error rate to 4.8 percent. (*Payment error rate* reflects both overpayments and underpayments.) The following definitions apply to the type of errors identified in the table.

The categories are insufficient documentation, nonresponse, medically unnecessary, incorrect coding, and other.

- Insufficient documentation relates to the documentation provided to CMS by the provider. This is the documentation in the actual health record. For FY Year 5, this category referred to physician-generated documentation used to code Evaluation and Management (E/M) services. This category also related to facility billing under the Medicare and Medicaid program.
- The nonresponse category means that the provider was requested to submit documentation but documentation was not received.
- The medically unnecessary category relates to services coded that do not meet requirements after being reviewed by CMS staff.
- Upcoding or downcoding is associated with the incorrect coding category. This is based on the review of the health record documentation.
- The other category refers to providers' claims not meeting benefit requirements.

Facilities and providers can focus on these issues by providing information to CMS when requested and ensuring that health record documentation meets the level of service or procedure coded. Meeting requirements for medical necessity and proper code assignment are measures that facilities and providers can use to impact future data.

Type of Error	Year 1	Year 2	Year 3	Year 4	Year 5
Insufficient Documentation	19.2%	30.5%	20.1%	45.0%	43.7%
Nonresponse	17.2%	12.4%	8.5%	18.5%	29.7%
Medically Unnecessary	43.0%	43.2%	57.1%	21.7%	17.2%
Incorrect Coding	14.7%	17.0%	14.3%	12.1%	7.7%
Other	5.9%	-3.1%	0.0%	2.7%	1.6%
Total	100%	100.0%	100.0%	100.0%	100.0%

Courtesy of the Centers for Medicare & Medicaid Services, www.cms.gov

FIGURE 20-3 **Percentage of net errors by category for each fiscal year**

Instructions

Review the Year 5 report entitled "Percentage of Net Errors by Category for Each Fiscal Year" (Figure 20-3) and answer the following questions.

1. Compare Year 4 to Year 5 data. Did CMS providers improve their documentation in Year 5? In which category did CMS providers fail to show improvement for Year 5?

   ____

2. According to Year 2 data, which is the major area of concern for health care facilities?
   a. Incorrect coding
   b. Insufficient documentation
   c. Medically unnecessary care
   d. No response/no documentation
3. Use the Year 3 through Year 5 data to calculate the percentage of increase or decrease for the category of incorrect coding. Has this category seen improvement in the last two fiscal years? ______________
4. Review the Year 5 data and identify where net errors improved.

   ____

5. When comparing Year 4 to Year 5 data, is there an increase or a decrease in coding errors? Calculate the percentage increase or decrease in coding errors for the period Year 4 to Year 5.

   ____

ASSIGNMENT 20.4 – AMBULATORY PAYMENT CLASSIFICATIONS

Objectives

At the conclusion of this assignment, the student should be able to:

- Explain the ambulatory payment classification prospective payment system.
- Use ambulatory payment classification grouper software to determine reimbursement amounts.

Overview

Ambulatory payment classification (APC) grouper software is used to assign an APC to each CPT and/or HCPCS level II code reported on an outpatient claim, as well as to ICD-10-CM codes, as appropriate.

Outpatient code editor (OCE) software is used in conjunction with the APC grouper to identify Medicare claims edits and assign APC groups to reported codes.

The Balanced Budget Act of 1997 legislated implementation of the outpatient prospective payment system (OPPS), which uses ambulatory payment classifications (APCs) to reimburse hospital outpatient services. Outpatient health care services are organized clinically and according to resources required. A reimbursement rate is established for each APC, and depending on services provided, hospitals can be paid for more than one APC per encounter, with second and subsequent APCs discounted at 50 percent.

Instructions

Review each case and assign the ICD-10-CM and CPT codes. Then use ambulatory payment classification (APC) grouper software to determine the correct reimbursement amount.

NOTE:

Ask your instructor for information about the availability of APC grouper software at your school.

1. A 60-year-old female presented to the hospital outpatient surgical unit for repair of an umbilical hernia, which was performed via an open approach in Operating Room B. The patient had minimal blood loss and was sent to the recovery room in good condition. The patient was discharged home later that same day.
   a. Assign the ICD-10-CM code(s) to the first-listed diagnosis. Assign the CPT code(s) to the procedure(s).
      FIRST-LISTED DIAGNOSIS CODE: ________
      PROCEDURE CODE: ________
   b. Enter the patient's CPT procedure code(s) in APC grouper software. Review the APC grouper results and answer the following question:
      To which APC does this patient group? ________
2. A 55-year-old male presented to the hospital outpatient surgical unit for a cystoscopy. The patient's complaint was hematuria. A transurethral diagnostic cystoscopy was performed. No acute or abnormal findings were determined to be the cause of his hematuria. The patient was sent to the recovery room in good condition and was discharged later that same day.
   a. Assign the ICD-10-CM code(s) to the first-listed diagnosis. Assign the CPT code(s) to the procedure(s).
      FIRST-LISTED DIAGNOSIS CODE: ________
      PROCEDURE CODE: ________
   b. Enter the patient's CPT code(s) in APC grouper software. Review the APC grouper results and answer the following question:
      To which APC does this patient group? ________
3. A 45-year-old female complained of fatigue and underwent a laboratory blood test that revealed elevated T_3 and T_4 levels. The patient underwent a fine-needle aspiration biopsy of her thyroid as an outpatient. The patient experienced minimal blood loss and was discharged home at the conclusion of the procedure.
   a. Assign the ICD-10-CM code(s) to the first-listed diagnosis and the additional diagnosis. Assign the CPT code(s) to the procedure(s).
      FIRST-LISTED DIAGNOSIS CODE: ________
      ADDITIONAL DIAGNOSIS CODE: ________
      PROCEDURE CODE: ________
   b. Enter the patient's CPT code(s) in APC grouper software. Review the APC grouper results and answer the following question:
      To which APC does this patient group? ________

4. An 80-year-old gentleman presented to the hospital outpatient surgical unit for the removal of a cortical senile cataract from his left eye. The patient underwent an extracapsular cataract extraction with anterior chamber intraocular lens (IOL) implant insertion. There were no problems, and the patient was sent to the recovery room in good condition. He was later discharged home to be followed in the office.
   a. Assign the ICD-10-CM code(s) to the first-listed diagnosis. Assign the CPT and HCPCS level II code(s) to the procedure(s).
      FIRST-LISTED DIAGNOSIS CODE: ______________
      PROCEDURE CODE: ______________
      PROCEDURE CODE (HCPCS LEVEL II ANTERIOR CHAMBER IOL IMPLANT SUPPLY): ______________
   b. Enter the patient's CPT and HCPCS level II code(s) in APC grouper software. Review the APC grouper results and answer the following question:

      To which APC does this patient group? ______________

5. A 67-year-old female underwent a laparoscopic cholecystectomy for cholelithiasis with acute cholecystitis. The patient also had an intraoperative cholangiogram performed. The patient had minimal blood loss and was discharged home later that day.
   a. Assign the ICD-10-CM code(s) to the first-listed diagnosis and the additional diagnoses. Assign the CPT code(s) to the procedure(s).
      FIRST-LISTED DIAGNOSIS CODE: ______________
      ADDITIONAL DIAGNOSIS CODE: ______________
      ADDITIONAL DIAGNOSIS CODE: ______________
      PROCEDURE CODE: ______________
   b. Enter the patient's CPT procedure code(s) in APC grouper software. Review the APC grouper results and answer the following question:

      To which APC does this patient group? ______________

ASSIGNMENT 20.5 – INTERPRETING DIAGNOSIS-RELATED GROUPS DECISION TREES

Objectives

At the conclusion of this assignment, the student should be able to:

- Interpret a diagnosis-related group (DRG) decision tree.
- Differentiate between medical partitioning and surgical partitioning DRG decision trees.
- Determine which DRG is assigned when a secondary diagnosis such as a complication and/or comorbidity is documented in the patient record.

Overview

Diagnoses and procedures are grouped according to a particular DRG, and DRG decision trees (Figures 20-4 and 20-5) visually represent the process of assigning a DRG within a medical diagnostic category (MDC). The decision trees use a flowchart design to facilitate the decision-making logic for assigning a DRG. ICD-10-CM diagnosis codes are grouped according to a medical partitioning DRG decision tree, and ICD-10-CM diagnosis and ICD-10-PCS surgical procedure codes are grouped according to a surgical partitioning DRG decision tree. (Only ICD-10-CM diagnosis codes are grouped according to medical partitioning DRG decision trees, while ICD-10-CM and ICD-10-PCS codes are grouped according to surgical partitioning DRG decision trees.) DRGs with associated comorbidities and/or complications (CC) require increased utilization of hospital resources, and reimbursement for such DRGs is increased. Although just one CC can change a *DRG without CC* to a *DRG with CC*, a number of stand-alone DRGs are not affected by the presence or absence of CCs (e.g., DRG 014, Specific Cerebrovascular Disorders except Transient Ischemic Attack). For stand-alone DRGs, the DRG (and reimbursement amount) will change (and increase) *only if* the principal diagnosis is changed or a significant surgical procedure is reported.

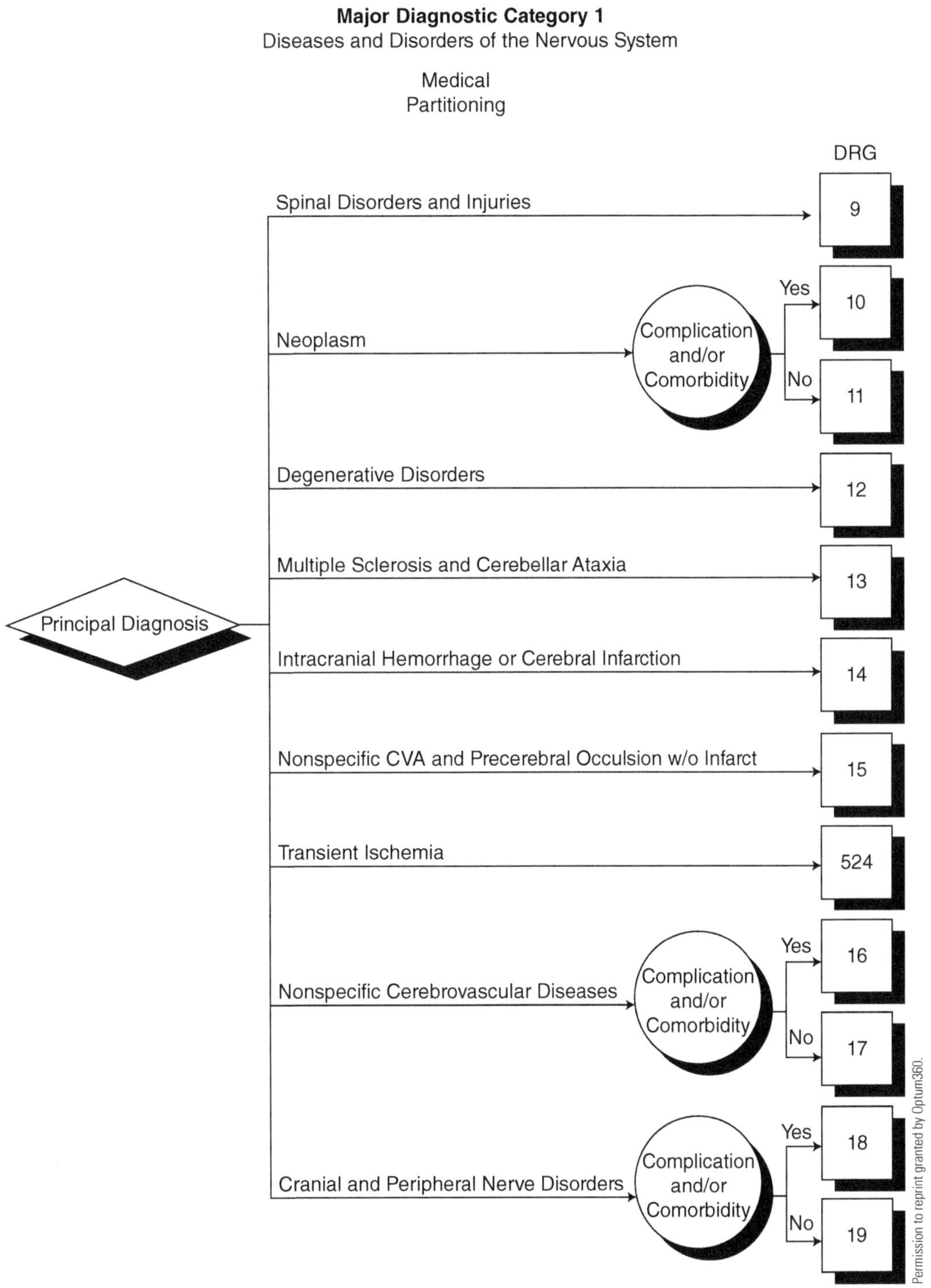

FIGURE 20-4 Medical partitioning DRG decision tree

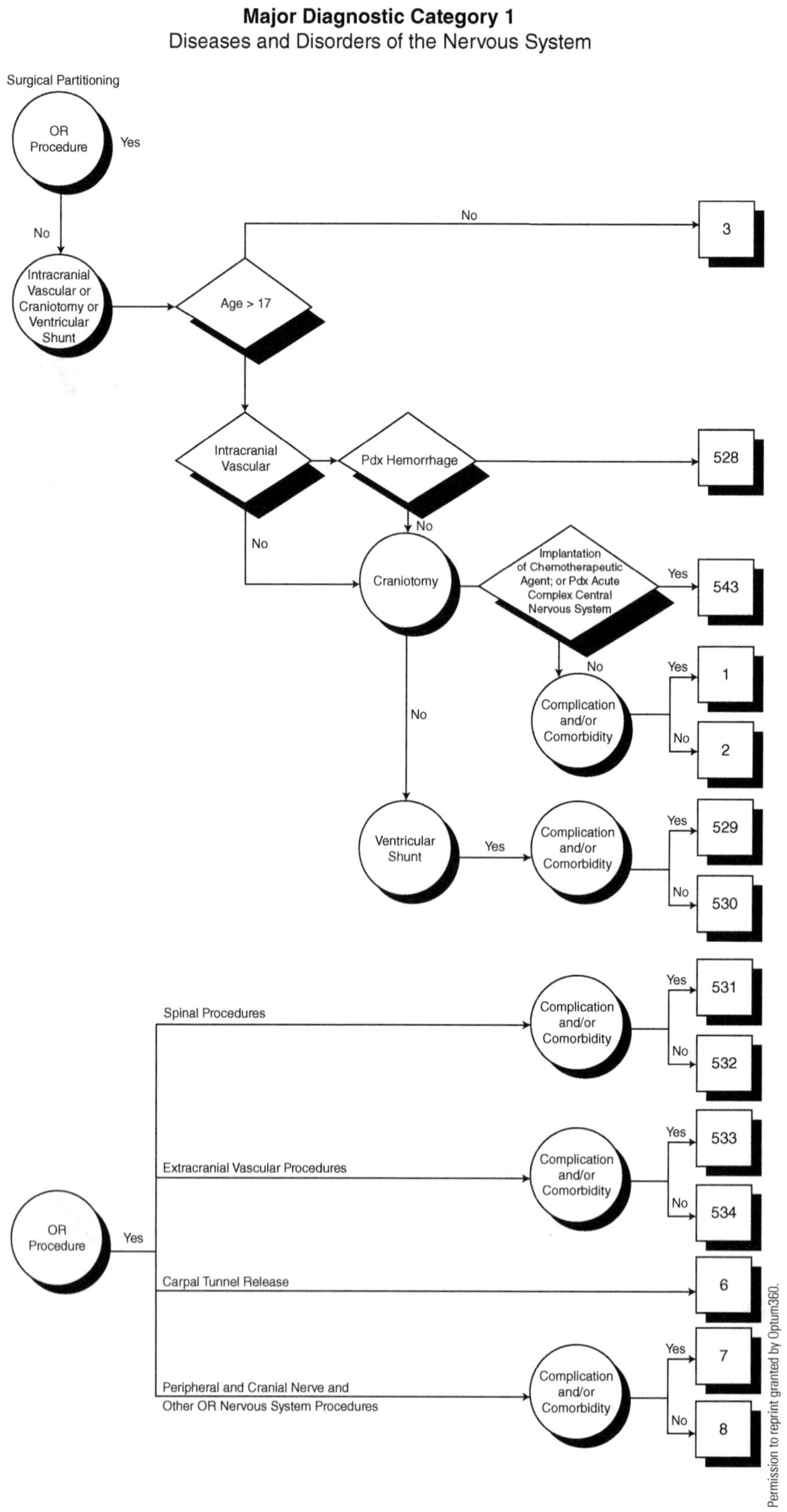

FIGURE 20-5 Surgical partitioning DRG decision tree

Instructions

Answer questions 1 through 5 to interpret the medical partitioning DRG decision tree (Figure 20-4).

EXAMPLE: Which neoplasm DRG is assigned to a patient whose provider has documented a complication and/or comorbidity?

ANSWER: DRG 10.

1. Which DRG is assigned when a code for "intracranial hemorrhage" is reported as the patient's principal diagnosis and no comorbidity or complication codes are reported?

 ____

2. Which DRG is assigned when a code for "cranial and peripheral nerve disorders" is reported as the principal diagnosis and no comorbidity or complication codes are reported?

 ____

3. Which DRG is assigned when a code for "cranial disorder" is reported as the principal diagnosis and a "hypothyroidism" code is reported as a comorbidity?

 ____

4. Which DRG is assigned when a code for "neoplasm of the nervous system" is reported as the principal diagnosis and no codes are reported for comorbidities or complications?

 ____

5. Which DRG is assigned when a code for "cerebrovascular disease" is reported as the principal diagnosis and no comorbidity or complication codes are reported?

 ____

Instructions

Answer questions 6 through 10 to interpret the surgical partitioning DRG decision tree (Figure 20-5).

6. Which DRG is assigned when a code for "carpal tunnel release" is reported as the principal procedure and no comorbidity or complication codes are reported?

 ____

7. Which DRG is assigned when a code for "spinal procedure" is reported as the principal procedure and a "postoperative renal insufficiency" code is reported as a complication?

 ____

8. Which DRG is assigned when a code for "craniotomy" is reported as the principal procedure performed on a 16-year-old patient and no comorbidity or complication codes are reported?

 ____

9. Which DRG is assigned when a code for "extracranial vascular procedure" is reported as the principal procedure and a "rheumatic heart disease" code is reported as a comorbidity?

 ____

10. Which DRG is assigned when a code for "insertion of a ventricular shunt" for a 68-year-old patient is reported as the principal procedure and a "postoperative cerebrovascular accident" code is reported as a complication?

 ____

ASSIGNMENT 20.6 – ASSIGNING DIAGNOSIS-RELATED GROUPS

Objectives

At the conclusion of this assignment, the student should be able to:

- Review case scenarios and identify the principal diagnosis, comorbidities, complications, principal procedure, and other significant procedures.
- Assign ICD-10-CM and ICD-10-PCS codes to diagnoses and procedures, respectively.
- Use grouper software to determine a diagnosis-related group (DRG).
- Identify the major diagnostic category (MDC) for each DRG.

Overview

Diagnosis-related groups (DRGs) are assigned to acute care hospital cases using grouper software to report the patient's age, gender, discharge status, principal diagnosis, up to eight additional diagnoses, the principal procedure, and up to five additional procedures. One DRG is assigned to each inpatient stay, and all DRGs are organized into one of 25 major diagnostic categories (MDCs).

Instructions

Review each case scenario below and identify the principal diagnosis, comorbidities, complications, principal procedure, and other significant procedures. Assign ICD-10-CM and ICD-10-PCS codes to each diagnosis and procedure, respectively. Enter patient information and ICD-10-CM and ICD-10-PCS codes into DRG grouper software and answer the questions.

NOTE:

Ask your instructor for information about the availability of DRG grouper software at your school.

1. Martha Robbins is admitted directly to the hospital with the complaint of severe dyspnea. Mrs. Robbins is 75 years old and has a history of hypertensive renal disease and diabetes mellitus controlled with insulin. Upon examination, she is noted to have edema of her legs and feet. Radiographic films indicate fluid in her lungs. Her albumin level is .5 grams per decaliter, and her creatinine level is 3.0 milligrams per decaliter. Sputum culture is positive for *Klebsiella pneumoniae*. Her blood pressure upon admission is 155/100. She is diagnosed with acute left ventricular heart failure, acute exacerbation of hypertensive renal disease, and pneumonia due to *Klebsiella pneumoniae*. Antihypertensive medications, antibiotics, insulin, Zocor, and intravenous diuretics are administered, and her diet is restricted for sodium and fluid. Three days later, she is discharged home in an improved condition.

   DISCHARGE DIAGNOSES: Acute left ventricular heart failure. Hypertensive heart and renal disease, stage 2. Pneumonia due to *Klebsiella pneumoniae*. Hyperlipidemia. Type 2 diabetes mellitus.

   a. Assign ICD-10-CM codes to the principal diagnosis of congestive heart failure and comorbidities. (No procedures were performed.)

      PRINCIPAL DIAGNOSIS CODE: ____________
      COMORBIDITY CODE: ____________
      COMORBIDITY CODE: ____________
      COMORBIDITY CODE: ____________
      COMORBIDITY CODE: ____________
      COMORBIDITY CODE: ____________

b. Enter the patient's age, gender, discharge status, and assigned ICD-10-CM and ICD-10-PCS codes in the DRG grouper software. Review the DRG grouper results and answer the following questions:
What is the MDC number? ______________
What is the DRG number and description? ______________

2. Mr. Browne is a 66-year-old man with a history of cerebrovascular accident who is seen in the emergency department for complaints of chest pain and oral phase dysphagia. He is noted to have a temperature of 101 degrees upon examination. He is admitted as a hospital inpatient for further evaluation and treatment. Mr. Browne has a history of type 2 diabetes mellitus and hypertension. Lab tests include a white blood cell count with differential and a chest x-ray. Results reveal that Mr. Browne has pneumonia, and a sputum culture is ordered. The sputum culture results are negative. A percutaneous endoscopic gastrostomy (PEG tube) is inserted to assist with his nutrition, which is difficult due to his dysphagia. He is administered respiratory therapy for the pneumonia. His feeding is done via the PEG tube. His oral antihypertensive and diabetic medications are continued as an inpatient. After several days he is discharged to a skilled nursing facility for further care.

FINAL DIAGNOSES: Viral pneumonia. Oral phase dysphagia due to previous cerebrovascular accident (CVA). Type 2 diabetes mellitus. Hypertension.

PROCEDURE: Insertion of percutaneous endoscopic gastrostomy (PEG tube).

a. Assign ICD-10-CM codes to the principal diagnosis of viral pneumonia and comorbidities. Assign an ICD-10-PCS code to the principal procedure.
PRINCIPAL DIAGNOSIS CODE: ______________
COMORBIDITY CODE: ______________
COMORBIDITY CODE: ______________
COMORBIDITY CODE: ______________
PRINCIPAL PROCEDURE CODE: ______________

b. Enter the patient's age, gender, discharge status, and assigned ICD-10-CM and ICD-10-PCS codes in the DRG grouper software. Review the DRG grouper results and answer the following questions:
What is the MDC number? ______________
What is the DRG number and description? ______________

3. A patient is admitted through the emergency department (ED) with the chief complaint of nosebleeds. The patient also complains of facial pain on the right side of her face and head. Patient is a 67-year-old female with a history of diabetes mellitus, hypertension (HTN), and epistaxis 10 years ago (status postcauterization) who has presented to the ED twice in the last five hours for right nasal epistaxis. Positive profuse bleeding is noted at times. During the first visit at 10:50 P.M., the patient was administered Neo-Synephrine drops and sent home. During the second visit at 4 A.M., the right nostril was packed with gauze soaked in lidocaine with epinephrine, and the patient's bleeding resolved. Right epistaxis was treated with balloon therapy and at present is under control. Patient was admitted for further treatment and consultation with the ear, nose, and throat specialist. Patient was administered Xanax 0.25 mg by mouth for anxiety, Dilaudid 0.5 mg intravenously every three hours as needed for facial pain, and prophylactic Cleocin 600 mg intravenously every eight hours. The first dose was at 4:40 A.M. today. Her hypertension was treated with Lasix 20 mg and Tenormin 50 mg by mouth daily. For her hyperlipidemia, she received Zocor 10 mg by mouth daily. She received Diabinese 100 mg daily for her type 2 diabetes mellitus. The patient then underwent endoscopic control of right epistaxis with cautery done for her condition. Postoperatively, her red blood cell count, hemoglobin, and hematocrit were low. She was diagnosed with blood-loss anemia and received 2 units of packed red blood cells (nonautologous). She was discharged on day four of this admission with an order for home health services.

FINAL DIAGNOSES: Epistaxis. Acute posthemorrhagic anemia. Type 2 diabetes mellitus. Hypertension. Hyperlipidemia.

PROCEDURES: Endoscopic control of right epistaxis with cautery. Transfusion with packed red blood cells.

a. Assign ICD-10-CM codes to the principal diagnosis and comorbidities. Based on ICD-10-CM coding guidelines, sequence the diagnoses in the correct order. Assign ICD-10-PCS codes to the principal procedure and additional procedure.

PRINCIPAL DIAGNOSIS CODE: __________
COMORBIDITY CODE: __________
COMORBIDITY CODE: __________
COMORBIDITY CODE: __________
COMORBIDITY CODE: __________
PRINCIPAL PROCEDURE CODE: __________
ADDITIONAL PROCEDURE CODE: __________
ADDITIONAL PROCEDURE CODE: __________
ADDITIONAL PROCEDURE CODE: __________

b. Enter the patient's age, gender, discharge status, and ICD-10-CM and ICD-10-PCS codes in the DRG grouper software. Review the DRG grouper results and answer the following questions:

What is the MDC number? __________
What is the DRG number and description? __________

4. A 45-year-old female is admitted to the hospital with the chief complaint of severe left arm pain. This patient has a history of end stage renal failure, and she has an arteriovenous graft in her left arm for dialysis access. The patient's end stage renal failure is due to hypertensive renal disease. She receives dialysis on Tuesday, Thursday, and Saturday. The patient was seen, evaluated, and scheduled for surgery. Postoperative diagnosis was end stage renal failure with left upper extremity arteriovenous graft stenosis. Procedures performed are fluoroscopy of dialysis fistula (high osmolar), left upper extremity, and declotting of arteriovenous graft, left upper extremity with percutaneous infusion of urokinase. Postprocedurally, the patient had a run of sinus tachycardia that was treated with medication. Postprocedurally, her blood pressure was 163/100. She was administered intravenous antihypertensive medication for this. She was discharged on day two in an improved condition with instructions to follow up with her nephrologist at the renal clinic.

FINAL DIAGNOSES: Severe left arm pain due to left upper extremity arteriovenous graft stenosis. Hypertensive renal disease with end stage renal failure. Postprocedural sinus tachycardia.

PROCEDURES: Percutaneous declotting of arteriovenous graft, left upper extremity, with percutaneous infusion of urokinase. Fluoroscopy of dialysis fistula (high osmolar).

a. Assign ICD-10-CM codes to the principal diagnosis and comorbidities. Based on ICD-10-CM coding guidelines, sequence the diagnoses in the correct order. Assign ICD-10-PCS codes to the principal procedure and additional procedure.

PRINCIPAL DIAGNOSIS CODE: __________
COMORBIDITY CODE: __________
COMORBIDITY CODE: __________
COMORBIDITY CODE: __________
COMORBIDITY CODE: __________
COMPLICATION CODE: __________
PRINCIPAL PROCEDURE CODE: __________
ADDITIONAL PROCEDURE CODE: __________
ADDITIONAL PROCEDURE CODE: __________

b. Enter the patient's age, gender, discharge status, and assigned ICD-10-CM and ICD-10-PCS codes in the DRG grouper software. Review the DRG grouper results and answer the following questions:

What is the MDC number? __________
What is the DRG number and description? __________

5. An 85-year-old man presents with the complaint of shortness of breath and fatigue. Both of these symptoms have become worse over the past month. The patient is an active man and works with his son and grandson in a real estate business. These symptoms are preventing him from working. His past medical history includes bypass grafting 12 years ago. The patient is admitted for further workup and treatment. Diagnostic testing reveals that the patient has aortic valve stenosis. This is confirmed by catheterization. A right and left cardiac catheterization confirms that the patient's previous bypass graft is working well. Surgery for aortic valve replacement with synthetic substitute is performed. Postoperatively, the patient's gout was exacerbated in his right foot. He does have a history of this condition. Oral medication is given to treat the gout, and on postoperative day four, the patient is discharged home in an improved condition.

   FINAL DIAGNOSES: Aortic stenosis. Previous bypass graft surgery. Gout, right foot.

   PROCEDURES: Aortic valve replacement (open approach). Right and left cardiac catheterization (percutaneous approach).

   a. Assign ICD-10-CM codes to the principal diagnosis and comorbidities. Based on ICD-10-CM coding guidelines, sequence the diagnoses in the correct order. Assign ICD-10-PCS codes to the principal procedure and additional procedure.

      PRINCIPAL DIAGNOSIS CODE: __________
      COMORBIDITY CODE: __________
      COMORBIDITY CODE: __________
      PRINCIPAL PROCEDURE CODE: __________
      ADDITIONAL PROCEDURE CODE: __________

   b. Enter the patient's age, gender, discharge status, and assigned ICD-10-CM codes in the DRG grouper software. Review the DRG grouper results and answer the following questions:

      What is the MDC number? __________
      What is the DRG number and description? __________

REVIEW

Multiple Choice

Circle the most appropriate response.

1. Which has been replaced with Medicare administrative contractors?
   a. Fiscal intermediaries
   b. Medicare Part B
   c. Providers
   d. Third-party payers
2. The Uniform Bill 2004 (UB-04) replaced the ___________ in 2007.
   a. CMS-1450
   b. CMS-1500
   c. UB-82
   d. UB-92
3. Individuals who enroll in ___________ establish tax-exempt accounts.
   a. BlueCross BlueShield
   b. consumer-directed health plans
   c. Medicare and/or Medicaid
   d. workers' compensation
4. A major advantage of a health savings account (HSA) when compared to other types of consumer-directed health plans (CDHP) is that the HSA:
   a. allows unused balances to be rolled over to the next year.
   b. is combined with zero deductible insurance plans.
   c. is funded by private or government insurance coverage.
   d. is regulated by the Internal Revenue Service (IRS).
5. A third-party administrator (TPA) provides ___________ services.
   a. benefit design, claims processing, and utilization review
   b. claims management, medical necessity review, and financing
   c. ICD-10-CM, ICD-10-PCS, and HCPCS/CPT coding and provider billing
   d. regulatory, medical oversight, and national/regional coverage
6. An active duty member of the U.S. Army would be covered by the ___________ health plan.
   a. CHAMPUS
   b. CHAMPVA
   c. FEHBP
   d. TRICARE
7. A patient with the principal diagnosis of nontraumatic stupor and coma would be assigned to which DRG? (Refer to Figure 20-6.)
   a. 23
   b. 27
   c. 28
   d. 29
8. A 25-year-old patient with a principal diagnosis of seizures and headaches but no complications or comorbidities would be assigned to which DRG? (Refer to Figure 20-6.)
   a. 24
   b. 25
   c. 26
   d. 27
9. As part of its forecasting for the upcoming fiscal year, West Lake Hospital noted that the hospital treated 200 inpatients grouped to DRG 127 last fiscal year (Table 20-1). The hospital expects to treat the same number of inpatients for DRG 127 during the next fiscal year. Use the data in Table 20-1 to calculate the anticipated reimbursement amount for DRG 127.
   a. $947,600
   b. $954,200
   c. $1,136,400
   d. $2,854,600

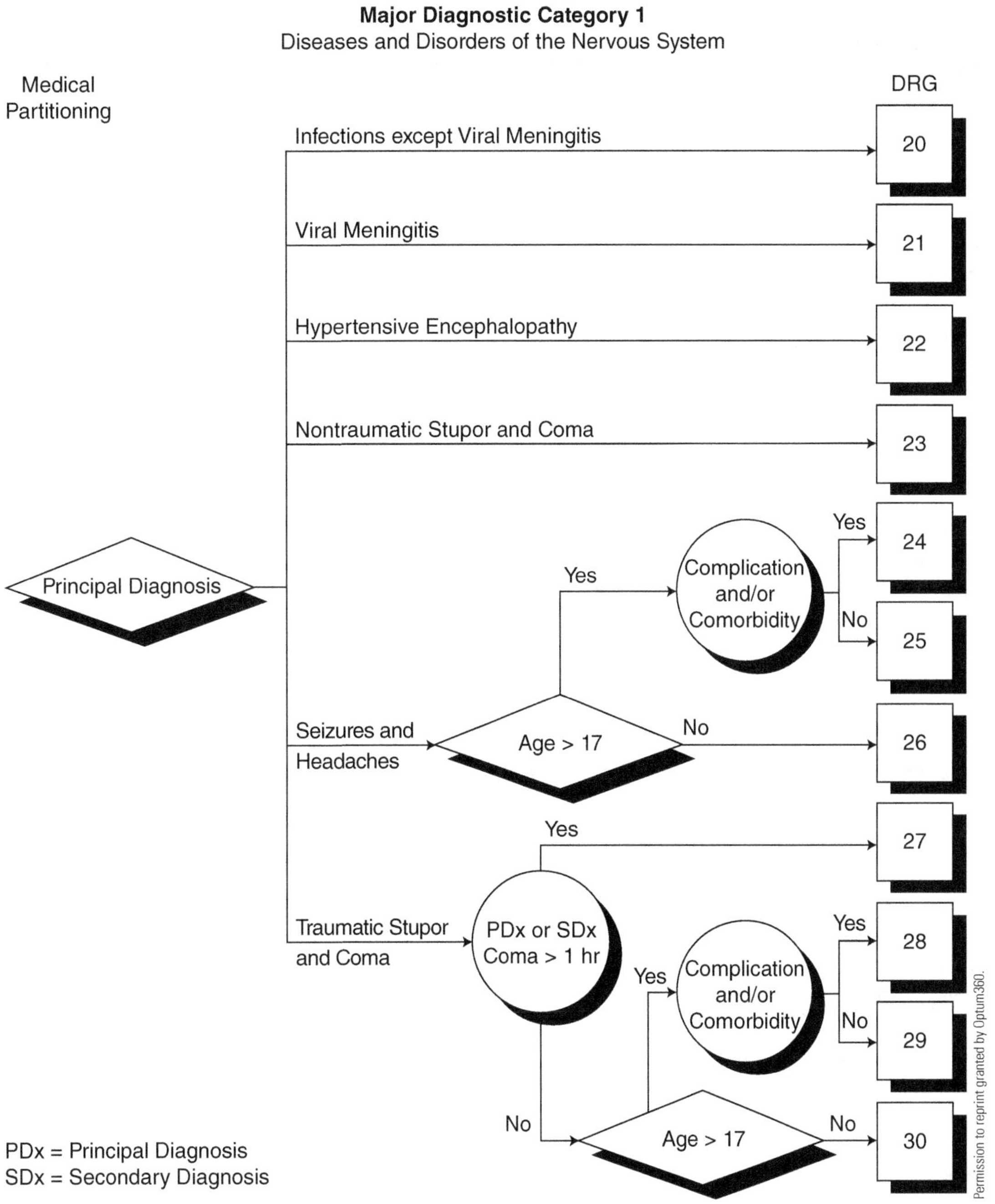

FIGURE 20-6 **Major diagnostic category 1 (diseases and disorders of the nervous system) DRG decision tree**

10. Locate West Lake Hospital's average cost to care for a patient assigned to DRG 127 (Table 20-1) and compare it to the average DRG reimbursement amount. If the hospital admits 200 patients next year who are assigned to DRG 127, the hospital will ___________.
    a. break even
    b. increase revenue
    c. show a profit
    d. take a loss

TABLE 20-1 Data for DRG 127 and DRG 089 from CMS MedPar File

West Lake Hospital, West Lake, US 12345				
Diagnosis-Related Group (DRG)	Average Length of Stay (days)	Average Actual Charges[1]	Average DRG Reimbursement Amount[2]	Average Cost[3]
127—Heart failure and shock	5.32	$14,273	$4,738	$5,682
089—Pneumonia and pleurisy age > 17 with complication and/or comorbidities	5.92	$14,003	$4,771	$5,623

[1]"Average actual charges" is based on what the hospital charges for inpatient services. (Think of this as retail charges.)
[2]"Average DRG reimbursement amount" is the actual payment the hospital received from the payer (e.g., Medicare) for inpatient services.
[3]"Average cost" is based on what it cost the hospital to provide inpatient services. (Think of this as wholesale costs.)

Courtesy of the Centers for Medicare & Medicaid Services, www.cms.gov

11. Compare the PAR and nonPAR fees located in Table 20-2. Upon review, it is noted that the ___________.
    a. fees are all the same for PAR and nonPAR
    b. limiting charge is less than the PAR fee
    c. nonPAR fee is greater than the PAR fee
    d. PAR fee is greater than the nonPAR fee

TABLE 20-2 Medicare Physician Fee Schedule (MPFS) for CPT Codes

CPT E/M Code	Participating Provider (PAR) Fee[1]	Nonparticipating Provider (nonPAR) Fee[2]	Limiting Charge[3]
99211	$26.34	$25.02	$28.77
99212	$45.18	$42.92	$49.36
99213	$63.10	$59.95	$68.94
99214	$97.91	$93.01	$106.96
99215	$142.12	$135.01	$155.26

[1]A participating provider (PAR) accepts as payment in full whatever Medicare reimburses for services provided.
[2]A nonparticipating provider (nonPAR) does not accept as payment in full whatever Medicare reimburses for services provided and is subject to limiting charges.
[3]The nonPAR's "limiting charge" is calculated by reducing the PAR fee by 5 percent and then multiplying it by 15 percent; the patient is responsible for paying the nonPAR whatever Medicare did not reimburse for services provided up to the limiting charge.

Courtesy of the Centers for Medicare & Medicaid Services, www.cms.gov

12. Dr. Williams, a nonparticipating provider, is updating his superbill for the upcoming year. For CPT codes 99213 and 99214, Dr. Williams plans to charge $75 and $125, respectively. As a coding specialist, you advise Dr. Williams that the updated charges are ___________ when compared to the Table 20-2 fee schedule amounts for PAR and nonPAR providers.
    a. less than limiting charges
    b. less than PAR fees
    c. too high
    d. too low
13. Upon review of the data in Table 20-3, the average cost for CPT Radiology code 72193 is ___________ the average payment.
    a. greater than
    b. higher than
    c. lower than
    d. the same as

TABLE 20-3 Data for Radiology CPT Codes 74160 and 72193

CPT Code	CPT Code Description	Total Reimbursement Received	Average Charge	Average Cost	Average Payment	National Average Charge
74160	CT scan abdomen; with contrast	$2,756,296	$1,227	$200	$610	$1,144
72193	CT scan, pelvis; with contrast	$2,534,030	$1,306	$214	$653	$1,084

14. CPT radiology code 74160 (Table 20-3) has ____________.
    a. greater average costs than national average charges
    b. higher average payments than average costs
    c. lower total reimbursement received than code 72193
    d. the same national average charge as code 72193

15. Dr. Jones owns a home health agency with three other physicians; the agency is called Greenville Home Health Care. Dr. Jones is also on the emergency room staff at Mingo Valley Hospital. During the past 12 months, Dr. Jones has referred 150 patients to Greenville Home Health Care for home care. Of this group of 150 patients, 76 were Medicare recipients. Dr. Jones's practice of referring Medicare patients to Greenville Home Health Care is a violation of the ____________ legislation.
    a. ERISA
    b. HIPAA
    c. Stark I
    d. Stark II

16. A coding professional is employed at a local hospital where she codes medical records from a recent inpatient discharge day. Two patients in the group of records were diagnosed with pneumonia. The sputum culture results are inconclusive for the specific organism or type of pneumonia, so the coder reports a code for "pneumonia, unspecified" on each claim. DRG payment was $4,500 for each patient. Upon review, a coding consultant firm hired by the hospital changes the codes to "pneumonia due to *Klebsiella pneumoniae*" (even though there is no documentation of *Klebsiella pneumoniae* as having caused either patient's pneumonia). DRG payment increased to $9,500 for each patient. Which HIPAA provision was violated as a result of the change in the code?
    a. Abuse
    b. Fraud
    c. Privacy
    d. Security

17. A 65-year-old patient presents to the outpatient surgical suite for a bilateral cystourethroscopy. The CPT codes reported on the claim are 52290 and 53020. The code descriptors are as follows:

    ```
    52290 Cystourethroscopy; with ureteral meatotomy, unilateral or bilateral
    53020 Meatotomy, cutting of meatus (separate procedure); except infant
    ```

    Upon review by the payer, only code 52290 was allowed. The original incorrect coding of the case violates which HIPAA provision?
    a. Abuse
    b. Fraud
    c. Privacy
    d. Security

18. A physician office releases the names and addresses of patients recently diagnosed with depression to a pharmaceutical representative, who sends each patient an informational flyer about a new antidepressive drug along with a coupon for $5 off a new prescription. This action would be considered a violation of which HIPAA provision?
    a. Abuse
    b. Fraud
    c. Privacy
    d. Security

19. A patient was seen in the emergency department (ED) of a local medical center with the admitting diagnosis of hip pain and laceration of forehead. This patient had been involved in a motor vehicle crash immediately prior to the visit to the ED, and repair of the forehead laceration was done in the ED. The patient was then admitted to the medical center for further workup. After study, it is determined that the patient had a fracture of the neck of the femur, which was reduced by surgery during the hospital stay. While recovering from his surgery, the patient suffered an acute myocardial infarction (AMI). The patient was discharged to a rehabilitation facility five days after admission. When this patient's case is coded, it is grouped to DRG 468 (extensive operating room procedure unrelated to the principal diagnosis), which has a relative weight of 3.9472 and an average length of stay of 13.2 days. The principal diagnosis on this case was incorrectly designated as acute myocardial infarction. The correct principal diagnosis based on UHDDS guidelines should have been fracture of neck of femur, which would have caused the case to be grouped to DRG 236, defined as "fractures of hip and pelvis." DRG 236 has a relative weight of 0.7544 and an average length of stay of 4.7 days. The financial impact of this claim is that the hospital would be reimbursed a(n):
    a. higher rate for DRG 236.
    b. identical rate for DRGs 468 and 236.
    c. lower rate for DRG 236.
    d. lower rate for DRG 468.
20. HIPAA established standard code sets to be used for electronic data interchange (EDI). Which would be in compliance with HIPAA for reporting of medical services?
    a. A hospital pharmacy reports NDC codes for inpatient and outpatient drug transactions.
    b. A hospital reports ICD-10-CM/PCS codes for outpatient diagnoses and procedures and services.
    c. A hospital reports ICD-10-CM/PCS codes for inpatient diagnoses and procedures.
    d. A physician reports ICD-10-CM codes for office diagnoses and procedures and services.

APPENDIX

A

Ambulatory Surgery Unit Coding Cases (ASUCase001–010)

INSTRUCTIONS

Enter ICD-10-CM and CPT/HCPCS level II codes (and modifiers) in the "Codes" column on the Ambulatory Surgery Face Sheet. Before coding ambulatory surgery unit cases, review the definitions listed below.

- **Admission diagnosis:** Condition assigned to the patient upon admission to the facility (e.g., hospital outpatient department or ambulatory surgery center); coded according to ICD-10-CM.
- **First-listed diagnosis:** Condition treated or investigated during the relevant episode of care; coded according to ICD-10-CM. **NOTE:** When there is no definitive diagnosis, the first-listed diagnosis is the main symptom, abnormal finding, or problem.
- **Secondary diagnosis:** Condition(s) that coexist during the relevant episode of care and that affect the treatment provided to the patient; coded according to ICD-10-CM. **NOTE:** Assign ICD-10-CM codes to secondary diagnoses only if one or more of the following are documented in the patient's record: clinical evaluation of the condition, therapeutic treatment of the condition, and diagnostic procedures performed to evaluate the condition.
- **First-listed procedure:** Procedure that has the highest payment associated with it; coded according to CPT and HCPCS level II. **NOTE:** Do not confuse *first-listed procedure* with *principal procedure*.
- **Secondary procedure:** Procedure(s) that are less complex than the first-listed procedure; coded according to CPT and HCPCS level II. Third-party payers usually discount payment of secondary procedures by 50 percent.

NOTE:

A secondary procedure that does not add significant time or complexity to the patient's care or is considered an integral part of the first-listed procedure is called an *incidental procedure*. Examples include an incidental appendectomy, lysis of adhesions, and scar revision. When an incidental procedure is performed, payers reimburse for the first-listed procedure and no payment is made for the incidental procedure (even if assigned a CPT or HCPCS level II code).

NOTE:

ASUCase009 does not contain an operative report. There is enough information in the other reports in that record to assign diagnosis and procedure codes.

ASUCase001

Global Care Medical Center
100 Main St, Alfred NY 14802
(607) 555-1234

Ambulatory Surgery Face Sheet

PATIENT INFORMATION:

NAME:	WINGATE, Samantha	**PATIENT NUMBER:**	ASUCase001
ADDRESS:	535 S Main St	**DATE OF BIRTH:**	02-15-YYYY
CITY:	Belmont	**AGE:**	52
STATE:	NY	**GENDER:**	Female
ZIP CODE:	14813	**ORGAN DONOR:**	Yes
TELEPHONE:	585-555-2222	**DATE OF ADMISSION:**	02-20-YYYY

ADMITTING INFORMATION:

SURGEON:	Martin Hande, M.D.	**SERVICE:**	Neurosurgery
PRIMARY CARE PROVIDER:	Sandra Homacker, M.D.	**FINANCIAL CLASS:**	Workers' Compensation (WC)

		CODES
ADMITTING DIAGNOSIS:	Right carpal tunnel syndrome	
FIRST-LISTED DIAGNOSIS:	Right carpel tunnel syndrome	
SECONDARY DIAGNOSES:	Flexor tenosynovitis of palm and wrist	
FIRST-LISTED PROCEDURE:	Decompression of right carpal tunnel	
SECONDARY PROCEDURES:		

SURGEON'S SIGNATURE Reviewed and Approved: Martin Hande MD ATP-B-S:02:1001261385: Martin Hande MD (Signed: 2/20/YYYY 2:20:44 PM EST)

Global Care Medical Center
100 Main St, Alfred NY 14802
(607) 555-1234

Consent for Operation(s) and/or Procedure(s) and Anesthesia

PERMISSION. I hereby authorize Dr. Martin Hande, M.D., or associates of his/her choice at the Global Care Medical Center (the "Hospital") to perform upon Samantha Wingate the following operation(s) and/or procedure(s): Decompression or right carpal tunnel, epineurolysis of median nerve and individual motor branch decompression. Multiple flexor tenosynovectomies of palm and wrist, including such photography, videotaping, televising or other observation of the operation(s)/procedure(s) as may be purposeful for the advance of medical knowledge and/or education, with the understanding that the patient's identity will remain anonymous.

EXPLANATION OF PROCEDURE, RISKS, BENEFITS, ALTERNATIVES. Dr. Martin Hande, M.D. has fully explained to me the nature and purposes of the operation(s)/procedures named above and has also informed me of expected benefits and complications, attendant discomforts and risks that may arise, as well as possible alternatives to the proposed treatment. I have been given an opportunity to ask questions and all my questions have been answered fully and satisfactorily.

UNFORESEEN CONDITIONS. I understand that during the course of the operation(s) or procedure(s), unforeseen conditions may arise which necessitate procedures in addition to or different from those contemplated. I, therefore, consent to the performance of additional operations and procedures which the above named physician or his/her associates or assistants may consider necessary.

ANESTHESIA. I further consent to the administration of such anesthesia as may be considered necessary by the above-named physician or his/her associates or assistants. I recognize that there are always risks to life and health associated with anesthesia. Such risks have been fully explained to me and I have been given an opportunity to ask questions and all my questions have been answered fully and satisfactorily.

SPECIMENS. Any organs or tissues surgically removed may be examined and retained by the Hospital for medical, scientific or educational purposes and such tissues or parts may be disposed of in accordance with accustomed practice and applicable Stale laws and/or regulations.

NO GUARANTEES. I acknowledge that no guarantees or assurances have been made to me concerning the operations(s) or procedure(s) described above.

MEDICAL DEVICE TRACKING. I hereby authorize the release of my Social Security number to the manufacturer of the medical device(s) I receive, if applicable, in accordance with federal law and regulations which may be used to help locate me if a need arises with regard to this medical device. I release The Global Care Medical Center from any liability that might result from the release of this information.*

UNDERSTANDING OF THIS FORM. I confirm that I have read this form, fully understand its contents, and that all blank spaces above have been completed prior to my signing. I have crossed out any paragraphs above that do not pertain to me.

	Signature	Print Name
Patient /Relative/Guardian*	*Samantha Wingate*	Samantha Wingate
Relationship, if other than patient signed:		
Witness:		
Date:	02-20-YYYY	

*The signature of the patient must be obtained unless the patient is an unemancipated minor under the age of 18 or is otherwise incompetent to sign.

PHYSICIAN'S CERTIFICATION. I hereby certify that I have explained the nature, purpose, benefits, risks of and alternatives to the operation(s)/procedure(s), have offered to answer any questions and have fully answered all such questions. I believe that the patient (relative/guardian) fully understands what I have explained and answered.

PHYSICIAN: Reviewed and Approved: Martin Hande MD ATP-B-S:02:1001261385: Martin Hande MD (Signed: 2/20/YYYY 2:20:44 PM EST)

Signature

Global Care Medical Center
100 Main St, Alfred NY 14802
(607) 555-1234

Ambulatory Surgery Operative Report

PATIENT INFORMATION:

NAME:	WINGATE, Samantha	**PATIENT NUMBER:**	ASUCase001
DATE OF SURGERY:	02-20-YYYY	**SURGEON:**	Martin Hande, M.D.

PREOPERATIVE DIAGNOSIS: Right carpal tunnel syndrome.

POSTOPERATIVE DIAGNOSIS: Same, plus flexor tenosynovitis of the palm and wrist.

PROCEDURES: Decompression of the right carpal tunnel.

OPERATIVE PROCEDURES AND PATHOLOGICAL FINDINGS:

This white female has had bilateral carpal tunnel syndrome, slightly greater on the left than on the right for an undetermined period of time. The patient is deaf. She also had bilateral thumb arthritis. It was elected not to address the latter problem at the present time. She had quite classic symptoms without any history of any rheumatoid type arthritis. Nerve conduction studies showed significant prolongation of the median nerve conduction times on both sides. She also had bilateral thenar atrophy. Her more symptomatic left side was done in June. At surgery, multiple flexor tenosynovitis was found. She underwent resection of the tenosynovitis along with carpal tunnel decompression. Pathology report did not show a rheumatoid etiology for the tenosynovitis. Plan was to decompress her right side today. She has full extension of her fingers and possibly a slight diminution in flexion related to some degenerative arthritis.

DESCRIPTION OF PROCEDURE:

Under satisfactory right IV block, prep and drape was performed. Using 4½ loupe magnification, standard incision was made, which was carried down through the superficial palmar fascia. One proximal crossing branch of the median palmar cutaneous nerve was identified and preserved. Battery operated cautery was utilized to control some small bleeding points. The superficial palmar fascia and then the transverse carpal ligament were divided in a distal to proximal direction. The distal wrist fascia was decompressed. Inspection of the canal revealed a quite large median nerve with a subligamentous motor branch going into a tight hiatus. This was decompressed. Further inspection of the canal revealed a picture reminiscent of the left side. Most of the flexor tendons were involved in the tenosynovitis. Systematic flexor tenosynovectomy was then performed down to the level of the lumbrical, removing the tenosynovium. Two of the deep flexors, namely those to the ring and little fingers, had some area of tendon erosions on them. These were excised. This involved the small portion of the tendon and in no way weakened it. The incision was extended 4 to 5 cm to allow some removal of additional tenosynovium in the wrist. After completing this, the median nerve was reinspected. There was a moderate hourglass deformity and a longitudinal epineurolysis was performed on the ulnar border. The wound was then thoroughly irrigated with saline. The skin was closed with interrupted 4-0 nylon suture. A Xeroform bulky gauze dressing was applied along with a volar splint out to the PIP joints, putting the wrist in a neutral position. The tourniquet was released. Tourniquet time was a little over one hour. There was good color in the fingers. The patient tolerated the procedure quite well and was sent to the ASU for recovery.

SURGEON'S SIGNATURE
MH: MAG
DD: 2-20-YYYY DT: 2-20-YYYY

Reviewed and Approved: Martin Hande Black MD ATP-B-S:02:1001261385: Martin Hande MD (Signed: 2/20/YYYY 2:20:44 PM EST)
Martin Hande, M.D.

Global Care Medical Center
100 Main St, Alfred NY 14802
(607) 555-1234

Ambulatory Surgery Pathology Report

PATIENT INFORMATION:

NAME:	WINGATE, Samantha	**PATIENT NUMBER:**	ASUCase001
DATE:	02-20-YYYY	**DATE OF SURGERY:**	02-20-YYYY
PATHOLOGIST:	Peter Frank, M.D.	**SURGEON:**	Martin Hande, M.D.

CLINICAL DIAGNOSIS AND HISTORY:

Carpal tunnel syndrome. No history of rheumatoid arthritis.

TISSUE(S) SUBMITTED:

SYNOVIUM, right hand.

GROSS DESCRIPTION:

Specimen is received in fixative and consists of multiple yellow-tan, rubbery, irregular connective tissue fragments, 4 × 2 × 1 cm in aggregate.

MICROSCOPIC DESCRIPTION:

1 microscopic slide examined.

DIAGNOSIS:

Chronic inflammation and fibrosis, tenosynovium, clinically, right hand.

PATHOLOGIST'S SIGNATURE:
PF : ygc

Reviewed and Approved: Peter Frank MD ATP-B-S:02:1001261385:
Peter Frank MD (Signed: 2/20/YYYY 2:20:44 PM EST)

DD: 2-20-YYYY DT: 2-20-YYYY **Peter Frank, M.D.**

ASUCase002

Global Care Medical Center
100 Main St, Alfred NY 14802
(607) 555-1234

Ambulatory Surgery Face Sheet

PATIENT INFORMATION:

NAME:	FLINTSTONE, Wilma	**PATIENT NUMBER:**	ASUCase002
ADDRESS:	124 W. East Avenue	**DATE OF BIRTH:**	02-13-YYYY
CITY:	Hornell	**AGE:**	23
STATE:	NY	**GENDER:**	Female
ZIP CODE:	14843	**ORGAN DONOR:**	No
TELEPHONE:	555-555-0486	**DATE OF ADMISSION:**	07-24-YYYY

ADMITTING INFORMATION:

SURGEON:	Frank Bowser, M.D.	**SERVICE:**	Gynecology
PRIMARY CARE PROVIDER:	Curtis Herrneckar, M.D.	**FINANCIAL CLASS:**	Blue Cross (BC)

		CODES
ADMITTING DIAGNOSIS:	Mild cervical dysplasia	
FIRST-LISTED DIAGNOSIS:	Mild cervical dysplasia	
SECONDARY DIAGNOSES:	Right vaginal cyst	
FIRST-LISTED PROCEDURE:	Laser vaporization (cauterization) ablation of cervix	
SECONDARY PROCEDURES:	Excision of vaginal wall cyst	

SURGEON'S SIGNATURE Reviewed and Approved: Frank Bowser MD ATP-B-S:02:1001261385: Frank Bowser MD (Signed: 7/24/YYYY 2:20:44 PM EST)

Global Care Medical Center
100 Main St, Alfred NY 14802
(607) 555-1234

Consent for Operation(s) and/or Procedure(s) and Anesthesia

PERMISSION. I hereby authorize Dr. Frank Bowser, M.D., or associates of his/her choice at the Global Care Medical Center (the "Hospital") to perform upon Wilma Flintstone

the following operation(s) and/or procedure(s): Laser vaporization cone

Drainage of vaginal cyst; Brush vaporization of cervix

including such photography, videotaping, televising or other observation of the operation(s)/procedure(s) as may be purposeful for the advance of medical knowledge and/or education, with the understanding that the patient's identity will remain anonymous.

EXPLANATION OF PROCEDURE, RISKS, BENEFITS, ALTERNATIVES. Dr. Frank Bowser, M.D.

has fully explained to me the nature and purposes of the operation(s)/procedures named above and has also informed me of expected benefits and complications, attendant discomforts and risks that may arise, as well as possible alternatives to the proposed treatment. I have been given an opportunity to ask questions and all my questions have been answered fully and satisfactorily.

UNFORESEEN CONDITIONS. I understand that during the course of the operation(s) or procedure(s), unforeseen conditions may arise which necessitate procedures in addition to or different from those contemplated. I, therefore, consent to the performance of additional operations and procedures which the above-named physician or his/her associates or assistants may consider necessary.

ANESTHESIA. I further consent to the administration of such anesthesia as may be considered necessary by the above-named physician or his/her associates or assistants. I recognize that there are always risks to life and health associated with anesthesia. Such risks have been fully explained to me and I have been given an opportunity to ask questions and all my questions have been answered fully and satisfactorily.

SPECIMENS. Any organs or tissues surgically removed may be examined and retained by the Hospital for medical, scientific or educational purposes and such tissues or parts may be disposed of in accordance with accustomed practice and applicable State laws and/ or regulations.

NO GUARANTEES. I acknowledge that no guarantees or assurances have been made to me concerning the operation(s) or procedure(s) described above.

MEDICAL DEVICE TRACKING. I hereby authorize the release of my Social Security number to the manufacturer of the medical device(s) I receive, if applicable, in accordance with federal law and regulations which may be used to help locate me if a need arises with regard to this medical device. I release The Global Care Medical Center from any liability that might result from the release of this information.*

UNDERSTANDING OF THIS FORM. I confirm that I have read this form, fully understand its contents, and that all blank spaces above have been completed prior to my signing. I have crossed out any paragraphs above that do not pertain to me.

Patient /Relative/Guardian*: *Wilma Flintstone* (Signature) — Wilma Flintstone (Print Name)

Relationship, if other than patient signed: ____________

Witness: ____________ (Signature) ____________ (Print Name)

Date: 07-24-YYYY

*The signature of the patient must be obtained unless the patient is an unemancipated minor under the age of 18 or is otherwise incompetent to sign.

PHYSICIAN'S CERTIFICATION. I hereby certify that I have explained the nature, purpose, benefits, risks of and alternatives to the operation(s)/ procedure(s), have offered to answer any questions and have fully answered all such questions. I believe that the patient (relative/guardian) fully understands what I have explained and answered.

PHYSICIAN: Reviewed and Approved: Frank Bowser MD ATP-B-S:02:1001261385: Frank Bowser MD (Signed: 7/24/YYYY 2:20:44 PM EST)

Signature

Global Care Medical Center
100 Main St, Alfred NY 14802
(607) 555-1234

Ambulatory Surgery Operative Report

PATIENT INFORMATION:

NAME:	FLINTSTONE, Wilma	**PATIENT NUMBER:**	ASUCase002
DATE OF SURGERY:	07-24-YYYY		
SURGEON:	Frank Bowser, M.D.	**ASSISTANT SURGEON:**	Nurse

PREOPERATIVE DIAGNOSIS: Cervical dysplasia and right vaginal wall cyst.

POSTOPERATIVE DIAGNOSIS: Cervical dysplasia and right vaginal wall cyst.

PROCEDURES: Cervical laser ablation; excision of vaginal wall cyst.

INDICATIONS AND PATHOLOGICAL FINDINGS:

Indications: The patient is a 23-year-old gravida 0 who had a Pap smear in April YYYY showing slight dysplasia. She had a colposcopy on June 2, YYYY, with biopsy showing extensive lesion with slight dysplasia. She was also noted to have a large right vaginal wall cyst, cultures of which were negative.

Findings: Examination under anesthesia revealed a right vaginal wall cyst measuring 3 × 5 cm, uterus was within normal limits, adnexa was normal, and no masses were palpated. Findings also included cervical dysplasia and sebaceous right vaginal wall cyst.

DESCRIPTION OF PROCEDURE:

The patient was taken to the operating room and placed in the dorsal lithotomy position and general anesthesia was induced. The perineum was prepped. Examination under anesthesia revealed the above findings. A speculum was placed in the vagina. Cervix and right vaginal wall were well visualized. A 3 mm incision was made at the center of the vaginal cyst using electrocautery. The incision was extended using blade and stretched with a Crile. A thick sebaceous mucoid substance oozed from the cyst. The remainder of the contents of the cyst was expressed using a Kelly and fingers.

Then 3% acetic acid was placed on the cervix. An area of dysplasia 1 cm around the cervical os was noted. Then 14 cc of 1 amp Pitressin and 50 cc of normal saline were injected into the cervix with good hemostasis. The area of cervical dysplasia was ablated 7 cm deep using a CO_2 laser at 40 watts. The rest of the cervix was brushed using a 20 watt CO2 laser. Good hemostasis was noted throughout the procedure. The speculum was then removed from the vagina, anesthesia was reversed, and the patient was taken to the post anesthesia care unit in satisfactory condition. Estimated blood loss was 25 cc. Cultures were sent of the vaginal cyst contents.

SURGEON'S SIGNATURE

Reviewed and Approved: Frank Bowser MD ATP-B-S:02:1001261385: Frank Bowser MD (Signed: 7/24/YYYY 2:20:44 PM EST)

FB: ygc

DD: 7-24-YYYY

Frank Bowser, M.D.

DT: 7-28-YYYY

GLOBAL CARE MEDICAL CENTER
100 Main St, Alfred NY 14802
(607) 555-1234

Ambulatory Surgery Laboratory Data

PATIENT NAME:	FLINTSTONE, Wilma	**PATIENT NUMBER:**	ASUCase002
LOCATION:	ASU	**ASU PHYSICIAN:**	Frank Bowser, M.D.
SPECIMEN COLLECTED:	Blood	**SPECIMEN RECEIVED:**	Blood

Test	Result	Flag	Reference
Glucose	105		**82-115 mg/dl**
BUN	15		**8-25 mg/dl**
Creatinine	1.0		**0.9-1.4 mg/dl**
Sodium	138		**135-145 mmol/L**
Potassium	3.7		**3.6-5.0 mmol/L**
Chloride	101		**99-110 mmol/L**
CO_2	23		**21-31 mmol/L**
Calcium	8.8		**8.6-10.2 mg/dl**
WBC	9.9		**4.5-11.0 thous/UL**
RBC	5.2		**5.2-5.4 mill/UL**
HGB	11.9		**11.7-16.1 g/dl**
HCT	38		**35.0-47.0 %**
Platelets	175		**140-400 thous/UL**
PT	12.0		**11.0-13.0 seconds**

** END OF REPORT **

ASUCase003

Global Care Medical Center
100 Main St, Alfred NY 14802
(607) 555-1234

Ambulatory Surgery Face Sheet

PATIENT INFORMATION:

NAME:	MARTINI, James	**PATIENT NUMBER:**	ASUCase003
ADDRESS:	2 Elm Street	**DATE OF BIRTH:**	08-26-YYYY
CITY:	Norwich	**AGE:**	32
STATE:	WV	**GENDER:**	M
ZIP CODE:	18949	**ORGAN DONOR:**	No
TELEPHONE:	555-555-3942	**DATE OF ADMISSION:**	07-10-YYYY

ADMITTING INFORMATION:

SURGEON:	Absalom Fuse, M.D.	**SERVICE:**	Anesthesiology
PRIMARY CARE PROVIDER:	Henry Pfutter, M.D.	**FINANCIAL CLASS:**	Workers' Compensation (WC)

		CODES
ADMITTING DIAGNOSIS:	Right L3-L4 radiculopathy	
FIRST-LISTED DIAGNOSIS:	Right L3-L4 radiculopathy	
SECONDARY DIAGNOSIS:	Myofascial pain, right lower lumbar paraspinal muscles	
FIRST-LISTED PROCEDURE:	Epidural (caudal) therapeutic block	
SECONDARY PROCEDURES:		

SURGEON'S SIGNATURE Reviewed and Approved: Absalom Fuse MD ATP-B-S:02:1001261385: Absalom Fuse MD (Signed: 7/10/YYYY 2:20:44 PM EST)

Global Care Medical Center
100 Main St, Alfred NY 14802
(607) 555-1234

Consent for Operation(s) and/or Procedure(s) and Anesthesia

PERMISSION. I hereby authorize Dr. Absalom Fuse, M.D., or associates of his/her choice at the Global Care Medical Center (the "Hospital") to perform upon James Martini the following operation(s) and/or procedure(s): Epidural (caudal) therapeutic block

including such photography, videotaping, televising or other observation of the operation(s)/procedure(s) as may be purposeful for the advance of medical knowledge and/or education, with the understanding that the patient's identity will remain anonymous.

EXPLANATION OF PROCEDURE, RISKS, BENEFITS, ALTERNATIVES. Dr. Absalom Fuse, M.D. has fully explained to me the nature and purposes of the operation(s)/procedures named above and has also informed me of expected benefits and complications, attendant discomforts and risks that may arise, as well as possible alternatives to the proposed treatment. I have been given an opportunity to ask questions and all my questions have been answered fully and satisfactorily.

UNFORESEEN CONDITIONS. I understand that during the course of the operation(s) or procedure(s), unforeseen conditions may arise which necessitate procedures in addition to or different from those contemplated. I, therefore, consent to the performance of additional operations and procedures which the above-named physician or his/her associates or assistants may consider necessary.

ANESTHESIA. I further consent to the administration of such anesthesia as may be considered necessary by the above-named physician or his/her associates or assistants. I recognize that there are always risks to life and health associated with anesthesia. Such risks have been fully explained to me and I have been given an opportunity to ask questions and all my questions have been answered fully and satisfactorily.

SPECIMENS. Any organs or tissues surgically removed may be examined and retained by the Hospital for medical, scientific or educational purposes and such tissues or parts may be disposed of in accordance with accustomed practice and applicable State laws and/or regulations.

NO GUARANTEES. I acknowledge that no guarantees or assurances have been made to me concerning the operation(s) or procedure(s) described above.

MEDICAL DEVICE TRACKING. I hereby authorize the release of my Social Security number to the manufacturer of the medical device(s) I receive, if applicable, in accordance with federal law and regulations which may be used to help locate me if a need arises with regard to this medical device. I release The Global Care Medical Center from any liability that might result from the release of this information.*

UNDERSTANDING OF THIS FORM. I confirm that I have read this form, fully understand its contents, and that all blank spaces above have been completed prior to my signing. I have crossed out any paragraphs above that do not pertain to me.

Patient/Relative/Guardian*: *James Martini* (Signature) — James Martini (Print Name)

Relationship, if other than patient signed: ______

Witness: ______ (Signature) ______ (Print Name)

Date: 07-10-YYYY

*The signature of the patient must be obtained unless the patient is an unemancipated minor under the age of 18 or is otherwise incompetent to sign.

PHYSICIAN'S CERTIFICATION. I hereby certify that I have explained the nature, purpose, benefits, risks of and alternatives to the operation(s)/procedure(s), have offered to answer any questions and have fully answered all such questions. I believe that the patient (relative/guardian) fully understands what I have explained and answered.

PHYSICIAN: Reviewed and Approved: Absalom Fuse MD ATP-B-S:02:1001261385: Absalom Fuse MD (Signed: 7/10/YYYY 2:20:44 PM EST)

Signature

Global Care Medical Center
100 Main St, Alfred NY 14802
(607) 555-1234

Ambulatory Surgery Progress Notes

NAME:	MARTINI, James	**PATIENT NUMBER:**	ASUCase003
DATE OF BIRTH:	08-26-YYYY	**DATE OF ADMISSION:**	07-10-YYYY

DATE	**Progress Note:**
07-10-YYYY	Patient injured his lower back lifting a patient on May 15 of this past year and diagnosed with right L3-L4 radiculopathy, with secondary myofascial pain in the right lower lumbar paraspinal muscles. He was treated with physical therapy, pain medication, and a TENS unit. Patient states that he still experiences occasional pain even after this treatment. Previous lumbar myelogram showed mild spinal stenosis at L4-L5 and a CT of the lumbar spine showed mild to moderate acquired spinal stenosis at L4-L5. Patient was prepped and epidural (caudal) therapeutic block administered at L4-L5. The procedure was well tolerated, and the patient was discharged from recovery in satisfactory condition to follow up in the office next week. He was instructed to do no lifting the first week post-procedure, and is restricted to no more than 25 pounds thereafter.

SURGEON'S SIGNATURE Reviewed and Approved: Absalom Fuse MD ATP-B-S:02:1001261385: Absalom Fuse MD (Signed: 7/10/YYYY 2:20:44 PM EST)

ASUCase004

Global Care Medical Center
100 Main St, Alfred NY 14802
(607) 555-1234

Ambulatory Surgery Face Sheet

PATIENT INFORMATION:

NAME:	JUNE, April Mae	**PATIENT NUMBER:**	ASUCase004
ADDRESS:	1930 Washington Street	**DATE OF BIRTH:**	06-15-YYYY
CITY:	Androsa	**AGE:**	28
STATE:	VA	**GENDER:**	Female
ZIP CODE:	18038	**ORGAN DONOR:**	No
TELEPHONE:	555-555-3908	**DATE OF ADMISSION:**	07-24-YYYY

ADMITTING INFORMATION:

SURGEON:	Frank Bowser, M.D.	**SERVICE:**	Gynecology
PRIMARY CARE PROVIDER:	Henrietta Davis, M.D.	**FINANCIAL CLASS:**	Blue Cross (BC)

		CODES
ADMITTING DIAGNOSIS:	Chronic pelvic pain	
FIRST-LISTED DIAGNOSIS:	Primary infertility	
SECONDARY DIAGNOSIS:	Chronic pelvic pain	
FIRST-LISTED PROCEDURE:	Diagnostic laparoscopy	
SECONDARY PROCEDURES:		

SURGEON'S SIGNATURE Reviewed and Approved: Frank Bowser MD ATP-B-S:02:1001261385: Frank Bowser MD (Signed: 7/24/YYYY 2:20:44 PM EST)

Global Care Medical Center
100 Main St, Alfred NY 14802
(607) 555-1234

Consent for Operation(s) and/or Procedure(s) and Anesthesia

PERMISSION. I hereby authorize Dr. Frank Bowser, M.D., or associates of his/her choice at the Global Care Medical Center (the "Hospital") to perform upon. April Mae June

the following operation(s) and/or procedure(s): diagnostic laparoscopy

including such photography, videotaping, televising or other observation of the operation(s)/procedure(s) as may be purposeful for the advance of medical knowledge and/or education, with the understanding that the patient's identity will remain anonymous.

EXPLANATION OF PROCEDURE, RISKS, BENEFITS, ALTERNATIVES. Dr. Frank Bowser, M.D.

has fully explained to me the nature and purposes of the operation(s)/procedures named above and has also informed me of expected benefits and complications, attendant discomforts and risks that may arise, as well as possible alternatives to the proposed treatment. I have been given an opportunity to ask questions and all my questions have been answered fully and satisfactorily.

UNFORESEEN CONDITIONS. I understand that during the course of the operation(s) or procedure(s), unforeseen conditions may arise which necessitate procedures in addition to or different from those contemplated. I, therefore, consent to the performance of additional operations and procedures which the above-named physician or his/her associates or assistants may consider necessary.

ANESTHESIA. I further consent to the administration of such anesthesia as may be considered necessary by the above-named physician or his/her associates or assistants. I recognize that there are always risks to life and health associated with anesthesia. Such risks have been fully explained to me and I have been given an opportunity to ask questions and all my questions have been answered fully and satisfactorily.

SPECIMENS. Any organs or tissues surgically removed may be examined and retained by the Hospital for medical, scientific or educational purposes and such tissues or parts may be disposed of in accordance with accustomed practice and applicable State laws and/or regulations.

NO GUARANTEES. I acknowledge that no guarantees or assurances have been made to me concerning the operation(s) or procedure(s) described above.

MEDICAL DEVICE TRACKING. I hereby authorize the release of my Social Security number to the manufacturer of the medical device(s) I receive, if applicable, in accordance with federal law and regulations which may be used to help locate me if a need arises with regard to this medical device. I release The Global Care Medical Center from any liability that might result from the release of this information.*

UNDERSTANDING OF THIS FORM. I confirm that I have read this form, fully understand its contents, and that all blank spaces above have been completed prior to my signing. I have crossed out any paragraphs above that do not pertain to me.

Patient/Relative/Guardian* *April Mae June* (Signature) April Mae June (Print Name)

Relationship, if other than patient signed: ______________________

Witness: ______________ (Signature) ______________ (Print Name)

Date: 07-24-YYYY

*The signature of the patient must be obtained unless the patient is an unemancipated minor under the age of 18 or is otherwise incompetent to sign.

PHYSICIAN'S CERTIFICATION. I hereby certify that I have explained the nature, purpose, benefits, risks of and alternatives to the operation(s)/ procedure(s), have offered to answer any questions and have fully answered all such questions. I believe that the patient (relative/ guardian) fully understands what I have explained and answered.

PHYSICIAN: Reviewed and Approved: Frank Bowser MD ATP-B-S:02:1001261385:
Frank Bowser MD (Signed: 7/24/YYYY 2:20:44 PM EST)

Signature

Global Care Medical Center
100 Main St, Alfred NY 14802
(607) 555-1234

Ambulatory Surgery Operative Report

PATIENT INFORMATION:

NAME:	JUNE, April Mae	**PATIENT NUMBER:**	ASUCase004
DATE OF SURGERY:	07-24-YYYY		
SURGEON:	Frank Bowser, M.D.	**ASSISTANT SURGEON:**	Mary Joseph, M.D.

PREOPERATIVE DIAGNOSIS: Chronic pelvic pain, primary infertility

POSTOPERATIVE DIAGNOSIS: Chronic pelvic pain, primary infertility

PROCEDURES: Examination under anesthesia, diagnostic laparoscopy

FINDINGS:

Examination under anesthesia revealed a retroverted uterus which was about 6 weeks size. The left and right adnexa were palpable and felt to be about 5 cm in diameter on both sides. The uterus was not very mobile at all. On examination under laparoscopy, her uterus was smooth and globular and reverted, as well as retroflexed. The left fallopian tube was visualized from the cornua to the fimbriated end and appeared normal. The left ovary was 3×4 cm. The right fallopian tube was also visualized from the cornua to the fimbriated end and appeared to have clubbing but was otherwise normal. The right ovary was 4×5 cm with a cyst evident. She had bilateral patent fallopian tubes. Laparoscopic examination showed her hepatic capsule to be grossly smooth and a slightly dilated gallbladder. The appendix could not be visualized secondary to bowel.

DESCRIPTION OF PROCEDURE:

The patient is brought to the operating room and placed in a dorsal lithotomy position and she was induced under general anesthesia. We then did an examination under anesthesia after emptying the bladder of about 50 cc of clear yellow urine. The cervix was visualized and affixed to a single-tooth tenaculum. We then fixed a Rubin's cannula onto the single-tooth tenaculum on the abdomen in the usual fashion utilizing Betadine and sterile drapes. A small infraumbilical incision was made through which a Veress needle was passed. The abdomen was insufflated with 4 liters of carbon dioxide at 7 to 8 mmHg. The infraumbilical incision was than extended and laparoscopic trocar and sleeve were inserted into the pneumoperitoneum without any problem. Camera with light source was admitted into the abdomen under direct visualization, and there was no overt trauma. We then placed a secondary suprapubic trocar under direct visualization. A blunt probe was placed into that part and we then did a survey of the abdomen with the above-mentioned findings. We then did a hydrotubation of the uterus with methylene blue in normal saline. There was spillage seen on both fallopian tubes and there was no dilatation noted. At this point, the surgery was terminated and all vaginal instruments, as well as laparoscopic instruments, were removed. The secondary trocar was removed under direct visualization. The incision was then closed with 4-0 Vicryl in a vertical mattress fashion as was the suprapubic incision. The wounds were dressed with Band-Aids, and the patient was brought to the PACU in good condition.

SURGEON'S SIGNATURE

Reviewed and Approved: Frank Bowser MD ATP-B-S:02:1001261385: Frank Bowser MD (Signed: 7/24/YYYY 2:20:44 PM EST)

FB:mag

Frank Bowser, M.D.

DD: 07-24-YYYY DT: 07-24-YYYY

Global Care Medical Center
100 Main St, Alfred NY 14802
(607) 555-1234

Ambulatory Surgery Laboratory Data

PATIENT NAME:	JUNE, April Mae	**PATIENT NUMBER:**	ASUCase004
LOCATION:	ASU	**ASU PHYSICIAN:**	Frank Bowser, M.D.
DATE:	07-24-YYYY	**SPECIMEN:**	Blood

Test	Result	Flag	Reference
Glucose	105		82-115 mg/dl
BUN	15		8-25 mg/dl
Creatinine	1.0		0.9-1.4 mg/dl
Sodium	138		135-145 mmol/L
Potassium	3.7		3.6-5.0 mmol/L
Chloride	101		99-110 mmol/L
CO_2	23		21-31 mmol/L
Calcium	8.8		8.6-10.2 mg/dl
WBC	9.9		4.5-11.0 thous/UL
RBC	5.3		5.2-5.4 mill/UL
HGB	11.9		11.7-16.1 g/dl
HCT	38		35.0-47.0 %
Platelets	175		140-400 thous/UL
PT	12.0		11.0-13.0 seconds

** END OF REPORT **

ASUCase005

Global Care Medical Center
100 Main St, Alfred NY 14802
(607) 555-1234

Ambulatory Surgery Face Sheet

PATIENT INFORMATION:

NAME:	SNOWFLAKE, Suzie	**PATIENT NUMBER:**	ASUCase005
ADDRESS:	5439 Jones Parkway	**DATE OF BIRTH:**	06-04-YYYY
CITY:	Sparrowville	**AGE:**	39
STATE:	WV	**GENDER:**	Female
ZIP CODE:	45685	**ORGAN DONOR:**	N
TELEPHONE:	555-555-0009	**DATE OF ADMISSION:**	07-23-YYYY

ADMITTING INFORMATION:

SURGEON:	Frank Bowser, M.D.	**SERVICE:**	Gynecology
PRIMARY CARE PROVIDER:	Joanne Oaks, M.D.	**FINANCIAL CLASS:**	Blue Cross (BC)

		CODES
ADMITTING DIAGNOSIS:	Sterilization	
FIRST-LISTED DIAGNOSIS:	Desires surgical sterilization	
SECONDARY DIAGNOSES:		
FIRST-LISTED PROCEDURE:	Bilateral tubal ligation with fallopian tube rings	
SECONDARY PROCEDURES:		

SURGEON'S SIGNATURE Reviewed and Approved: Frank Bowser MD ATP-B-S:02:1001261385: Frank Bowser MD (Signed: 7/23/YYYY 2:20:44 PM EST)

Global Care Medical Center
100 Main St, Alfred NY 14802
(607) 555-1234

Consent for Operation(s) and/or Procedure(s) and Anesthesia

PERMISSION. I hereby authorize Dr. Frank Bowser, M.D., or associates of his/her choice at the Global Care Medical Center (the "Hospital") to perform upon Suzie Snowflake the following operation(s) and/or procedure(s): Bilateral tubal ligation with fallopian tube rings including such photography, videotaping, televising or other observation of the operation(s)/procedure(s) as may be purposeful for the advance of medical knowledge and/or education, with the understanding that the patient's identity will remain anonymous.

EXPLANATION OF PROCEDURE, RISKS, BENEFITS, ALTERNATIVES. Dr. Frank Bowser, M.D. has fully explained to me the nature and purposes of the operation(s)/procedures named above and has also informed me of expected benefits and complications, attendant discomforts and risks that may arise, as well as possible alternatives to the proposed treatment. I have been given an opportunity to ask questions and all my questions have been answered fully and satisfactorily.

UNFORESEEN CONDITIONS. I understand that during the course of the operation(s) or procedure(s), unforeseen conditions may arise which necessitate procedures in addition to or different from those contemplated. I, therefore, consent to the performance of additional operations and procedures which the above-named physician or his/her associates or assistants may consider necessary.

ANESTHESIA. I further consent to the administration of such anesthesia as may be considered necessary by the above-named physician or his/her associates or assistants. I recognize that there are always risks to life and health associated with anesthesia. Such risks have been fully explained to me and I have been given an opportunity to ask questions and all my questions have been answered fully and satisfactorily.

SPECIMENS. Any organs or tissues surgically removed may be examined and retained by the Hospital for medical, scientific or educational purposes and such tissues or parts may be disposed of in accordance with accustomed practice and applicable State laws and/or regulations.

NO GUARANTEES. I acknowledge that no guarantees or assurances have been made to me concerning the operation(s) or procedure(s) described above.

MEDICAL DEVICE TRACKING. I hereby authorize the release of my Social Security number to the manufacturer of the medical device(s) I receive, if applicable, in accordance with federal law and regulations which may be used to help locate me if a need arises with regard to this medical device. I release The Global Care Medical Center from any liability that might result from the release of this information.*

UNDERSTANDING OF THIS FORM. I confirm that I have read this form, fully understand its contents, and that all blank spaces above have been completed prior to my signing. I have crossed out any paragraphs above that do not pertain to me.

Patient /Relative/Guardian* *Suzie Snowflake* (Signature) Suzie Snowflake (Print Name)

Relationship, if other than patient signed: ____________________

Witness: ____________________ (Signature) ____________________ (Print Name)

Date: 07-23-YYYY

*The signature of the patient must be obtained unless the patient is an unemancipated minor under the age of 18 or is otherwise incompetent to sign.

PHYSICIAN'S CERTIFICATION. I hereby certify that I have explained the nature, purpose, benefits, risks of and alternatives to the operation(s)/ procedure(s), have offered to answer any questions and have fully answered all such questions. I believe that the patient (relative/guardian) fully understands what I have explained and answered.

PHYSICIAN: Reviewed and Approved: Frank Bowser MD ATP-B-S:02:1001261385: Frank Bowser MD (Signed: 7/23/YYYY 2:20:44 PM EST)

Signature

Global Care Medical Center
100 Main St, Alfred NY 14802
(607) 555-1234

Ambulatory Surgery Operative Report

PATIENT INFORMATION:

NAME:	SNOWFLAKE, Suzie	**PATIENT NUMBER:**	ASUCase005
DATE OF SURGERY:	07-23-YYYY		
SURGEON:	Frank Bowser, M.D.	**ASSISTANT SURGEON:**	Georgia Peach, M.D.

PREOPERATIVE DIAGNOSIS: Desires surgical sterilization.

POSTOPERATIVE DIAGNOSIS: Desires surgical sterilization.

PROCEDURES: Bilateral tubal ligation with fallopian tube rings.

INDICATIONS AND FINDINGS:

Indications: The patient is a 39-year-old female on lithium who is unable to discontinue this medication and does not desire to become pregnant while on the medication. The patient therefore desires surgical sterilization.

Findings: Examination under anesthesia reveals a normal size uterus, anteverted, palpated. A small myoma was palpated on the right side. No other unusual masses were noted. On laparoscopy, normal tubes and ovaries were noted. A pedunculated myoma of approximately 2 to 3 cm in diameter was noted on the right posterior wall of the uterus and a myoma was noted on the left posterior wall.

DESCRIPTION OF PROCEDURE:

The patient is brought into the operating room and placed in the dorsal lithotomy position. After good anesthesia was achieved, the bladder was emptied using a straight catheter and examination under anesthesia was performed which revealed the previously mentioned results of an anteverted uterus of normal size with a myoma noted on the right side. No adnexal masses or other abnormalities were noted. The vaginal vault was prepped with Betadine scrub and solution and rinsed. A pack was placed on the anterior lip of the cervix and a Rubin cannula was introduced into the cervical os. The abdomen was then prepped and draped in the usual sterile manner. A 1.5 cm incision was made subumbilically and the Veress needle was introduced into the incision. CO_2 gas was insufflated into the abdomen. High flow and low pressure were noted. Once adequate pneumoperitoneum was achieved, the Veress needle was removed and a 10 mm trocar was introduced into the incision. The laparoscopic camera was placed in the trocar sheath confirming intra-abdominal position. A second incision was made in the midline approximately 3 fingerbreadths above the pubic symphysis. An 8 mm trocar was introduced through the incision under direct visualization. The fallopian tube ring applicator was introduced through the trocar sheath. Inspection of the abdomen revealed a normal size uterus with pedunculated myoma on the right posterior wall of the uterus and a second myoma was noted on the left posterior side. Normal tubes and ovaries were noted. The fallopian tube rings were placed on the proximal tubes bilaterally without problem. Good blanching of the knuckles was noted. The abdominal instruments were then removed and the incisions were closed with 4-0 Vicryl. The vaginal instruments were removed. Good hemostasis of the cervix was noted when the tenaculum was removed. Anesthesia was reversed, and the patient was transferred to the PACU in satisfactory condition. Estimated blood loss was 10 cc.

SURGEON'S SIGNATURE Reviewed and Approved: Frank Bowser MD ATP-B-S:02:1001261385: Frank Bowser MD (Signed: 7/23/YYYY 2:20:44 PM EST)

FB: mag **Frank Bowser, M.D.**

DD: 07-23-YYYY DT: 07-24-YYYY

Global Care Medical Center
100 Main St, Alfred NY 14802
(607) 555-1234

Ambulatory Surgery Laboratory Data

PATIENT NAME:	SNOWFLAKE, Suzie	**PATIENT NUMBER:**	ASUCase005
LOCATION:	ASU	**ASU PHYSICIAN:**	Frank Bowser, M.D.
DATE:	07-23-YYYY	**SPECIMEN:**	Blood

Test	Result	Flag	Reference
Glucose	105		82-115 mg/dl
BUN	15		8-25 mg/dl
Creatinine	1.0		0.9-1.4 mg/dl
Sodium	138		135-145 mmol/L
Potassium	3.7		3.6-5.0 mmol/L
Chloride	101		99-110 mmol/L
CO_2	23		21-31 mmol/L
Calcium	8.8		8.6-10.2 mg/dl
WBC	9.9		4.5-11.0 thous/UL
RBC	5.3		5.2-5.4 mill/UL
HGB	11.9		11.7-16.1 g/dl
HCT	38		35.0-47.0 %
Platelets	175		140-400 thous/UL
PT	12.0		11.0-13.0 seconds

** END OF REPORT **

ASUCase006

Global Care Medical Center
100 Main St, Alfred NY 14802
(607) 555-1234

Ambulatory Surgery Face Sheet

PATIENT INFORMATION:

NAME:	PELLIZZI, Danielle	**PATIENT NUMBER:**	ASUCase006
ADDRESS:	P.O. Box 1490	**DATE OF BIRTH:**	08-26-YYYY
CITY:	Rochester	**AGE:**	25
STATE:	NY	**GENDER:**	Female
ZIP CODE:	14652	**ORGAN DONOR:**	N
TELEPHONE:	555-555-4584	**DATE OF ADMISSION:**	07-24-YYYY

ADMITTING INFORMATION:

SURGEON:	Frank Bowser, M.D.	**SERVICE:**	Gynecology
FAMILY PHYSICIAN:	Jonathan Johnson, M.D.	**FINANCIAL CLASS:**	Blue Cross (BC)

		CODES
ADMITTING DIAGNOSIS:	Incompetent cervix	
FIRST-LISTED DIAGNOSIS:	Incompetent cervix	
SECONDARY DIAGNOSES:	Pregnancy at 13 weeks	
FIRST-LISTED PROCEDURE:	McDonald suture × 2	
SECONDARY PROCEDURES:		

SURGEON'S SIGNATURE Reviewed and Approved: Frank Bowser MD ATP-B-S:02:1001261385: Frank Bowser MD (Signed: 7/24/YYYY 2:20:44 PM EST)

Global Care Medical Center
100 Main St, Alfred NY 14802
(607) 555-1234

Consent for Operation(s) and/or Procedure(s) and Anesthesia

PERMISSION. I hereby authorize Dr. Frank Bowser, M.D., or associates of his/her choice at the Global Care Medical Center (the "Hospital") to perform upon Danielle Pellizzi

the following operation(s) and/or procedure(s): McDonald suture × 2

including such photography, videotaping, televising or other observation of the operation(s)/procedure(s) as may be purposeful for the advance of medical knowledge and/or education, with the understanding that the patient's identity will remain anonymous.

EXPLANATION OF PROCEDURE, RISKS, BENEFITS, ALTERNATIVES. Dr. Frank Bowser, M.D. has fully explained to me the nature and purposes of the operation(s)/procedures named above and has also informed me of expected benefits and complications, attendant discomforts and risks that may arise, as well as possible alternatives to the proposed treatment. I have been given an opportunity to ask questions and all my questions have been answered fully and satisfactorily.

UNFORESEEN CONDITIONS. I understand that during the course of the operation(s) or procedure(s), unforeseen conditions may arise which necessitate procedures in addition to or different from those contemplated. I, therefore, consent to the performance of additional operations and procedures which the above-named physician or his/her associates or assistants may consider necessary.

ANESTHESIA. I further consent to the administration of such anesthesia as may be considered necessary by the above-named physician or his/her associates or assistants. I recognize that there are always risks to life and health associated with anesthesia. Such risks have been fully explained to me and I have been given an opportunity to ask questions and all my questions have been answered fully and satisfactorily.

SPECIMENS. Any organs or tissues surgically removed may be examined and retained by the Hospital for medical, scientific or educational purposes and such tissues or parts may be disposed of in accordance with accustomed practice and applicable State laws and/or regulations.

NO GUARANTEES. I acknowledge that no guarantees or assurances have been made to me concerning the operation(s) or procedure(s) described above.

MEDICAL DEVICE TRACKING. I hereby authorize the release of my Social Security number to the manufacturer of the medical device(s) I receive, if applicable, in accordance with federal law and regulations which may be used to help locate me if a need arises with regard to this medical device. I release The Global Care Medical Center from any liability that might result from the release of this information.*

UNDERSTANDING OF THIS FORM. I confirm that I have read this form, fully understand its contents, and that all blank spaces above have been completed prior to my signing. I have crossed out any paragraphs above that do not pertain to me.

Patient /Relative/Guardian* *Danielle Pellizzi* (Signature) Danielle Pellizzi (Print Name)

Relationship, if other than patient signed:

Witness: (Signature) (Print Name)

Date: 07-24-YYYY

*The signature of the patient must be obtained unless the patient is an unemancipated minor under the age of 18 or is otherwise incompetent to sign.

PHYSICIAN'S CERTIFICATION. I hereby certify that I have explained the nature, purpose, benefits, risks of and alternatives to the operation(s)/ procedure(s), have offered to answer any questions and have fully answered all such questions. I believe that the patient (relative/ guardian) fully understands what I have explained and answered.

PHYSICIAN: Reviewed and Approved: Frank Bowser MD ATP-B-S:02:1001261385:
Frank Bowser MD (Signed: 7/24/YYYY 2:20:44 PM EST)

Signature

Global Care Medical Center
100 Main St, Alfred NY 14802
(607) 555-1234

Ambulatory Surgery Operative Report

PATIENT INFORMATION:

NAME:	PELLIZZI, Danielle	**PATIENT NUMBER:**	ASUCase006
DATE OF SURGERY:	07-24-YYYY		
SURGEON:	Frank Bowser, M.D.	**ASSISTANT SURGEON:**	Henry Shutt, M.D.

PREOPERATIVE DIAGNOSIS: Cervical incompetence.

POSTOPERATIVE DIAGNOSIS: Cervical incompetence.

PROCEDURES: McDonald suture (cerclage).

INDICATIONS:

The patient is a 25-year-old white female who is at 13 weeks gestation right now with an EDC of February 3, YYYY. She had a history of a 23½ week loss of twins secondary to cervical incompetence. She also has a history of PPD which was positive in 1990 and a one-year history of INH therapy. Because of the cervix having fingertip dilatation now, the decision was made with the patient to go along with cervical cerclage in hopes to salvage the pregnancy.

DESCRIPTION OF PROCEDURE:

The patient was brought to the operating room and placed in a dorsal lithotomy position after epidural anesthetic was placed. The epidural anesthetic then required 3 attempts and after waiting for 45 minutes for the epidural to take effect and finding no vulvar or vaginal relief from discomfort, the decision was made to go onward with a general anesthetic. She required general by mask, and at this point we were able to expose the cervix. The cervix was then grasped with 2 sponge forceps and a 2 Ethibond suture was placed in a McDonald cerclage fashion circumferentially around the cervix. This was done with 2 separate sutures, both being tightened down with multiple knots on the suture. The cervix was closed at the end of the procedure and the end of the suture was cut leaving a good 2-inch length for visualization. The vagina was cleaned up. Blood loss was less than 10 cc. Complications: None. There was a good hemostasis and the patient was then brought to the PACU in good condition.

SURGEON'S SIGNATURE

Reviewed and Approved: Frank Bowser MD ATP-B-S:02:1001261385: Frank Bowser MD (Signed: 7/24/YYYY 2:20:44 PM EST)

Frank Bowser, M.D.

FB:LMB
DD: 07-24-YYYY
DT: 07-29-YYYY

Global Care Medical Center
100 Main St, Alfred NY 14802
(607) 555-1234

Ambulatory Surgery Laboratory Data

PATIENT NAME:	PELLIZZI, Danielle	**PATIENT NUMBER:**	ASUCase006
LOCATION:	ASU	**ASU PHYSICIAN:**	Frank Bowser, M.D.
DATE:	07-24-YYYY	**SPECIMEN:**	Blood

Test	Result	Flag	Reference
Glucose	105		82-115 mg/dl
BUN	15		8-25 mg/dl
Creatinine	1.0		0.9-1.4 mg/dl
Sodium	138		135-145 mmol/L
Potassium	3.7		3.6-5.0 mmol/L
Chloride	101		99-110 mmol/L
CO_2	23		21-31 mmol/L
Calcium	8.8		8.6-10.2 mg/dl
WBC	9.9		4.5-11.0 thous/UL
RBC	5.4		5.2-5.4 mill/UL
HGB	11.9		11.7-16.1 g/dl
HCT	38		35.0-47.0 %
Platelets	175		140-400 thous/UL
PT	12.0		11.0-13.0 seconds

** END OF REPORT **

ASUCase007

Global Care Medical Center
100 Main St, Alfred NY 14802
(607) 555-1234

Ambulatory Surgery Face Sheet

PATIENT INFORMATION:

NAME:	FEENEY, Shirley	**PATIENT NUMBER:**	ASUCase007
ADDRESS:	1 Milwaukee Drive	**DATE OF BIRTH:**	04-13-yyyy
CITY:	Jonesville	**AGE:**	35
STATE:	NY	**GENDER:**	Female
ZIP CODE:	14856	**ORGAN DONOR:**	N
TELEPHONE:	555-555-4300	**DATE OF ADMISSION:**	07-21-YYYY

ADMITTING INFORMATION:

SURGEON:	Frank Bowser, M.D.	**SERVICE:**	Gynecology
PRIMARY CARE PROVIDER:	Ima N. Payne, M.D.	**FINANCIAL CLASS:**	Blue Cross (BC)

		CODES
ADMITTING DIAGNOSIS:	Condyloma acuminata of vulva	
FIRST-LISTED DIAGNOSIS:	Condyloma acuminata of vulva	
SECONDARY DIAGNOSES:		
FIRST-LISTED PROCEDURE:	Vulvectomy, simple (partial)	
SECONDARY PROCEDURES:		

SURGEON'S SIGNATURE Reviewed and Approved: Frank Bowser MD ATP-B-S:02:1001261385: Frank Bowser MD (Signed: 7/21/YYYY 2:20:44 PM EST)

Global Care Medical Center
100 Main St, Alfred NY 14802
(607) 555-1234

Consent for Operation(s) and/or Procedure(s) and Anesthesia

PERMISSION. I hereby authorize Dr. Frank Bowser, M.D., or associates of his/her choice at the Global Care Medical Center (the "Hospital") to perform upon Shirley Feeney

the following operation(s) and/or procedure(s): Vulvectomy, simple (partial)

including such photography, videotaping, televising or other observation of the operation(s)/procedure(s) as may be purposeful for the advance of medical knowledge and/or education, with the understanding that the patient's identity will remain anonymous.

EXPLANATION OF PROCEDURE, RISKS, BENEFITS, ALTERNATIVES. Dr. Frank Bowser, M.D. has fully explained to me the nature and purposes of the operation(s)/procedures named above and has also informed me of expected benefits and complications, attendant discomforts and risks that may arise, as well as possible alternatives to the proposed treatment. I have been given an opportunity to ask questions and all my questions have been answered fully and satisfactorily.

UNFORESEEN CONDITIONS. I understand that during the course of the operation(s) or procedure(s), unforeseen conditions may arise which necessitate procedures in addition to or different from those contemplated. I, therefore, consent to the performance of additional operations and procedures which the above-named physician or his/her associates or assistants may consider necessary.

ANESTHESIA. I further consent to the administration of such anesthesia as may be considered necessary by the above-named physician or his/her associates or assistants. I recognize that there are always risks to life and health associated with anesthesia. Such risks have been fully explained to me and I have been given an opportunity to ask questions and all my questions have been answered fully and satisfactorily.

SPECIMENS. Any organs or tissues surgically removed may be examined and retained by the Hospital for medical, scientific or educational purposes and such tissues or parts may be disposed of in accordance with accustomed practice and applicable State laws and/or regulations.

NO GUARANTEES. I acknowledge that no guarantees or assurances have been made to me concerning the operation(s) or procedure(s) described above.

MEDICAL DEVICE TRACKING. I hereby authorize the release of my Social Security number to the manufacturer of the medical device(s) I receive, if applicable, in accordance with federal law and regulations which may be used to help locate me if a need arises with regard to this medical device. I release The Global Care Medical Center from any liability that might result from the release of this information.*

UNDERSTANDING OF THIS FORM. I confirm that I have read this form, fully understand its contents, and that all blank spaces above have been completed prior to my signing. I have crossed out any paragraphs above that do not pertain to me.

	Signature	Print Name
Patient /Relative/Guardian*	*Shirley Feeney*	Shirley Feeney
Relationship, if other than patient signed:		
Witness:		
Date:	07-21-YYYY	

*The signature of the patient must be obtained unless the patient is an unemancipated minor under the age of 18 or is otherwise incompetent to sign.

PHYSICIAN'S CERTIFICATION. I hereby certify that I have explained the nature, purpose, benefits, risks of and alternatives to the operation(s)/procedure(s), have offered to answer any questions and have fully answered all such questions. I believe that the patient (relative/guardian) fully understands what I have explained and answered.

PHYSICIAN: Reviewed and Approved: Frank Bowser MD ATP-B-S:02:1001261385: Frank Bowser MD (Signed: 7/21/YYYY 2:20:44 PM EST)

Signature

Global Care Medical Center
100 Main St, Alfred NY 14802
(607) 555-1234

Ambulatory Surgery Operative Report

PATIENT INFORMATION:

NAME:	FEENEY, Shirley	**PATIENT NUMBER:**	ASUCase007
DATE OF SURGERY:	07-21-YYYY		
SURGEON:	Frank Bowser, M.D.	**ASSISTANT SURGEON:**	None

PREOPERATIVE DIAGNOSIS: Condyloma acuminata of vulva.

POSTOPERATIVE DIAGNOSIS: Condyloma acuminata of vulva.

PROCEDURES: Vulvectomy, simple (partial)

INDICATIONS:

The patient is a 35-year-old nulligravida admitted for excision of condyloma of the vulva. She had a history of papillomatosis, which were excised in 1988. In May, raised papillomatous lesions were noted extending from the clitoris on the left inferiorly, approximately 2 cm and 0.5 cm wide. Biopsies were obtained which confirmed condyloma and marked dysplasia extending to the lateral margins. The patient was admitted for further excision. Pap smear was negative.

DESCRIPTION OF PROCEDURE:

With the patient in the dorsal lithotomy position, the vagina was prepped and draped in the usual fashion. Acetic acid was applied and the abnormal area of condylomatous changes was easily demarcated. This area was infiltrated, after further prep with Betadine, with 10 cc of 1% Xylocaine. The entire lesion was excised in elliptical fashion with a 5 mm margin on either side. Hemostasis was obtained with the Bovie, and skin edges were approximated with a continuous locked suture of 4-0 Vicryl. Hemostasis was adequate and the patient went to Recovery.

SURGEON'S SIGNATURE

Reviewed and Approved: Frank Bowser MD ATP-B-S:02:1001261385: Frank Bowser MD (Signed: 7/21/YYYY 2:20:44 PM EST)

Frank Bowser, M.D.

FB: ygc

DD: 07-21-YYYY

DT: 07-21-YYYY

Global Care Medical Center
100 Main St, Alfred NY 14802
(607) 555-1234

Ambulatory Surgery Laboratory Data

Patient Name:	FEENEY, Shirley	**Patient Number:**	ASUCase007
Location:	ASU	**ASU Physician:**	Frank Bowser, M.D.
Date:	07-21-YYYY	**Specimen:**	Blood

Test	Result	Flag	Reference
Glucose	105		82-115 mg/dl
BUN	15		8-25 mg/dl
Creatinine	1.0		0.9-1.4 mg/dl
Sodium	138		135-145 mmol/L
Potassium	3.7		3.6-5.0 mmol/L
Chloride	101		99-110 mmol/L
CO_2	23		21-31 mmol/L
Calcium	8.8		8.6-10.2 mg/dl
WBC	9.9		4.5-11.0 thous/UL
RBC	5.4		5.2-5.4 mill/UL
HGB	11.9		11.7-16.1 g/dl
HCT	38		35.0-47.0 %
Platelets	175		140-400 thous/UL
PT	12.0		11.0-13.0 seconds

** END OF REPORT **

ASUCase008

Global Care Medical Center
100 Main St, Alfred NY 14802
(607) 555-1234

Ambulatory Surgery Face Sheet

PATIENT INFORMATION:

NAME:	PITTS, Sally	**PATIENT NUMBER:**	ASUCase008
ADDRESS:	24 Truman Avenue	**DATE OF BIRTH:**	03-15-yyyy
CITY:	Paris	**AGE:**	24
STATE:	NY	**GENDER:**	Female
ZIP CODE:	14753	**ORGAN DONOR:**	N
TELEPHONE:	555-555-9982	**DATE OF ADMISSION:**	07-21-YYYY

ADMITTING INFORMATION:

SURGEON:	Frank Bowser, M.D.	**SERVICE:**	Gynecology
PRIMARY CARE PROVIDER:	Jack Frost, M.D.	**FINANCIAL CLASS:**	Blue Cross (BC)

		CODES
ADMITTING DIAGNOSIS:	Ovarian cyst, left	
FIRST-LISTED DIAGNOSIS:	Left ovarian cyst	
SECONDARY DIAGNOSES:		
FIRST-LISTED PROCEDURE:	Operative laparoscopy with left ovarian cystectomy	
SECONDARY PROCEDURES:		

SURGEON'S SIGNATURE Reviewed and Approved: Frank Bowser MD ATP-B-S:02:1001261385: Frank Bowser MD (Signed: 7/21/YYYY 2:20:44 PM EST)

Global Care Medical Center
100 Main St, Alfred NY 14802
(607) 555-1234

Consent for Operation(s) and/or Procedure(s) and Anesthesia

PERMISSION. I hereby authorize Dr. Frank Bowser, M.D., or associates of his/her choice at the Global Care Medical Center (the "Hospital") to perform upon Sally Pitts

the following operation(s) and/or procedure(s): Operative laparoscopy with left ovarian cystectomy

including such photography, videotaping, televising or other observation of the operation(s)/procedure(s) as may be purposeful for the advance of medical knowledge and/or education, with the understanding that the patient's identity will remain anonymous.

EXPLANATION OF PROCEDURE, RISKS, BENEFITS, ALTERNATIVES. Dr. Frank Bowser, M.D. has fully explained to me the nature and purposes of the operation(s)/procedures named above and has also informed me of expected benefits and complications, attendant discomforts and risks that may arise, as well as possible alternatives to the proposed treatment. I have been given an opportunity to ask questions and all my questions have been answered fully and satisfactorily.

UNFORESEEN CONDITIONS. I understand that during the course of the operation(s) or procedure(s), unforeseen conditions may arise which necessitate procedures in addition to or different from those contemplated. I, therefore, consent to the performance of additional operations and procedures which the above-named physician or his/her associates or assistants may consider necessary.

ANESTHESIA. I further consent to the administration of such anesthesia as may be considered necessary by the above-named physician or his/her associates or assistants. I recognize that there are always risks to life and health associated with anesthesia. Such risks have been fully explained to me and I have been given an opportunity to ask questions and all my questions have been answered fully and satisfactorily.

SPECIMENS. Any organs or tissues surgically removed may be examined and retained by the Hospital for medical, scientific or educational purposes and such tissues or parts may be disposed of in accordance with accustomed practice and applicable State laws and/or regulations.

NO GUARANTEES. I acknowledge that no guarantees or assurances have been made to me concerning the operation(s) or procedure(s) described above.

MEDICAL DEVICE TRACKING. I hereby authorize the release of my Social Security number to the manufacturer of the medical device(s) I receive, if applicable, in accordance with federal law and regulations which may be used to help locate me if a need arises with regard to this medical device. I release The Global Care Medical Center from any liability that might result from the release of this information.*

UNDERSTANDING OF THIS FORM. I confirm that I have read this form, fully understand its contents, and that all blank spaces above have been completed prior to my signing. I have crossed out any paragraphs above that do not pertain to me.

	Signature	Print Name
Patient /Relative/Guardian*	*Sally Pitts*	Sally Pitts
Relationship, if other than patient signed:		
Witness:		
Date:	07-21-YYYY	

*The signature of the patient must be obtained unless the patient is an unemancipated minor under the age of 18 or is otherwise incompetent to sign.

PHYSICIAN'S CERTIFICATION. I hereby certify that I have explained the nature, purpose, benefits, risks of and alternatives to the operation(s)/procedure(s), have offered to answer any questions and have fully answered all such questions. I believe that the patient (relative/guardian) fully understands what I have explained and answered.

PHYSICIAN: Reviewed and Approved: Frank Bowser MD ATP-B-S:02:1001261385: Frank Bowser MD (Signed: 7/21/YYYY 2:20:44 PM EST)

Signature

Global Care Medical Center
100 Main St, Alfred NY 14802
(607) 555-1234

Ambulatory Surgery Operative Report

PATIENT INFORMATION:

NAME:	PITTS, Sally	**PATIENT NUMBER:**	ASUCase008
DATE OF SURGERY:	07-21-YYYY		
SURGEON:	Frank Bowser, M.D.	**ASSISTANT SURGEON:**	Sunny Morning, M.D.

PREOPERATIVE DIAGNOSIS: Persistent left ovarian cyst.

POSTOPERATIVE DIAGNOSIS: Persistent left ovarian cyst.

PROCEDURES: Operative laparoscopy with left ovarian cystectomy.

OPERATIVE PROCEDURES AND PATHOLOGICAL FINDINGS:

Indications: The patient is a 25-year-old white female, gravida 1, para 1, with persistent ovarian cyst throughout her recent pregnancy. On ultrasound the cyst was measured to 6.4 × 5.1 × 4.8 cm. Postpartum the cyst was still present; therefore, laparoscopy was planned.

Findings: Examination under anesthesia revealed a smooth, regular mass in the posterior cul-de-sac and uterus that was anteverted and normal in size. Laparoscopy revealed a normal-appearing right adnexa and uterus; however, the left adnexa was significant for a 6 × 5 cm cyst with a smooth white capsule adjacent to the distal end of the left ovary. The fimbriated end of the tube was adherent along the capsule of the cyst.

DESCRIPTION OF PROCEDURE:

The patient was taken to the operating room and general anesthesia was induced. The patient was placed in the dorsal lithotomy position. The perineum was prepped and bladder catheterized. Examination under anesthesia performed with the above findings noted. Anterior and posterior speculums were placed. The anterior lip of the cervix was grasped with a single-tooth tenaculum. The Rubin cannula was inserted. The abdomen was prepped and draped in sterile fashion. An infraumbilical incision was made and the Veress needle inserted. Abdomen was distended with CO_2. A laparoscopic 10 mm trocar was inserted and intra-abdominal placement was confirmed. A second incision was made suprapubically in the midline and another 10 mm trocar was placed under direct visualization. A probe was inserted and the pelvis and abdomen explored with the above-noted findings. In addition, there was a normal-appearing appendix. A third port was placed in the lower right quadrant with a 5 mm trocar inserted under direct visualization. Using the Babcocks to elevate the left cyst, a needle cyst aspirator was placed into the cyst and approximately 40 cc of clear to serous-appearing fluid was obtained. The cyst was deflated and no abnormalities along the cyst wall were noted. Using a laser on continuous watt, set at 15, a 1.5 cm incision was made along the cyst. The cyst wall was grasped with a grasper and using traction, the cyst wall was pulled in its entirety from the ovary. A 3 mm area of tissue was still adhered to the ovary containing the vessel and this was cauterized using bipolar and lysed. There was no bleeding at the bed of the cyst. The cyst wall was removed and sent to pathology. The pelvis was irrigated with 100 cc normal saline and again good hemostasis was noted. The abdomen was deflated; instruments were removed. The incisions were dosed with buried subcuticular stitches of 4-0 Vicryl. Instruments were removed from the vagina. Anesthesia was reversed and patient was sent to Recovery in satisfactory condition. Estimated blood loss was negligible.

SURGEON'S SIGNATURE
FB: ygc

Reviewed and Approved: Frank Bowser MD ATP-B-S:02:1001261385: Frank Bowser MD (Signed: 7/21/YYYY 2:20:44 PM EST)

DD: 07-21-YYYY DT: 07-23-YYYY **Frank Bowser, M.D.**

Global Care Medical Center
100 Main St, Alfred NY 14802
(607) 555-1234

Ambulatory Surgery Laboratory Data

PATIENT NAME:	PITTS, Sally	**PATIENT NUMBER:**	ASUCase008
LOCATION:	ASU	**ASU PHYSICIAN:**	Frank Bowser, M.D.
DATE:	07-21-YYYY	**SPECIMEN:**	Blood

Test	Result	Flag	Reference
Glucose	105		82-115 mg/dl
BUN	15		8-25 mg/dl
Creatinine	1.0		0.9-1.4 mg/dl
Sodium	138		135-145 mmol/L
Potassium	3.7		3.6-5.0 mmol/L
Chloride	101		99-110 mmol/L
CO_2	23		21-31 mmol/L
Calcium	8.8		8.6-10.2 mg/dl
WBC	9.9		4.5-11.0 thous/UL
RBC	5.3		5.2-5.4 mill/UL
HGB	11.9		11.7-16.1 g/dl
HCT	38		35.0-47.0 %
Platelets	175		140-400 thous/UL
PT	12.0		11.0-13.0 seconds

** END OF REPORT **

ASUCase009

Global Care Medical Center
100 Main St, Alfred NY 14802
(607) 555-1234

Ambulatory Surgery Face Sheet

PATIENT INFORMATION:

NAME:	SPRINGS, Hope	**PATIENT NUMBER:**	ASUCase009
ADDRESS:	90 Washington Street	**DATE OF BIRTH:**	09-23-YYYY
CITY:	West Winfield	**AGE:**	30
STATE:	NY	**GENDER:**	Female
ZIP CODE:	14500	**ORGAN DONOR:**	N
TELEPHONE:	555-555-9999	**DATE OF ADMISSION:**	07-23-YYYY

ADMITTING INFORMATION:

SURGEON:	Rusty Gates, M.D.	**SERVICE:**	Orthopedics
PRIMARY CARE PROVIDER:	Fred Stryker, M.D.	**FINANCIAL CLASS:**	Blue Cross (BC)

		CODES
ADMITTING DIAGNOSIS:	Admission for removal of surgical hip screw (implant)	
FIRST-LISTED DIAGNOSIS:	Admission for removal of surgical hip screw (implant)	
SECONDARY DIAGNOSES:		
FIRST-LISTED PROCEDURE:	Removal of hip screw (implant)	
SECONDARY PROCEDURES:		

SURGEON'S SIGNATURE Reviewed and Approved: Rusty Gates MD ATP-B-S:02:1001261385: Rusty Gates MD (Signed: 7/23/YYYY 2:20:44 PM EST)

Global Care Medical Center
100 Main St, Alfred NY 14802
(607) 555-1234

Consent for Operation(s) and/or Procedure(s) and Anesthesia

PERMISSION. I hereby authorize Dr. Rusty Gates, M.D., or associates of his/her choice at the Global Care Medical Center (the "Hospital") to perform upon Hope Springs the following operation(s) and/or procedure(s): Removal hip screw (implant)

including such photography, videotaping, televising or other observation of the operation(s)/procedure(s) as may be purposeful for the advance of medical knowledge and/or education, with the understanding that the patient's identity will remain anonymous.

EXPLANATION OF PROCEDURE, RISKS, BENEFITS, ALTERNATIVES. Dr. Rusty Gates, M.D. has fully explained to me the nature and purposes of the operation(s)/procedures named above and has also informed me of expected benefits and complications, attendant discomforts and risks that may arise, as well as possible alternatives to the proposed treatment. I have been given an opportunity to ask questions and all my questions have been answered fully and satisfactorily.

UNFORESEEN CONDITIONS. I understand that during the course of the operation(s) or procedure(s), unforeseen conditions may arise which necessitate procedures in addition to or different from those contemplated. I, therefore, consent to the performance of additional operations and procedures which the above-named physician or his/her associates or assistants may consider necessary.

ANESTHESIA. I further consent to the administration of such anesthesia as may be considered necessary by the above-named physician or his/her associates or assistants. I recognize that there are always risks to life and health associated with anesthesia. Such risks have been fully explained to me and I have been given an opportunity to ask questions and all my questions have been answered fully and satisfactorily.

SPECIMENS. Any organs or tissues surgically removed may be examined and retained by the Hospital for medical, scientific or educational purposes and such tissues or parts may be disposed of in accordance with accustomed practice and applicable State laws and/or regulations.

NO GUARANTEES. I acknowledge that no guarantees or assurances have been made to me concerning the operation(s) or procedure(s) described above.

MEDICAL DEVICE TRACKING. I hereby authorize the release of my Social Security number to the manufacturer of the medical device(s) I receive, if applicable, in accordance with federal law and regulations which may be used to help locate me if a need arises with regard to this medical device. I release The Global Care Medical Center from any liability that might result from the release of this information.*

UNDERSTANDING OF THIS FORM. I confirm that I have read this form, fully understand its contents, and that all blank spaces above have been completed prior to my signing. I have crossed out any paragraphs above that do not pertain to me.

Patient/Relative/Guardian*: *Hope Springs* (Signature) — Hope Springs (Print Name)

Relationship, if other than patient signed: ______________________

Witness: ______________ (Signature) — ______________ (Print Name)

Date: 07-23-YYYY

*The signature of the patient must be obtained unless the patient is an unemancipated minor under the age of 18 or is otherwise incompetent to sign.

PHYSICIAN'S CERTIFICATION. I hereby certify that I have explained the nature, purpose, benefits, risks of and alternatives to the operation(s)/procedure(s), have offered to answer any questions and have fully answered all such questions. I believe that the patient (relative/guardian) fully understands what I have explained and answered.

PHYSICIAN: Reviewed and Approved: Rusty Gates MD ATP-B-S:02:1001261385: Rusty Gates MD (Signed: 7/23/YYYY 2:20:44 PM EST)

Signature

Global Care Medical Center
100 Main St, Alfred NY 14802
(607) 555-1234

Ambulatory Surgery Operative Report

PATIENT INFORMATION:

NAME:	SPRINGS, Hope	**PATIENT NUMBER:**	ASUCase009
DATE OF SURGERY:	07-23-YYYY		
SURGEON:	Rusty Gates, M.D.	**ASSISTANT SURGEON:**	Fred Stryker, MD

PREOPERATIVE DIAGNOSIS: Removal of surgical hip screw (implant).

POSTOPERATIVE DIAGNOSIS: Removal of surgical hip screw (implant).

PROCEDURES: Removal of hip screw (implant).

DESCRIPTION OF PROCEDURE:

The patient was taken to the operating room and general anesthesia was administered. The right hip was prepped and draped in the normal sterile manner. An incision was made overlying the site of the implant at the right hip. Deep dissection was carried down to visualize the implant, below the muscle level, within bone. Instruments were used to remove the implant from the bone. All bleeders were identified, cut, clamped, and cauterized. Incision was extended to level of periosteum. Dissection was carried down to level of hip screw, which was identified and removed intact. The screw was sent to pathology for examination. The area was copiously flushed with sterile saline. Periosteal and capsular tissues were approximated with 3-0 Vicryl sutures. Subcutaneous tissues were approximated with 4-0 Vicryl sutures. Skin edges were approximated with 5-0 Prolene. After layer suturing, Steri-strips were applied and incision was covered with Xeroform and copious amounts of fluff and Kling. Anesthesia was reversed and patient was sent to Recovery in satisfactory condition. Estimated blood loss was negligible.

SURGEON'S SIGNATURE
FB:YGC
DD:07-23-YYYY
DT: 07-23-YYYY

Reviewed and Approved: Rusty Gates MD ATP-B-S:02:1001261385: Rusty Gates MD (Signed: 7/21/YYYY 2:20:44 PM EST)
Rusty Gates, M.D.

Global Care Medical Center
100 Main St, Alfred NY 14802
(607) 555-1234

Ambulatory Surgery Pathology Report

PATIENT INFORMATION:

NAME:	SPRINGS, Hope	**PATIENT NUMBER:**	ASUCase009
DATE:	07-25-YYYY	**DATE OF SURGERY:**	07-23-YYYY
PATHOLOGIST:	Peter Frank, M.D.	**SURGEON:**	Rusty Gates, M.D.

CLINICAL DIAGNOSIS AND HISTORY:

S/P right hip osteotomy.

TISSUE(S) SUBMITTED:

Tissue and bone, right hip.

GROSS DESCRIPTION:

Specimen is received in fixative and consists of multiple irregular pieces of bone that are 3.5 × 2 × 1 cm. The largest dense cortical piece is 2.5 × 0.8 × 0.6 cm. Also present is an ellipse of dark gray-black skin, 8 × 0.6 cm. It has a slightly raised, longitudinal, wrinkled scar with dense tissue in the dermis.

MICROSCOPIC DESCRIPTION:

2 microscopic slides examined.

DIAGNOSIS:

Scar of skin, bone with intramedullary fibrosis and degenerated fibrocartilage, clinically right hip area.

PATHOLOGIST'S SIGNATURE

Reviewed and Approved: Peter Frank MD ATP-B-S:02:1001261385: Peter Frank MD (Signed: 7/23/YYYY 2:20:44 PM EST)

Peter Frank, M.D.

PF: ygc

DD: 07-25-YYYY

DT: 07-27-YYYY

Global Care Medical Center
100 Main St, Alfred NY 14802
(607) 555-1234

Ambulatory Surgery Laboratory Data

PATIENT NAME:	SPRINGS, Hope	**PATIENT NUMBER:**	ASUCase009
LOCATION:	ASU	**ASU PHYSICIAN:**	Rusty Gates, M.D.
DATE:	07-23-YYYY	**SPECIMEN:**	Blood

Test	Result	Flag	Reference
Glucose	105		**82-115 mg/dl**
BUN	15		**8-25 mg/dl**
Creatinine	1.0		**0.9-1.4 mg/dl**
Sodium	138		**135-145 mmol/L**
Potassium	3.7		**3.6-5.0 mmol/L**
Chloride	101		**99-110 mmol/L**
CO_2	23		**21-31 mmol/L**
Calcium	8.8		**8.6-10.2 mg/dl**
WBC	9.9		**4.5-11.0 thous/UL**
RBC	5.4		**5.2-5.4 mill/UL**
HGB	11.9		**11.7-16.1 g/dl**
HCT	38		**35.0-47.0 %**
Platelets	175		**140-400 thous/UL**
PT	12.0		**11.0-13.0 seconds**

** END OF REPORT **

ASUCase010

Global Care Medical Center
100 Main St, Alfred NY 14802
(607) 555-1234

Ambulatory Surgery Face Sheet

PATIENT INFORMATION:

NAME:	SNOW, Chrissy	**PATIENT NUMBER:**	ASUCase010
ADDRESS:	5908 Jefferson Road	**DATE OF BIRTH:**	10-22-yyyy
CITY:	Richfield Springs	**AGE:**	39
STATE:	NY	**GENDER:**	Female
ZIP CODE:	13468	**ORGAN DONOR:**	N
TELEPHONE:	555-555-5554	**DATE OF ADMISSION:**	07-23-YYYY

ADMITTING INFORMATION:

SURGEON:	Rusty Gates, M.D.	**SERVICE:**	Orthopedics
PRIMARY CARE PROVIDER:	Charlie Hoffmann, M.D.	**FINANCIAL CLASS:**	Blue Cross (BC)

		CODES
ADMITTING DIAGNOSIS:	Left middle trigger finger (acquired)	
FIRST-LISTED DIAGNOSIS:	Left middle trigger finger (acquired)	
SECONDARY DIAGNOSES:		
FIRST-LISTED PROCEDURE:	Incision of tendon sheath, left middle trigger finger	
SECONDARY PROCEDURES:		

SURGEON'S SIGNATURE Reviewed and Approved: Rusty Gates MD ATP-B-S:02:1001261385: Rusty Gates MD (Signed: 7/23/YYYY 2:20:44 PM EST)

Global Care Medical Center
100 Main St, Alfred NY 14802
(607) 555-1234

Consent for Operation(s) and/or Procedure(s) and Anesthesia

PERMISSION. I hereby authorize Dr. Rusty Gates, M.D., or associates of his/her choice at the Global Care Medical Center (the "Hospital") to perform upon Chrissy Snow

the following operation(s) and/or procedure(s): Tenolysis

the following operation(s) and/or procedure

including such photography, videotaping, televising or other observation of the operation(s)/procedure(s) as may be purposeful for the advance of medical knowledge and/or education, with the understanding that the patient's identity will remain anonymous.

EXPLANATION OF PROCEDURE, RISKS, BENEFITS, ALTERNATIVES. Dr. Rusty Gates, M.D. has fully explained to me the nature and purposes of the operation(s)/procedures named above and has also informed me of expected benefits and complications, attendant discomforts and risks that may arise, as well as possible alternatives to the proposed treatment. I have been given an opportunity to ask questions and all my questions have been answered fully and satisfactorily.

UNFORESEEN CONDITIONS. I understand that during the course of the operation(s) or procedure(s), unforeseen conditions may arise which necessitate procedures in addition to or different from those contemplated. I, therefore, consent to the performance of additional operations and procedures which the above-named physician or his/her associates or assistants may consider necessary.

ANESTHESIA. I further consent to the administration of such anesthesia as may be considered necessary by the above-named physician or his/her associates or assistants. I recognize that there are always risks to life and health associated with anesthesia. Such risks have been fully explained to me and I have been given an opportunity to ask questions and all my questions have been answered fully and satisfactorily.

SPECIMENS. Any organs or tissues surgically removed may be examined and retained by the Hospital for medical, scientific or educational purposes and such tissues or parts may be disposed of in accordance with accustomed practice and applicable State laws and/or regulations.

NO GUARANTEES. I acknowledge that no guarantees or assurances have been made to me concerning the operation(s) or procedure(s) described above.

MEDICAL DEVICE TRACKING. I hereby authorize the release of my Social Security number to the manufacturer of the medical device(s) I receive, if applicable, in accordance with federal law and regulations which may be used to help locate me if a need arises with regard to this medical device. I release The Global Care Medical Center from any liability that might result from the release of this information.*

UNDERSTANDING OF THIS FORM. I confirm that I have read this form, fully understand its contents, and that all blank spaces above have been completed prior to my signing. I have crossed out any paragraphs above that do not pertain to me.

	Signature	Print Name
Patient /Relative/Guardian*	*Chrissy Snow*	Chrissy Snow
Relationship, if other than patient signed:		
Witness:		
Date:	07-23-YYYY	

*The signature of the patient must be obtained unless the patient is an unemancipated minor under the age of 18 or is otherwise incompetent to sign.

PHYSICIAN'S CERTIFICATION. I hereby certify that I have explained the nature, purpose, benefits, risks of and alternatives to the operation(s)/procedure(s), have offered to answer any questions and have fully answered all such questions. I believe that the patient (relative/guardian) fully understands what I have explained and answered.

PHYSICIAN: Reviewed and Approved: Rusty Gates MD ATP-B-S:02:1001261385: Rusty Gates MD (Signed: 7/23/YYYY 2:20:44 PM EST)

Signature

Global Care Medical Center
100 Main St, Alfred NY 14802
(607) 555-1234

Ambulatory Surgery Operative Report

PATIENT INFORMATION:

NAME:	SNOW, Chrissy	**PATIENT NUMBER:**	ASUCase010
DATE OF SURGERY:	07-23-YYYY		
SURGEON:	Rusty Gates, M.D.	**ASSISTANT SURGEON:**	None

PREOPERATIVE DIAGNOSIS: Left middle trigger finger.

POSTOPERATIVE DIAGNOSIS: Left middle trigger finger.

PROCEDURES: Incision of tendon sheath, left middle trigger finger.

DESCRIPTION OF PROCEDURE:

Under satisfactory IV block anesthesia, the patient was prepped and draped in the usual fashion. A transverse incision was made parallel to the distal palmar crease overlying the middle finger and the wound was then deepened by sharp dissection and blunt dissection being very careful to preserve all blood vessels intact and not to disturb the neurovascular bundle. The flexor tendon sheath was identified and divided longitudinally for a distance of approximately 1/5 cm. There was no bow stringing of the flexor tendon following this and there was good gliding motion of the flexor tendon passively without any obstruction. The patient then had closure of the subcutaneous tissue with an interrupted 4-0 plain catgut suture, and the skin was approximated with 3 interrupted 4-0 nylon vertical mattress sutures. Betadine ointment and dry sterile dressing was applied. Bulky hand dressing was applied. The patient, having tolerated the procedure well, had the tourniquet released without any untoward effects and was returned to ASU in satisfactory condition.

SURGEON'S SIGNATURE

Reviewed and Approved: Rusty Gates MD ATP-B-S:02:1001261385: Rusty Gates MD (Signed: 7/23/YYYY 2:20:44 PM EST)

RG: ygc

Rusty Gates, M.D.

DD: 07-23-YYYY

DT: 07-23-YYYY

GLOBAL CARE MEDICAL CENTER
100 Main St, Alfred NY 14802
(607) 555-1234

Ambulatory Surgery Laboratory Data

PATIENT NAME:	SNOW, Chrissy	**PATIENT NUMBER:**	ASUCase010
LOCATION:	ASU	**ASU PHYSICIAN:**	Rusty Gates, M.D.
DATE:	07-23-YYYY	**SPECIMEN:**	Blood

Test	Result	Flag	Reference
Glucose	105		82-115 mg/dl
BUN	15		8-25 mg/dl
Creatinine	1.0		0.9-1.4 mg/dl
Sodium	138		135-145 mmol/L
Potassium	3.7		3.6-5.0 mmol/L
Chloride	101		99-110 mmol/L
CO_2	23		21-31 mmol/L
Calcium	8.8		8.6-10.2 mg/dl
WBC	9.9		4.5-11.0 thous/UL
RBC	5.4		5.2-5.4 mill/UL
HGB	11.9		11.7-16.1 g/dl
HCT	38		35.0-47.0 %
Platelets	175		140-400 thous/UL
PT	12.0		11.0-13.0 seconds

** END OF REPORT **

APPENDIX B

Emergency Department Coding Cases (EDCase001–010)

INSTRUCTIONS

Enter ICD-10-CM and CPT/HCPCS level II codes (and modifiers) in the "ICD Codes" and "CPT/HCPCS Level II Codes" rows on the Emergency Department Record. Before coding emergency department records, review the definitions listed below.

- **Admission diagnosis:** Condition assigned to the patient upon admission to the facility (e.g., hospital outpatient department or ambulatory surgery center); coded according to ICD-10-CM.
- **First-listed diagnosis:** Condition treated or investigated during the relevant episode of care; coded according to ICD-10-CM. **NOTE:** When there is no definitive diagnosis, the first-listed diagnosis is the main symptom, abnormal finding, or problem.
- **Secondary diagnosis:** Condition(s) that coexist during the relevant episode of care and that affect the treatment provided to the patient; coded according to ICD-10-CM. **NOTE:** Assign ICD-10-CM codes to secondary diagnoses only if one or more of the following are documented in the patient's record: clinical evaluation of the condition, therapeutic treatment of the condition, and diagnostic procedures performed to evaluate the condition.
- **First-listed procedure:** Procedure that has the highest payment associated with it; coded according to CPT and HCPCS level II. **NOTE:** Do not confuse *first-listed procedure* with *principal procedure*.
- **Secondary procedure:** Procedure(s) that are less complex than the first-listed procedure; coded according to CPT and HCPCS level II. Third-party payers usually discount payment of secondary procedures by 50 percent.

NOTE:

A secondary procedure that does not add significant time or complexity to the patient's care or is considered an integral part of the first-listed procedure is called an *incidental procedure.* Examples include an incidental appendectomy, lysis of adhesions, and scar revision. When an incidental procedure is performed, payers reimburse for the first-listed procedure and no payment is made for the incidental procedure (even if assigned a CPT or HCPCS level II code).

EDCase001

Global Care Medical Center
100 Main St, Alfred NY 14802
(607) 555-1234

Emergency Department Record

PATIENT INFORMATION:

NAME:	CAMERON, Adam E.	**PATIENT NUMBER:**	EDCase001
ADDRESS:	4 Blue Spruce	**ADMISSION DATE & TIME:**	03-09-YYYY 1610
CITY:	Brockport	**DISCHARGE DATE & TIME:**	03-09-YYYY 1630
STATE:	NY	**CONDITION ON DISCHARGE:**	
ZIP CODE:	14420	☑ Satisfactory	❒ AMA
TELEPHONE:	585-637-2524	❒ Home	❒ DOA
		❒ Inpatient Admission	❒ Code Blue
GENDER:	Male	❒ Transfer to: ___________	❒ Died
DATE OF BIRTH:	05-09-YYYY	☑ Instruction Sheet Given	

NURSING DOCUMENTATION:

ALLERGIES: ☑ No ❒ Yes **EXPLAIN:** No known allergies.

CURRENT MEDICATIONS: ☑ No ❒ Yes **EXPLAIN:** Last tetanus toxoid more than 10 years ago.

BP: 122/80 **P:** 76 **R:** 24 **T:** 98.8

CC:

HPI: Small two-inch puncture wound noted on the lateral aspect below right knee. No drainage noted.

CONDITION: Puncture wound, right lower leg with nail today.

ASSESSMENT: Dr. Beeson cleansed wound with pHisoHex.

SIGNATURE OF NURSE: Reviewed and Approved: Marilyn Hillman RN ATP-B-S:02:1001261385: Marilyn Hillman RN (Signed: 3/9/YYYY 2:20:44 PM EST)

ICD CODES:					
CPT/HCPCS LEVEL II CODES:					

Global Care Medical Center
100 Main St, Alfred NY 14802
(607) 555-1234

Emergency Department Physician Documentation

PATIENT NAME:	CAMERON, Adam E.	**PATIENT NUMBER:**	EDCase001
LOCATION:	Emergency Room	**ED PHYSICIAN:**	Jon W. Beeson, M. D.
DATE OF SERVICE:	03-09-YYYY	**DATE OF BIRTH:**	05-09-YYYY

Physician Notes:

Patient punctured right lateral calf with rusty nail while working in his wood shop at home. Last tetanus over 10 years ago. Small two-inch puncture wound. No erythema, ecchymosis, or peripheral vascular involvement.

DIAGNOSIS: Puncture wound of right calf. Wound cleaned.

Physician Orders:

Tetanus and diphtheria toxoid 0.5 ml administered, IM, left deltoid.

DISCHARGE INSTRUCTIONS: Ice left arm (tetanus injection). Aspirin, 2 tablets, every four hours. Return if signs of infection are noted in calf.

SIGNATURE OF ED PHYSICIAN: Reviewed and Approved: Jon Beeson MD ATP-B-S: 02:1001261385: Jon Beeson MD (Signed: 3/9/YYYY 2:20:44 PM EST)

EDCase002

Global Care Medical Center
100 Main St, Alfred NY 14802
(607) 555-1234

Emergency Department Record

PATIENT INFORMATION:

NAME:	DEEDS, Mary Jean	**PATIENT NUMBER:**	EDCase002
ADDRESS:	57 Carrington Place	**ADMISSION DATE & TIME:**	02-08-YYYY 1230
CITY:	East Rochester	**DISCHARGE DATE & TIME:**	02-08-YYYY 1330
STATE:	NY	**CONDITION ON DISCHARGE:**	
ZIP CODE:	14445	☑ Satisfactory	❒ AMA
TELEPHONE:	585-383-4190	❒ Home	❒ DOA
		❒ Inpatient Admission	❒ Code Blue
GENDER:	Female	❒ Transfer to: ___________	❒ Died
DATE OF BIRTH:	10-19-YYYY	☑ Instruction Sheet Given	

NURSING DOCUMENTATION:

ALLERGIES: ❒ No ❒ Yes **EXPLAIN:**

CURRENT MEDICATIONS: ☑ No ❒ Yes **EXPLAIN:**

BP: **P:** **R:** **T:** 97.4

CC:

HPI:

CONDITION: Laceration, right index finger, on glass. Patient was washing dishes at home, and she dropped a glass and cut her finger.

ASSESSMENT:

SIGNATURE OF NURSE: Reviewed and Approved: Marilyn Hillman RN ATP-B-S:02:1001261385: Marilyn Hillman RN (Signed: 2/8/YYYY 2:20:44 PM EST)

ICD CODES:					
CPT/HCPCS LEVEL II CODES:					

Global Care Medical Center
100 Main St, Alfred NY 14802
(607) 555-1234

Emergency Department Physician Documentation

PATIENT NAME:	DEEDS, Mary Jean	**PATIENT NUMBER:**	EDCase002
LOCATION:	Emergency Room	**ED PHYSICIAN:**	Jon W. Beeson, M. D.
DATE OF SERVICE:	02-08-YYYY	**DATE OF BIRTH:**	10-19-YYYY

Physician Notes:

Four months pregnant. Patient was washing dishes at home and dropped a glass and cut her finger. Examination of the right index finger revealed 4 cm circular, flapped laceration over the right proximal phalanx. There was no tendon injury.

Patient was advised about possibility of devitalization of flap and possible requirement for plastic graft.

Wound approximated with 4-0 silk stitches, #6. Tetanus and diphtheria booster. Penicillin 250 mg poqid × 7 days.

DIAGNOSIS: Laceration, right index finger.

Physician Orders:

Tetanus and diphtheria toxoid administered IM in right deltoid at 13:20.

DISCHARGE INSTRUCTIONS: Keep wound dry and check closely.

SIGNATURE OF ED PHYSICIAN: Reviewed and Approved: Jon Beeson MD ATP-B-S: 02:1001261385: Jon Beeson MD (Signed: 2/8/YYYY 2:20:44 PM EST)

EDCase003

Global Care Medical Center
100 Main St, Alfred NY 14802
(607) 555-1234

Emergency Department Record

PATIENT INFORMATION:

NAME:	ZONE, Paula R.	**PATIENT NUMBER:**	EDCase003
ADDRESS:	36 Ryan Road	**ADMISSION DATE & TIME:**	08-09-YYYY 2005
CITY:	Webster	**DISCHARGE DATE & TIME:**	08-09-YYYY 2103
STATE:	NY	**CONDITION ON DISCHARGE:**	
ZIP CODE:	14580	☑ Satisfactory	❐ AMA
TELEPHONE:	585-342-0990	❐ Home	❐ DOA
		❐ Inpatient Admission	❐ Code Blue
GENDER:	Female	❐ Transfer to: ___________	❐ Died
DATE OF BIRTH:	09-10-YYYY	☑ Instruction Sheet Given	

NURSING DOCUMENTATION:

ALLERGIES: ☑ No ❐ Yes **EXPLAIN:** NKA

CURRENT MEDICATIONS: ☑ No ❐ Yes **EXPLAIN:**

BP: 100/70 **P:** 108 **R:** 16 **T:** 99

CC:

HPI:

CONDITION: Laceration, flexor carpi ulnaris tendon, right wrist (at home) on glass.

ASSESSMENT: Bleeding controlled. Two larger lacerations, right wrist.

SIGNATURE OF NURSE: Reviewed and Approved: Marilyn Hillman RN ATP-B-S:02:1001261385: Marilyn Hillman RN (Signed: 8/9/YYYY 2:20:44 PM EST)

ICD CODES:					
CPT/HCPCS LEVEL II CODES:					

Global Care Medical Center
100 Main St, Alfred NY 14802
(607) 555-1234

Emergency Department Physician Documentation

PATIENT NAME:	ZONE, Paula R.	**PATIENT NUMBER:**	EDCase003
LOCATION:	Emergency Room	**ED PHYSICIAN:**	Jon W. Beeson, M. D.
DATE OF SERVICE:	08-09-YYYY	**DATE OF BIRTH:**	09-10-YYYY

Physician Notes:

Patient is a 35-year-old female who stuck her right hand through a glass window at home, sustaining several lacerations particularly about the right wrist.

A 4 centimeter lacerated flexor carpi ulnaris tendon, right, was noted upon further evaluation. It was repaired with a figure-of-eight 3-0 Vicryl suture, and skin was closed with interrupted 4-0 Prolene.

Dry sterile dressings were applied, the wrist was splinted with a plastic splint, and the patient was administered a tetanus and diphtheria toxoid booster. She was started on ampicillin for four days as prophylaxis against infection. She is to return on Thursday for a dressing change.

Diagnosis: Laceration, flexor carpi ulnaris tendon, 4 centimeters.

Physician Orders:

1/2 cubic centimeter tetanus and diphtheria toxoid, IM, right deltoid.

Discharge instructions: Return Thursday for dressing change.

SIGNATURE OF ED PHYSICIAN: Reviewed and Approved: Jon Beeson MD ATP-B-S:02:1001261385: Jon Beeson MD (Signed: 8/9/YYYY 2:20:44 PM EST)

Jon W. Beeson, M.D.

EDCase004

Global Care Medical Center
100 Main St, Alfred NY 14802
(607) 555-1234

Emergency Department Record

PATIENT INFORMATION:

NAME:	GOODRICH, Lyle	**PATIENT NUMBER:**	EDCase004
ADDRESS:	645 Beverly Drive	**ADMISSION DATE & TIME:**	08-10-YYYY 1820
CITY:	Victor	**DISCHARGE DATE & TIME:**	08-10-YYYY 1930
STATE:	NY	**CONDITION ON DISCHARGE:**	
ZIP CODE:	14564	☑ Satisfactory	☐ AMA
TELEPHONE:	585-924-1221	☐ Home	☐ DOA
		☐ Inpatient Admission	☐ Code Blue
GENDER:	Male	☑ Transfer to: Victor ER	☐ Died
DATE OF BIRTH:	08-30-YYYY	☑ Instruction Sheet Given	

NURSING DOCUMENTATION:

ALLERGIES: ☐ No ☑ Yes **EXPLAIN:**

CURRENT MEDICATIONS: ☑ No ☐ Yes **EXPLAIN:** Last tetanus. > 5 years

BP: 120/80 **P:** 88 **R:** 20 **T:**

CC:

HPI: LOC – ambulating well – alert & oriented. Laceration under eyelid.

CONDITION: Broomstick by L eye.

ASSESSMENT: Dr. Beeson spoke with Dr. Tyson in Victor. Dr. Tyson will meet with patient in Victor ER. Vision OD 20/30-1

SIGNATURE OF NURSE: Reviewed and Approved: Donna Smith RN ATP-B-S:02:1001261385: Donna Smith RN (Signed: 8/10/YYYY 2:20:44 PM EST)

ICD CODES:					
CPT/HCPCS LEVEL II CODES:					

Global Care Medical Center
100 Main St, Alfred NY 14802
(607) 555-1234

Emergency Department Physician Documentation

PATIENT NAME:	GOODRICH, Lyle	**PATIENT NUMBER:**	EDCase004
LOCATION:	Emergency Room	**ED PHYSICIAN:**	Jon W. Beeson, M. D.
DATE OF SERVICE:	08-10-YYYY	**DATE OF BIRTH:**	08-30-YYYY

Physician Notes:

S: Patient is an 18-year-old white male who had the end of a broomstick jammed into his eye while horsing around at home with his younger brother. The patient arrived in the ED with a laceration of the lower lid and blurred vision.

O: The patient has a 3 cm laceration which begins at the medial canthus, extending through the tear duct there, circling beneath the lower lid and then re-entering laterally and extending down through the lid margin inferiorly to a point where it disappears. Pupils are equal, round and reactive to light; extraocular muscles are intact. Vision in that eye is 20/60. He normally has 20/20 vision. There is slight steaminess of the anterior chamber and funduscopic exam does not visualize the optic disc or cup due to a hazy, diffuse and blurred redness through the ophthalmoscope. This may represent bleeding in the posterior chamber. There is no foreign body and no bleeding at present. There is no reason to suspect a fracture of the supraorbital or infraorbital rim at this point.

A: Laceration, left lower eyelid; possible posterior chamber hyphema.

P: Dr. Tyson was called and suggested we send the patient down to his office right away. Tetanus and diphtheria toxoid 0.5 cc administered IM, left deltoid.

Physician Orders:

Tetanus and diphtheria toxoid, 0.5 cc, left deltoid (IM).

DISCHARGE INSTRUCTIONS: Transfer to Victor.

SIGNATURE OF ED PHYSICIAN Reviewed and Approved: Jon Beeson MD ATP-B-S: 02:1001261385: Jon Beeson MD (Signed:8/10/YYYY 2:20:44 PM EST)

Jon W. Beeson, M.D.

EDCase005

Global Care Medical Center
100 Main St, Alfred NY 14802
(607) 555-1234

Emergency Department Record

PATIENT INFORMATION:

NAME:	TAYLOR, Lonnie W.	**PATIENT NUMBER:**	EDCase005
ADDRESS:	6278 Mission Road	**ADMISSION DATE & TIME:**	02-08-YYYY 1210
CITY:	Henrietta	**DISCHARGE DATE & TIME:**	02-08-YYYY 1330
STATE:	NY	**CONDITION ON DISCHARGE:**	
ZIP CODE:	14467	☑ Satisfactory	☐ AMA
TELEPHONE:	585-334-8567	☐ Home	☐ DOA
		☐ Inpatient Admission	☐ Code Blue
GENDER:	Male	☐ Transfer to: ___________	☐ Died
DATE OF BIRTH:	04-01-YYYY	☑ Instruction Sheet Given	

NURSING DOCUMENTATION:

ALLERGIES: ☐ No ☐ Yes **EXPLAIN:**

CURRENT MEDICATIONS: ☐ No ☐ Yes **EXPLAIN:**

BP: 180/110 **P:** 72 **R:** 20 **T:** 98.8

CC: Complains of severe pain on movement.

HPI: While driving a snowmobile, the patient states he flew off and landed on his right ribs and right shoulder.

CONDITION:

ASSESSMENT:

SIGNATURE OF NURSE: Reviewed and Approved: Donna Smith RN ATP-B-S:02:1001261385: Donna Smith RN (Signed: 2/8/YYYY 2:20:44 PM EST)

ICD CODES:					
CPT/HCPCS LEVEL II CODES:					

Global Care Medical Center
100 Main St, Alfred NY 14802
(607) 555-1234

Emergency Department Physician Documentation

PATIENT NAME:	TAYLOR, Lonnie W.	**PATIENT NUMBER:**	EDCase005
LOCATION:	Emergency Room	**ED PHYSICIAN:**	Jon W, Beeson, M. D.
DATE OF SERVICE:	02-08-YYYY	**DATE OF BIRTH:**	04-01-YYYY

Physician Notes:

HISTORY: Patient complains of severe pain on movement. He says while he was snowmobiling, he flew off the snowmobile and landed on his right ribs and right shoulder.

EXAMINATION:

GENERAL: Middle-aged white male.

HEAD: Normocephalic.
EENT: Within normal limits.
RIGHT SHOULDER: Pain on abduction of right arm. Positive for deformity over mid-shaft right clavicle.
CHEST: Positive tenderness to palpation on right post ribs.
LUNGS: Clear.

X-RAY, RIGHT CLAVICLE: Fracture, right clavicle shaft. X-RAY, RIBS: Nondisplaced fractures of right second, third and fourth ribs.

TREATMENT: Tylenol #3, q4h prn. Disposition #30. Copy of film to accompany patient. Clavicle brace sling applied.

DIAGNOSIS: Fracture, shaft of right clavicle. Nondisplaced fractures of the right second, third and fourth ribs in the anterior axillary line. Contusion of ribs, right, × 3.

Physician Orders:

X-ray, right shoulder, right clavicle, right ribs × 3.

DISCHARGE INSTRUCTIONS: Brace sling. Follow up with family MD in one wk.

SIGNATURE OF ED PHYSICIAN: Reviewed and Approved: Jon Beeson MD ATP-B-S:02:1001261385: Jon Beeson MD (Signed: 2/8/YYYY 2:20:44 PM EST)

Global Care Medical Center
100 Main St, Alfred NY 14802
(607) 555-1234

Emergency Department Physician Documentation

PATIENT NAME:	TAYLOR, Lonnie W.	**PATIENT NUMBER:**	EDCase005
LOCATION:	Emergency Room	**ED PHYSICIAN:**	Dr. Jon W. Beeson
DATE OF SERVICE:	02-08-YYYY	**DATE OF BIRTH:**	04-01-YYYY

Radiology Report

Reason for exam: snowmobile accident on a snowmobile trail located at a vacation resort.

Technical data: pain axillary (mid.) ribs, rt. Clavicle.

RIGHT SHOULDER: Multiple views reveal the shoulder to be normal.

RIGHT CLAVICLE: Complete x-ray reveals comminuted, essentially nondisplaced fracture of the shaft of the right clavicle.

RIGHT RIBS: Two views reveal essentially nondisplaced fracture of the right second, third and fourth ribs in the anterior axillary line. There is also some thickening of the pleura in this region suggesting associated hemorrhage. The heart and lungs are normal.

SIGNATURE OF RADIOLOGIST **Philip Rogers**

DD: 02-08-YYYY **Philip Rogers, M.D., Radiologist**

DT: 02-09-YYYY

EDCase006

Global Care Medical Center
100 Main St, Alfred NY 14802
(607) 555-1234

Emergency Department Record

PATIENT INFORMATION:

NAME:	GILLISH, Herbert	**PATIENT NUMBER:**	EDCase006
ADDRESS:	7701 Huddlestone Way	**ADMISSION DATE & TIME:**	02-09-YYYY 0120
CITY:	Webster	**DISCHARGE DATE & TIME:**	02-09-YYYY 0230
STATE:	NY	**CONDITION ON DISCHARGE:**	
ZIP CODE:	14580	☑ Satisfactory	☐ AMA
TELEPHONE:	585-670-0231	☐ Home	☐ DOA
		☐ Inpatient Admission	☐ Code Blue
GENDER:	Male	☐ Transfer to: ___________	☐ Died
DATE OF BIRTH:	11-07-YYYY	☑ Instruction Sheet Given	

NURSING DOCUMENTATION:

ALLERGIES: ☑ No ☐ Yes **EXPLAIN:** NKA

CURRENT MEDICATIONS: ☑ No ☐ Yes **EXPLAIN:** NONE

BP: **P:** 88 **R:** 16 **T:** 98

CC:

HPI:

CONDITION: Laceration R knee

ASSESSMENT: 1 1/2 - 2 yrs. last tetanus

SIGNATURE OF NURSE: Reviewed and Approved: Donna Smith RN ATP-B-S:02:1001261385: Donna Smith RN (Signed: 2/9/YYYY 2:20:44 PM EST)

ICD CODES:					

CPT/HCPCS LEVEL II CODES:					

Global Care Medical Center
100 Main St, Alfred NY 14802
(607) 555-1234

Emergency Department Physician Documentation

Patient Name:	GILLISH, Herbert	**Patient Number:**	EDCase006
Location:	Emergency Room	**ED Physician:**	Jon W. Beeson, M. D.
Date of Service:	02-09-YYYY	**Date of Birth:**	11-07-YYYY

Physician Notes:

V-shaped laceration, right knee 1.5 cm × 1.5 cm. Patient states he injured his knee at home when he slipped and fell down his front steps.

Irrigated vigorously with normal saline solution.

8.0 cc 1% Xylocaine administered. Intermediate repair involved placement of #3-4-0 chromic deep suture and #10-3-0 Prolene simple interrupted suture placed. Antibiotic ointment applied. Adaptic, pressure dressing, and Ace wrap applied.

DIAGNOSIS: V-shaped laceration, right knee, 1.5 cm × 1.5 cm.

Physician Orders:

X-ray, right knee. Tetanus and diphtheria, left deltoid, IM. +3 suture.

Signature of ED Physician Reviewed and Approved: Jon Beeson MD ATP-B-S:02:1001261385: Jon Beeson MD (Signed:8/10/YYYY 2:20:44 PM EST)

Global Care Medical Center
100 Main St, Alfred NY 14802
(607) 555-1234

Emergency Department Physician Documentation

PATIENT NAME:	GILLISH, Herbert	**PATIENT NUMBER:**	EDCase006
LOCATION:	Emergency Room	**ED PHYSICIAN:**	Dr. Jon W. Beeson
DATE OF SERVICE:	02-09-YYYY	**DATE OF BIRTH:**	11-07-YYYY

Radiology Report

Reason for exam: Laceration to R knee

Technical data: laceration distal to (anterior) patella. No foreign body.
02-09-YYYY RIGHT KNEE: 3 views reveal no bony abnormality. The joint space is normal.
Conclusion: Normal right knee.

SIGNATURE OF RADIOLOGIST **Philip Rogers**

DD: 02-09-YYYY
DT: 02-10-YYYY

Philip Rogers, M.D., Radiologist

EDCase007

Global Care Medical Center
100 Main St, Alfred NY 14802
(607) 555-1234

Emergency Department Record

PATIENT INFORMATION:

NAME:	JONES, Jason E.	**PATIENT NUMBER:**	EDCase007
ADDRESS:	56 Maple Lane	**ADMISSION DATE & TIME:**	02-09-YYYY 1700
CITY:	Brockport	**DISCHARGE DATE & TIME:**	02-09-YYYY 1740
STATE:	NY	**CONDITION ON DISCHARGE:**	
ZIP CODE:	14420	☑ Satisfactory	☐ AMA
TELEPHONE:	585-637-1010	☐ Home	☐ DOA
		☐ Inpatient Admission	☐ Code Blue
GENDER:	Male	☐ Transfer to: ___________	☐ Died
DATE OF BIRTH:	03-26-YYYY	☑ Instruction Sheet Given	

NURSING DOCUMENTATION:

ALLERGIES: ☐ No ☑ Yes **EXPLAIN:** Penicillin

CURRENT MEDICATIONS: ☑ No ☐ Yes **EXPLAIN:** T.T. w/in 2 years

BP: 170/110 **P:** 80 **R:** 20 **T:** 98.7

CC:

HPI:

CONDITION: Fell on ice Feb 9, lacerated chin.

ASSESSMENT: Small laceration on chin. No LOC. States "stiffness of jaw," Negative for any other injury.

SIGNATURE OF NURSE: Reviewed and Approved: Marilyn Hillman RN ATP-B-S:02:1001261385: Marilyn Hillman RN (Signed: 2/9/YYYY 2:20:44 PM EST)

ICD CODES:					
CPT/HCPCS LEVEL II CODES:					

Global Care Medical Center
100 Main St, Alfred NY 14802
(607) 555-1234

Emergency Department Physician Documentation

PATIENT NAME:	JONES, Jason E.	**PATIENT NUMBER:**	EDCase007
LOCATION:	Emergency Room	**ED PHYSICIAN:**	Jon W. Beeson, M. D.
DATE OF SERVICE:	02-09-YYYY	**DATE OF BIRTH:**	03-26-YYYY

Physician Notes:

This 22-year-old white male slipped on the ice on his driveway at his house and struck his chin against a pipe. He presents now with a laceration on the chin. The patient denies any loss of consciousness but he does have a slight amount of jaw discomfort. With motion, however, he has no pain or tenderness.

Physical exam reveals an alert, cooperative 22-year-old white male with a 1.5 cm jagged laceration on his chin. The patient has full range of motion of the jaw and no discomfort with forced biting on either side. The neck is supple and nontender. The wound was cleaned with Betadine, anesthetized with 1% Carbocaine and irrigated copiously with normal saline. It was closed with five #6-0 nylon sutures.

The patient was instructed to keep the wound clean and dry and to return in four days for suture removal; return sooner if any evidence of infection should occur.

DIAGNOSIS: 1 ½ cm laceration, chin.

Physician Orders:

6-0 nylon sutures.

DISCHARGE INSTRUCTIONS: Keep clean and dry.

SIGNATURE OF ED PHYSICIAN: Reviewed and Approved: Jon Beeson MD ATP-B-S:02:1001261385: Jon Beeson MD (Signed:2/9/YYYY 2:20:44 PM EST)

Jon W. Beeson, M.D.

EDCase008

Global Care Medical Center
100 Main St, Alfred NY 14802
(607) 555-1234

Emergency Department Record

PATIENT INFORMATION:

NAME:	Hauset, Jennifer L.	**PATIENT NUMBER:**	EDCase008
ADDRESS:	2233 Mill Street	**ADMISSION DATE & TIME:**	10-13-YYYY 2350
CITY:	Pittsford	**DISCHARGE DATE & TIME:**	10-14-YYYY 0158
STATE:	NY	**CONDITION ON DISCHARGE:**	
ZIP CODE:	14534	☑ Satisfactory	❒ AMA
TELEPHONE:	585-264-9876	❒ Home	❒ DOA
		❒ Inpatient Admission	❒ Code Blue
GENDER:	Female	❒ Transfer to: ___________	❒ Died
DATE OF BIRTH:	06-27-YYYY	☑ Instruction Sheet Given	

NURSING DOCUMENTATION:

ALLERGIES: ☑ No ❒ Yes **EXPLAIN:**

CURRENT MEDICATIONS: ☑ No ❒ Yes **EXPLAIN:** None. Unsure about tetanus status.

BP: 128/70 **P:** 108 **R:** 28 **T:** 97.4

CC: Scalp lacerations. Headache.

HPI: Pt. was the passenger in a MVA a short time ago. Was wearing a seatbelt. Thinks she may have been unconscious momentarily. Has a 2 inch laceration behind the right ear and a 3 inch laceration in the left parietal area. Also has multiple abrasions on the right forearm and on the dorsal right thigh.

CONDITION: Motor vehicle accident. Lacerations to scalp. Headache.

TREATMENT: Tetanus and diphtheria toxoid administered.

SIGNATURE OF NURSE: Reviewed and Approved: Marilyn Hillman RN ATP-B-S:02:1001261385: Marilyn Hillman RN (Signed: 10/14/YYYY 2:20:44 PM EST)

ICD CODES:					
CPT/HCPCS LEVEL II CODES:					

Global Care Medical Center
100 Main St, Alfred NY 14802
(607) 555-1234

Emergency Department Physician Documentation

PATIENT NAME:	Hauset, Jennifer L.	**PATIENT NUMBER:**	EDCase008
LOCATION:	Emergency Room	**ED PHYSICIAN:**	Preston Treeline, M.D.
DATE OF SERVICE:	10-13-YYYY	**DATE OF BIRTH:**	06-27-YYYY

Physician Notes:

18-year-old involved in a motor vehicle accident as a passenger on Highway 101 and apparently was wearing full seat restraints at the time. The patient was able to crawl out of the car There was no firm history of any loss of consciousness although she apparently was dazed for a minute or two. She remembers all the events surrounding the accident. There is no amnesia, and she is oriented ×3 in the ER. Although there were numerous scrapes and contusions about the extremities, particularly the right arm, and the left leg, there was no evidence of any long bone fractures. There is no tenderness along the c-spine and she had a good range of pain-free motion of the c-spine. She had a laceration bilaterally in the parietal area of the scalp. There was no drainage from the ears. The PERRLA extraocular eye movements are intact. No evidence of any loose teeth and no evidence of any facial bone fractures. No pain on rib compression. Heart NSR, she moved the upper extremities freely and easily through a full range of motion. No evidence of any abdominal injury, and no pain or tenderness on palpation. Compression of the pelvis did not produce any discomfort, no pain along the thoracic or lumbar spine. She had a full range of motion in lower extremities. No nausea or vomiting, denies any headache, although she complains of pain along the laceration. Hair was shaved about the margins of the wounds which were then washed and infiltrated with lidocaine and sutured with interrupted 3-0 Ethilon sutures. Complete skull x-rays were negative for fractures. Patient denies any dizziness. She was ambulatory and walked to the bathroom without difficulty and was allowed to go home with her grandmother with instructions to have the wound checked in 2-3 days, sutures out in 8 days. Head injury sheet was dispensed and she is to return if any of the outlined symptoms should occur.

DIAGNOSIS: Contusion, dorsal right thigh. Abrasion, right forearm. Two lacerations of scalp totaling 12.7 centimeters.

Physician Orders:

Nugauge; extra sutures. Skull x-rays. Small ice packs. Tylenol tabs 325 mg p.o. Tetanus and diphtheria toxoid, left deltoid, IM.

SIGNATURE OF ED PHYSICIAN:

```
Reviewed and Approved: Preston Treeline MD
ATP-B-S: 02:1001261385: Preston Treeline MD
(Signed: 2/9/YYYY 2:20:44 PM EST)
```

Preston Treeline, M.D.

Global Care Medical Center 100 Main St, Alfred NY 14802 (607) 555-1234		**Emergency Department Physician Documentation**	
PATIENT NAME:	Hauset, Jennifer L.	**PATIENT NUMBER:**	EDCase008
LOCATION:	Emergency Room	**ED PHYSICIAN:**	Preston Treeline, M.D.
DATE OF SERVICE:	10-13-YYYY	**DATE OF BIRTH:**	06-27-YYYY

RADIOLOGY REPORT:

Reason for exam: MVA

COMPLETE SKULL X-RAY: Four views of the skull show no evidence of any fractures. Incidentally, the patient has a 2 mm radiopaque density projected over the left angle of the mandible. This could conceivably represent either a stone in the parotid gland or some radiopaque debris on the patient's skin or clothing.

SIGNATURE OF RADIOLOGIST: Reviewed and Approved: Philip Rogers MD ATP-B-S:02:1001261385: Philip Rogers MD (Signed:10/14/YYYY 2:20:44 PM EST)

DD: 10-13-YYYY
DT: 10-14-YYYY

Philip Rogers, M.D., Radiologist

EDCase009

Global Care Medical Center
100 Main St, Alfred NY 14802
(607) 555-1234

Emergency Department Record

PATIENT INFORMATION:

NAME:	UNGER, Betty	**PATIENT NUMBER:**	EDCase009
ADDRESS:	Route 96	**ADMISSION DATE & TIME:**	10-02-YYYY 1645
CITY:	Victor	**DISCHARGE DATE & TIME:**	10-02-YYYY 1721
STATE:	NY	**CONDITION ON DISCHARGE:**	
ZIP CODE:	14564	☑ Satisfactory	❒ AMA
TELEPHONE:	585-924-0123	❒ Home	❒ DOA
		❒ Inpatient Admission	❒ Code Blue
GENDER:	Female	❒ Transfer to: ___________	❒ Died
DATE OF BIRTH:	03-29-YYYY	☑ Instruction Sheet Given	

NURSING DOCUMENTATION:

ALLERGIES: ☑ No ❒ Yes **EXPLAIN:** NKA

CURRENT MEDICATIONS: ☑ No ❒ Yes **EXPLAIN:** None. Last tetanus shot 6-7 years ago.

BP: 124/80 **P:** 88 **R:** 20 **T:** 98.4

CC:

HPI:

CONDITION: 2 lacerations: left arm on exposed furniture nail of couch and right 3rd knuckle on pointed end of a knife while washing dishes, 0900, 10-02-YYYY.

ASSESSMENT: Approximately ¾ - 1" laceration, 3rd knuckle, right hand.
1" laceration, left forearm Occurred 0900 this a.m.

SIGNATURE OF NURSE: Reviewed and Approved: Marilyn Hillman RN ATP-B-S:02:1001261385: Marilyn Hillman RN (Signed: 10/2/YYYY 2:20:44 PM EST)

ICD CODES:					
CPT/HCPCS LEVEL II CODES:					

Global Care Medical Center
100 Main St, Alfred NY 14802
(607) 555-1234

Emergency Department Physician Documentation

PATIENT NAME:	UNGER, Betty	**PATIENT NUMBER:**	EDCase009
LOCATION:	Emergency Room	**ED PHYSICIAN:**	Preston Treeline, M.D.
DATE OF SERVICE:	10-2-YYYY	**DATE OF BIRTH:**	03-29-YYYY

Physician Notes:

S: 23-year-old white female who lacerated her right hand and left forearm in separate incidents at home.

O: Patient has shallow laceration of the right 3rd MP joint. It was closed well with Betadine and infiltrated with 1% Xylocaine and closed with 4-0 silk. She has a 1.5 cm laceration of the left forearm too, which was also cleaned with Betadine and infiltrated with 1 % Xylocaine and closed with 4-0 silk.

A: 1.5 cm laceration (injured on exposed furniture nail of her couch), and 1.5 cm laceration of right third finger (injured on pointed end of a knife while washing dishes in her kitchen).

P: Per infection and suture guidelines.

DIAGNOSIS: Two 1.5 cm lacerations of right third finger and left forearm.

Physician Orders:

SIGNATURE OF ED PHYSICIAN:

```
Reviewed and Approved: Preston Treeline MD
ATP-B-S: 02:1001261385: Preston Treeline MD
(Signed: 10/2/YYYY 2:20:44 PM EST)
```

Preston Treeline, M.D.

EDCase010

Global Care Medical Center
100 Main St, Alfred NY 14802
(607) 555-1234

Emergency Department Record

PATIENT INFORMATION:

NAME:	WASHBURN, Chris	**PATIENT NUMBER:**	EDCase010
ADDRESS:	709 Hawthorne Way	**ADMISSION DATE & TIME:**	10-13-YYYY 1040
CITY:	Henrietta	**DISCHARGE DATE & TIME:**	10-13-YYYY 1110
STATE:	NY	**CONDITION ON DISCHARGE:**	
ZIP CODE:	14467	☑ Satisfactory	☐ AMA
TELEPHONE:	585-334-2265	☐ Home	☐ DOA
		☐ Inpatient Admission	☐ Code Blue
GENDER:	Male	☐ Transfer to: ___________	☐ Died
DATE OF BIRTH:	09-27-YYYY	☑ Instruction Sheet Given	

NURSING DOCUMENTATION:

ALLERGIES: ☑ No ☐ Yes **EXPLAIN:** NKA

CURRENT MEDICATIONS: ☐ No ☑ Yes **EXPLAIN:** Antibiotic

BP: 120/80 **P:** 88 **R:** 18 **T:** 97.4

CC:

HPI:

CONDITION: Recheck laceration, left lower leg. (Patient previously gored by pig on his farm.)

ASSESSMENT: Dressing fell off this morning. Drain also fell out. Continues to have some bloody drainage.

SIGNATURE OF NURSE: Reviewed and Approved: Donna Smith RN ATP-B-S:02:1001261385: Donna Smith RN (Signed: 10/13/YYYY 2:20:44 PM (EST)

ICD CODES:					
CPT/HCPCS LEVEL II CODES:					

Global Care Medical Center
100 Main St, Alfred NY 14802
(607) 555-1234

Emergency Department Physician Documentation

PATIENT NAME:	WASHBURN, Chris	**PATIENT NUMBER:**	EDCase010
LOCATION:	Emergency Room	**ED PHYSICIAN:**	Benjamin Baker, M. D.
DATE OF SERVICE:	10-13-YYYY	**DATE OF BIRTH:**	09-27-YYYY

Physician Notes:

This patient returns for recheck of laceration, left lower leg, because the dressing fell off this morning and the drain fell out at the same time. Patient was seen in the ED last week, and laceration was sutured at that time.

Laceration looks good. Drain removed with dressing. Patient to return in 9 days for suture removal; sooner if any signs of infection develop.

DIAGNOSIS: Recheck laceration.

Physician Orders:

DISCHARGE INSTRUCTIONS: Keep clean and dry.

SIGNATURE OF ED PHYSICIAN: Reviewed and Approved: Benjamin Baker MD ATP-B-S:02:1001261385: Benjamin Baker (Signed: 10/13/YYYY 2:20:44 PM EST)

APPENDIX

C

Physician Office Coding Cases (POCase001–010)

INSTRUCTIONS

Enter ICD-10-CM codes in the "Code" column of the "Diagnosis Information" section and enter CPT/HCPCS level II codes (and modifiers) in the "Code" column of the "Procedure Information" section. Before coding physician office records, review the definitions listed below.

- **Admission diagnosis:** Condition assigned to the patient upon admission to the facility (e.g., hospital outpatient department or ambulatory surgery center); coded according to ICD-10-CM.
- **First-listed diagnosis:** Condition treated or investigated during the relevant episode of care; coded according to ICD-10-CM. **NOTE:** When there is no definitive diagnosis, the first-listed diagnosis is the main symptom, abnormal finding, or problem.
- **Secondary diagnosis:** Condition(s) that coexist during the relevant episode of care and that affect the treatment provided to the patient; coded according to ICD-10-CM. **NOTE:** Assign ICD-10-CM codes to secondary diagnoses only if one or more of the following are documented in the patient's record: clinical evaluation of the condition, therapeutic treatment of the condition, and diagnostic procedures performed to evaluate the condition.
- **First-listed procedure:** Procedure that has the highest payment associated with it; coded according to CPT and HCPCS level II. **NOTE:** Do not confuse *first-listed procedure* with *principal procedure*.
- **Secondary procedure:** Procedure(s) that are less complex than the first-listed procedure; coded according to CPT and HCPCS level II. Third-party payers usually discount payment of secondary procedures by 50 percent.

NOTE:

A secondary procedure that does not add significant time or complexity to the patient's care or is considered an integral part of the first-listed procedure is called an *incidental procedure*. Examples include an incidental appendectomy, lysis of adhesions, and scar revision. When an incidental procedure is performed, payers reimburse for the first-listed procedure and no payment is made for the incidental procedure (even if assigned a CPT or HCPCS level II code).

NOTE:

Each patient in the physician office cases is an *established patient*.

POCase001

Global Care Medical Center
100 Main St, Alfred NY 14802
(607) 555-1234

Physician Office Record

EIN:	12-345678	**NPI:**	987CBA321
BCBS PIN:	GC2222		
BCBS GRP:	1234-P		

Patient Information:

Name:	TIBBS, Carmine	**Patient Number:**	POCase001
Address:	4590 Canyon Road	**Admission Date & Time:**	08-26-YYYY
City:	Hornell	**Primary Insurance Plan:**	BCBS of WNY
State:	NY	**Primary Insurance Plan ID #:**	088674322
Zip Code:	14843	**Secondary Insurance Plan:**	
Telephone:	607-324-1289	**Secondary Insurance Plan ID #:**	
Gender:	Male	**Occupation:**	Machinist
Date of Birth:	07-07-YYYY	**Name of Employer:**	Alstom

Diagnosis Information

	Diagnosis	Code		Diagnosis	Code
1.	Bipolar disorder, manic type		5.		
2.			6.		
3.			7.		
4.			8.		

Procedure Information

	Description of Procedure or Service	Date	Code	Charge
1.	Level 2 E/M visit			
2.				
3.				
4.				
5.				

Special Notes:

Global Care Medical Center
100 Main St, Alfred NY 14802
(607) 555-1234

Physician Office Record

PATIENT NAME:	TIBBS, Carmine	**PATIENT NUMBER:**	POCase008
DATE OF SERVICE:	08-26-YYYY	**DATE OF BIRTH:**	07-07-YYYY

NURSING DOCUMENTATION:

MEDICATIONS ALLERGIES/REACTIONS: **None**

CURRENT MEDICATIONS Lithium 1,500 mg

BP: 130/80 **P:** 84 **R:** **T:** **WT:** 265

CC: Patient states he feels well today. Was seen in outpatient psych today.

PMH: Bipolar disorder, manic type.

NOTES: Veteran here for scheduled appointment. Voices no concerns.

SIGNATURE OF NURSE: Reviewed and Approved: Jeanette Allen RN ATP-B-S:02:1001261385: Jeanette Allen RN (Signed: 8/26/YYYY 2:20:44 PM EST)

PHYSICIAN DOCUMENTATION:

Notes: HISTORY: Patient seen today for regular appointment. He appears relaxed, cooperative, and coherent. No evidence of recurrent manic behavior. He is a 46-year-old, divorced twice, Navy veteran, who served as a machinist mate in non-combat situation. He has been suffering from bipolar disorder, manic type, and takes medication, lithium 1,500 mg a day, which seems effective.

He has been employed at Alstom plant as a machinist for nine years, full time.

Mental Status Exam: He has been doing very well with the current medication. No evidence of memory loss or any psychotic behavior. His affect is appropriate, and mood is stable, insight and judgment are good. He is not considered a danger to himself or others.

DIAGNOSIS: Bipolar disorder, manic type.

PLAN: Continue lithium 1,500 mg a day.

SIGNATURE OF PROVIDER: Reviewed and Approved: Raymond Massey MD ATP-B-S:02:1001261385: Raymond Massey MD (Signed: 8/26/YYYY 2:20:44 PM EST)

Raymond E. Massey, M.D.
Psychiatrist

POCase002

Global Care Medical Center
100 Main St, Alfred NY 14802
(607) 555-1234

EIN: 12-345678
BCBS PIN: GC2222
BCBS GRP: 1234-P

Physician Office Record

NPI: 987CBA321

PATIENT INFORMATION:

NAME:	MAYNARD, Homer	**PATIENT NUMBER:**	POCase002
ADDRESS:	345 Maple Street	**ADMISSION DATE & TIME:**	09-01-YYYY
CITY:	Riverdale	**PRIMARY INSURANCE PLAN:**	Medicare
STATE:	NY	**PRIMARY INSURANCE PLAN ID #:**	455678344A
ZIP CODE:	14882	**SECONDARY INSURANCE PLAN:**	BCBS OF WNY
TELEPHONE:	818-992-7884	**SECONDARY INSURANCE PLAN ID #:**	45567834
GENDER:	Male	**OCCUPATION:**	Retired
DATE OF BIRTH:	11-19-YYYY	**NAME OF EMPLOYER:**	

DIAGNOSIS INFORMATION

Diagnosis	Code	Diagnosis	Code
1. Osteoarthritis		5.	
2. Difficulty walking		6.	
3.		7.	
4.		8.	

PROCEDURE INFORMATION

Description of Procedure or Service	Date	Code	Charge
1. Level 2 E/M visit			
2.			
3.			
4.			
5.			

SPECIAL NOTES:

Global Care Medical Center
100 Main St, Alfred NY 14802
(607) 555-1234

Physician Office Record

Patient Name:	MAYNARD, Homer	**Patient Number:**	POCase002
Date of Service:	09-01-YYYY	**Date of Birth:**	11-19-YYYY

Nursing Documentation:

Medications Allergies/Reactions: **None**

Current Medications: Sertraline

BP: 110/60 **P:** 72 **R:** **T:** 96.7 **WT:** 201

CC: Reports problems with balance.

PMH: Degenerative joint disease.

Notes: Came here for a regular appointment today.

Signature of Nurse: Reviewed and Approved: Jeanette Allen RN ATP-B-S:02:1001261385: Jeanette Allen RN (Signed: 9/1/YYYY 2:20:44 PM EST)

Physician Documentation:

Notes: Patient seen for regular appointment today. He is pleasant, cooperative, and coherent. Reports he is still having some problems with balance. He walks with the cane, which is helpful. He reports that taking regular Tylenol produces the same result as previous medications. We will also add glucosamine chondroitin sulfate to his daily regimen. Follow-up in 3 months, sooner if any new concerns.

DIAGNOSIS: Degenerative joint disease. Difficulty walking.

Signature of Provider: Reviewed and Approved: Raymond Massey MD ATP-B-S:02:1001261385: Raymond Massey MD (Signed: 9/1/YYYY 2:20:44 PM EST)

Raymond E. Massey, M.D.

POCase003

Global Care Medical Center
100 Main St, Alfred NY 14802
(607) 555-1234

EIN: 12-345678
BCBS PIN: GC2222
BCBS GRP: 1234-P

Physician Office Record

NPI: 987CBA321

PATIENT INFORMATION:

NAME:	GLEASON, James	**PATIENT NUMBER:**	POCase003
ADDRESS:	24 Hawthorne Street	**ADMISSION DATE & TIME:**	08-24-YYYY
CITY:	Hornell	**PRIMARY INSURANCE PLAN:**	Medicare
STATE:	NY	**PRIMARY INSURANCE PLAN ID #:**	055152760A
ZIP CODE:	14843	**SECONDARY INSURANCE PLAN:**	GHI Medigap
TELEPHONE:	607-324-1234	**SECONDARY INSURANCE PLAN ID #:**	055152760
GENDER:	Male	**OCCUPATION:**	Retired
DATE OF BIRTH:	01-28-YYYY	**NAME OF EMPLOYER:**	

DIAGNOSIS INFORMATION

Diagnosis	Code	Diagnosis	Code
1. Diabetes mellitus, type 2		5.	
2. Hyperlipidemia		6.	
3.		7.	
4.		8.	

PROCEDURE INFORMATION

Description of Procedure or Service	Date	Code	Charge
1. Level 2 E/M visit			
2.			
3.			
4.			
5.			

SPECIAL NOTES:

Global Care Medical Center
100 Main St, Alfred NY 14802
(607) 555-1234

Physician Office Record

Patient Name:	GLEASON, James	**Patient Number:**	POCase003
Date of Service:	08-24-YYYY	**Date of Birth:**	01-28-YYYY

Nursing Documentation:

Medications Allergies/Reactions: **None**

Current Medications: Glucophage, Lipitor.

BP: 120/78 **P:** 72 **R:** **T:** 96.9 **WT:** 178

CC: Recheck.

PMH: Diabetes mellitus, type 2. Hyperlipidemia.

Notes: Veteran here for scheduled appointment. Voices no concerns.

Signature of Nurse: Reviewed and Approved: Jeanette Allen RN ATP-B-S:02:1001261385: Jeanette Allen RN (Signed: 8/24/YYYY 2:20:44 PM EST)

Physician Documentation:

Notes: This is a 78-year-old white male veteran who is seen for his regular appointment. He has a long-standing history with diabetes mellitus, type 2. His condition has been stable. He used to complain about a sleeping problem, but no longer complains of sleeping problems. He remains stable on Glucophage and was recently prescribed Lipitor for hyperlipidemia, and both were refilled today.

DIAGNOSIS: Diabetes mellitus, type 2, controlled. Hyperlipidemia.

PLAN: Continue medications as prescribed.

Signature of Provider: Reviewed and Approved: Raymond Massey MD ATP-B-S:02:1001261385: Raymond Massey MD (Signed: 8/24/YYYY 2:20:44 PM EST)

Raymond E. Massey, M.D.

POCase004

Global Care Medical Center
100 Main St, Alfred NY 14802
(607) 555-1234

Physician Office Record

EIN:	12-345678
BCBS PIN:	GC2222
BCBS GRP:	1234-P

NPI: 987CBA321

PATIENT INFORMATION:

NAME:	CONSTANTINE, Connie	**PATIENT NUMBER:**	POCase004
ADDRESS:	8989 Wiggley Road	**ADMISSION DATE & TIME:**	08-26-YYYY
CITY:	Hornell	**PRIMARY INSURANCE PLAN:**	GHI
STATE:	NY	**PRIMARY INSURANCE PLAN ID #:**	239095674
ZIP CODE:	14843	**SECONDARY INSURANCE PLAN:**	
TELEPHONE:	607-324-3232	**SECONDARY INSURANCE PLAN ID #:**	
GENDER:	Female	**OCCUPATION:**	Bus Driver
DATE OF BIRTH:	03-09-YYYY	**NAME OF EMPLOYER:**	Hornell School District

DIAGNOSIS INFORMATION

	Diagnosis	Code		Diagnosis	Code
1.	Anger reaction		5.		
2.	Possible reaction to prednisone		6.		
3.	Crohn's disease		7.		
4.			8.		

PROCEDURE INFORMATION

	Description of Procedure or Service	Date	Code	Charge
1.	Level 2 E/M visit			
2.				
3.				
4.				
5.				

SPECIAL NOTES:

Global Care Medical Center
100 Main St, Alfred NY 14802
(607) 555-1234

Physician Office Record

Patient Name:	CONSTANTINE, Connie	**Patient Number:**	POCase004
Date of Service:	08-26-YYYY	**Date of Birth:**	03-09-YYYY

Nursing Documentation:

Medications Allergies/Reactions: **None**

Current Medications: Prednisone

CC: Feelings of anger

PMH: Crohn's disease

Signature of Nurse: Reviewed and Approved: Jeanette Allen RN ATP-B-S:02:1001261385: Jeanette Allen RN (Signed: 8/26/YYYY 2:20:44 PM EST)

Physician Documentation:

Notes: Patient is under treatment for Crohn's disease with prednisone, which she began taking recently for a flare-up of symptoms. She is presently taking 15 milligrams twice daily. The patient reports feelings of extreme anger related to a recent break-in and vandalization of her family cabin. After investigation by police, the situation has not resolved as the patient expected. The patient states she is still experiencing unusually extreme anger about the break-in incident in addition to the same level of anger in reaction to some other minor situations. For example, She went into a rage when she was required to wait a long time in line at the bank. She is embarrassed by her behavior and says, in the past, she has reacted to such situations with mild annoyance instead of the extreme anger she now feels. She asked if the increased and unusual feelings of anger might be related to the prednisone. I explained that this could be a possibility.

PLAN: Follow-up in two weeks for recheck of symptoms, at which time if her symptoms remain the same, we will discuss reducing the prednisone dosage or switching her to another medication entirely.

Signature of Provider: Reviewed and Approved: Raymond Massey MD ATP-B-S:02:1001261385: Raymond Massey MD (Signed: 8/26/YYYY 2:20:44 PM EST)

Raymond E. Massey, M.D.

POCase005

Global Care Medical Center
100 Main St, Alfred NY 14802
(607) 555-1234

EIN: 12-345678
BCBS PIN: GC2222
BCBS GRP: 1234-P

Physician Office Record

NPI: 987CBA321

PATIENT INFORMATION:

NAME:	BRONTE, Betty	**PATIENT NUMBER:**	POCase005
ADDRESS:	77 Sunset Blvd.	**ADMISSION DATE & TIME:**	09-02-YYYY
CITY:	Hornell	**PRIMARY INSURANCE PLAN:**	BCBS of WNY
STATE:	NY	**PRIMARY INSURANCE PLAN ID #:**	291837241
ZIP CODE:	14843	**SECONDARY INSURANCE PLAN:**	
TELEPHONE:	607-324-1290	**SECONDARY INSURANCE PLAN ID #:**	
GENDER:	Female	**OCCUPATION:**	Reporter
DATE OF BIRTH:	04-17-YYYY	**NAME OF EMPLOYER:**	Evening Tribune

DIAGNOSIS INFORMATION

Diagnosis	Code	Diagnosis	Code
1. Premenopausal menorrhagia		5.	
2.		6.	
3.		7.	
4.		8.	

PROCEDURE INFORMATION

Description of Procedure or Service	Date	Code	Charge
1. Level 2 E/M visit			
2.			
3.			
4.			
5.			

SPECIAL NOTES:

Global Care Medical Center
100 Main St, Alfred NY 14802
(607) 555-1234

Physician Office Record

Patient Name: BRONTE, Betty
Patient Number: POCase005
Date of Service: 02-09-YYYY
Date of Birth: 04-17-YYYY

Nursing Documentation:

Medications Allergies/Reactions: None

Current Medications: Glucophage, Lipitor

BP: 140/100 **P:** 94 **R:** **T:** **WT:** 300 **OVS:**

CC: Excessive menstruation, tiredness, and tearfulness

PMH: Depression

Notes:

Signature of Nurse: Reviewed and Approved: Jeanette Allen RN ATP-B-S:02:1001261385: Jeanette Allen RN (Signed: 9/2/YYYY 2:20:44 PM EST)

Physician Documentation:

Notes: Mrs. Bronte is an established patient who was seen for complaints of excessive menses, tiredness, and tearfulness. She states her menstruation has become irregular as compared with the past. She has had 12 consecutive days of heavy bleeding, with no signs of decrease. She reports feeling more tired than usual with no new stressors nor increased feelings of depression. She is also seeing Tammy Titus for psychotherapy, which she states is very helpful. The medications are also very helpful to her, and she is feeling much less depressed. I explained to her that she is going through early menopause. We will order lab work to check estrogen levels and follicle stimulating hormone levels. The patient is inactive sexually and does not worry about getting pregnant, in view of taking medications. She is alert oriented × 3, no abnormalities of thought content or thought process. She states that she has never had any suicidal thoughts. Return for recheck in 1 month.

Signature of Provider: Reviewed and Approved: Raymond Massey MD ATP-B-S:02:1001261385: Raymond Massey MD (Signed: 9/2/YYYY 2:20:44 PM EST)

Raymond E. Massey, M.D.

POCase006

Global Care Medical Center
100 Main St, Alfred NY 14802
(607) 555-1234

Physician Office Record

EIN:	12-345678
BCBS PIN:	GC2222
BCBS GRP:	1234-P

NPI: 987CBA321

Patient Information:

Name:	HALL, Harry	**Patient Number:**	POCase006
Address:	999 Appian Way	**Admission Date & Time:**	08-16-YYYY
City:	Hornell	**Primary Insurance Plan:**	Medicare
State:	NY	**Primary Insurance Plan ID #:**	444569090A
Zip Code:	14843	**Secondary Insurance Plan:**	United Health Medigap
Telephone:	607-324-1110	**Secondary Insurance Plan ID #:**	444569090
Gender:	Male	**Occupation:**	Retired
Date of Birth:	01-21-YYYY	**Name of Employer:**	

Diagnosis Information

Diagnosis	Code	Diagnosis	Code
1. Coronary artery disease		5. Depression	
2. Cerebrovascular disease		6.	
3. Esophageal reflux		7.	
4. Hyperlipidemia		8.	

Procedure Information

Description of Procedure or Service	Date	Code	Charge
1. Level 3 E/M visit			
2.			
3.			
4.			
5.			

Special Notes:

Global Care Medical Center
100 Main St, Alfred NY 14802
(607) 555-1234

Physician Office Record

Patient Name:	HALL, Harry	**Patient Number:**	POCase006
Date of Service:	08-16-YYYY	**Date of Birth:**	01-21-YYYY

Nursing Documentation:

Medications Allergies/Reactions: **None**

Current Medications: Cimetidine

BP: 122/70 **P:** 60 **R:** 18 **T:** **WT:** 183 **HEENT:** Within Normal Limits

CC: Feels very sad and depressed all the time and has absolutely no energy.

PMH: Hyperlipidemia, coronary artery disease, cerebrovascular disease, esophageal reflux, and depression.

Notes: Patient says he is feeling tired all the time and no energy.

Signature of Nurse: Reviewed and Approved: Jeanette Allen RN ATP-B-S:02:1001261385: Jeanette Allen RN (Signed: 8/16/YYYY 2:20:44 PM EST)

Physician Documentation:

Notes: Mr. Hall has the following problems: Hyperlipidemia, coronary artery disease (CAD}, cerebrovascular disease (CVD), esophageal reflux.

HPI: Mr. Hall is an 80-year-old white male who was last seen in June of this year for the above problems. At that time the patient was placed on cimetidine twice a day and fluoxetine 10 mg a day. There are no labs done on this patient as of yet. He comes in today without any new complaints, except for his original complaint of feeling very sad and depressed all of the time and having absolutely no energy.

PE: Today on examination the patient was 57 inches tall, weighed 183 lbs. Blood pressure: 122/70. Pulse: 60 per minute. Respiration: 18 per minute. HEENT: Basically within normal limits. He wears glasses for visual acuity. He has hearing aids bilaterally. NECK: Supple. Trachea is midline. Thyroid not palpable. LUNGS: Clear to A&P. HEART: sounds were regular without murmur or ectopic beat noted. ABDOMEN: slightly obese. It was nontender. There was no gross organomegaly noted. His bowel sounds were normal. EXTREMITIES: The lower extremities were present. He had good circulation with some very mild edema around the ankles.

ASSESSMENT: As stated above in the problem list.

PLAN: I would like to see this patient back in three months time. He will have labs requested in the next two to three weeks. We will check his blood chemistries and hemogram to monitor CAO, CVD, and hyperlipidemia. I also want to get fecults times three. I will see him in three months. He will continue his CAD and CVD medications, along with cimetidine 400 mg which he will take just once a day at nighttime. He is also taking lovastatin for his hyperlipidemia 40 mg a day. He has used blocks under the head of his bed which has relieved his nighttime heartburn. I would advise him to continue doing this, as well as taking the Cimetidine at bedtime. He is being referred as stated to psychiatry for follow up, and I will see him in three months.

Signature of Provider: Reviewed and Approved: Raymond Massey MD ATP-B-S:02:1001261385: Raymond Massey MD (Signed: 8/16/YYYY 2:20:44 PM EST)

Raymond E. Massey, M.D.

POCase007

Global Care Medical Center
100 Main St, Alfred NY 14802
(607) 555-1234

Physician Office Record

EIN:	12-345678	**NPI:**	987CBA321
BCBS PIN:	GC2222		
BCBS GRP:	1234-P		

Patient Information:

Name:	HAMILTON, George	**Patient Number:**	POCase007
Address:	35 Sunnyside Drive	**Admission Date & Time:**	08-24-YYYY
City:	Hornell	**Primary Insurance Plan:**	Medicare
State:	NY	**Primary Insurance Plan ID #:**	079336943
Zip Code:	14843	**Secondary Insurance Plan:**	BCBS Medigap
Telephone:	607-324-7766	**Secondary Insurance Plan ID #:**	079336943
Gender:	Male	**Occupation:**	Retired
Date of Birth:	08-12-YYYY	**Name of Employer:**	

Diagnosis Information

Diagnosis	Code	Diagnosis	Code
1. Gait disorder		5.	
2. Cervical spondylosis		6.	
3. Peripheral neuropathy		7.	
4.		8.	

Procedure Information

Description of Procedure or Service	Date	Code	Charge
1. Level 2 E/M visit			
2.			
3.			
4.			
5.			

Special Notes:

Global Care Medical Center
100 Main St, Alfred NY 14802
(607) 555-1234

Physician Office Record

PATIENT NAME:	HAMILTON, George	**PATIENT NUMBER:**	POCase007
DATE OF SERVICE:	08-24-YYYY	**DATE OF BIRTH:**	08-12-YYYY

NURSING DOCUMENTATION:

MEDICATIONS ALLERGIES/REACTIONS: None

CURRENT MEDICATIONS: warfarin, digoxin, verapamil

BP: **P:** **R:** **T:** **LMP:** **OVS:**

CC:

PMH:

NOTES:

SIGNATURE OF NURSE: Reviewed and Approved: Jeanette Allen RN ATP-B-S:02:1001261385: Jeanette Allen RN (Signed: 8/24/YYYY 2:20:44 PM EST)

PHYSICIAN DOCUMENTATION:

Notes:

S: Patient returns for recheck of gait instability; there is no change in gait instability; when he had head CT and had to lie quietly with neck extended, gait instability much more for 20-30 minutes after test; meds - warfarin, digoxin, verapamil.

O: Alert, ataxic gait with foot slapping and instability on tandem, mild distal weakness and wasting, barely detectable DTRs, impaired vibration below hips, impaired position sense in toes; head CT revealed diffuse atrophic changes; EMG revealed distal demyelinating axonal neuropathy. GHb and TSH unremarkable.

A: Gait disorder with central/peripheral components in context of cervical spondylosis and peripheral neuropathy.

P: B12/folate [I can find no evidence in chart these have ever been done], revisit one month.

SIGNATURE OF PROVIDER: Reviewed and Approved: Phyllis Neumann MD ATP-B-S:02:1001261385: Phyllis Neumann MD (Signed: 8/24/YYYY 2:20:44 PM EST)

Phyllis A. Neumann, M.D.

POCase008

Global Care Medical Center
100 Main St, Alfred NY 14802
(607) 555-1234

Physician Office Record

EIN:	12-345678	**NPI:**	987CBA321
BCBS PIN:	GC2222		
BCBS GRP:	1234-P		

PATIENT INFORMATION:

NAME:	TRUMAN, Leonard	**PATIENT NUMBER:**	POCase008
ADDRESS:	78909 Holmes Road	**ADMISSION DATE & TIME:**	08-17-YYYY
CITY:	Hornell	**PRIMARY INSURANCE PLAN:**	Medicare
STATE:	NY	**PRIMARY INSURANCE PLAN ID #:**	020443413A
ZIP CODE:	14843	**SECONDARY INSURANCE PLAN:**	Medicare
TELEPHONE:	607-324-3333	**SECONDARY INSURANCE PLAN ID #:**	UHI Medigap
GENDER:	Male	**OCCUPATION:**	Retired
DATE OF BIRTH:	06-20-YYYY	**NAME OF EMPLOYER:**	

DIAGNOSIS INFORMATION

Diagnosis	Code	Diagnosis	Code
1. Distal mononeuropathy, right lower extremity		5.	
2. Paresthesias		6.	
3.		7.	
4.		8.	

PROCEDURE INFORMATION

Description of Procedure or Service	Date	Code	Charge
1. Level 2 E/M service			
2.			
3.			
4.			
5.			

SPECIAL NOTES:

Global Care Medical Center
100 Main St, Alfred NY 14802
(607) 555-1234

Physician Office Record

PATIENT NAME:	TRUMAN, Leonard	**PATIENT NUMBER:**	POCase008
DATE OF SERVICE:	08-17-YYYY	**DATE OF BIRTH:**	06-20-YYYY

NURSING DOCUMENTATION:

MEDICATIONS ALLERGIES/REACTIONS: **None**

CURRENT MEDICATIONS: amitriptyline

BP: **P:** **R:** **T:** **LMP:** **OVS:**

CC:

PMH:

NOTES:

SIGNATURE OF NURSE: Reviewed and Approved: Karla Herrslip RN ATP-B-S:02:1001261385: Karla Herrslip RN (Signed: 8/17/YYYY 2:20:44 PM EST)

PHYSICIAN DOCUMENTATION:

Notes:

S: Some improvement in paresthesias since amitriptyline started, though he is using it only sporadically.

O: As per previous visit, most notable findings being moderate distal weakness of right lower extremity, antalgic gait, diminished ankle jerks, impaired vibratory sensation below knees, and low stocking sensory impairment.

A: Distal mononeuropathy, right lower extremity, with symptomatic response to prescribed amitriptyline.

P: Suggested he take amitriptyline daily each evening as originally prescribed. Reassess in 4 months.

SIGNATURE OF PROVIDER: Reviewed and Approved: Phyllis Neumann MD ATP-B-S:02:1001261385: Phyllis Neumann MD (Signed: 8/17/YYYY 2:20:44 PM EST)

Phyllis A. Neumann, M.D.

POCase009

Global Care Medical Center
100 Main St, Alfred NY 14802
(607) 555-1234

Physician Office Record

EIN:	12-345678	**NPI:**	987CBA321
BCBS PIN:	GC2222		
BCBS GRP:	1234-P		

PATIENT INFORMATION:

NAME:	BILLSON, William	**PATIENT NUMBER:**	POCase009
ADDRESS:	33 Redwood Road	**ADMISSION DATE & TIME:**	08-24-YYYY
CITY:	Hornell	**PRIMARY INSURANCE PLAN:**	Medicare
STATE:	NY	**PRIMARY INSURANCE PLAN ID #:**	112672345A
ZIP CODE:	14843	**SECONDARY INSURANCE PLAN:**	BCBS Medigap
TELEPHONE:	607-324-3555	**SECONDARY INSURANCE PLAN ID #:**	112672345
GENDER:	Male	**OCCUPATION:**	Retired
DATE OF BIRTH:	06-06-YYYY	**NAME OF EMPLOYER:**	

DIAGNOSIS INFORMATION

Diagnosis	Code	Diagnosis	Code
1. Essential tremor		5.	
2. Hypertensive vascular disease		6.	
3. Bilateral cerebral artery occlusion with cerebral infarction		7.	
4.		8.	

PROCEDURE INFORMATION

Description of Procedure or Service	Date	Code	Charge
1. Level 2 E/M visit			
2.			
3.			
4.			
5.			

SPECIAL NOTES:

Global Care Medical Center
100 Main St, Alfred NY 14802
(607) 555-1234

Physician Office Record

Patient Name:	BILLSON, William	**Patient Number:**	POCase009
Date of Service:	08-24-YYYY	**Date of Birth:**	06-06-YYYY

Nursing Documentation:

Medications Allergies/Reactions: None

Current Medications: fexofenadine, clonazepam, desipramine, trazodone. terazosin, nifedipine, lovastatin, captopril, beclomethasone, timolol drops

BP: 144/90 **P:** **R:** **T:** **WT:** **OVS:**

CC: Tremor

PMH: Essential tremor; bilateral cerebral artery occlusion with cerebral infarction secondary to hypertensive vascular disease.

Notes: Patient voices no additional complaints today. Alert.

Signature of Nurse: Reviewed and Approved: Karla Herrslip RN ATP-B-S:02:1001261385: Karla Herrslip RN (Signed: 8/24/YYYY 2:20:44 PM EST)

Physician Documentation:

Notes:

S: Upon recheck, tremor remains under control, manifest mainly during fine manipulations; no symptoms of TIA; schedule for right knee replacement at SMH next month; meds: fexofenadine, ASA BID, clonazepam 1 mg QID, desipramine 150 mg/day, trazodone 100 mg hs, terazosin, nifedipine, lovastatin, captopril, beclomethasone, timolol drops.

O: BP 144/90, alert, impaired tongue motility, antalgic gait, impaired RAMs [L>R], no tremor, left hyper-reflexia, + snout reflexes and jaw jerk.

A: Essential tremor, responsive to primidone. Bilateral cerebral artery occlusion with cerebral infarction secondary to hypertensive vascular disease. Hypertension.

P: Continue primidone 125 mg BID; revisit 4 months.

Signature of Provider: Reviewed and Approved: Phyllis Neumann MD ATP-B-S:02:1001261385: Phyllis Neumann MD (Signed: 8/24/YYYY 2:20:44 PM EST)

Phyllis A. Neumann, M.D.

POCase010

Global Care Medical Center
100 Main St, Alfred NY 14802
(607) 555-1234

EIN: 12-345678
BCBS PIN: GC2222
BCBS GRP: 1234-P

Physician Office Record

NPI: 987CBA321

PATIENT INFORMATION:

NAME:	YARROW, Melvin	**PATIENT NUMBER:**	POCase010
ADDRESS:	12 Painter Street	**ADMISSION DATE & TIME:**	08-26-YYYY
CITY:	Alfred	**PRIMARY INSURANCE PLAN:**	Medicare
STATE:	NY	**PRIMARY INSURANCE PLAN ID #:**	573908899
ZIP CODE:	14802	**SECONDARY INSURANCE PLAN:**	Medicaid
TELEPHONE:	607-587-0101	**SECONDARY INSURANCE PLAN ID #:**	23562879
GENDER:	Male	**OCCUPATION:**	Retired
DATE OF BIRTH:	05-22-YYYY	**NAME OF EMPLOYER:**	

DIAGNOSIS INFORMATION

Diagnosis	Code	Diagnosis	Code
1. Onychomycosis		5.	
2. Hyperkeratoses		6.	
3. Type 1 diabetes mellitus with		7.	
4. polyneuropathy		8.	

PROCEDURE INFORMATION

Description of Procedure or Service	Date	Code	Charge
1. Debridement, mycotic toenails (more than five)			
2. Paring of digital hyperkeratoses, third and fourth toes, right foot			
3.			
4.			
5.			

SPECIAL NOTES:

Global Care Medical Center
100 Main St, Alfred NY 14802
(607) 555-1234

Physician Office Record

Patient Name:	YARROW, Melvin	**Patient Number:**	POCase010
Date of Service:	08-26-YYYY	**Date of Birth:**	05-22-YYYY

Nursing Documentation:

Medications Allergies/Reactions: None

Current Medications:

BP: **P:** **R:** **T:** **WT:** **OVS:**

CC: Mycotic toenails.

PMH: Onychomycosis, diabetes type1 with neuropathy, hyperkeratoses.

Notes: Patient has no other concerns today.

Signature of Nurse: Reviewed and Approved: Albert Molina RN ATP-B-S:02:1001261385: Albert Molina RN (Signed: 8/26/YYYY 2:20:44 PM EST)

Physician Documentation:

Notes: DIAGNOSES: Onychomycosis Hyperkeratoses. Type 1 diabetes mellitus with polyneuropathy.

Follow-up diabetic maintenance-care was provided with debridement of 10 mycotic toenails and paring of digital hyperkeratoses, third and fourth toes, right foot. Mr. Yarrow has an ulcer on the right heel, which is under the care of Dr. Hoffman. When first examining Mr. Yarrow this morning, dried blood was noted on all toes of the left foot. Mr. Yarrow admits lo attempting nail-care yesterday evening and apparently created a mild laceration of the second toenail, left foot. There is an intact scab formation this morning. No further treatment is needed.

The Plastizote chukka-style boots that were dispensed in April are comfortable, and patient likes them very much. No other concerns.

Return to Clinic in six weeks.

Signature of Provider: Reviewed and Approved: H.W. Pocket MD ATP-B-S:02:1001261385: H.W. Pocket MD (Signed: 8/26/YYYY 2:20:44 PM EST)

H.W. Pocket, M.D.

APPENDIX

D

Inpatient Coding Cases (IPCase001–010)

INSTRUCTIONS

Enter ICD-10-CM diagnosis codes and ICD-10-PCS procedure codes in the "ICD Code" column on the Inpatient Face Sheet. Before coding inpatient records in Appendix D, review the definitions listed below.

- **Admission diagnosis:** Condition assigned to the patient upon admission to the facility (e.g., hospital outpatient department or ambulatory surgery center) and coded according to ICD-10-CM.
- **Principal diagnosis:** Condition established after study that resulted in the patient's admission to the hospital.

NOTE:

When there is no definitive diagnosis, assign codes to signs, symptoms, and abnormal findings, selecting one as the principal diagnosis code (because there is always just one principal diagnosis).

- **Secondary diagnosis:** Includes comorbidities and complications coded according to ICD-10-CM.
  - **Comorbidity:** Any condition that coexists during the relevant episode of care *and affects treatment provided to the patient.*
  - **Complication:** Any condition that arises during the relevant episode of care *and affects treatment provided to the patient.*

NOTE:

Assign ICD-10-CM codes to secondary diagnoses *only if one or more of the following are documented in the patient's record*: clinical evaluation of the condition, therapeutic treatment of the condition, diagnostic procedures performed to evaluate the condition, and documentation that secondary diagnosis impacted inpatient care.

- **Principal procedure:** Procedure performed for therapeutic rather than diagnostic purposes or procedure performed that is most closely related to the principal diagnosis or procedure performed to treat a complication. This is coded according to ICD-10-PCS.
- **Secondary procedure:** Additional procedure(s) performed for therapeutic or diagnostic purposes coded according to ICD-10-PCS.

IPCase001

Global Care Medical Center
100 Main St, Alfred NY 14802
(607) 555-1234
Hospital No. 999

Inpatient Face Sheet

Patient Name and Address	Gender	Race	Marital Status	Patient No.
LONG, BETH	F	W	M	IPCase001
4983 REED STREET	**Date of Birth**	**Age**	**Maiden Name**	**Occupation**
ALMOND, NY 14804	12/17/YYYY	30	Short	Clerk

Admission Date	Time	Discharge Date	Time	Length of Stay	Telephone Number
04/26/YYYY	1350	04/30/YYYY	1150	04 DAYS	(607) 555-3319

Guarantor Name and Address	Next of Kin Name and Address
LONG, BERNIE	LONG, BERNIE
4983 REED STREET	4983 REED STREET
ALMOND, NY 14804	ALMOND, NY 14804

Guarantor Telephone No.	Relationship to Patient	Next of Kin Telephone Number	Relationship to Patient
(607) 555-3319	Husband	(607) 555-3319	Husband
Admitting Physician	**Service**	**Admit Type**	**Room Number/Bed**
John Black, MD			369

Attending Physician	Admitting Diagnosis
John Black, MD	Fever of undetermined origin

Primary Insurer	Policy and Group Number	Secondary Insurer	Policy and Group Number

Diagnoses and Procedures	ICD Code
Principal Diagnosis	
Acute Pyelonephritis due to *E. coli.*	
Secondary Diagnoses	
Dehydration	
Principal Procedure	
Secondary Procedures	

Discharge Instructions

Activity: ❐ Bed rest ❐ Light ❐ Usual ❐ Unlimited ❐ Other:

Diet: ❐ Regular ❐ Low Cholesterol ❐ Low Salt ❐ ADA ❐ _____ Calorie

Follow-Up: ☒ Call for appointment ❐ Office appointment on _____ ❐ **Other:** To be seen for a follow-up in office in one week

Special Instructions: None

Attending Physician Authentication: Reviewed and Approved: John Black MD
ATP-B-S:02:1001261385: John Black MD
(Signed: 4/30/YYYY 2:20:44 PM EST)

LONG, BETH	Admission: 04/26/YYYY	**Consent to Admission**
IPCase001	DOB: 12/17/YYYY	
Dr. BLACK	ROOM: 369	

I, Beth Long hereby consent to admission in the Global Care Medical Center (GCMC), and I further consent to such routine hospital care, diagnostic procedures, and medical treatment that the medical and professional staff of GCMC may deem necessary or advisable. I authorize the use of medical information obtained about me as specified above and the disclosure of such information to my referring physician(s). This form has been fully explained to me, and I understand its contents. I further understand that no guarantees have been made to me as to the results of treatments or examinations done at the GCMC.

Reviewed and Approved: Beth Long
ATP-B-S:02:1001261385: Beth Long
(Signed: 4/26/YYYY 2:12:05 PM EST)

Signature of Patient

Signature of Parent/Legal Guardian for Minor

Relationship to Minor

Reviewed and Approved: Andrea Witteman
ATP-B-S:02:1001261385: Andrea Witteman
(Signed: 4/26/YYYY 2:12:05 PM EST)

WITNESS: Global Care Medical Center Staff Member

Consent To Release Information For Reimbursement Purposes

In order to permit reimbursement, upon request, the Global Care Medical Center (GCMC) may disclose such treatment information pertaining to my hospitalization to any corporation, organization, or agent thereof, which is, or may be liable under contract to the GCMC or to me, or to any of my family members or other person, for payment of all or part of the GCMC's charges for services rendered to me (e.g. the patient's health insurance carrier). I understand that the purpose of any release of information is to facilitate reimbursement for services rendered. In addition, in the event that my health insurance program includes utilization review of services provided during this admission. I authorize GCMC to release information as is necessary to permit the review. This authorization will expire once the reimbursement for services rendered is complete.

Reviewed and Approved: Beth Long
ATP-B-S:02:1001261385: Beth Long
(Signed: 4/26/YYYY 2:14:17 PM EST)

Signature of Patient

Signature of Parent/Legal Guardian for Minor

Relationship to Minor

Reviewed and Approved: Andrea Witteman
ATP-B-S:02:1001261385: Andrea Witteman
(Signed: 4/26/YYYY 2:16:24 PM EST)

WITNESS: Global Care Medical Center Staff Member

Global Care Medical Center ■ 100 Main St, Alfred NY 14802 ■ (607) 555-1234

LONG, BETH	Admission: 04/26/YYYY	**Advance Directive**
IPCase001	DOB: 12/17/YYYY	
Dr. BLACK	ROOM: 369	

Your answers to the following questions will assist your Physician and the Hospital to respect your wishes regarding your medical care. This information will become a part of your medical record.

	Yes	No	Patient's Initials
1. Have you been provided with a copy of the information called "Patient Rights Regarding Health Care Decision"?	X		
2. Have you prepared a "Living Will"? If yes, please provide the Hospital with a copy for your medical record.		X	
3. Have you prepared a Durable Power of Attorney for Health Care? If yes, please provide the Hospital with a copy for your medical record.		X	
4. Have you provided this facility with an Advance Directive on a prior admission and is it still in effect? If yes, Admitting Office to contact Medical Records to obtain a copy for the medical record.		X	
5. Do you desire to execute a Living Will/Durable Power of Attorney? If yes, refer to in order: a. Physician b. Social Service c. Volunteer Service		X	

Hospital Staff Directions: Check when each step is completed.

1. ✓ Verify the above questions were answered and actions taken where required.
2. ✓ If the "Patient Rights" information was provided to someone other than the patient, state reason:

____

______________________ ______________________

Name of Individual Receiving Information **Relationship to Patient**

3. ✓ If information was provided in a language other than English, specify language and method.
4. ✓ Verify patient was advised on how to obtain additional information on Advance Directives.
5. ✓ Verify the Patient/Family Member/Legal Representative was asked to provide the Hospital with a copy of the Advanced Directive which will be retained in the medical record.

File this form in the medical record, and give a copy to the patient.

____

Name of Patient/Name of Individual giving information if different from Patient

Reviewed and Approved: Beth Long
ATP-B-S:02:1001261385: Beth Long
(Signed: 4/26/YYYY 2:35:05 PM EST)

Signature of Patient **Date**

Reviewed and Approved: Andrea Witteman
ATP-B-S:02:1001261385: Andrea Witteman
(Signed: 4/26/YYYY 2:35:47 PM EST)

Signature of Hospital Representative **Date**

Global Care Medical Center ■ 100 Main St, Alfred NY 14802 ■ (607) 555-1234

LONG, BETH	Admission: 04/26/YYYY	**Discharge Summary**
IPCase001	DOB: 12/17/YYYY	
Dr. BLACK	ROOM: 369	

ADMISSION DATE: 04/26/YYYY DISCHARGE DATE: 04/30/YYYY

ADMISSION DIAGNOSIS: Fever of undetermined origin.

DISCHARGE DIAGNOSIS: Acute pyelonephritis due to *E. coli.*

SUMMARY: This 30 year old white female had high fever off and on for several days prior to admission without any localizing signs or symptoms. Preliminary studies done as an outpatient were unremarkable except to indicate an infection some place. She was ultimately seen in the office, temperature was 103 to 104. She was becoming dehydrated, washed out, weak, tired, and she was admitted for further workup and evaluation.

Workup included a chest x-ray, which was normal. Intravenous pyelogram was also normal. Blood culture report was normal. Urine culture grew out *Escherichia coli* greater than 100,000 colonies. Throat culture was normal. One blood culture did finally grow out an alpha strep viridans.

I talked to Dr. Burke about this and we decided on the basis of her clinical condition and the fact that this did not grow on all bottles it was more likely a contaminate. Urine showed a specific gravity of 1.010, albumin 1+, sugar and acetone were negative, white blood cells 6 to 8, and red blood cells 1 to 2. White count 13,100, Hemoglobin 12, hematocrit 35.1, segmental cells 81, lymphocytes 11, monocytes 5, eosinophils 1, bands 2. Mononucleosis test was negative. Alkaline phosphatase 127, blood sugar 125, sodium 142, potassium 4.7, carbon dioxide 30, chloride 104, cholesterol 119, serum glutamic oxaloacetic transaminase 41, lactate dehydrogenase 151, creatinine 0.9, calcium 9.8, phosphorus 3.3, bilirubin 0.6, total protein 6.8, albumin 4.0, uric acid 6.5. Electrocardiogram was reported as normal.

She was started on intravenous fluids, intravenous Keflex, her temperature remained elevated for approximately 48 hours and now has been normal for the last 48 to 72 hours. She feels better, hydration is better, eating better, no urinary symptoms. She's being discharged at this time on Keflex 500 mg four times per day, increased fluid intake. To be seen in follow up in the office in 1 week.

DD:04/30/YYYY

Reviewed and Approved: John Black MD
ATP-B-S:02:1001261385: John Black MD
(Signed: 5/1/YYYY 2:24:44 PM EST)

DT:05/01/YYYY

Physician Authentication

GLOBAL CARE MEDICAL CENTER ■ 100 MAIN ST, ALFRED NY 14802 ■ (607) 555-1234

LONG, BETH	Admission: 04/26/YYYY	**History & Physical Exam**
IPCase001	DOB: 12/17/YYYY	
Dr. BLACK	ROOM: 369	

ADMISSION DIAGNOSIS: Fever undetermined etiology, pyelonephritis, dehydration, and possible urinary tract infection.

CHIEF COMPLAINT: Chills and fever, and just feels lousy for the last 5 days.

HISTORY OF PRESENT ILLNESS: The patient began to run a temperature on Sunday, had no other complaints whatsoever. She has not felt like eating for the past 5 days and only taking in fluids and aspirin. She was seen in the office on 4/24 with 98 degree temperature but she had just taken aspirin. At that time physical exam was negative but she had an 18,300 white count. The white count was repeated the next day and found to be 13,400 with temperature elevated at 102-103 unless she was taking Aspirin. She was seen in the office again today, continues to feel lousy and now she has some pain in the left upper flank area posteriorly, she is being admitted to the hospital for a workup with a temperature of 103.

FAMILY HISTORY: Negative for cancer, tuberculosis, diabetes, she has a brother with mild epilepsy.

PAST HISTORY: She has only been admitted for delivery of her 2 children, otherwise she has always been in excellent health without any problems. She smokes 15-20 cigarettes a day and has done so for the last 15 years. She doesn't drink. She uses no other drugs.

SOCIAL HISTORY: She lives at home with her husband and 2 children. There are no apparent problems.

REVIEW OF SYSTEMS: Normal except for the history of the present problem.

GENERAL: Shows a cooperative young lady. She shows no pain. She is 30 years old. WEIGHT: 113 lb. TEMPERATURE: 103 oral PULSE: 102 RESPIRATIONS: 18

SKIN: Pink, warm, dry, no evidence of rash or jaundice.

BeenT: Head symmetrical. No masses or abnormalities. Eyes react to light and accommodation. Extraocular movements are normal. Sclera is clear. Ears, tympanic membranes are not injected. Mouth and throat are negative. NECK: Supple. No lymph nodes felt. No thyromegaly.

CHEST: Clear to percussion and auscultation. HEART: Normal sinus rhythm. Not enlarged.

ABDOMEN: Soft. She is tender under the left costal margin with no enlargement of any organs. She has pain to percussion in left upper flank area.

PELVIC & RECTAL: Deferred.

EXTREMITIES: Normal. Peripheral pulses are normal.

DD: 04/26/YYYY

Reviewed and Approved: John Black MD
ATP-B-S:02:1001261385: John Black MD
(Signed: 4/26/YYYY 2:24:24 PM EST)

DT: 04/26/YYYY

Physician Authentication

GLOBAL CARE MEDICAL CENTER ■ 100 MAIN ST, ALFRED NY 14802 ■ (607) 555-1234

LONG, BETH	Admission: 04/26/YYYY	**Progress Notes**
IPCase001	DOB: 12/17/YYYY	
Dr. BLACK	ROOM: 369	

Date	Time	Physician's signature required for each order. (Please skip one line between dates.)
04/27/YYYY	1450	Chief complaint: left flank pain; fever. Diagnosis: pyelonephritis; dehydration; rule out renal calculus. Plan of Treatment: Admit. Hydration with intravenous Ancef. Reviewed and Approved: John Black MD ATP-B-S:02:1001261385: John Black MD (Signed: 4/27/YYYY 2:50:55 PM EST)
04/28/YYYY	1110	Alpha strep in blood culture. Not viridans, clinically. Improving. Has genitourinary infection; urinary tract infection. Reviewed and Approved: John Black MD ATP-B-S:02:1001261385: John Black MD (Signed: 4/28/YYYY 11:14:07 AM EST)
04/29/YYYY	1140	Patient feels better; still complains of left flank and back pain. SUBJECTIVE: Afebrile vital signs. OBJECTIVE: HEAD/EYES/EARS/NOSE/THROAT: Tympanic membrane of left ear somewhat dull yellowish. Throat: slight erythema. Heart: regular rate and rhythm, without murmur. Back: positive left costovertebral angle tenderness. Abdomen: mild left upper quadrant. ASSESSMENT/PLAN: 1) Probable left pyelonephritis. Rule out stone. 2) Positive streptococcal bacteremia. Possibly secondary to pyelonephritis. Possible other source? Abscess - doubt. Intravenous pyelogram is okay. Reviewed and Approved: John Black MD ATP-B-S:02:1001261385: John Black MD (Signed: 4/29/YYYY 11:40:32 AM EST)

GLOBAL CARE MEDICAL CENTER ■ 100 MAIN ST, ALFRED NY 14802 ■ (607) 555-1234

LONG, BETH	Admission: 04/26/YYYY	**Doctors' Orders**
IPCase001	DOB: 12/17/YYYY	
Dr. BLACK	ROOM: 369	

Date	Time	Physician's signature required for each order. (Please skip one line between dates.)
04/26/YYYY	1400	Complete blood count and mononucleosis test, Urinalysis. Urine for culture and sensitivity. Throat Culture. Blood culture every one-half hour times two until next temperature increases to 101 degrees. Chest x-ray done as outpatient. Electrocardiogram. SCG #2. Electrolytes. Full liquids as tolerated. Intravenous fluids, 50-100 cubic centimeters per hour. Tylenol 2 tabs every 4 to 6 hours as needed for elevated temperature. Ancef 500 milligrams intravenous every 6 hours (after cultures are obtained) History and physical examination report dictated. Reviewed and Approved: John Black MD ATP-B-S:02:1001261385: John Black MD (Signed: 04/26/YYYY 2:04:00 PM EST)
04/27/YYYY	1110	Please schedule for intravenous pyelogram, Monday morning. Soft diet as tolerated. Strain urine. Reviewed and Approved: John Black MD ATP-B-S:02:1001261385: John Black MD (Signed: 4/27/YYYY 11:24:52 AM EST)
04/29/YYYY	1515	Discontinue intravenous fluids in morning. Discontinue Ancef in morning. Start on Keflex, 500 milligrams four times per day in morning on April 30. Reviewed and Approved: John Black MD ATP-B-S:02:1001261385: John Black MD (Signed: 4/29/YYYY 3:24:00 PM EST)
04/30/YYYY	1315	Discharge to home. Reviewed and Approved: John Black MD ATP-B-S:02:1001261385: John Black MD (Signed: 4/30/YYYY 1:16:32 PM EST)

GLOBAL CARE MEDICAL CENTER ■ 100 MAIN ST, ALFRED NY 14802 ■ (607) 555-1234

LONG, BETH	Admission: 04/26/YYYY	**Laboratory Data**
IPCase001	DOB: 12/17/YYYY	
Dr. BLACK	ROOM: 369	

SPECIMEN COLLECTED: 04/26/YYYY SPECIMEN RECEIVED: 04/26/YYYY

TEST	RESULT	FLAG	REFERENCE
URINALYSIS			
DIPSTICK ONLY			
COLOR	YELLOW		
SPECIFIC GRAVITY	1.010		≤ 1.030
GLUCOSE	NEGATIVE		≤ 125 mg/dl
BILIRUBIN	NEGATIVE		≤ 0.8 mg/dl
KETONE	TRACE		≤ 10 mg/dl
BLOOD	TRACE		0.06 mg/dl hgb
PH	6.5		5-8.0
PROTEIN	NORMAL		≤ 30 mg/dl
UROBILINOGEN	NORMAL		≤ −1 mg/dl
NITRITES	NEGATIVE		NEG
LEUKOCYTE	NEGATIVE		≤ 15 WBC/hpf
WHITE BLOOD CELLS	6-8/hpf	**H**	≤ 5/hpf
RED BLOOD CELLS	1-2/hpf		≤ 5/hpf
BACTERIA	MANY	**H**	1+(≤ 20/hpf)
URINE PREGNANCY TEST	Negative		

≤ = less than or equal to

≥ = greater than or equal to

mg/dl = milligrams per deciliter

hgb = hemoglobin

/hpf = per high power field

End of Report

GLOBAL CARE MEDICAL CENTER ■ 100 MAIN ST, ALFRED NY 14802 ■ (607) 555-1234

LONG, BETH	Admission: 04/26/YYYY	**Laboratory Data**
IPCase001	DOB: 12/17/YYYY	
Dr. BLACK	ROOM: 369	

SPECIMEN COLLECTED: 04/26/YYYY 1450 **SPECIMEN RECEIVED:** 04/29/YYYY 1814

TEST	**RESULT**
BACTERIOLOGY	**OTHER ROUTINE CULTURES**
SOURCE:	Blood Cultures
SMEAR ONLY:	
CULTURE	
1st PRELIMINARY	No bacteria seen at 24 hours.
2nd PRELIMINARY	
FINAL REPORT	Strep viridans

SENSITIVITIES

R = Resistant

S = Sensitive

1.	S	AMIKACIN			NITROFURANTOIN
		AMPICILLIN	1.	R	PENICILLIN G
		CARBENICILLIN			POLYMYXIN B
		CEFAMANDOLE			SULFISOXAZOLE
		CEFOXITIN	1.	S	TETRACYCLINE
1.	R	CEPHALOTHIN			TRIMETHOPRIM
1.	S	CHLORAMPHENICOL	1.	S	VANCOMYCIN
1.	S	CLINDAMYCIN			
1.	S	ERYTHROMYCIN			
1.	S	GENTAMICIN			
		KANAMYCIN			
1.	S	METHICILLIN			
		NALIDIXIC ACID			

GLOBAL CARE MEDICAL CENTER ■ 100 MAIN ST, ALFRED NY 14802 ■ (607) 555-1234

LONG, BETH Admission: 04/26/YYYY

IPCase001 DOB: 12/17/YYYY

Dr. BLACK ROOM: 369

Laboratory Data

SPECIMEN COLLECTED: 04/26/YYYY 1504 SPECIMEN RECEIVED: 04/29/YYYY 1814

TEST	RESULT
BACTERIOLOGY	OTHER ROUTINE CULTURES
SOURCE:	Blood culture
SMEAR ONLY:	
CULTURE	
1st PRELIMINARY	No bacteria seen at 24 hours
2nd PRELIMINARY	No growth seen on 24 hour subculture
FINAL REPORT	

End of Report

GLOBAL CARE MEDICAL CENTER ■ 100 MAIN ST, ALFRED NY 14802 ■ (607) 555-1234

LONG, BETH	Admission: 04/26/YYYY	**Laboratory Data**
IPCase001	DOB: 12/17/YYYY	
Dr. BLACK	ROOM: 369	

SPECIMEN COLLECTED: 04/26/YYYY 1450 SPECIMEN RECEIVED: 04/26/YYYY 1746

BLOOD CHEMISTRY

TEST	REFERENCE		RESULT
ACID PHOSPHATASE	0.0-0.8 U/I		
ALKALINE PHOSPHATASE	50-136 U/I		127
AMYLASE	23-85 U/I		
LIPASE	4-24 U/I		
GLUCOSE FASTING	70-110 mg/dl		
GLUCOSE	Time collected		125
BUN	7-22 mg/dl		
SODIUM	136-147 mEq/l		142
POTASSIUM	3.7-5.1 mEq/l		4.7
CARBON DIOXIDE	24-32 mEq/1		30
CHLORIDE	98-108 mEq/l		104
CHOLESTEROL	120-280 mg/dl		119
SERUM GLUTAMATE PYRUVATE TRANSAMINASE	3-36 U/I		
SERUM GLUTAMIC OXALOCETIC TRANSAMINASE	M-27-47 U/I	F-22-37 U/I	41
CREATININE KINASE	H-35-232 U/I	F-21-215 U/I	
LACTATE DEHYDROGENASE	100-190 U/I		151
CREATININE	M-0.8-1.3 mg/dl	F-0.6-1.0 mg/dl	0.9
CALCIUM	8.7-10.2 mg/dl		9.8
PHOSPHORUS	2.5-4.9 mg/dl		3.3
BILIRUBIN-DIRECT	0.0-0.4 mg/dl		
BILIRUBIN-TOTAL	Less than 1.5 mg/dl		0.6
TOTAL PROTEIN	6.4-8.2 g/dl		6.8
ALBUMIN	3.4-5.0 g/dl		4.0
URIC ACID	M-3.8-7.1 mg/dl	F-2.6-5.6 mg/dl	6.5
TRIGLYCERIDE	30-200 mg/dl		

U/I = International Units
g/dl = grams per deciliter
mEq = milliequivalent per deciliter
mg/dl = milligrams per deciliter

GLOBAL CARE MEDICAL CENTER ■ 100 MAIN ST, ALFRED NY 14802 ■ (607) 555-1234

LONG, BETH	Admission: 04/26/YYYY	**Laboratory Data**
IPCase001	DOB: 12/17/YYYY	
Dr. BLACK	ROOM: 369	

SPECIMEN COLLECTED: 04/26/YYYY 1505 SPECIMEN RECEIVED: 04/28/YYYY 1957

TEST	RESULT					
BACTERIOLOGY	OTHER ROUTINE CULTURES					
SOURCE:	Urine					
SMEAR ONLY:	1+ white blood cells, 4+ gram negative rods					
CULTURE						
1st PRELIMINARY	1. CC = >100,000 *Escherichia coli*					
2nd PRELIMINARY						
FINAL REPORT	1. CC = >100,000 *Escherichia coli*					
SENSITIVITIES	1.	S	AMIKACIN	1.	S	NITROFURANTOIN
R = Resistant	1.	R	AMPICILLIN			PENICILLIN G
S = Sensitive	1.	R	CARBENICILLIN			POLYMYXIN B
> = greater than	1.	S	CEFAMANDOLE	1.	R	SULFISOXAZOLE
	1.	S	CEFOXITIN	1.	R	TETRACYCLINE
	1.	S	CEPHALOTHIN	1.	S	TRIMETHOPRIM
	1.	R	CHLORAMPHENICOL			VANCOMYCIN
			CLINDAMYCIN			
			ERYTHROMYCIN			
	1.	S	GENTAMICIN			
			KANAMYCIN			
			METHICILLIN			
			NALIDIXIC ACID			

GLOBAL CARE MEDICAL CENTER ■ 100 MAIN ST, ALFRED NY 14802 ■ (607) 555-1234

LONG, BETH Admission: 04/26/YYYY
IPCase001 DOB: 12/17/YYYY
Dr. BLACK ROOM: 369

Laboratory Data

TIME IN: 04/26/YYYY 1450 TIME OUT: 04/26/YYYY 1746

COMPLETE BLOOD COUNTS DIFFERENTIAL

TEST	RESULT	FLAG	REFERENCE
WHITE BLOOD CELL	13.1		4.5-11.0 thou/ul
RED BLOOD CELL	3.99		5.2-5.4 milliliter/upper limit
HEMOGLOBIN	12.0		11.7-16.1 grams per deciliter
HEMATOCRIT	35.1		35.0-47.0 %
MEAN CORPUSCULAR VOLUME	87.9		85-99 factor level
MEAN CORPUSCULAR HEMOGLOBIN	30.2		
MEAN CORPUSCULAR HEMOGLOBIN CONCENTRATION	34.3		33-37
RED CELL DISTRIBUTION WIDTH			11.4-14.5
PLATELETS	355		130-400 thou/ul
SEGMENTED CELLS %	81		
LYMPHOCYTES %	11		20.5-51.1
MONOCYTES %	5		1.7-9.3
EOSINOPHILS %	1		
BAND CELLS %	2		

Thou/ul = thousand upper limit

End of Report

GLOBAL CARE MEDICAL CENTER ■ 100 MAIN ST, ALFRED NY 14802 ■ (607) 555-1234

LONG, BETH	Admission: 04/26/YYYY	**Radiology Report**
IPCase001	DOB: 12/17/YYYY	
Dr. BLACK	ROOM: 369	

Date of X-ray: 04/29/YYYY

REASON: Fever of unknown origin.

TECHNICAL DATA: No known allergies. 100 milliliter infusion through intravenous - no reaction noted.

INTRAVENOUS PYELOGRAM: A plain film taken prior to the intravenous pyelogram shows no shadows of urological significance.

Following the intravenous injection of contrast material, serial films including anterior-posterior and oblique views show that both kidneys are normal in size and configuration. The right kidney is slightly ptotic and there is some buckling of the right proximal ureter. However, I do not think that this finding is clinically significant. The visualized course of the distal ureters are both normal. The bladder is well visualized on a delayed film and is within normal limits. There is a small amount of urinary residual on the post voiding film.

CONCLUSION: Essentially normal intravenous pyelogram.

DD:04/29/YYYY Reviewed and Approved: Randall Cunningham MD
ATP-B-S:02:1001261385: Randall Cunningham MD
(Signed:4/29/YYYY 2:24:44 PM EST)

DT:04/29/YYYY

Global Care Medical Center ■ 100 Main St, Alfred NY 14802 ■ (607) 555-1234

LONG, BETH	Admission: 04/26/YYYY	**EKG Report**
IPCase001	DOB: 12/17/YYYY	
Dr. BLACK	ROOM: 369	

Date of Electrocardiogram: 04/26/YYYY   Time of Electrocardiogram:1600

Rate 90

PR .12

QRSD .68

QT .32

QTC

-- Axis --

P

QRS

T

Sinus rhythm normal.

Reviewed and Approved: Dr. Steven J. Chambers, M.D.
ATP-B-S:02:1001261385: Dr. Steven J. Chambers, M.D. (Signed:4/29/YYYY 2:24:44 PM EST)

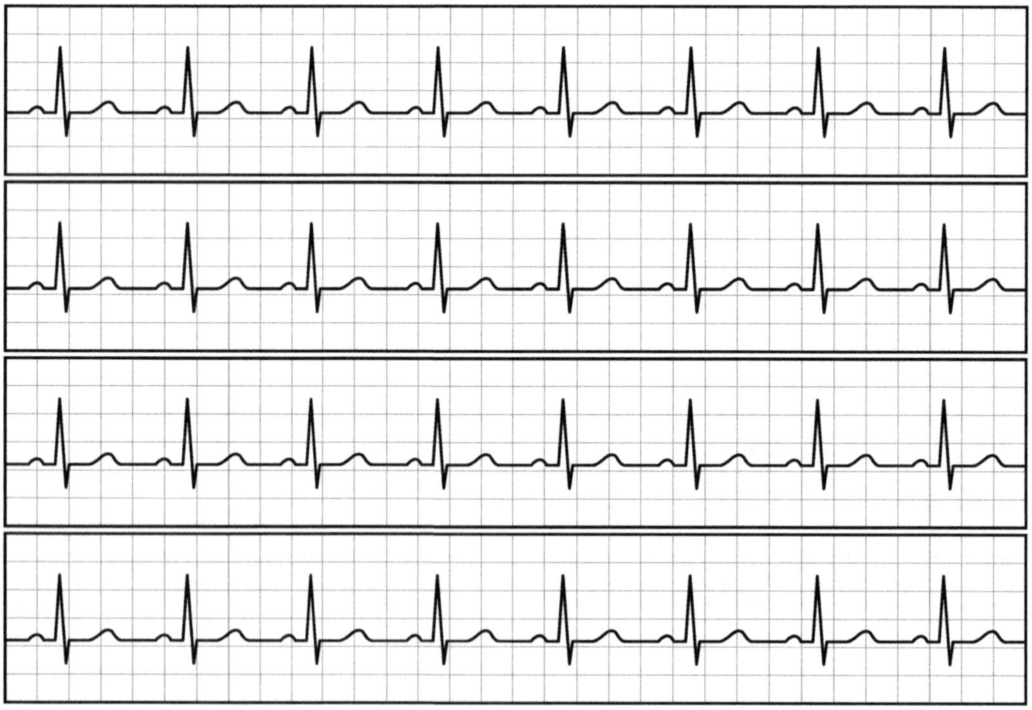

Global Care Medical Center ■ 100 Main St, Alfred NY 14802 ■ (607) 555-1234

LONG, BETH	Admission: 04/26/YYYY	**Graphic Chart**
IPCase001	DOB: 12/17/YYYY	
Dr. BLACK	ROOM: 369	

DAY IN HOSPITAL	1						2						3						4					
DATE	04/26/YYYY						04/27/YYYY						04/28/YYYY						04/29/YYYY					
PULSE (•) / TEMP (X)	0400	0800	1200	1600	2000	2400	0400	0800	1200	1600	2000	2400	0400	0800	1200	1600	2000	2400	0400	0800	1200	1600	2000	2400
140 / 106																								
130 / 105																								
120 / 104																								
110 / 103																								
100 / 102					X				X															
90 / 101				•	•		X		•	•	X		•	•							•			
80 / 100			X			•	•	•			•	•	X	X	•			•	•	•		•		
70 / 99						X		X							X	•	•					X		
60 / 98.6			•	X						X		X				X	X	X	X		X			
50 / 98																				X				
40 / 97																								
30 / 96																								
20 / 95																								
RESPIRATION			20	20	16	20	20	18	16	20	20	20	20	18	16	16	20	18	16	20	18	18		

BLOOD PRESSURE																
	0800		1600	110/65	0800	110/70	1600	112/68	0800	100/70	1600	110/70	0800	108/68	1600	
	1200	102/60	2000	90/60	1200	90/65	2000	110/69	1200	110/70	2000	105/68	1200	95/72	2000	

WEIGHT 5'8"	141#											
DIET	Full liquid			Full liquid			Soft			Soft		
APPETITE		50%	50%	100%	100%	30%	90%	75%	100%	100%	100%	80%
BATH	Self			Self			Self			Self		
INTAKE/OUTPUT	7-3	3-11	11-7	7-3	3-11	11-7	7-3	3-11	11-7	7-3	3-11	11-7
INTAKE: ORAL FLUIDS		600	100	650	1350	200	600	1170	100	850	440	
INTAKE: IV FLUIDS		500	600	650	850	550	650	650	1050	700	600	
INTAKE: BLOOD												
INTAKE: 8-HOUR TOTAL		1100	700	1250	2200	750	1250	1820	1150	1550	1040	
INTAKE: 24-HOUR TOTAL	1800			4200			4220			2590		
OUTPUT: URINE		800	600	1100	750	650	700	1175	700	1000	900	
OUTPUT: STOOL				2 loose								
OUTPUT: EMESIS												
OUTPUT: NASOGASTRIC												
OUTPUT: 8-HOUR TOTAL		800	600	1100	750	650	700	1175	700	1000	900	
OUTPUT: 24-HOUR TOTAL	1400			2500			2575			1900		

GLOBAL CARE MEDICAL CENTER ■ 100 MAIN ST, ALFRED NY 14802 ■ (607) 555-1234

LONG, BETH	Admission: 04/26/YYYY	
IPCase001	DOB: 12/17/YYYY	**Graphic Chart**
Dr. BLACK	ROOM: 369	

DAY IN HOSPITAL	5				
DATE	04/30/YYYY				

PULSE (•)	TEMP (X)	0400	0800	1200	1600	2000	2400	0400	0800	1200	1600	2000	2400	0400	0800	1200	1600	2000	2400	0400	0800	1200	1600	2000	2400
140	106																								
130	105																								
120	104																								
110	103																								
100	102																								
90	101																								
80	100			X																					
70	99																								
60	98.6			•																					
50	98																								
40	97																								
30	96																								
20	95																								
RESPIRATION				20																					

BLOOD PRESSURE	0800 / 1200: 102/60; 1600 / 2000			
WEIGHT 5'8"	141#			
DIET	Full liquid			
APPETITE	50%			
BATH	Self			
INTAKE/OUTPUT	7-3			
INTAKE: ORAL FLUIDS				
INTAKE: IV FLUIDS				
INTAKE: BLOOD				
INTAKE:				
INTAKE: 8-HOUR TOTAL				
INTAKE: 24-HOUR TOTAL				
OUTPUT: URINE				
OUTPUT: STOOL				
OUTPUT: EMESIS				
OUTPUT: N-G				
OUTPUT:				
OUTPUT: 8-HOUR TOTAL				
OUTPUT: 24-HOUR TOTAL				

GLOBAL CARE MEDICAL CENTER ■ 100 MAIN ST, ALFRED NY 14802 ■ (607) 555-1234

LONG, BETH Admission: 04/26/YYYY
IPCase001 DOB: 12/17/YYYY
Dr. BLACK ROOM: 369

Medication Administration Record

SPECIAL INSTRUCTIONS:

MEDICATION (dose and route)	**DATE:** 04/26 TIME	INITIALS	**DATE:** 04/27 TIME	INITIALS	**DATE:** 04/28 TIME	INITIALS	**DATE:** 04/29 TIME	INITIALS
Ancef 500 mg IV q6°	0600	--	0600	--	0600	JD	0600	JD
(started before	1200	--	1200	VS	1200	JD	1200	HF
cultures obtained)	1800	OR	1800	HF	1800	OR	1800	OR
	2400	JD	2400	OR	2400	OR	2400	OR
mg = milligrams								
IV = intravenous								
PRN Medications:								
Tylenol 2 tabs by mouth	1930	OR	0435	JD	0520	JD	0600	JD
daily 4 to 6 hours as			1100	VS			1230	HF
needed for increased			1830	HF				
temperature								
PRN = as needed								

INITIALS	SIGNATURE AND TITLE	INITIALS	SIGNATURE AND TITLE	INITIALS	SIGNATURE AND TITLE
VS	Vera South, RN	GPW	G. P. Well, RN		
OR	Ora Richards, RN	PS	P. Small, RN		
JD	Jane Dobbs, RN				
HF	H.Figgs, RN				

GLOBAL CARE MEDICAL CENTER ■ 100 MAIN ST, ALFRED NY 14802 ■ (607) 555-1234

LONG, BETH Admission: 04/26/YYYY
IPCase001 DOB: 12/17/YYYY
Dr. BLACK ROOM: 369

Medication Administration Record

SPECIAL INSTRUCTIONS:

	DATE: 04/30		DATE:		DATE:		DATE:	
MEDICATION (dose and route)	**TIME**	**INITIALS**	**TIME**	**INITIALS**	**TIME**	**INITIALS**	**TIME**	**INITIALS**
Keflex 500 milligram	0800	HF						
four times a day								

INITIALS	SIGNATURE AND TITLE	INITIALS	SIGNATURE AND TITLE	INITIALS	SIGNATURE AND TITLE
VS	Vera South, RN	GPW	G. P. Well, RN		
OR	Ora Richards, RN	PS	P. Small, RN		
JD	Jane Dobbs, RN				
HF	H.Figgs, RN				

GLOBAL CARE MEDICAL CENTER ■ 100 MAIN ST, ALFRED NY 14802 ■ (607) 555-1234

LONG, BETH	Admission: 04/26/YYYY	
IPCase001	DOB: 12/17/YYYY	**Intravenous Therapy Record**
Dr. BLACK	ROOM: 369	

Time	Solution & Amount	Medication Added	Injection Site & Mode	Rate	IV & CVP	Site Changed q 48 Hours	Nurse's Initials	Remarks
4/27 1400	1000 cubic centimeter	none	#209 Cathalin left arm	100 cubic centimeter per hour			JD	
4/28 0100	1000 cubic centimeter	none	added	100 cubic centimeter per hour			HF	
4/28 1300	1000 cubic centimeter	none	same	100 cubic centimeter per hour			JD	
4/29 2400	1000 cubic centimeter	----	----	100 cubic centimeter per hour			OR	
4/29 1330	Intravenous site	sore	Discontinued				JD	
4/29 1340	1000 cubic centimeter	none	#209 Cathalin left antecubital	100 cubic centimeter per hour			JD	
4/30 2400	1000 cubic centimeter			100 cubic centimeter per hour			OR	
4/30 0900	1000 cubic centimeter			100 cubic centimeter per hour			HF	
4/30 2200	1000 cubic centimeter			100 cubic centimeter per hour			VS	
4/31 0750	Intravenous discontinued						HF	150 cubic centimeters remaining in bag.
								Needle removed intact.
								No signs of infiltration or redness at site.

Nurse's Signature	Vera South RN (VS)	Ora Richards RN (OR)
	H. Figgs RN (HF)	Jane Dobbs RN (JD)

GLOBAL CARE MEDICAL CENTER ■ 100 MAIN ST, ALFRED NY 14802 ■ (607) 555-1234

LONG, BETH	Admission: 04/26/YYYY	**Patient Property Record**
IPCase001	DOB: 12/17/YYYY	
Dr. BLACK	ROOM: 369	

I understand that while the facility will be responsible for items deposited in the safe. I must be responsible for all items retained by me at the bedside. (Dentures kept at the bedside will be labeled, but the facility cannot assure responsibility for them.) I also recognize that the hospital cannot be held responsible for items brought in to me after this form has been completed and signed.

Reviewed and Approved: Beth Long
ATP-B-S:02:1001261385: Beth Long
(Signed: 4/26/YYYY 2:24:44 PM EST)

Signature of Patient

Reviewed and Approved: Andrea Witteman
ATP-B-S:02:1001261385: Andrea Witteman
(Signed: 4/26/YYYY 1:44:00 PM EST)

Signature of Witness

I have no money or valuables that I wish to deposit for safekeeping. I do not hold the facility responsible for any other money or valuables that I am retaining or will have brought in to me. I have been advised that it is recommended that I retain no more than $5.00 at the bedside.

Reviewed and Approved: Beth Long
ATP-B-S:02:1001261385: Beth Long
(Signed: 4/26/YYYY 1:46:44 PM EST)

Signature of Patient

Reviewed and Approved: Andrea Witteman
ATP-B-S:02:1001261385: Andrea Witteman
(Signed: 4/26/YYYY 1:48:28 PM EST)

Signature of Witness

I have deposited valuables in the facility safe. The envelope number is ________________.

Signature of Patient

Signature of Person Accepting Property

I understand that medications I have brought to the facility will be handled as recommended by my physician. This may include storage, disposal, or administration.

Signature of Patient

Signature of Witness

GLOBAL CARE MEDICAL CENTER ■ 100 MAIN ST, ALFRED NY 14802 ■ (607) 555-1234

LONG, BETH	Admission: 04/26/YYYY	
IPCase001	DOB: 12/17/YYYY	**Nurses' Notes**
Dr. BLACK	ROOM: 369	

DATE	TIME	TREATMENTS & MEDICATIONS	TIME	NURSES' NOTES
4/26/YYYY			1400	A 30 year old female admitted to room 369 services of Dr. Black. Oriented to room and call system. Urine culture sent to lab.
				Reviewed and Approved: V. South, RN ATP-B-S:02:1001261385: V. South, RN (Signed: 4/26/YYYY 2:00:10 PM EST)
4/26/YYYY			1430	Resting in bed.
				Reviewed and Approved: V. South, RN ATP-B-S:02:1001261385: V. South, RN (Signed: 4/26/YYYY 2:30:23 PM EST)
			1530	Resting comfortably in bed. Intravenous infusing well. Temperature decreased to 99°.
				Reviewed and Approved: V. South, RN ATP-B-S:02:1001261385: V. South, RN (Signed: 4/26/YYYY 3:31:00 PM EST)
	1930	Tylenol, 2 tablets by mouth for increased temperature.	2000	Vitals taken. Temperature increased to 103.
				Reviewed and Approved: O. Richards, RN ATP-B-S:02:1001261385: O. Richards, RN (Signed: 4/26/YYYY 8:04:05 PM EST)
			2045	Refused backrub. States she gets chilled and then too warm. Face is flushed at present.
				Reviewed and Approved: O. Richards, RN ATP-B-S:02:1001261385: O. Richards, RN (Signed: 4/26/YYYY 8:45:44 PM EST)
			2215	Appears asleep. Respirations even.
				Reviewed and Approved: O. Richards, RN ATP-B-S:02:1001261385: O. Richards, RN (Signed: 4/26/YYYY 10:15:17 PM EST)
	2330	Temperature 100.1. Pulse 80. Respirations 16.	2330	Sleeping. Awakened for vital signs.
				Reviewed and Approved: J. Dobbs, RN ATP-B-S:02:1001261385: J. Dobbs, RN (Signed: 4/27/YYYY 11:30:34 PM EST)
4/27/YYYY		Saturday	0200	Sleeping. Respirations even.
				Reviewed and Approved: J. Dobbs, RN ATP-B-S:02:1001261385: J. Dobbs, RN (Signed: 4/27/YYYY 2:24:20 AM EST)
	0405	102.7 - 100 - 20	0415	Awake. Vital signs taken. Skin warm to touch.
				Reviewed and Approved: J. Dobbs, RN ATP-B-S:02:1001261385: J. Dobbs, RN (Signed: 4/27/YYYY 4:15:04 AM EST)
	0430	Tylenol tabs 2 by mouth for increased temperature.		Intravenous infusing well.
				Reviewed and Approved: J. Dobbs, RN ATP-B-S:02:1001261385: J. Dobbs, RN (Signed: 4/27/YYYY 4:31:44 AM EST)
			0600	Resting quietly. Skin cooler.
	0600	Temperature - 100.2		Reviewed and Approved: J. Dobbs, RN ATP-B-S:02:1001261385: J. Dobbs, RN (Signed: 4/27/YYYY 6:00:02 AM EST)

GLOBAL CARE MEDICAL CENTER ■ 100 MAIN ST, ALFRED NY 14802 ■ (607) 555-1234

LONG, BETH	Admission: 04/26/YYYY	**Nurses' Notes**
IPCase001	DOB: 12/17/YYYY	
Dr. BLACK	ROOM: 369	

DATE	TIME	TREATMENTS & MEDICATIONS	TIME	NURSES' NOTES
			0730	Temperature decreased. Vital signs stable. States feels better. Intravenous infusing well. Voiding without difficulty.
				Reviewed and Approved: J. Dobbs, RN ATP-B-S:02:1001261385: J. Dobbs, RN (Signed: 4/27/YYYY 7:30:16 AM EST)
4/27/YYYY			0800	Ate all of breakfast.
				Reviewed and Approved: V. South, RN ATP-B-S:02:1001261385: V. South, RN (Signed: 4/27/YYYY 8:00:41 AM EST)
			0830	Patient took shower with bag over intravenous site.
				Reviewed and Approved: V. South, RN ATP-B-S:02:1001261385: V. South, RN (Signed: 4/27/YYYY 8:30:28 AM EST)
			1000	Move well. Walking to day room to smoke.
				Reviewed and Approved: V. South, RN ATP-B-S:02:1001261385: V. South, RN (Signed: 4/27/YYYY 10:01:03 AM EST)
	1130	Temperature 104	1130	Complains of chills. Temperature increased. Lying in bed.
				Reviewed and Approved: V. South, RN ATP-B-S:02:1001261385: V. South, RN (Signed: 4/27/YYYY 11:30:44 AM EST)
			1700	Up as desired to smoke. Supper taken fair.
				Reviewed and Approved: O. Richards, RN ATP-B-S:02:1001261385: O. Richards, RN (Signed: 4/27/YYYY 5:00:17 PM EST)
			1800	Complains of feeling 'shaky' and felt fever coming on. Temperature = 102. Charge notified and patient given Tylenol 2 tabs.
				Reviewed and Approved: O. Richards, RN ATP-B-S:02:1001261385: O. Richards, RN (Signed: 4/27/YYYY 6:02:41 PM EST)
			2000	Patient complains of 'sweats.' Patient's skin moist & warm.
				Temperature = 100.3. Encouraged to drink fluids. Voiding well. No sediment or stones strained from urine.
				Reviewed and Approved: O. Richards, RN ATP-B-S:02:1001261385: O. Richards, RN (Signed: 4/27/YYYY 8:00:10 PM EST)
			2200	Awake. No stones strained from urine.
				Temperature at 2200 - 98.4. Skin less diaphoretic.
				Reviewed and Approved: O. Richards, RN ATP-B-S:02:1001261385: O. Richards, RN (Signed: 4/27/YYYY 10:00:51 PM EST)
4/27/YYYY	2330	Temperature 98.1. Pulse 72. Respirations 20.	2330	Awake. Reading. No complaints offered. Intravenous infusing well.
				Reviewed and Approved: J. Dobbs, RN ATP-B-S:02:1001261385: J. Dobbs, RN (Signed: 4/27/YYYY 11:30:16 AM EST)

GLOBAL CARE MEDICAL CENTER ■ 100 MAIN ST, ALFRED NY 14802 ■ (607) 555-1234

LONG, BETH	Admission: 04/26/YYYY	**Nurses' Notes**
IPCase001	DOB: 12/17/YYYY	
Dr. BLACK	ROOM: 369	

DATE	TIME	TREATMENTS & MEDICATIONS	TIME	NURSES' NOTES
4/28/YYYY		Sunday	0200	Sleeping at present.
				Reviewed and Approved: J. Dobbs, RN ATP-B-S:02:1001261385: J. Dobbs, RN (Signed: 4/28/YYYY 2:00:35 AM EST)
			0500	Awakened for vital signs. Temperature increased.
				Reviewed and Approved: J. Dobbs, RN ATP-B-S:02:1001261385: J. Dobbs, RN (Signed: 4/28/YYYY 5:02:00 AM EST)
	0520	Tylenol tabs 2 by mouth for increased temperature.		Medicated. Intravenous infusing well.
				Reviewed and Approved: J. Dobbs, RN ATP-B-S:02:1001261385: J. Dobbs, RN (Signed: 4/28/YYYY 5:20:18 AM EST)
			0630	Sleeping at present.
				Reviewed and Approved: J. Dobbs, RN ATP-B-S:02:1001261385: J. Dobbs, RN (Signed: 4/28/YYYY 6:30:16 AM EST)
			0730	Awake for vitals. Ambulatory in hall. Ate 90% of breakfast. To bathroom for shower. Sitting out of bed in a chair.
				Reviewed and Approved: V. South, RN ATP-B-S:02:1001261385: V. South, RN (Signed: 4/28/YYYY 7:30:00 AM EST)
			1200	Ate 75% of lunch. Ambulatory. To day room to smoke.
				Reviewed and Approved: V. South, RN ATP-B-S:02:1001261385: V. South, RN (Signed: 4/28/YYYY 12:03:00 PM EST)
			1400	All urine strained. No calculi noted.
				Reviewed and Approved: V. South, RN ATP-B-S:02:1001261385: V. South, RN (Signed: 4/28/YYYY 2:00:40 PM EST)
			1530	In day room visiting. Vitals taken. Intravenous infusing well.
				Reviewed and Approved: V. South, RN ATP-B-S:02:1001261385: V. South, RN (Signed: 4/28/YYYY 3:30:04 PM EST)
4/28/YYYY			1830	Ambulatory as desired,
				Reviewed and Approved: O. Richards, RN ATP-B-S:02:1001261385: O. Richards, RN (Signed: 4/28/YYYY 6:30:35 PM EST)
		Sunday	1930	Vitals taken. Temperature decreased. Preparation effective.
				Reviewed and Approved: O. Richards, RN ATP-B-S:02:1001261385: O. Richards, RN (Signed: 4/28/YYYY 7:30:06 PM EST)
		No calculi noted	2030	Refused backrub. Clear juice taken.
				Reviewed and Approved: O. Richards, RN ATP-B-S:02:1001261385: O. Richards, RN (Signed: 4/28/YYYY 8:30:17 PM EST)
		Large amount white sediment.	2200	Resting in bed. Awake. Television on.
				Reviewed and Approved: O. Richards, RN ATP-B-S:02:1001261385: O. Richards, RN (Signed: 4/28/YYYY 10:00:44 PM EST)

GLOBAL CARE MEDICAL CENTER ■ 100 MAIN ST, ALFRED NY 14802 ■ (607) 555-1234

LONG, BETH	Admission: 04/26/YYYY	**Nurses' Notes**
IPCase001	DOB: 12/17/YYYY	
Dr. BLACK	ROOM: 369	

DATE	TIME	TREATMENTS & MEDICATIONS	TIME	NURSES' NOTES
	2330	Temperature 99.4. Pulse 92. Respirations 20.	2330	Awake. Resting quietly. Intravenous infusing well. Vital signs taken.
				Reviewed and Approved: J. Dobbs, RN ATP-B-S:02:1001261385: J. Dobbs, RN (Signed: 4/28/YYYY 11:30:16 PM EST)
4/29/YYY		Monday	0200	Sleeping at present.
				Reviewed and Approved: J. Dobbs, RN ATP-B-S:02:1001261385: J. Dobbs, RN (Signed: 4/29/YYYY 2:00:42 AM EST)
	0400	Temperature 97.3. Pulse 80. Respirations 16.	0400	Sleeping. Skin warm & dry.
				Reviewed and Approved: J. Dobbs, RN ATP-B-S:02:1001261385: J. Dobbs, RN (Signed: 4/29/YYYY 4:00:10 AM EST)
	0545	Tylenol, 2 tablets by mouth for headache.	0630	Out of bed to bathroom for self morning care. Ready for X-rays.
				Reviewed and Approved: J. Dobbs, RN ATP-B-S:02:1001261385: J. Dobbs, RN (Signed: 4/29/YYYY 6:30:44 AM EST)
			0730	Vital signs stable. Temperature decreased. Denies discomfort.
				Reviewed and Approved: V. South, RN ATP-B-S:02:1001261385: V. South, RN (Signed: 4/29/YYYY 7:30:00 AM EST)
			0800	Took all of clear liquids for breakfast.
				Reviewed and Approved: V. South, RN ATP-B-S:02:1001261385: V. South, RN (Signed: 4/29/YYYY 8:03:00 AM EST)
			1000	Down for test. Intravenous infusing well.
				Reviewed and Approved: V. South, RN ATP-B-S:02:1001261385: V. South, RN (Signed: 4/29/YYYY 10:00:47 AM EST)
			1200	Took all of lunch.
				Reviewed and Approved: V. South, RN ATP-B-S:02:1001261385: V. South, RN (Signed: 4/29/YYYY 12:03:00 PM EST)
			1400	Resting quietly in bed at this time. Had better day.
				Reviewed and Approved: V. South, RN ATP-B-S:02:1001261385: V. South, RN (Signed: 4/29/YYYY 2:03:00 PM EST)
4/29/YYYY	1511	Monday	1530	Resting, watching TV. Intravenous infusing.
				Reviewed and Approved: O. Richards, RN ATP-B-S:02:1001261385: O. Richards, RN (Signed: 4/29/YYYY 3:30:44 PM EST)
			1600	Denies any discomfort. Temperature decreased. Ambulatory in hall to day room.
				Reviewed and Approved: O. Richards, RN ATP-B-S:02:1001261385: O. Richards, RN (Signed: 4/29/YYYY 4:01:13 PM EST)
			1730	Patient took 60% of supper.
				Reviewed and Approved: O. Richards, RN ATP-B-S:02:1001261385: O. Richards, RN (Signed: 4/29/YYYY 5:30:55 PM EST)

GLOBAL CARE MEDICAL CENTER ■ 100 MAIN ST, ALFRED NY 14802 ■ (607) 555-1234

LONG, BETH	Admission: 04/26/YYYY	**Nurses' Notes**
IPCase001	DOB: 12/17/YYYY	
Dr. BLACK	ROOM: 369	

DATE	TIME	TREATMENTS & MEDICATIONS	TIME	NURSES' NOTES
4/29/YYYY		Monday	1800	Ambulatory to day room.
				Reviewed and Approved: O. Richards, RN ATP-B-S:02:1001261385: O. Richards, RN (Signed: 4/30/YYYY 6:00:44 PM EST)
			1900	Resting on bed; husband in. Intravenous infusing.
				Reviewed and Approved: O. Richards, RN ATP-B-S:02:1001261385: O. Richards, RN (Signed: 4/30/YYYY 7:00:03 PM EST)
			2000	Bedtime care refused.
				Reviewed and Approved: O. Richards, RN ATP-B-S:02:1001261385: O. Richards, RN (Signed: 4/30/YYYY 8:00:49 PM EST)
			2215	Patient resting, watching television. Had a good evening.
				Reviewed and Approved: O. Richards, RN ATP-B-S:02:1001261385: O. Richards, RN (Signed: 4/30/YYYY 10:15:33 PM EST)
4/29/YYYY		Monday	2400	Asleep. Intravenous infusing well at 100/hr.
				Reviewed and Approved: J. Dobbs, RN ATP-B-S:02:1001261385: J. Dobbs, RN (Signed: 4/30/YYYY 1:04:44 AM EST)
			0200	Continues to sleep.
				Reviewed and Approved: J. Dobbs, RN ATP-B-S:02:1001261385: J. Dobbs, RN (Signed: 4/30/YYYY 2:00:00 AM EST)
	0400	Temperature 97.8. No evidence of calculi in urine.	0400	Continues to sleep.
				Reviewed and Approved: J. Dobbs, RN ATP-B-S:02:1001261385: J. Dobbs, RN (Signed: 4/30/YYYY 4:00:12 AM EST)
			0600	Slept well.
				Reviewed and Approved: J. Dobbs, RN ATP-B-S:02:1001261385: J. Dobbs, RN (Signed: 4/30/YYYY 6:00:44 AM EST)
4/30/YYYY		Tuesday	0730	Awake and alert. Skin pink and warm to touch. Respirations 16 per minute and even.
				Reviewed and Approved: J. Dobbs, RN ATP-B-S:02:1001261385: J. Dobbs, RN (Signed: 4/30/YYYY 7:30:26 AM EST)
			0750	Intravenous discontinued needle intact. See flow sheet.
				Reviewed and Approved: V. South, RN ATP-B-S:02:1001261385: V. South, RN (Signed: 4/30/YYYY 7:50:47 AM EST)
			0800	Patient resting quietly.
				Reviewed and Approved: V. South, RN ATP-B-S:02:1001261385: V. South, RN (Signed: 4/30/YYYY 8:00:00 AM EST)
			0930	Patient states she has no pain.
				Reviewed and Approved: V. South, RN ATP-B-S:02:1001261385: V. South, RN (Signed: 4/30/YYYY 9:30:00 AM EST)
			0945	Ambulatory to day room.
				Reviewed and Approved: V. South, RN ATP-B-S:02:1001261385: V. South, RN (Signed: 4/30/YYYY 9:45:47 AM EST)

GLOBAL CARE MEDICAL CENTER ■ 100 MAIN ST, ALFRED NY 14802 ■ (607) 555-1234

LONG, BETH Admission: 04/26/YYYY
IPCase001 DOB: 12/17/YYYY
Dr. BLACK ROOM: 369

Nurses' Notes

DATE	TIME	TREATMENTS & MEDICATIONS	TIME	NURSES' NOTES
4/30/YYYY			1015	Strained urine. No signs or calculi 800 cubic centimeters.
				Reviewed and Approved: V. South, RN ATP-B-S:02:1001261385: V. South, RN (Signed: 4/30/YYYY 10:15:11 AM EST)
			1130	Returned to room.
				Reviewed and Approved: V. South, RN ATP-B-S:02:1001261385: V. South, RN (Signed: 4/30/YYYY 11:30:33 AM EST)
			1150	Discharged to home.
				Reviewed and Approved: V. South, RN ATP-B-S:02:1001261385: V. South, RN (Signed: 4/30/YYYY 11:50:40 AM EST)

GLOBAL CARE MEDICAL CENTER ■ 100 MAIN ST, ALFRED NY 14802 ■ (607) 555-1234

LONG, BETH
IPCase001
Dr. BLACK

Admission: 04/26/YYYY
DOB: 12/17/YYYY
ROOM: 369

Nursing Discharge Status Summary

1.	AFEBRILE:	X	Yes		No				
2.	WOUND:		Clean/Dry		Reddened	Infected		NA	
3.	PAIN FREE:	X	Yes		No	If "No," describe:			
4.	POST-HOSPITAL INSTRUCTION SHEET GIVEN TO PATIENT/FAMILY:						Yes	X	No
	If NO, complete lines 5 – 8 below.								
5.	DIET:	X	Regular		Other (Describe):				
6.	ACTIVITY:	X	Normal		Light		Limited		Bed rest
7.	MEDICATIONS:	Prescriptions given to patient.							
8.	INSTRUCTIONS GIVEN TO PATIENT/FAMILY:				Appointment as needed.				
9.	PATIENT/FAMILY verbalize understanding of instructions:					X	Yes		No
10.	DISCHARGED at	1150	Via:	X	Wheelchair		Stretcher		Ambulance Co.
	Accompanied by:	Vera South, RN				to	Front desk		
	COMMENTS:								

GLOBAL CARE MEDICAL CENTER ■ 100 MAIN ST, ALFRED NY 14802 ■ (607) 555-1234

IPCase002

Global Care Medical Center
100 Main St, Alfred NY 14802
(607) 555-1234
Hospital No. 999

Inpatient Face Sheet

Patient Name and Address	Gender	Race	Marital Status	Patient No.
TIDD, JUDY	F	W	S	IPCase002
1227 MAIN STREET	**Date of Birth**	**Age**	**Maiden Name**	**Occupation**
ALMOND, NY 14804	02/08/YYYY	63	Tidd	Landscape Architect

Admission Date	Time	Discharge Date	Time	Length of Stay	Telephone Number
09/24/YYYY	08:35	09/26/YYYY	10:00	02 DAY	(607)555-5535

Guarantor Name and Address		Next of Kin Name and Address	
TIDD, JUDY 1227 MAIN STREET ALMOND, NY 14804		TIDD, GEORGE 1225 MAIN STREET ALMOND, NY 14804	
Guarantor Telephone No.	**Relationship to Patient**	**Next of Kin Telephone Number**	**Relationship to Patient**
(607) 555-5535	Self	(607)555-6986	Brother
Admitting Physician	**Service**	**Admit Type**	**Room Number/Bed**
Philip Newman, MD			254
Attending Physician	**Admitting Diagnosis**		
Philip Newman, MD	Cataract right eye		
Primary Insurer	**Policy and Group Number**	**Secondary Insurer**	**Policy and Group Number**
NA	NA	NA	NA

Diagnoses and Procedures	ICD Code
Principal Diagnosis	
Cataract of the right eye	
Secondary Diagnoses	
Chronic obstructive pulmonary disease	
Principal Procedure	
Extracapsular cataract extraction with implantation of a synthetic substitute,16 diopter posterior chamber lens (Sinskey style posterior chamber lens) in the ciliary sulcus.	
Secondary Procedures	

Discharge Instructions

Activity: ❒ Bedrest ❒ Light ❒ Usual ❒ Unlimited ❒ Other:

Diet: ❒ Regular ❒ Low Cholesterol ❒ Low Salt ❒ ADA ❒ ____ Calorie

Follow-Up: ❒ Call for appointment ❒ Office appointment on ____ ❒ Other:

Special Instructions: None

Attending Physician Authentication:	Reviewed and Approved: Philip Newman MD ATP-B-S:02:1001261385: Philip Newman MD (Signed: 09/24/YYYY 9:04:26 AM EST)

TIDD, JUDY	Admission: 09/24/YYYY	**Consent to Admission**
IPCase002	DOB: 02/08/YYYY	
Dr. NEWMAN	ROOM: 254	

I, Judy Tidd hereby consent to admission to the Global Care Medical Center (GCMC), and I further consent to such routine hospital care, diagnostic procedures, and medical treatment that the medical and professional staff of GCMC may deem necessary or advisable. I authorize the use of medical information obtained about me as specified above and the disclosure of such information to my referring physician(s). This form has been fully explained to me, and I understand its contents. I further understand that no guarantees have been made to me as to the results of treatments or examinations done at the GCMC.

Reviewed and Approved: Judy Tidd
ATP-B-S:02:1001261385: Judy Tidd
(Signed: 09/24/YYYY 8:45:05 PM EST)

Signature of Patient

Signature of Parent/Legal Guardian for Minor

Relationship to Minor

Reviewed and Approved: Andrea Witteman
ATP-B-S:02:1001261385: Andrea Witteman
(Signed: 9/24/YYYY 8:46:34 PM EST)

WITNESS: Global Care Medical Center Staff Member

Consent To Release Information For Reimbursement Purposes

In order to permit reimbursement, upon request, the Global Care Medical Center (GCMC) may disclose such treatment information pertaining to my hospitalization to any corporation, organization, or agent thereof, which is, or may be liable under contract to the GCMC or to me, or to any of my family members or other person, for payment of all or part of the GCMC's charges for services rendered to me (e.g. the patient's health insurance carrier). I understand that the purpose of any release of information is to facilitate reimbursement for services rendered. In addition, in the event that my health insurance program includes utilization review of services provided during this admission. I authorize GCMC to release information as is necessary to permit the review. This authorization will expire once the reimbursement for services rendered is complete.

Reviewed and Approved: Judy Tidd
ATP-B-S:02:1001261385: Judy Tidd
(Signed: 09/24/YYYY 8:47:05 PM EST)

Signature of Patient

Signature of Parent/Legal Guardian for Minor

Relationship to Minor

Reviewed and Approved: Andrea Witteman
ATP-B-S:02:1001261385: Andrea Witteman
(Signed: 9/24/YYYY 8:47:56 PM EST)

WITNESS: Global Care Medical Center Staff Member

Global Care Medical Center ■ 100 Main St, Alfred NY 14802 ■ (607) 555-1234

TIDD, JUDY	Admission: 09/24/YYYY	**Advance Directive**
IPCase002	DOB: 02/08/YYYY	
Dr. NEWMAN	ROOM: 254	

Your answers to the following questions will assist your Physician and the Hospital to respect your wishes regarding your medical care. This information will become a part of your medical record.

		Yes	No	Patient's Initials
1.	Have you been provided with a copy of the information called "Patient Rights Regarding Health Care Decision"?	X		
2.	Have you prepared a "Living Will"? If yes, please provide the Hospital with a copy for your medical record.		X	
3.	Have you prepared a Durable Power of Attorney for Health Care? If yes, please provide the Hospital with a copy for your medical record.		X	
4.	Have you provided this facility with an Advance Directive on a prior admission and is it still in effect? If yes, Admitting Office to contact Medical Records to obtain a copy for the medical record.		X	
5.	Do you desire to execute a Living Will/Durable Power of Attorney? If yes, refer to in order: a. Physician b. Social Service c. Volunteer Service		X	

Hospital Staff Directions: Check when each step is completed.

1. ✓ Verify the above questions were answered and actions taken where required.
2. ✓ If the "Patient Rights" information was provided to someone other than the patient, state reason:

____

______________________ ______________________

Name of Individual Receiving Information **Relationship to Patient**

3. ✓ If information was provided in a language other than English, specify language and method.
4. ✓ Verify patient was advised on how to obtain additional information on Advance Directives.
5. ✓ Verify the Patient/Family Member/Legal Representative was asked to provide the Hospital with a copy of the Advanced Directive which will be retained in the medical record.

File this form in the medical record, and give a copy to the patient.

____

Name of Patient/Name of Individual giving information if different from Patient

Reviewed and Approved: Judy Tidd
ATP-B-S:02:1001261385: Judy Tidd
(Signed: 09/24/YYYY 8:51:05 PM EST)

Signature of Patient **Date**

Reviewed and Approved: Andrea Witteman
ATP-B-S:02:1001261385: Andrea Witteman
(Signed: 09/24/YYYY 8:52:47 PM EST)

Signature of Hospital Representative **Date**

Global Care Medical Center ■ 100 Main St, Alfred NY 14802 ■ (607) 555-1234

TIDD, JUDY	Admission: 09/24/YYYY	**Discharge Summary**
IPCase002	DOB: 02/08/YYYY	
Dr. NEWMAN	ROOM: 254	

ADMISSION DATE: 9-24-YYYY DISCHARGE DATE: 09/26/YYYY

ADMISSION DIAGNOSIS: Cataract, right eye.

DISCHARGE DIAGNOSIS: Cataract, right eye. Chronic obstructive pulmonary disease.

OPERATION: Extracapsular cataract extraction with peripheral iridectomy and implantation of a synthetic substitute, 16 diopter Sinskey style lens in the posterior chamber in the ciliary sulcus of the right eye.

SURGEON: Dr. Newman DATE: 9-25-YY COMPLICATIONS: None

SUMMARY: The patient underwent the above procedure without complications and was discharged to be followed up in the office.

Laboratory values: Protime 13.6, control time 11.6. Partial thromboplastin time was normal. Glucose was 140. WBC 4.5, hematocrit 33.5, hemoglobin 11.1 and platelets 129,000. Urine showed 1+ mucus threads.

Chest x-ray shows no evidence of active cardiopulmonary disease.

Electrocardiogram was abnormal-nonspecific ST changes similar to 4-18-YYYY.

DD: 09/27/YYYY

Reviewed and Approved: Philip Newman MD
ATP-B-S:02:1001261385: Philip Newman MD
(Signed: 09/27/YYYY 10:24:44 PM EST)

DT: 09/27/YYYY

Physician Authentication

GLOBAL CARE MEDICAL CENTER ■ 100 MAIN ST, ALFRED NY 14802 ■ (607) 555-1234

TIDD, JUDY	Admission: 09/24/YYYY	**History & Physical Exam**
IPCase002	DOB: 02/08/YYYY	
Dr. NEWMAN	ROOM: 254	

CHIEF COMPLAINT: Bilateral decrease in vision especially in the right eye.

HISTORY OF PRESENT ILLNESS: Mrs. Tidd is a 63 year old woman who has had very poor vision in the right eye for some time which was the result of a cataract and is finding increasing difficulty functioning because of cataract developing in her other eye at this time. Allergies: Sulfa.

FAMILY HISTORY: She has a brother who had retinal detachment.

SOCIAL HISTORY: She denies smoking or drinking alcohol.

REVIEW OF SYSTEMS: Neuro - negative. Eye, ear, nose and throat - bilateral decrease in vision as well as occasional sinus problems. Cardiovascular negative. Pulmonary - she has had chronic obstructive pulmonary disease, treated with medication. Gastrointestinal- she had history of liver biopsy in the past. Genitourinary - occasional frequent urination and history of kidney infections in the past. Gynecologic - negative. Endocrine - negative. Hematologic - she has a history of platelet disorder for which she had a splenectomy in 19YY to increase her platelets. Skin - negative.

PAST MEDICAL HISTORY: covered in review of systems.

BLOOD PRESSURE: 140/76 PULSE: 72 RESPIRATIONS:16

NEUROLOGICAL: Negative.

NECK: Negative.

COR: S-1, S-2 without murmur, gallop or rub.

CHEST: Clear.

ABDOMEN: Negative.

EXTREMITIES: Shows 1+ pedal edema.

Head Ears Eyes Nose Throat: Bilateral cataracts right eye greater than left eye.

IMPRESSION: Bilateral cataracts, right eye greater than the left.

PLAN: Cataract extraction with implant of synthetic substitute in the right eye.

DD: 09/25/YYYY

Reviewed and Approved: Phil Newman MD
ATP-B-S:02:1001261385: Phil Newman MD
(Signed: 09/26/YYYY 2:24:44 PM EST)

DT: 09/26/YYYY

Physician Authentication

GLOBAL CARE MEDICAL CENTER ■ 100 MAIN ST, ALFRED NY 14802 ■ (607) 555-1234

TIDD, JUDY	Admission: 09/24/YYYY	**Progress Notes**
IPCase002	DOB: 02/08/YYYY	
Dr. NEWMAN	ROOM: 254	

Date	Time	Physician's signature required for each order. (Please skip one line between dates.)
09/24/YYYY	0935	CHIEF COMPLAINT: Decreased vision in right eye DIAGNOSIS: Cataract of the right eye Confirmed __X__ Provisional ______ DISCHARGE PLAN: Home. No services needed. Reviewed and Approved: Phil Newman MD ATP-B-S:02:1001261385: Phil Newman MD (Signed: 09/25/YYYY 10:40:55 AM EST)
09/24/YYYY	0935	Pre-op clearance 1600 Physical examination pending. Reviewed and Approved: Phil Newman MD ATP-B-S:02:10012613S5: Phil Newman MD (Signed: 09/24/YYYY 9:40:55 AM EST)
09/25/YYYY	0900	Pre-anesthesia; PS gr 3 tablets for local. Reviewed and Approved: Don Galloway MD ATP-B-S:02:1001261385: Don Galloway MD (Signed: 09/25/YYYY 10:05:42 AM EST)
09/25/YYYY	Op note	Extracapsular cataract extraction with peripheral iridectomy, right eye. No operative or anesthetic complications. **IOLAB INTRAOCULAR LENS** 707G 16.0 **MODEL** **DIOPTERS** PC, SIHSHEY, AHG. SL LOOPS, LASERIDCE. 14MM **CONTROL NO** 030884 707G 6190 **Patient Label** REV 7-78 Reviewed and Approved: Phil Newman MD ATP-B-S:02:1001261385: Phil Newman MD (Signed: 09/25/YYYY 1:40:55 PM EST)
09/26/YYYY	0900	Preop right eye 20/70. Postop right eye 20/40. Minimal edema inferiorly. Follow up in the office. Patient discharged with Maxitrol 4 times daily. Reviewed and Approved: Phil Newman MD ATP-B-S:02:1001261385: Phil Newman MD (Signed: 09/26/YYYY 11:19:34 AM EST)

Global Care Medical Center ■ 100 Main St, Alfred NY 14802 ■ (607) 555-1234

TIDD, JUDY	Admission: 09/24/YYYY	**Doctors' Orders**
IPCase002	DOB: 02/08/YYYY	
Dr. NEWMAN	ROOM: 254	

Date	Time	Physician's signature required for each order. (Please skip one line between dates.)
09/24/YYYY	0930	Date of surgery 09/25/YYYY. Platelets, protime, PTT, complete blood count. Electrolytes. Blood urea nitrogen and glucose. Urinalysis. Electrocardiogram. Chest x-ray (done 09/24/YYYY). Pre-op lab to chart. Nothing by mouth after midnight. Void on call to Operating Room. Garamycin eye solution right eye. One drop every 10 minutes 4 times. Begin at 0615. Homatropine 2% right eye. Neosynephrine 2.5% right eye. Garamycin eye solution, 1 drop each eye every 2 hours while awake. Activities as desired. Vital signs every shift. Reviewed and Approved: Phil Newman MD ATP-B-S:02:1001261385: Phil Newman MD (Signed: 09/24/YYYY 10:45:00 AM EST)
09/24/YYYY	2100	Dalmane 15 milligrams half strength Potassium chloride 30 milliequivalents, 3 times today. Reviewed and Approved: Phil Newman MD ATP-B-S:02:1001261385: Phil Newman MD (Signed: 09/24/YYYY 22:03:44 PM EST)

GLOBAL CARE MEDICAL CENTER ■ 100 MAIN ST, ALFRED NY 14802 ■ (607) 555-1234

TIDD, JUDY Admission: 09/24/YYYY
IPCase002 DOB: 02/08/YYYY
Dr. NEWMAN ROOM: 254

Doctors' Orders

Date	Time	Physician's signature required for each order. (Please skip one line between dates.)
09/25/YYYY	0835	Apply Honan intra-ocular pressure reducer to right eye on arrival in operating room voice order Dr. Newman at 0840. Reviewed and Approved: Phil Newman MD ATP-B-S:02:1001261385: Phil Newman MD (Signed: 09/25/YYYY 10:11:12 AM EST)
09/25/YYYY	1115	Vital signs every half hour for 2 hours then every hour for two hours then every shift. Activity advance to as tolerated. Diet advance to regular as tolerated. Lanoxin 0.125 milligrams by mouth once a day. Lasix 20 milligrams by mouth once a day. Tolectin 1 by mouth three times daily. Dalmane 15 milligrams by mouth at bedtime. Maxitrol ophthalmological ointment, apply once a day in right eye. Label to give to patient at discharge. Reviewed and Approved: Phil Newman MD ATP-B-S:02:1001261385: Phil Newman MD (Signed: 09/25/YYYY 12:24:27 PM EST)
09/25/YYYY	2100	Milk of Magnesia and Cascara half strength. Voice orders. Reviewed and Approved: Phil Newman MD ATP-B-S:02:1001261385: Phil Newman MD (Signed: 09/25/YYYY 22:11:12 PM EST)
09/26/YYYY	1000	Discharge. Reviewed and Approved: Phil Newman MD ATP-B-S:02:1001261385: Phil Newman MD (Signed: 09/26/YYYY 10:45:00 AM EST)

GLOBAL CARE MEDICAL CENTER ■ 100 MAIN ST, ALFRED NY 14802 ■ (607) 555-1234

TIDD, JUDY	Admission: 09/24/YYYY	**Laboratory Data**
IPCase002	DOB: 02/08/YYYY	
Dr. NEWMAN	ROOM: 254	

SPECIMEN COLLECTED: 09/24/YYYY 0900 **SPECIMEN RECEIVED:** 09/24/YYYY 1037

HEMATOLOGY

	PLATELET COUNT	NORMAL 130-400 × 10^3			
	BLEEDING TIME	NORMAL 1-4 MINUTES		Pt:	SEC.
X	PROTIME	CONTROL:	11.6 SECONDS	Pt:	13.6 SECONDS
X	PTT	NORMAL:	<32 SECONDS	Pt:	24 SECONDS
	FIBRINDEX	CONTROL:		Pt:	
	FIBRINOGEN	NORMAL:		Pt:	
	F.D.P.	NORMAL:		Pt:	
	CLOT RETRACTION	NORMAL:	30-65%	Pt:	%
	CLOT LYSIS	24 hr:		48 hr:	

End of Report

GLOBAL CARE MEDICAL CENTER ■ 100 MAIN ST, ALFRED NY 14802 ■ (607) 555-1234

TIDD, JUDY Admission: 09/24/YYYY
IPCase002 DOB: 02/08/YYYY
Dr. NEWMAN ROOM: 254

Laboratory Data

SPECIMEN COLLECTED: 09/24/YYYY 0900 SPECIMEN RECEIVED: 09/24/YYYY 1555

URINALYSIS

TEST	RESULT	FLAG	REFERENCE
DIPSTICK ONLY			
COLOR	Yellow		5-8.0
Ph.	6.5		≤ 1.030
SP. GR.	1.015		
ALBUMIN	Negative		
SUGAR	Negative		≤ 10 mg/dl
ACETONE	Negative		
BILIRUBIN	Negative		≤ 0.8 mg/dl
BLOOD	Negative		0.06 mg/dl hgb
REDUCING			≤ −1 mg/dl
EPITH:	Rare		
W.B.C.:	0-2/hpf		≤ 5/hpf
R.B.C.:	Rare		≤ 5/hpf
BACT.:			1+ (≤ 20/hpf)
CASTS.:			
CRYSTALS:			

1+ mucus threads

End of Report

GLOBAL CARE MEDICAL CENTER ■ 100 MAIN ST, ALFRED NY 14802 ■ (607) 555-1234

TIDD, JUDY	Admission: 09/24/YYYY	**Laboratory Data**
IPCase002	DOB: 02/08/YYYY	
Dr. NEWMAN	ROOM: 254	

SPECIMEN COLLECTED: 09/24/YYYY 0900 SPECIMEN RECEIVED: 09/24/YYYY 1037

BLOOD CHEMISTRY I

TEST	REFERENCE		RESULT	
ACID PHOS	0.0-0.8 U/I			
ALK. PHOS	50-136 U/I			
AMY LASE	23-85 U/I			
LIPASE	4-24 U/I			
GLUCOSE FAST	70-110 mg/dl			
GLUCOSE	Time collected	1 ½	140	X
BUN	7-22 mg/dl		15	X
SODIUM	136-147 mEq/l		141	
POTASSIUM	3.7-5.1 mEq/l		3.5	
CO_2	24-32 mEq /l		30	
CHLORIDE	98-108 mEq/1		108	
CHOLESTEROL	120-280 mg/dl			
SGP-T	3-36 U/I			
SGO-T	M-27-47 U/I	F-22-37 U/I		
CK	M-35-232 U/I	F-21-215 U/I		
LDH	100-190 U/I			
CREATININE	M-0.8-1.3 mg/dl	F-0.6-1.0 mg/dl		
CALCIUM	8.7-10.2 mg/dl			
PHOSPHORUS	2.5-4.9 mg/dl			
BILIRUBIN-DIRECT	0.0-0.4 mg/dl			
BILIRUBIN-TOTAL	Less than 1.5 mg/dl			
TOTAL PROTEIN	6.4-8.2 g /dl			
ALBUMIN	3.4-5.0 g/dl			
URIC ACID	M-3.8-7.1 mg/dl	F-2.6-5.6 mg/dl		
TRIGLYCERIDE	30-200 mg/dl			

GLOBAL CARE MEDICAL CENTER ■ 100 MAIN ST, ALFRED NY 14802 ■ (607) 555-1234

TIDD, JUDY Admission: 09/24/YYYY
IPCase002 DOB: 02/08/YYYY
Dr. NEWMAN ROOM: 254

Laboratory Data

TIME IN: 09/24/YYYY 0905 TIME OUT: 09/24/YYYY 1036

CBC S DIFF

TEST	RESULT	FLAG	REFERENCE
WBC	4.5		4.5-11.0 thous/UL
RBC	3.52		5.2-5.4 mill/UL
HGB	11.8		11.7-16.1 g/dl
HCT	35.5		35.0-47.0 %
MCV	94.9		85-99 fL.
MCH	31.7		
MCHC	33.4		33-37
RDW			11.4-14.5
PTL	129		130-400 thous/UL
SEGS %	31		
LYMPH %	47		20.5-51.1
MONO %	6		1.7-9.3
EOS %	14		
BASO %	2		
BAND %			
GRAN %			42.2-75.2
LYMPH $\times 10^3$			1.2-3.4
MONO $\times 10^3$			0.11-0.59
GRAN $\times 10^3$			1.4-6.5
EOS $\times 10^3$			0.0-0.7
BASO $\times 10^3$			0.0-0.2
ANISO			

End of Report

GLOBAL CARE MEDICAL CENTER ■ 100 MAIN ST, ALFRED NY 14802 ■ (607) 555-1234

TIDD, JUDY	Admission: 09/24/YYYY	**Consent for Operation(s) and/or Procedure(s) and Anesthesia**
IPCase002	DOB: 02/08/YYYY	
Dr. NEWMAN	ROOM: 254	

PERMISSION. I hereby authorize Dr. Newman, or associates of his/her choice at the Global Care Medical Center (the "Hospital") to perform upon Judy Tidd

the following operation(s) and/or procedure(s): Extraction of right cataract with lens implantation

including such photography, videotaping, televising or other observation of the operation(s)/procedure(s) as may be purposeful for the advance of medical knowledge and/or education, with the understanding that the patient's identity will remain anonymous.

EXPLANATION OF PROCEDURE, RISKS, BENEFITS, ALTERNATIVES. Dr. Newman

has fully explained to me the nature and purposes of the operation(s)/procedures named above and has also informed me of expected benefits and complications, attendant discomforts and risks that may arise, as well as possible alternatives to the proposed treatment. I have been given an opportunity to ask questions and all my questions have been answered fully and satisfactorily.

UNFORESEEN CONDITIONS. I understand that during the course of the operation(s) or procedure(s), unforeseen conditions may arise which necessitate procedures in addition to or different front those contemplated. I, therefore, consent to the performance of additional operations and procedures which the above-named physician or his/her associates or assistants may consider necessary.

ANESTHESIA. I further consent to the administration of such anesthesia as may he considered necessary by the above-named physician or his/her associates or assistants. I recognize that there are always risks to life and health associated with anesthesia. Such risks haw been fully explained to me and I have been given an opportunity to ask questions and all my questions have been answered fully and satisfactorily.

SPECIMENS. Any organs or tissues surgically removed may be examined and retained by the Hospital for medical, scientific or educational purposes and such tissues or parts may be disposed of in accordance with accustomed practice and applicable State laws and/or regulations.

NO GUARANTEES. I acknowledge that no guarantees or assurances have been made to me concerning the operation(s) or procedure(s) described above.

MEDICAL DEVICE TRACKING. I hereby authorize the release of my Social Security number to the manufacturer of the medical device(s) I receive, if applicable, in accordance with federal law and regulations which may be used to help locate me if a need arises with regard to this medical device. I release The Global Care Medical Center from any liability that might result from the release of this information.*

UNDERSTANDING OF THIS FORM. I confirm that I have read this form, fully understand its contents, and that all blank spaces above have been completed prior to my signing. I have crossed out any paragraphs above that do not pertain to me.

Patient/ Relative/Guardian*

Reviewed and Approved: Judy Tidd
ATP-B-S:02:1001261385: Judy Tidd
(Signed: 09/24/YYYY 4:51:05 PM EST)

Signature

Relationship, if other than patient signed:

Witness:

Reviewed and Approved: William Preston
ATP-B-S:02:1001261385: William Preston
(Signed: 09/24/YYYY 4:52:47 PM EST)

Signature

Date 09-24-YYYY

*The signature of the patient must be obtained unless the patient is an unemancipated minor under the age of 18 or is otherwise incompetent to sign.

PHYSICIAN'S CERTIFICATION. I hereby certify that I have explained the nature, purpose, benefits, risks of and alternatives to the operation(s)/ procedure(s), have offered to answer any questions and have fully answered all such questions. I believe that the patient (relative/guardian) fully understands what I have explained and answered.

PHYSICIAN: Reviewed and Approved:
Philip Newman MD
ATP-B-S:02:1001261385:
Philip Newman MD
(Signed: 09/24/YYYY 5:24:44 PM EST)

Signature

09/24/YYYY

Date

GLOBAL CARE MEDICAL CENTER ■ 100 MAIN ST, ALFRED NY 14802 ■ (607) 555-1234

TIDD, JUDY	Admission: 09/24/YYYY	**Operative Report**
IPCase002	DOB: 02/08/YYYY	
Dr. NEWMAN	ROOM: 254	

PREOPERATIVE DIAGNOSIS: Cataract right eye.

POSTOPERATIVE DIAGNOSIS: Same.

OPERATION PERFORMED: Extra Capsular Cataract extraction with implantation of a replacement synthetic substitute 16-diopter posterior chamber lens (a Sinskey style posterior chamber lens) ciliary sulcus.

SURGEON: Dr. Newman

DATE: 09/25/YYYY

COMPLICATIONS: None.

ANESTHESIA: Local.

OPERATIVE NOTE: A Honan balloon was placed on the right eye for half-an-hour at 35 millimeters of Mercury pressure. The patient was then prepped and draped in the usual fashion and an O'Brien block and a retrobulbar injection of Marcaine and Lidocaine and Wydase were performed on the right. The lid speculum was inserted, superior rectus suture was placed. A fornix-based flap was made; limbal hemostasis was obtained with bipolar cautery. A corneal groove was made with a 64 Beaver blade and a microsharp entered the anterior chamber. Healon was injected into the anterior chamber and an anterior capsulotomy was performed. The wound was enlarged with corneal scleral scissors to the right and to the left and 8-0 silk 10 o'clock and 2 o'clock sutures were placed. Nucleus expression was performed without difficulty and temporary sutures were tied. Site irrigation aspiration was performed and Kratz scratcher was used to polish the posterior capsule. The 16-diopter implant was inspected, irrigated and Healon placed on the implant and in the anterior chamber. The implant was then inserted with the inferior Haptic beneath the iris at 6 o'clock into the sulcus, avoiding the capsule. The superior Haptic was then likewise placed beneath the iris at 12 o'clock. The lens was rotated to approximately 9 and 3 o'clock positions with excellent centration. The peripheral iridectomy was performed. Balanced salt solution was irrigated to remove the Healon and the wound closed with interrupted 10-0 Nylon sutures, the knots of which were buried. The superior rectus suture was removed. Maxitrol ointment was placed on the eye and a patch and shield placed on the eye.

DD:09-25-YYYY

Reviewed and Approved:
Philip Newman MD
ATP-B-S:02:1001261385:
Philip Newman MD
(Signed: 09/26/YYYY 5:24:44 PM EST)

Physician Name

DT:09-26-YYYY

Global Care Medical Center ■ 100 Main St, Alfred NY 14802 ■ (607) 555-1234

TIDD, JUDY Admission: 09/24/YYYY
IPCase002 DOB: 02/08/YYYY
Dr. NEWMAN ROOM: 254

Pathology Report

Date of Surgery: 09-25-YYYY

OPERATION: Extraction of right cataract with lens implantation.

SPECIMEN: Cataract

GROSS: The specimen submitted as "cataract right eye" consists of a discoid lens measuring .8 cm in greatest dimension.

GROSS DIAGNOSIS ONLY: Lens, clinically right eye.

DD:09-25-YYYY

Reviewed and Approved:
Marcus Aurelius, MD
ATP-B-S:02:1001261385:
Marcus Aurelius, MD
(Signed: 09/26/YYYY 5:24:44 PM EST)

DT:09-26-YYYY

GLOBAL CARE MEDICAL CENTER ■ 100 MAIN ST, ALFRED NY 14802 ■ (607) 555-1234

TIDD, JUDY	Admission: 09/24/YYYY	**Radiology Report**
IPCase002	DOB: 02/08/YYYY	
Dr. NEWMAN	ROOM: 254	

Date of x-ray: 09/24/YYYY

REASON: Pre operative

TECHNICAL DATA: No chest complaints.

CHEST: Posteroanterior and lateral views show no evidence of any active cardiopulmonary disease. There is a rather severe compression fracture of the lower thoracic spine which was present on the previous chest x-ray of 4-8-YYYY. The patient also appears to have some degree of chronic obstructive pulmonary disease.

CONCLUSION: chronic obstructive pulmonary disease. Old compression fracture of the lower thoracic spine.

DD:09/24/YYYY

Reviewed and Approved:
Randall Cunningham, MD
ATP-B-S:02:1001261385:
Randall Cunningham, MD
(Signed: 09/26/YYYY 5:24:44 PM EST)

DT:09/24/YYYY

TIDD, JUDY	Admission: 09/24/YYYY	**EKG Report**
IPCase002	DOB: 02/08/YYYY	
Dr. NEWMAN	ROOM: 254	

Date of EKG: 09/24/YYYY Time of EKG: 1005

Rate 80

PR 16

QRSD .08

QT .38

QTC

-- Axis --

P

QRS

T

Abnormal: Non specific ST changes similar to 04/18/YYYY

Reviewed and Approved:
Steven J. Chambers, MD
ATP-B-S:02:1001261385:
Marcus Aurelius, MD
(Signed: 09/26/YYYY 5:24:44 PM EST)
Steven J. Chambers, MD

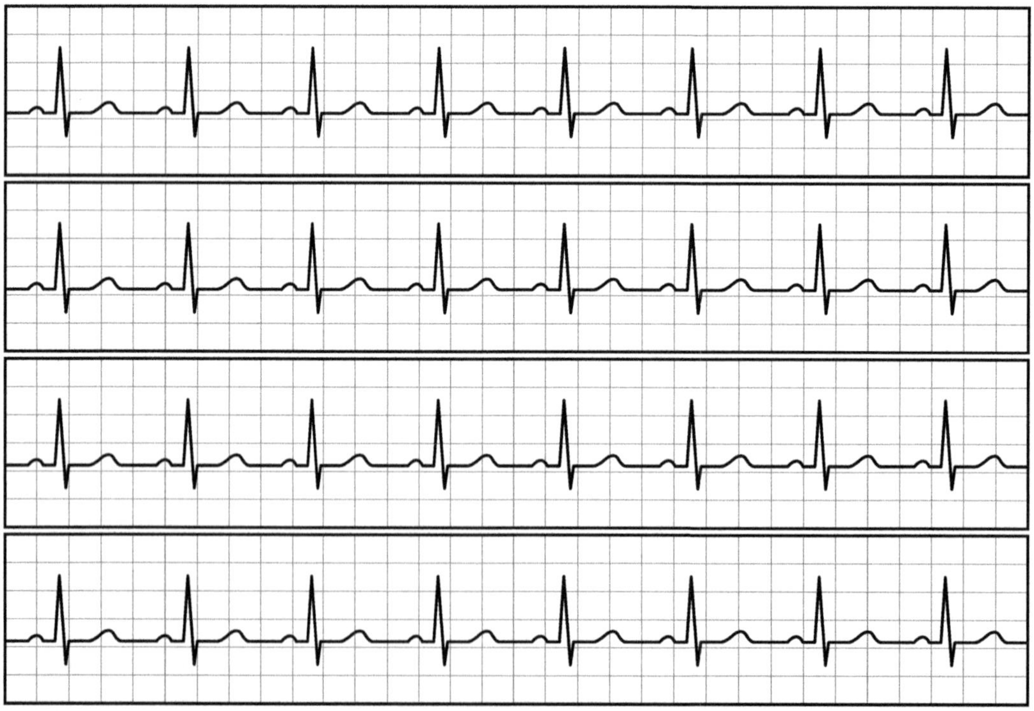

GLOBAL CARE MEDICAL CENTER ■ 100 MAIN ST, ALFRED NY 14802 ■ (607) 555-1234

TIDD, JUDY	Admission: 09/24/YYYY	**Medication Administration Record**
IPCase002	DOB: 02/08/YYYY	
Dr. NEWMAN	ROOM: 254	

Special Instructions:

Medication (dose and route)	Date: 09/24 Time	Initials	Date: 09/25 Time	Initials	Date: 09/26 Time	Initials	Date: Time	Initials
Garamycin eye solution 1 gtt ou q2h	0800	VS	0800	VS	0800	HF		
Ka Cl 30 meq 3x today	0600	GPW	0600	GPW	0600	GPW		
Maxitrol ophthalmic ointment, apply qid OD	1800	JD	1800	OR	D/c			
PRN Medications:								
Dalmane 15 mg	0800	JD	0800	JD	0800	HF	0800	HF
Milk of magnesia + cascara	0800	JD	0800	JD	D/C			

Initials	Signature and Title	Initials	Signature and Title	Initials	Signature and Title
VS	Vera South, RN	GPW	G. P. Well, RN		
OR	Ora Richards, RN				
JD	Jane Dobbs, RN				
HF	H.Figgs, RN				

Global Care Medical Center ■ 100 Main St, Alfred NY 14802 ■ (607)555-1234

TIDD, JUDY IPCase002 Dr. NEWMAN	Admission: 09/24/YYYY DOB: 02/08/YYYY ROOM: 254	**Nurses' Notes**

DATE	TIME	TREATMENTS & MEDICATIONS	TIME	NURSES' NOTES
09/24/YYYY			1000	This 63 year old white female admitted to room 254 under the services of Dr. Newman for removal cataract right eye with implant. Alert skin warm and dry to the touch. Legs edematous. Temperature 97.7 Pulse 76 Respiration 12 Blood Pressure 144/90 Reviewed and Approved: V. South, RN ATP-B-S:02:1001261385: V. South, RN (Signed: 09/24/YYYY 10:01:03 AM EST)
			1230	Ate 75% of regular lunch. Reviewed and Approved: V. South, RN ATP-B-S:02:1001261385: V. South, RN (Signed: 09/24/YYYY 12:35:41 PM EST)
			1340	Voided urine specimen collected and taken to lab. Reviewed and Approved: V. South, RN ATP-B-S:02:1001261385: V. South, RN (Signed: 09/24/YYYY 01:45:28 PM EST)
			1400	To Dr. Newman's office via wheelchair. Reviewed and Approved: V. South, RN ATP-B-S:02:1001261385: V. South, RN (Signed: 09/24/YYYY 02:06:03 PM EST)
			1530	Down to Dr. Pagell's office. Reviewed and Approved: V. South, RN ATP-B-S:02:1001261385: V. South, RN (Signed: 09/24/YYYY 03:40:44 PM EST)
			1600	Brought back from Dr. Pagell's office via wheelchair. Reviewed and Approved: O. Richards, RN ATP-B-S:02:1001261385: O. Richards, RN (Signed: 09/24/YYYY 04:04:00 PM EST)
			1630	Appetite good ate supper. Reviewed and Approved: O. Richards, RN ATP-B-S:02:1001261385: O. Richards, RN (Signed: 09/24/YYYY 04:32:41 PM EST)
			1730	In bed resting. Up to bathroom voiding every 2 hours. Reviewed and Approved: O. Richards, RN ATP-B-S:02:1001261385: O. Richards, RN (Signed: 09/24/YYYY 05:34:10 PM EST)
			1830	Ambulating in hall to day room. Reviewed and Approved: O. Richards, RN ATP-B-S:02:1001261385: O. Richards, RN (Signed: 09/24/YYYY 06:32:51 PM EST)
			1930	Back in bed dozing. Reviewed and Approved: J. Dobbs, RN ATP-B-S:02:1001261385: J. Dobbs, RN (Signed: 09/24/YYYY 07:33:16 PM EST)
			2030	Up to bathroom and washed self. Reviewed and Approved: J. Dobbs, RN ATP-B-S:02:1001261385: J. Dobbs, RN (Signed: 09/24/YYYY 08:35:44 PM EST)
			2130	Sitting up in bed drinking Pepsi. Reviewed and Approved: J. Dobbs, RN ATP-B-S:02:1001261385: J. Dobbs, RN (Signed: 09/24/YYYY 09:35:07 PM EST)

GLOBAL CARE MEDICAL CENTER ■ 100 MAIN ST, ALFRED NY 14802 ■ (607)555-1234

TIDD, JUDY	Admission: 09/24/YYYY	**Nurses' Notes**
IPCase002	DOB: 02/08/YYYY	
Dr. NEWMAN	ROOM: 254	

DATE	TIME	TREATMENTS & MEDICATIONS	TIME	NURSES' NOTES
09/24/YYYY			2230	Lying quietly in bed. Refused back rub and said she would like to try to sleep without her sleeping pill. Reviewed and Approved: J. Dobbs, RN ATP-B-S:02:1001261385: J. Dobbs, RN (Signed: 09/24/YYYY 10:30:16 PM EST)
			2245	Resting quietly. Voiced no complaints. Reviewed and Approved: J. Dobbs, RN ATP-B-S:02:1001261385: J. Dobbs, RN (Signed: 09/24/YYYY 10:47:41 PM EST)
09/24/YYYY		Nothing by mouth for operating room	2330	Resting quietly in bed without complaints. Reviewed and Approved: J. Dobbs, RN ATP-B-S:02:1001261385: J. Dobbs, RN (Signed: 09/24/YYYY 11:32:41 PM EST)
09/25/YYYY		Tuesday	0100-0500	Sleeping with respiration easy and regular on hourly checks. Reviewed and Approved: J. Dobbs, RN ATP-B-S:02:1001261385: J. Dobbs, RN (Signed: 09/25/YYYY 05:02:00 PM EST)
		96-72-16 140/60	0515	Awake out of bed to bathroom to void. Vital signs taken, out of bed ambulated in hall to tub room for self AM care for surgery. Reviewed and Approved: J. Dobbs, RN ATP-B-S:02:1001261385: J. Dobbs, RN (Signed: 09/25/YYYY 05:17:00 AM EST)
			0600	Resting quietly in bed without complaints. Reviewed and Approved: J. Dobbs, RN ATP-B-S:02:1001261385: J. Dobbs, RN (Signed: 09/25/YYYY 06:04:00 AM EST)

GLOBAL CARE MEDICAL CENTER ■ 100 MAIN ST, ALFRED NY 14802 ■ (607)555-1234

TIDD, JUDY	Admission: 09/24/YYYY	**Patient Property Record**
IPCase002	DOB: 02/08/YYYY	
Dr. NEWMAN	ROOM: 254	

I understand that while the facility will be responsible for items deposited in the safe. I must be responsible for all items retained by me at the bedside. (Dentures kept at the bedside will be labeled, but the facility cannot assure responsibility for them.) I also recognize that the hospital cannot be held responsible for items brought in to me after this form has been completed and signed.

Reviewed and Approved: Judy Tidd — 09/24/YYYY
ATP-B-S:02:1001261385: Judy Tidd
(Signed: 09/24/YYYY 10:24:44 AM EST)

Signature of Patient — **Date**

Reviewed and Approved: Andrea Witteman — 09/24/YYYY
ATP-B-S:02:1001261385: Andrea Witteman
(Signed: 09/24/YYYY 10:26:44 AM EST)

Signature of Witness — **Date**

I have no money or valuables that I wish to deposit for safekeeping. I do not hold the facility responsible for any other money or valuables that I am retaining or will have brought in to me.

I have been advised that it is recommended that I retain no more than $5.00 at the bedside.

Reviewed and Approved: Judy Tidd — 09/24/YYYY
ATP-B-S:02:1001261385: Judy Tidd
(Signed: 09/24/YYYY 10:27:44 AM EST)

Signature of Patient — **Date**

Reviewed and Approved: Andrea Witteman — 09/24/YYYY
ATP-B-S:02:1001261385: Andrea Witteman
(Signed: 09/24/YYYY 10:28:44 AM EST)

Signature of Witness — **Date**

I have deposited valuables in the facility safe. The envelope number is ____________.

Signature of Patient — **Date**

Signature of Person Accepting Property — **Date**

I understand that medications I have brought to the facility will be handled as recommended by my physician. This may include storage, disposal, or administration.

Signature of Patient — **Date**

Signature of Witness — **Date**

GLOBAL CARE MEDICAL CENTER ■ 100 MAIN ST, ALFRED NY 14802 ■ (607) 555-1234

IPCase003

Global Care Medical Center
100 Main St, Alfred NY 14802
(607) 555-1234
Hospital No. 999

Inpatient Face Sheet

Patient Name and Address				Gender	Race	Marital Status	Patient No.
RAY, PAM 380, HOWE ROAD ALMOND, NY 14804				F	W	S	IPCase003
				Date of Birth	**Age**	**Maiden Name**	**Occupation**
				02/08/YYYY	63	NA	Cleaner
Admission Date	**Time**	**Discharge Date**	**Time**	**Length of Stay**	**Telephone Number**		
04/18/YYYY	1253	04/20/YYYY	1515	02 DAYS	(607) 555-3319		

Guarantor Name and Address		Next of Kin Name and Address	
RAY, PAM 380, HOWE ROAD ALMOND, NY 14804		RAY, MATT 380, HOWE ROAD ALMOND, NY 1480	
Guarantor Telephone No.	**Relationship to Patient**	**Next of Kin Telephone Number**	**Relationship to Patient**
(607) 555-3319		(607) 555-3319	Brother
Admitting Physician	**Service**	**Admit Type**	**Room Number/Bed**
Harold Dunn, MD			
Attending Physician	**Admitting Diagnosis**		
Harold Dunn, MD	Advanced periodontal disease		
Primary Insurer	**Policy and Group Number**	**Secondary Insurer**	**Policy and Group Number**
NA	NA	NA	NA

Diagnoses and Procedures	ICD Code
Principal Diagnosis	
Diseased and carious mandibular teeth.	
Secondary Diagnoses	
Hypertrophied alveolar process. Thrombocyotopenic purpura. Congestive heart failure. Cirrhosis. Arteriosclerotic heart disease. Chronic alcoholism.	
Principal Procedure	
Extraction of 6 mandibular teeth, right-side. Mandibular alveolectomy.	
Secondary Procedures	

Discharge Instructions

Activity: ❒ Bed rest ❒ Light ❒ Usual ❒ Unlimited ❒ Other:

Diet: ❒ Regular ❒ Low Cholesterol ❒ Low Salt ❒ ADA ❒ ____Calorie

Follow-Up: ☒ Call for appointment ❒ Office appointment on ____ ❒ Other: To be seen for a follow-up in office in one week

Special Instructions: None

Attending Physician Authentication: Reviewed and Approved: Harold Dunn MD
ATP-B-S:02:1001261385: Harold Dunn MD
(Signed: 4/18/YYYY 2:20:44 PM EST)

RAY, PAM	Admission: 04/18/YYYY	**Consent to Admission**
IPCase003	DOB: 02/08/YYYY	
Dr. DUNN	ROOM: 244	

I, Pam Ray hereby consent to admission to the Global Care Medical Center (GCMC), and I further consent to such routine hospital care, diagnostic procedures, and medical treatment that the medical and professional staff of GCMC may deem necessary or advisable. I authorize the use of medical information obtained about me as specified above and the disclosure of such information to my referring physician(s). This form has been fully explained to me, and I understand its contents. I further understand that no guarantees have been made to me as to the results of treatments or examinations done at the GCMC.

Reviewed and Approved: Pam Ray
ATP-B-S:02:1001261385: Pam Ray
(Signed: 4/18/YYYY 2:12:05 PM EST)

Signature of Patient

Signature of Parent/Legal Guardian for Minor

Relationship to Minor

Reviewed and Approved: Andrea Witteman
ATP-B-S:02:1001261385: Andrea Witteman
(Signed: 4/18/YYYY 2:12:05 PM EST)

WITNESS: Global Care Medical Center Staff Member

Consent To Release Information For Reimbursement Purposes

In order to permit reimbursement, upon request, the Global Care Medical Center (GCMC) may disclose such treatment information pertaining to my hospitalization to any corporation, organization, or agent thereof, which is, or may be liable under contract to the GCMC or to me, or to any of my family members or other person, for payment of all or part of the GCMC's charges for services rendered to me (e.g. the patient's health insurance carrier). I understand that the purpose of any release of information to facilitate reimbursement for services rendered. In addition, in the event that my health insurance program includes utilization review of services provided during this admission. I authorize GCMC to release information as is necessary to permit the review. This authorization will expire once the reimbursement for services rendered is complete.

Reviewed and Approved: Pam Ray
ATP-B-S:02:1001261385: Pam Ray
(Signed: 4/18/YYYY 2:14:17 PM EST)

Signature of Patient

Signature of Parent/Legal Guardian for Minor

Relationship to Minor

Reviewed and Approved: Andrea Witteman
ATP-B-S:02:1001261385: Andrea Witteman
(Signed: 4/18/YYYY 2:16:24 PM EST)

WITNESS: Global Care Medical Center Staff Member

Global Care Medical Center ■ 100 Main St, Alfred NY 14802 ■ (607) 555-1234

RAY, PAM	Admission: 04/18/YYYY	**Advance Directive**
IPCase003	DOB: 02/08/YYYY	
Dr. DUNN	ROOM: 244	

Your answers to the following questions will assist your Physician and the Hospital to respect your wishes regarding your medical care. This information will become a part of your medical record.

	Yes	No	Patient's Initials
1. Have you been provided with a copy of the information called "Patient Rights Regarding Health Care Decision"?	X		
2. Have you prepared a "Living Will"? If yes, please provide the Hospital with a copy for your medical record.		X	
3. Have you prepared a Durable Power of Attorney for Health Care? If yes, please provide the Hospital with a copy for your medical record.		X	
4. Have you provided this facility with an Advance Directive on a prior admission and is it still in effect? If yes, Admitting Office to contact Medical Records to obtain a copy for the medical record.		X	
5. Do you desire to execute a Living Will/Durable Power of Attorney? If yes, refer to in order: a. Physician b. Social Service c. Volunteer Service		X	

Hospital Staff Directions: Check when each step is completed.

1. ✓ Verify the above questions were answered and actions taken where required.
2. ✓ If the "Patient Rights" information was provided to someone other than the patient, state reason:

____

______________________ ______________________

Name of Individual Receiving Information **Relationship to Patient**

3. ✓ If information was provided in a language other than English, specify language and method.
4. ✓ Verify patient was advised on how to obtain additional information on Advance Directives.
5. ✓ Verify the Patient/Family Member/Legal Representative was asked to provide the Hospital with a copy of the Advanced Directive which will be retained in the medical record.

Fill this form in the medical record, and give a copy to the patient.

____

Name of Patient/Name of Individual giving information if different from Patient

Reviewed and Approved: Pam Ray
ATP-B-S:02:1001261385: Pam Ray
(Signed: 4/18/YYYY 2:35:05 PM EST)

Signature of Patient **Date**

Reviewed and Approved: Andrea Witteman
ATP-B-S:02:1001261385: Andrea Witteman
(Signed: 4/18/YYYY 2:35:47 PM EST)

Signature of Hospital Representative **Date**

Global Care Medical Center ■ 100 Main St, Alfred NY 14802 ■ (607) 555-1234

RAY, PAM	Admission: 04/18/YYYY	**Discharge Summary**
IPCase003	DOB: 02/08/YYYY	
Dr. DUNN	ROOM: 244	

ADMISSION DATE: 04/18/YYYY

DISCHARGE DATE: 04/20/YYYY

ADMISSION DIAGNOSIS: Diseased and carious mandibular teeth.

DISCHARGE DIAGNOSIS: Same, plus hypertrophied alveolar process, congestive heart failure, thrombocytopenic purpura, cirrhosis, arteriosclerotic heart disease, and chronic alcoholism.

OPERATION: Extraction of 6 right-side mandibular teeth, mandibular alveolectomy.
SURGEON: Dunn
DATE: 04/19/YYYY
COMPLICATIONS: None.

SUMMARY: Pam Ray was admitted to the hospital for removal of her six abscessed mandibular teeth under general anesthesia. She had hypertrophied alveolar process, and she was very medically compromised because of CHF, thrombocytopenic purpura, cirrhosis, and ASHD. Medications for CHF, thrombocytopenic purpura, cirrhosis, and ASHD were continued during her inpatient stay.

Electrocardiogram showed nonspecific ST segment changes. Her urinalysis was normal. Her PTT and prothrombin times were normal. Hemoglobin 13.5 grams %, hematocrit 40 volume % and white count 6,800 with 30 segmented cells, 51 lymphocytes, 14 monocytes, 3 eosinophils and 2 basophils.

She tolerated her surgery well. She had sutures put in her gum. She had significant swelling of her mandible area and lip. She also complained of pains in the left lower quadrant but no diarrhea and no guarding or rigidity and no elevation of the white count, so no further studies were done at this time. She was kept overnight because of her medically compromised condition. She is being discharged now to continue her Lasix and Lanoxin, and she will be seen in the office in three days for follow-up care.

DD:04/20/YYYY

Reviewed and Approved: Harold Dunn MD
ATP-B-S:02:1001261385: Harold Dunn MD
(Signed: 4/20/YYYY 2:20:44 PM EST)

DT:04/21/YYYY

Physician Name

GLOBAL CARE MEDICAL CENTER ■ 100 MAIN ST, ALFRED NY 14802 ■ (607) 555-1234

RAY, PAM	Admission: 04/18/YYYY	**History & Physical Exam**
IPCase003	DOB: 02/08/YYYY	
Dr. DUNN	ROOM: 244	

4/18/YYYY

ADMITTING DIAGNOSIS: Diseased and carious mandibular teeth. CHIEF COMPLAINT: Mouth pain, infected teeth

HISTORY OF PRESENT ILLNESS: Pam Ray has been having pain, discomfort and bleeding from her mandible where a bridge has been attached to her few remaining lower teeth on the right side of her mouth. This has been quite bothersome through several months and she has been seeing her dentist but a solution has not been easily attained and she was seen in the office here. I referred her to Dr. Black for reevaluation and he plans to remove her teeth under general anesthesia.

PAST MEDICAL HISTORY: Significant in that she had thrombocytopenic purpura many years ago and had a splenectomy. She has had no significant bleeding problems since that time but has been avoiding all salicylates and many medications for fear they may cause bleeding. She has had two hernia repairs however without difficulty and she also has a history of heavy alcohol ingestion through the years up until about January YYYY and she maintains that she now is not drinking at all and I have no reason to doubt her statement.

FAMILY HISTORY: No known diabetes, heart disease or tuberculosis. SOCIAL HISTORY: She is employed at a local plant nursery and does some cleaning and maintenance work. She does not smoke and participates in AA for chronic alcoholism,

REVIEW OF SYSTEMS: Cardiorespiratory system: No chest pain, no cough or cold, no ankle swelling or edema, though she has had congestive failure with leg and ankle swelling in the past. Gastrointestinal system: She is very slim but has had no recent weight change. Her bowel movements have been normal. She has no specific food intolerances. Genitourinary system: No frequency or burning with urination. Musculoskeletal system: She complains of some numbness and paresthesias in her legs and hands that is of an intermittent and erratic nature.

GENERAL: Thin, elderly white female in moderate distress with pain in her mandible and around her lower teeth. VITAL SIGNS: Temperature 98, pulse 74, respirations 16, blood pressure 154/90.

EENT: Eyes: Pupils round, regular and equal; react to light and accommodation. Ears, Nose and Throat: Normal. Teeth: Lower remaining mandibular teeth in poor repair and gingivitis is present. NECK: Supple, thyroid is not enlarged, no carotid bruits.

HEART: Normal sinus rhythm, no murmurs. LUNGS: Clear to auscultation and percussion. BREASTS: Soft and atrophic with no masses palpable.

EXTREMITIES: No edema; the peripheral pulses are decreased but present bilaterally, no edema is present at this time. No objective motor or sensory deficit is elicited.

DD: 04/18/YYYY

Reviewed and Approved: Harold Dunn MD
ATP-B-S:02:1001261385: Harold Dunn MD
(Signed: 4/20/YYYY 2:20:44 PM EST)

DT: 04/19/YYYY

Physician Name

GLOBAL CARE MEDICAL CENTER ■ 100 MAIN ST, ALFRED NY 14802 ■ (607) 555-1234

RAY, PAM	Admission: 04/18/YYYY	**Consultation Report**
IPCase003	DOB: 02/08/YYYY	
Dr. DUNN	ROOM: 244	

S. Anderson, DPM

Dr. Black asked me to see Ms. Ray since I was to see her on Friday morning in my office for follow-up of a removal of an infected ingrown toenail and drainage of the abscess that was present. This was on her right great toe. I evaluated the toe today. There is a small eschar present. The toe is healing very well. The patient does complain of some tenderness yet present in the toe. This would be likely with the process which was present-the infection and the abscess in that border. The nail was significantly ingrown and as noted this would be the reason for some discomfort yet. As noted above, the op site is healing very well and I told her that she should contact me as needed.

Thank you very much for the opportunity to see Ms. Ray.

DD: 04/20/YYYY

Reviewed and Approved: S. Anderson DPM
ATP-B-S:02:1001261385: S. Anderson DPM
(Signed: 4/20/YYYY 2:20:44 PM EST}

DT: 04/23/YYYY

Physician Name

GLOBAL CARE MEDICAL CENTER ■ 100 MAIN ST, ALFRED NY 14802 ■ (607) 555-1234

RAY, PAM	Admission: 04/18/YYYY	**Progress Notes**
IPCase003	DOB: 02/08/YYYY	
Dr. DUNN	ROOM: 244	

Date	Time	Physician's signature required for each order. (Please skip one line between dates.)
04/18/YYYY	1352	CHIEF COMPLAINT: Jaw pain. DIAGNOSIS: Diseased teeth and gums. History of thrombocytopenic purpura with splenectomy. History of alcoholism. History of congestive heart failure, PLAN OF TREATMENT: Dental extractions. Confirmed _X__ Provisional____________. DISCHARGE PLAN: Home. No services needed. Reviewed and Approved: Harold Dunn MD ATF-B-S:02:1001261385: Harold Dunn MD (Signed: 4/18/YYYY 3:21:00 PM EST)
04/18/YYYY	2100	Pre-Op Care: 2125 63 year old female Plan general anesthesia Physical exam pending. Reviewed and Approved: Jon Black DDS ATP-B-S:02:1001261385: Jon Black DDS (Signed: 4/18/YYYY 21:20:44 PM EST)
04/19/YYYY	1000	General anesthesia. 6 extractions and alveolectomy. To Recovery Room in good condition. Reviewed and Approved: Jon Black DDS ATP-B-S:02:1001261385: Jon Black DDS (Signed: 4/19/YYYY 10:03:30 AM EST)
04/19/YYYY	1200	Recovery uneventful. Appointment given for 04/24 Prescription: Tylenol #2 x 10 1 every four hours as needed. Discharge diagnosis: infected teeth; hypertrophied alveolar process. Greatly medically compromised patient. Reviewed and Approved: Jon Black DDS ATP-B-S:02:1001261385: Jon Black DDS (Signed: 4/19/YYYY 12:03:30 AM EST)
04/19/YYYY	1512	Podiatry: recovering from infected ingrown toenail right - 1 medial border. Healing very well. Advised to contact me as needed. Thank you! Reviewed and Approved: S. Anderson DPM ATP-B-S:02:1001261385: S. Anderson DPM (Signed: 4/19/YYYY 15:14:00 PM EST)

GLOBAL CARE MEDICAL CENTER ■ 100 MAIN ST, ALFRED NY 14802 ■ (607) 555-1234

RAY, PAM	Admission: 04/18/YYYY	**Doctors' Orders**
IPCase003	DOB: 02/08/YYYY	
Dr. DUNN	ROOM: 244	

Date	Time	Physician's signature required for each order. (Please skip one line between dates.)
04/18/YYYY	1000	1) Admit service Dr. Dunn, Black 2) Chest X-Ray (done 04/18/YYYY) 3) Electrocardiogram 4) Complete blood count, urinalysis, Protime, PTT 5) Dr. Dunn for history and physical and medical orders 6) Regular diet - nothing by mouth after midnight 7) Dalmane 30 milligrams by mouth at bedtime 8) Robinul 0.2 milligrams intramuscular 1° pre-op 9) Vistaril 50 milligrams intramuscular 1° pre-op Reviewed and Approved: Jon Black DDS ATP-B-S:02:1001261385: Jon Black DDS (Signed: 4/18/YYYY 10:09:30 AM EST)
04/18/YYYY	1200	History and physical dictated. OK general anesthesia. Lanoxin 0.125 milligrams by mouth daily. Reviewed and Approved: Harold Dunn MD ATP-B-S:02:1001261385: Harold Dunn MD (Signed: 4/18/YYYY 12:11:17 PM EST)
		Lasix 40 milligrams by mouth daily. Codeine with Tylenol ½ grain by mouth 4 times a day as needed for pain or Tylenol #3. Reviewed and Approved: Harold Dunn MD ATP-B-S:02:1001261385: Harold Dunn MD (Signed: 4/18/YYYY 12:11:17 PM EST)
04/19/YYYY	0700	Call Dr. Anderson to see patient today. Reviewed and Approved: Jon Black DDS ATP-B-S:02:1001261385: Jon Black DDS (Signed: 4/19/YYYY 10:09:30 AM EST)
04/19/YYYY	1000	1) Ice to chin 2) Remove oral pack in Recovery Room 3) Liquid diet 4) Dr. Dunn for medical orders 5) Tylenol #2 by mouth every 4 hours as needed 6) Discharged from Recovery Room at 1055 Reviewed and Approved: Jon Black DDS ATP-B-S:02:1001261385: Jon Black DDS (Signed: 4/19/YYYY 10:09:30 AM EST)

GLOBAL CARE MEDICAL CENTER ■ 100 MAIN ST, ALFRED NY 14802 ■ (607) 555-1234

RAY, PAM	Admission: 04/18/YYYY	**Doctors' Orders**
IPCase003	DOB: 02/08/YYYY	
Dr. DUNN	ROOM: 244	

Date	Time	Physician's signature required for each order. (Please skip one line between dates.)
04/19/YYYY	1100	Resume: Lanoxin 0.125 milligrams daily start today Lasix 40 milligrams daily start today Reviewed and Approved: Harold Dunn MD ATP-B-S:02:1001261385: Harold Dunn MD (Signed: 4/19/YYYY 11:16:27 AM EST)
04/19/YYYY	1200	Discharge tomorrow at discretion of Dr. Dunn To report to my office 04/24 Reviewed and Approved: Jon Black DDS ATP-B-S:02:1001261385: Jon Black DDS (Signed: 4/19/YYYY 12:03:45 PM EST)
04/19/YYYY	1230	Nubain 10 milligrams intramuscular now Reviewed and Approved: Harold Dunn MD ATP-B-S:02:1001261385: Harold Dunn MD (Signed: 4/19/YYYY 12:33:52 PM EST)
04/19/YYYY	1800	Dalmane 30 milligrams by mouth at bedtime Reviewed and Approved: Harold Dunn MD ATP-B-S:02:1001261385: Harold Dunn MD (Signed: 4/19/YYYY 18:04:26 PM EST)
04/20/YYYY	0700	Discharge Reviewed and Approved: Harold Dunn MD ATP-B-S:02:1001261385: Harold Dunn MD (Signed: 4/20/YYYY 07:06:00 AM EST)

GLOBAL CARE MEDICAL CENTER ■ 100 MAIN ST, ALFRED NY 14802 ■ (607) 555-1234

RAY, PAM	Admission: 04/18/YYYY	**Laboratory Data**
IPCase003	DOB: 02/08/YYYY	
Dr. DUNN	ROOM: 244	

SPECIMEN COLLECTED: 04/18/YYYY 1315 SPECIMEN RECEIVED: 04/18/YYYY 1402

HEMATOLOGY II

	PLATELET COUNT	NORMAL 130-400 × 10^3		
	BLEEDING TIME	NORMAL 1-4 MINUTES	Pt:	SEC.
X	PROTIME	CONTROL: 12.5 SEC.	Pt:	12.8 SEC.
X	PTT	NORMAL: <32 SEC.	Pt:	22 SEC.
	FIBRINDEX	CONTROL:	Pt:	
	FIBRINOGEN	NORMAL:	Pt:	
	F.D.P.	NORMAL:	Pt:	
	CLOT RETRACTION	NORMAL 30-65%	Pt: %	
	CLOT LYSIS	24hr:	48 hr:	

COMMENTS:

End of Report

GLOBAL CARE MEDICAL CENTER ■ 100 MAIN ST, ALFRED NY 14802 ■ (607) 555-1234

RAY, PAM	Admission: 04/18/YYYY	**Laboratory Data**
IPCase003	DOB: 02/08/YYYY	
Dr. DUNN	ROOM: 244	

TIME IN: 04/18/YYYY 1315 TIME OUT: 04/18/YYYY 1503

CBC S DIFFERENTIAL

TEST	RESULT	FLAG	REFERENCE
WBC	6.8		4.5-11.0 thous/UL
RBC	5.22		5.2-5.4 mill/UL
HGB	13.5		11.7-16.1 g/dl
HCT	39.6		35.0-47.0 %
MCV	93.9		85-99 fL.
MCH	32.1		
MCHC	34.2		33-37
RDW			11.4-14.5
PTL	135.		130-400 thous/UL
SEGS %	30		
LYMPH %	51		20.5-51.1
MONO %	9.0		1.7-9.3
EOS %	3		
BASO %	2		
BAND %			
GRAN %			42.2-75.2
LYMPH × 10^3			1.2-3.4
MONO × 10^3			0.11-0.59
GRAN × 10^3			1.4-6.5
EOS × 10^3			0.0-0.7
BASO × 10^3			0.0-0.2
ANISO			

End of Report

GLOBAL CARE MEDICAL CENTER ■ 100 MAIN ST, ALFRED NY 14802 ■ (607) 555-1234

RAY, PAM	Admission: 04/18/YYYY	**Laboratory Data**
IPCase003	DOB: 02/08/YYYY	
Dr. DUNN	ROOM: 244	

SPECIMEN COLLECTED:	04/18/YYYY 1315	SPECIMEN RECEIVED:	04/18/YYYY 1341

URINALYSIS

TEST	RESULT	FLAG	REFERENCE
DIPSTICK ONLY			
COLOR	Straw		
Ph.	6.5		5-8.0
SP. GR.	1.011		≤ 1.030
ALBUMIN	Neg		
SUGAR	Neg		≤ 10 mg/dl
ACETONE	Neg		
BILIRUBIN	Neg		≤ 0.8 mg/dl
BLOOD	Neg		0.06 mg/dl hgb
REDUCING			≤ -1 mg/dl
EPITH:	2+		
W.B.C.:	Occasional		≤ 5/hpf
R.B.C.:	-		≤ 5/hpf
BACT.:	Few		1 + (≤ 20/hpf)
CASTS.:	-		
CRYSTALS:	-		

End of Report

GLOBAL CARE MEDICAL CENTER ■ 100 MAIN ST, ALFRED NY 14802 ■ (607) 555-1234

RAY, PAM	Admission: 04/18/YYYY	**Consent for Operation(s) and/or Procedure(s) and Anesthesia**
IPCase003	DOB: 02/08/YYYY	
Dr. DUNN	ROOM: 244	

PERMISSION. I hereby authorize Dr. Dunn , or associates of his/her choice at the Global Care Medical Center (the "Hospital") to perform upon Pam Ray the following operation(s) and/or procedure(s): Extraction of 6 mandibular teeth, right-side, mandibular alveolectomy including such photography, videotaping, televising or other observation of the operation(s)/procedure(s) as may be purposeful for the advance of medical knowledge and/or education, with the understanding that the patient's identity will remain anonymous.

EXPLANATION OF PROCEDURE, RISKS, BENEFITS, ALTERNATIVES. Dr. Dunn has fully explained to me the nature and purposes of the operation(s)/procedures named above and has also informed me of expected benefits and complications, attendant discomforts and risks that may arise, as well as possible alternatives to the proposed treatment. I have been given an opportunity to ask questions and all my questions have been answered fully and satisfactorily.

UNFORESEEN CONDITIONS. I understand that during the course of the operation(s) or procedure(s), unforeseen conditions may arise which necessitate procedures in addition to or different from those contemplated. I, therefore, consent to the performance of additional operations and procedures which the above-named physician or his/her associates or assistants may consider necessary.

ANESTHESIA. I further consent to the administration of such anesthesia as may be considered necessary by the above-named physician or his/her associates or assistants. I recognize that there are always risks to life and health associated with anesthesia. Such risks have been fully explained to me and I have been given an opportunity to ask questions and all my questions have been answered fully and satisfactorily.

SPECIMENS. Any organs or tissues surgically removed may be examined and retained by the Hospital for medical, scientific or educational purposes and such tissues or parts may be disposed of in accordance with accustomed practice and applicable State laws and/or regulations.

NO GUARANTEES. I acknowledge that no guarantees or assurances have been made to me concerning the operation(s) or procedure(s) described above.

MEDICAL DEVICE TRACKING. I hereby authorize the release of my Social Security number to the manufacturer of the medical device(s) I receive, if applicable, in accordance with federal law and regulations which may be used to help locate me if a need arises with regard to this medical device. I release The Global Care Medical Center from any liability that might result from the release of this information.*

UNDERSTANDING OF THIS FORM. I confirm that I have read this form, fully understand its contents, and that all blank spaces above have been completed prior to my signing. I have crossed out any paragraphs above that do not pertain to me.

Patient/ Relative/Guardian*

Reviewed and Approved: Pam Ray
ATP-B-S:02:1001261385: Pam Ray
(Signed: 04/18/YYYY 2:12:05 PM EST)

Signature

Pam Ray

Print Name

Relationship, if other than patient signed:

Witness:

Reviewed and Approved: William Preston
ATP-B-S:02:1001261385: William Preston
(Signed: 04/18/YYYY 2:13:00 PM EST)

Signature

William Preston

Print Name

Date: 04/18/YYYY

*The signature of the patient must be obtained unless the patient is an unemancipated minor under the age of 18 or is otherwise incompetent to sign.

PHYSICIAN'S CERTIFICATION. I hereby certify that I have explained the nature, purpose, benefits, risks of and alternatives to the operation(s)/ procedure(s), have offered to answer any questions and have fully answered all such questions. I believe That the patient (relative/guardian) fully understands what I have explained and answered.

PHYSICIAN:

Reviewed and Approved: Harold Dunn MD
ATP-B-S:02:1001261385: Harold Dunn MD
(Signed: 4/18/YYYY 2:20:44 PM EST)

Signature

04/18/YYYY

Date

GLOBAL CARE MEDICAL CENTER ■ 100 MAIN ST, ALFRED NY 14802 ■ (607) 555-1234

RAY, PAM Admission: 04/18/YYYY
IPCase003 DOB: 02/08/YYYY
Dr. DUNN ROOM: 244

Operative Report

PREOPERATIVE DIAGNOSIS:6 abscessed mandibular teeth, right-side, hypertrophied alveolar process, extremely medically compromised patient.

POSTOPERATIVE DIAGNOSIS:6 infected mandibular teeth, right-side, hypertrophied mandibular alveolar process.

OPERATION PERFORMED: Extraction of 6 mandibular teeth, mandibular alveolectomy, right-side.

SURGEON: Black ASSISTANT: DATE: 04/19/YYYY

ANESTHESIA: General and Xylocaine infiltration.

OPERATIVE NOTE: Following induction of general anesthesia the buccal sulcus was infiltrated with Lidocaine anesthesia. Approximately 2 cc of Lidocaine 1% was used. The remaining 6 teeth on the right-side of the mouth were then removed with forceps and the mucoperiosteal flap was made exposing alveolar process. This was trimmed with rongeurs and filed smooth with bone file. The tissue flaps were then trimmed with scissors, approximated and closed with blanket 3-0 silk suture. Minimal bleeding occurred during the procedure. The patient was then recovered and returned to the Recovery Room in good condition with 1 oral pack in place.

DD: 04/20/YYYY

Reviewed and Approved: Jon Black DDS
ATP-B-S:02:1001261385: Jon Black DDS
(Signed: 4/20/YYYY 2:20:44 PM EST)

Physician Name

DT: 04/23/YYYY

GLOBAL CARE MEDICAL CENTER ■ 100 MAIN ST, ALFRED NY 14802 ■ (607) 555-1234

RAY, PAM Admission: 04/18/YYYY
IPCase003 DOB: 02/08/YYYY
Dr. DUNN ROOM: 244

Pathology Report

Date of Surgery: 04/19/YYYY

OPERATION: Extraction of teeth.

SPECIMEN: teeth

GROSS: The specimen consists of 6 teeth.

GROSS DIAGNOSIS ONLY: TEETH (6)

DD:4/20/YYYY Reviewed and Approved: Marc Reynolds, Pathologist
ATP-B-S:02:1001261385: Marc Reynolds, Pathologist
DT:04/20/YYYY (Signed: 4/20/YYYY 2:20:44 PM EST)

GLOBAL CARE MEDICAL CENTER ■ 100 MAIN ST, ALFRED NY 14802 ■ (607) 555-1234

RAY, PAM Admission: 04/18/YYYY
IPCase003 DOB: 02/08/YYYY
Dr. DUNN ROOM: 244

Recovery Room Record

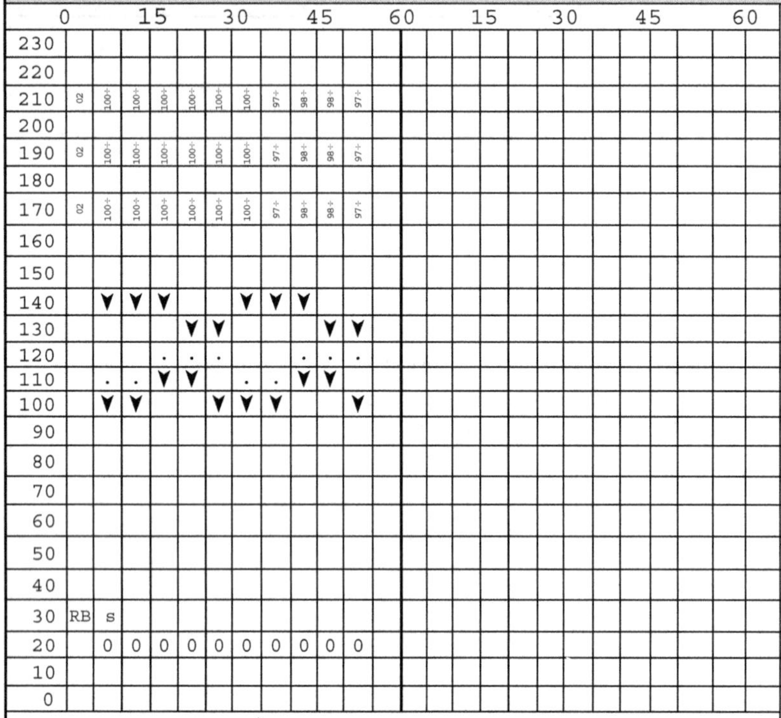

↑ hermoscan probe, Oral mode q9 adm.

Date: 04-19/YYYY Time: 0955
Operation: extraction
Anesthesia: General
Airway: N/A
O_2 Used: ☐ Yes ☒ No
Route:

Time	Medications	Site

Intake	Amount
650 cc D5L R Left hand	
IV discontinued at 1050	
Needle out intact	
Total	50 cc

Output	Amount
Catheter N/A	
Levine N/A	
Hemovac N/A	
Total	

Discharge Status

Room: 0244 Time: 1055
Condition: Satisfactory
Transferred by: Stretcher
R.R. Nurse:
Rev& App: Mary Crawford, RN
ATP-B-S:02:1001261385: Mary Crawford, RN
(Signed: 4/19/YYYY 10:56:00 AM EST)

Post Anesthesia Recovery Score		Adm	30 min	1 hr	2 hr	Disch
Moves 4 extremities voluntarily or on command (2) Moves 2 extremities voluntarily or on command (1) Moves 0 extremities voluntarily or on command (0)	Activity	2	2	2		2
Able to deep breathe and cough freely (2) Dyspnea or limited breathing (1) Apneic (0)	Respiration	2	2	2		2
BP ± 20% of preanesthetic level BP + 20% of preanesthetic level BP + 50% of preanesthetic level	Circulation 140/70	2	2	2		2
Fully awake (2) Arouseable on calling (1) Not responding (0)	Consciousness	2	2	2		2
Pink (2) Pale, dusky, blQTChy, jaundiced, other (1) Cyanotic (0)	Color	2	2	2		2

Preop Visit:

Postop Visit:

Comments & Observation:

Oral pack removed at 1005. Ice applied to chin no active bleeding. 1030 patient states "feels like she's swallowing blood" - area clotted. Pressure pack applied to determined ooze. 1040 pack removed. Small stain. No active bleeding noted ice removed at discharge.

Reviewed and Approved: Mary Crawford, RN
ATP-B-S:02:1001261385: Mary Crawford, RN
(Signed: 4/19/YYYY 10:56:00 AM EST)

Signature of Recovery Room Nurse

Global Care Medical Center ■ 100 Main St, Alfred NY 14802 ■ (607)555-1234

RAY, PAM Admission: 04/18/YYYY
IPCase003 DOB: 02/08/YYYY
Dr. DUNN ROOM: 244

Medication Administration Record

SPECIAL INSTRUCTIONS: Allergic to Sulfa and Demerol

MEDICATION (dose and route)	DATE: 04-18 TIME	INITIALS	DATE: 04-19 TIME	INITIALS	DATE: 04-20 TIME	INITIALS	DATE: TIME	INITIALS
Lanoxin 0.125 mg by mouth daily			0800	JD	0800	JD		
Lasix 40mg by mouth daily			0800	JD	0800	JD		
Single Orders & Pre-Ops								
Dalmane 30 mg by mouth at bedtime	2100	VS						
Vistaril 50 mg intramuscular 1° pre op			Pre-op	VS				
Robinul 0.2 mg 1° pre-op			Pre-op	VS				
Nubain 10 mg intramuscular now			1300	HF				
Dalmane 30 mg at bedtime			2200	PS				
PRN Medications:								
Tylenol with codeine ½ grain four times a day as needed	1140	JD						
Tylenol #2 by mouth four times a day as needed	2040	PS	1245	HF				

INITIALS	SIGNATURE AND TITLE	INITIALS	SIGNATURE AND TITLE	INITIALS	SIGNATURE AND TITLE
VS	Vera South, RN	GPW	G.P.Well, RN		
OR	Ora Richards, RN	PS	P.Small, RN		
JD	Jane Dobbs, RN				
HF	H.Figgs, RN				

GLOBAL CARE MEDICAL CENTER ■ 100 MAIN ST, ALFRED NY 14802 ■ (607)555-1234

RAY, PAM	Admission: 04/18/YYYY	**EKG Report**
IPCase003	DOB: 02/08/YYYY	
Dr.DUNN	ROOM: 244	

Date of EKG: 04/18/YYYY Time of EKG: 1345

Rate 70

PR .12

QRSD .08

QT .40

QTC

-- Axis --

P

QRS

T

Sinus rhythm: Nonspecific ST wave changes since 04/09/YYYY

Reviewed and Approved:
Bella Kaplan,MD
ATP-B-S:02:1001261385:
Bella Kaplan,MD
(Signed: 04/19/YYYY 8:54:14 PM EST)

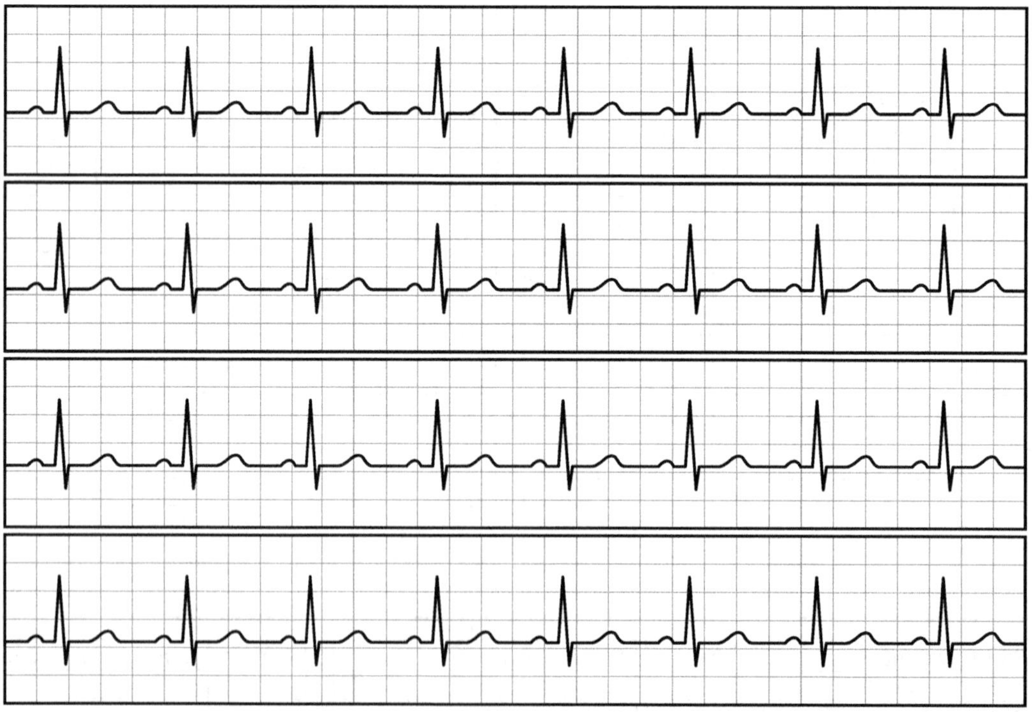

Global Care Medical Center ■ 100 Main St, Alfred NY 14802 ■ (607) 555-1234

RAY, PAM
IPCase003
Dr. DUNN

Admission: 04/10/YYYY
DOB: 02/08/YYYY
ROOM: 244

Nurses' Notes

DATE	TIME	TREATMENTS & MEDICATIONS	TIME	NURSES' NOTES
04/18/YYYY			1345	A 63 year old white female admitted to room 244A for mouth surgery in morning. Allergic to sulfa and Demerol. Reviewed and Approved: V. South, RN ATP-B-S:02:1001261385: V. South, RN (Signed: 04/18/YYYY 13:49:41 PM EST)
			1430	Comfortable without complaint. Reviewed and Approved: V. South, RN ATP-B-S:02:1001261385: V. South, RN (Signed: 04/18/YYYY 14:32:23 PM EST)
04/18/YYYY			1600	Resting quietly. Asked to soak toe in tepid water as was advised by Dr. Anderson who treated her recently. Reviewed and Approved: O. Richards, RN ATP-B-S:02:1001261385: O. Richards, RN (Signed: 04/18/YYYY 16:04:20 PM EST)
			1700	Ate only 30% of regular diet at bedside, sore mouth cannot chew. Reviewed and Approved: O. Richards, RN ATP-B-S:02:1001261385: O. Richards, RN (Signed: 04/18/YYYY 17:04:00 PM EST)
			1830	Resting quietly, napping at times. Reviewed and Approved: O. Richards, RN ATP-B-S:02:1001261385: O. Richards, RN (Signed: 04/18/YYYY 18:32:06 PM EST)
			2000	Snack of ice cream, vital signs taken. Reviewed and Approved: O. Richards, RN ATP-B-S:02:1001261385: O. Richards, RN (Signed: 04/18/YYYY 20:04:04 PM EST)
	2040	Tylenol with codeine ½ grain by mouth for pain	2100	Up as needed for self PM care, back rub given settled into bed Reviewed and Approved: O. Richards, RN ATP-B-S:02:1001261385: O. Richards, RN (Signed: 04/18/YYYY 21:07:220 PM EST)
			2200	Resting quietly not yet sleep Reviewed and Approved: O. Richards, RN ATP-B-S:02:1001261385: O. Richards, RN (Signed: 04/18/YYYY 22:14:33 PM EST)
04/19/YYYY		Thursday	2400	Awake without complaints. Nothing by mouth for operating room in the morning. Reviewed and Approved: Sandy Oates, RN ATP-B-S:02:1001261385: Sandy Oates, RN (Signed: 04/19/YYYY 00:12:08 AM EST)
			0300	Sleeping. Reviewed and Approved: Sandy Oates, RN ATP-B-S:02:1001261385: Sandy Oates, RN (Signed: 04/19/YYYY 03:04:17 AM EST)

GLOBAL CARE MEDICAL CENTER ■ 100 MAIN ST, ALFRED NY 14802 ■ (607)555-1234

RAY, PAM	Admission: 04/18/YYYY	**Nurses' Notes**
IPCase003	DOB: 02/08/YYYY	
Dr. DUNN	ROOM: 244	

DATE	TIME	TREATMENTS & MEDICATIONS	TIME	NURSES' NOTES
04/19/YYYY		Thursday	0600	Awake, no complaints. Reviewed and Approved: Sandy Oates, RN ATP-B-S:02:1001261385: Sandy Oates, RN (Signed: 04/19/YYYY 06:07:45 AM EST)
04/19/YYYY	0700	Thursday	0730	Awake - vital signs taken nothing by mouth for surgery. Reviewed and Approved: V. South, RN ATP-B-S:02:1001261385: V. South, RN (Signed: 04/19/YYYY 07:30:30 AM EST)
			0915	To Operating Room via stretcher. Reviewed and Approved: V. South, RN Reviewed and Approved: V. South, RN ATP-B-S:02:1001261385: V. South, RN (Signed: 04/19/YYYY 09:15:18 AM EST)
04/19/YYYY			1100	Returned from Operating Room fully awake. Post operation vital signs started. Ice to chin; sipping on Pepsi Reviewed and Approved: V. South, RN ATP-B-S:02:1001261385: V. South, RN (Signed: 04/19/YYYY 11:09:24 AM EST)
	1215			Up to bathroom with help-voided Reviewed and Approved: V. South, RN ATP-B-S:02:1001261385: V. South, RN (Signed: 04/19/YYYY 12:15:41 PM EST)
	1300	Nubain 10 milligrams intramuscular	1230	Clear liquid lunch taken well. Reviewed and Approved: V. South, RN ATP-B-S:02:1001261385: V. South, RN (Signed: 04/19/YYYY 13:00:41 PM EST)
			1430	Resting in bed without complaints. Vital signs finished. Reviewed and Approved: V. South, RN ATP-B-S:02:1001261385: V. South, RN (Signed: 04/19/YYYY 14:49:41 PM EST)
04/19/YYYY			1530	Vital signs taken. Complains of difficulty with speech and discomfort in front jaw. Reviewed and Approved: O. Richards, RN ATP-B-S:02:1001261385: O. Richards, RN (Signed: 04/19/YYYY 15:34:30 PM EST)
			1630	Sitting up, visitor here. Reviewed and Approved: O. Richards, RN ATP-B-S:02:1001261385: O. Richards, RN (Signed: 04/19/YYYY 16:35:43 PM EST)
			1730	85% of diet taken at supper. Reviewed and Approved: O. Richards, RN ATP-B-S:02:1001261385: O. Richards, RN (Signed: 04/19/YYYY 17:32:11 PM EST)

GLOBAL CARE MEDICAL CENTER ■ 100 MAIN ST, ALFRED NY 14802 ■ (607)555-1234

RAY, PAM Admission: 04/10/YYYY
IPCase003 DOB: 02/08/YYYY
Dr. DUNN ROOM: 244

Nurses' Notes

DATE	TIME	TREATMENTS & MEDICATIONS	TIME	NURSES' NOTES
04/19/YYYY			1830	Very little blood noted. Reviewed and Approved: O. Richards, RN ATP-B-S:02:1001261385: O. Richards, RN (Signed: 04/19/YYYY 18:31:22 PM EST)
			2000	Vital signs taken. Reviewed and Approved: O. Richards, RN ATP-B-S:02:1001261385: O. Richards, RN (Signed: 04/19/YYYY 20:07:27 PM EST)
			2100	Refused evening care. Reviewed and Approved: O. Richards, RN ATP-B-S:02:1001261385: O. Richards, RN (Signed: 04/19/YYYY 21:06:28 PM EST)
04/19/YYYY			2200	States she is unable to see well due to cataracts but refuses any night light. Voiding. Reviewed and Approved: O. Richards, RN ATP-B-S:02:1001261385: O. Richards, RN (Signed: 04/19/YYYY 22:02:35 PM EST)
04/20/YYYY		Friday	2400	Sleeping soundly, skin warm and dry. No apparent new bleeding from mouth. Ice off at present. Reviewed and Approved: Sandy Oates, RN ATP-B-S:02:1001261385: Sandy Oates, RN (Signed: 04/20/YYYY 00:1 :17 PM EST)
			0300	Awake. Wanting to gargle with salt water and rinse out her mouth. No complaints. Face slightly edematous and ecchymotic. Reviewed and Approved: Sandy Oates, RN ATP-B-S:02:1001261385: Sandy Oates, RN (Signed: 04/20/YYYY 03:12:22 AM EST)
			0600	Awake. Up to take bath; no complaints. Reviewed and Approved: Sandy Oates, RN ATP-B-S:02:1001261385: Sandy Oates, RN (Signed: 04/20/YYYY 06:02:44 AM EST)
04/20/YYYY	0700-1500	Friday	0730	Awake. Vital signs taken. No complaints. Reviewed and Approved: V. South, RN ATP-B-S:02:1001261385: V. South, RN (Signed: 04/20/YYYY 07:32:32 AM EST)
			0830	Full liquid breakfast taken well. Reviewed and Approved: V. South, RN ATP-B-S:02:1001261385: V. South, RN (Signed: 04/20/YYYY 08:34:08 AM EST)
04/20/YYYY			0930	Ice to face, resting in bed. Reviewed and Approved: V. South, RN ATP-B-S:02:1001261385: V. South, RN (Signed: 04/20/YYYY 09:32:10 AM EST)

GLOBAL CARE MEDICAL CENTER ■ 100 MAIN ST, ALFRED NY 14802 ■ (607)555-1234

RAY, PAM	Admission: 04/18/YYYY	**Nurses' Notes**
IPCase003	DOB: 02/08/YYYY	
Dr. DUNN	ROOM: 244	

DATE	TIME	TREATMENTS & MEDICATIONS	TIME	NURSES' NOTES
04/20/YYYY			1030	Rinsed mouth with warm salt water. Reviewed and Approved: V. South, RN ATP-B-S:02:1001261385: V. South, RN (Signed: 04/20/YYYY 10:31:18 AM EST)
			1100	Visitor in - no complaints. Reviewed and Approved: V. South, RN ATP-B-S:02:1001261385: V. South, RN (Signed: 04/20/YYYY 11:01:09 AM EST)
		Full liquid	1230	Lunch taken well. Reviewed and Approved: V. South, RN ATP-B-S:02:1001261385: V. South, RN (Signed: 04/20/YYYY 12:32:32 AM EST)
			1300	Complains still hungry-ordered up applesauce & pudding for her to eat. Reviewed and Approved: V. South, RN ATP-B-S:02:1001261385: V. South, RN (Signed: 04/20/YYYY 13:14:28 AM EST)
			1430	Resting without complaints. Reviewed and Approved: V. South, RN ATP-B-S:02:1001261385: V. South, RN (Signed: 04/20/YYYY 14:36:15 AM EST)
			1515	Discharged. Reviewed and Approved: V. South, RN ATP-B-S:02:1001261385: V. South, RN (Signed: 04/20/YYYY 15:15:15 AM EST)

GLOBAL CARE MEDICAL CENTER ■ 100 MAIN ST, ALFRED NY 14802 ■ (607)555-1234

RAY, PAM	Admission: 04/18/YYYY		**Nursing Discharge Status Summary**
IPCase003	DOB: 02/08/YYYY		
Dr. DUNN	ROOM: 244		

1.	AFEBRILE:	X	Yes		No					
2.	WOUND:	X	Clean/Dry		Reddened		Infected		NA	
3.	PAIN FREE:	X	Yes		No	If "No," describe:				
4.	POST-HOSPITAL INSTRUCTION SHEET GIVEN TO PATIENT/FAMILY:							Yes	X	No
	If NO, complete lines 5 – 8 below.									
5.	DIET:	X	Regular		Other (Describe):					
6.	ACTIVITY:	X	Normal		Light		Limited		Bed rest	
7.	MEDICATIONS:	As instructed by Dr. Dunn								
8.	INSTRUCTIONS GIVEN TO PATIENT/FAMILY:				As ordered by Dr. Dunn					
9.	PATIENT/FAMILY verbalize understanding of instructions:					X	Yes		No	
10.	DISCHARGED at	1510	Via:		Wheelchair		Stretcher		Ambulance Co.	
				X	Ambulatory					
	Accompanied by:	Vera South, RN					to	Front desk		
	COMMENTS:									
	DATE:	04/20/YYYY								
	SIGNATURE:	Reviewed and Approved: V. South, RN ATP-B-S:02:1001261385: V. South, RN (Signed: 04/20/YYYY 15:15:15 AM EST)								

GLOBAL CARE MEDICAL CENTER ■ 100 MAIN ST, ALFRED NY 14802 ■ (607) 555-1234

RAY, PAM	Admission: 04/18/YYYY	**Patient Property Record**
IPCase003	DOB: 02/08/YYYY	
Dr. DUNN	ROOM: 244	

I understand that while the facility will be responsible for items deposited in the safe. I must be responsible for all items retained by me at the bedside. (Dentures kept at the bedside will be labeled, but the facility cannot assure responsibility for them.) I also recognize that the hospital cannot be held responsible for items brought in to me after this form has been completed and signed.

Reviewed and Approved: Pam Ray
ATP-B-S:02:1001261385: Pam Ray
(Signed: 04/18/YYYY 10:26:44 AM EST) — 04/18/YYYY

Signature of Patient — **Date**

Reviewed and Approved: Andrea Witteman
ATP-B-S:02:1001261385: Andrea Witteman
(Signed: 04/18/YYYY 10:27:44 AM EST — 04/18/YYYY

Signature of Witness — **Date**

I have no money or valuables that I wish to deposit for safekeeping. I do not hold the facility responsible for any other money or valuables that I am retaining or will have brought in to me. I have been advised that it is recommended that I retain no more than $5.00 at the bedside.

Reviewed and Approved: Pam Ray
ATP-B-S:02:1001261385: Pam Ray
(Signed: 04/18/YYYY 10:28:44 AM EST) — 04/18/YYYY

Signature of Patient — **Date**

Reviewed and Approved: Andrea Witteman
ATP-B-S:02:1001261385: Andrea Witteman
(Signed: 04/18/YYYY 10:29:44 AM EST — 04/18/YYYY

Signature of Witness — **Date**

I have deposited valuables in the facility safe. The envelope number is ________________.

Signature of Patient — **Date**

Signature of Person Accepting Property — **Date**

I understand that medications I have brought to the facility will be handled as recommended by my physician. This may include storage, disposal, or administration.

Signature of Patient — **Date**

Signature of Witness — **Date**

GLOBAL CARE MEDICAL CENTER ■ 100 MAIN ST, ALFRED NY 14802 ■ (607) 555-1234

IPCase004

Global Care Medical Center 100 Main St, Alfred NY 14802 (607) 555-1234 Hospital No. 999	**Inpatient Face Sheet**

Patient Name and Address	Gender	Race	Marital Status	Patient No.
SIMON, MYRNA 9145 ROCK ROAD ALMOND, NY 14804	F	W	S	IPCase004
	Date of Birth	**Age**	**Maiden Name**	**Occupation**
	02/08/YYYY	64		Retired

Admission Date	Time	Discharge Date	Time	Length of Stay	Telephone Number
09/11/YYYY	0930	09/12/YYYY	1400	1 DAY	(607) 555-5427

Guarantor Name and Address		Next of Kin Name and Address	
SIMON, MYRNA 9145 ROCK ROAD ALMOND, NY 14804		SIMON, MARTY 87 BRIDGE STREET ALMOND, NY 14804	
Guarantor Telephone No.	**Relationship to Patient**	**Next of Kin Telephone Number**	**Relationship to Patient**
(607) 555-5427	Self	(607) 555-3311	Brother
Admitting Physician	**Service**	**Admit Type**	**Room Number/Bed**
John Black, MD	Emergency	NA	0365
Admitting Physician	**Admitting Diagnosis**		
John Black, MD	Parkinson Disease		
Primary Insurer	**Policy and Group Number**	**Secondary Insurer**	**Policy and Group Number**
Medicare	34-471-9876	Medicaid	56739871

Diagnoses and Procedures	ICD Code
Principal Diagnosis	
Hypopotassemia	
Secondary Diagnoses	
Exacerbation of Parkinsonism Dehydration	
Principal Procedure	
Secondary Procedure	

Discharge Instructions

Activity: ☐ Bed rest ☒ Light ☐ Usual ☐ Unlimited ☐ Other:

Diet: ☒ Regular ☐ Low Cholesterol ☐ Low Salt ☐ ADA ☐ _____Calorie

Follow-Up: ☒ Call for appointment ☐ Office appointment on _____ ☐ Other:

Special Instruction: Appointment to see Dr. Kelly on Tuesday, 09/16 at 1045 in Outpatient Dept. at Global Care Medical Center.

Attending Physician Authentication:	Reviewed and Approved: John Black MD ATP-B-S:02:1001261385: John Black MD (Signed: 09/11/YYYY 12:00:44 PM EST)

SIMON, MYRNA	Admission: 09/11/YYYY	**Consent to Admission**
IPCase004	DOB: 02/08/YYYY	
Dr. BLACK	ROOM: 0365	

I, Myrna Simon hereby consent to admission in the Global Care Medical Center (GCMC), and I further consent to such routine hospital care, diagnostic procedures, and medical treatment that the medical and professional staff of GCMC may deem necessary or advisable. I authorize the use of medical information obtained about me as specified above and the disclosure of such information to my referring physician(s). This form has been fully explained to me, and I understand its contents. I further understand that no guarantees have been made to me as to the results of treatments or examinations done at the GCMC.

Reviewed and Approved: Myrna Simon
ATP-B-S:02:1001261385: Myrna Simon
(Signed: 9/11/YYYY 02:12:05 PM EST)

Signature of Patient

Signature of Parent/Legal Guardian for Minor

Relationship to Minor

Reviewed and Approved: Andrea Witteman
ATP-B-S:02:1001261385: Andrea Witteman
(Signed: 9/11/YYYY 02:12:05 PM EST)

WITNESS: Global Care Medical Center Staff Member

Consent To Release Information For Reimbursement Purposes

In order to permit reimbursement, upon request, the Global Care Medical Center (GCMC) may disclose such treatment information pertaining to my hospitalization to any corporation, organization, or agent thereof, which is, or may be liable under contract to the GCMC or to me, or to any of my family members or other person, for payment of all or part of the GCMC's charges for services rendered to me (e.g. the patient's health insurance carrier). I understand that the purpose of any release of information to facilitate reimbursement for services rendered. In addition, in the event that my health insurance program includes utilization review of services provided during this admission. I authorize GCMC to release information as is necessary to permit the review. This authorization will expire once the reimbursement for services rendered is complete.

Reviewed and Approved: Myrna Simon
ATP-B-S:02:1001261385: Myrna Simon
(Signed: 9/11/YYYY 02:14:17 PM EST)

Signature of Patient

Signature of Parent/Legal Guardian for Minor

Relationship to Minor

Reviewed and Approved: Andrea Witteman
ATP-B-S:02:1001261385: Andrea Witteman
(Signed: 9/11/YYYY 02:16:24 PM EST)

WITNESS: Global Care Medical Center Staff Member

GLOBAL CARE MEDICAL CENTER ■ 100 MAIN ST, ALFRED NY 14802 ■ (607) 555-1234

SIMON, MYRNA — Admission: 09/11/YYYY
IPCase004 — DOB: 02/08/YYYY
Dr. BLACK — ROOM: 0365

Advance Directive

Your answers to the following questions will assist your Physician and the Hospital to respect your wishes regarding your medical care. This information will become a part of your medical record.

	Yes	No	Patient's Initials
1. Have you been provided with a copy of the information called "Patient Rights Regarding Health Care Decision"?	X		
2. Have you prepared a "Living Will"? If yes, please provide the Hospital with a copy for your medical record.		X	
3. Have you prepared a Durable Power of Attorney for Health Care? If yes, please provide the Hospital with a copy for your medical record.		X	
4. Have you provided this facility with an Advance Directive on a prior admission and is it still in effect? If yes, Admitting Office to contact Medical Records to obtain a copy for the medical record.		X	
5. Do you desire to execute a Living Will/Durable Power of Attorney? If yes, refer to in order: a. Physician b. Social Service c. Volunteer Service		X	

Hospital Staff Directions: Check when each step is completed.

1. ✓ Verify the above questions were answered and actions taken where required.
2. ✓ If the "Patient Rights" information was provided to someone other than the patient, state reason:

____

Name of Individual Receiving Information — Relationship to Patient

3. ✓ If information was provided in a language other than English, specify language and method.
4. ✓ Verify patient was advised on how to obtain additional information on Advance Directives.
5. ✓ Verify the Patient/Family Member/Legal Representative was asked to provide the Hospital with a copy of the Advanced Directive which will be retained in the medical record.

File this form in the medical record, and give a copy to the patient.

Name of Patient/Name of Individual giving information if different from Patient

Reviewed and Approved: Myrna Simon
ATP-B-S:02:1001261385: Myrna Simon
(Signed: 9/11/YYYY 02:35:05 PM EST)

Signature of Patient — **Date**

Reviewed and Approved: Andrea Witteman
ATP-B-S:02:1001261385: Andrea Witteman
(Signed: 9/11/YYYY 02:35:47 PM EST)

Signature of Hospital Representative — **Date**

Global Care Medical Center ■ 100 Main St, Alfred NY 14802 ■ (607) 555-1234

SIMON, MYRNA	Admission: 09/11/YYYY	**Discharge Summary**
IPCase004	DOB: 02/08/YYYY	
Dr. BLACK	ROOM: 0365	

ADMISSION DATE: 09/11/YYYY   DISCHARGE DATE: 09/12/YYYY

ADMISSION DIAGNOSIS: Parkinsonism in acute exacerbation.

DISCHARGE DIAGNOSIS: Hypopotassemia, exacerbation of parkinsonism, and dehydration.

Ms. Simon was admitted to the hospital from the Emergency Room. She had apparently been falling, stumbling and staggering around her home for the last 2-3 days and finally was brought to the Emergency Room by her brother. She appeared quite weak and was therefore admitted for more thorough evaluation and treatment. She had bruises on her knees, elbows, feet and shins from her previous falls. She had previously been diagnosed as having parkinsonism and was taking Symmetrel for the condition. She also has a chronic wry neck on the left which gives her a lot of difficulty.

Examination here of the chest by x-ray revealed no abnormalities. An old compression fracture of T10 was noted. Sinuses also were within normal limits. Her Activated Partial Thromboplastin Time and Protimes were normal. Her urinalysis revealed a trace of blood, 1-2 red cells per high power field. Her potassium, however, was down at 3.1. Chlorides were normal at 100 and BUN was 6, sodium 145, blood sugar 90, calcium 8.5., hemoglobin 13.4%, hematocrit 39 vol.% and white count 7.10 with 64 segmented cells, 22 lymphocytes, 10 monocytes, 3 eosinophils, and 1 band cell.

She seems to improve, stabilize and become more confident while in the hospital. I walked her down the hall and back without assistance but she did hold onto the rail on the wall. I felt that use of a cane would be helpful to her. She lives in Pine Towers and has been ambulating up to the last few days without help or assistance. I have arranged for her to be seen by Dr. Kelly, neurologist, for re-evaluation on Tuesday, September 16th at 1045. She is being discharged at this time to use Symmetrel 100 mg. every 12 hours, Parafon Forte 1 pill 4 times daily as needed for muscle spasms, potassium 10 mEq. 1 pill 3 times daily. She has a sinus pill prescribed by Dr. Beach, Noludar 300 was prescribed by Dr. Beach, and she was cautioned to use only if it was absolutely necessary. She will be seen in our office at her discretion.

DD:09/12/YYYY

Reviewed and Approved: John Black MD
ATP-B-S:02:1001261385: John Black MD
(Signed: 09/12/YYYY 05:44:18 PM EST)

DT:09/18/YYYY

Physician Name

GLOBAL CARE MEDICAL CENTER ■ 100 MAIN ST, ALFRED NY 14802 ■ (607) 555-1234

SIMON, MYRNA	Admission: 09/11/YYYY	**History & Physical Exam**
IPCase004	DOB: 02/08/YYYY	
Dr. BLACK	ROOM: 0365	

DATE: 09/11/YYYY CHIEF COMPLAINT: Progressive unsteadiness of gait.

HISTORY OF PRESENT ILLNESS: This is one of multiple admissions for this 64 year old female whose past medical history is significant for parkinsonism, a bleeding disorder and cervical spondylolisthesis. She was in her usual state of fair health until the week prior to admission when she noted the onset of fever, chills, myalgias and nausea and associated with loose, brown, watery bowel movements without frank blood or melena. This abated after 2 days and she attributes this to a flu-like syndrome. Over the last 2 to 3 weeks she states that she has noted progressive unsteadiness of gait. She has fallen repeatedly at home. She also notes more increased tremor and diffuse muscular weakness. She states that she is unable to even write or make her own bed and she feels that these symptoms have been getting worse. The patient has had a history of parkinsonism and has been treated by Dr. Beach for this disorder. Other pertinent review: the patient notes the episodic occurrence of left hand numbness and tingling. She states that this does not occur in her right hand and she attributes this to her cervical disc disease. Also the patient has noted increasing sinus drainage and some sinus-type of headache associated with these symptoms. The patient denies any loss of consciousness, any orthostatic signs or symptoms. She denies any problems with speech or memory. She denies any problems with seizure-like activity.

PAST MEDICAL HISTORY: Childhood - unremarkable. Adulthood - the patient has a history of Parkinsonism, as stated above in the History of Present Illness. She has a history of chronic sinusitis. She has a history of cervical disc disease secondary to motor vehicle accident. She has a history of a bleeding disorder for which she underwent splenectomy. It sounds from her description as though this might be a bleeding disorder secondary to a platelet disorder such as the immune thrombocytopenia. In Five years ago, the patient underwent bilateral cataract removal with intraocular lens implantation. Medications - Symmetrel 100 milligrams by mouth twice a day, Parafon Forte 250 milligrams by mouth three times a day, Decongex 3 1 capsule by mouth twice a day, and Naludar 300 milligrams by mouth every night at bedtime. Allergies - the patient states she is allergic to sulfa drugs.

FAMILY HISTORY: Her mother's sister suffered from parkinsonism as did a distant great aunt. Her mother died at the age of 74 from a carcinoma of unknown type. Her father died in his 60's from myocardial Infarction and he also had emphysema. The patient has three brothers. History is positive for chronic obstructive pulmonary disease, myocardial infarction, and carcinoma of the colon. They suffered from no parkinsonism themselves. There is no history of anemia and no history of thyroid disease.

SOCIAL HISTORY: The patient has never smoked cigarettes or used tobacco in any form. She states that at one time she was a heavy drinker but presently drinks only socially approximately once per week and not to the point of being intoxicated.

REVIEW OF SYSTEMS: Head, eyes, ears, nose, throat - negative. Cardiopulmonary - negative. No shortness of breath, no cough, no hemoptysis. No sputum production. No pleuritic-type chest pain. No palpitations, edema, orthopnea, post nasal discharge, dyspnea on exercise, or shortness of breath. Abdominal - diarrhea as stated 2 days last week. The patient also gives a history of heartburn and a long-standing history of chronic constipation for which she takes laxatives daily. Genitourinary - no dysuria, frequency, hesitancy or hematuria. Neurological - as per History of Present Illness.

DD:09/11/YYYY
DT:09/12/YYYY

Page 1 continued
Physician Name

GLOBAL CARE MEDICAL CENTER ■ 100 MAIN ST, ALFRED NY 14802 ■ (607) 555-1234

SIMON, MYRNA	Admission: 09/11/YYYY	**History & Physical Exam**
IPCase004	DOB: 02/08/YYYY	
Dr. BLACK	ROOM: 0365	

Page 2 continuation

GENERAL: Reveals a well-developed cachectic-appearing elderly white female who appeared to be visibly anxious.

TEMPERATURE: 98.0 PULSE: 70 RESPIRATIONS: 20 BLOOD PRESSURE 150/90 WEIGHT: 108 pounds. No orthostatic changes were noted.

HEAD: General appearance about the head and neck. Although their appearance was normal in anatomically, during the examination the patient exhibited spastic-type movements with flexion of the neck. The patient seemed to be unaware that she was doing this, would be most closely described as a torticollis-type of movement which would be relaxed if you stated to the patient to relax herself. The patient was noted not to be making any lip smacking or any other abnormal head movements.

EYES EARS NOSE THROAT: Eyes - Left eye noted a superior iridectomy scar. Right eye noted artificial lens noted in the anterior chamber. Funduscopic examination was unremarkable. Pupils were somewhat irregular but reactive to light and accommodation. Extra-ocular muscles were intact with some lateral gaze nystagmus noted which was felt to be within normal limits. The patient was able to elevate and depress ocular movement as directed. Visual fields were noted to be intact bilaterally. Ears - Tympanic membranes were pearl gray and moist without exudates or fluid. No injection. Nose - large amounts of mucopurulent discharge noted bilaterally, mucosa appeared boggy. No mass lesions were noted. Some dry blood was also noted in the vault. Throat - the patient is edentulous. No mass lesions are noted in the oral pharynx. Throat was clear without injection, without exudates. No blood was noted.

BACK: Examination showed slight kyphosis noted. No costovertebral angle tenderness.

LUNG: Clear to auscultation and percussion bilaterally.

NECK: Supple without lymphadenopathy. Carotids were 2+ bilaterally without bruit. Thyroid gland was not palpable.

CARDIAC: No jugular venous distention, no hepatojugular reflux, S-1 and S-2 were normal, no S-3 or S-4. No murmurs, rubs or clicks were noted.

PERIPHERAL PULSES: 2+ bilaterally throughout with no bruit.

ABDOMEN: Scaphoid in appearance, soft, nontender, no guarding or rigidity, no rebound. kidneys not palpable. Spleen not palpable. Surgical scar was noted in the left upper quadrant. Liver edge was not palpable below the costal margin and not enlarged to percussion. No fluid wave was appreciated. No masses were palpable.

RECTAL & GYNECOLOGICAL: Deferred.

EXTREMITIES: Reveals clubbing of the upper extremity and the lower extremity. This was noted to be quite severe. No edema was noted. No cyanosis was noted.

DD:09/11/YYYY
DT:09/12/YYYY

Page 2 continued
Physician Name

Global Care Medical Center ■ 100 Main St, Alfred NY 14802 ■ (607) 555-1234

SIMON, MYRNA Admission: 09/11/YYYY
IPCase004 DOB: 02/08/YYYY
Dr. BLACK ROOM: 0365

History & Physical Exam

Page 3 continuation

NEUROLOGICAL: Mental status examination showed the patient appeared to be quite anxious, affect was somewhat flat although congruent at all times. Her memory was intact for distant memory, recent memory and immediate recall were noted to be intact bilaterally. Motor examination - there was decreased muscle bulk noted with atrophy noted of the interthenar and hypothenar muscle groups. Muscles were hypertonic with cogwheeling rigidity noted in the upper extremities. Strength was 3+- 4+ in all flexor and extensor groups out of 5+. A rest tremor was noted in the hands bilaterally. Deep tendon reflexes - the patient was felt to be diffusely hyperreflexic without spread, good return. No Babinski signs were noted. No Hoffman's signs were noted. Sensory examination - normal to pin prick and light touch. Cerebellar examination - no intentional tremor. Gait examination - patient was noted to have a shuffling gait with heal to toe walking noted. The patient was noted to step with the dorsiflexed foot. Gait was circumscribed shuffling and the patient was noted to be observing the movement of her feet at all times. Her gait was also noted to be quite unsteady with the patient continuing to fall to the right side.

ADMISSION DIAGNOSIS: 1. Parkinsonism, recent exacerbation of symptoms. 2. Bleeding disorder, platelet-type bleeding disorder, history of. 3. Sinusitis, probably bacterial in etiology. 4. Status post cataract removal with intraocular lens placement. 5. Status post gastroenteritis one week, probable viral etiology. 6. Cervical disc disease secondary to motor vehicle accident, clinically worsened.

DD:09/11/YYYY

Reviewed and Approved: John Black MD
ATP-B-S:02:1001261385: John Black MD
(Signed: 09/11/YYYY 12:05:44 PM EST)

DT:09/12/YYYY

Physician Name

GLOBAL CARE MEDICAL CENTER ■ 100 MAIN ST, ALFRED NY 14802 ■ (607) 555-1234

SIMON, MYRNA IPCase004 Dr. BLACK		Admission: 09/11/YYYY DOB: 02/08/YYYY ROOM: 0365 **Progress Notes**
Date	**Time**	**Physician's signature required for each order. (Please skip one line between dates.)**
09/11/YYYY	1030	CHIEF COMPLAINT: Falling – unsteady gait DIAGNOSIS: Parkinsonism - acute exacerbation Confirmed______ Provisional __X__ PLAN OF TREATMENT: Stabilize - treatment as needed DISCHARGE PLAN: Home. No services needed Reviewed and Approved: John Black MD ATP-B-S:02:1001261385: John Black MD (Signed: 09/11/YYYY 10:44: 32 AM EST)
09/12/YYYY	1100	Has appointment with Dr. Kelly for evaluation of obscure neurologic disease at 1045 09/16 in hospital outpatient department. Dr. Fletcher felt she had parkinsonism and she couldn't tolerate Sinemet therefore given Symmetrel with indifferent results. She is more stable today and can ambulate fairly well. I recommend use of a cane. She is discharged now to be reevaluated by Dr. Kelly 09/16. Continue Symmetrel. Reviewed and Approved: John Black MD ATP-B-S:02:1001261385: John Black MD (Signed: 09/12/YYYY 11:44:32 AM EST)
09/11/YYYY		Nutrition Diet Consult acknowledged. Patient receiving soft diet re: no dentures, sore mouth, neck pain, Parkinson's disease. Current weight 108 pounds usual at 113 pounds. 5 pound weight loss in 2 weeks. Obtained food likes and tolerances to incorporate into menu and plan to initiate milk shakes between meals to increase by mouth nutrition. To follow. Thanks. Reviewed and Approved: William Allan RD ATP-B-S:02:1001261385: William Allan RD (Signed: 09/11/YYYY 08:17:30 AM EST)

GLOBAL CARE MEDICAL CENTER ■ 100 MAIN ST, ALFRED NY 14802 ■ (607) 555-1234

SIMON, MYRNA IPCase004 Dr. BLACK	Admission: 09/11/YYYY DOB: 02/08/YYYY ROOM: 0365	**Progress Notes**

Date	Time	Physician's signature required for each order. (Please skip one line between dates.)
09/12/YYYY	1340	Medical Student Progress Note Subjective - Patient slept better than usual Objective - afebrile pulse 80 Blood Pressure 150/60 Heart: regular rate and rhythm without murmur Lungs: clear Abdomen: regular Neuro unchanged from admit Positive hypertonic Positive cogwheeling Positive torticollis Positive unsteady gait Assessment / Plan: (1) Parkinsonism - patient noted to have other nonparkinsonian features such as torticollis, and frequent falls may suggest Parkinson variant such as progressive supranuclear palsy; Shy-Drager syndrome or multisystem atrophy is likely. I feel neurological consult or transfer would be most helpful to clarify diagnosis and advise on treatment. Will confer with Dr. Black. Reviewed and Approved: Andrea Palmer RN ATP-B-S:02:1001261385: Andrea Palmer RN (Signed: 09/12/YYYY 01:45:30 PM EST) Reviewed and Approved: John Black MD ATP-B-S:02:1001261385: John Black MD (Signed: 09/12/YYYY 01:47:32 PM EST)

Global Care Medical Center ■ 100 Main St, Alfred NY 14802 ■ (607) 555-1234

SIMON, MYRNA IPCase004 Dr. BLACK	Admission: 09/11/YYYY DOB: 02/08/YYYY ROOM: 0365	**Doctors' Orders**

Date	Time	Physician's signature required for each order. (Please skip one line between dates.)
09/11/YYYY	1045	Complete blood count Urinalysis Admit to Dr. Black Regular diet Reviewed and Approved: John Black MD ATP-B-S:02:1001261385: John Black MD (Signed: 09/11/YYYY 10:55:15 AM EST)
09/11/YYYY	1300	Old records to the floor. Admit to service of Dr. Cooper. Diagnosis: Parkinsonism Condition: Stable Allergies: Sulfa Activity: Bathroom privileges with assistance only Patient must be assisted with all ambulation. Nursing: None Intravenous fluids. Diet: Consult dietary. Soft diet. Meds: Symmetrel 100 milligrams by mouth twice a day Parafon forte 250 milligrams by mouth twice a day Naludar 300 milligrams every night at bedtime Milk of Magnesia 30 cubic centimeters by mouth every morning Tylenol 2 tabs by mouth every 4 hours as needed for headache Colace 50 milligrams by mouth for constipation. Reviewed and Approved: Andrea Palmer RN ATP-B-S:02:1001261385: Andrea Palmer RN (Signed: 09/11/YYYY 01:46:12 PM EST) Reviewed and Approved: John Black MD ATP-B-S:02:1001261385: John Black MD (Signed: 09/11/YYYY 01:47:55 PM EST)

GLOBAL CARE MEDICAL CENTER ■ 100 MAIN ST, ALFRED NY 14802 ■ (607) 555-1234

SIMON, MYRNA	Admission: 09/11/YYYY	**Doctors' Orders**
IPCase004	DOB: 02/08/YYYY	
Dr. BLACK	ROOM: 0365	

Date	Time	Physician's signature required for each order. (Please skip one line between dates.)
09/11/YYYY	1340	LABS: Prothrombin time, Partial Thromboplastin Time Chest x-ray, sinus films Calcium and Magnesium levels History and physical done Reviewed and Approved: Andrea Palmer RN ATP-B-S:02:1001261385: Andrea Palmer RN (Signed: 09/11/YYYY 13:45:30 PM EST} Reviewed and Approved: John Black MD ATP-B-S:02:1001261385: John Black MD (Signed: 09/11/YYYY 01:47:32 PM EST)
09/11/YYYY	1610	Halcion 0.25 at bedtime Flexeril 10 milligrams three times a day start this evening Reviewed and Approved: John Black MD ATP-B-S:02:1001261385: John Black MD (Signed: 09/11/YYYY 04:17:03 PM EST)
09/12/YYYY	0750	Begin Klotrix 1 tab by mouth three times a day Clean catch urine for culture and sensitivity Lytes in morning Reviewed and Approved: Andrea Palmer RN ATP-B-S:02:1001261385: Andrea Palmer RN (Signed: 09/12/YYYY 07:59:30 AM EST)
09/12/YYYY	0850	Cane for use with all ambulation Reviewed and Approved: John Black MD ATP-B-S:02:1001261385: John Black MD (Signed: 09/12/YYYY 08:55:15 AM EST)
09/12/YYYY	1100	Discharge Reviewed and Approved: John Black MD ATP-B-S:02:1001261385: John Black MD (Signed: 09/12/YYYY 11:05:46 AM EST)

GLOBAL CARE MEDICAL CENTER ■ 100 MAIN ST, ALFRED NY 14802 ■ (607) 555-1234

SIMON, MYRNA Admission: 09/11/YYYY
IPCase004 DOB: 02/08/YYYY
Dr. BLACK ROOM: 0365

Radiology Report

Date of X-ray: 09/11/YYYY

REASON: Parkinson's disease

CHEST: Posteroanterior and lateral views reveal the heart and lungs to be normal. There is an old compression deformity of T10 which has been present for several years. There has been no significant change from the study of 6/30/YYYY.

CONCLUSION: Essentially normal chest.

SINUSES: Multiple views reveal the sinuses to be well developed and well aerated. No air fluid levels or mucosal thickening is seen.

CONCLUSION: Normal sinuses.

DD:09/11/YYYY

Reviewed and Approved: Randall Cunningham MD
ATP-B-S:02:1001261385: Randall Cunningham MD
(Signed:09/12/YYYY 14:24:44 PM EST)

DT:09/12/YYYY

GLOBAL CARE MEDICAL CENTER ■ 100 MAIN ST, ALFRED NY 14802 ■ (607) 555-1234

SIMON, MYRNA	Admission: 09/11/YYYY	**Laboratory Data**
IPCase004	DOB: 02/08/YYYY	
Dr. BLACK	ROOM: 0365	

SPECIMEN COLLECTED: 09/11/YYYY SPECIMEN RECEIVED: 09/11/YYYY

TEST	RESULT	FLAG	REFERENCE
URINALYSIS			
DIPSTICK ONLY			
COLOR	Yellow		
SP GRAVITY	1.007		≤ 1.030
GLUCOSE	Neg		≤ 125 mg/dl
BILIRUBIN	Neg		≤ 0.8 mg/dl
KETONE			≤ 10 mg/dl
BLOOD	Trace		0.06 mg/dl hgb
PH	7.5		5-8.0
PROTEIN			≤ 30 mg/dl
UROBILINOGEN			≤ −1 mg/dl
NITRITES			NEG
EPITHELIALS	2+		≤ 15 WBC/hpf
W.B.C.	1-2 per high powered field		≤ 5/hpf
R.B.C.	0-21 per high powered field		≤ 5/hpf
BACT.			1+ (≤ 20/hpf)
URINE PREGNANCY TEST			

End of Report

GLOBAL CARE MEDICAL CENTER ■ 100 MAIN ST, ALFRED NY 14802 ■ (607) 555-1234

SIMON, MYRNA	Admission: 09/11/YYYY	**Laboratory Data**
IPCase004	DOB: 02/08/YYYY	
Dr. BLACK	ROOM: 0365	

SPECIMEN COLLECTED:	09/11/YYYY	SPECIMEN RECEIVED:	09/11/YYYY
IN:	0814	OUT:	0850

BLOOD CHEMISTRY 1

TEST	REFERENCE		RESULT
ACID PHOSPHATASE	0.0-0.8 U/I		
ALKALINE PHOSPHATASE	50-136 U/I		
AMYLASE	23-85 U/I		
LIPASE	4-24 U/I		
GLUCOSE FASTING	70-110 mg/dl		90
GLUCOSE	Time collected		125
BUN	7-22 mg/dl		6
SODIUM	136-147 mEq/l		145
POTASSIUM	3.7-5.1 mEq/l		3.1
CARBON DIOXIDE	24-32 mEq/1		33
CHLORIDE	98-108 mEq/l		100
CHOLESTEROL	120-280 mg/dl		
SERUM GLUTAMATE PYRUVATE TRANSAMINASE	3-36 U/I		
SERUM GLUTAMIC OXALOCETIC TRANSAMINASE	M-27-47 U/I	F-22-37 U/I	
CREATININE KINASE	M-35-232 U/I	F-21-215 U/I	
LACTATE DEHYDROGENASE	100-190 U/I		
CREATININE	M-0.8-1.3 mg/dl	F-0.6-1.0 mg/dl	
CALCIUM	8.7-10.2 mg/dl		
PHOSPHORUS	2.5-4.9 mg/dl		
BILIRUBIN-DIRECT	0.0-0.4 mg/dl		
BILIRUBIN-TOTAL	Less than 1.5 mg/dl		
TOTAL PROTEIN	6.4-8.2 g/dl		
ALBUMIN	3.4-5.0 g/dl		
URIC ACID	M-3.8-7.1 mg/dl	F-2.6-5.6 mg/dl	
TRIGLYCERIDE	30-200 mg/dl		

U/I = International Units
g/dl = grams per deciliter
mEq = milliequivalent per deciliter
mg/dl = milligrams per deciliter

GLOBAL CARE MEDICAL CENTER ■ 100 MAIN ST, ALFRED NY 14802 ■ (607) 555-1234

SIMON, MYRNA	Admission: 09/11/YYYY	**Laboratory Data**
IPCase004	DOB: 02/08/YYYY	
Dr. BLACK	ROOM: 0365	

SPECIMEN COLLECTED: 09/12/YYYY 1315 SPECIMEN RECEIVED: 09/12/YYYY 1327

BACTERIOLOGY

TEST	RESULT
URINE CULTURE	Rare epithelial cells
(clean catch)	Rare gram positive rods
	Rare gram negative rods
	No growth at 48 hours.

End of Report

GLOBAL CARE MEDICAL CENTER ■ 100 MAIN ST, ALFRED NY 14802 ■ (607) 555-1234

SIMON, MYRNA	Admission: 09/11/YYYY	**Laboratory Data**
IPCase004	DOB: 02/08/YYYY	
Dr. BLACK	ROOM: 0365	

SPECIMEN COLLECTED: 09/11/YYYY 1600 SPECIMEN RECEIVED: 09/11/YYYY 1615

BLOOD CHEMISTRY

TEST	REFERENCE		RESULT
ACID PHOSPHATASE	0.0-0.8 U/I		
ALKALINE PHOSPHATASE	50-136 U/I		
AMYLASE	23-85 U/I		
LIPASE	4-24 U/I		
GLUCOSE FASTING	70-110 mg/dl		90
GLUCOSE	Time collected		
BUN	7-22 mg/dl		6
SODIUM	136-147 mEq/l		145
POTASSIUM	3.7-5.1 mEq/l		** 3.1 **
CARBON DIOXIDE	24-32 mEq/1		33
CHLORIDE	98-108 mEq/l		100
CHOLESTEROL	120-280 mg/dl		
SERUM GLUTAMATE PYRUVATE TRANSAMINASE	3-36 U/I M-27-47 U/I	F-22-37 U/I	
SERUM GLUTAMIC OXALOCETIC TRANSAMINASE			
CREATININE KINASE	M-35-232 U/I	F-21-215 U/I	
LACTATE DEHYDROGENASE	100-190 U/I		
CREATININE	M-0.8-1.3 mg/dl	F-0.6-1.0 mg/dl	
CALCIUM	8.7-10.2 mg/dl		8.5
PHOSPHORUS	2.5-4.9 mg/dl		
BILIRUBIN-DIRECT	0.0-0.4 mg/dl		
BILIRUBIN-TOTAL	Less than 1.5 mg/dl		
TOTAL PROTEIN	6.4-8.2 g/dl		
ALBUMIN	3.4-5.0 g/dl		
URIC ACID	M-3.8-7.1 mg/dl	F-2.6-5.6 mg/dl	
TRIGLYCERIDE	30-200 mg/dl		

U/I = International Units
g/dl = grams per deciliter
mEq = milliequivalent per deciliter
mg/dl = milligrams per deciliter

GLOBAL CARE MEDICAL CENTER ■ 100 MAIN ST, ALFRED NY 14802 ■ (607) 555-1234

SIMON, MYRNA Admission: 09/11/YYYY
IPCase004 DOB: 02/08/YYYY
Dr. BLACK ROOM: 0365

Laboratory Data

SPECIMEN COLLECTED:	09/11/YYYY	SPECIMEN RECEIVED:	09/11/YYYY
IN:	1300	OUT:	1310

BLOOD CHEMISTRY II

COMMENTS:

❑ BLOOD ALCOHOL
❑ DRUG SCREEN SEE ATTACHED RPT
❑ CARDIAC ISOENZYMES
❑ LDH ISOENZYMES
❑ CK ISOENZYMES
❑ PROTEIN ELECTROPHORESIS
❑ URINE PROTEIN ELECTROPHORESIS

GLUCOSE TOLERANCE

	BLOOD VALUE	URINE RESULTS
FASTING	90	
½ hr.		
1 hr.		
2 hr.		
3 hr.		
4 hr.		
5 hr.		

TEST

End of Report

GLOBAL CARE MEDICAL CENTER ■ 100 MAIN ST, ALFRED NY 14802 ■ (607) 555-1234

SIMON, MYRNA	Admission: 09/11/YYYY	**Laboratory Data**
IPCase004	DOB: 02/08/YYYY	
Dr. BLACK	ROOM: 0365	

SPECIMEN COLLECTED: 09/11/YYYY 1635 **SPECIMEN RECEIVED:** 09/11/YYYY 1645

HEMATOLOGY II

	PLATELET COUNT	NORMAL 130-400 × 10^3				
	BLEEDING TIME	NORMAL 1-4 MINUTES			Pt:	SEC.
X	PROTIME	CONTROL:	11.4	SEC.	Pt:	13.9 SEC.
X	PTT	NORMAL:	<32	SEC.	Pt:	27 SEC.
	FIBRINDEX	CONTROL:			Pt:	
	FIBRINOGEN	NORMAL:			Pt:	
	F.D.P.	NORMAL:			Pt:	
	CLOT RETRACTION	NORMAL:			Pt: %	
	CLOT LYSIS	24 hr:			48 hr:	

COMMENTS:

End of Report

GLOBAL CARE MEDICAL CENTER ■ 100 MAIN ST, ALFRED NY 14802 ■ (607) 555-1234

SIMON, MYRNA
IPCase004
Dr. BLACK

Admission: 09/11/YYYY
DOB: 02/08/YYYY
ROOM: 0365

Medication Administration Record

Special Instructions: Allergic to Sulfa

Medication (dose and route)	Date: 09/11 Time	Initials	Date: 09/12 Time	Initials	Date: 00/00 Time	Initials	Date: Time	Initials
Symmetrel 100 milligrams by mouth twice a day	0800	----	0800	JD				
	1600	OR						
Parafon Forte 250 milligrams by mouth four times a day	0800							
	1200							
	1600							
	2000							
Noludar 300 milligrams every night at bedtime	2100							
Milk of Magnesia 30 cubic centimeters by mouth every morning	0800	----	0800	JD				
Colace 50 milligrams by mouth daily	0800	----	0800	JD				
Halcion 0.25 milligrams by mouth at bedtime	2100	OR						
Flexeril 10 milligrams by mouth three times a day	0800	----	0800	JD				
	1300	----	1300	JD				
	1800	OR						
Klotrix 1 tab by mouth three times a day	0800	----	0800	-----				
	1300	----	1300	----				
	1800	----						
Single Orders & Pre-Ops								
PRN Medications:								
Tylenol two tabs by mouth four times a day as needed for headache								

Initials	Signature and Title	Initials	Signature and Title	Initials	Signature and Title
VS	Vera South, RN	GPW	G. P. Well, RN		
OR	Ora Richards, RN	PS	P. Small, RN		
JD	Jane Dobbs, RN				
HF	H. Figgs RN				

Global Care Medical Center ■ 100 Main St, Alfred NY 14802 ■ (607) 555-1234

SIMON, MYRNA IPCase004 Dr. BLACK	Admission: 09/11/YYYY DOB: 02/08/YYYY ROOM: 0365	**Nurses' Notes**

DATE	TIME	TREATMENTS & MEDICATIONS	TIME	NURSES' NOTES
09/11/YYYY		Thursday	0930	Patient admitted to Room 0365 via stretcher from the Emergency Room and skin warm and dry to touch. Lab work done before coming to the floor. Reviewed and Approved: V. South, RN ATP-B-S:02:1001261385: V. South, RN (Signed: 09/11/YYYY 09:31:03 AM EST)
			1045	Medical student in visiting with patient. Reviewed and Approved: V. south, RN ATP-B-S:02:1001261385: V. South, RN (Signed: 09/11/YYYY 10:47:41 AM EST)
			1050	Lying quietly in bed. Reviewed and Approved: V. South, RN ATP-B-S:02:1001261385: V. South, RN (Signed: 09/11/YYYY 10:52:28 AM EST)
			1215	Continues to rest quietly in bed. Reviewed and Approved: V. South, RN ATP-B-S:02:1001261385: V. South, RN (Signed: 09/11/YYYY 12:16:03 PM EST)
			1315	Urine obtained. Sent to the lab. Reviewed and Approved: V. South, RN ATP-B-S:02:1001261385: V. South, RN (Signed: 09/11/YYYY 01:20:44 PM EST)
			1445	Remains in bed sleeping quietly. No complaints at this time. Reviewed and Approved: V. South, RN ATP-B-S:02:1001261385: V. South, RN (Signed: 09/11/YYYY 02:47:00 PM EST)
			1630	Resting in bed. Blood work drawn. Skin warm and dry. No complaints at present. Reviewed and Approved: O. Richards, RN ATP-B-S:02:1001261385: O. Richards, RN (Signed: 09/11/YYYY 04:32:41 PM EST)
			1845	Ambulated to nurses' station. Complains of pain in her neck. Back to bed. Reviewed and Approved: O. Richards, RN ATP-B-S:02:1001261385: O. Richards, RN (Signed: 09/11/YYYY 06:50:10 PM EST)
			2000	Resting in bed. Refused bedtime care. Sleeping at present. Respirations even. Reviewed and Approved: O. Richards, RN ATP-B-S:02:1001261385: O. Richards, RN (Signed: 09/11/YYYY 08:02:51 PM EST)

GLOBAL CARE MEDICAL CENTER ■ 100 MAIN ST, ALFRED NY 14802 ■ (607) 555-1234

SIMON, MYRNA Admission: 09/11/YYYY
IPCase004 DOB: 02/08/YYYY
Dr. BLACK ROOM: 0365

Nurses' Notes

DATE	TIME	TREATMENTS & MEDICATIONS	TIME	NURSES' NOTES
			2400	Lying in bed with eyes closed. Appears to be sleeping. Skin is warm and dry, pink in color. Respirations easy at 20 per minute on room air. Four side rails up for safety. Reviewed and Approved: J. Dobbs, RN ATP-B-S:02:1001261385: J. Dobbs, RN (Signed: 09/12/YYYY 12:03:16 AM EST)
09/12/YYYY		Friday	0200	Remains asleep. Respirations even and regular on room air. Reviewed and Approved: J. Dobbs, RN ATP-B-S:02:1001261385: J. Dobbs, RN (Signed: 09/12/YYYY 02:02:44 AM EST)
			0400	Out of bed to void quantity sufficient in bathroom. Gait steady with assistance. Denies any complaints of pain or discomfort upon questioning. Reviewed and Approved: J. Dobbs, RN ATP-B-S:02:1001261385: J. Dobbs, RN (Signed: 09/12/YYYY 04:05:07 AM EST)
			0600	Out of bed to void quantity sufficient in bathroom. Assisted with ambulation. Resting easy on room air. No complaints voiced at this time. Reviewed and Approved: J. Dobbs, RN ATP-B-S:02:1001261385: J. Dobbs, RN (Signed: 09/12/YYYY 06:00:41 AM EST)
			0830	Patient sleeping and awakened for morning vitals. Reviewed and Approved: J. Dobbs, RN ATP-B-S: 02:1001261385: J. Dobbs, RN (Signed: 09/12/YYYY 08:32:00 AM EST)
			0900	Skin warm and dry to touch. Reviewed and Approved: V. South, RN ATP-B-S:02:1001261385: V. South, RN (Signed: 09/12/YYYY 09:02:00 AM EST)
			0930	Morning care at the bedside without assistance. Reviewed and Approved: V. South, RN ATP-B-S:02:1001261385: V. South, RN (Signed: 09/12/YYYY 09:33:00 AM EST)
			1000	Out of bed to bathroom and had assistance. Good bowel movement. Reviewed and Approved: V. South, RN ATP-B-S:02:1001261385: V. South, RN (Signed: 09/12/YYYY 10:04:00 AM EST)

GLOBAL CARE MEDICAL CENTER ■ 100 MAIN ST, ALFRED NY 14802 ■ (607) 555-1234

SIMON, MYRNA Admission: 09/11/YYYY
IPCase004 DOB: 02/08/YYYY
Dr. BLACK ROOM: 0365

Nurses' Notes

DATE	TIME	TREATMENTS & MEDICATIONS	TIME	NURSES' NOTES
09/12/YYYY		Friday	1120	Dr. Black was in to visit patient. Reviewed and Approved: V. South, RN ATP-B-S:02:1001261385: V. South, RN (Signed: 09/12/YYYY 11:22:03 AM EST)
			1215	Dr. Black gave patient a cane to take home for use. Reviewed and Approved: V. South, RN ATP-B-S:02:1001261385: V. South, RN (Signed: 09/12/YYYY 12:17:41 PM EST)
			1315	Culture and sensitivity urine was obtained and sent to the lab. Reviewed and Approved: V. South, RN ATP-B-S:02:1001261385: V. South, RN (Signed: 09/12/YYYY 01:22:28 PM EST)
			1400	Patient taken via wheelchair to front desk for discharge. Reviewed and Approved: V. South, RN ATP-B-S:02:1001261385: V. South, RN (Signed: 09/12/YYYY 02:03:00 PM EST)

GLOBAL CARE MEDICAL CENTER ■ 100 MAIN ST, ALFRED NY 14802 ■ (607) 555-1234

SIMON, MYRNA Admission: 09/11/YYYY
IPCase004 DOB: 02/08/YYYY
Dr. BLACK ROOM: 0365

Patient Property Record

I understand that while the facility will be responsible for items deposited in the safe. I must be responsible for all items retained by me at the bedside. (Dentures kept at the bedside will be labeled, but the facility cannot assure responsibility for them.) I also recognize that the hospital cannot be held responsible for items brought in to me after this form has been completed and signed.

Reviewed and Approved: Myrna Simon 09/11/YYYY
ATP-B-S:02:1001261385: Myrna Simon
(Signed: 9/11/YYYY 02:35:05 PM EST)

Signature of Patient **Date**

Reviewed and Approved: Andrea Witteman 09/11/YYYY
ATP-B-S:02:1001261385: Andrea Witteman
(Signed: 9/11/YYYY 02:37:22 PM EST)

Signature of Witness **Date**

I have no money or valuables that I wish to deposit for safekeeping. I do not hold the facility responsible for any other money or valuables that I am retaining or will have brought in to me.

I have been advised that it is recommended that I retain no more than $5.00 at the bedside.

Reviewed and Approved: Myrna Simon 09/11/YYYY
ATP-B-S:02:10012611385 : Myrna Simon
(Signed: 9/11 /YYYY 02:35:05 PM EST)

Signature of Patient **Date**

Reviewed and Approved: Andrea Witteman 09/11/YYYY
ATP-B-S:02:1001261385: Andrea Witteman
(Signed: 9/11/YYYY 02:39:38 PM EST)

Signature of Witness **Date**

I have deposited valuables in the facility safe. The envelope number is _________.

Signature of Patient **Date**

Signature of Person Accepting Property **Date**

I understand that medications I have brought to the facility will be handled as recommended by my physician. This may include storage, disposal, or administration.

Signature of Patient **Date**

Signature of Witness **Date**

Global Care Medical Center
100 Main St, Alfred NY 14802
(607) 555-1234

Emergency Department Record

PATIENT INFORMATION:

NAME:	Simon, Myrna	PATIENT NUMBER:	EDCase004
ADDRESS:	9145 Rock Road	ADMISSION DATE & TIME:	09/11/YYYY
CITY:	Almond	DISCHARGE DATE & TIME:	09/12/YYYY
STATE:	NY	CONDITION ON DISCHARGE:	
ZIP CODE:	14804	☑ Satisfactory	❒ AMA
TELEPHONE:	607-555-5427	❒ Home	❒ DOA
		☒ Impatient Admission	❒ Code Blue
GENDER:	F	❒ Transfer to: ___________	❒ Died
DATE OF BIRTH:	02/08/YYYY 64 years	❒ Instruction Sheet Given	

NURSING DOCUMENTATION:

ALLERGIES: ❒ No ☑ Yes EXPLAIN: Sulfa

CURRENT MEDICATIONS: ❒ No ☑ Yes Symmetrel, Decongex - 3, Parafon Forte, Noludar

BP: 174/90 P: 84 R: 16 T: 98.6

CC: Shaking and an extremely dry mouth

HPI:

CONDITION: Shakes.

ASSESSMENT: Patient states that she was shaky all night long, mouth dry, diarrhea for a few days-none this morning or yesterday. Has slight tremor of hands on arrival.

SIGNATURE OF PRIMARY CARE NURSE: Reviewed and Approved: Cindy Stevens RN
ATP-B-S:02:1001261385: Cindy Stevens RN
(Signed: 09/11/YYYY 08:15:56 AM EST)

ICD CODES:					

CPT/HCPCS LEVEL II CODES:					

Global Care Medical Center
100 Main St, Alfred NY 14802
(607) 555-1234

Emergency Department Physician Documentation

PATIENT NAME:	Simon, Myrna	**PATIENT NUMBER:**	EDCase004
LOCATION:		**ED PHYSICIAN:**	John Carter, MD
DATE OF SERVICE:	09/11/YYYY	**DATE OF BIRTH**	02/08/YYYY

PHYSICIAN NOTES:

64 year old brought to the Emergency Room complaining of shaking all night long and having an extremely dry mouth. She had diarrhea a few days ago although that subsided. At this time she feels weak and dizzy and generally has problems getting around to her apartment and is very concerned about falling and being able to get her meals, etc.

Physical Examination: reveals a patient who apparently has Parkinson's disease and does take Symmetrel as one of her medications. The mucous membranes of her mouth are extremely dry, ears are unremarkable. The eyes are unremarkable. Heart and lungs are unremarkable on auscultation. The abdomen is soft. She has a number of scars present, one an upper abdominal scar from apparently a splenectomy, and several hernia scars. A complete blood count, sequential multiplier analyzer 6, and urinalysis were ordered. The lab work was fairly unremarkable except for low potassium. It was felt that most of the symptoms that the patient has can be attributed to her medication. She seems to be somewhat dehydrated at this time and I feel she has not been having an adequate intake at home due to her difficulty in getting about. It was felt that perhaps a change in her medication would produce some improvement in her symptoms and this would have to be done on in patient basis. Also it may be time for the patient to be encouraged to consider a Nursing Home, since it seems to be more and more difficult for her to function on her own in her apt. Dr. Black was contacted, following which the patient was admitted to the hospital.

PHYSICIAN ORDERS:

Admit to nursing floor.

SIGNATURE OF ED PHYSICIAN Reviewed and Approved: John Carter MD
ATP-B-S: 02:1001261385: John Carter MD
(Signed: 09/12/YYYY 14:24:44 PM EST)

IPCase005

Global Care Medical Center 100 Main St, Alfred NY 14802 (607) 555-1234 Hospital No. 999	**Inpatient Face Sheet**

Patient Name and Address	Gender	Race	Marital Status	Patient No.
PIRE, SALLY 1122 CHERRY STREET ALMOND, NY 14804	F	W	S	IPCase005

Date of Birth	Age	Maiden Name	Occupation
06/23/YYYY	60	NA	Dog groomer

Admission Date	Time	Discharge Date	Time	Length of Stay	Telephone Number
07/31/YYYY	0950	08/05/YYYY	1145	05 DAYS	(607) 000-4397

Guarantor Name and Address	Next of Kin Name and Address
PIRE, SALLY 1122 CHERRY STREET ALMOND, NY 14804	PIRE, JACOB 556 MILL STREET ALMOND, NY 14804

Guarantor Telephone No.	Relationship to Patient	Next of Kin Telephone Number	Relationship to Patient
(607) 000-4397	Self	(607) 555-7676	BROTHER

Admitting Physician	Service	Admit Type	Room Number/Bed
John Black, MD	NA	NA	0253

Attending Physician	Admitting Diagnosis
John Black, MD	Acute and chronic alcoholism

Primary Insurer	Policy and Group Number	Secondary Insurer	Policy and Group Number
New Age Insurance	PW 6790456	NEBC	229162171

Diagnoses and Procedures	ICD Code
Principal Diagnosis	
Acute and chronic alcoholism	
Secondary Diagnoses	
Left wrist fracture	
Principal Procedure	
Secondary Procedures	

Discharge Instructions

Activity: ☐ Bed rest ☐ Light ☐ Usual ☐ Unlimited ☒ Other: As tolerated.

Diet: ☒ Regular ☐ Low Cholesterol ☐ Low Salt ☐ ADA ☐ ____Calorie

Follow-Up: ☐ Call for appointment ☐ Office appointment on ____ ☐ Other: N/A

Special Instructions:

Attending Physician Authentication:	Reviewed and Approved: John Black MD ATP-B-S:02:1001261385: John Black MD (Signed: 7/31/YYYY 10:00:00 AM EST)

PIRE, SALLY	Admission: 07/31/YYYY	**Consent to Admission**
IPCase005	DOB: 06/23/YYYY	
Dr. BLACK	ROOM: 0253	

I, Sally Pire hereby consent to admission to the Global Care Medical Center (GCMC), and I further consent to such routine hospital care, diagnostic procedures, and medical treatment that the medical and professional staff of GCMC may deem necessary or advisable. I authorize the use of medical information obtained about me as specified above and the disclosure of such information to my referring physician(s). This form has been fully explained to me, and I understand its contents. I further understand that no guarantees have been made to me as to the results of treatments or examinations done at the GCMC.

Reviewed and Approved: Sally Pire
ATP-B-S:02:1001261385: Sally Pire
(Signed: 07/31/YYYY 10:12:05 AM EST)

Signature of Patient

Signature of Parent/Legal Guardian for Minor

Relationship to Minor

Reviewed and Approved: Andrea Witteman
ATP-B-S:02:1001261385: Andrea Witteman
(Signed: 07/31/YYYY 10:12:05 AM EST)

WITNESS: Global Care Medical Center Staff Member

Consent To Release Information For Reimbursement Purposes

In order to permit reimbursement, upon request, the Global Care Medical Center (GCMC) may disclose such treatment information pertaining to my hospitalization to any corporation, organization, or agent thereof, which is, or may be liable under contract to the GCMC or to me, or to any of my family members or other person, for payment of all or part of the GCMC's charges for services rendered to me (e.g. the patient's health insurance carrier). I understand that the purpose of any release of information is to facilitate reimbursement for services rendered. In addition, in the event that my health insurance program includes utilization review of services provided during this admission. I authorize GCMC to release information as is necessary to permit the review. This authorization will expire once the reimbursement for services rendered is complete.

Reviewed and Approved: Sally Pire
ATP-B-S:02:1001261385: Sally Pire
(Signed: 07/31/YYYY 10:14:17 AM EST)

Signature of Patient

Signature of Parent/Legal Guardian for Minor

Relationship to Minor

Reviewed and Approved: Andrea Witteman
ATP-B-S:02:1001261385: Andrea Witteman
(Signed: 07/31/YYYY 10:16:24 AM EST)

WITNESS: Global Care Medical Center Staff Member

Global Care Medical Center ■ 100 Main St, Alfred NY 14802 ■ (607) 555-1234

PIRE, SALLY	Admission: 07/31/YYYY	**Advance Directive**
IPCase005	DOB: 06/23/YYYY	
Dr. BLACK	ROOM: 0253	

Your answers to the following questions will assist your Physician and the Hospital to respect your wishes regarding your medical care. This information will become a part of your medical record.

	Yes	No	Patient's Initials
1. Have you been provided with a copy of the information called "Patient Rights Regarding Health Care Decision"?	X		
2. Have you prepared a "Living Will"? If yes, please provide the Hospital with a copy for your medical record.		X	
3. Have you prepared a Durable Power of Attorney for Health Care? If yes, please provide the Hospital with a copy for your medical record.		X	
4. Have you provided this facility with an Advance Directive on a prior admission and is it still in effect? If yes, Admitting Office to contact Medical Records to obtain a copy for the medical record.		X	
5. Do you desire to execute a Living Will/Durable Power of Attorney? If yes, refer to in order: a. Physician b. Social Service c. Volunteer Service		X	

Hospital Staff Directions: Check when each step is completed.

1. ✓ Verify the above questions were answered and actions taken where required.
2. ✓ If the "Patient Rights" information was provided to someone other than the patient, state reason:

____

______________________ ______________________

Name of Individual Receiving Information **Relationship to Patient**

3. ✓ If information was provided in a language other than English, specify language and method.
4. ✓ Verify patient was advised on how to obtain additional information on Advance Directives.
5. ✓ Verify the Patient/Family Member/Legal Representative was asked to provide the Hospital with a copy of the Advanced Directive which will be retained in the medical record.

File this form in the medical record, and give a copy to the patient.

____

Name of Patient/Name of Individual giving information if different from Patient

Reviewed and Approved: Sally Pire
ATP-B-S:02:1001261385: Sally Pire
(Signed: 07/31/YYYY 10:35:05 AM EST)

Signature of Patient **Date**

Reviewed and Approved: Andrea Witteman
ATP-B-S:02:1001261385: Andrea Witteman
(Signed: 07/31/YYYY 10:35:47 AM EST)

____

Signature of Hospital Representative **Date**

Global Care Medical Center ■ 100 Main St, Alfred NY 14802 ■ (607) 555-1234

PIRE, SALLY Admission: 07/31/YYYY
IPCase005 DOB: 06/23/YYYY
Dr. BLACK ROOM: 0253

Discharge Summary

ADMISSION DATE: 07/31/YYYY DISCHARGE DATE: 08/05/YYYY

ADMISSION DIAGNOSIS: Acute and chronic alcoholism.

DISCHARGE DIAGNOSIS: Acute and chronic alcoholism.

SUMMARY: This is a 60-year-old female who had extensive workups recently because of an abnormal CAT scan of the abdomen. She had been in our hospital earlier this year, and had the scan done in another city. Had a repeat scan done at General. Finally she was sent to Dr. Miller at General, for further evaluation. Apparently his study was unremarkable. Since that period of time, we've lost track of her. Apparently she had some problems with alcoholism recently, ended up at the Snowy Owls Retreat in Florida because of her alcohol problems, and they, for some reason or other, felt that she should be transferred here. I'm not exactly sure why. She, in the interval time, had sustained a fracture of her left forearm and wrist. This is being cared for by Dr. Jones in Rochester. She's returning to see him in follow-up about that situation.

Her brief workup here included a chest x-ray which showed no evidence of any active pulmonary disease. There was noted a compression deformity of the lower thoracic spine representing old fractures, X-ray of the left wrist revealed a healing comminuted fracture of the distal radius, position alignment of fracture fragments in wrist joint appeared to be satisfactory. Her lab work included an alkaline phosphatase of 20, blood sugar 143, sodium 144, potassium 4.4, carbon dioxide 27, chloride 108, cholesterol 143, Serum glutamic oxaloacetic transaminase 48, Lactate dehydrogenase 310, creatinine 0.4, calcium 9.0, phosphorus 2.5, bilirubin 0.8, total protein 6.2, albumin 3.6, uric acid 2.7, Urine with a specific gravity of 1.005, albumin and sugar were negative. White count was 5,800, hemoglobin 13.4, hematocrit 39.3, segmented cells 49, lymphocytes 34, monocytes 12, eosinophils 4, and 1 band cell.

She was treated supportively here in the hospital. She developed no problems, no signs of delirium tremens. She was up, ambulatory, doing well and eating well. She is discharged at this time on no medications, other than Theragran M, 1 tablet twice a day.

DD:07/31/YYYY

Reviewed and Approved: John Black MD
ATP-B-S:02:1001261385: John Black MD
(Signed: 07/31/YYYY 05:44:18 PM EST)

DT:08/02/YYYY

Physician Name

GLOBAL CARE MEDICAL CENTER ■ 100 MAIN ST, ALFRED NY 14802 ■ (607) 555-1234

PIRE, SALLY	Admission: 07/31/YYYY	**History & Physical Exam**
IPCase005	DOB: 06/23/YYYY	
Dr. BLACK	ROOM: 0253	

ADMISSION DIAGNOSIS: Alcoholism, probably acute and chronic.

CHIEF COMPLAINT: Weak and referred over by General Hospital.

HISTORY OF PRESENT ILLNESS: This is a 60-year-old female who has had extensive workup and evaluation recently because of abnormal liver function studies. She was in this hospital in January where she manifested mildly abnormal liver function studies without definitive diagnosis. She had a past history of splenectomy and hypokalemia. She was discharged after workup for this evaluation and was sent to General Hospital in the city for scan of the abdomen. They were somewhat unsure about the scan at that time, but in light of her history, they reported it as normal. However, a repeat scan was done down at General where the study was reported as significantly abnormal, but without a specific diagnosis. Ultimately, she was referred to Dr. Miller, who did extensive studies, and apparently felt there was no acute process. During all of this time she denied any significant alcoholic intake, although we have been told otherwise by certain members of her family. In the past month to six weeks. I'm not sure what has happened. Apparently she tried to go back to work but was unable to. Subsequent to that she was in an altercation where she sustained a fracture of the left wrist. Subsequent to that she ended up at the Treatment Center in Florida and apparently they felt that she needed further hospitalization here from physical point of view for further stabilization.

PAST MEDICAL HISTORY: Pretty well explained in the above outline. In addition, she has had a splenectomy several years ago for an abnormal bleeding problem.

FAMILY HISTORY: Noncontributory.

SOCIAL HISTORY: She works as a licensed practical nurse type worker in a nursing home. She claims to be a nonsmoker and did claim to be a nondrinker, but we are quite sure now that she has had a rather heavy alcohol intake.

SYSTEMIC REVIEW: No cough, dyspnea, orthopnea on exertion. Appetite is good. No bowel or bladder problems.

VITAL SIGNS: Weight 113, Blood pressure 150/90, Pulse 80, Temperature 97.

SKIN: Warm and dry. Color good.

GENERAL: Clear. Eyes - pupils round, react and equal. Extraocular muscles are okay. Sclera clear; no evidence of any jaundice. Nose and throat are unremarkable. Hydration is adequate.

NECK: Supple, No nodes or thyroid abnormalities.

CHEST: Peripheral lung fields are clear.

HEART: Sounds are good. No significant murmurs are heard.

BREASTS: Free of masses.

ABDOMEN: No palpable megaly or masses. Well-healed scar in the left upper quadrant area.

PELVIC & RECTAL: Not done at this time.

EXTREMITIES: Warm, pulses good.

NEUROLOGIC & ORTHOPEDIC: Are okay.

DD: 07/31/YYYY

Reviewed and Approved: John Black MD
ATP-B-S:02:1001261385: John Black MD
(Signed: 07/31/YYYY 06:05:44 PM EST)

DT: 08/02/YYYY

Physician Name

GLOBAL CARE MEDICAL CENTER ■ 100 MAIN ST, ALFRED NY 14802 ■ (607) 555-1234

PIRE, SALLY Admission: 07/31/YYYY
IPCase005 DOB: 06/23/YYYY
Dr. BLACK ROOM: 0253

Progress Notes

Date	Time	Physician's signature required for each order. (Please skip one line between dates.)
07/31/YYYY	1050	CHIEF COMPLAINT: DIAGNOSIS: Acute and chronic alcoholism. PLAN OF TREATMENT: Alert alcohol treatment counseling staff about need for treatment. DISCHARGE PLAN: Home. No services needed Reviewed and Approved: John Black MD ATP-B-S:02:1001261385: John Black MD (Signed: 07/31/YYYY 10:54:32 AM EST)
07/31/YYYY	1100	Workup in progress. Apparent difficulty with alcoholism. Patient history a bit sketchy. Working diagnosis as stated. Possible cirrhosis. Reviewed and Approved: John Black MD ATP-B-S:02:1001261385: John Black MD (Signed: 07/31/YYYY 11:04:32 AM EST)
07/31/YYYY	1115	Recent wrist fracture; will ask Surgery to follow. Reviewed and Approved: John Black MD ATP-B-S:02:1001261385: John Black MD (Signed: 07/31/YYYY 11:17:30 AM EST)
08/01/YYYY	1000	No sign of delirium tremens. Appetite good. Reviewed and Approved: John Black MD ATP-B-S:02:1001261385: John Black MD (Signed: 08/01/YYYY 10:07:00 AM EST)
08/03/YYYY	1000	Doing well. Home Wednesday. Reviewed and Approved: John Black MD ATP-B-S:02:1001261385: John Black MD (Signed: 08/03/YYYY 10:05:07 AM EST)
08/04/YYYY	0930	Home Wednesday. Doing well. No further follow-up indicated. Reviewed and Approved: John Black MD ATP-B-S:02:1001261385: John Black MD (Signed: 08/04/YYYY 09:44:32 AM EST)

GLOBAL CARE MEDICAL CENTER ■ 100 MAIN ST, ALFRED NY 14802 ■ (607) 555-1234

PIRE, SALLY	Admission: 07/31/YYYY	**Doctors' Orders**
IPCase005	DOB: 06/23/YYYY	
Dr. BLACK	ROOM: 0253	

Date	Time	Physician's signature required for each order. (Please skip one line between dates.)
07/31/YYYY	1100	Complete blood count Urinalysis Lytes SCG II Chest X ray Regular diet Reviewed and Approved: John Black MD ATP-B-S:02:1001261385: John Black MD (Signed: 07/31/YYYY 11:03:12 AM EST)
07/31/YYYY	1115	Watch for delirium tremens. Repeat x-ray hand and wrist - left. Reviewed and Approved: John Black MD ATP-B-S:02:1001261385: John Black MD (Signed: 07/31/YYYY 11:18:44 AM EST)
07/31/YYYY	1130	Surgical consult - Dr. Taylor for fracture of arm. Valium 5 milligrams daily for nervousness Thiamine 100 milligrams intramuscular Theragran M 1 tab twice a day History and physical exam dictated. Surgical consult - regarding recent fracture of left wrist, Tylenol 1 or 2 tablets every 4-6 hours as needed for pain. Reviewed and Approved: John Black MD ATP-B-S:02:1001261385: John Black MD (Signed: 07/31/YYYY 11:38:00 AM EST)
08/01/YYYY	1100	May ambulate as desired. Reviewed and Approved: John Black MD ATP-B-S:02:1001261385: John Black MD (Signed: 08/01/YYYY 11:02:12 AM EST)
08/05/YYYY	1100	Discharge today. Reviewed and Approved: John Black MD ATP-B-S:02:1001261385: John Black MD (Signed: 08/05/YYYY 11:12:56 AM EST)

GLOBAL CARE MEDICAL CENTER ■ 100 MAIN ST, ALFRED NY 14802 ■ (607) 555-1234

PIRE, SALLY Admission: 07/31/YYYY
IPCase005 DOB: 06/23/YYYY
Dr. BLACK ROOM: 0253

Radiology Report

Date of X-ray: 07/31/YYYY

REASON: Repeat x-ray.

REPORT

07/31/YYYY LEFT Wrist: Posteroanterior, oblique and lateral views taken through plaster show a comminuted fracture of the distal radius. The position and alignment of the fracture fragments and of the wrist joint appear to be satisfactory.

LEFT HAND: Multiple views of the left hand show only the previously described fracture of the distal radius.

DD:07/31/YYYY

DT:08/01/YYYY

Reviewed and Approved: Randall Cunningham MD
ATP-B-S:02:1001261385: Randall Cunningham MD
(Signed: 07/31/YYYY 02:24:44 PM EST)

GLOBAL CARE MEDICAL CENTER ■ 100 MAIN ST, ALFRED NY 14802 ■ (607) 555-1234

PIRE, SALLY	Admission: 07/31/YYYY	**Radiology Report**
IPCase005	DOB: 06/23/YYYY	
Dr. BLACK	ROOM: 0253	

Date of X-ray: 07/31/YYYY

REASON: Cirrhosis.

07/31/YYYY
CHEST: Posteroanterior and lateral views show that the cardiothoracic ratio measures 13.8/26.2 cm. The pulmonary vascularity is normal, and there is no evidence of any active pulmonary disease. There is a compression deformity of the lower thoracic spine which appears to represent an old compression fracture.

DD:07/31/YYYY

Reviewed and Approved: Randall Cunningham MD
ATP-B-S:02:1001261385: Randall Cunningham MD
Signed: 07/31/YYYY 02:32:08 PM EST)

DT:08/01/YYYY

GLOBAL CARE MEDICAL CENTER ■ 100 MAIN ST, ALFRED NY 14802 ■ (607) 555-1234

PIRE, SALLY	Admission: 07/31/YYYY	**Laboratory Data**
IPCase005	DOB: 06/23/YYYY	
Dr. BLACK	ROOM: 0253	

SPECIMEN COLLECTED:	07/31/YYYY	SPECIMEN RECEIVED:	07/31/YYYY
IN:	1242	OUT:	1810

BLOOD CHEMISTRY 1

TEST	REFERENCE		RESULT
ACID PHOSPHATASE	0.0-0.8 U/I		
ALKALINE PHOSPHATASE	50-136 U/I		20.0
AMYLASE	23-85 U/I		
LIPASE	4-24 U/I		
GLUCOSE FASTING	70-110 mg/dl		143
GLUCOSE	Time collected		
BUN	7-22 mg/dl		
SODIUM	136-147 mEq/l		144
POTASSIUM	3.7-5.1 mEq/l		4.4
CARBON DIOXIDE	24-32 mEq/1		27
CHLORIDE	98-108 mEq/l		108
CHOLESTEROL	120-280 mg/dl		143
SERUM GLUTAMATE PYRUVATE TRANSAMINASE	3-36 U/I		
SERUM GLUTAMIC OXALOCETIC TRANSAMINASE	M-27-47 U/I	F-22-37 U/I	48
CREATININE KINASE	M-35-232 U/I	F-21-215 U/I	
LACTATE DEHYDROGENASE	100-190 U/I		310
CREATININE	M-0.8-1.3 mg/dl	F-0.6-1.0 mg/dl	0.4
CALCIUM	8.7-10.2 mg/dl		9.0
PHOSPHORUS	2.5-4.9 mg/dl		2.5
BILIRUBIN-DIRECT	0.0-0.4 mg/dl		
BILIRUBIN-TOTAL	Less than 1.5 mg/dl		0.8
TOTAL PROTEIN	6.4-8.2 g/dl		6.2
ALBUMIN	3.4-5.0 g/dl		3.6
URIC ACID	M-3.8-7.1 mg/dl	F-2.6-5.6 mg/dl	2.7
TRIGLYCERIDE	30-200 mg/dl		

U/I = International Units
g/dl = grams per deciliter
mEq = milliequivalent per deciliter
mg/dl = milligrams per deciliter

GLOBAL CARE MEDICAL CENTER ■ 100 MAIN ST, ALFRED NY 14802 ■ (607) 555-1234

PIRE, SALLY	Admission: 07/31/YYYY	**Laboratory Data**
IPCase005	DOB: 06/23/YYYY	
Dr. BLACK	ROOM: 0253	

SPECIMEN COLLECTED: 07/31/YYYY SPECIMEN RECEIVED: 07/31/YYYY

TEST	RESULT	FLAG	REFERENCE
URINALYSIS			
DIPSTICK ONLY			
COLOR	straw		
SP GRAVITY	1.005		≤ 1.030
ALBUMIN	negative		≤ 125 mg/dl
BILIRUBIN	negative		≤ 0.8 mg/dl
SUGAR	negative		≤ 10 mg/dl
BLOOD	negative		0.06 mg/dl hgb
PH	6.5		5-8.0
ACETONE	negative		≤ 30 mg/dl
UROBILINOGEN			≤ -1 mg/dl
NITRITES			NEG
LEUKOCYTE			≤ 15 WBC/hpf
W.B.C.	rare		≤ 5/hpf
R.B.C.			≤ 5/hpf
BACT.			1+(≤ 20/hpf)
URINE PREGNANCY TEST			

End of Report

GLOBAL CARE MEDICAL CENTER ■ 100 MAIN ST, ALFRED NY 14802 ■ (607) 555-1234

PIRE, SALLY	Admission: 07/31/YYYY	**Laboratory Data**
IPCase005	DOB: 06/23/YYYY	
Dr. BLACK	ROOM: 0253	

TIME IN: 07/31/YYYY 1241 TIME OUT: 07/31/YYYY 1604

COMPLETE BLOOD COUNTS DIFFERENTIAL

TEST	RESULT	FLAG	REFERENCE
WHITE BLOOD CELL	5.8		4.5-11.0 thou/ul
RED BLOOD CELL	4.07		5.2-5.4 milliliter/upper limit
HEMOGLOBIN	13.4		11.7-16.1 grams per deciliter
HEMATOCRIT	39.3		35.0-47.0 %
MEAN CORPUSCULAR VOLUME	96.4		85-99 factor level
MEAN CORPUSCULAR HEMOGLOBIN	32.8		
MEAN CORPUSCULAR HEMOGLOBIN CONCENTRATION	34.0		33-37
RED CELL DISTRIBUTION WIDTH			11.4-14.5
PLATELETS	145		130-400 thou/ul
SEGMENTED CELLS %	49		
LYMPHOCYTES %	34		20.5-51.1
MONOCYTES %	12		1.7-9.3
EOSINOPHILS %	4		
BAND CELLS %	1		

Thou/ul = thousand upper limit

End of Report

GLOBAL CARE MEDICAL CENTER ■ 100 MAIN ST, ALFRED NY 14802 ■ (607) 555-1234

PIRE, SALLY Admission: 07/31/YYYY
IPCase005 DOB: 06/23/YYYY
Dr. BLACK ROOM: 0253

Graphic Chart

DAY IN HOSPITAL		1						2						3						4					
DATE		07/31/YYYY						08/01/YYYY						08/02/YYYY						08/03/YYYY					
PULSE (•)	TEMP (X)	0400	0800	1200	1600	2000	2400	0400	0800	1200	1600	2000	2400	0400	0800	1200	1600	2000	2400	0400	0800	1200	1600	2000	2400
140	106																								
130	105																								
120	104																								
110	103																								
100	102																								
90	101																								
80	100			X																					
70	99									•											•		•		
60	98.6			•											•				•						
50	98																								
40	97																								
30	96																								
20	95																								
RESPIRATION				20																					

	1 (07/31/YYYY)	2 (08/01/YYYY)	3 (08/02/YYYY)	4 (08/03/YYYY)
BLOOD PRESSURE	0800 / 1600 / 1200 50/100 / 2000	140/86	132/80	118/80
WEIGHT	113#			
DIET	Regular			
APPETITE	90%			
BATH	Self			
INTAKE/OUTPUT				
INTAKE: ORAL FLUIDS				
INTAKE: IV FLUIDS				
INTAKE: BLOOD				
INTAKE: 8 HOUR TOTAL				
INTAKE: 24 HOUR TOTAL				
OUTPUT: URINE				
OUTPUT: STOOL				
OUTPUT: EMESIS				
OUTPUT: N-G				
OUTPUT: 8 HOUR TOTAL				
OUTPUT: 24 HOUR TOTAL				

GLOBAL CARE MEDICAL CENTER ■ 100 MAIN ST, ALFRED NY 14802 ■ (607)555-1234

PIRE, SALLY	Admission: 07/31/YYYY	**Graphic Chart**
IPCase005	DOB: 06/23/YYYY	
Dr. BLACK	ROOM: 0253	

DAY IN HOSPITAL	4	5		
DATE	08/04/YYYY	08/05/YYYY		

PULSE (•)	TEMP (X)	0400	0800	1200	1600	2000	2400	0400	0800	1200	1600	2000	2400	0400	0800	1200	1600	2000	2400	0400	0800	1200	1600	2000	2400
140	106																								
130	105																								
120	104																								
110	103																								
100	102																								
90	101																								
80	100			X																					
70	99																								
60	98.6			•																					
50	98																								
40	97																								
30	96																								
20	95																								
RESPIRATION				20																					

BLOOD PRESSURE	0800		1600			
	1200	150/100	2000			
WEIGHT	113#					
DIET	Regular					
APPETITE		90%				
BATH	Self					
INTAKE/OUTPUT						
INTAKE – ORAL FLUIDS	X					
INTAKE – IV FLUIDS	0					
INTAKE – BLOOD	0					
INTAKE –	0					
INTAKE – 8 HOUR TOTAL						
INTAKE – 24 HOUR TOTAL						
OUTPUT – URINE	X					
OUTPUT – STOOL	0					
OUTPUT – EMESIS	1					
OUTPUT – N-G						
OUTPUT –						
OUTPUT – 8 HOUR TOTAL						
OUTPUT – 24 HOUR TOTAL						

GLOBAL CARE MEDICAL CENTER ■ 100 MAIN ST, ALFRED NY 14802 ■ (607)555-1234

PIRE, SALLY Admission: 07/31/YYYY
IPCase005 DOB: 06/23/YYYY
Dr. BLACK ROOM: 0253

Medication Administration Record

Special Instructions: Allergic to Sulfa / Demerol

Medication (dose and route)	**Date:** 07/31 **Time**	**Initials**	**Date:** 08/01 **Time**	**Initials**	**Date:** 08/02 **Time**	**Initials**	**Date:** 08/03 **Time**	**Initials**
Theragran M 1 tablet twice a day.	0800	----	0800	JD	0800	JD	0800	JD
	1600	OR	1600	OR	1600	OR	1600	OR
Single Orders & Pre-Ops								
Thiamine 100 milligrams intramuscular	1800	OR						
PRN Medications:								
Valium 5 milligrams daily as needed for nerves	2200	OR	2000	OR				
Tylenol 1 or 2 tablets every 4-6 hours as needed for pain	1800	OR	2400	JD	0130	JD	0800	JD
			0800	VS	0815	VS		
			1200	VS	2000	OR		
			1600	OR				

Initials	**Signature and Title**	**Initials**	**Signature and Title**	**Initials**	**Signature and Title**
VS	Vera South, RN	GPW	G. P. Well, RN		
OR	Ora Richards, RN	PS	P. Small, RN		
JD	Jane Dobbs, RN				
HF	H.Figgs, RN				

Global Care Medical Center ■ 100 Main St, Alfred NY 14802 ■ (607)555-1234

FIRE, SALLY	Admission: 07/31/YYYY	**Medication Administration Record**
IPCase005	DOB: 06/23/YYYY	
Dr. BLACK	ROOM: 0253	

SPECIAL INSTRUCTIONS: Allergic to Sulfa/Demerol

MEDICATION (dose and route)	DATE: 08/04 TIME	INITIALS	DATE: 08/05 TIME	INITIALS	DATE: 00/00 TIME	INITIALS	DATE: 00/00 TIME	INITIALS
Theragran M 1 tablet twice a day.	0800	VS	0800	VS				
	1600	OR	1600	OR				
Single Orders & Pre-Ops								
PRN Medications:								
Tylenol 1 or 2 tablets every 4-6 hours as needed for pain	0630	JD	0800	VS				
	1015	VS						

INITIALS	SIGNATURE AND TITLE	INITIALS	SIGNATURE AND TITLE	INITIALS	SIGNATURE AND TITLE
VS	Vera South, RN	GPW	G. P. Well, RN		
OR	Ora Richards, RN	PS	P. Small, RN		
JD	Jane Dobbs, RN				
HF	H.Figgs, RN				

GLOBAL CARE MEDICAL CENTER ■ 100 MAIN ST, ALFRED NY 14802 ■ (607)555-1234

PIRE, SALLY	Admission: 07/31/YYYY	**Nurses' Notes**
IPCase005	DOB: 06/23/YYYY	
Dr. BLACK	ROOM: 0253	

DATE	TIME	TREATMENTS & MEDICATIONS	TIME	NURSES' NOTES
07/31/YYYY		Friday	1030	Admission of 60-year-old white female with fractured left wrist with cast on but it has been split the full length because of edema. Done by doctor. Patient having large amount of pain. Patient requests to see a dentist here at the hospital because of having so many problems with them. Reviewed and Approved: V. South, RN ATP-B-S:02:1001261385: V. South, RN (Signed: 07/31/YYYY 10:31:03 AM EST)
07/31/YYYY			1200	Regular diet taken and retained. Appetite good. Still complains of pain in left arm. Reviewed and Approved: V. South, RN ATP-B-S:02:1001261385: V. South, RN (Signed: 07/31/YYYY 12:07:41 PM EST)
			1500	Dr. Black in to examine the patient. New orders noted. Reviewed and Approved: V. South, RN ATP-B-S:02:1001261385: V. South, RN (Signed: 07/31/YYYY 03:02:28 PM EST)
07/31/YYYY			1600	To x-ray and returned. Complains of pain in left arm. Resting. Reviewed and Approved: O. Richards, RN ATP-B-S:02:1001261385: O. Richards, RN (Signed: 07/31/YYYY 04:16:03 PM EST)
			1800	Diet taken fair. Resting. Reviewed and Approved: O. Richards, RN ATP-B-S:02:1001261385: O. Richards, RN (Signed: 07/31/YYYY 06:10:44 PM EST)
	2000	98.6 - 100-20 140/90	2000	Resting. Reviewed and Approved: O. Richards, RN ATP-B-S:02:1001261385: O. Richards, RN (Signed: 07/31/YYYY 08:04:00 PM EST)
	2040	Tylenol 1 tablet	2100	Bedtime care given. Reviewed and Approved: O. Richards, RN ATP-B-S:02:1001261385: O. Richards, RN (Signed: 07/31/YYYY 09:02:41 PM EST)
	2200	Valium 5 milligrams	2200	Resting. Reviewed and Approved: O. Richards, RN ATP-B-S:02:1001261385: O. Richards, RN (Signed: 07/31/YYYY 10:05:10 PM EST)

GLOBAL CARE MEDICAL CENTER ■ 100 MAIN ST, ALFRED NY 14802 ■ (607)555-1234

PIRE, SALLY	Admission: 07/31/YYYY	**Nurses' Notes**
IPCase005	DOB: 06/23/YYYY	
Dr. BLACK	ROOM: 0253	

DATE	TIME	TREATMENTS & MEDICATIONS	TIME	NURSES' NOTES
08/01/YYYY	11-7	Saturday Tylenol 1 tablet	2400	Complains of pain. Medicated with Tylenol 1 tablet. Left arm elevated on a pillow. Hand warm to touch. Color good. Good blanching. States "It feels prickly." No numbness. Reviewed and Approved: J. Dobbs, RN ATP-B-S:02:1001261385: J. Dobbs, RN (Signed: 08/01/YYYY 12:03:16 AM EST)
			0300	Continues to sleep. Reviewed and Approved: J. Dobbs, RN ATP-B-S:02:1001261385: J. Dobbs, RN (Signed: 08/01/YYYY 03:02:44 AM EST)
			0600	Slept at long intervals. Reviewed and Approved: J. Dobbs, RN ATP-B-S:02:1001261385: J. Dobbs, RN (Signed: 08/01/YYYY 06:05:07 AM EST)
08/01/YYYY		97.7 76-20 140/86	0730	Awake. Fingers warm and pink on left hand. Ambulated to bathroom. Returned to bed. Reviewed and Approved: J. Dobbs, RN ATP-B-S:02:1001261385: J. Dobbs, RN (Signed: 08/01/YYYY 07:32:41 AM EST)
		Dr. Black in.	0800	Breakfast taken well. Reviewed and Approved: V. South, RN ATP-B-S:02:1001261385: V. South, RN (Signed: 08/01/YYYY 08:02:30 AM EST)
			0900	Dr. in 0930. Reviewed and Approved: V. South, RN ATP-B-S:02:1001261385: V. South, RN (Signed: 08/01/YYYY 09:05:10 AM EST)
			1000	Ambulated in hall to tub room. Self morning care with assistance. Reviewed and Approved: V. South, RN ATP-B-S:02:1001261385: V. South, RN (Signed: 08/01/YYYY 10:02:50 AM EST)
			1030	Returned to room. Out of bed in chair. Morning spent napping on bed. Reviewed and Approved: V. South, RN ATP-B-S:02:1001261385: V. South, RN (Signed: 08/01/YYYY 10:32:00 AM EST)
			1215	Lunch taken well. Reviewed and Approved: V. South, RN ATP-B-S:02:1001261385: V. South, RN (Signed: 08/01/YYYY 12:16:00 PM EST)
			1330	Afternoon spent resting/napping at intervals. Reviewed and Approved: V. South, RN ATP-B-S:02:1001261385: V. South, RN (Signed: 08/01/YYYY 01:32:00 PM EST)

GLOBAL CARE MEDICAL CENTER ■ 100 MAIN ST, ALFRED NY 14802 ■ (607)555-1234

PIRE, SALLY	Admission: 07/31/YYYY	**Nurses' Notes**
IPCase005	DOB: 06/23/YYYY	
Dr. BLACK	ROOM: 0253	

DATE	TIME	TREATMENTS & MEDICATIONS	TIME	NURSES' NOTES
08/01/YYYY	1511		1530	Patient resting quietly with left arm elevated on a pillow. Complains of pain in her left lower arm. Reviewed and Approved: V. South, RN ATP-B-S:02:1001261385: V. South, RN (Signed: 08/01/YYYY 03:32:00 PM EST)
			1630	Out of bed in chair for dinner. Ambulated well by self. Ambulated in hall twice and tolerated well. Reviewed and Approved: O. Richards, RN ATP-B-S:02:1001261385: O. Richards, RN (Signed: 08/01/YYYY 04:33:00 PM EST)
			1715	Appetite was good. Reviewed and Approved: O. Richards, RN ATP-B-S:02:1001261385: O. Richards, RN (Signed: 08/01/YYYY 05:17:00 PM EST)
			1830–1930	Visitors in to see. Reviewed and Approved: O. Richards, RN ATP-B-S:02:1001261385: O. Richards, RN (Signed: 08/01/YYYY 07:31:03 PM EST)
			2000	Back to bed and watching television. Reviewed and Approved: O. Richards, RN ATP-B-S:02:1001261385: O. Richards, RN (Signed: 08/01/YYYY 08:07:41 PM EST)
			2030	Refused bedtime care. Reviewed and Approved: O. Richards, RN ATP-B-S:02:1001261385: O. Richards, RN (Signed: 08/01/YYYY 08:32:28 PM EST)
			2200	Patient stated her arm felt better since it had been taped earlier in the afternoon. Reviewed and Approved: O. Richards, RN ATP-B-S:02:1001261385: O. Richards, RN (Signed: 08/01/YYYY 10:00:03 PM EST)
			2230	Resting quietly with eyes closed. Reviewed and Approved: O. Richards, RN ATP-B-S:02:1001261385: O. Richards, RN (Signed: 08/01/YYYY 10:32:44 PM EST)
08/02/YYYY	11-7	Sunday	2400	Awake resting with eyes closed. Cast on left wrist. Hand warm to touch. Color good. Patient stated that arm feels "prickly." Reviewed and Approved: J. Dobbs, RN ATP-B-S:02:1001261385: J. Dobbs, RN (Signed: 08/02/YYYY 12:04:00 AM EST)
		Tylenol 2 tablets	0130	Complains of arm pain. Given Tylenol 2 tablets. Reviewed and Approved: J. Dobbs, RN ATP-B-S:02:1001261385: J. Dobbs, RN (Signed: 08/02/YYYY 01:33:10 AM EST)

Global Care Medical Center ■ 100 Main St, Alfred NY 14802 ■ (607)555-1234

PIRE, SALLY	Admission: 07/31/YYYY	**Nurses' Notes**
IPCase005	DOB: 06/23/YYYY	
Dr. BLACK	ROOM: 0253	

DATE	TIME	TREATMENTS & MEDICATIONS	TIME	NURSES' NOTES
			0300	Appears to be sleeping. Reviewed and Approved: J. Dobbs, RN ATP-B-S:02:1001261385: J. Dobbs, RN (Signed: 08/02/YYYY 03:00:00 AM EST)
			0600	Remains asleep. Left arm elevated on a pillow. Hand warm and color good. Reviewed and Approved: J. Dobbs, RN ATP-B-S:02:1001261385: J. Dobbs, RN (Signed: 08/02/YYYY 06:32:41 AM EST)
08/02/YYYY		98 - 68 20 132/86	0730	Awake. Ambulated to bathroom as needed. Cast intact. Fingers warm and pink. Reviewed and Approved: V. South, RN ATP-B-S:02:1001261385: V. South, RN (Signed: 08/02/YYYY 07:37:11 AM EST)
			0800	Breakfast taken well. Ambulated to tub room. Reviewed and Approved: V. South, RN ATP-B-S:02:1001261385: V. South, RN (Signed: 08/02/YYYY 08:02:00 AM EST)
			0830	Self care done. Reviewed and Approved: V. South, RN ATP-B-S:02:1001261385: V. South, RN (Signed: 08/02/YYYY 08:32:00 AM EST)
			0900	Morning spent watching television and reading without complaints. Reviewed and Approved: V. South, RN ATP-B-S:02:1001261385: V. South, RN (Signed: 08/02/YYYY 09:04:20 AM EST)
		Dr. Black is in.	1215	Lunch taken well. Reviewed and Approved: V. South, RN ATP-B-S:02:1001261385: V. South, RN (Signed: 08/02/YYYY 12:16:00 PM EST)
			1300	Afternoon spent visiting and watching television without complaints. Reviewed and Approved: V. South, RN ATP-B-S:02:1001261385: V. South, RN (Signed: 08/02/YYYY 01:06:34 PM EST)
08/02/YYYY			1600	Up walking in hall without complaints. Reviewed and Approved: O. Richards, RN ATP-B-S:02:1001261385: O. Richards, RN (Signed: 08/02/YYYY 04:03:00 PM EST)
			1800	Diet taken well. Reviewed and Approved: O. Richards, RN ATP-B-S:02:1001261385: O. Richards, RN (Signed: 08/02/YYYY 06:00:00 PM EST)

GLOBAL CARE MEDICAL CENTER ■ 100 MAIN ST, ALFRED NY 14802 ■ (607)555-1234

PIRE, SALLY	Admission: 07/31/YYYY	**Nurses' Notes**
IPCase005	DOB: 06/23/YYYY	
Dr. BLACK	ROOM: 0253	

DATE	TIME	TREATMENTS & MEDICATIONS	TIME	NURSES' NOTES
	2000	99.2 96 - 20 150/90	2000	Bedtime snack. Visiting with roommate. Self bedtime care. Reviewed and Approved: O. Richards, RN ATP-B-S:02:1001261385: O. Richards, RN (Signed: 08/02/YYYY 08:02:49 PM EST)
			2200	Resting. Reviewed and Approved: O. Richards, RN ATP-B-S:02:1001261385: O. Richards, RN (Signed: 08/02/YYYY 10:07:13 PM EST)
08/03/YYYY	11-7	Monday	2400	Appears to be sleeping. Left arm elevated on a pillow. Hand warm and pink. Reviewed and Approved: J. Dobbs, RN ATP-B-S:02:1001261385: J. Dobbs, RN (Signed: 08/03/YYYY 12:04:00 AM EST)
			0300	Continues to sleep. Reviewed and Approved: J. Dobbs, RN ATP-B-S:02:1001261385: J. Dobbs, RN (Signed: 08/03/YYYY 03:03:45 AM EST)
			0600	Remains asleep. Respirations easy. Left hand elevated on a pillow. Fingers warm and pink. No complaints offered. Reviewed and Approved: J. Dobbs, RN ATP-B-S:02:1001261385: J. Dobbs, RN (Signed: 08/03/YYYY 06:04:20 AM EST)
08/03/YYYY			0730	Awake and out of bed as desired. To shower for self morning care. Reviewed and Approved: V. South, RN ATP-B-S:02:1001261385: V. South, RN (Signed: 08/03/YYYY 07:33:12 AM EST)
			0800	Appetite good. Reviewed and Approved: V. South, RN ATP-B-S:02:1001261385: V. South, RN (Signed: 08/03/YYYY 08:06:50 AM EST)
			1000	Comfortable without complaints at present. Reviewed and Approved: V. South, RN ATP-B-S:02:1001261385: V. South, RN (Signed: 08/03/YYYY 10:03:34 AM EST)
			1200	Appetite good. Reviewed and Approved: V. South, RN ATP-B-S:02:1001261385: V. South, RN (Signed: 08/03/YYYY 12:05:00 PM EST)
			1430	Comfortable without complaints at present. Reviewed and Approved: V. South, RN ATP-B-S:02:1001261385: V. South, RN (Signed: 08/03/YYYY 02:33:10 PM EST)

GLOBAL CARE MEDICAL CENTER ■ 100 MAIN ST, ALFRED NY 14802 ■ (607)555-1234

PIRE, SALLY	Admission: 07/31/YYYY	**Nurses' Notes**
IPCase005	DOB: 06/23/YYYY	
Dr. BLACK	ROOM: 0253	

DATE	TIME	TREATMENTS & MEDICATIONS	TIME	NURSES' NOTES
08/03/YYYY	3-11	Monday	1530-1630	Resting quietly. No complaints offered. Reviewed and Approved: O. Richards, RN ATP-B-S:02:1001261385: O. Richards, RN (Signed: 08/03/YYYY 04:32:49 PM EST)
			1700	Appetite good at supper. Reviewed and Approved: O. Richards, RN ATP-B-S:02:1001261385: O. Richards, RN (Signed: 08/03/YYYY 05:07:13 PM EST)
		99.1 - 84 - 18 118/78	1830-1930	Vital signs taken; sitting up watching television and visiting with roommate. Reviewed and Approved: O. Richards, RN ATP-B-S:02:1001261385: O. Richards, RN (Signed: 08/03/YYYY 06:37:23 PM EST)
			2030	Bedtime care given; snack taken well. Reviewed and Approved: O. Richards, RN ATP-B-S:02:1001261385: O. Richards, RN (Signed: 08/03/YYYY 08:32:00 PM EST)
			2200	Quiet; no complaints. Reviewed and Approved: O. Richards, RN ATP-B-S:02:1001261385: O. Richards, RN (Signed: 08/03/YYYY 10:02:00 PM EST)
08/04/YYYY	11-7	Tuesday	2400	Appears to be sleeping. Respirations easy. Reviewed and Approved: J. Dodds, RN ATP-B-S:02:1001261385: J. Dodds, RN (Signed: 08/04/YYYY 12:04:20 AM EST)
			0300	Continues to sleep. Reviewed and Approved: J. Dodds, RN ATP-B-S:02:1001261385: J. Dodds, RN (Signed: 08/04/YYYY 03:06:47 AM EST)
			0600	Left hand in cast elevated on a pillow. Hand warm. Color good. Reviewed and Approved: J. Dodds, RN ATP-B-S:02:1001261385: J. Dodds, RN (Signed: 08/04/YYYY 06:02:17 AM EST)
08/04/YYYY			0730	Awake and out of bed as desired. Tub bath taken. Reviewed and Approved: V. South, RN ATP-B-S:02:1001261385: V. South, RN (Signed: 08/04/YYYY 07:33:10 AM EST)
			0800	Appetite good. Reviewed and Approved: V. South, RN ATP-B-S:02:1001261385: V. South, RN (Signed: 08/04/YYYY 08:02:00 AM EST)

GLOBAL CARE MEDICAL CENTER ■ 100 MAIN ST, ALFRED NY 14802 ■ (607)555-1234

PIRE, SALLY	Admission: 07/31/YYYY			Nurses' Notes
IPCase005	DOB: 06/23/YYYY			
Dr. BLACK	ROOM: 0253			

DATE	TIME	TREATMENTS & MEDICATIONS	TIME	NURSES' NOTES
			1000	Out of bed as desired. Walking in hall. Cast patent. No complaints offered. Reviewed and Approved: V. South, RN ATP-B-S:02:1001261385: V. South, RN (Signed: 08/04/YYYY 10:04:49 AM EST)
			1200	Appetite good. Reviewed and Approved: O. Richards, RN ATP-B-S:02:1001261385: O. Richards, RN (Signed: 08/04/YYYY 12:01:13 PM EST)
			1430	Comfortable without complaints at present. Reviewed and Approved: O. Richards, RN ATP-B-S:02:1001261385: O. Richards, RN (Signed: 08/04/YYYY 02:33:18 PM EST)
08/04/YYYY			1630	Resting quietly. No complaints offered. Reviewed and Approved: O. Richards, RN ATP-B-S:02:1001261385: O. Richards, RN (Signed: 08/04/YYYY 04:31:55 PM EST)
			1700	Appetite good at supper. Reviewed and Approved: O. Richards, RN ATP-B-S:02:1001261385: O. Richards, RN (Signed: 08/04/YYYY 05:01:09 PM EST)
			1830	Comfortable. Sitting up watching television and visiting with roommate. Reviewed and Approved: O. Richards, RN ATP-B-S:02:1001261385: O. Richards, RN (Signed: 08/04/YYYY 06:31:44 PM EST)
			2030	Bedtime care given; snack taken well. Reviewed and Approved: O. Richards, RN ATP-B-S:02:1001261385: O. Richards, RN (Signed: 08/04/YYYY 08:32:11 PM EST)
08/04/YYYY	2330	Tuesday	2330	Appears to be to sleeping soundly. Reviewed and Approved: J. Dodds, RN ATP-B-S:02:1001261385: J. Dodds, RN (Signed: 08/04/YYYY 11:36:34 PM EST)
08/05/YYYY		Wednesday	0100	Continues to sleep soundly. Reviewed and Approved: J. Dodds, RN ATP-B-S:02:1001261385: J. Dodds, RN (Signed: 08/05/YYYY 01:03:00 AM EST)
			0230	Remains asleep. Reviewed and Approved: J. Dodds, RN ATP-B-S:02:1001261385: J. Dodds, RN (Signed: 08/05/YYYY 02:32:17 AM EST)

GLOBAL CARE MEDICAL CENTER ■ 100 MAIN ST, ALFRED NY 14802 ■ (607)555-1234

PIRE, SALLY   Admission: 07/31/YYYY
IPCase005   DOB: 06/23/YYYY
Dr. BLACK   ROOM: 0253

Nurses' Notes

DATE	TIME	TREATMENTS & MEDICATIONS	TIME	NURSES' NOTES
			0400	Sleeping. Reviewed and Approved: J. Dodds, RN ATP-B-S:02:1001261385: J. Dodds, RN (Signed: 08/05/YYYY 04:02:49 AM EST)
			0630	Had good night. Slept. Reviewed and Approved: V. South, RN ATP-B-S:02:1001261385: V. South, RN (Signed: 08/05/YYYY 06:33:56 AM EST)
08/05/YYYY	7-3		0730	Awake and alert without distress. Voices no complaints. Self morning care done. Showered. Reviewed and Approved: V. South, RN ATP-B-S:02:1001261385: V. South, RN (Signed: 08/05/YYYY 07:31:14 AM EST)
			0830	Diet taken and tolerated well. Ambulating in hallway. Reviewed and Approved: V. South, RN ATP-B-S:02:1001261385: V. South, RN (Signed: 08/05/YYYY 08:33:57 AM EST)
			1030	Ready to go home. Reviewed and Approved: V. South, RN ATP-B-S:02:1001261385: V. South, RN (Signed: 08/05/YYYY 10:33:45 AM EST)
			1145	Discharged to front lobby. To home with family. Reviewed and Approved: V. South, RN ATP-B-S:02:1001261385: V. South, RN (Signed: 08/05/YYYY 11:47:23 AM EST)

GLOBAL CARE MEDICAL CENTER ■ 100 MAIN ST, ALFRED NY 14802 ■ (607)555-1234

PIRE, SALLY	Admission: 07/31/YYYY	**Nursing Discharge Status Summary**
IPCase005	DOB: 06/23/YYYY	
Dr. BLACK	ROOM: 0253	

1.	AFEBRILE:	X	Yes		No	140/80 98 - 80 - 20				
2.	WOUND:		Clean/Dry		Reddened		Infected			NA X
3.	PAIN FREE:		Yes	X	No	If "No," describe: Requires Tylenol as needed.				
4.	POST-HOSPITAL INSTRUCTION SHEET GIVEN TO PATIENT/FAMILY:							Yes	X	No
	If NO, complete lines 5-8 below.									
5.	DIET:	X	Regular		Other (Describe):					
6.	ACTIVITY:	X	Normal		Light		Limited			Bed rest
7.	MEDICATIONS:	None								
8.	INSTRUCTIONS GIVEN TO PATIENT/FAMILY:				As ordered by Dr. Black					
9.	PATIENT/FAMILY verbalize understanding of instructions:					X	Yes			No
10.	DISCHARGED at	1145	Via:		Wheelchair		Stretcher			Ambulance Co.
				X	Ambulatory					
	Accompanied by:	Vera South, RN				to	Front lobby			
	COMMENTS:	To front lobby. Ambulated with assistant to home with family.								
		Cast on left arm.								
	DATE:	08/05/YYYY								
	SIGNATURE:	Reviewed and Approved: V. South, RN ATP-B-S:02:1001261385: V. South, RN (Signed: 08/05/YYYY 11:47:15 AM EST)								

GLOBAL CARE MEDICAL CENTER ■ 100 MAIN ST, ALFRED NY 14802 ■ (607) 555-1234

PIRE, SALLY Admission: 07/31/YYYY
IPCase005 DOB: 06/23/YYYY
Dr. BLACK ROOM: 0253

Patient Property Record

I understand that while the facility will be responsible for items deposited in the safe. I must be responsible for all items retained by me at the bedside. (Dentures kept at the bedside will be labeled, but the facility cannot assure responsibility for them.) I also recognize that the hospital cannot be held responsible for items brought in to me after this form has been completed and signed.

Reviewed and Approved: Sally Pire
ATP-B-S:02:1001261385: Sally Pire
(Signed: 07/31/YYYY 10:35:05 AM EST) — 07/31/YYYY

Signature of Patient — **Date**

Reviewed and Approved: Andrea Witteman
ATP-B-S:02:1001261385: Andrea Witteman
(Signed: 07/31/YYYY 10:37:22 AM EST) — 07/31/YYYY

Signature of Witness — **Date**

I have no money or valuables that I wish to deposit for safekeeping. I do not hold the facility responsible for any other money or valuables that I am retaining or will have brought in to me.

I have been advised that it is recommended that I retain no more than $5.00 at the bedside.

Reviewed and Approved: Sally Pire
ATP-B-S:02:1001261385: Sally Pire
(Signed: 07/31/YYYY 10:35:05 AM EST) — 07/31/YYYY

Signature of Patient — **Date**

Reviewed and Approved: Andrea Witteman
ATP-B-S:02:1001261385: Andrea Witteman
(Signed: 07/31/YYYY 10:39:38 AM EST) — 07/31/YYYY

Signature of Witness — **Date**

I have deposited valuables in the facility safe. The envelope number is__________.

Signature of Patient — **Date**

Signature of Person Accepting Property — **Date**

I understand that medications I have brought to the facility will be handled as recommended by my physician. This may include storage, disposal, or administration.

Signature of Patient — **Date**

Signature of Witness — **Date**

GLOBAL CARE MEDICAL CENTER ■ 100 MAIN ST, ALFRED NY 14802 ■ (607) 555-1234

IPCase006

Global Care Medical Center
100 Main St, Alfred NY 14802
(607) 555-1234
Hospital No. 999

Inpatient Face Sheet

Patient Name and Address				Gender	Race	Marital Status		Patient No.
PIRE, SALLY 1122 CHERRY STREET ALMOND, NY 14804				F	W	S		IPCase006
				Date of Birth		**Age**	**Maiden Name**	**Occupation**
				06/23/YYYY		60	NA	Dog groomer
Admission Date	**Time**	**Discharge Date**	**Time**	**Length of Stay**		**Telephone Number**		
06-30-YYYY	12:45	07-07-YYYY	10:00	07 DAYS		(607) 000-4397		

Guarantor Name and Address		Next of Kin Name and Address	
PIRE, SALLY 1122 CHERRY STREET ALMOND, NY 14804		PIRE, JACOB 556 MILL STREET ALMOND, NY 14804	
Guarantor Telephone No.	**Relationship to Patient**	**Next of Kin Telephone Number**	**Relationship to Patient**
(607) 000-4397	Self	(607) 555-7676	BROTHER
Admitting Physician	**Service**	**Admit Type**	**Room Number/Bed**
John Black, MD	ME	NA	0371
Attending Physician	**Admitting Diagnosis**		
John Black, MD	Pneumonia		
Primary Insurer	**Policy and Group Number**	**Secondary Insurer**	**Policy and Group Number**
New Age Insurance	PW 6790456	NEBC	229162171

Diagnoses and Procedures	ICD Code
Principal Diagnosis	
Pneumonia due to *Enterobacter cloacae* gram-negative anaerobe	
Secondary Diagnoses	
Arteriosclerotic cardiovascular disease	
Principal Procedure	
Secondary Procedures	

Discharge Instructions

Activity: ❒ Bed rest ❒ Light ❒ Usual ❒ Unlimited ☒ Other: As tolerated.

Diet: ☒ Regular ❒ Low Cholesterol ❒ Low Salt ❒ ADA ❒ ____Calorie

Follow-Up: ❒ Call for appointment ☒ Office appointment on 07-14 ❒ Other:

Special Instructions:

Attending Physician Authentication: Reviewed and Approved: John Black MD
ATP-B-S: 02:1001261385: John Black MD
(Signed: 06/30/YYYY 01:00:00 PM EST)

PIRE, SALLY	Admission: 06/30/YYYY	**Consent to Admission**
IPCase006	DOB: 06/23/YYYY	
Dr. BLACK	ROOM: 0371	

I, Sally Pire hereby consent to admission to the Global Care Medical Center (GCMC), and I further consent to such routine hospital care, diagnostic procedures, and medical treatment that the medical and professional staff of GCMC may deem necessary or advisable. I authorize the use of medical information obtained about me as specified above and the disclosure of such information to my referring physician(s). This form has been fully explained to me, and I understand its contents. I further understand that no guarantees have been made to me as to the results of treatments or examinations done at the GCMC.

Reviewed and Approved: Sally Pire
ATP-B-S:02:1001261385: Sally Pire
(Signed: 06/30/YYYY 01:45:05 PM EST)

Signature of Patient

Signature of Parent/Legal Guardian for Minor

Relationship to Minor

Reviewed and Approved: Andrea Witteman
ATP-B-S:02:1001261385: Andrea Witteman
(Signed: 06/30/YYYY 01:45:05 PM EST)

WITNESS: Global Care Medical Center Staff Member

Consent To Release Information For Reimbursement Purposes

In order to permit reimbursement, upon request, the Global Care Medical Center (GCMC) may disclose such treatment information pertaining to my hospitalization to any corporation, organization, or agent thereof, which is, or may be liable under contract to the GCMC or to me, or to any of my family members or other person, for payment of all or part of the GCMC's charges for services rendered to me (e.g. the patient's health insurance carrier). I understand that the purpose of any release of information is to facilitate reimbursement for services rendered. In addition, in the event that my health insurance program includes utilization review of services provided during this admission, I authorize GCMC to release information as is necessary to permit the review. This authorization will expire once the reimbursement for services rendered is complete.

Reviewed and Approved: Sally Pire
ATP-B-S:02:1001261385: Sally Pire
(Signed: 06/30/YYYY 01:47:05 PM EST)

Signature of Patient

Signature of Parent/Legal Guardian for Minor

Relationship to Minor

Reviewed and Approved: Andrea Witteman
ATP-B-S:02:1001261385: Andrea Witteman
(Signed: 06/30/YYYY 01:48:05 PM EST)

WITNESS: Global Care Medical Center Staff Member

GLOBAL CARE MEDICAL CENTER ■ 100 MAIN ST, ALFRED NY 14802 ■ (607) 555-1234

PIRE, SALLY	Admission: 06/30/YYYY	**Advance Directive**
IPCase001	DOB: 06/23/YYYY	
Dr. BLACK	ROOM: 0371	

Your answers to the following questions will assist your Physician and the Hospital to respect your wishes regarding your medical care. This information will become a part of your medical record.

	Yes	No	Patient's Initials
1. Have you been provided with a copy of the information called "Patient Rights Regarding Health Care Decision"?	X		
2. Have you prepared a "Living Will"? If yes, please provide the Hospital with a copy for your medical record.		X	
3. Have you prepared a Durable Power of Attorney for Health Care? If yes, please provide the Hospital with a copy for your medical record.		X	
4. Have you provided this facility with an Advance Directive on a prior admission and is it still in effect? If yes, Admitting Office to contact Medical Records to obtain a copy for the medical record.		X	
5. Do you desire to execute a Living Will/Durable Power of Attorney? If yes, refer to in order: a. Physician b. Social Service c. Volunteer Service		X	

Hospital Staff Directions: Check when each step is completed.

1. ✓ Verify the above questions were answered and actions taken where required.
2. ✓ If the "Patient Rights" information was provided to someone other than the patient, state reason:

Name of Individual Receiving Information **Relationship to Patient**

3. ✓ If information was provided in a language other than English, specify language and method.
4. ✓ Verify patient was advised on how to obtain additional information on Advance Directives.
5. ✓ Verify the Patient/Family Member/Legal Representative was asked to provide the Hospital with a copy of the Advanced Directive which will be retained in the medical record.

File this form in the medical record, and give a copy to the patient.

Name of Patient/Name of Individual giving information if different from Patient

Reviewed and Approved: Sally Pire
ATP-B-S:02:1001261385: Sally Pire
(Signed: 06/30/YYYY 01:48:05 PM EST)

Signature of Patient **Date**

Reviewed and Approved: Andrea Witteman
ATP-B-S:02:1001261385: Andrea Witteman
(Signed: 06/30/YYYY 01:49:05 PM EST)

Signature of Hospital Representative **Date**

Global Care Medical Center ■ 100 Main St, Alfred NY 14802 ■ (607) 555-1234

PIRE, SALLY Admission: 06/30/YYYY
IPCase006 DOB: 06/23/YYYY
Dr. BLACK ROOM: 0371

Discharge Summary

ADMISSION DATE: 06/30/YYYY DISCHARGE DATE: 07/07/YYYY

ADMISSION DIAGNOSIS: 1. Pneumonia; 2. Arteriosclerotic cardiovascular disease; 3. Past history of alcoholism; 4. Past history of hypokalemia.

DISCHARGE DIAGNOSES: Pneumonia due to *Enterobacter cloacae* gram-negative anaerobe. Arteriosclerotic cardiovascular disease.

SUMMARY: This is a 60-year-old white female who has been doing fairly well recently until the onset of an upper respiratory infection with a cough, recurrent chills, sweats, fever. She tried to work, was unable to. Her temperature went to 102. Chest x-ray showed a pneumonia, and I felt that she should be admitted for further evaluation and treatment.

Workup has included a chest x-ray which revealed a small area of infiltrate in the lingual of the right side compatible with an acute pneumonia; a follow-up study is suggested. Repeat chest x-ray showed bilateral pneumonia, clearing; however, there was a remaining area of consolidation in the lateral portion of the middle lobe. Her urine showed a specific gravity of 1.015, albumin and sugar were negative, white blood cells rare, red blood cells 0-6. White count 15,000. Hemoglobin 11.8, hematocrit 34.8, segmented cells 52, lymphocytes 18, monocytes 12, eosinophils 3, and 5 band cells. Complete blood count was normal. Sodium 137, potassium 3.4, carbon dioxide 27, chloride 97, alkaline phosphatase 10.4, blood sugar 81, cholesterol 138, Serum glutamic oxaloacetic transaminase 42, Lactate dehydrogenase 260, creatinine 0.4, calcium 8.3, phosphorus 2.2, bilirubin 1.2, total protein 6.1, albumin 3.2, uric acid 0.5. Sputum culture grew out a 1+ enterobacter. Cardiogram was reported as showing sinus tachycardia; this later slowed down clinically.

She was started originally on Ampicillin 500 milligrams, four times a day, Intermittent positive pressure breathing. She was continued on her Lanoxin 0.125 a day, Lasix 20 milligrams a day, Klotrix tablets 1 tablet three times a day. Her temperature stayed up, her Ampicillin was stopped, and she was switched to Erythromycin 500 milligrams, four times a day. Now her temperature has been normal for 48 hours. She feels better, and her cough has lessened. She is up ambulatory, and she is anxious to go home. She is being discharged at this time on E-Mycin 333 milligrams, three times a day and Afrin nasal spray. She will continue on her Lanoxin 0.125 milligrams a day, Lasix 20 milligrams a day, and should be seen in follow-up in the office early next week.

DD: 06/30/YYYY

DT: 07/01/YYYY

Reviewed and Approved: John Black MD
ATP-B-S:02:1001261385: John Black MD
(Signed: 06/30/YYYY 05:44:18 PM EST)

Physician Name

GLOBAL CARE MEDICAL CENTER ■ 100 MAIN ST, ALFRED NY 14802 ■ (607) 555-1234

PIRE, SALLY	Admission: 06/30/YYYY	**History & Physical Exam**
IPCase006	DOB: 06/23/YYYY	
Dr. BLACK	ROOM: 0371	

ADMISSION DIAGNOSIS: 1. Pneumonia; 2. Arteriosclerotic cardiovascular disease; 3. Past history of alcoholism; 4. Past history of hypokalemia.

CHIEF COMPLAINT: Shortness of breath.

HISTORY OF PRESENT ILLNESS: This is a 60-year-old female who has been in the hospital on two occasions within the past year or two. Her last admission was related to some problems with alcohol. Prior to that she had been in with some abnormal liver function studies that were later evaluated at Strong. Recently she's been doing fairly well until a few days ago when she had the onset of upper respiratory symptoms. She continued to work. She now is coughing, having chills, fever, and sweats. She was seen and evaluated in the office this morning. She had fever of 102. We referred her over for a chest x-ray which showed pneumonia of the left lung field, and she subsequently was admitted for further investigation, evaluation, and treatment.

PAST MEDICAL HISTORY: As mentioned, she's had some problems with alcohol in the past. She had a fractured wrist recently. She also has recently been put on Lanoxin and Lasix, apparently for arteriosclerotic cardiovascular problems. Subsequent to her second admission in YYYY, she was referred to General Hospital for further evaluation and treatment of her abnormal liver function studies. It was determined at that time that she did not have an active process.

FAMILY HISTORY: Noncontributory.

SOCIAL HISTORY: She works as a nurse's aide. She's a moderate smoker. Denies heavy drinking, but we are not quite sure about that.

REVIEW OF SYSTEMS: She has hacking cough, slight dyspnea on exertion, 2 pillow orthopnea, no hemoptysis. Appetite has been fair. She denies any specific bowel or bladder symptomatology.

PHYSICAL EXAMINATION: VITAL SIGNS: Temperature 102. Pulse 90, Respirations 24.

SKIN: Warm, dry.

EYES: Pupils round, reactive and equal. Extraocular muscles intact. Sclera clear; no evidence of any jaundice. Nose and throat are unremarkable.

NECK: Supple. No nodes or thyroid abnormalities.

CHEST: Scattered rales and rhonchi at both mid-lung fields. HEART: Sounds are somewhat distant. No significant murmurs are heard. BREASTS: Soft and free of masses.

ABDOMEN: No palpable organomegaly or masses. No cerebrovascular accident tenderness or bruits. Bowel sounds normally active.

PELVIC: Not done. RECTAL: Not done.

EXTREMITIES: Warm, pulses good.

NEUROLOGIC: Okay.

Reviewed and Approved: John Black MD
ATP-B-S:02:1001261385 John Black MD
(Signed: 06/30/YYYY 06:05:44 PM EST)

DD: 06/30/YYYY

DT: 07/01/YYYY

Physician Name

GLOBAL CARE MEDICAL CENTER ■ 100 MAIN ST, ALFRED NY 14802 ■ (607) 555-1234

PIRE, SALLY	Admission: 06/30/YYYY	**Progress Notes**
IPCase006	DOB: 06/23/YYYY	
Dr. BLACK	ROOM: 0371	

Date	Time	Physician's signature required for each order. (Please skip one line between dates.)
06/30/YYYY	1300	CHIEF COMPLAINT: Shortness of breath. DIAGNOSIS: 1) Pneumonia. 2) Arteriosclerotic cardiovascular disease. Confirmed _______ Provisional __X__ PLAN OF TREATMENT: Admit for evaluation and treatment. Reviewed and Approved: John Black MD ATP-B-S:02:1001261385: John Black MD (Signed: 06/30/YYYY 01:47:02 PM EST)
06/30/YYYY	1800	Intermittent positive pressure breathing ordered four times a day and saline for 48 hours. Started at 1730. Patient tolerated well. Slight production with cough, sputum clear in color. Reviewed and Approved: Rose Markam, CPT ATP-B-S:02:1001261385: Rose Markam, CPT (Signed: 06/30/YYYY 06:07:22 PM EST)
07/01/YYYY	0800	Intermittent positive pressure breathing treatment given at 0700. Non-productive cough noted. Reviewed and Approved: Shelly White CPT ATP-B-S:02:1001261385: Shelly White CPT (Signed: 07/01/YYYY 08:17:30 AM EST)
07/01/YYYY	1000	Intermittent positive pressure breathing treatment given at 1000. Tolerated well. Reviewed and Approved: Shelly White CPT ATP-B-S:02:1001261385: Shelly White CPT (Signed: 07/01/YYYY 10:06:00 AM EST)
07/01/YYYY	1300	Intermittent positive pressure breathing treatment given at 1300. Good treatment. Reviewed and Approved: Shelly White CPT ATP-B-S: 02:1001261385: Shelly White CPT (Signed: 07/01/YYYY) 01:17:30 PM EST)

GLOBAL CARE MEDICAL CENTER ■ 100 MAIN ST, ALFRED NY 14802 ■ (607) 555-1234

PIRE, SALLY Admission: 06/30/YYYY
IPCase006 DOB: 06/23/YYYY
Dr. BLACK ROOM: 0371

Progress Notes

Date	Time	Physician's signature required for each order. (Please skip one line between dates.)
07/01/YYYY	1600	Intermittent positive pressure breathing treatment given at 1600. Tolerated well. Reviewed and Approved: Rose Markam, CPT ATP-B-S:02:1001261385: Rose Markam, CPT (Signed: 07/01/YYYY 04:10:30 PM EST)
07/01/YYYY	1900	Still feels "lousy." Temperature up. Reviewed and Approved: John Black MD ATP-B-S:02:1001261385: John Black MD (Signed: 07/01/YYYY 07:07:42 PM EST)
07/02/YYYY	1000	Intermittent positive pressure breathing treatment not given at 0700. Therapist busy in Intensive Care Unit. 1000 tolerated. Reviewed and Approved: Shelly White CPT ATP-B-S: 02:1001261385: Shelly White CPT (Signed: 07/02/YYYY 10:06:00 AM EST)
07/02/YYYY	1300	Intermittent positive pressure breathing treatment given. Some production. Reviewed and Approved: Shelly White CPT ATP-B-S:02:1001261385: Shelly White CPT (Signed: 07/02/YYYY 01:17:30 PM EST)
07/02/YYYY	1600	Intermittent positive pressure breathing treatment given at 1600. Tolerated. Reviewed and Approved: Rose Markam, CPT ATP-B-S:02:1001261385: Rose Markam, CPT (Signed: 07/02/YYYY 04:06:00 PM EST)
07/02/YYYY	1900	Hydration good. Not much appetite. Reviewed and Approved: John Black MD ATP-B-S:02:1001261385: John Black MD (Signed: 07/02/YYYY 07:07:42 PM EST)
07/03/YYYY	0800	Temperature still up. Will switch to erythromycin. Still ambulatory as tolerated. Reviewed and Approved: John Black MD ATP-B-S:02:1001261385: John Black MD (Signed: 07/03/YYYY 08:07:42 AM EST)

GLOBAL CARE MEDICAL CENTER ■ 100 MAIN ST, ALFRED NY 14802 ■ (607) 555-1234

PIRE, SALLY	Admission: 06/30/YYYY	**Progress Notes**
IPCase006	DOB: 06/23/YYYY	
Dr. BLACK	ROOM: 0371	

Date	Time	Physician's signature required for each order. (Please skip one line between dates.)
07/03/YYYY	1030	Intermittent positive pressure breathing treatment with normal saline four times a day for 48 hours started at 1030. Tolerated well. No cough noted. Reviewed and Approved: Shelly White CPT ATP-B-S:02:1001261385: Shelly White CPT (Signed: 07/03/YYYY 10:36:00 AM EST)
07/03/YYYY	1300	Intermittent positive pressure breathing treatment at 1300. Tolerated well. Reviewed and Approved: Shelly White CPT ATP-b-S:02:1001261385: Shelly White CPT (Signed: 07/03/YYYY 01:06:45 PM EST)
07/03/YYYY	1700	Intermittent positive pressure breathing treatment at 1700. Tolerated well. Reviewed and Approved: Rose Markam, CPT ATP-B-S:02:1001261385: Rose Markam, CPT (Signed: 07/03/YYYY 05:03:00 PM EST)
07/04/YYYY	0700	Feels better. Temperature coming down. Reviewed and Approved : John Black MD ATP-B-S:02:1001261385: John Black MD (Signed: 07/04/YYYY 07:02:30 AM EST)
07/04/YYYY	0700	Intermittent positive pressure breathing treatment at 0700. Tolerated well. No cough. Reviewed and Approved: Shelly White CPT ATP-B-S:02:1001261385: Shelly White CPT (Signed: 07/04/YYYY 07:06:45 AM EST)
07/04/YYYY	1000	Intermittent positive pressure breathing treatment at 1000. Tolerated. Reviewed and Approved: Shelly White CPT ATP-B-S:02:1001261385: Shelly White CPT (Signed: 07/04/YYYY 10:02:17 AM EST)
07/04/YYYY	1300	Intermittent positive pressure breathing treatment at 1300. Tolerated well. No cough. Reviewed and Approved: Shelly White CPT ATP-B-S:02:1001261385: Shelly White CPT (Signed: 07/04/YYYY 01:06:45 PM EST)

GLOBAL CARE MEDICAL CENTER ■ 100 MAIN ST, ALFRED NY 14802 ■ (607) 555-1234

PIRE, SALLY	Admission: 06/30/YYYY	**Progress Notes**
IPCase006	DOB: 06/23/YYYY	
Dr. BLACK	ROOM: 0371	

Date	Time	Physician's signature required for each order. (Please skip one line between dates.)
07/04/YYYY	1800	Intermittent positive pressure breathing treatment at 1800. Tolerated well. No cough. Reviewed and Approved: Rose Markam, CPT ATP-B-S:02:1001261385: Rose Markam, CPT (Signed: 07/04/YYYY 06:01:25 PM EST)
07/05/YYYY	0700	Intermittent positive pressure breathing treatment at 0700. Tolerated well. Dry cough released completion of 48 hours. Reviewed and Approved: Shelly White CPT ATP-B-S:02:1001261385: Shelly White CPT (Signed: 07/05/YYYY 07:07:45 AM EST)
07/05/YYYY	0800	Dry cough. Fever down. Improving with intermittent positive pressure breathing treatments. Serous otitis left ear. Reviewed and Approved: John Black MD ATP-B-S:02:1001261385: John Black MD (Signed: 07/05/YYYY 08:02:30 AM EST)
07/06/YYYY	0800	Afebrile. Regaining strength. Home tomorrow if chest x-ray warrants. Reviewed and Approved: John Black MD ATP-B-S:02:1001261385: John Black MD (Signed: 07/06/YYYY 08:06:45 AM EST)

GLOBAL CARE MEDICAL CENTER ■ 100 MAIN ST, ALFRED NY 14802 ■ (607) 555-1234

PIRE, CALLY Admission: 06/30/YYYY
IPCase006 DOB: 06/23/YYYY
Dr. BLACK ROOM: 0371

Doctors' Orders

Date	Time	Physician's signature required for each order. (Please skip one line between dates.)
06-30-YYYY	1530	Complete blood count Urinalysis Chest X-ray done as outpatient. Get report. Electrocardiogram SCG II Electrolytes Sputum for culture and sensitivity Regular diet Aspirin, grain 10 every four hours for elevated temperature Bed rest with bathroom privileges Intermittent positive pressure breathing with saline four times a day for 48 hours Ampicillin 500 milligrams four times a day for 7 days History and physical exam dictated. Lanoxin, 0.125 milligram daily Lasix, 20 milligrams daily Klotrix one tablet three times a day Reviewed and Approved: John Black MD ATP-B-S:02:1001261385: John Black MD (Signed: 06/30/YYYY 03:33:12 PM EST)
07/01/YYYY	1115	Tylenol one or two tablets every four to six hours as needed for fever. Reviewed and Approved: John Black MD ATP-B-S: 02:1001261385: John Black MD (Signed: 07/01/YYYY 11:18:44 AM EST)
07/01/YYYY	1515	Dalmane 15 milligrams every bedtime as needed for sleep. Reviewed and Approved: John Black MD ATP-B-S:02:1001261385: John Black MD (Signed: 07/01/YYYY 03:20:00 PM EST)
07/03/YYYY	0930	Discontinue Ampicillin. Erythromycin 500 milligrams every six hours for 5 days. Intermittent positive pressure breathing with saline four times a day for 48 hours Reviewed and Approved: John Black MD ATP-B-S:02:1001261385: John Black MD (Signed: 07/03/YYYY 09:32:12 AM EST)

GLOBAL CARE MEDICAL CENTER ■ 100 MAIN ST, ALFRED NY 14802 ■ (607) 555-1234

PIRE, SALLY	Admission: 06/30/YYYY	**Doctors' Orders**
IPCase006	DOB: 06/23/YYYY	
Dr. BLACK	ROOM: 0371	

Date	Time	Physician's signature required for each order. (Please skip one line between dates.)
07/04/YYYY	0800	Chest X-ray and Complete blood count scheduled for 07/05. Reviewed and Approved: John Black MD ATP-B-S:02:1001261385: John Black MD (Signed: 07/04/YYYY 08:05:23 AM EST)
07/05/YYYY	1330	Dimetapp Extentabs one tablet now then twice daily. Reviewed and Approved: John Black MD ATP-B-S:02:1001261385: John Black MD (Signed: 07/05/YYYY 03:40:44 PM EST)
07/06/YYYY	1315	Afrin nasal spray - 2 squeezes in each nostril every 12 hours. Reviewed and Approved: John Black MD ATP-B-S:02:1001261385: John Black MD (Signed: 07/06/YYYY 03:20:00 PM EST)
07/07/YYYY	0900	Discharge. Reviewed and Approved: John Black MD ATP-B-S:02:1001261385: John Black MD (Signed: 07/07/YYYY 09:02:12 AM EST)

GLOBAL CARE MEDICAL CENTER ■ 100 MAIN ST, ALFRED NY 14802 ■ (607) 555-1234

PIRE, SALLY Admission: 06/30/YYYY
IPCase006 DOB: 06/23/YYYY
Dr. BLACK ROOM: 0371

Radiology Report

Date of X-ray: 06/30/YYYY REASON: Pneumonia

TECHNICAL DATA: Posteroanterior and lateral.

CHEST: Posteroanterior and lateral views reveal partial clearing of the lingular pneumonia since 06/30/YYYY. There is now an area of consolidation in the lateral portion of the middle lobe. The lungs otherwise appear clear.

CONCLUSION: Bilateral pneumonia.

DD: 06/30/YYYY Reviewed and Approved: Randall Cunningham MD
DT: 07/01/YYYY ATP-B-S:02:1001261385: Randall Cunningham MD
(Signed: 06/30/YYYY 02:24:44 PM EST)

GLOBAL CARE MEDICAL CENTER ■ 100 MAIN ST, ALFRED NY 14802 ■ (607) 555-1234

PIRE, SALLY	Admission: 06/30/YYYY	**Radiology Report**
IPCase006	DOB: 06/23/YYYY	
Dr. BLACK	ROOM: 0371	

Date of X-ray: 06/30/YYYY

REASON: Rule out Pneumonia.

TECHNICAL DATA: Please call.

06/30/YYYY

CHEST: Posteroanterior and lateral views reveal a small area of infiltrate in the lingual which has appeared since the study of 07/31/YYYY. This would be compatible with an acute pneumonia and a follow-up study is suggested. The heart is of normal size and the lungs otherwise appear clear. There is an old fracture in the lower thoracic spine and several old healing left rib fractures.

DD: 06/30/YYYY Reviewed and Approved: Randall Cunningham MD
DT: 07/01/YYYY ATP-B-S:02:1001261385: Randall Cunningham MD
(Signed: 06/30/YYYY 02:32:08 PM EST)

GLOBAL CARE MEDICAL CENTER ■ 100 MAIN ST, ALFRED NY 14802 ■ (607) 555-1234

PIRE, SALLY	Admission: 06/30/YYYY	**Laboratory Data**
IPCase006	DOB: 06/23/YYYY	
Dr. BLACK	ROOM: 0371	

SPECIMEN COLLECTED:	06/30/YYYY	SPECIMEN RECEIVED:	06/30/YYYY
IN:	1614	OUT:	1749

BLOOD CHEMISTRY 1

TEST	REFERENCE		RESULT
ACID PHOSPHATASE	0.0-0.8 U/I		
ALKALINE PHOSPHATASE	50-136 U/I		
AMYLASE	23-85 U/I		
LIPASE	4-24 U/I		
GLUCOSE FASTING	70-110 mg/dl		
GLUCOSE	Time collected		
BUN	7-22 mg/dl		
SODIUM	136-147 mEq/l		137
POTASSIUM	3.7-5.1 mEq/l		**3.4**
CARBON DIOXIDE	24-32 mEq/1		27
CHLORIDE	98-108 mEq/l		97
CHOLESTEROL	120-280 mg/dl		
SERUM GLUTAMATE PYRUVATE TRANSAMINASE	3-36 U/I		
SERUM GLUTAMIC OXALOCETIC TRANSAMINASE	M-27-47 U/I	F-22-37 U/I	
CREATININE KINASE	M-35-232 U/I	F-21-215 U/I	
LACTATE DEHYDROGENASE	100-190 U/I		
CREATININE	M-0.8-1.3 mg/dl	F-0.6-1.0 mg/dl	
CALCIUM	8.7-10.2 mg/dl		
PHOSPHORUS	2.5-4.9 mg/dl		
BILIRUBIN-DIRECT	0.0-0.4 mg/dl		
BTLIRUBIN-TOTAL	Less than 1.5 mg/dl		
TOTAL PROTEIN	6.4-8.2 g/dl		
ALBUMIN	3.4-5.0 g/dl		
URIC ACID	M-3.8-7.1 mg/dl	F-2.6-5.6 mg/dl	
TRIGLYCERIDE	30-200 mg/dl		

U/I = International Units
g/dl = grams per deciliter
mEq = milliequivalent per deciliter
mg/dl = milligrams per deciliter

GLOBAL CARE MEDICAL CENTER ■ 100 MAIN ST, ALFRED NY 14802 ■ (607) 555-1234

PIRE, SALLY	Admission: 06/30/YYYY	**Laboratory Data**
IPCase006	DOB: 06/23/YYYY	
Dr. BLACK	ROOM: 0371	

SPECIMEN COLLECTED:	06/30/YYYY	SPECIMEN RECEIVED:	07/01/YYYY
IN:	2322	OUT:	1032

BLOOD CHEMISTRY 1

TEST	REFERENCE		RESULT
ACID PHOSPHATASE	0.0-0.8 U/I		
ALKALINE PHOSPHATASE	50-136 U/I		**10.4**
AMYLASE	23-85 U/I		
LIPASE	4-24 U/I		
GLUCOSE FASTING	70-110 mg/dl		81
GLUCOSE	Time collected		
BUN	7-22 mg/dl		
SODIUM	136-147 mEq/l		
POTASSIUM	3.7-5.1 mEq/l		
CARBON DIOXIDE	24-32 mEq/l		
CHLORIDE	98-108 mEq/l		
CHOLESTEROL	120-280 mg/dl		138
SERUM GLUTAMATE PYRUVATE TRANSAMINASE	3-36 U/I		
SERUM GLUTAMIC OXALOCETIC TRANSAMINASE	M-27-47 U/I	F-22-37 U/I	42
CREATININE KINASE	M-35-232 U/I	F-21-215 U/I	
LACTATE DEHYDROGENASE	100-190 U/I		**260**
CREATININE	M-0.8-1.3 mg/dl	F-0.6-1.0 mg/dl	**0.4**
CALCIUM	8.7-10.2 mg/dl		**8.3**
PHOSPHORUS	2.5-4.9 mg/dl		**2.2**
BILIRUBIN-DIRECT	0.0-0.4 mg/dl		
BTLIRUBIN-TOTAL	Less than 1.5 mg/dl		1.2
TOTAL PROTEIN	6.4-8.2 g/dl		**6.1**
ALBUMIN	3.4-5.0 g/dl		**3.2**
URIC ACID	M-3.8-7.1 mg/dl	F-2.6-5.6 mg/dl	**0.5**
TRIGLYCERIDE	30-200 mg/dl		

U/I = International Units
g/dl = grams per deciliter
mEq = milliequivalent per deciliter
mg/dl = milligrams per deciliter

GLOBAL CARE MEDICAL CENTER ■ 100 MAIN ST, ALFRED NY 14802 ■ (607) 555-1234

PIRE, SALLY Admission: 06/30/YYYY
IPCase006 DOB: 06/23/YYYY
Dr. BLACK ROOM: 0371

Laboratory Data

SPECIMEN COLLECTED: 06/30/YYYY SPECIMEN RECEIVED: 06/30/YYYY

TEST	RESULT	FLAG	REFERENCE
URINALYSIS			
DIPSTICK ONLY			
COLOR	Yellow clear		
SP GRAVITY	1.015		≤ 1.030
ALBUMIN	negative		≤ 125 mg/dl
BILIRUBIN	negative		≤ 0.8 mg/dl
SUGAR	negative		≤ 10 mg/dl
BLOOD	moderate		0.06 mg/dl hgb
PH	7.5		5-8.0
ACETONE	negative		≤ 30 mg/dl
UROBILINOGEN			≤ −1 mg/dl
NITRITES			NEG
LEUKOCYTE			≤ 15 WBC/hpf
W.B.C.	rare		≤ 5/hpf
R.B.C.	0-6/hpf		≤ 5/hpf
BACT.			1+(≤ 20/hpf)
URINE PREGNANCY TEST			

End of Report

GLOBAL CARE MEDICAL CENTER ■ 100 MAIN ST, ALFRED NY 14802 ■ (607) 555-1234

PIRE, SALLY   Admission: 06/30/YYYY
IPCase006   DOB: 06/23/YYYY
Dr. BLACK   ROOM: 0371

Laboratory Data

TIME IN: 06/30/YYYY 1614   TIME OUT: 06/30/YYYY 1749

COMPLETE BLOOD COUNTS DIFFERENTIAL

TEST	RESULT	FLAG	REFERENCE
WHITE BLOOD CELL	15.1		4.5 - 11.0 thou/ul
RED BLOOD CELL	3.69		5.2-5.4 milliliter/ upper limit
HEMOGLOBIN	11.8		11.7-16.1 grams per deciliter
HEMATOCRIT	34.8		35.0-47.0 %
MEAN CORPUSCULAR VOLUME	94.3		85-99 factor level
MEAN CORPUSCULAR HEMOGLOBIN	32.1		
MEAN CORPUSCULAR HEMOGLOBIN CONCENTRATION	34.0		33-37
RED CELL DISTRIBUTION WIDTH			11.4-14.5
PLATELETS	143		130-400 thou/ul
SEGMENTED CELLS %	52		
LYMPHOCYTES %	18		20.5-51.1
MONOCYTES %	12		1.7-9.3
EOSINOPHILS %	3		
BAND CELLS %	5		

Thou/ul= thousand upper limit

COMMENTS: Few target cells

End of Report

GLOBAL CARE MEDICAL CENTER ■ 100 MAIN ST, ALFRED NY 14802 ■ (607) 555-1234

PIRE, SALLY Admission: 06/30/YYYY
IPCase006 DOB: 06/23/YYYY
Dr. BLACK ROOM: 0371

Laboratory Data

TIME IN: 07/04/YYYY 1052 TIME OUT: 07/05/YYYY 1029

COMPLETE BLOOD COUNTS DIFFERENTIAL

TEST	RESULT	FLAG	REFERENCE
WHITE BLOOD CELL	4.9		4.5-11.0 thou/ul
RED BLOOD CELL	4.06		5.2-5.4 milliliter/ upper limit
HEMOGLOBIN	12.8		11.7-16.1 grams per deciliter
HEMATOCRIT	37.7		35.0-47.0 %
MEAN CORPUSCULAR VOLUME	93		85-99 factor level
MEAN CORPUSCULAR HEMOGLOBIN	31.7		
MEAN CORPUSCULAR HEMOGLOBIN CONCENTRATION	34.1		33-37
RED CELL DISTRIBUTION WIDTH			11.4-14.5
PLATELETS	242		130-400 thou/ul
SEGMENTED CELLS %	44		
LYMPHOCYTES %	27		20.5-51.1
MONOCYTES %	6		1.7-9.3
EOSINOPHILS %	14		
BAND CELLS %	8		

Thou/ul= thousand upper limit

COMMENTS: Occasional target cells

End of Report

GLOBAL CARE MEDICAL CENTER ■ 100 MAIN ST, ALFRED NY 14802 ■ (607) 555-1234

PIRE, SALLY	Admission: 06/30/YYYY	**Laboratory Data**
IPCase006	DOB: 06/23/YYYY	
Dr. BLACK	ROOM: 0371	

SPECIMEN COLLECTED: 07-02-YYYY **SPECIMEN RECEIVED:** 07-06-YYYY

TEST	**RESULT**
BACTERIOLOGY	
SOURCE:	**Sputum**
SMEAR ONLY:	1+ gram positive cocci; rare white blood cells
CULTURE	
1st PRELIMINARY	1+ gram negative rod
2nd PRELIMINARY	
OTHER ROUTINE CULTURES	
FINAL REPORT	1+ *Enterobacter cloacae*
SENSITIVITIES	

End of Report

GLOBAL CARE MEDICAL CENTER ■ 100 MAIN ST, ALFRED NY 14802 ■ (607) 555-1234

PIRE, SALLY	Admission: 06/30/YYYY	**EKG Report**
IPCase006	DOB: 06/23/YYYY	
Dr. BLACK	ROOM: 0371	

Date of EKG: 06/30/YYYY **Time of EKG** 1005

Rate	112
PR	12
QRSD	.08
QT	.32
QTC	

-- Axis --

P
QRS
T

Sinus tachycardia. Myocardial changes of inferior ischemia progressive from 01/09/YYYY. Occasional premature ventricular contraction.

Reviewed and Approved:
Bella Kaplan, MD
ATP-B-S:02:1001261385:
Bella Kaplan, MD
(Signed: 07/01/YYYY 5:24:44 PM EST)

Referred by: **Unconfirmed**

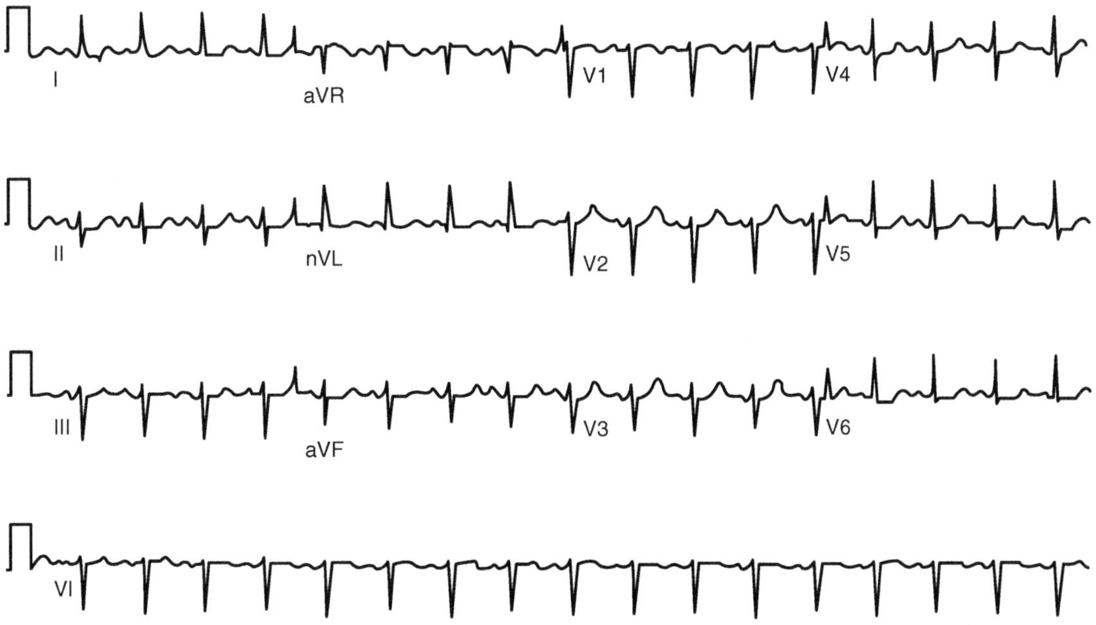

PIRE, SALLY
IPCase006
Dr. BLACK

Admission: 06/30/YYYY
DOB: 06/23/YYYY
ROOM: 0371

Medication Administration Record

Special Instructions: Allergic to Aspirin

Medication (dose and route)	**Date:** 07/04 **Time**	**Initials**	**Date:** 07/05 **Time**	**Initials**	**Date:** 07/06 **Time**	**Initials**	**Date:** 07/07 **Time**	**Initials**
Erythromycin 500 milligrams every 6 hours for 5 days	0600	JD	0600	JD	0600	JD	0600	JD
	1200	VS	1200	VS	1200	VS	1200	----
	1800	OR	1800	OR	1800	OR	1800	----
	2400	JD	2400	JD	2400	JD	2400	----
Lanoxin 0.125 milligrams daily	0800	VS	0800	VS	0800	VS	0800	VS
Lasix 20 milligram daily	0800	VS	0800	VS	0800	VS	0800	VS
Klotrix 1 tablet three times a day	0800	VS	0800	VS	0800	VS	0800	VS
	1300	VS	1300	VS	1300	VS	1300	----
	1800	OR	1800	OR	1800	OR	1800	----
Dimetapp Extentabs			0800	VS	0800	VS	0800	VS
			2000	OR	2000	OR		
Afrin nasal spray 2 squeezes each nostril every 12 hours					0800	----	0800	VS
					2000	OR	2000	----
PRN Medications:								
Tylenol 1 or 2 tablets every 4-6 hours as needed for Pain	0830	JD						
Dalmane 15 milligrams every bedtime as needed for sleep			2200	OR	2230	OR		

Initials	**Signature and Title**	**Initials**	**Signature and Title**	**Initials**	**Signature and Title**
VS	Vera South, RN	GPW	G. P. Well, RN		
OR	Ora Richards, RN	PS	P.Small, RN		
JD	Jane Dobbs, RN				
HF	H. Figgs, RN				

Global Care Medical Center ■ 100 Main St, Alfred NY 14802 ■ (607)555-1234

PIRE, SALLY Admission: 06/30/YYYY
IPCase006 DOB: 06/23/YYYY
Dr. BLACK ROOM: 0371

Nurses' Notes

DATE	TIME	TREATMENTS & MEDICATIONS	TIME	NURSES' NOTES
06/30/YYYY	1530	Wednesday Aspirin 10 grain for elevated temperature.	1515	Resting in bed. Reminded patient to save sputum for specimen and urine for specimen. Reviewed and Approved: V. South, RN ATP-B-S:02:1001261385: V. South, RN (Signed: 06/30/YYYY 03:31:03 PM EST)
	1700	Regular diet	1700	Ate fair amount at dinner. Reviewed and Approved: O. Richards, RN ATP-B-S: 02:1001261385: O. Richards, RN (Signed: 06/30/YYYY 05:07:41 PM EST)
	1930	101-104-20 126/70 Aspirin 10 grain for elevated temperature. Urine specimen sent to lab.	1900	Resting in bed. Reviewed and Approved: O. Richards, RN ATP-B-S:02:1001261385: O. Richards, RN (Signed: 06/30/YYYY 07:31:41 PM EST)
			2000	Evening care given. Reviewed and Approved: O. Richards, RN ATP-B-S:02:1001261385: O. Richards, RN (Signed: 06/30/YYYY 08:06:03 PM EST)
			2230	Resting quietly in bed. Reviewed and Approved: O. Richards, RN ATP-B-S:02:1001261385: O. Richards, RN (Signed: 06/30/YYYY 10:33:44 PM EST)
07/01/YYYY	2400	Thursday 100.2-100-20 Aspirin 10 grain for elevated temperature.	2400	Awake. Mild cough. Coughs occasionally. Reviewed and Approved: J. Dobbs, RN ATP-B-S:02:1001261385: J. Dobbs, RN (Signed: 07/01/YYYY 12:03:16 AM EST)
			0300	Sleeping. Reviewed and Approved: J. Dobbs, RN ATP-B-S:02:1001261385: J. Dobbs, RN (Signed: 07/01/YYYY 03:08:22 AM EST)
	0600 0615	101.2-96-20 Aspirin 10 grain for elevated temperature.	0600	Awake for temperature, pulse, and respirations. Slept well most of the night. Medicine for elevated temperature. Reviewed and Approved: J. Dobbs, RN ATP-B-S:02:1001261385: J. Dobbs, RN (Signed: 07/01/YYYY 06:03:16 AM EST)
07/01/YYYY			0700	Appetite good for breakfast, Regular diet. Non-productive cough noted. Reviewed and Approved: J. Dobbs, RN ATP-B-S:02:1001261385: J. Dobbs, RN (Signed: 07/01/YYYY 07:05:33 AM EST)
			1200	Lunch taken and tolerated well. Resting quietly in bed. Reviewed and Approved: V. South, RN ATP-B-S:02:1001261385: V. South, RN (Signed: 07/01/YYYY 12:16:00 PM EST)

GLOBAL CARE MEDICAL CENTER ■ 100 MAIN ST, ALFRED NY 14802 ■ (607) 555-1234

PIRE, SALLY Admission: 06/30/YYYY
IPCase006 DOB: 06/23/YYYY
Dr. BLACK ROOM: 0371

Nurses' Notes

DATE	TIME	TREATMENTS & MEDICATIONS	TIME	NURSES' NOTES
07/01/YYYY	1511 1530	Temperature 102.2 Tylenol 2 tablets for elevated temperature.	1515	Resting in bed. Skin warm and moist. Reviewed and Approved: V. South, RN ATP-B-S:02:1001261385: V. South, RN (Signed: 07/01/YYYY 03:36:00 PM EST)
	1700	Regular diet.	1700	Ate moderate amount at dinner. Reviewed and Approved: O. Richards, RN ATP-B-S:02:1001261385: O. Richards, RN (Signed: 07/01/YYYY 05:05:12 PM EST)
	1900	100.3-100-20 120/60	1900	Resting in bed. Taking fluids well. Coughing no sputum for specimen. Reviewed and Approved: O. Richards, RN ATP-B-S:02:1001261385: O. Richards, RN (Signed: 07/01/YYYY 07:05:07 PM EST)
	1950	Tylenol 2 tablets for elevated temperature.	2000	Evening care given. Reviewed and Approved: O. Richards, RN ATP-B-S:02:1001261385: O. Richards, RN (Signed: 07/01/YYYY 08:02:41 PM EST)
			2230	Resting quietly in bed. Non-productive cough noted. Reviewed and Approved: O. Richards, RN ATP-B-S:02:1001261385: O. Richards, RN (Signed: 07/01/YYYY 10:32:01 PM EST)
07/02/YYYY	2400	Friday 99-100-24	2400	Sleeping on first rounds. Awakened for temperature, pulse, and respirations. Reviewed and Approved: J. Dobbs, RN ATP-B-S:02:1001261385: J. Dobbs, RN (Signed: 07/02/YYYY 12:04:00 AM EST)
			0600	Slept well through most of the night. Reviewed and Approved: J. Dobbs, RN ATP-B-S:02:1001261385: J. Dobbs, RN (Signed: 07/02/YYYY 06:08:44 AM EST)
		Tylenol 2 tablets given by mouth.	0730	Awake. Vitals stable. Elevated temperature 101.8. Encouraged to drink fluids. Reviewed and Approved: V. South, RN ATP-B-S:02:1001261385: V. South, RN (Signed: 07/02/YYYY 07:32:00 AM EST)
			0800	Breakfast taken fair. Bathroom without assistance. Self morning care. Reviewed and Approved: V. South, RN ATP-B-S:02:1001261385: V. South, RN (Signed: 07/02/YYYY 08:04:22 AM EST)
	0900	Dr. Black is in.	0900	Patient working on sputum. Face appears slightly flushed and eyes very bright. Reviewed and Approved: V. South, RN ATP-B-S:02:1001261385: V. South, RN (Signed: 07/02/YYYY 09:02:13 AM EST)

GLOBAL CARE MEDICAL CENTER ■ 100 MAIN ST, ALFRED NY 14802 ■ (607) 555-1234

PIRE, SALLY	Admission: 06/30/YYYY	**Nurses' Notes**
IPCase006	DOB: 06/23/YYYY	
Dr. BLACK	ROOM: 0371	

DATE	TIME	TREATMENTS & MEDICATIONS	TIME	NURSES' NOTES
07/02/YYYY			1200	Lunch taken fair. Reviewed and Approved: V. South, RN ATP-B-S:02:1001261385: V. South, RN (Signed: 07/02/YYYY 12:02:17 PM EST)
			1400	Resting. Still working on sputum specimen. Reviewed and Approved: O. Richards, RN ATP-B-S:02:1001261385: O. Richards, RN (Signed: 07/02/YYYY 02:03:00 PM EST)
07/02/YYYY		Temperature 101	1530	Resting quietly in bed. Temperature elevated. States not coughing up as much as previously. Reviewed and Approved: O. Richards, RN ATP-B-S:02:1001261385: O. Richards, RN (Signed: 07/02/YYYY 03:32:50 PM EST)
			1730	Diet taken poorly. Reviewed and Approved: O. Richards, RN ATP-B-S:02:1001261385: O. Richards, RN (Signed: 07/02/YYYY 05:31:03 PM EST)
		99.9-64-20 144/70	1930	Vitals taken. Complained of ears feeling very "full." Working at sputum collection. Reviewed and Approved: O. Richards, RN ATP-B-S:02:1001261385: O. Richards, RN (Signed: 07/02/YYYY 07:37:41 PM EST)
			2030	Bedtime care given. No productive cough noted. Reviewed and Approved: O. Richards, RN ATP-B-S:02:1001261385: O. Richards, RN (Signed: 07/02/YYYY 08:32:28 PM EST)
			2215	Out of bed to bathroom. Back to bed. Comfortable. Reviewed and Approved: O. Richards, RN ATP-B-S:02:1001261385: O. Richards, RN (Signed: 07/02/YYYY 10:16:03 PM EST)
07/03/YYYY		Saturday	2400	Awakened. Asked for Tylenol for headache. Reviewed and Approved: J. Dobbs, RN ATP-B-S:02:1001261385: J. Dobbs, RN (Signed: 07/03/YYYY 12:04:00 AM EST)
			0600	Slept well throughout the night. Reviewed and Approved: J. Dobbs, RN ATP-B-S:02:1001261385: J. Dobbs, RN (Signed: 07/03/YYYY 06:04:00 AM EST)
			0730	To bathroom for self morning care and returned to room. Reviewed and Approved: V. South, RN ATP-B-S:02:1001261385: V. South, RN (Signed: 07/03/YYYY 07:37:11 AM EST)

GLOBAL CARE MEDICAL CENTER ■ 100 MAIN ST, ALFRED NY 14802 ■ (607) 555-1234

PIRE, SALLY	Admission: 06/30/YYYY	**Nurses' Notes**
IPCase006	DOB: 06/23/YYYY	
Dr. BLACK	ROOM: 0371	

DATE	TIME	TREATMENTS & MEDICATIONS	TIME	NURSES' NOTES
07/03/YYYY			1200	Out of bed in chair for lunch. Ate well. Reviewed and Approved: V. South, RN ATP-B-S:02:1001261385: V. South, RN (Signed: 07/03/YYYY 12:06:00 PM EST)
			1400	Resting quietly. No complaints offered. Reviewed and Approved: O. Richards, RN ATP-B-S:02:1001261385: O. Richards, RN (Signed: 07/03/YYYY 02:02:20 PM EST)
			1530	Resting in bed visiting with family. Offers no complaint of discomfort at present. Reviewed and Approved: O. Richards, RN ATP-B-S:02:1001261385: O. Richards, RN (Signed: 07/03/YYYY 03:32:40 PM EST)
			1700	Ate very poor regular diet. Reviewed and Approved: O. Richards, RN ATP-B-S: 02:1001261385: O. Richards, RN (Signed: 07/03/YYYY 05:02:40 PM EST)
	1930	Temperature 101.2	1900	Sleeping soundly. Reviewed and Approved: O. Richards, RN ATP-B-S:02:1001261385: O. Richards, RN (Signed: 07/03/YYYY 07:32:40 PM EST)
	2020	Tylenol 2 tablets for elevated temperature.	2030	Bedtime care given. Temperature elevated a little. Reviewed and Approved: O. Richards, RN ATP-B-S:02:1001261385: O. Richards, RN (Signed: 07/03/YYYY 08:31:34 PM EST)
			2200	Appears to be sleeping. Reviewed and Approved: O. Richards, RN ATP-B-S:02:1001261385: O. Richards, RN (Signed: 07/03/YYYY 10:03:00 PM EST)
07/04/YYYY	2400	Sunday 97.7-76-24	2400	Sleeping on first rounds. Awakened for temperature, pulse, and respirations. Reviewed and Approved: J. Dobbs, RN ATP-B-S:02:1001261385: J. Dobbs, RN (Signed: 07/04/YYYY 12:01:00 AM EST)
			0300	Sleeping. Reviewed and Approved: J. Dobbs, RN ATP-B-S:02:1001261385: J. Dobbs, RN (Signed: 07/04/YYYY 03:02:20 AM EST)
			0600	Slept well most of the night. Still sounds congested. Reviewed and Approved: J. Dobbs, RN ATP-B-S: 02:1001261385: J. Dobbs, RN (Signed: 07/04/YYYY 06:05:46 AM EST)

GLOBAL CARE MEDICAL CENTER ■ 100 MAIN ST, ALFRED NY 14802 ■ (607) 555-1234

PIRE, SALLY	Admission: 06/30/YYYY	**Nurses' Notes**
IPCase006	DOB: 06/23/YYYY	
Dr. BLACK	ROOM: 0371	

DATE	TIME	TREATMENTS & MEDICATIONS	TIME	NURSES' NOTES
07/04/YYYY	0800	Dr. Black is in.	0800	Breakfast taken well. Self morning care taken in bathroom. Reviewed and Approved: J. Dobbs, RN ATP-B-S:02:1001261385: J. Dobbs, RN (Signed: 07/04/YYYY 08:05:46 AM EST)
			1000	Out of bed sitting in chair, watching television. No cough noted. Reviewed and Approved: V. South, RN ATP-B-S:02:1001261385: V. South, RN (Signed: 07/04/YYYY 10:07:13 AM EST)
			1200	Lunch taken well. Reviewed and Approved: V. South, RN ATP-B-S: 02:1001261385: V. South, RN (Signed: 07/04/YYYY 12:04:00 PM EST)
			1400	Resting quietly. Reviewed and Approved: V. South, RN ATP-B-S: 02:1001261385: V. South, RN (Signed: 07/04/YYYY 02:03:45 PM EST)
07/04/YYYY		Temperature 99.6	1530	Awake resting quietly in bed, complains of being hungry and requested coffee and cookies-given to her. Reviewed and Approved: O. Richards, RN ATP-B-S: 02:1001261385: O. Richards, RN (Signed: 07/04/YYYY 03:34:20 PM EST)
			1700	Ate very good dinner. Resting quietly. Reviewed and Approved: O. Richards, RN ATP-B-S: 02:1001261385: O. Richards, RN (Signed: 07/04/YYYY 05:33:12 PM EST)
	2030	Temperature 99.8 Tylenol 2 tablets for elevated temperature.	2000	Complains of being cold. Temperature elevated. Given more blankets. Reviewed and Approved: O. Richards, RN ATP-B-S: 02:1001261385: O. Richards, RN (Signed: 07/04/YYYY 08:36:50 PM EST)
			2200	Appears to be sleeping soundly. Reviewed and Approved: O. Richards, RN ATP-B-S: 02:1001261385: O. Richards, RN (Signed: 07/04/YYYY 10:03:34 PM EST)
07/05/YYYY	2400	Monday 96.9-88-16	2400	Sleeping on first rounds. Awakened for temperature, pulse, and respirations. Skin warm and moist, Pajamas changed and made comfortable. Reviewed and Approved: J. Dobbs, RN ATP-B-S: 02:1001261385: J. Dobbs, RN (Signed: 07/05/YYYY 12:05:00 AM EST)
			0300	Sleeping soundly. Reviewed and Approved: J. Dobbs, RN ATP-B-S: 02:1001261385: J. Dobbs, RN (Signed: 07/05/YYYY 03:03:10 AM EST)

GLOBAL CARE MEDICAL CENTER ■ 100 MAIN ST, ALFRED NY 14802 ■ (607) 555-1234

PIRE, SALLY IPCase006 Dr. BLACK	Admission: 06/30/YYYY DOB: 06/23/YYYY ROOM: 0371	**Nurses' Notes**

DATE	TIME	TREATMENTS & MEDICATIONS	TIME	NURSES' NOTES
07/05/YYYY		Monday	0600	Slept well most of the night. Still sounds congested. Reviewed and Approved: J. Dobbs, RN ATP-B-S: 02:1001261385: J. Dobbs, RN (Signed: 07/05/YYYY 06:02:49 AM EST)
			0730	Morning vitals taken. Reviewed and Approved: V. South, RN ATP-B-S: 02:1001261385: V. South, RN (Signed: 07/05/YYYY 07:37:13 AM EST)
			0800	Breakfast taken fairly well. Reviewed and Approved: V. South, RN ATP-B-S: 02:1001261385: V. South, RN (Signed: 07/05/YYYY 08:02:23 AM EST)
			0830	Self morning care in the bathroom. Reviewed and Approved: V. South, RN ATP-B-S: 02:1001261385: V. South, RN (Signed: 07/05/YYYY 08:32:00 AM EST)
			1000-1100	Patient our in chair sitting for most of the morning. Reviewed and Approved: V. South, RN ATP-B-S: 02:1001261385: V. South, RN (Signed: 07/05/YYYY 11:02:00 AM EST)
			1200	Dr. Black is in. Patient take lunch fairly well. Reviewed and Approved: V. South, RN ATP-B-S:02:1001261385: V. South, RN (Signed: 07/05/YYYY 12:04:20 PM EST)
			1300-1400	Patient resting quietly in bed and offered no complaints. Had a fairly good day. Reviewed and Approved: V. South, RN ATP-B-S : 02:1001261385: V. South, RN (Signed: 07/05/YYYY 02:01:46 PM EST)
			1530	Resting quietly in bed. Reviewed and Approved: O. Richards, RN ATP-B-S:02:1001261385: O. Richards, RN (Signed: 07/05/YYYY 03:32:17 PM EST)
			1700	Ate well at dinner. Reviewed and Approved: O. Richards, RN ATP-B-S: 02:1001261385: O. Richards, RN (Signed: 07/05/YYYY 05:03:10 PM EST)
			1900	Up and about in room. Reviewed and Approved: O. Richards, RN ATP-B-S: 02:1001261385: O. Richards, RN (Signed: 07/05/YYYY 07:02:00 PM EST)

GLOBAL CARE MEDICAL CENTER ■ 100 MAIN ST, ALFRED NY 14802 ■ (607) 555-1234

PIRE, SALLY	Admission: 06/30/YYYY	**Nurses' Notes**
IPCase006	DOB: 06/23/YYYY	
Dr. BLACK	ROOM: 0371	

DATE	TIME	TREATMENTS & MEDICATIONS	TIME	NURSES' NOTES
07/05/YYYY		Monday	2000	Evening care given. Voiding quantity sufficient in bathroom. Reviewed and Approved: O. Richards, RN ATP-B-S: 02:1001261385: O. Richards, RN (Signed: 07/05/YYYY 08:02:00 PM EST)
			2230	Resting in bed. Reviewed and Approved: O. Richards, RN ATP-B-S: 02:1001261385: O. Richards, RN (Signed: 07/05/YYYY 10:32:50 PM EST)
07/06/YYYY		Tuesday	2400	Asleep on rounds. Respirations sound a little full. Side rails up. No complaints. Reviewed and Approved: J. Dodds, RN ATP-B-S: 02:1001261385: J. Dodds, RN (Signed: 07/06/YYYY 12:02:49 AM EST)
			0300	Continues to sleep. Reviewed and Approved: J. Dodds, RN ATP-B-S: 02:1001261385: J. Dodds, RN (Signed: 07/06/YYYY 03:04:09 AM EST)
			0600	Remains sleeping this morning. No cough noted. Reviewed and Approved: J. Dodds, RN ATP-B-S: 02:1001261385: J. Dodds, RN (Signed: 07/06/YYYY 06:02:19 AM EST)
07/06/YYYY	0800	98.9-92-20 132/78 Regular diet	0800	Self morning care in bathroom. Ate well for breakfast. No complaints. Occasional harsh cough noted. Reviewed and Approved: V. South, RN ATP-B-S: 02:1001261385: V. South, RN (Signed: 07/06/YYYY 08:12:55 AM EST)
	1200	Regular diet Temperature 97.2	1200	Ate well for lunch. Ambulated as desired. Reviewed and Approved: V. South, RN ATP-B-S: 02:1001261385: V. South, RN (Signed: 07/06/YYYY 12:05:45 PM EST)
	1430	Dr. Black in.	1430	Comfortable day. Reviewed and Approved: V. South, RN ATP-B-S: 02:1001261385: V. South, RN (Signed: 07/06/YYYY 02:32:55 PM EST)
07/06/YYYY			1530	Resting in bed. Reviewed and Approved: O. Richards, RN ATP-B-S: 02:1001261385: O. Richards, RN (Signed: 07/06/YYYY 03:32:17 PM EST)
	1700	Regular diet.	1700	Ate well at dinner. Reviewed and Approved: O. Richards, RN ATP-B-S: 02:1001261385: O. Richards, RN (Signed: 07/06/YYYY 05:02:17 PM EST)

GLOBAL CARE MEDICAL CENTER ■ 100 MAIN ST, ALFRED NY 14802 ■ (607) 555-1234

PIRE, SALLY	Admission: 06/30/YYYY	**Nurses' Notes**
IPCase006	DOB: 06/23/YYYY	
Dr. BLACK	ROOM: 0371	

DATE	TIME	TREATMENTS & MEDICATIONS	TIME	NURSES' NOTES
07/06/YYYY		Tuesday	1900	Up and about in room. Reviewed and Approved: O. Richards, RN ATP-B-S: 02:1001261385: O. Richards, RN (Signed: 07/06/YYYY 07:02:17 PM EST)
	1930	99.3-80-20 100/64	2000	Evening care given. Took bedtime snack Reviewed and Approved: O. Richards, RN ATP-B-S: 02:1001261385: O. Richards, RN (Signed: 07/06/YYYY 08:01:34 PM EST)
			2230	Resting quietly in bed. Reviewed and Approved: O. Richards, RN ATP-B-S: 02:1001261385: O. Richards, RN (Signed: 07/06/YYYY 10:34:06 PM EST)
07/07/YYYY	11-7	Wednesday	2400	Asleep on rounds. No complaints. Respirations sounding more clear. Side rails up. Reviewed and Approved: J. Dobbs, RN ATP-B-S: 02:1001261385: J. Dobbs, RN (Signed: 07/07/YYYY 12:03:07 AM EST)
			0300	Continues to sleep. Reviewed and Approved: J. Dobbs, RN ATP-B-S: 02:1001261385: J. Dobbs, RN (Signed: 07/07/YYYY 03:01:17 AM EST)
			0600	Slept fairly well throughout the night. Respirations clear. No complaints. Reviewed and Approved: J. Dobbs, RN ATP-B-S: 02:1001261385: J. Dobbs, RN (Signed: 07/07/YYYY 06:05:38 AM EST)
07/07/YYYY			0730	Awake. Vitals stable. Anxious for discharge. Reviewed and Approved: J. Dobbs, RN ATP-B-S: 02:1001261385: J. Dobbs, RN (Signed: 07/07/YYYY 07:33:27 AM EST)
			0800	Took breakfast well - appetite good. Reviewed and Approved: V. South, RN ATP-B-S: 02:1001261385: V. South, RN (Signed: 07/07/YYYY 08:04:53 AM EST)
		Dr. Black in. Discharged to home.	0900	Morning care done. No complaints. Reviewed and Approved: V. South, RN ATP-B-S: 02:1001261385: V. South, RN (Signed: 07/07/YYYY 09:02:12 AM EST)
			1000	Discharged to home. Instructions given to patient. Reviewed and Approved: V. South, RN ATP-B-S: 02:1001261385: V. South, RN (Signed: 07/07/YYYY 10:02:23 AM EST)

GLOBAL CARE MEDICAL CENTER ■ 100 MAIN ST, ALFRED NY 14802 ■ (607) 555-1234

PIRE, SALLY Admission: 06/30/YYYY
IPCase006 DOB: 06/23/YYYY
Dr. BLACK ROOM: 0371

Nursing Discharge Status Summary

1.	AFEBRILE:	X	Yes			No 140/80 98 - 80 - 20			
2.	WOUND:		Clean/Dry		Reddened		Infected		NA X
3.	PAIN FREE:		Yes	X	No	If "No," describe: Requires Tylenol as needed.			
4.	POST-HOSPITAL INSTRUCTION SHEET GIVEN TO PATIENT/FAMILY:						Yes	X	No
	If NO, complete lines 5-8 below.								
5.	DIET:	X	Regular		Other (Describe):				
6.	ACTIVITY:	X	Normal		Light		Limited		Bed rest
7.	MEDICATIONS:	None							
8.	INSTRUCTIONS GIVEN TO PATIENT/FAMILY:				As ordered by Dr. Black				
9.	PATIENT/FAMILY verbalize understanding of instructions:					X	Yes		No
10.	DISCHARGED at	1000	Via:		Wheelchair		Stretcher		Ambulance Co.
				X	Ambulatory				
	Accompanied by:	Vera South, RN				to	Front lobby		
	COMMENTS:	To front lobby. Ambulated with assistant to home with family.							
	DATE:	07/07/YYYY							
	SIGNATURE:	Reviewed and Approved: V. South, RN ATP-B-S: 02:1001261385: V. South, RN (Signed: 07/07/YYYY 10:02:15 AM EST)							

GLOBAL CARE MEDICAL CENTER ■ 100 MAIN ST, ALFRED NY 14802 ■ (607) 555-1234

PIRE, SALLY Admission: 06/30/YYYY
IPCase006 DOB: 06/23/YYYY
Dr. BLACK ROOM: 0371

Patient Property Record

I understand that while the facility will be responsible for items deposited in the safe, I must be responsible for all items retained by me at the bedside. (Dentures kept at the bedside will be labeled, but the facility cannot assure responsibility for them.) I also recognize that the hospital cannot be held responsible for items brought in to me after this form has been completed and signed.

Reviewed and Approved: Sally Pire
ATP-B-S: 02:1001261385: Sally Pire
(Signed: 06/30/YYYY 01:35:05 PM EST) — 06/30/YYYY

Signature of Patient — **Date**

Reviewed and Approved: Andrea Witteman
ATP-B-S:02:1001261385: Andrea Witteman
(Signed: 06/30/YYYY 01:37:23 PM EST) — 06/30/YYYY

Signature of Witness — **Date**

I have no money or valuables that I wish to deposit for safekeeping. I do not hold the facility responsible for any other money or valuables that I am retaining or will have brought in to me. I have been advised that it is recommended that I retain no more than $5.00 at the bedside.

Reviewed and Approved: Sally Pire
ATP-B-S: 02:1001261385: Sally Pire
(Signed: 06/30/YYYY EST) 01:38:00 PM — 06/30/YYYY

Signature of Patient — **Date**

Reviewed and Approved: Andrea Witteman
ATP-B-S:02:1001261385: Andrea Witteman
(Signed: 06/30/YYYY EST) 01:39:18 PM — 06/30/YYYY

Signature of Witness — **Date**

I have deposited valuables in the facility safe. The envelope number is _________.

Signature of Patient — **Date**

Signature of Person Accepting Property — **Date**

I understand that medications I have brought to the facility will be handled as recommended by my physician. This may include storage, disposal, or administration.

Signature of Patient — **Date**

Signature of Witness — **Date**

GLOBAL CARE MEDICAL CENTER ■ 100 MAIN ST, ALFRED NY 14802 ■ (607) 555-1234

IPCase007

Global Care Medical Center
100 Main St, Alfred NY 14802
(607) 555-1234
Hospital No. 999

Inpatient Face Sheet

Patient Name and Address	Gender	Race	Marital Status	Patient No.
LATES, LONNIE 2 BUCK ROAD ALMOND, NY 14804	F	W	S	IPCase007

Date of Birth	Age	Maiden Name	Occupation
02/08/YYYY	64	NA	Housekeeper

Admission Date	Time	Discharge Date	Time	Length of Stay	Telephone Number
05/10/YYYY	1530	05/14/YYYY	1745	04 DAYS	(607) 000-2644

Guarantor Name and Address	Next of Kin Name and Address
LATES, LONNIE 2 BUCK ROAD ALMOND, NY 14804	LATES, JONATHAN 4983 REED STREET ALMOND, NY 14804

Guarantor Telephone No.	Relationship to Patient	Next of Kin Telephone Number	Relationship to Patient
(607) 000-2644	Self	(607) 000-5621	Brother

Admitting Physician	Service	Admit Type	Room Number/Bed
John Chase, MD	ME	NA	367

Attending Physician	Admitting Diagnosis
John Black, MD	Parkinson's Disease, rule out cerebral vascular insufficiency

Primary Insurer	Policy and Group Number	Secondary Insurer	Policy and Group Number

Diagnoses and Procedures	ICD Code
Principal Diagnosis	
Parkinsonism	
Secondary Diagnoses	
Left hip pain Hypokalemia	
Principal Procedure	
Secondary Procedures	

Discharge Instructions

Activity: ☐ Bed rest ☒ Light ☐ Usual ☐ Unlimited ☐ Other:

Diet: ☐ Regular ☐ Low Cholesterol ☐ Low Salt ☐ ADA ☒ Soft

Follow-Up: ☒ Call for appointment ☐ Office appointment on 05/17/YYYY 12:40 p.m. (Friday) with Dr. Black.

Special Instructions: None.

Attending Physician Authentication: Reviewed and Approved: John Black MD
ATP-B-S:02:1001261385: John Black MD
(Signed: 05/10/YYYY 04:20:44 PM EST)

LATES, LONNIE Admission: 05/10/YYYY
IPCase007 DOB: 02/08/YYYY
Dr. BLACK ROOM: 367

Consent to Admission

I, Lonnie Lates hereby consent to admission to the Global Care Medical Center (GCMC), and I further consent to such routine hospital care, diagnostic procedures, and medical treatment that the medical and professional staff of GCMC may deem necessary or advisable. I authorize the use of medical information obtained about me as specified above and the disclosure of such information to my referring physician(s). This form has been fully explained to me, and I understand its contents. I further understand that no guarantees have been made to me as to the results of treatments or examinations done at the GCMC.

Reviewed and Approved: Lonnie Lates
ATP-B-S:02:1001261385: Lonnie Lates
(Signed: 05/10/YYYY 04:32:05 PM EST)

Signature of Patient

Signature of Parent/Legal Guardian for Minor

Relationship to Minor

Reviewed and Approved: Andrea Witteman
ATP-B-S:02:1001261385: Andrea Witteman
(Signed: 05/10/YYYY 04:32:05 PM EST)

WITNESS: Global Care Medical Center Staff Member

Consent To Release Information For Reimbursement Purposes

In order to permit reimbursement, upon request, the Global Care Medical Center (GCMC) may disclose such treatment information pertaining to my hospitalization to any corporation, organization, or agent thereof, which is, or may be liable under contract to the GCMC or to me, or to any of my family members or other person, for payment of all or part of the GCMC's charges for services rendered to me (e.g. the patient's health insurance carrier). I understand that the purpose of any release of information to facilitate reimbursement for services rendered. In addition, in the event that my health insurance program includes utilization review of services provided during this admission, I authorize GCMC to release information as is necessary to permit the review. This authorization will expire once the reimbursement for services rendered is complete.

Reviewed and Approved: Lonnie Lates
ATP-B-S:02:1001261385: Lonnie Lates
(Signed: 05/10/YYYY 04:34:17 PM EST)

Signature of Patient

Signature of Parent/Legal Guardian for Minor

Relationship to Minor

Reviewed and Approved: Andrea Witteman
ATP-B-S:02:1001261385: Andrea Witteman
(Signed: 05/10/YYYY 04:36:24 PM EST)

WITNESS: Global Care Medical Center Staff Member

Global Care Medical Center ■ 100 Main St, Alfred NY 14802 ■ (607) 555-1234

LATES, LONNIE	Admission: 05/10/YYYY	**Advance Directive**
IPCase007	DOB: 02/08/YYYY	
Dr. BLACK	ROOM: 367	

Your answers to the following questions will assist your Physician and the Hospital to respect your wishes regarding your medical care. This information will become a part of your medical record.

	Yes	No	Patient's Initials
1. Have you been provided with a copy of the information called "Patient Rights Regarding Health Care Decision"?	X		
2. Have you prepared a "Living Will"? If yes, please provide the Hospital with a copy for your medical record.		X	
3. Have you prepared a Durable Power of Attorney for Health Care? If yes, please provide the Hospital with a copy for your medical record.		X	
4. Have you provided this facility with an Advance Directive on a prior admission and is it still in effect? If yes, Admitting Office to contact Medical Records to obtain a copy for the medical record.		X	
5. Do you desire to execute a Living Will/Durable Power of Attorney? If yes, refer to in order: a. Physician b. Social Service c. Volunteer Service		X	

Hospital Staff Directions: Check when each step is completed

1. ✓ Verify the above questions were answered and actions taken where required.
2. ✓ If the "Patient Rights" information was provided to someone other than the patient, state reason:

____

Name of Individual Receiving Information **Relationship to Patient**

3. ✓ If information was provided in a language other than English, specify language and method.
4. ✓ Verify patient was advised on how to obtain additional information on Advance Directives.
5. ✓ Verify the Patient/Family Member/Legal Representative was asked to provide the Hospital with a copy of the Advanced Directive which will be retained in the medical record.

File this form in the medical record, and give a copy to the patient.

Name of Patient/Name of Individual giving information if different from Patient

Reviewed and Approved: Lonnie Lates
ATP-B-S:02:1001261385 Lonnie Lates
(Signed: 05/10/YYYY 04:35:05 PM EST)

Signature of Patient **Date**

Reviewed and Approved: Andrea Witteman
ATP-B-S:02:1001261385 Andrea Witteman
(Signed: 05/10/YYYY 04:35:47 PM EST)

Signature of Hospital Representative **Date**

Global Care Medical Center ■ 100 Main St, Alfred NY 14802 ■ (607) 555-1234

LATES, LONNIE   Admission: 05/10/YYYY
IPCase007   DOB: 02/08/YYYY
Dr. BLACK   ROOM: 367

Discharge Summary

ADMISSION DATE: 05/10/YYYY   DISCHARGE DATE: 05/14/YYYY

ADMISSION DIAGNOSIS: Parkinsonism versus cerebrovascular accident versus viral syndrome.

DISCHARGE DIAGNOSIS: Acute parkinsonism, left hip pain, hypokalemia, constipation, insomnia, allergic to sulfonamides.

SUMMARY: Ms. Lates is a 64-year-old white female who presented to the Emergency Room on the day of admission with a history of progressive weakness and instability over two or three days prior to admission. On the day of admission, she had numerous episodes of falling that happened without any onset of weakness or dizziness. She did remark that she was very unstable, and it was very difficult for her to get back up again, and she had marked weakness at that time. She had been seen by Dr. Black and Dr. Flight, a neurologist in Rochester, with a tentative diagnosis of Parkinson's disease in the past. She had been tried on Sinemet which caused more instability and staggering and was later switched to Symmetrel 100 milligrams twice a day which she tolerated well. However, when she recently ran out of this, she continued to do well, and they decided to just see how she did without any medication. However, in the few days prior to admission, she got rapidly worse. Of note-she has a past medical history of alcohol abuse and has been recently known to drink although she denies this.

On medical exam in the Emergency Room, her neurological exam was intact, and she had no ataxia of the upper extremities or lower extremities on testing in bed. However, when she stood up to walk, she was very unsteady and especially didn't seem to be able to move forward without falling forward or to the right or left. She had a negative Romberg sign, however. Neurological exam failed to show any focal neurological deficits. There was a mild degree of cogwheeling in the left arm on flexion and extension.

Her admission electrocardiogram showed nonspecific ST wave changes similar to September last year. Chemistry studies revealed elevated liver enzymes with a serum glutamic oxaloacetic transaminase of 70, lactate dehydrogenase 325 but a total bilirubin of only 1.3. These abnormalities have been noted and evaluated in the past. She was also noted to be slightly hypokalemic with a potassium of 3.3 which responded to Klotrix by mouth and came up to 3.6 on the second hospital day. Blood alcohol level was 0. Complete blood count on admission showed a white count of 6,700 with 35 segmented cells, 56 lymphocytes, 5 monocytes, 4 eosinophils, and occasional atypical lymph. Hematocrit was 34.2 with mean cell volume 95.5 and mean cell hemoglobin concentration of 34.2. Platelet count was 141,000. Of note-the patient in the past has had thrombocytopenic purpura. Her sedimentation rate on admission was 2. Blood gases in the Emergency Room were obtained, and her hydrogen ion concentration was 7.446, PCO2 was 43.3, partial pressure of oxygen 71.1 on room air. Urinalysis was essentially normal except for a trace of blood and amorphous phosphate crystals in moderate amounts in the urine. An x-ray was obtained of the left hip to rule out fracture, and there was none. Chest x-ray showed no significant active cardiopulmonary disease. She had numerous healing rib fractures and an old deformity of the glenoid on the right to be secondary to an old fracture and a compression fracture of T-11. All these were felt to be old and not caused by her recent falls.

Continued on next page

DD: 05/10/YYYY

DT: 05/11/YYYY   **Physician Authentication**

GLOBAL CARE MEDICAL CENTER ■ 100 MAIN ST, ALFRED NY 14802 ■ (607) 555-1234

LATES, LONNIE Admission: 05/10/YYYY
IPCase007 DOB: 02/08/YYYY
Dr. BLACK ROOM: 367

Discharge Summary

Page 2 continued:

When patient was admitted, she was started on Symmetrel 100 milligrams twice a day and observed closely for neurological changes. She improved markedly over the first 48 hours of admission with no other treatment except for the Symmetrel. Her neurological exam remained stable, and she developed no focal signs. She remained afebrile, and vital signs remained stable. She did have some trouble in the hospital complaining of constipation and difficulty sleeping, although she had good response to an enema, and the nurses' notes documented that at least on one night she slept quite well. She also ate fairly well while in the hospital. On the day prior to discharge, a repeat complete blood count was obtained which showed a white count of 5,800 hematocrit 37.7 and there were 36% segmented cells, 41% lymphocytes, 6 monocytes, 4 eosinophils. She was experiencing no symptoms of rash or allergy. She was discharged on the fourth hospital day in much improved condition. She was able to ambulate easily in the hall, and she will be seen in follow-up by Dr. Black in his office this coming Friday.

Discharge medications include Symmetrel 100 milligrams twice a day, Halcion .25 milligrams by mouth every night at bedtime as needed for sleep, and Metamucil one tablespoon in a glass of milk or juice per day.

Pending labs before this dictation is complete is B 12 and Folate levels which will probably come back toward the end of the week.

DD: 05/10/YYYY

Reviewed and Approved: John Black MD
ATP-B-S:02:1001261385: John Black MD
(Signed: 5/10/YYYY 04:14:44 PM EST)

Physician Authentication

DT: 05/11/YYYY

GLOBAL CARE MEDICAL CENTER ■ 100 MAIN ST, ALFRED NY 14802 ■ (607) 555-1234

LATES, LONNIE	Admission: 05/10/YYYY	**History & Physical Exam**
IPCase007	DOB: 02/08/YYYY	
Dr. BLACK	ROOM: 367	

CHIEF COMPLAINT: Frequent falls, dizziness and weakness of rapid onset.

HISTORY OF PRESENT ILLNESS: The patient is a 64-year-old white female who presented to the Emergency Room today with the story that over the past month or so she has had progressive weakness and episodes of dizziness. On the day prior to admission, she became very weak and was having difficulty walking and was falling frequently in her apartment. These episodes of falling happened without any sudden onset of weakness but more from instability. She was also dizzy and had difficulty getting herself back in bed or back in a chair. She denies any palpitations, chest pain, shortness of breath, change in her vision, unilateral weakness or numbness. She has been followed by Dr. Black and seen by Dr. Flight, a neurologist at Strong, for her Parkinson's disease. She has been tried on Sinemet which caused instability and staggering and was later changed to Symmetrel 100 milligrams twice a day which she tolerated well, but when she ran out of the medication, she felt just as well as when she had been on it, so it was decided to keep her off for awhile. She also has complained of insomnia and restlessness at night not associated with depression or anxiety. She has no history of cerebrovascular disease or cardiovascular disease.

PAST MEDICAL HISTORY: Significant for her Parkinson's disease, status post left inguinal hernia repair and diaphragmatic hernia repair. She was also status post splenectomy for diagnosis of thrombocytopenia and has a history of alcoholism and hepatitis in the past. She also has been hospitalized for pneumonia. She does not smoke; she reports that she does not currently drink alcohol - she has an allergy to Sulfa medications. She is currently on no medication at all. She was in the hospital for a lens implant that was unsuccessful last year.

SOCIAL HISTORY: She lives by herself in Rose Apartments. Her brother lives just out of town. His name is Jonathan.

REVIEW OF SYSTEMS: Negative for nausea, vomiting, hematemesis, hemoptysis; she has not had any melena or bleeding per rectum. She does tend to be somewhat constipated but this is not a new problem. She denies any pedal edema, orthopnea or dyspnea on exertion. She has no paroxysmal nocturnal dyspnea. She also denies headaches or sudden changes in her vision.

FAMILY HISTORY: Significant for an aunt who died of Parkinson's disease, a mother who died of colon cancer, and patient's brother was also operated on for colon cancer.

GENERAL: The patient is an elderly, slim, white female in no acute distress. She is alert and oriented times 3. She is cooperative with the exam. BLOOD PRESSURE: 160/92 TEMPERATURE: 99.9 orally PULSE: 96 RESPIRATIONS: 9-12 and somewhat deep. She is in no respiratory distress

EENT: Pupils are equal, round, and reactive to light and accommodation. Extraocular movements are full. Fields are intact to confrontation. Right disc was visualized and was sharp. Left funduscopic exam was difficult secondary to patient's inability to cooperate. Mouth and pharynx were clear. Patient was edentulous with dentures not in. Tympanic membranes were normal bilaterally.

DD: 05/10/YYYY

Continued on next page

DT: 05/11/YYYY

Physician Authentication

GLOBAL CARE MEDICAL CENTER ■ 100 MAIN ST, ALFRED NY 14802 ■ (607) 555-1234

LATES, LONNIE   Admission: 05/10/YYYY
IPCase007   DOB: 02/08/YYYY
Dr. BLACK   ROOM: 367

History & Physical Exam

Page 2 continued

NECK: Supple, without thyromegaly or adenopathy.

LUNGS: Clear to auscultation.

CARDIAC: Reveals rapid, regular rate without clicks, rubs, or murmurs. No carotid bruits.

BREASTS: Without masses, dimpling, or discharge. Adnexa were free of masses.

ABDOMEN : Soft and nontender with normal bowel sounds throughout. She had a right upper quadrant scar and left inguinal scar.

EXTREMITIES: There were bilateral femoral bruits but pulses distally were 2+ and equal. She had no varicosities or edema. Deep tendon reflexes were 2+ and equal and toes were down going bilaterally. She had full range of motion at the knee and hip without rigidity or cogwheeling. She did have a mild degree of cogwheeling in the left arm on flexion and extension but none detected in the right arm. Her strength in her upper extremities was about 4 out of 5 and in her lower extremities about 3 out of 5. Her left hip was sore deep inside specifically on external rotation and so that was x-rayed which is pending at this time.

NEUROLOGICAL: Extraocular movements were full. Cranial nerves 2-12 were grossly intact and she was intact to light touch and motor testing throughout. Toes were down going bilaterally. She had a negative Romberg sign but on attempting to ambulate was very uncertain and hesitant and tended to lean forward over the feet. Blood gases obtained in the Emergency Room showed a hydrogen ion concentration of 7.46, PC0 2 of 43, and a partial pressure of oxygen of 71 on room air. Complete blood count showed a white count of 6,700, hematocrit of 34.2% and platelet count of 141,000. She had 35 segmented cells, 56 lymphocytes, 5 monocytes, 4 eosinophils and an occasional atypical lymph. Her blood alcohol level was 0 and her SCG II was remarkable for a potassium of 3.3, serum glutamic oxaloacetic transaminase of 70 and lactic dehydrogenase of 325 and a normal bilirubin. Electrocardiogram was also within normal limits.

ASSESSMENT: 64-year-old woman with progressive onset of weakness and vertigo and tendency to fall. This could be secondary to parkinsonism, cerebral basilar, vertebral basal insufficiency or viral syndrome given patient's slightly abnormal differential and elevated temperature.

PLAN: Admit her and start her back on her Symmetrel 100 milligrams twice a day in case this represents an acute exacerbation of her parkinsonism. She will be put to bed rest and observed closely. Her electrolyte abnormalities were corrected. We will also follow her liver enzymes.

DD: 05/10/YYYY

Reviewed and Approved: John Black MD
ATP-B-S:02:1001261385: John Black MD
(Signed: 05/10/YYYY 04:24:44 PM EST)

DT: 05/11/YYYY

Physician Authentication

GLOBAL CARE MEDICAL CENTER ■ 100 MAIN ST, ALFRED NY 14802 ■ (607) 555-1234

LATES, LONNIE Admission: 05/10/YYYY
IPCase007 DOB: 02/08/YYYY
Dr. BLACK ROOM: 367

Progress Notes

Date	Time	Physician's signature required for each order. (Please skip one line between dates.)
05/10/YYYY	1600	Chief complaint: Frequent falls and weakness. Diagnosis: Sudden onset of weakness, vertigo, and gait ataxia. Rule out parkinsonism. Rule out cerebrovascular accident. Rule out viral syndrome. Confirmed ______ Provisional __X__ Plan of Treatment: Admit, observe, and treat as appropriate. DISCHARGE PLAN: Refer to Patient Services for: Evaluation - may require placement Reviewed and Approved: John Black MD ATP-B-S: 02 :1001261385: John Black MD (Signed: 05/10/YYYY 04:50:55 PM EST)
05/11/YYYY	1100	Patient is usually a heavy drinker and almost always denies it. May be a factor. Always has abnormal liver function study in long past history and multiple workups for same. Reviewed and Approved: John Black MD ATP-B-S:02:1001261385: John Black MD (Signed: 5/11/YYYY 11:14:07 AM EST)
05/12/YYYY	1100	Subjective: Patient feeling better. Still complains of inability to sleep. However feels stronger and able to ambulate without support. Complains of constipation. Objective: Vital signs stable and afebrile. Lungs: clear. Cardiac: regular rate and rhythm without murmur. Extremities: without edema. Patient ambulated to door and back without stumbling or ataxia. Assessment: Improved gait and strength. Admission symptoms likely due to Parkinson's disease. Plan: Enema for constipation if no results with Milk of Magnesia. Discontinue if discharged in the morning. Reviewed and Approved: John Black MD ATP-B-S:02 :1001261385: John Black MD (Signed: 05/12/YYYY 11:40:32 AM EST)

GLOBAL CARE MEDICAL CENTER ■ 100 MAIN ST, ALFRED NY 14802 ■ (607) 555-1234

LATES, LONNIE IPCase007 Dr. BLACK	Admission: 05/10/YYYY DOB: 02/08/YYYY ROOM: 367	**Progress Notes**

Date	Time	Physician's signature required for each order. (Please skip one line between dates.)
05/13/YYYY	1100	Patient receiving regular no added salt diet as ordered. 64-year-old female, height: 5 foot, 3 inches weight: 110 pounds. Ideal Body Weight 115 + 10%. Albumin = 3.0. Has been eating well. Reviewed and Approved: C.T. Connor, Dietitian ATP-B-S:02:1001261385: C.T. Connor, Dietitian (Signed: 05/13/YYYY 11:40:32 AM EST) Social Services request for evaluation acknowledged. Reviewed and Approved: V. South, RN ATP-B-S:02:1001261385: V. South, RN (Signed: 05/13/YYYY 11:12:16 AM EST)
05/14/YYYY	1130	Subjective: Patient ambulating in halls without difficulty. Only complains of constipation and nausea although she had a good bowel movement with enema yesterday. Objective: Vital signs stable and afebrile. Lungs: clear. Cardiac: regular rate and rhythm. Extremities: without edema. Skin: without rash. Assessment: Doing well with recovery from apparent parkinsonism crisis. Plan: Discharge today. Follow up with Dr. Black on Friday. Reviewed and Approved: John Black MD ATP-B-S:02:1001261385: John Black MD (Signed: 05/14/YYYY 11:40:50 AM EST)
05/14/YYYY	1730	Patient discharged home today. Patient will be followed by North Point Home Care Services for now. Reviewed and Approved: O. Richards, RN ATP-B-S:02:1001261385: O. Richards, RN (Signed: 05/14/YYYY 05:30:12 PM EST)

GLOBAL CARE MEDICAL CENTER ■ 100 MAIN ST, ALFRED NY 14802 ■ (607) 555-1234

LATES, LONNIE IPCase007 Dr. BLACK	Admission: 05/10/YYYY DOB: 02/08/YYYY ROOM: 367	**Doctors' Orders**

Date	Time	Physician's signature required for each order. (Please skip one line between dates.)
05/10/YYYY	1625	Admit. Bed rest. Diet: 4 grains sodium diet. Neuro checks every 4 hours for 48 hours. Arterial blood gases on right arm. Urinalysis. Chest x-ray and left hip. Morning lab lytes, erythrocyte sedimentation rate. Klotrix by mouth twice a day for three days. Colace 100 milligrams by mouth twice a day. Restoril 15 milligrams by mouth at bedtime as needed for sleep. Symmetrel 100 milligrams by mouth twice a day. Reviewed and Approved: John Chase MD ATP-B-S:02:1001261385: John Chase MD (Signed: 05/10/YYYY 04:42:00 PM EST)
05/10/YYYY	1640	Cold compresses to relieve tension. Tylenol 1 or 2 tablets by mouth every 4 hours as needed for pain. Reviewed and Approved: John Chase MD ATP-B-S:02:1001261385: John Chase MD (Signed: 05/10/YYYY 04:45:52 PM EST)
05/11/YYYY	0830	Neuro parameters: Blood Pressure: Greater than 190/100 Lower than 100/60 Pulse: Greater than 120 Lower than 60 Temperature: Greater than 101 Lower than 97 Respirations: Greater than 30 Lower than 10 Reviewed and Approved: John Black MD ATP-B-S:02:1001261385: John Black MD (Signed: 05/11/YYYY 08:34:00 AM EST)
05/12/YYYY	1045	Milk of Magnesia as needed for constipation. Discontinue neuro checks. Out of bed as desired. Discontinue Restoril. Meprobamate 400 milligrams at bedtime as needed for sleep for 5 days. Reviewed and Approved: John Black MD ATP-B-S:02:1001261385: John Black MD (Signed: 05/12/YYYY 11:06:52 AM EST)

GLOBAL CARE MEDICAL CENTER ■ 100 MAIN ST, ALFRED NY 14802 ■ (607) 555-1234

LATES, LONNIE IPCase007 Dr. BLACK	Admission: 05/10/YYYY DOB: 02/08/YYYY ROOM: 367	**Doctors' Orders**

Date	Time	Physician's signature required for each order. (Please skip one line between dates.)
05/12/YYYY	2225	B12 - folate level Complete blood count in morning. Reviewed and Approved: John Chase MD ATP-B-S:02:1001261385: John Chase MD (Signed: 05/12/YYYY 10:45:52 PM EST)
05/13/YYYY	1100	Change diet to dental soft-encourage patient to eat. Discontinue Meprobamate. Start Halcion 0.25 milligrams by mouth every bedtime as needed for sleep. Patient may have tap water enema if no significant response to Milk of Magnesia by noon tomorrow. Check stool for occult blood. Reviewed and Approved: John Chase MD ATP-B-S:02:1001261385: John Chase MD (Signed: 05/13/YYYY 11:05:29 AM EST)
05/14/YYYY	1100	Patient to be discharged today. Please make follow-up appointment with Dr. Black on Friday. Please arrange for ambulance service to take patient home. Ask social worker to arrange for Meals on Wheels for patient. Chart dictated 05/14/YYYY Reviewed and Approved: John Chase MD ATP-B-S:02:1001261385: John Chase MD (Signed: 05/14/YYYY 11:07:44 AM EST)

GLOBAL CARE MEDICAL CENTER ■ 100 MAIN ST, ALFRED NY 14802 ■ (607) 555-1234

LATES, LONNIE	Admission: 05/10/YYYY	**Laboratory Data**
IPCase007	DOB: 02/08/YYYY	
Dr. BLACK	ROOM: 367	

SPECIMEN COLLECTED: 05/10/YYYY SPECIMEN RECEIVED: 05/10/YYYY

TEST	RESULT	FLAG	REFERENCE
URINALYSIS			
DIPSTICK ONLY			
COLOR	Slightly cloudy yellow		
SP GRAVITY	1.010		≤ 1.030
ALBUMIN	Negative		≤ 125 mg/dl
BILIRUBIN	Negative		≤ 0.8 mg/dl
ACETONE	Negative		≤ 10 mg/dl
BLOOD	Slight trace		0.06 mg/dl hgb
PH	8		5-8.0
PROTEIN			≤ 30 mg/dl
SUGAR	Negative		NEG
NITRITES			NEG
LEUKOCYTE			≤ 15 WBC/hpf
W.B.C.	rare		≤ 5/hpf
R.B.C.	----		≤ 5/hpf
BACT.	few		1+(≤ 20/hpf)
URINE PREGNANCY TEST			

End of Report

GLOBAL CARE MEDICAL CENTER ■ 100 MAIN ST, ALFRED NY 14802 ■ (607) 555-1234

LATES, LONNIE Admission: 05/10/YYYY
IPCase007 DOB: 02/08/YYYY
Dr. BLACK ROOM: 367

Laboratory Data

TIME IN: 05/10/YYYY 1352 TIME OUT: 05/10/YYYY 1402

COMPLETE BLOOD COUNTS DIFFERENTIAL

TEST	RESULT	FLAG	REFERENCE
WHITE BLOOD CELL	6.7		4.5-11.0 thou/ul
RED BLOOD CELL	3.58		5.2-5.4 milliliter/upper limit
HEMOGLOBIN	11.7		11.7-16.1 grams per deciliter
HEMATOCRIT	34.2		35.0-47.0 %
MEAN CORPUSCULAR VOLUME	95.5		85-99 factor level
MEAN CORPUSCULAR HEMOGLOBIN	32.7		
MEAN CORPUSCULAR HEMOGLOBIN CONCENTRATION	34.2		33-37
RED CELL DISTRIBUTION WIDTH			11.4-14.5
PLATELETS	141		130-400 thou/ul
SEGMENTED CELLS %	35		
LYMPHOCYTES %	56		20.5-51.1
MONOCYTES %	5		1.7-9.3
EOSINOPHILS %	4		
BAND CELLS %	Occasional		
ATYPICAL LYMPH			

Thou/ul= thousand upper limit

COMMENTS: Occasional target cells

End of Report

GLOBAL CARE MEDICAL CENTER ■ 100 MAIN ST, ALFRED NY 14802 ■ (607) 555-1234

LATES, LONNIE	Admission: 05/10/YYYY	**Laboratory Data**
IPCase007	DOB: 02/08/YYYY	
Dr. BLACK	ROOM: 367	

TIME IN: 05/13/YYYY 0720 **TIME OUT:** 05/13/YYYY

COMPLETE BLOOD COUNTS DIFFERENTIAL

TEST	RESULT	FLAG	REFERENCE
WHITE BLOOD CELL	5.8		4.5-11.0 thou/ul
RED BLOOD CELL	3.90		5.2-5.4 milliliter/upper limit
HEMOGLOBIN	12.9		11.7-16.1 grams per deciliter
HEMATOCRIT	37.7		35.0-47.0 %
MEAN CORPUSCULAR VOLUME	96.6		85-99 factor level
MEAN CORPUSCULAR HEMOGLOBIN	33.2		
MEAN CORPUSCULAR HEMOGLOBIN CONCENTRATION	34.3		33-37
RED CELL DISTRIBUTION WIDTH			11.4-14.5
PLATELETS	154		130-400 thou/ul
SEGMENTED CELLS %	36		
LYMPHOCYTES %	41		20.5-51.1
MONOCYTES %	6		1.7-9.3
EOSINOPHILS %	4		
BAND CELLS %			

Thou/ul = thousand upper limit

End of Report

GLOBAL CARE MEDICAL CENTER ■ 100 MAIN ST, ALFRED NY 14802 ■ (607) 555-1234

LATES, LONNIE | Admission: 05/10/YYYY
IPCase007 | DOB: 02/08/YYYY
Dr.BLACK | ROOM: 367

Radiology Report

Date of X-ray: 05/10/YYYY

REASON: Admission

TECHNICAL DATA: Anterior-posterior and lateral elevated on stretcher. Patient has had multiple falls on left hip.

LEFT HIP: Anterior-posterior and lateral views show no evidence of any fractures.

Chest: Posteroanterior and lateral views show no evidence of any active pulmonary infiltrate. The cardiac silhouette appears to be slightly enlarged but I think this is most likely due to the fact that it was an anterior-posterior film. There are moderate to severe osteoporotic changes noted and there is a deformity of the glenoid on the right side which is probably secondary to a very old fracture. There are multiple healing rib fractures on the left side posteriorly and there appear to be 2 or 3 healing rib fractures on the right side of the thorax anteriorly. None of these fractures appears fresh. There is an old compression fracture of T11 as well.

CONCLUSION: Multiple old healing rib fractures. No evidence of any active cardiopulmonary disease.

DD: 05/11/YYYY

Reviewed and Approved: Randall Cunningham MD
ATP-B-S:02:1001261385: Randall Cunningham MD
(Signed:05/11/YYYY 2:24:44 PM EST)

DT: 05/11/YYYY

Physician Authentication

GLOBAL CARE MEDICAL CENTER ■ 100 MAIN ST, ALFRED NY 14802 ■ (607) 555-1234

LATES, LONNIE	Admission: 05/10/YYYY	**EKG Report**
IPCase007	DOB: 02/08/YYYY	
Dr. BLACK	ROOM: 367	

Date of Electrocardiogram: 05/10/YYYY Time of Electrocardiogram: 1657

Rate	95	
PR	.16	Abnormal: nonspecific ST changes similar to 09/24/YYYY.
QRSD	.08	
QT	.36	
QTC		
-- Axis --		
P		
QRS		
T		

Reviewed and Approved: Dr. Steven J. Chambers, M.D.
ATP-B-S:02:1001261385: Dr. Steven J. Chambers, M.D.
(Signed:05/10/YYYY 2:24:44 PM EST)

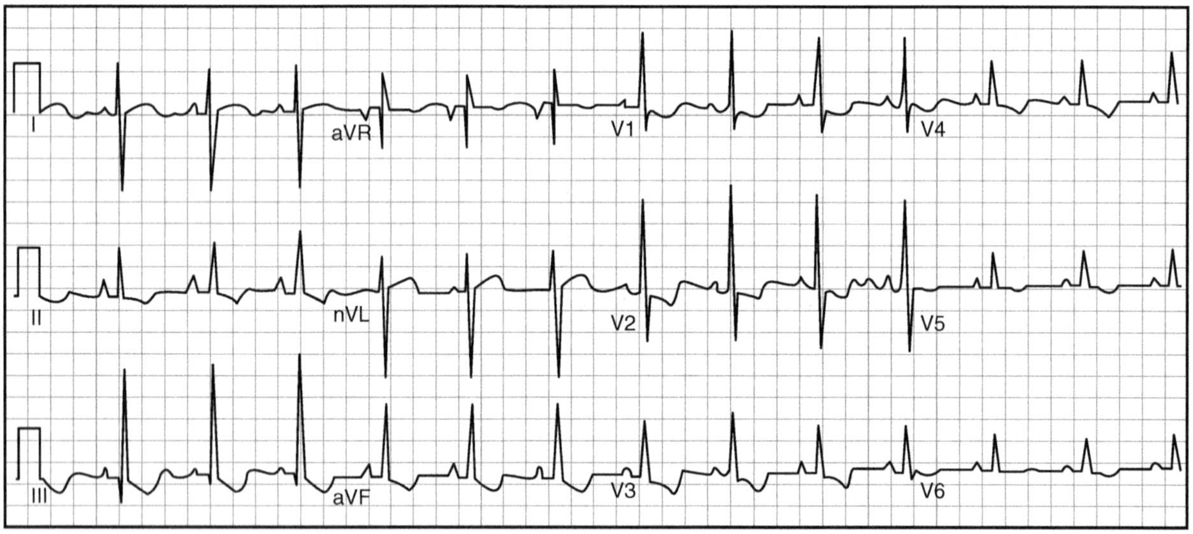

GLOBAL CARE MEDICAL CENTER ■ 100 MAIN ST, ALFRED NY 14802 ■ (607) 555-1234

LATES, LONNIE Admission: 05/10/YYYY
IPCase007 DOB: 02/08/YYYY
Dr. BLACK ROOM: 367

Graphic Chart

DAY IN HOSPITAL	1						2						3						4					
DATE	05/10/YYYY						05/11/YYYY						05/12/YYYY						0/YYYY					
PULSE (•) / TEMP (X)	0400	0800	1200	1600	2000	2400	0400	0800	1200	1600	2000	2400	0400	0800	1200	1600	2000	2400	0400	0800	1200	1600	2000	2400
140 / 106																								
130 / 105																								
120 / 104																								
110 / 103																								
100 / 102																								
90 / 101							•	•	•															
80 / 100				•		•				•	•	•		•										
70 / 99					•X	X							•											
60 / 98.6				X			X			X	X													
50 / 98									X															
40 / 97												X	X	X										
30 / 96								X																
20 / 95																								
RESPIRATION				16	18		16	20	24	20	20	20	16	24										

	Day 1			Day 2			Day 3			Day 4		
BLOOD PRESSURE	0800	1600	146/82	0800 152/80	1600	136/70	0800 120/50	1600		0800	1600	
	1200	2000	122/60	1200 150/80	2000	168/70	1200	2000		1200	2000	
WEIGHT 5'3"	110 #											
DIET	4 Gram Salt			4 Gram Salt			4 Gram Salt			4 Gram Salt		
APPETITE			75%	100%	100%	25%	100%	100%	100%	100%	100%	25%
BATH				Self			Self			Self		
INTAKE/OUTPUT												
INTAKE: ORAL FLUIDS												
INTAKE: IV FLUIDS												
INTAKE: BLOOD												
INTAKE:												
INTAKE: 8-HOUR TOTAL												
INTAKE: 24-HOUR TOTAL												
OUTPUT: URINE												
OUTPUT: STOOL												
OUTPUT: EMESIS												
OUTPUT: NASOGASTRIC												
OUTPUT:												
OUTPUT: 8-HOUR TOTAL												
OUTPUT: 24-HOUR TOTAL												

GLOBAL CARE MEDICAL CENTER ■ 100 MAIN ST, ALFRED NY 14802 ■ (607) 555-1234

LATES, LONNIE   Admission: 05/10/YYYY
IPCase007   DOB: 02/08/YYYY
Dr. BLACK   ROOM: 367

Medication Administration Record

SPECIAL INSTRUCTIONS: Allergic to Sulfa

MEDICATION (dose and route)	DATE: 05/10 TIME	INITIALS	DATE: 05/11 TIME	INITIALS	DATE: 05/12 TIME	INITIALS	DATE: 05/13 TIME	INITIALS
Klotrix 1 tablet by mouth two times a day for three days	0800	----	0800	VS	0800	VS	0800	VS
	1600	OR	1600	OR	1600	OR	1600	----
Colace 100 milligrams by mouth two times a day	0800	----	0800	VS	0800	VS	0800	VS
	1600	OR	1600	OR	1600	OR	1600	OR
Symmetrel 100 milligrams by mouth two times a day	0800	----	0800	VS	0800	VS	0800	VS
	1600	OR	1600	OR	1600	OR	1600	OR
	0800	----	0800	VS	0800	VS	0800	VS
	1300	----	1300	VS	1300	VS	1300	VS
	1800	OR	1800	OR	1800	OR	1800	OR
Erythromycin 500 milligrams every 6 hours for 5 days.	0600	----		----		----	0600	----
	1200	----		----		----	1200	VS
	1800	----		----		----	1800	OR
	2400	----		----		----	2400	JD
Single Orders								
PRN Medications								
Restoril 15 milligrams by mouth every bedtime as needed for sleep.	2110	OR	2130	OR				
Tylenol 1 or 2 tablets by mouth every 4 hours as needed for pain.					0115	JD	0130	JD
Milk of Magnesia 30 cc by mouth as needed for constipation.					1400	OR		
Meprobamate 400 milligrams by mouth every bedtime as needed for sleep for 5 days					2140	OR		
Halcion 0.25 milligrams by mouth every bedtime as needed for sleep.							2200	JD

INITIALS	SIGNATURE AND TITLE	INITIALS	SIGNATURE AND TITLE	INITIALS	SIGNATURE AND TITLE
VS	Vera South, RN	GPW	G. P. Well, RN		
OR	Ora Richards, RN	PS	P. Small, RN		
JD	Jane Dobbs, RN				
HF	H. Figgs, RN				

GLOBAL CARE MEDICAL CENTER ■ 100 MAIN ST, ALFRED NY 14802 ■ (607) 555-1234

LATES, LONNIE Admission: 05/10/YYYY
IPCase007 DOB: 02/08/YYYY
Dr. BLACK ROOM: 367

Medication Administration Record

SPECIAL INSTRUCTIONS: Allergic to Sulfa

MEDICATION (dose and route)	DATE: 05/14 TIME	INITIALS	DATE: TIME	INITIALS	DATE: TIME	INITIALS	DATE: TIME	INITIALS
Colace 100 milligrams by mouth two times a day	0800	VS						
	1600	OR						
Symmetrel 100 milligrams by mouth two times a day	0800	VS						
	1600	OR						
Single Orders								
PRN Medications								
Tylenol 1 or 2 tablets by mouth every 4 hours as needed for pain.	0230	JD						
Milk of Magnesia 30 cc by mouth as needed for constipation.	0345	JD						

INITIALS	SIGNATURE AND TITLE	INITIALS	SIGNATURE AND TITLE	INITIALS	SIGNATURE AND TITLE
VS	Vera South, RN	GPW	G. P. Well, RN		
OR	Ora Richards, RN	PS	P. Small, RN		
JD	Jane Dobbs, RN				
HF	H. Figgs, RN				

GLOBAL CARE MEDICAL CENTER ■ 100 MAIN ST, ALFRED NY 14802 ■ (607) 555-1234

LATES, LONNIE	Admission: 05/10/YYYY	
IPCase007	DOB: 02/08/YYYY	**Nurses' Notes**
Dr. BLACK	ROOM: 367	

DATE	TIME	TREATMENTS & MEDICATIONS	TIME	NURSES' NOTES
05/10/YYYY	1635	98.7 - 80 - 16 - 146/82 Allergic to Sulfa Neuro checks every four hours. "See neuro sheet."	1635	Admitted to 367 services of Dr. Black. Weak, color pale. "Red areas to left elbow and lower arm from falling at home," patient stated. Reviewed and Approved: V. South, RN ATP-B-S:02:1001261385: V. South, RN (Signed: 5/10/YYYY 04:35:10 PM EST)
			1700	Diet taken 75% at bedside without difficulty. Reviewed and Approved: O. Richards, RN ATP-B-S:02:1001261385: O. Richards, RN (Signed: 05/10/YYYY 05:04:05 PM EST)
			1900	Out of bed with help to bathroom. Voided quantity sufficient and returned to bed. Reviewed and Approved: O. Richards, RN ATP-B-S:02:1001261385: O. Richards, RN (Signed: 05/10/YYYY 07:07:11 PM EST)
			2030	Vital signs and evening care given. Reviewed and Approved: O. Richards, RN ATP-B-S:02:1001261385: O. Richards, RN (Signed: 05/10/YYYY 08:37:33 PM EST)
			2130	Asleep. Reviewed and Approved: O. Richards, RN ATP-B-S:02:1001261385: O. Richards, RN (Signed: 05/10/YYYY 09:34:33 PM EST)
			2245	Out of bed to bathroom - wandering in hall. Returned patient to her bed. Reoriented bed down position with side rails up. Reviewed and Approved: O. Richards, RN ATP-B-S:02:1001261385: O. Richards, RN (Signed: 05/10/YYYY 11:47:02 PM EST)
05/11/YYYY		Saturday	2400	Resting quietly in bed without complaints. Reviewed and Approved: J. Dobbs, RN ATP-B-S:02:1001261385: J. Dobbs, RN (Signed: 05/11/YYYY 12:03:28 AM EST)
	0100	98 - 96 - 16 150/100	0100	Sleeping with snoring respirations. Neuro checks done. Left corner of mouth drooped left hand grasp weaker than right. Wiggles toes on command but can't press foot against nurse's hands. Reviewed and Approved: J. Dobbs, RN ATP-B-S:02:1001261385: J. Dobbs, RN (Signed: 05/11/YYYY 01:03:28 AM EST)

GLOBAL CARE MEDICAL CENTER ■ 100 MAIN ST, ALFRED NY 14802 ■ (607) 555-1234

LATES, LONNIE	Admission: 05/10/YYYY	**Nurses' Notes**
IPCase007	DOB: 02/08/YYYY	
Dr. BLACK	ROOM: 367	

DATE	TIME	TREATMENTS & MEDICATIONS	TIME	NURSES' NOTES
05/10/YYYY		Saturday	0130	Sleeping with snoring respirations. Reviewed and Approved: J. Dobbs, RN ATP-B-S:02:1001261385: J. Dobbs, RN (Signed: 05/11/YYYY 01:34:16 AM EST)
			0200	Awake. Complains of not being able to sleep. Reviewed and Approved: J. Dobbs, RN ATP-B-S:02:1001261385: J. Dobbs, RN (Signed: 05/11/YYYY 02:02:56 AM EST)
			0250	Found walking to bathroom without assistance. Patient had climbed out of bed over side rails - all side rails were up. Reviewed and Approved: J. Dobbs, RN ATP-B-S:02:1001261385: J. Dobbs, RN (Signed: 05/11/YYYY 02:52:23 AM EST)
	0500	97.4 - 88 16 144/100	0330-0530	Sleeping with respirations easy and regular. All 4 side rails up. Reviewed and Approved: J. Dobbs, RN ATP-B-S:02:1001261385: J. Dobbs, RN (Signed: 05/11/YYYY 05:33:12 AM EST)
			0600	Sleeping at present and respirations easy and regular. Reviewed and Approved: J. Dobbs, RN ATP-B-S:02:1001261385: J. Dobbs, RN (Signed: 05/11/YYYY 06:05:33 AM EST).
05/11/YYYY		Saturday	0730	Patient asleep upon arrival. Easily awakened. Vital signs taken with neuro vital signs stable. Hand grasps equal, patient is oriented times three, out of bed to bathroom to void quantity sufficient in bathroom. Gait is fine. Patient has a pleasant affect this morning. Voiced no complaints. Appetite excellent at breakfast. Patient did own self care at bedside. Reviewed and Approved: V. South, RN ATP-B-S:02:1001261385: V. South, RN (Signed: 05/11/YYYY 07:30:28 AM EST)
			1300	Appetite good at lunch. Resting in bed at present time. Reviewed and Approved: V. South, RN ATP-B-S:02:1001261385: V. South, RN (Signed: 05/11/YYYY 01:02:11 PM EST)
			1440	Patient sleeping well at present time. Had no complaints today. Appears very tired. Reviewed and Approved: V. South, RN ATP-B-S:02:1001261385: V. South, RN (Signed: 05/11/YYYY 02:04:11 PM EST)

GLOBAL CARE MEDICAL CENTER ■ 100 MAIN ST, ALFRED NY 14802 ■ (607) 555-1234

LATES, LONNIE	Admission: 05/10/YYYY	
IPCase007	DOB: 02/08/YYYY	**Nurses' Notes**
Dr. BLACK	ROOM: 367	

DATE	TIME	TREATMENTS & MEDICATIONS	TIME	NURSES' NOTES
05/11/YYYY		Saturday	1530	Sleeping. Reviewed and Approved: O. Richards, RN ATP-B-S:02:1001261385: O. Richards, RN (Signed: 05/11/YYYY 03:31:29 PM EST)
			1730	25% of diet taken - visitor with patient. Reviewed and Approved: O. Richards, RN ATP-B-S:02:1001261385: O. Richards, RN (Signed: 05/11/YYYY 05:34:19 PM EST)
			1800-2000	To bathroom to void and returned to bed. Reviewed And Approved: O. Richards, RN ATP-B-S:02:1001261385: O. Richards, RN (Signed: 05/11/YYYY 08:01:33 PM EST)
			2100-2200	Bedtime care given. Sleeping off and on most of the evening. Does not initiate any conversation. Reviewed and Approved: O. Richards, RN ATP-B-S:02:1001261385: O. Richards, RN (Signed: 05/11/YYYY 10:11:45 PM EST)
05/12/YYYY		Sunday	2400	Neuro vitals done, stable. Refer to neuro sheet; patient back to sleep. Reviewed and Approved: J. Dobbs, RN ATP-B-S:02:1001261385: J. Dobbs, RN (Signed: 05/12/YYYY 12:02:16 AM EST)
	0100	Tylenol 2 tablets by mouth	0100	Complains of sleeplessness, already had sleeping pill. Reviewed and Approved: J. Dobbs, RN ATP-B-S:02:1001261385: J. Dobbs, RN (Signed: 05/12/YYYY 01:02:36 AM EST)
			0200	Asleep. Reviewed and Approved: J. Dobbs, RN ATP-B-S:02:1001261385: J. Dobbs, RN (Signed: 05/12/YYYY 02:03:41 AM EST)
			0400	Awake. Reviewed and Approved: J. Dobbs, RN ATP-B-S:02:1001261385: J. Dobbs, RN (Signed: 05/12/YYYY 04:00:16 AM EST)
			0600	Slept very little. Reviewed and Approved: J. Dobbs, RN ATP-B-S:02:1001261385: J. Dobbs, RN (Signed: 05/12/YYYY 06:00:06 AM EST)
			0800	Sleeping upon arrival. Voiced no complaints. Vital signs stable, out of bed to bathroom to void quantity sufficient in bathroom. Gait steady, appetite good, ate 100% of breakfast. Out of bed to bathroom to do total self care. Reviewed and Approved: V. South, RN ATP-B-S:02:1001261385: V. South, RN (Signed: 05/12/YYYY 08:03:00 AM EST)

GLOBAL CARE MEDICAL CENTER ■ 100 MAIN ST, ALFRED NY 14802 ■ (607) 555-1234

LATES, LONNIE Admission: 05/10/YYYY
IPCase007 DOB: 02/08/YYYY
Dr. BLACK ROOM: 367

Nurses' Notes

DATE	TIME	TREATMENTS & MEDICATIONS	TIME	NURSES' NOTES
05/13/YYYY		Milk of Magnesia 30 cc by mouth given for constipation.	1000-1200	Dozing at intervals throughout morning. Out of bed to ambulate to dayroom. Gait remains steady. Has a slow propulsive gait. Appetite good at lunch. Ate 100% of meal. Resting in bed with no complaints. Reviewed and Approved: V. South, RN ATP-B-S:02:1001261385: V. South, RN (Signed: 05/12/YYYY 12:02:10 PM EST)
			1330	Patient resting in bed watching television. Reviewed and Approved: V. South, RN ATP-B-S:02:1001261385: V. South, RN (Signed: 05/12/YYYY 01:32:29 PM EST)
			1430	Complains of basilar neck pain that doesn't radiate anywhere. Able to move all extremities well. No numbness noted in peripheral. Patient stated "I had this problem before. It is my vertebrae that are deteriorating." Does not request any pain medication. Reviewed and Approved: V. South, RN ATP-B-S:02:1001261385: V. South, RN (Signed: 05/12/YYYY 02:32:14 PM EST)
05/12/YYYY	3-11	Sunday	1530	Resting in bed. Talking with visitors. Reviewed and Approved: O. Richards, RN ATP-B-S:02:1001261385: O. Richards, RN (Signed: 05/12/YYYY 03:30:44 PM EST)
			1730	Patient took 100% of supper. Reviewed and Approved: O. Richards, RN ATP-B-S:02:1001261385: O. Richards, RN (Signed: 05/12/YYYY 05:30:32 PM EST)
			1900	Resting quietly at this time. Reviewed and Approved: O. Richards, RN ATP-B-S:02:1001261385: O. Richards, RN (Signed: 05/12/YYYY 07:02:59 PM EST)
			2000	Bedtime care given. Reviewed and Approved: O. Richards, RN ATP-B-S:02:1001261385: O. Richards, RN (Signed: 05/12/YYYY 08:03:37 PM EST)
			2200	Patient sleeping at this time. Had a good evening. Reviewed and Approved: O. Richards, RN ATP-B-S:02:1001261385: O. Richards, RN (Signed: 05/12/YYYY 10:10:47 PM EST)
05/13/YYYY		Monday	2400	Asleep. Reviewed and Approved: J. Dobbs, RN ATP-B-S:02:1001261385: J. Dobbs, RN (Signed: 05/13/YYYY 12:02:16 AM EST)

GLOBAL CARE MEDICAL CENTER ■ 100 MAIN ST, ALFRED NY 14802 ■ (607) 555-1234

LATES, LONNIE	Admission: 05/10/YYYY	
IPCase007	DOB: 02/08/YYYY	**Nurses' Notes**
Dr. BLACK	ROOM: 367	

DATE	TIME	TREATMENTS & MEDICATIONS	TIME	NURSES' NOTES
05/13/YYYY		Monday	0200	Asleep. Reviewed and Approved: J. Dobbs, RN ATP-B-S:02:1001261385: J. Dobbs, RN (Signed: 05/13/YYYY 02:03:55 AM EST)
			0400	Continues to sleep. Reviewed and Approved: J. Dobbs, RN ATP-B-S:02:1001261385: J. Dobbs, RN (Signed: 05/13/YYYY 04:04:25 AM EST)
			0600	Slept well. Reviewed and Approved: J. Dobbs, RN ATP-B-S:02:1001261385: J. Dobbs, RN (Signed: 05/13/YYYY 06:00:17 AM EST)
05/13/YYYY	7-3		0730	Awake, vital signs taken. No complaints. To bathroom as desired voiding quantity sufficient. Gait appears unsteady this morning. Reviewed and Approved: V. South, RN ATP-B-S:02:1001261385: V. South, RN (Signed: 05/13/YYYY 07:32:00 AM EST)
			0800	Out of bed to chair for breakfast. Ate well. Reviewed and Approved: V. South, RN ATP-B-S:02:1001261385: V. South, RN (Signed: 05/13/YYYY 08:02:00 AM EST)
			0930	Dr. Chase in to see patient. Assisted with morning care at bedside. Reviewed and Approved: V. South, RN ATP-B-S:02:1001261385: V. South, RN (Signed: 05/13/YYYY 09:34:10 AM EST)
			1030	Ambulated most of the morning. Back and forth in hall. Complains of bowels not moving. Reviewed and Approved: V. South, RN ATP-B-S:02:1001261385: V. South, RN (Signed: 05/13/YYYY 10:32:57 AM EST)
			1300	Tap water enema given with good results. Reviewed and Approved: V. South, RN ATP-B-S:02:1001261385: V. South, RN (Signed: 05/13/YYYY 01:02:13 PM EST)
			1430	Comfortable at present. Reviewed and Approved: V. South, RN ATP-B-S:02:1001261385: V. South, RN (Signed: 05/13/YYYY 02:32:57 PM EST)
05/13/YYYY			1530	Out of bed to bathroom and ambulated in hall - full length. Reviewed and Approved: O. Richards, RN ATP-B-S:02:1001261385: O. Richards, RN (Signed: 05/13/YYYY 03:30:44 PM EST)
			1700	Diet taken well. 25% Reviewed and Approved: O. Richards, RN ATP-B-S:02:1001261385: O. Richards, RN (Signed: 05/13/YYYY 05:04:44 PM EST)

GLOBAL CARE MEDICAL CENTER ■ 100 MAIN ST, ALFRED NY 14802 ■ (607) 555-1234

LATES, LONNIE	Admission: 05/10/YYYY	
IPCase007	DOB: 02/08/YYYY	**Nurses' Notes**
Dr. BLACK	ROOM: 367	

DATE	TIME	TREATMENTS & MEDICATIONS	TIME	NURSES' NOTES
5/13/YYYY			2000	Vital signs and evening care given. Ambulated well in hall and recreation room. Voided quantity sufficient. Reviewed and Approved: O. Richards, RN ATP-B-S:02:1001261385: O. Richards, RN (Signed: 05/13/YYYY 08:01:00 PM EST)
			2200	Asleep. Reviewed and Approved: O. Richards, RN ATP-B-S:02:1001261385: O. Richards, RN (Signed: 05/13/YYYY 10:02:34 PM EST)
05/14/YYYY		Tuesday	2400	Asleep. Reviewed and Approved: J. Dobbs, RN ATP-B-S:02:1001261385: J. Dobbs, RN (Signed: 05/14/YYYY 12:03:55 AM EST)
	0230	Tylenol tabs 2 by mouth	0200	Complained of sleeplessness. Reviewed and Approved: J. Dobbs, RN ATP-B-S:02:1001261385: J. Dobbs, RN (Signed: 05/14/YYYY 02:03:18 AM EST)
	0400	Milk of Magnesia 30 cc by mouth.	0400	Complained of constipation, very upset, laxative and prune juice given. Reviewed and Approved: J. Dobbs, RN ATP-B-S:02:1001261385: J. Dobbs, RN (Signed: 05/14/YYYY 04:04:18 AM EST)
			0420	Pacing the hall. Complains of constipation. Reviewed and Approved: J. Dobbs, RN ATP-B-S:02:1001261385: J. Dobbs, RN (Signed: 05/14/YYYY 04:22:19 AM EST)
			0600	Poor night. Complained of constipation. Reviewed and Approved: J. Dobbs, RN ATP-B-S:02:1001261385: J. Dobbs, RN (Signed: 05/14/YYYY 06:00:55 AM EST)
			0730	Vital signs stable. Ambulated to bathroom per self. Reviewed and Approved: V. South, RN ATP-B-S:02:1001261385: V. South, RN (Signed: 05/14/YYYY 07:32:00 AM EST)
			0800	Ate 100% of breakfast. Reviewed and Approved: V. South, RN ATP-B-S:02:1001261385: V. South, RN (Signed: 05/14/YYYY 08:02:45 AM EST)
			0830	Morning care done per self. Reviewed and Approved: V. South, RN ATP-B-S:02:1001261385: V. South, RN (Signed: 05/14/YYYY 08:32:00 AM EST)

Global Care Medical Center ■ 100 Main St, Alfred NY 14802 ■ (607) 555-1234

LATES, LONNIE IPCase007 Dr. BLACK	Admission: 05/10/YYYY DOB: 02/08/YYYY ROOM: 367	**Nurses' Notes**

DATE	TIME	TREATMENTS & MEDICATIONS	TIME	NURSES' NOTES
05/14/YYYY		Tuesday	0900	Had hair done. Reviewed and Approved: V. South, RN ATP-B-S:02:1001261385: V. South, RN (Signed: 05/14/YYYY 09:32:00 AM EST)
			1100	Walking in the hall waiting to go home. Reviewed and Approved: V. South, RN ATP-B-S:02:1001261385: V. South, RN (Signed: 05/14/YYYY 11:02:40 AM EST)
			1200	Ate good lunch. Reviewed and Approved: V. South, RN ATP-B-S:02:1001261385: V. South, RN (Signed: 05/14/YYYY 12:03:16 PM EST)
			1430	Walking halls waiting to go home. Reviewed and Approved: V. South, RN ATP-B-S:02:1001261385: V. South, RN (Signed: 05/14/YYYY 02:32:44 PM EST)
			1530	Ambulating freely in hallway. Reviewed and Approved: O. Richards, RN ATP-B-S:02:1001261385: O. Richards, RN (Signed: 05/14/YYYY 03:30:44 PM EST)
			1730	Out of bed in chair for supper. Reviewed and Approved: O. Richards, RN ATP-B-S:02:1001261385: O. Richards, RN (Signed: 05/14/YYYY 05:30:18 PM EST)
			1745	Home by ambulance. See discharge summary sheet. Reviewed and Approved: O. Richards, RN ATP-B-S:02:1001261385: O. Richards, RN (Signed: 05/14/YYYY 05:47:00 PM EST)

GLOBAL CARE MEDICAL CENTER ■ 100 MAIN ST, ALFRED NY 14802 ■ (607) 555-1234

Global Care Medical Center
100 Main St, Alfred NY 14802
(607) 555-1234

Emergency Department Record

PATIENT INFORMATION:

NAME:	LATES, LONNIE	**PATIENT NUMBER:**	IPCase007
ADDRESS:	2 Buck Road	**ADMISSION DATE & TIME:**	05/10/YYYY 1530
CITY:	Almond	**DISCHARGE DATE & TIME:**	05/14/YYYY 1745
STATE:	New York	**CONDITION ON DISCHARGE:**	
ZIP CODE:	14804	☐ Satisfactory	☐ AMA
TELEPHONE:	(607) 000-2644	☐ Home	☐ DOA
		☑ Inpatient Admission	☐ Code Blue
GENDER:	F	☐ Transfer to: ___________	☐ Died
DATE OF BIRTH:	02/08/YYYY	☐ Instruction Sheet Given	

NURSING DOCUMENTATION:

ALLERGIES: ☐ No ☑ Yes **EXPLAIN:** Allergic to Sulfa

CURRENT MEDICATIONS: ☑ No ☐ Yes

BP: 160/92 **P:** 96 **R:** 9-12 **T:** 99.9

CC: Dizziness; complains of pain near left hip. No visible bruise.

HPI: Parkinson's disease.

CONDITION: Dizzy

ASSESSMENT: Multiple bruises from several falls today; every time stood up got very dizzy and fell. Patient couldn't keep her balance. Color - pink.

SIGNATURE OF PRIMARY CARE NURSE: Reviewed and Approved: Cindy Stevens, RN
ATP-B-S:02:1001261385: Cindy Stevens, RN
(Signed: 05/10/YYYY 03:58:40 PM EST)

ICD CODES:					
CPT/HCPCS LEVEL II CODES:					

Global Care Medical Center
100 Main St, Alfred NY 14802
(607) 555-1234

Emergency Department Physician Documentation

Patient Name:	LATES, LONNIE	**Patient Number:**	IPCase007
Location:	Emergency Room	**ED Physician:**	Dr. John Chase
Date of Service:	05/10/YYYY	**Date of Birth:**	02/08/YYYY

Physician Notes:

Symptoms: This 64-year-old female who apparently has been diagnosed with Parkinson's disease is currently on no medications, presented in the Emergency Room complaining of numerous falls and multiple bruises. Patient also is an alcoholic, but she states she has not had any alcohol in a year or two. Patient states that over the past few days, she felt extremely weak when she stood up; when she tried to walk, she stumbled, and then she fell approximately 20 times last night because she could not keep her balance. Patient does complain of vertigo. There has been no nausea or vomiting, no cough, patient's appetite has been poor.

Physical exam: This 64-year-old female is alert, she is oriented X 3, and her mental status seems appropriate. Pupils equal round and reactive. Extraocular eye movements are intact. There is no evidence of nystagmus. Tympanic membranes are clear, the neck is supple, with no bruits, lungs clear, heart regular rate and rhythm, with 2 out of 6 systolic murmur best at the apex. Abdomen soft and nontender. Neurological exam showed patient has average muscle strength which is symmetrical bilaterally. Sensation intact. Reflexes are somewhat hyperactive, plantar reflexes downgoing bilaterally. Romberg patient does sway but she does not actually lose balance. When she walks, she has a shuffling gait and is extremely unsteady but does not favor one direction or the other. She has a mild tremor, but there is no rigidity. Finger to nose movement is extremely slow, but she is able to do this. Complete blood count is basically unremarkable. SCGII shows elevation of the liver enzymes. Electrocardiogram shows normal sinus rhythm with no acute changes. Ethanol level was negative.

Diagnosis: Ataxia and vertigo. Uncertain etiology. Rule out exacerbation of Parkinson's disease. Rule out basilar vertebral cerebral vascular accident, rule out acute labyrinthitis.

Treatment: Patient was admitted by Dr. Chase for further evaluation and treatment.

Physician Orders:

Signature of ED Physician Reviewed and Approved: John Chase MD
ATP-B-S:02:1001261385: John Chase MD
(Signed: 05/10/YYYY 03:59:52 PM EST)

LATES, LONNIE	Admission: 05/10/YYYY		**Nursing Discharge Status Summary**
IPCase007	DOB: 02/08/YYYY		
Dr. BLACK	ROOM: 367		

1.	AFEBRILE:	X	Yes		No					
2.	WOUND:		CLEAN/DRY		Reddened		Infected			NA
3.	PAIN FREE:	X	Yes		No	If "No," describe:				
4.	POST-HOSPITAL INSTRUCTION SHEET GIVEN TO PATIENT/FAMILY:							Yes	X	No
	If NO, complete lines 5-8 below.									
5.	DIET:		Regular	X	Other (Describe): Soft					
6.	ACTIVITY:	X	Normal		Light		Limited		Bed rest	
7.	MEDICATIONS:	Symmetrel 100 milligrams 1 tablet by mouth every 12 hours; Halcion .25 milligrams one at bedtime if needed to sleep; Metamucil 1 tablespoon in a glass of milk or juice each day.								
8.	INSTRUCTIONS GIVEN TO PATIENT/FAMILY:				Call for appointment with Dr. Black for 05/17/YYYY at 12:40 pm					
9.	PATIENT/FAMILY verbalize understanding of instructions:					X	Yes		No	
10.	DISCHARGED at	1745	Via:	X	Wheelchair		Stretcher	X	Ambulance Co.	
	Accompanied by:	Reviewed and Approved: O. Richards, RN ATP-B-S:02:1001261385: O. Richards, RN (Signed: 05/14/YYYY 05:47:03 PM EST)				to	Front desk			
	COMMENTS:									

GLOBAL CARE MEDICAL CENTER ■ 100 MAIN ST, ALFRED NY 14802 ■ (607) 555-1234

LATES, LONNIE Admission: 05/10/YYYY
IPCase007 DOB: 02/08/YYYY
Dr. BLACK ROOM: 367

Patient Property Record

I understand that while the facility will be responsible for items deposited in the safe, I must be responsible for all items retained by me at the bedside. (Dentures kept at the bedside will be labeled, but the facility cannot assure responsibility for them.) I also recognize that the hospital cannot be held responsible for items brought in to me after this form has been completed and signed.

Reviewed and Approved: Lonnie Lates
ATP-B-S:02:1001261385: Lonnie Lates
(Signed: 05/10/YYYY 1:43:44 PM EST)

Signature of Patient

Reviewed and Approved: Andrea Witteman
ATP-B-S:02:1001261385: Andrea Witteman
(Signed: 05/10/YYYY 1:44:00 PM EST)

Signature of Witness

I have no money or valuables that I wish to deposit for safekeeping. I do not hold the facility responsible for any other money or valuables that I am retaining or will have brought in to me. I have been advised that it is recommended that I retain no more than $5.00 at the bedside.

Reviewed and Approved: Lonnie Lates
ATP-B-S:02:1001261385: Lonnie Lates
(Signed: 05/10/YYYY 1:46:44 PM EST)

Signature of Patient

Reviewed and Approved: Andrea Witteman
ATP-B-S:02:1001261385: Andrea Witteman
(Signed: 05/10/YYYY 1:48:28 PM EST)

Signature of Witness

I have deposited valuables in the facility safe. The envelope number is ________________.

Signature of Patient

Signature of Person Accepting Property

I understand that medications I have brought to the facility will be handled as recommended by my physician. This may include storage, disposal, or administration.

Signature of Patient

Signature of Witness

Global Care Medical Center ■ 100 Main St, Alfred NY 14802 ■ (607) 555-1234

IPCase008

Global Care Medical Center
100 Main St, Alfred NY 14802
(607) 555-1234
Hospital No. 999

Inpatient Face Sheet

Patient Name and Address	Gender	Race	Marital Status	Patient No.
SEGER, SAM	M	W	M	IPCase008
306 N. EAST STREET	**Date of Birth**	**Age**	**Maiden Name**	**Occupation**
ALMOND, NY 14804	06/08/YYYY	61	N/A	Grocer

Admission Date	Time	Discharge Date	Time	Length of Stay	Telephone Number
11-11-YYYY	21:30	11-22-YYYY	10:20	11 DAYS	(607)000-1398

Guarantor Name and Address	Next of Kin Name and Address
SEGER, SAM 306 N. EAST STREET ALMOND, NY 14804	SEGER, SANDY 306 N. EAST STREET ALMOND, NY 14804

Guarantor Telephone No.	Relationship to Patient	Next of Kin Telephone Number	Relationship to Patient
(607)000-1398	Self	(607)000-1398	Wife
Admitting Physician	**Service**	**Admit Type**	**Room Number/Bed**
John Chase, MD			369
Attending Physician	**Admitting Diagnosis**		
John Black, MD	Infected abdominal wound		
Primary Insurer	**Policy and Group Number**	**Secondary Insurer**	**Policy and Group Number**
Blue Cross of WNY	7894590345	Medicare	1402-8879

Diagnoses and Procedures	ICD Code
Principal Diagnosis	
Infected abdominal wound and massive cellulitis due to *Escherichia coli* and *Bacteroides fragilis*	
Secondary Diagnoses	
Candidiasis of the mouth History of colon cancer	
Principal Procedure	
Incision and drainage, with packing, of right lower quadrant subcutaneous wound infection.	
Secondary Procedures	

Discharge Instructions

Activity: ❒ Bedrest ❒ Light ❒ Usual ❒ Unlimited ❒ Other:

Diet: ❒ Regular ❒ Low Cholesterol ❒ Low Salt ❒ ADA ❒ ____Calorie

Follow-Up: ❒ Call for appointment ❒ Office appointment on ____ ❒ Other:

Special Instructions: None

Attending Physician Authentication: Reviewed and Approved: John Black MD
ATP-B-S:02:1001261385: John Black MD
(Signed: 11/11/YYYY 10:35:26 PM EST)

SEGER, SAM	Admission: 11/11/YYYY	**Consent to Admission**
IPCase008	DOB: 06/08/YYYY	
Dr. BLACK	ROOM: 369	

I, Sam Seger hereby consent to admission in the Global Care Medical Center (GCMC), and I further consent to such routine hospital care, diagnostic procedures, and medical treatment that the medical and professional staff of GCMC may deem necessary or advisable. I authorize the use of medical information obtained about me as specified above and the disclosure of such information to my referring physician(s). This form has been fully explained to me, and I understand its contents. I further understand that no guarantees have been made to me as to the results of treatments or examinations done at the GCMC.

Reviewed and Approved: Sam Seger
ATP-B-S:02:1001261385: Sam Seger
(Signed: 11/11/YYYY 10:45:05 PM EST)

Signature of Patient

Signature of Parent/Legal Guardian for Minor

Relationship to Minor

Reviewed and Approved: Andrea Witteman
ATP-B-S:02:1001261385: Andrea Witteman
(Signed: 11/11/YYYY 10:46:34 PM EST)

WITNESS: Global Care Medical Center Staff Member

Consent To Release Information For Reimbursement Purposes

In order to permit reimbursement, upon request, the Global Care Medical Center (GCMC) may disclose such treatment information pertaining to my hospitalization to any corporation, organization, or agent thereof, which is, or may be liable under contract to the GCMC or to me, or to any of my family members or other person, for payment of all or part of the GCMC's charges for services rendered to me (e.g. the patient's health insurance carrier). I understand that the purpose of any release of information is to facilitate reimbursement for services rendered. In addition, in the event that my health insurance program includes utilization review of services provided during this admission. I authorize GCMC to release information as is necessary to permit the review. This authorization will expire once the reimbursement for services rendered is complete.

Reviewed and Approved: Sam Seger
ATP-B-S:02:1001261385: Sam Seger
(Signed: 11/11/YYYY 10:47:05 PM EST)

Signature of Patient

Signature of Parent/Legal Guardian for Minor

Relationship to Minor

Reviewed and Approved: Andrea Witteman
ATP-B-S:02:1001261385: Andrea Witteman
(Signed: 11/11/YYYY 10:47:56 PM EST)

WITNESS: Global Care Medical Center Staff Member

Global Care Medical Center ■ 100 Main St, Alfred NY 14802 ■ (607) 555-1234

SEGER, SAM	Admission: 11/11/YYYY	**Advance Directive**
IPCase008	DOB: 06/08/YYYY	
Dr. BLACK	ROOM: 369	

Your answers to the following questions will assist your Physician and the Hospital to respect your wishes regarding your medical care. This information will become a part of your medical record.

	Yes	No	Patient's Initials
1. Have you been provided with a copy of the information called "Patient Rights Regarding Health Care Decision"?	X		
2. Have you prepared a "Living Will"? If yes, please provide the Hospital with a copy for your medical record.		X	
3. Have you prepared a Durable Power of Attorney for Health Care? If yes, please provide the Hospital with a copy for your medical record.		X	
4. Have you provided this facility with an Advance Directive on a prior admission and is it still in effect? If yes, Admitting Office to contact Medical Records to obtain a copy for the medical record.		X	
5. Do you desire to execute a Living Will/Durable Power of Attorney? If yes, refer to in order: a. Physician b. Social Service c. Volunteer Service		X	

Hospital Staff Directions: Check when each step is completed.

1. ✓ Verify the above questions were answered and actions taken where required.
2. ✓ If the "Patient Rights" information was provided to someone other than the patient, state reason:

____

______________________ ______________________

Name of Individual Receiving Information **Relationship to Patient**

3. ✓ If information was provided in a language other than English, specify language and method.
4. ✓ Verify patient was advised on how to obtain additional information on Advance Directives.
5. ✓ Verify the Patient/Family Member/Legal Representative was asked to provide the Hospital with a copy of the Advanced Directive which will be retained in the medical record.

Fill this form in the medical record, and give a copy to the patient

____

Name of Patient/Name of Individual giving information if different from Patient

Reviewed and Approved: Sam Seger
ATP-B-S:02:1001261385: Sam Seger
(Signed: 11/11/YYYY 10:51:05 PM EST)

Signature of Patient **Date**

Reviewed and Approved: Andrea Witteman
ATP-B-S:02:1001261385: Andrea Witteman
(Signed: 11/11/YYYY 10:52:47 PM EST)

Signature of Hospital Representative **Date**

Global Care Medical Center ■ 100 Main St, Alfred NY 14802 ■ (607) 555-1234

SEGER, SAM	Admission: 11/11/YYYY	**Discharge Summary**
IPCase008	DOB: 06/08/YYYY	
Dr. BLACK	ROOM: 369	

ADMISSION DATE: 11/11/YYYY DISCHARGE DATE: 11/22/YYYY

ADMISSION DIAGNOSIS: Secondarily infected right lower quadrant incision.

DISCHARGE DIAGNOSIS: Same, due to *Escherichia coli* and *Bacteroides fragilis*. Candidiasis, mouth.

OPERATION: Incision and drainage, with packing, of right lower quadrant subcutaneous wound infection.

SURGEON: Dr. Henson DATE: 11/15/YYYY COMPLICATIONS: None

SUMMARY: Patient is a 61-year-old male who recently had an appendectomy because the appendix had a fecalith in it, and he had had low anterior bowel resection, with radiotherapy, to the pelvis a year plus ago, and we were afraid the chance was high that he might get acute appendicitis with abscess, that we decided to do an appendectomy electively. The appendectomy was done, and the radiotherapied bowel reacted and he ended up with a bowel obstruction which required further surgery, and nutritionally, while this was all healing, he went downhill and had to recover. He did recover slowly and was discharged. However, not many days after discharge, with his incisions both healing well, he began to get sore in the right lower quadrant appendectomy incision and was seen in the Emergency Room with an obvious secondary wound infection in that incision. This was opened in the Emergency Room and drained by Dr. Sizemore, and the patient was admitted and placed on IV antibiotics. This was over the weekend. When I saw him on Monday morning, I believed this still needed to be opened up more. There had been essentially no change in the PMH and H&P from his last admission, except that he had some redness along the right flank and lateral wall, along with this obvious secondary wound infection, and it was felt at the time that he may have secondary cellulites in that area.

Laboratory work revealed normal hemoglobin, hematocrit, and white blood count, with a slight left shift. He was treated appropriately, and by the time I saw him I felt it could be opened up some more and drained further and packed and took him to the operating room and did this without problem under local anesthetic. Since that time, irrigations have been with strong Betadine solution, and then with half-strength peroxide every 4 hours. The redness in the flank went away. The incision still continues with some purulent drainage in the morning mostly, but I suspect this was the night shift, from what the patient says, was not really irrigating this as vigorously as I'd like them to, and it has been fine during the day. The packing was pulled 24 hours later, and irrigations were begun, and since then he is slowly recovering nutritionally; I put him on a high-calorie, high-protein-type diet, encouraged ambulation and moving around, with physical therapy. He has done well, and I think he is ready to go home at this point. Both he and his wife know how to irrigate this. His temperature went down, and the curve has been down since; he has been afebrile for the past 48 hours. The Keflex has been

DD: 11/22/YYYY
DT: 11/22/YYYY

continued on page 2

Physician Authentication

SEGER, SAM Admission: 11/11/YYYY

IPCase008 DOB: 06/08/YYYY

Dr. BLACK ROOM: 369

Discharge Summary

Page two continuation

stopped, and he really has done well from that standpoint. His abdominal incision looks good. The staples were removed from that during this hospitalization, and the rest of the abdominal wall seems to be healing nicely. He is being discharged with adequate instructions to see me next Tuesday and his family doctor sometime thereafter. With all the antibiotics he has been on for this problem in the last month or two, he has been on broad spectrum antibiotics at various periods of time, and he did develop what appeared to be oral candidiasis; this was treated and will continue to be treated until the 14 days, and this should be at least a week after the antibiotics are discontinued, so his mouth is healing up nicely.

DD: 11/22/YYYY

DT: 11/22/YYYY

Reviewed and Approved: John Black MD
ATP-B-S:02:1001261385: John Black MD
(Signed: 11/22/YYYY 10:24:44 PM EST)

Physician Authentication

GLOBAL CARE MEDICAL CENTER ■ 100 MAIN ST, ALFRED NY 14802 ■ (607) 555-1234

SEGER, SAM Admission: 11/11/YYYY
IPCase008 DOB: 06/08/YYYY
Dr. BLACK ROOM: 369

History & Physical Exam

CHIEF COMPLAINT AND HISTORY OF PRESENT ILLNESS: This 61-year-old male is admitted to the hospital from the Emergency Room with a fever of 102, tender, red abdomen on the right side over his McBurney wound and the lateral flank area. He appears very ill, obviously has a cellulitis. The swelling over the flank area on the right almost looks like a paranephric type of abscess. He is fluctuant over the McBurney wound which was aspirated and purulent foul-smelling pus was obtained and sent to the Lab for culture and sensitivity, both aerobic and anaerobic. He was admitted to the hospital directly from the Emergency Room.

PAST MEDICAL HISTORY: His previous history is that he had originally, 2 years ago, a colectomy for malignancy and followed by radiation therapy. He then had an interval appendectomy done a few weeks ago. Following this he developed a severe ileus, what was thought to be mechanical obstruction requiring a secondary operation in 6 days. No definite mechanical obstruction was found at that time, but the bowel was quite thickened. It did not seem to respond in the normal manner. Following this he remained in the hospital for 2 more weeks and was very slow to regain peristaltic sounds. At the time of discharge 2 days ago, he did complain of some swelling and redness in the posterior right flank and lateral area, but it was not thought to be too significant at that time. He went home and has gradually worsened and this evening came in quite ill with his markedly swollen right flank and the McBurney wound with obvious infection.

The remainder of history is unchanged from previous admission.

GENERAL: Reveals a 61-year-old male, appearing quite ill.

HEAD and Neck: Normal.

EYES, EARS, NOSE and THROAT: Eyes - pupils are round, regular and equal, and react to light and accommodation. Extraocular movements are normal. Ears - externally negative.

CHEST: Normal cage, no lag. Lung fields clear to auscultation.

LUNGS: Regular in rate, rhythm, and force, without murmurs.

ABDOMEN: Obese. Linear incision of the abdomen still has clips in place and appears to be healing well, did not appear to be infected; however, the McBurney wound is quite reddened, and I detect a fluctuant area toward the center. The whole right flank is swollen, reddened, pitting edema, almost like an erysipelas or a paranephric abscess in this area. However, under 1% Carbocaine anesthesia, a tiny incision was made over the fluctuant area and an abundant amount of purulent material was obtained, 2 drains were placed into the area, and the pus was sent to the lab for culture and sensitivity.

continued on page 2

DD: 11/12/YYYY
DT: 11/12/YYYY

Physician Authentication

GLOBAL CARE MEDICAL CENTER ■ 100 MAIN ST, ALFRED NY 14802 ■ (607) 555-1234

SEGER, SAM Admission: 11/11/YYYY
IPCase008 DOB: 06/08/YYYY
Dr. BLACK ROOM: 369

History & Physical Exam

Page 2 continuation

GENITALIA: Normal.

RECTAL: Deferred.

EXTREMITIES: Negative.

REFLEXES: Physiological.

IMPRESSION: Overwhelming abdominal wall infection, cellulitis, and purulent abscess pointing over McBurney area but also in the lateral flank, seemed to be a deep-seated infection.

Reviewed and Approved: Kathleen Hepburn MD
ATP-B-S:02:1001261385: Kathleen Hepburn MD
(Signed: 11/12/YYYY 11:06:34 AM EST)

DD: 11/12/YYYY

DT: 11/12/YYYY

Physician Authentication

SEGER, SAM Admission: 11/11/YYYY
IPCase008 DOB: 06/08/YYYY
Dr. BLACK ROOM: 369

Progress Notes

Date	Time	Physician's signature required for each order. (Please skip one line between dates.)
11/11/YYYY	2235	Chief complaint: Fever with malaise. Pain from large swollen right flank area and appendectomy wound. Diagnosis: Pus from appendectomy wound obtained by aspiration and sent to laboratory for culture and sensitivity. Massive cellulites and deep infection right lateral abdominal wall. Appendectomy wound area. Plan of Treatment: Admitted for intravenous antibiotic management; drainage by incision and drainage as needed. DISCHARGE PLAN: Home. No services needed. Reviewed and Approved: John Black MD ATP-B-S:02:1001261385: John Black MD (Signed: 11/11/YYYY 10:50:55 PM EST)
11/11/YYYY	2315	Wound still draining as needed. Patient is afebrile; abdomen soft and non-tender with good bowel sounds. Bowels moving without problem. Will take to operating room and open drain site up a little more. Reviewed and Approved: John Black MD ATP-B-S:02:1001261385: John Black MD (Signed: 11/11/YYYY 11:17:22 PM EST)
11/12/YYYY	0930	Temperature 99.2 this morning. More purulent drainage from drain site but considerable edema, flank and right abdomen. Patient is very ill. Reviewed and Approved: Kathleen Hepburn MD ATP-B-S:02:1001261385: Kathleen Hepburn MD (Signed: 11/12/YYYY 09:37:56 AM EST)
11/13/YYYY	1015	Drainage still profuse. Seems better today. Reviewed and Approved: Kathleen Hepburn MD ATP-B-S:02:1001261385: Kathleen Hepburn MD (Signed: 11/13/YYYY 10:17:56 AM EST)

GLOBAL CARE MEDICAL CENTER ■ 100 MAIN ST, ALFRED NY 14802 ■ (607) 555-1234

SEGER, SAM	Admission: 11/11/YYYY	**Progress Notes**
IPCase008	DOB: 06/08/YYYY	
Dr. BLACK	ROOM: 369	

Date	Time	Physician's signature required for each order. (Please skip one line between dates.)
11/14/YYYY	1100	Vital signs reveal low-grade temperature. Pus noted from drain site. Will begin half strength hydrogen peroxide irrigation vigorously and discontinue intravenous antibiotics. The major bacteria is *E. coli,* as I suspected and oral Velosef should treat it adequately. Mouth mucus is reddened and sore, dry. Will begin oral mycostatin as probably is Candida as he was on antibiotics for some time recently. We need to build him up nutritionally. Reviewed and Approved: John Black MD ATP-B-S:02:1001261385: John Black MD (Signed: 11/14/YYYY 11:02:29 AM EST)
11/15/YYYY	0715	Drain site opened, wound irrigated with Betadine and packed with Iodoform gauze. Tolerated well. Reviewed and Approved: John Black MD ATP-B-S:02:1001261385: John Black MD (Signed: 11/15/YYYY 07:16:19 AM EST)
11/16/YYYY	0930	Iodoform drain removed and will begin irrigation again. Abdomen incision healing well. Everything decreasing in right flank area. Progressing. Reviewed and Approved: John Black MD ATP-B-S:02:1001261385: John Black MD (Signed: 11/16/YYYY 09:31:29 AM EST)
11/17/YYYY	0900	Fall on floor, accidentally yesterday. Reviewed and Approved: John Black MD ATP-B-S:02:1001261385: John Black MD (Signed: 11/17/YYYY 09:01:54 AM EST)
11/17/YYYY	0930	Vital signs intact, afebrile this morning. Less drainage-irrigation helping considerably. Mouth Candida is clearing up. He looks and feels much better. Still need to monitor nitrogen balance. Reviewed and Approved: John Black MD ATP-B-S:02:1001261385: John Black MD (Signed: 11/17/YYYY 09:31:54 AM EST)

GLOBAL CARE MEDICAL CENTER ■ 100 MAIN ST, ALFRED NY 14802 ■ (607) 555-1234

SEGER, SAM IPCase008 Dr. BLACK	Admission: 11/11/YYYY DOB: 06/08/YYYY ROOM: 369	**Progress Notes**

Date	Time	Physician's signature required for each order. (Please skip one line between dates.)
11/18/YYYY	1530	Vital signs intact, afebrile. All staples removed from mid-line incision, that wound is healing well. Still getting purulence from right lower quadrant wound-but irrigations are beginning to clear it up. Reviewed and Approved: John Black MD ATP-B-S:02:1001261385: John Black MD (Signed: 11/18/YYYY 03:36:35 PM EST)
11/19/YYYY	0855	Draining from right lower quadrant drain site. Wound looks clean, afebrile. Reviewed and Approved: Kathleen Hepburn MD ATP-B-S:02:1001261385: Kathleen Hepburn MD (Signed: 11/19/YYYY 08:59:40 AM EST)
11/20/YYYY	0830	Afebrile. No complaints. Bowels moving. Reviewed and Approved: Kathleen Hepburn MD ATP-B-S:02:1001261385: Kathleen Hepburn MD (Signed: 11/20/YYYY 08:32:22 AM EST)
11/21/YYYY	1300	Vital signs intact, afebrile this afternoon. Wound looks clean. Patient is gaining strength. Reviewed and Approved: John Black MD ATP-B-S:02:1001261385: John Black MD (Signed: 11/21/YYYY 01:36:35 PM EST)
11/22/YYYY	0930	Vital signs intact, afebrile. Abdomen soft. Both he and his wife can do the irrigation. May go home today. Reviewed and Approved: John Black MD ATP-B-S:02:1001261385: John Black MD (Signed: 11/22/YYYY 09:36:01 AM EST)

GLOBAL CARE MEDICAL CENTER ■ 100 MAIN ST, ALFRED NY 14802 ■ (607) 555-1234

SEGER, SAM	Admission: 11/11/YYYY	**Doctors' Orders**
IPCase008	DOB: 06/08/YYYY	
Dr. BLACK	ROOM: 369	

Date	Time	Physician's signature required for each order. (Please skip one line between dates.)
11/11/YYYY	2240	1. Culture and sensitivities from pus of abdominal wall abscess 2. Continue pHisoHex compresses to right abdominal wall - lateral and posterior 3. Patient may require slight modification to lateral position to apply compress 4. Meloxin GM 2 every six hours intravenous 5. Ampicillin gm 1 every six hours intravenous 6. Keep intravenous open for antibiotics 7. Isolation in private room. 8. Demerol 50 milligrams every 4 hours as needed for pain or 9. Tylenol plus codeine #3 2 tablets every 4 hours as needed for pain 10. Dalmane 30 milligrams bedtime 11. Complete blood count 12. Metamucil 3 tablespoons in glass of water or orange juice three times a day. 13. Diet as tolerated and desired 14. Change dressings as needed. 15. Old chart Reviewed and Approved: John Black MD ATP-S-S:02:1001261385: John Black MD (Signed: 11/11/YYYY 10:45:00 PM EST)
11/12/YYYY	0930	Continue intravenous and antibiotic Reviewed and Approved: Kathleen Hepburn MD ATP-B-S:02:1001261385: Kathleen Hepburn MD (Signed: 11/12/YYYY 09:31:20 AM EST)
11/13/YYYY	1015	Continue intravenous and antibiotic Reviewed and Approved: Kathleen Hepburn MD ATP-B-S:02:1001261385: Kathleen Hepburn MD (Signed: 11/13/YYYY 10:18:44 AM EST)
11/13/YYYY	1900	Phenergan 50 milligrams intramuscular every 4 hours as needed for nausea. Reviewed and Approved: O. Richards, RN ATP-B-S:02:1001261385: O. Richards, RN (Signed: 11/13/YYYY 07:02:17 PM EST)

GLOBAL CARE MEDICAL CENTER ■ 100 MAIN ST, ALFRED NY 14802 ■ (607) 555-1234

SEGER, SAM	Admission: 11/11/YYYY	**Doctors' Orders**
IPCase008	DOB: 06/08/YYYY	
Dr. BLACK	ROOM: 369	

Date	Time	Physician's signature required for each order. (Please skip one line between dates.)
11/14/YYYY	0900	1. House diet as desired. 2. Motrin 600 milligrams by mouth every 6 hours as needed for milder pain 3. May use heating pad or hot water bottle. 4. Discontinue Meloxin, Ampicillin 5. Discontinue intravenous when tolerated.--?? 6. By mouth fluids 7. Give Velosef 250 milligrams by mouth 4 times a day 8. Irrigate drain site vigorously 4 times a day half strength hydrogen peroxide. 9. Give Mycostatin oral suspension 5 cc by mouth 4 times a day with half dose in each side of mouth, retain as long as possible before swallowing. 10. Ascorbic acid 500 milligrams by mouth 4 times a day. 11. Multivitamin 1 tablet by mouth twice a day. 12. Discontinue isolation. 13. Out of bed as desired. 14. Give patient milk shakes, etc. or other high-calorie, high-protein supplements, as desired. Reviewed and Approved: John Black MD ATP-S-S:02:1001261385: John Black MD (Signed: 11/14/YYYY 09:24:20 AM EST)
11/15/YYYY	0710	1. Ambulate in halls, especially after irrigation. 2. Make irrigation every 6 hours. Reviewed and Approved: John Black MD ATP-B-S:02:1001261385: John Black MD (Signed: 11/15/YYYY 07:16:17 AM EST)
11/15/YYYY	1210	1. Discontinue irrigation until reorder. 2. Motrin 600 milligrams by mouth every 6 hours as needed for pain (milder). 3. Give Talwin 1 tablet by mouth every 6 hours as needed for more severe pain. Reviewed and Approved: John Black MD ATP-B-S:02:1001261385: John Black MD (Signed: 11/15/YYYY 12:15:31 AM EST)
11/16/YYYY	0930	1. Dalmane 30 milligrams by mouth every evening at bedtime as needed for sleep. 2. Begin irrigation every 4 hours with half strength hydrogen peroxide vigorously (all over cavity). Reviewed and Approved: John Black MD ATP-B-S:02:1001261385: John Black MD (Signed: 11/16/YYYY 09:36:23 AM EST)

GLOBAL CARE MEDICAL CENTER ■ 100 MAIN ST, ALFRED NY 14802 ■ (607) 555-1234

SEGER, SAM	Admission: 11/11/YYYY	**Doctors' Orders**
IPCase008	DOB: 06/08/YYYY	
Dr. BLACK	ROOM: 369	

Date	Time	Physician's signature required for each order. (Please skip one line between dates.)
11/17/YYYY	0930	Change irrigation to a strong Betadine solution in normal saline solution (25 centimeters in 500 cc normal saline solution) and do every 4 hours. Reviewed and Approved: John Black MD ATP-B-S:02:1001261385: John Black MD (Signed: 11/17/YYYY 09:34:29 AM EST)
11/18/YYYY	1530	Begin then half strength hydrogen peroxide irrigation every 4 hours. Reviewed and Approved: John Black MD ATP-B-S:02:1001261385: John Black MD (Signed: 11/18/YYYY 03:16:17 PM EST)
11/19/YYYY	0855	May have low enema if necessary. Reviewed and Approved: John Black MD ATP-B-S:02:1001261385: John Black MD (Signed: 11/19/YYYY 08:59:31 AM EST)
11/21/YYYY	1300	1. Discontinue Keflex. 2. See primary care doctor in 2 weeks and me on next Tuesday. Reviewed and Approved: John Black MD ATP-B-S:02:1001261385: John Black MD (Signed: 11/21/YYYY 01:02:54 PM EST)
11/22/YYYY	0930	May be discharged today. Reviewed and Approved: John Black MD ATP-B-S:02:1001261385: John Black MD (Signed: 11/22/YYYY 09:36:23 AM EST)

GLOBAL CARE MEDICAL CENTER ■ 100 MAIN ST, ALFRED NY 14802 ■ (607) 555-1234

SEGER, SAM	Admission: 11/11/YYYY	**Laboratory Data**
IPCase008	DOB: 06/08/YYYY	
Dr. BLACK	ROOM: 369	

TIME IN: 11/11/YYYY 2302 TIME OUT: 11/11/YYYY 2316

CBC S DIFF

TEST	RESULT	FLAG	REFERENCE
WBC	9.7		4.5-11.0 thous/UL
RBC	3.85		5.2-5.4 mill/UL
HGB	12.0		11.7-16.1 g/dl
HCT	35.3		35.0-47.0 %
MCV	91.6		85-99 fL.
MCH	31.1		
MCHC	33.9		33-37
RDW			11.4-14.5
PTL	501.		130-400 thous/UL
SEGS %	83		
LYMPH %	5		20.5-51.1
MONO %	8		1.7-9.3
EOS %			
BASO %			
BAND %	4		
GRAN %			42.2-75.2
LYMPH $\times 10^3$			1.2-3.4
MONO $\times 10^3$			0.11-0.59
GRAN $\times 10^3$			1.4-6.5
EOS $\times 10^3$			0.0-0.7
BASO $\times 10^3$			0.0-0.2
ANISO			

End of Report

GLOBAL CARE MEDICAL CENTER ■ 100 MAIN ST, ALFRED NY 14802 ■ (607) 555-1234

SEGER, SAM	Admission: 11/11/YYYY	**Laboratory Data**
IPCase008	DOB: 06/08/YYYY	
Dr. BLACK	ROOM: 369	

TIME IN: 11/14/YYYY 0307 TIME OUT: 11/14/YYYY 1033

CBC S DIFF

TEST	RESULT	FLAG	REFERENCE
WBC	9.1		4.5-11.0 thous/UL
RBC	3.53		5.2-5.4 mill/UL
HGB	11.1		11.7-16.1 g/dl
HCT	32.2		35.0-47.0 %
MCV	91.1		85-99 fL.
MCH	31.5		
MCHC	34.5		33-37
RDW			11.4-14.5
PTL	456.		130-400 thous/UL
SEGS %	74		
LYMPH %	10		20.5-51.1
MONO %	3		1.7-9.3
EOS %			
METAS %	1		
BAND %	12		
GRAN %			42.2-75.2
LYMPH × 10^3			1.2-3.4
MONO × 10^3			0.11-0.59
GRAN × 10^3			1.4-6.5
EOS × 10^3			0.0-0.7
BASO × 10^3			0.0-0.2
ANISO			

End of Report

GLOBAL CARE MEDICAL CENTER ■ 100 MAIN ST, ALFRED NY 14802 ■ (607) 555-1234

SEGER, SAM	Admission: 11/11/YYYY	**Laboratory Data**
IPCase008	DOB: 06/08/YYYY	
Dr. BLACK	ROOM: 369	

SPECIMEN COLLECTED: 11/11/YYYY 2200 **SPECIMEN RECEIVED:** 11/11/YYYY 2330

TEST	RESULT
BACTERIOLOGY	OTHER ROUTINE CULTURES
SOURCE:	Wound (abdomen)
SMEAR ONLY:	3+ white blood cells, 4+ gram negative rods 1+ gram positive cocci
CULTURE	
1st PRELIMINARY	6 2+ gram negative rods
2nd PRELIMINARY	
FINAL REPORT	1. 2+ *E coli*
	2. 4+ *Bacteroides fragilis*

SENSITIVITIES	1.	S	AMIKACIN	1.	S	NITROFURANTOIN
R = Resistant	1.	S	AMPICILLIN			PENICILLIN G
S = Sensitive	1.	S	CARBENICILLIN			POLYMYXIN B
> = greater than	1.	S	CEFAMANDOLE	1.	S	SULFISOXAZOLE
	1.	S	CEFOXITIN	1.	S	TETRACYCLINE
	1.	S	CEPHALOTHIN	1.	S	TRIMETHOPRIM
	1.	S	CHLORAMPHENICOL			VANCOMYCIN
			CLINDAMYCIN			
			ERYTHROMYCIN			
	1.	S	GENTAMICIN			
			KANAMYCIN			
			METHICILLIN			
			NALIDIXIC ACID			

GLOBAL CARE MEDICAL CENTER ■ 100 MAIN ST, ALFRED NY 14802 ■ (607) 555-1234

SEGER, SAM	Admission: 11/11/YYYY	**Laboratory Data**
IPCase008	DOB: 06/08/YYYY	
Dr. BLACK	ROOM: 369	

SPECIMEN COLLECTED: 11/13/YYYY 0800 SPECIMEN RECEIVED : 11/13/YYYY 1047

URINALYSIS

TEST	RESULT	FLAG	REFERENCE
DIPSTICK ONLY			
COLOR	Amber		
Ph.	6.0		5-8.0
SP. GR.	1.027		≤ 1.030
ALBUMIN	Negative		
SUGAR	Negative		≤ 10 mg/dl
ACETONE	Negative		
BILIRUBIN	Negative		≤ 0.8 mg/dl
BLOOD	Negative		0.06 mg/dl hgb
REDUCING			≤ -1 mg/dl
EPITH:	Rare		
W.B.C.:	Rare		≤ 5/hpf
R.B.C.:			≤ 5/hpf
BACT.:	Few		1+(≤ 20/hpf)
CASTS:			
CRYSTALS:	Rare Calcium Oxalate		

End of Report

GLOBAL CARE MEDICAL CENTER ■ 100 MAIN ST, ALFRED NY 14802 ■ (607) 555-1234

SEGER, SAM	Admission: 11/11/YYYY	**Consent for Operation(s) and/or Procedure(s) and Anesthesia**
IPCase008	DOB: 06/08/YYYY	
Dr. BLACK	ROOM: 369	

PERMISSION. I hereby authorize Dr. Henson, or associates of his/her choice at the Global Care Medical Center (the "Hospital") to perform upon Sam Seger

the following operation(s) and/or procedure(s): Incision and drainage of the old appendectomy incision secondary wound infection, including such photography, videotaping, televising or other observation of the operation(s)/procedure(s) as may be purposeful for the advance of medical knowledge and/or education, with the understanding that the patient's identity will remain anonymous.

EXPLANATION OF PROCEDURE, RISKS, BENEFITS, ALTERNATIVES. Dr. Henson

has fully explained to me the nature and purposes of the operation(s)/procedures named above and has also informed me of expected benefits and complications, attendant discomforts and risks that may arise, as well as possible alternatives to the proposed treatment. I have been given an opportunity to ask questions and all my questions have been answered fully and satisfactorily.

UNFORESEEN CONDITIONS. I understand that during the course of the operation(s) or procedure(s) unforeseen conditions may arise which necessitate procedures in addition to or different from those contemplated. I. therefore, consent to the performance of additional operations and procedures which the above-named physician or his/her associates or assistants may consider necessary.

ANESTHESIA. I further consent to the administration of such anesthesia as may be considered necessary by the above-named physician or his/her associates or assistants. I recognize that there are always risks to life and health associated with anesthesia. Such risks have been fully explained to me and I have been given an opportunity to ask questions and all my questions have been answered fully and satisfactorily.

SPECIMENS. Any organs or tissues surgically removed may be examined and retained by the Hospital for medical, scientific or educational purposes and such tissues or parts may be disposed of in accordance with accustomed practice and applicable State laws and/or regulations.

NO GUARANTEES. I acknowledge that no guarantees or assurances have been made to me concerning the operation(s) or procedure(s) described above.

MEDICAL DEVICE TRACKING. I hereby authorize the release of my Social Security number to the manufacturer of the medical device(s) I receive, if applicable, in accordance with federal law and regulations which may be used to help locate me if a need arises with regard to this medical device. I release The Global Care Medical Center from any liability that might result from the release of this information.*

UNDERSTANDING OF THIS FORM. I confirm that I have read this form, fully understand its contents, and that all blank spaces above have been completed prior to my signing. I have crossed out any paragraphs above that do not pertain to me.

Patient/Relative/Guardian*

Reviewed and Approved: San Seger
ATP-B-S:02:1001261385: Sam Seger
(Signed:11/11/YYYY 4:51:05 PM EST)

Signature

Relationship, if other than patient signed:

Witness

Reviewed and Approved: William Preston
ATP-B-S:02:1001261385: William Preston
(Signed:11/11/YYYY 4:52:47 PM EST)

Signature

Date 11/11/YYYY

*The signature of the patient must be obtained unless the patient is an unemancipated minor under the age of 18 or is otherwise incompetent to sign.

PHYSICIAN'S CERTIFICATION. I hereby certify that I have explained the nature, purpose, benefits, risks of and alternatives to the operation(s)/procedure(s), have offered to answer any questions and have fully answered all such questions. I believe that the patient (relative/guardian) fully understands what I have explained and answered.

PHYSICIAN:

Reviewed and Approved: Gregory Henson MD
ATP-B-S:02:1001261385: Gregory Henson MD
(Signed: 11/11/YYYY 5:24:44 PM EST)

Signature

11/11/YYYY

Date

GLOBAL CARE MEDICAL CENTER ■ 100 MAIN ST, ALFRED NY 14802 ■ (607) 555-1234

SEGER, SAM
IPCase008
Dr.BLACK

Admission: 11/11/YYYY
DOB: 06/08/YYYY
ROOM: 369

Operative Report

PREOPERATIVE DIAGNOSIS: Secondary wound infection of appendectomy incision.

POSTOPERATIVE DISGNOSIS: Same

OPERATION PERFORMED: Further incision and drainage of old appendectomy incision secondary wound infection.

SURGEON: Dr. Henson ASSISTANT: N/A DATE: 11/15/YYYY

ANESTHESIA: Local anesthesia. DRAINS: Iodoform gauze. COMPLICATIONS: None

OPERATIVE NOTE: The patient was brought into the Outpatient Operating Room and after adequate prepping of this right lower quadrant incision that he developed a secondary wound infection of the subcutaneous tissue was adequately prepped. An incision and drainage procedure was previously performed on the wound by Dr. Sizemore. I put some local anesthetic around the recent incision and drainage site and proceeded to use a knife blade to open this up, so it is about 2 ½ centimeters long, opened it nicely, irrigated the subcutaneous tissue where the infection is with some good strong Betadine solution and packed the cavity with Iodoform gauze. The patient tolerated the procedure well, and he left the Operating Room for his room in satisfactory condition.

DD: 11/15/YYYY

Reviewed and Approved:
Gregory Henson MD
ATP-B-S:02:1001261385:
Gregory Henson MD
(Signed: 11/15/YYYY 5:24:44 PM EST)

Physician Authentication

DT: 11/15/YYYY

GLOBAL CARE MEDICAL CENTER ■ 100 MAIN ST, ALFRED NY 14802 ■ (607) 555-1234

SEGER, SAM	Admission: 11/11/YYYY	**Medication Administration Record**
IPCase008	DOB: 06/08/YYYY	
Dr. BLACK	ROOM: 369	

SPECIAL INSTRUCTIONS: N/A

MEDICATION (dose and route)	**DATE:** 11/12 **TIME**	**INITIALS**	**DATE:** 11/13 **TIME**	**INITIALS**	**DATE:** 11/14 **TIME**	**INITIALS**	**DATE:** 11/15 **TIME**	**INITIALS**
Meloxin 2 grams every 6 hours	2400	JD	2400	JD	2400	JD		
TV	0600	JD	0600	JD	0600	JD		
	1200	VS	1200	VS				
Ampicillin 1 gram every 6 hours	2400	JD	2400	JD	2400	JD		
TV	0600	JD	0600	JD	0600	JD		
	1200	VS	1200	VS				
	1800	OR	1800	OR				
Metamucil in glass of water or orange juice three times a day	0800	VS	0800	VS	0800	VS	0800	VS
	1300	VS	1300	VS	1300	VS	1300	VS
	1800	OR	1800	OR	1800	OR	1800	OR
Dalmane 30 milligrams at bedtime	2100	OR	2100	OR	2100	OR	2100	OR
Velosef 250 milligrams by mouth four times a day.	0800	----	0800	----	0800	VS	0800	
	1200	----	1200	----	1200	VS	1200	VS
	1600	----	1600	----	1600	OR	1600	OR
	2000	----	2000	----	2000	OR	2000	OR
Mycostatin oral suspension 5 centimeters by mouth 4 times a day - give ½ dose in each side of mouth - retain as long as possible before swallowing	0800	----	0800	----	0800	----	0800	VS
	1200	----	1200	----	1200	VS	1200	VS
	1600	----	1600	----	1600	OR	1600	OR
	2000	----	2000	----	2000	OR	2000	OR
Ascorbic acid 500 milligrams by mouth 4 times a day.	0800	----	0800	----	0800	----	0800	VS
	1200	----	1200	----	1200	VS	1200	VS
	1600	----	1600	----	1600	OR	1600	OR
	2000	----	2000	----	2000	OR	2000	OR
Multivitamin 1 tablet by mouth twice a day.	0800	----	0800	----	0800	----	0800	VS
	1600	----	1600	----	1600	OR	1600	OR

INITIALS	**SIGNATURE AND TITLE**	**INITIALS**	**SIGNATURE AND TITLE**	**INITIALS**	**SIGNATURE AND TITLE**
VS	Vera South, RN	GPW	G.P.Well, RN		
OR	Ora Richards, RN	PS	P.Small, RN		
JD	Jane Dobbs, RN				
HF	H.Figgs, RN				

GLOBAL CARE MEDICAL CENTER ■ 100 MAIN ST, ALFRED NY 14802 ■ (607) 555-1234

SEGER, SAM	Admission: 11/11/YYYY	**Medication Administration Record**
IPCase008	DOB: 06/08/YYYY	
Dr. BLACK	ROOM: 369	

SPECIAL INSTRUCTIONS: N/A

MEDICATION (dose and route)	DATE: 11/12 TIME	INITIALS	DATE: 11/13 TIME	INITIALS	DATE: 11/14 TIME	INITIALS	DATE: 11/15 TIME	INITIALS
PRN Medications								
Demerol 50 milligrams every 4 hours as needed for pain.	error	error						
Tylenol with codeine #3 2 tablets every 4 hours as needed for pain.	0015							
	1600							
	2000							
					1400	OR		
Phenergan 50 milligrams intramuscular every 4 hours as needed for nausea	1900	----	OR					
	2345	----	JD		2140	OR		
Motrin 600 milligrams by mouth every 6 hours as for needed for milder pain.	1030	----	1030	----	1030		1030	OR
Talwin 1 tablet by mouth every 6 hours as needed for more severe pain.	1210	----	1210	----	1210	----	1210	VS
	1915	----	1915	----	1915	----	1915	OR
Dalmane 30 milligrams by mouth every bedtime as needed for sleep.								

INITIALS	SIGNATURE AND TITLE	INITIALS	SIGNATURE AND TITLE	INITIALS	SIGNATURE AND TITLE
VS	Vera South, RN	GPW	G.P.Well, RN		
OR	Ora Richards, RN	PS	P.Small, RN		
JD	Jane Dobbs, RN				
HF	H.Figgs, RN				

GLOBAL CARE MEDICAL CENTER ■ 100 MAIN ST, ALFRED NY 14802 ■ (607) 555-1234

SEGER, SAM	Admission: 11/11/YYYY	**Medication Administration Record**
IPCase008	DOB: 06/08/YYYY	
Dr. BLACK	ROOM: 369	

SPECIAL INSTRUCTIONS: N/A

MEDICATION (dose and route)	**DATE:** 11/16 **TIME**	**INITIALS**	**DATE:** 11/17 **TIME**	**INITIALS**	**DATE:** 11/18 **TIME**	**INITIALS**	**DATE:** 11/19 **TIME**	**INITIALS**
Metamucil in glass of water or orange juice three times a day	0800	VS	0800	VS	0800	VS	0800	VS
	1300	VS	1300	VS	1300	VS	1300	VS
	1800	OR	1800	OR	1800	OR	1800	OR
Dalmane 30 milligrams at bedtime	2100	OR	2100	OR	2100	OR	2100	OR
Velosef 250 milligrams by mouth four times a day.	0800	VS	0800	VS	0800	VS	0800	
	1200	VS	1200	VS	1200	VS	1200	VS
	1600	OR	1600	OR	1600	OR	1600	OR
	2000	OR	2000	OR	2000	OR	2000	OR
Mycostatin oral suspension 5 centimeters by mouth 4 times a day - give ½ dose in each side of mouth - retain as long as possible before swallowing	0800	VS	0800	VS	0800	VS	0800	VS
	1200	VS	1200	VS	1200	VS	1200	VS
	1600	OR	1600	OR	1600	OR	1600	OR
	2000	OR	2000	OR	2000	OR	2000	OR
Ascorbic acid 500 milligrams by mouth 4 times a day.	0800	VS	0800	VS	0800		0800	VS
	1200	VS	1200	VS	1200	VS	1200	VS
	1600	OR	1600	OR	1600	OR	1600	OR
	2000	OR	2000	OR	2000	OR	2000	OR
Multivitamin 1 tablet by mouth twice a day.	0800	VS	0800	VS	0800	VS	0800	VS
	1600	OR	1600	OR	1600	OR	1600	OR

INITIALS	**SIGNATURE AND TITLE**	**INITIALS**	**SIGNATURE AND TITLE**	**INITIALS**	**SIGNATURE AND TITLE**
VS	Vera South, RN	GPW	G.P. Well, RN		
OR	Ora Richards,RN	PS	P. Small, RN		
JD	Jane Dobbs, RN				
HF	H. Figgs, RN				

GLOBAL CARE MEDICAL CENTER ■ 100 MAIN ST, ALFRED NY 14802 ■ (607) 555-1234

SEGER, SAM	Admission: 11/11/YYYY	**Medication Administration Record**
IPCase008	DOB: 06/08/YYYY	
Dr. BLACK	ROOM: 369	

Special Instructions: N/A

Medication (dose and route)	Date: 11/16 Time	Initials	Date: 11/17 Time	Initials	Date: 11/18 Time	Initials	Date: 11/19 Time	Initials
PRN Medications								
Talwin 1 tablet by mouth every 6 hours as needed for more severe pain.	2100	OR	2050	OR	2045	OR		

Initials	Signature and Title	Initials	Signature and Title	Initials	Signature and Title
VS	Vera South, RN	GPW	G. P. Well, RN		
OR	Ora Richards, RN	PS	P. Small, RN		
JD	Jane Dobbs, RN				
HF	H. Figgs, RN				

Global Care Medical Center ■ 100 Main St, Alfred NY 14802 ■ (607) 555-1234

SEGER, SAM
IPCase008
Dr. BLACK

Admission: 11/11/YYYY
DOB: 06/08/YYYY
ROOM: 369

Medication Administration Record

Special Instructions: N/A

Medication (dose and route)	Date: 11/20 Time	Initials	Date: 11/21 Time	Initials	Date: 11/22 Time	Initials	Date: Time	Initials
Metamucil in glass of water or orange juice three times a day	0800	VS	0800	VS	0800	VS		
	1300	VS	1300	VS	1300			
	1800	OR	1800	OR	1800			
Dalmane 30 milligrams at bedtime	2100	OR	2100	OR	2100			
Velosef 250 milligrams by mouth four times a day.	0800	VS	0800	VS	0800			
	1200	VS	1200		1200			
	1600	OR	1600		1600			
	2000	OR	2000		2000			
Mycostatin oral suspension 5 centimeters by mouth 4 times a day - give ½ dose in each side of mouth - retain as long as possible before swallowing	0800	VS	0800	VS	0800	VS		
	1200	VS	1200	VS	1200			
	1600	OR	1600	OR	1600			
	2000	OR	2000	OR	2000			
Ascorbic acid 500 milligrams by mouth 4 times a day.	0800	VS	0800	VS	0800	VS		
	1200	VS	1200	VS	1200			
	1600	OR	1600	OR	1600			
	2000	OR	2000	OR	2000			
Multivitamin 1 tablet by mouth twice a day.	0800	VS	0800	VS	0800	VS		
	1600	OR	1600	OR	1600			

Initials	Signature and Title	Initials	Signature and Title	Initials	Signature and Title
VS	Vera South, RN	GPW	G. P. Well, RN		
OR	Ora Richards, RN	PS	P. Small, RN		
JD	Jane Dobbs, RN				
HF	H. Figgs, RN				

Global Care Medical Center ■ 100 Main St, Alfred NY 14802 ■ (607) 555-1234

SEGER, SAM IPCase008 Dr. BLACK	Admission: 11/11/YYYY DOB: 06/08/YYYY ROOM: 369	**Nurses' Notes**

DATE	TIME	TREATMENTS & MEDICATIONS	TIME	NURSES' NOTES
11/11/YYYY	2325	101.8 - 100 - 24 100/60 W and S isolation	2325	61-year-old male admitted to Room 369 via stretcher from Emergency Room. Oriented to room and call light system. Intravenous infusing. Continuous pHisoHex compresses to abdomen. Reviewed and Approved: J. Dobbs, RN ATP-B-S:02:1001261385: J. Dobbs, RN (Signed: 11/11/YYYY 11:33:16 PM EST)
11/12/YYYY	0015	Dalmane 30 milligrams Tylenol #3 2 tablets by mouth	0015	Given for sleep and abdominal discomfort. Reviewed and Approved: J. Dobbs, RN ATP-B-S:02:1001261385: J. Dobbs, RN (Signed: 11/12/YYYY 12:18:46 AM EST)
			0130	Sleeping appears comfortable. Reviewed and Approved: J. Dobbs, RN ATP-B-S:02:1001261385: J. Dobbs, RN (Signed: 11/12/YYYY 01:32:10 AM EST)
			0230	Sleeping. Has not voided. Reviewed and Approved: J. Dobbs, RN ATP-B-S:02:1001261385: J. Dobbs, RN (Signed: 11/12/YYYY 02:32:00 AM EST)
			0430	Sleeping. Reviewed and Approved: J. Dobbs, RN ATP-B-S:02:1001261385: J. Dobbs, RN (Signed: 11/12/YYYY 04:34:20 AM EST)
			0630	Slept well. States he feels rested. Reviewed and Approved: J. Dobbs, RN ATP-B-S:02:1001261385: J. Dobbs, RN (Signed: 11/12/YYYY 06:32:09 AM EST)
		W and S isolation	0730	Sleeping soundly. Awakened for vital signs. Complained of being cold. Blanket applied. Reviewed and Approved: V. South, RN ATP-B-S:02:1001261385: V. South, RN (Signed: 11/12/YYYY 07:33:03 AM EST)
			0800	Breakfast taken fairly. Reviewed and Approved: V. South, RN ATP-B-S:02:1001261385: V. South, RN (Signed: 11/12/YYYY 08:03:26 AM EST)
			0930	Dr. Black in to see patient. Copious amount of drainage released by Dr. Black. Wound packed. Continuous pHisoHex compresses onto wound. Reviewed and Approved: V. South, RN ATP-B-S:02:1001261385: V. South, RN (Signed: 11/12/YYYY 09:32:18 AM EST)

GLOBAL CARE MEDICAL CENTER ■ 100 MAIN ST, ALFRED NY 14802 ■ (607) 555-1234

SEGER, SAM IPCase008 Dr. BLACK	Admission: 11/11/YYYY DOB: 06/08/YYYY ROOM: 369	**Nurses' Notes**

DATE	TIME	TREATMENTS & MEDICATIONS	TIME	NURSES' NOTES
11/12/YYYY			1030	Refused morning care. Urinal emptied for 300 cc of dark-amber colored urinalysis. Intravenous infusing at RVO rate. Reviewed and Approved: V. South, RN ATP-B-S:02:1001261385: V. South, RN (Signed: 11/12/YYYY 10:33:15 AM EST)
			1200	Lunch taken poorly. Patient picked at tray. Forcing fluids. Reviewed and Approved: V. South, RN ATP-B-S:02:1001261385: V. South, RN (Signed: 11/12/YYYY 12:05:44 PM EST)
			1400	Warm compress reapplied. Reviewed and Approved: V. South, RN ATP-B-S:02:1001261385: V. South, RN (Signed: 11/12/YYYY 02:03:56 PM EST)
			1430	Appears to be napping quietly. Respirations easy and regular. Color - pale. Reviewed and Approved: V. South, RN ATP-B-S:02:1001261385: V. South, RN (Signed: 11/12/YYYY 02:34:28 PM EST)
11/12/YYYY			1530	Resting quietly. Intravenous infusing well, pHisoHex compress changed. Reviewed and Approved: O. Richards, RN ATP-B-S:02:1001261385: O. Richards, RN (Signed: 11/12/YYYY 03:32:41 PM EST)
			1730	Diet taken poorly. Drinking ice tea. Reviewed and Approved: O. Richards, RN ATP-B-S:02:1001261385: O. Richards, RN (Signed: 11/12/YYYY 05:32:13 PM EST)
			1930	Evening vital signs taken. Reviewed and Approved: O. Richards, RN ATP-B-S:02:1001261385: O. Richards, RN (Signed: 11/12/YYYY 07:34:56 PM EST)
			2000	Dressing change with large amount of liquid drainage. Intravenous infusing well. Voided 600 cc of dark amber urine. Reviewed and Approved: O. Richards, RN ATP-B-S:02:1001261385: O. Richards, RN (Signed: 11/12/YYYY 08:03:47 PM EST)
			2200	Sleeping. Intravenous infusing well. Reviewed and Approved: O. Richards, RN ATP-B-S:02:1001261385: O. Richards, RN (Signed: 11/12/YYYY 10:06:35 PM EST)

GLOBAL CARE MEDICAL CENTER ■ 100 MAIN ST, ALFRED NY 14802 ■ (607) 555-1234

CEDER, SAM Admission: 11/11/YYYY
IPCase008 DOB: 06/08/YYYY
Dr. BLACK ROOM: 369

Nurses' Notes

DATE	TIME	TREATMENTS & MEDICATIONS	TIME	NURSES' NOTES
11/13/YYYY	2400	Sunday 100.2 - 100 - 24 Tylenol with codeine 2 tablets	2400	Awake on first rounds. Intravenous infusing at 90 cc an hour. W and S isolation maintained. No complaints at present time. Dressing to wound right side of abdomen in place. Continuous pHisoHex compress to wound. Reviewed and Approved: J. Dobbs, RN ATP-B-S:02:1001261385: J. Dobbs, RN (Signed: 11/13/YYYY 12:00:56 AM EST)
			0300	Sleeping. Reviewed and Approved: J. Dobbs, RN ATP-B-S:02:1001261385: J. Dobbs, RN (Signed: 11/13/YYYY 03:01:16 AM EST)
	0400	97.6 - 92 - 20	0600	Slept very well. No complaints during the night. Reviewed and Approved: J. Dobbs, RN ATP-B-S:02:1001261385: J. Dobbs, RN (Signed: 11/13/YYYY 06:04:25 AM EST)
11/13/YYYY			0730	Awakened for morning vitals. Reviewed and Approved: V. South, RN ATP-B-S:02:1001261385: V. South, RN (Signed: 11/13/YYYY 07:31:03 AM EST)
			0800	Diet taken well. Sleeping. Reviewed and Approved: V. South, RN ATP-B-S:02:1001261385: V. South, RN (Signed: 11/13/YYYY 08:04:22 AM EST)
			0930	Did partial bath - finished via nurse. Reviewed and Approved: V. South, RN ATP-B-S:02:1001261385: V. South, RN (Signed: 11/13/YYYY 09:31:16 AM EST)
			1015	Dressing changed. Reviewed and Approved: V. South, RN ATP-B-S:02:1001261385: V. South, RN (Signed: 11/13/YYYY 10:18:03 AM EST)
			1100	Family visiting. Patient stated vision blurry. Reviewed and Approved: V. South, RN ATP-B-S:02:1001261385: V. South, RN (Signed: 11/13/YYYY 11:02:48 AM EST)
		Temperature 100	1200	pHisoHex compresses to wound. Drank well for lunch. Temperature elevated. Reviewed and Approved: V. South, RN ATP-B-S:02:1001261385: V. South, RN (Signed: 11/13/YYYY 12:04:26 PM EST)

GLOBAL CARE MEDICAL CENTER ■ 100 MAIN ST, ALFRED NY 14802 ■ (607) 555-1234

SEGER, SAM IPCase008 Dr. BLACK	Admission: 11/11/YYYY DOB: 06/08/YYYY ROOM: 369			**Nurses' Notes**
DATE	**TIME**	**TREATMENTS & MEDICATIONS**	**TIME**	**NURSES' NOTES**
11/13/YYYY			1315	Out of bed to chair for bed making. Reviewed and Approved: V. South, RN ATP-B-S:02:1001261385: V. South, RN (Signed: 11/13/YYYY 01:18:19 PM EST)
			1430	Sleeping. Reviewed and Approved: V. South, RN ATP-B-S:02:1001261385: V. South, RN (Signed: 11/13/YYYY 02:34:04 PM EST)
11/13/YYYY			1530	Dressing changed for moderate amount of purulent drainage. pHisoHex soaks applied. Voided 300 cc of tea-colored urine. Reviewed and Approved: O. Richards, RN ATP-B-S:02:1001261385: O. Richards, RN (Signed: 11/13/YYYY 03:37:23 PM EST)
			1730	Diet taken poorly. Reviewed and Approved: O. Richards, RN ATP-B-S:02:1001261385: O. Richards, RN (Signed: 11/13/YYYY 05:33:20 PM EST)
	1900	Phenergan 50 milligrams intravenous.	1900	Complained of nausea. Reviewed and Approved: O. Richards, RN ATP-B-S:02:1001261385: O. Richards, RN (Signed: 11/13/YYYY 07:03:20 PM EST)
			2015	Vomited 100 cc brown liquid. Reviewed and Approved: O. Richards, RN ATP-B-S:02:1001261385: O. Richards, RN (Signed: 11/13/YYYY 08:18:56 PM EST)
			2100-2200	Resting - Intravenous infusing - Continued pHisoHex soaks. Reviewed and Approved: O. Richards, RN ATP-B-S:02:1001261385: O. Richards, RN (Signed: 11/13/YYYY 10:02:05 PM EST)
	2300-0700 2345	Phenergan 50 milligrams given intramuscularly.	2345	Resting. Intravenous infusing well. Complained of nausea. Reviewed and Approved: J. Dobbs, RN ATP-B-S:02:1001261385: J. Dobbs, RN (Signed: 11/13/YYYY 11:47:00 PM EST)
11/14/YYYY			2400	Continued pHisoHex soaks on. Temperature - 100 - Pulse -100 - Respirations 20. Reviewed and Approved: J. Dobbs, RN ATP-B-S:02:1001261385: J. Dobbs, RN (Signed: 11/14/YYYY 12:04:00 AM EST)

Global Care Medical Center ■ 100 Main St, Alfred NY 14802 ■ (607) 555-1234

CECER, CAM IPCase008 Dr. BLACK	Admission: 11/11/YYYY DOB: 06/08/YYYY ROOM: 369	**Nurses' Notes**

DATE	TIME	TREATMENTS & MEDICATIONS	TIME	NURSES' NOTES
11/14/YYYY			0300	Resting quietly without complaints. Reviewed and Approved: J. Dobbs, RN ATP-B-S:02:1001261385: J. Dobbs, RN (Signed: 11/14/YYYY 03:04:46 AM EST)
			0400	Awakened for vital signs. Temperature - 100 - Pulse - 100 - Respirations 24. Voided 400 cc amber-colored urine. Reviewed and Approved: J. Dobbs, RN ATP-B-S:02:1001261385: J. Dobbs, RN (Signed: 11/14/YYYY 04:07:36 AM EST)
			0530	Out of bed to bathroom with assistance. Large brown formed bowel movement noted in bathroom. Back to bed with assistance. Made comfortable. Reviewed and Approved: J. Dobbs, RN ATP-B-S:02:1001261385: J. Dobbs, RN (Signed: 11/14/YYYY 05:31:38 AM EST)
			0600	Large amount of yellow purulent drainage noted on dressing change. Reviewed and Approved: J. Dobbs, RN ATP-B-S:02:1001261385: J. Dobbs, RN (Signed: 11/14/YYYY 06:05:46 AM EST)
			0630	Sleeping. Intravenous infusing well. Continued pHisoHex soaks on to right abdomen wall. No complaints. Reviewed and Approved: J. Dobbs, RN ATP-B-S:02:1001261385: J. Dobbs, RN (Signed: 11/14/YYYY 06:34:08 AM EST)
			0800	Ate 30% of breakfast. Bed bath. Out of bed in chair. Warm soaks to abdomen wound. Purulent drainage from wound. Reviewed and Approved: V. South, RN ATP-B-S:02:1001261385: V. South, RN (Signed: 11/14/YYYY 08:02:12 AM EST)
			1100	Dr. Black in. Wound irrigated with half strength peroxide. Reviewed and Approved: V. South, RN ATP-B-S:02:1001261385: V. South, RN (Signed: 11/14/YYYY 11:04:58 AM EST)
			1200	Ate 20% of lunch. Wife in. Wound irrigated. Out of bed in chair. Reviewed and Approved: V. South, RN ATP-B-S:02:1001261385: V. South, RN (Signed: 11/14/YYYY 12:07:18 PM EST)

GLOBAL CARE MEDICAL CENTER ■ 100 MAIN ST, ALFRED NY 14802 ■ (607) 555-1234

SEGER, SAM IPCase008 Dr. BLACK	Admission: 11/11/YYYY DOB: 06/08/YYYY ROOM: 369	**Nurses' Notes**

DATE	TIME	TREATMENTS & MEDICATIONS	TIME	NURSES' NOTES
11/14/YYYY	1430	Hot water bottle to abdomen.	1430	Intravenous discontinued. Visiting with wife. Isolation discontinued per order. Reviewed and Approved: V. South, RN ATP-B-S:02:1001261385: V. South, RN (Signed: 11/14/YYYY 02:34:39 PM EST)
	1600	Temperature 99.4	1600	Very lethargic. Very foul smell coming from abdomen area. Irrigation of half strength hydrogen peroxide done. Dry sterile dressing applied. Large amount of pus material from incision. Reviewed and Approved: O. Richards, RN ATP-B-S:02:1001261385: O. Richards, RN (Signed: 11/14/YYYY 04:10:12 PM EST)
	1700	Regular diet	1700	Ate poorly for supper. Hot water bottle to flank area. Reviewed and Approved: O. Richards, RN ATP-B-S:02:1001261385: O. Richards, RN (Signed: 11/14/YYYY 05:06:30 PM EST)
			2000	Irrigation of wound area done with half strength hydrogen peroxide done. Dry sterile dressing applied. Large amount of purulent drainage oozing from incision site. Bedtime care and backrub given. Took bedtime snack poorly, hot water bottle to incision area and flank, right thigh, hip and flank reddened and hot to touch. Reviewed and Approved: O. Richards, RN ATP-B-S:02:1001261385: O. Richards, RN (Signed: 11/14/YYYY 08:12:00 PM EST)
			2230	Slept most of shift. Arouses easily, but very lethargic. Reviewed and Approved: O. Richards, RN ATP-B-S:02:1001261385: O. Richards, RN (Signed: 11/14/YYYY 10:32:10 PM EST)
11/15/YYYY	11-7 2400	98.6 - 96 - 24	2400	Patient awakened to have vital signs taken. Dressing clean and intact. Patient denied any complaints. Reviewed and Approved: J. Dobbs, RN ATP-B-S:02:1001261385: J. Dobbs, RN (Signed: 11/15/YYYY 12:02:56 AM EST)
	0400	97.6	0400	Awakened to have temperature taken. Denied any complaints. Reviewed and Approved: J. Dobbs, RN ATP-B-S:02:1001261385: J. Dobbs, RN (Signed: 11/15/YYYY 04:03:17 AM EST)

GLOBAL CARE MEDICAL CENTER ■ 100 MAIN ST, ALFRED NY 14802 ■ (607) 555-1234

SEGER, SAM
IPCase008
Dr. BLACK

Admission: 11/11/YYYY
DOB: 06/08/YYYY
ROOM: 369

Nurses' Notes

DATE	TIME	TREATMENTS & MEDICATIONS	TIME	NURSES' NOTES
11/15/YYYY			0630	Patient awakened to have vital signs taken. Denied any complaints. Reviewed and Approved: J. Dobbs, RN ATP-B-S:02:1001261385: J. Dobbs, RN (Signed: 11/15/YYYY 06:33:09 AM EST)
			0715-0930	Dr. Henson is in. Breakfast taken fair. Wife with patient. At 0930 to operating room via stretcher. Reviewed and Approved: V. South, RN ATP-B-S:02:1001261385: V. South, RN (Signed: 11/15/YYYY 09:35:28 AM EST)
			1000	Returned to room. 4 X 4 dressing intact on abdomen wound. Complains of pain in abdomen. Wife with patient. Refused morning care at present time. Reviewed and Approved: V. South, RN ATP-B-S:02:1001261385: V. South, RN (Signed: 11/15/YYYY 10:03:50 AM EST)
			1200	Lunch taken fair. Fed by wife. Reviewed and Approved: V. South, RN ATP-B-S:02:1001261385: V. South, RN (Signed: 11/15/YYYY 12:06:03 PM EST)
11/17/YYYY			0800	Ate fairly well at breakfast. No complaints offered. Resting quietly afterwards. Reviewed and Approved: V. South, RN ATP-B-S:02:1001261385: V. South, RN (Signed: 11/17/YYYY 08:00:44 AM EST)
			0930	To bathroom for self morning Care. Wound irrigated with half strength hydrogen peroxide with very little drainage noted. Dressing had moderate amount of brownish drainage on it. Reviewed and Approved: V. South, RN ATP-B-S:02:1001261385: V. South, RN (Signed: 11/17/YYYY 09:32:17 AM EST)
			1100	Out of bed walking in hall with help, then returned to bed. Reviewed and Approved: V. South, RN ATP-B-S:02:1001261385: V. South, RN (Signed: 11/17/YYYY 11:04:40 AM EST)
			1200	Ate well at lunch. Reviewed and Approved: V. South, RN ATP-B-S:02:1001261385: V. South, RN (Signed: 11/17/YYYY 12:06:55 PM EST)

GLOBAL CARE MEDICAL CENTER ■ 100 MAIN ST, ALFRED NY 14802 ■ (607) 555-1234

SEGER, SAM IPCase008 Dr. BLACK	Admission: 11/11/YYYY DOB: 06/08/YYYY ROOM: 369	**Nurses' Notes**

DATE	TIME	TREATMENTS & MEDICATIONS	TIME	NURSES' NOTES
11/17/YYYY			1315	Wound irrigated with normal saline and Betadine for large amount of purulent drainage expressed. Patient dressed and out of bed, walking in hall with nurse. Reviewed and Approved: V. South, RN ATP-B-S:02:1001261385: V. South, RN (Signed: 11/17/YYYY 01:19:25 PM EST)
			1400	Encouraged to sit up in chair but returned to bed in about 15 minutes. Resting quietly. Reviewed and Approved: V. South, RN ATP-B-S:02:1001261385: V. South, RN (Signed: 11/17/YYYY 02:02:57 PM EST)
11/17/YYYY	3-11	Thursday	1530	Resting quietly in bed. Dressing dry and intact. A foul odor noted around abdomen area. Reviewed and Approved: O. Richards, RN ATP-B-S:02:1001261385: O. Richards, RN (Signed: 11/17/YYYY 03:35:07 PM EST)
			1730	Appetite good. Ate everything. Reviewed and Approved: O. Richards, RN ATP-B-S:02:1001261385: O. Richards, RN (Signed: 11/17/YYYY 05:32:27 PM EST)
			1900	Incision irrigated with Betadine and hydrogen peroxide solution with yellowish green drainage. Dressing changed. Reviewed and Approved: O. Richards, RN ATP-B-S:02:1001261385: O. Richards, RN (Signed: 11/17/YYYY 07:12:52 PM EST)
			2100	Bedtime care refused. Reviewed and Approved: O. Richards, RN ATP-B-S:02:1001261385: O. Richards, RN (Signed: 11/17/YYYY 09:02:00 PM EST)
			2200	Sleeping normally. Reviewed and Approved: O. Richards, RN ATP-B-S:02:1001261385: O. Richards, RN (Signed: 11/17/YYYY 10:04:59 PM EST)
11/18/YYYY	2300-0700		2400	Awakened for Temperature, Pulse, and Respirations - Temperature - 97.2, Pulse 62, Respirations 16. Reviewed and Approved: J. Dobbs, RN ATP-B-S:02:1001261385: J. Dobbs, RN (Signed: 11/18/YYYY 12:03:17 AM EST)
			0030	Wound irrigated with normal saline and Betadine. Large amount of greenish-yellow purulent drainage noted. Dry sterile dressing applied. Reviewed and Approved: J. Dobbs, RN ATP-B-S:02:1001261385: J. Dobbs, RN (Signed: 11/18/YYYY 12:34:00 AM EST)

GLOBAL CARE MEDICAL CENTER ■ 100 MAIN ST, ALFRED NY 14802 ■ (607) 555-1234

SEGER, SAM IPCase008 Dr. BLACK	Admission: 11/11/YYYY DOB: 06/08/YYYY ROOM: 369	**Nurses' Notes**

DATE	TIME	TREATMENTS & MEDICATIONS	TIME	NURSES' NOTES
11/18/YYYY			0200	Sleeping soundly. Appears comfortable. Reviewed and Approved: J. Dobbs, RN ATP-B-S:02:1001261385: J. Dobbs, RN (Signed: 11/18/YYYY 02:04:00 AM EST)
			0400	Temperature 97.6, Pulse 96, Respirations 16. No complaints. Reviewed and Approved: J. Dobbs, RN ATP-B-S:02:1001261385: J. Dobbs, RN (Signed: 11/18/YYYY 04:10:43 AM EST)
			0430	Wound irrigated with normal saline and Betadine. Moderate amount of greenish-yellow drainage noted. Dry sterile dressing applied. Reviewed and Approved: J. Dobbs, RN ATP-B-S:02:1001261385: J. Dobbs, RN (Signed: 11/18/YYYY 04:35:13 AM EST)
			0630	Sleeping soundly. Had a good night. Reviewed and Approved: J. Dobbs, RN ATP-B-S:02:1001261385: J. Dobbs, RN (Signed: 11/18/YYYY 06:38:01 AM EST)
			0800	Ate fairly well at breakfast. No complaints offered. Dr. Henson in. Resting in morning after breakfast. Reviewed and Approved: V. South, RN ATP-B-S:02:1001261385: V. South, RN (Signed: 11/18/YYYY 08:00:44 AM EST)
			0945	Irrigation to wound done with Betadine solution with large amount purulent drainage obtained. Redressed with 4 X 4's. Morning care in bathroom with help from wife. Out of bed in hall with much encouragement. Does not want to move. Reviewed and Approved: V. South, RN ATP-B-S:02:1001261385: V. South, RN (Signed: 11/18/YYYY 09:45:01 AM EST)
			1045	Resting in bed. Reviewed and Approved: V. South, RN ATP-B-S:02:1001261385: V. South, RN (Signed: 11/18/YYYY 10:46:41 AM EST)
			1200	Out of bed in chair for lunch. Ate poorly. Reviewed and Approved: V. South, RN ATP-B-S:02:1001261385: V. South, RN (Signed: 11/18/YYYY 12:04:02 PM EST)
			1300	Resting in bed. Reviewed and Approved: V. South, RN ATP-B-S:02:1001261385: V. South, RN (Signed: 11/18/YYYY 01:03:03 PM EST)

GLOBAL CARE MEDICAL CENTER ■ 100 MAIN ST, ALFRED NY 14802 ■ (607) 555-1234

SEGER, SAM IPCase008 Dr. BLACK	Admission: 11/11/YYYY DOB: 06/08/YYYY ROOM: 369	**Nurses' Notes**

DATE	TIME	TREATMENTS & MEDICATIONS	TIME	NURSES' NOTES
11/18/YYYY			1345	Irrigation to wound done with less drainage obtained. Redressed. Reviewed and Approved: V. South, RN ATP-B-S:02:1001261385: V. South, RN (Signed: 11/18/YYYY 01:45:05 PM EST)
			1400	Out of bed walking in hall with nurse. Encouraged to sit in chair but returned to bed shortly. Reviewed and Approved: V. South, RN ATP-B-S:02:1001261385: V. South, RN (Signed: 11/18/YYYY 02:00:12 PM EST)
11/18/YYYY	1530	Dr. Black is in.	1530	Staples removed. Sterile dressing applied to incision area. Wound irrigation done with moderate amount of drainage obtained. Wife observed. Reviewed and Approved: O. Richards, RN ATP-B-S:02:1001261385: O. Richards, RN (Signed: 11/18/YYYY 03:32:18 PM EST)
			1630	Out of bed ambulating in hall with wife. Reviewed and Approved: O. Richards, RN ATP-B-S:02:1001261385: O. Richards, RN (Signed: 11/18/YYYY 04:33:27 PM EST)
			1900	Had many visitors in. Reviewed and Approved: O. Richards, RN ATP-B-S:02:1001261385: O. Richards, RN (Signed: 11/18/YYYY 07:01:29 PM EST)
			2000	Wound irrigation done. Small amount of purulent drainage noted. Reviewed and Approved: O. Richards, RN ATP-B-S:02:1001261385: O. Richards, RN (Signed: 11/18/YYYY 08:06:18 PM EST)
			2030	Bedtime care given. Reviewed and Approved: O. Richards, RN ATP-B-S:02:1001261385: O. Richards, RN (Signed: 11/18/YYYY 08:37:19 PM EST)
	2045	Talwin 1 tablet for pain.	2130	Resting quietly at present. Reviewed and Approved: O. Richards, RN ATP-B-S:02:1001261385: O. Richards, RN (Signed: 11/18/YYYY 09:32:09 PM EST)
11/19/YYYY	2400	Saturday 98.2 - 92 - 16 Wound irrigation every 4 hours	2400	Sleeping. K pad to right side of abdomen. Rouses easily. Irrigation to wound. Purulent drainage noted from wound, small amount. Reviewed and Approved: J. Dobbs, RN ATP-B-S:02:1001261385: J. Dobbs, RN (Signed: 11/19/YYYY 12:05:00 AM EST)

GLOBAL CARE MEDICAL CENTER ■ 100 MAIN ST, ALFRED NY 14802 ■ (607) 555-1234

CEDAR, SAM IPCase008 Dr. BLACK	Admission: 11/11/YYYY DOB: 06/08/YYYY ROOM: 369	**Nurses' Notes**

DATE	TIME	TREATMENTS & MEDICATIONS	TIME	NURSES' NOTES
11/19/YYYY			0400	Sleeping soundly. Awakens easily. Wound irrigation done. Reviewed and Approved: J. Dobbs, RN ATP-B-S:02:1001261385: J. Dobbs, RN (Signed: 11/19/YYYY 04:04:00 AM EST)
			0600	Slept well. No complaints during the night. Reviewed and Approved: J. Dobbs, RN ATP-B-S:02:1001261385: J. Dobbs, RN (Signed: 11/19/YYYY 06:10:46 AM EST)
11/19/YYYY			0730	Awakened for morning vitals. Reviewed and Approved: V. South, RN ATP-B-S:02:1001261385: V. South, RN (Signed: 11/19/YYYY 07:35:13 AM EST)
			0800	Breakfast taken well. Regular diet. Reviewed and Approved: V. South, RN ATP-B-S:02:1001261385: V. South, RN (Signed: 11/19/YYYY 08:05:55 AM EST)
			0930	Irrigation of drain site with half strength hydrogen peroxide. Mostly clear return with yellow tinge on top of hydrogen peroxide "froth." Dry, sterile dressing on. Bathroom for self morning care. Reviewed and Approved: V. South, RN ATP-B-S:02:1001261385: V. South, RN (Signed: 11/19/YYYY 09:33:44 AM EST)
			1000	Ambulating in hall. Walks fair. Wife states she thinks he seems stronger. Reviewed and Approved: V. South, RN ATP-B-S:02:1001261385: V. South, RN (Signed: 11/19/YYYY 10:02:01 AM EST)
			1200	Regular diet taken fair. Reviewed and Approved: V. South, RN ATP-B-S:02:1001261385: V. South, RN (Signed: 11/19/YYYY 12:01:41 PM EST)
			1315	Irrigation of drain site with half strength hydrogen peroxide. Mostly clear return as above. Ambulating in hall with wife's assistance. Back to bed. Reviewed and Approved: V. South, RN ATP-B-S:02:1001261385: V. South, RN (Signed: 11/19/YYYY 01:19:02 PM EST)
			1400	Appears asleep at present. Bioclusive intact. Reviewed and Approved: V. South, RN ATP-B-S:02:1001261385: V. South, RN (Signed: 11/19/YYYY 02:03:03 PM EST)

GLOBAL CARE MEDICAL CENTER ■ 100 MAIN ST, ALFRED NY 14802 ■ (607) 555-1234

SEGER, SAM IPCase008 Dr. BLACK	Admission: 11/11/YYYY DOB: 06/08/YYYY ROOM: 369			**Nurses' Notes**
DATE	**TIME**	**TREATMENTS & MEDICATIONS**	**TIME**	**NURSES' NOTES**
11/19/YYYY			1530	Awake for vital signs. Wife with. Reviewed and Approved: O. Richards, RN ATP-B-S:02:1001261385: O. Richards, RN (Signed: 11/19/YYYY 03:32:18 PM EST)
			1600	Irrigation of drain site with half strength hydrogen peroxide with mostly clear return with yellow froth. Dry, sterile dressing applied with K pad on top. Reviewed and Approved: O. Richards, RN ATP-B-S:02:1001261385: O. Richards, RN (Signed: 11/19/YYYY 04:00:10 PM EST)
			1700	Refused to eat my supper. Reviewed and Approved: O. Richards, RN ATP-B-S:02:1001261385: O. Richards, RN (Signed: 11/19/YYYY 05:02:18 PM EST)
			1900	Resting quietly in bed watching television. Reviewed and Approved: O. Richards, RN ATP-B-S:02:1001261385: O. Richards, RN (Signed: 11/19/YYYY 07:01:29 PM EST)
			2000	Vital signs taken. Instructed he should drink more fluids. Reviewed and Approved: O. Richards, RN ATP-B-S:02:1001261385: O. Richards, RN (Signed: 11/19/YYYY 08:04:00 PM EST)
			2200	Irrigation of drain site with moderate amount of pus from wound site. Dry, sterile dressing applied with K pad. Drank a glass of Pepsi. Reviewed and Approved: O. Richards, RN ATP-B-S:02:1001261385: O. Richards, RN (Signed: 11/19/YYYY 10:06:18 PM EST)
11/20/YYYY	2400	Sunday 99 - 96 - 24 Wound irrigation every 4 hours	2400	Sleeping on first rounds. Temperature Pulse and Respirations taken. Wound irrigation done with small amount purulent drainage noted. Dry, sterile dressing placed over wound. K pad continuous to right side of abdomen. Bioclusive dressing to incision dry and intact. Reviewed and Approved: J. Dobbs, RN ATP-B-S:02:1001261385: J. Dobbs, RN (Signed: 11/20/YYYY 12:05:00 AM EST)
			0300	Sleeping at present. Reviewed and Approved: O. Richards, RN ATP-B-S:02:1001261385: O. Richards, RN (Signed: 11/20/YYYY 03:01:0 AM EST)

Global Care Medical Center ■ 100 Main St, Alfred NY 14802 ■ (607) 555-1234

OEGER, SAM IPCase008 Dr. BLACK	Admission: 11/11/YYYY DOB: 06/08/YYYY ROOM: 369	**Nurses' Notes**

DATE	TIME	TREATMENTS & MEDICATIONS	TIME	NURSES' NOTES
11/20/YYYY	0400	Wound irrigation 98 - 100 - 20	0400	Wound irrigation done. Large amount of purulent drainage on old dressing. Dry, sterile dressing put on wound. K pad continuous to right side of abdomen. Reviewed and Approved: J. Dobbs, RN ATP-B-S:02:1001261385: J. Dobbs, RN (Signed: 11/20/YYYY 04:04:00 AM EST)
			0600	Appears lethargic and has slept well most of the night. Fluids encouraged. Nurse has to stand and help patient drink water. Abdomen not as distended as few days ago. Reviewed and Approved: J. Dobbs, RN ATP-B-S:02:1001261385: J. Dobbs, RN (Signed: 11/20/YYYY 06:04:13 AM EST)
11/20/YYYY			0730	Awakened for vital signs. Reviewed and Approved: J. Dobbs, RN ATP-B-S:02:1001261385: J. Dobbs, RN (Signed: 11/20/YYYY 07:38:01 AM EST)
			0800	Ate good breakfast. Reviewed and Approved: V. South, RN ATP-B-S:02:1001261385: V. South, RN (Signed: 11/20/YYYY 08:00:44 AM EST)
			0900	Wound irrigation done by wife with half strength hydrogen peroxide and saline with moderate amount of purulent drainage. Reviewed and Approved: V. South, RN ATP-B-S:02:1001261385: V. South, RN (Signed: 11/20/YYYY 09:03:01 AM EST)
	0930	Dr. Black is in.	0930	Morning care given in bathroom with assistance. Reviewed and Approved: V. South, RN ATP-B-S:02:1001261385: V. South, RN (Signed: 11/20/YYYY 09:32:41 AM EST)
			0940	Out of bed. Walked in hallway. Reviewed and Approved: V. South, RN ATP-B-S:02:1001261385: V. South, RN (Signed: 11/20/YYYY 09:42:02 AM EST)
			1000	Back in room. Sitting in chair. Reviewed and Approved: V. South, RN ATP-B-S:02:1001261385: V. South, RN (Signed: 11/20/YYYY 10:03:03 AM EST)
			1030	Back in bed resting. Reviewed and Approved: V. South, RN ATP-B-S:02:1001261385: V. South, RN (Signed: 11/20/YYYY 10:33:29 AM EST)

GLOBAL CARE MEDICAL CENTER ■ 100 MAIN ST, ALFRED NY 14802 ■ (607) 555-1234

SEGER, SAM IPCase008 Dr. BLACK	Admission: 11/11/YYYY DOB: 06/08/YYYY ROOM: 369	**Nurses' Notes**

DATE	TIME	TREATMENTS & MEDICATIONS	TIME	NURSES' NOTES
11/20/YYYY			1200	Out of bed in chair for lunch. Reviewed and Approved: V. South, RN ATP-B-S:02:1001261385: V. South, RN (Signed: 11/20/YYYY 12:01:05 PM EST)
			1300	Out of bed walking in hallway. Reviewed and Approved: V. South, RN ATP-B-S:02:1001261385: V. South, RN (Signed: 11/20/YYYY 01:00:12 PM EST)
			1400	Wound irrigation done by wife with half strength hydrogen peroxide and saline with return of clear foamy drainage. Resting quietly in bed. Reviewed and Approved: V. South, RN ATP-B-S:02:1001261385: V. South, RN (Signed: 11/20/YYYY 02:01:52 PM EST)
	1600	Temperature 96.3	1530	Resting quietly in bed. Wife and visitors in at bedside. Reviewed and Approved: O. Richards, RN ATP-B-S:02:1001261385: O. Richards, RN (Signed: 11/20/YYYY 03:33:27 PM EST)
			1730	Patient refused supper. States he was not hungry. Reviewed and Approved: O. Richards, RN ATP-B-S:02:1001261385: O. Richards, RN (Signed: 11/20/YYYY 05:31:29 PM EST)
			1815	Irrigation to right side done with half strength hydrogen peroxide and saline with milky colored foamy liquid returned. Reviewed and Approved: O. Richards, RN ATP-B-S:02:1001261385: O. Richards, RN (Signed: 11/20/YYYY 06:18:18 PM EST)
			1900	Resting quietly in bed. Television on. Reviewed and Approved: O. Richards, RN ATP-B-S:02:1001261385: O. Richards, RN (Signed: 11/20/YYYY 07:00:19 PM EST)
			2000	Bedtime care given. Reviewed and Approved: O. Richards, RN ATP-B-S:02:1001261385: O. Richards, RN (Signed: 11/20/YYYY 08:02:09 PM EST)
			2200	Resting quietly at present. Television. Reviewed and Approved: O. Richards, RN ATP-B-S:02:1001261385: O. Richards, RN (Signed: 11/20/YYYY 10:05:00 PM EST)

GLOBAL CARE MEDICAL CENTER ■ 100 MAIN ST, ALFRED NY 14802 ■ (607) 555-1234

SEGER, SAM IPCase008 Dr. BLACK	Admission: 11/11/YYYY DOB: 06/08/YYYY ROOM: 369			**Nurses' Notes**
DATE	**TIME**	**TREATMENTS & MEDICATIONS**	**TIME**	**NURSES' NOTES**
11/21/YYYY	11-7	Monday	2400	Awakened for treatment. Right wound irrigated with half strength hydrogen peroxide. K pad to right side. Reviewed and Approved: J. Dobbs, RN ATP-B-S:02:1001261385: J. Dobbs, RN (Signed: 11/21/YYYY 12:04:00 AM EST)
			0300	Sleeping soundly. Reviewed and Approved: J. Dobbs, RN ATP-B-S:02:1001261385: J. Dobbs, RN (Signed: 11/21/YYYY 03:04:13 AM EST)
			0400	Wound irrigated with half strength hydrogen peroxide. Dressing changed for moderate amount greenish yellow drainage. Reviewed and Approved: J. Dobbs, RN ATP-B-S:02:1001261385: J. Dobbs, RN (Signed: 11/21/YYYY 04:00:01 AM EST)
			0600	Slept quietly throughout night. Reviewed and Approved: J. Dobbs, RN ATP-B-S:02:1001261385: J. Dobbs, RN (Signed: 11/21/YYYY 06:05:21 AM EST)
21/11/YYYY			0730	Awakened for vitals. Regular diet taken fairly well sitting in chair. Ambulated in hall with wife. Wound irrigated as ordered. Dry, sterile dressing applied. Moderate amount of dark greenish drainage on dressing. Out of bed to bathroom for self morning care. Ambulated in hall with wife. Reviewed and Approved: V. South, RN ATP-B-S:02:1001261385: V. South, RN (Signed: 11/21/YYYY 07:33:01 AM EST)
			1200	Sitting in chair for lunch. Appetite fair. Reviewed and Approved: V. South, RN ATP-B-S:02:1001261385: V. South, RN (Signed: 11/21/YYYY 12:00:41 PM EST)
			1330	Resting in bed. K pad to right side. Reviewed and Approved: V. South, RN ATP-B-S:02:1001261385: V. South, RN (Signed: 11/21/YYYY 01:32:02 PM EST)
			1415	Irrigation done by wife. Dry, sterile dressing applied. Reviewed and Approved: V. South, RN ATP-B-S:02:1001261385: V. South, RN (Signed: 11/21/YYYY 02:18:03 PM EST)
			1440	Ambulated in hall with wife. Reviewed and Approved: V. South, RN ATP-B-S:02:1001261385: V. South, RN (Signed: 11/21/YYYY 02:41:29 PM EST)

GLOBAL CARE MEDICAL CENTER ■ 100 MAIN ST, ALFRED NY 14802 ■ (607) 555-1234

SEGER, SAM IPCase008 Dr. BLACK	Admission: 11/11/YYYY DOB: 06/08/YYYY ROOM: 369	**Nurses' Notes**

DATE	TIME	TREATMENTS & MEDICATIONS	TIME	NURSES' NOTES
11/21/YYYY			1530	Vital signs taken. Resting in bed without complaints. Visitors with patient. Reviewed and Approved: O. Richards, RN ATP-B-S:02:1001261385: O. Richards, RN (Signed: 11/21/YYYY 03:32:05 PM EST)
			1700	Diet taken very poor for supper. Reviewed and Approved: O. Richards, RN ATP-B-S:02:1001261385: O. Richards, RN (Signed: 11/21/YYYY 05:02:09 PM EST)
			1800	Wound irrigation with dark green drainage. Ambulated in halls with nurse. Became very weak. Reviewed and Approved: O. Richards, RN ATP-B-S:02:1001261385: O. Richards, RN (Signed: 11/21/YYYY 06:05:45 PM EST)
			2000	Vitals taken. Bedtime care given. Reviewed and Approved: O. Richards, RN ATP-B-S:02:1001261385: O. Richards, RN (Signed: 11/21/YYYY 08:00:27 PM EST)
			2200	Appears to be sleeping. Reviewed and Approved: O. Richards, RN ATP-B-S:02:1001261385: O. Richards, RN (Signed: 11/21/YYYY 10:03:29 PM EST)
11/22/YYYY	2300- 0700		2400	Sleeping soundly. Awakened for vital signs. Temperature - 97.5 Pulse - 92 Respirations 20. Reviewed and Approved: J. Dobbs, RN ATP-B-S:02:1001261385: J. Dobbs, RN (Signed: 11/22/YYYY 12:00:18 AM EST)
			0100	Wound irrigated with half strength hydrogen peroxide. Dry, sterile dressing applied. Large amount of purulent greenish-yellow drainage noted on old dressing and around wound. Reviewed and Approved: J. Dobbs, RN ATP-B-S:02:1001261385: J. Dobbs, RN (Signed: 11/22/YYYY 01:00:19 AM EST)
			0230	Sleeping soundly. Respirations easy. Reviewed and Approved: J. Dobbs, RN ATP-B-S:02:1001261385: J. Dobbs, RN (Signed: 11/22/YYYY 02:30:14 AM EST)
			0430	Awakened. Temperature - 96.7 Pulse - 84 Respirations - 20. Wound irrigated with half strength hydrogen peroxide. Moderate amount of greenish drainage noted. Reviewed and Approved: J. Dobbs, RN ATP-B-S:02:1001261385: J. Dobbs, RN (Signed: 11/22/YYYY 04:33:45 AM EST)

GLOBAL CARE MEDICAL CENTER ■ 100 MAIN ST, ALFRED NY 14802 ■ (607) 555-1234

SEGER, SAM IPCase008 Dr. BLACK	Admission: 11/11/YYYY DOB: 06/08/YYYY ROOM: 369	**Nurses' Notes**

DATE	TIME	TREATMENTS & MEDICATIONS	TIME	NURSES' NOTES
11/22/YYYY	11-7		0630	Sleeping soundly at present. Had a quiet night. Reviewed and Approved: J. Dobbs, RN ATP-B-S:02:1001261385: J. Dobbs, RN (Signed: 11/22/YYYY 06:34:00 AM EST)
			0730	Awake and vitals stable. K pad to abdomen incision. Reviewed and Approved: V. South, RN ATP-B-S:02:1001261385: V. South, RN (Signed: 11/22/YYYY 07:34:13 AM EST)
			0800	Breakfast taken well. Reviewed and Approved: V. South, RN ATP-B-S:02:1001261385: V. South, RN (Signed: 11/22/YYYY 08:04:33 AM EST)
			0900	Wife in. Wife irrigated would. Did procedure well. Reviewed and Approved: V. South, RN ATP-B-S:02:1001261385: V. South, RN (Signed: 11/22/YYYY 09:00:27 AM EST)
			0930	Morning care done. Instructions reviewed with patient and wife. No questions verbalized. Reviewed and Approved: V. South, RN ATP-B-S:02:1001261385: V. South, RN (Signed: 11/22/YYYY 09:34:19 AM EST)
			1020	Discharged. Reviewed and Approved: V. South, RN ATP-B-S:02:1001261385: V. South, RN (Signed: 11/22/YYYY 10:24:08 AM EST)

GLOBAL CARE MEDICAL CENTER ■ 100 MAIN ST, ALFRED NY 14802 ■ (607) 555-1234

Global Care Medical Center
100 Main St, Alfred NY 14802
(607) 555-1234

Emergency Department Record

Patient Information:

Name:	SEGER, SAM	**Patient Number:**	IPCase008
Address:	306 N. East St.	**Admission Date & Time:**	11/11/YYYY 2130
City:	Almond	**Discharge Date & Time:**	11/22/YYYY 1020
State:	New York	**Condition on Discharge:**	
Zip Code:	14804		
Telephone:	(607) 000-1398		
Gender:	M		
Date of Birth:	06/08/YYYY		

Condition on Discharge:

- ☐ Satisfactory
- ☐ Home
- ☑ Inpatient Admission
- ☐ Transfer to: ___________
- ☐ Instruction Sheet Given
- ☐ AMA
- ☐ DOA
- ☐ Code Blue
- ☐ Died

Nursing Documentation:

Allergies: ☑ No ☐ Yes **Explain:** NKA

Current Medications: ☑ No ☐ Yes

BP: 160/92 **P:** 96 **R:** 9-12 **T:** 102

CC: Fever with malaise

HPI: Complains of redness and swelling on incision line

Condition: Possible abdominal infection

Assessment: Admit

Signature of Primary Care Nurse: Reviewed and Approved: Cindy Stevens, RN
ATP-B-S:02:1001261385: Cindy Stevens, RN
(Signed: 11/11/YYYY 11:58:40 PM EST)

ICD Codes:					
CPT/HCPCS Level II Codes:					

Global Care Medical Center
100 Main St, Alfred NY 14802
(607) 555-1234

Emergency Department Physician Documentation

PATIENT NAME:	SEGER, SAM	**PATIENT NUMBER:**	IPCase008
LOCATION:	Emergency Room	**ED PHYSICIAN:**	Dr. John Chase
DATE OF SERVICE:	11/11/YYYY	**DATE OF BIRTH:**	06/08/YYYY

Physician Notes:

Temperature 102. Massive infection, McBurney's wound and lateral flank. Incision and drainage with evidence of large amount of purulent material. Culture and sensitivity of wound taken. Placed on Meloxin.

Diagnosis: Massive abdominal wall infection.

Physician Orders:

Dry sterile dressing

Complete Blood Count

Wound culture and sensitivity

500 cc Norm M D5

Irrigation and drainage

SIGNATURE OF ED PHYSICIAN

Reviewed and Approved: John Chase MD
ATP-B-S:02:1001261385: John Chase MD
(Signed: 11/11/YYYY 11:59:52 PM EST)

SEGER, SAM Admission: 11/11/YYYY
IPCase008 DOB: 06/08/YYYY
Dr. BLACK ROOM: 369

Nursing Discharge Status Summary

1.	AFEBRILE:	X	Yes		No				
2.	WOUND:		Clean/Dry		Reddened		Infected	X	
3.	PAIN FREE:	X	Yes		No	If "No," describe:			
4.	POST-HOSPITAL INSTRUCTION SHEET GIVEN TO PATIENT/FAMILY:						Yes	X	No
	If NO, complete lines 5-8 below.								
5.	DIET:		Regular	X	Other (Describe): Soft				
6.	ACTIVITY:		Normal		Light	X	Limited		Bed rest
7.	MEDICATIONS:								
8.	INSTRUCTIONS GIVEN TO PATIENT/FAMILY:				Irrigation and drainage to wound area. Apply dry sterile dressing.				
9.	PATIENT/FAMILY verbalize understanding of instructions:					X	Yes		No
10.	DISCHARGED at	1020	Via:	X	Wheelchair		Stretcher	X	Ambulance Co.
	Accompanied by:	Reviewed and Approved: V. South, RN ATP-B-S:02:1001261385: V. South, RN (Signed: 05/14/YYYY 10:47:03 AM EST)				to	Front desk		
	COMMENTS:	See follow-up doctor in 2 weeks and see me next Tuesday.							

GLOBAL CARE MEDICAL CENTER ■ 100 MAIN ST, ALFRED NY 14802 ■ (607) 555-1234

SEGER, SAM Admission: 11/11/YYYY
IPCase008 DOB: 06/08/YYYY
Dr. BLACK ROOM: 369

Patient Property Record

I understand that while the facility will be responsible for items deposited in the safe. I must be responsible for all items retained by me at the bedside. (Dentures kept at the bedside will be labeled, but the facility cannot assure responsibility for them.) I also recognize that the hospital cannot be held responsible for items brought in to me after this form has been completed and signed.

Reviewed and Approved: Sam Seger 11/11/YYYY
ATP-B-S:02:1001261385: Sam Seger
(Signed: 11/11/YYYY 09:24:44 PM EST)

Signature of Patient **Date**

Reviewed and Approved: Andrea Witteman
ATP-B-S:02:1001261385: Andrea Witteman 11/11/YYYY
(Signed: 11/11/YYYY 09:26:44 PM EST)

Signature of Witness **Date**

I have no money or valuables that I wish to deposit for safekeeping. I do not hold the facility responsible for any other money or valuables that I am retaining or will have brought in to me.

I have been advised that it is recommended that I retain no more than $5.00 at the bedside.

Reviewed and Approved: Sam Seger 11/11/YYYY
ATP-B-S:02:1001261385: Sam Seger
(Signed: 11/11/YYYY 09:27:44 PM EST)

Signature of Patient **Date**

Reviewed and Approved: Andrea Witteman
ATP-B-S:02:1001261385: Andrea Witteman 11/11/YYYY
(Signed: 11/11/YYYY 09:28:44 PM EST)

Signature of Witness **Date**

I have deposited valuables in the facility safe. The envelope number is ________________.

Signature of Patient **Date**

Signature of Person Accepting Property **Date**

I understand that medications I have brought to the facility will be handled as recommended by my physician. This may include storage, disposal, or administration.

Signature of Patient **Date**

Signature of Witness **Date**

GLOBAL CARE MEDICAL CENTER ■ 100 MAIN ST, ALFRED NY 14802 ■ (607) 555-1234

IPCase009

Global Care Medical Center
100 Main St, Alfred NY 14802
(607) 555-1234
Hospital No. 999

Inpatient Face Sheet

Patient Name and Address			Gender	Race	Marital Status		Patient No.
SHELTON, RENEE			F	W	S		IPCase009
9457 PARK STREET			Date of Birth		Age	Maiden Name	Occupation
ALMOND, NY 14804			03/31/YYYY		17	N/A	Student
Admission Date	Time	Discharge Date	Time	Length of Stay		Telephone Number	
09/18/YYYY	22:50	09/21/YYYY	09:45	03 DAYS		(607) 000-7176	

Guarantor Name and Address	Next of Kin Name and Address
SHELTON, RHONDA 9457 PARK STREET ALMOND, NY 14804	SHELTON, RHONDA 9457 PARK STREET ALMOND, NY 14804

Guarantor Telephone No.	Relationship to Patient	Next of Kin Telephone Number	Relationship to Patient
(607) 000-7176	Mother	(607) 000-7176	Mother
Admitting Physician	**Service**	**Admit Type**	**Room Number/Bed**
BEN KING, MD			322
Attending Physician	**Admitting Diagnosis**		
JOHN BLACK, MD	Seizure disorder		
Primary Insurer	**Policy and Group Number**	**Secondary Insurer**	**Policy and Group Number**

Diagnoses and Procedures	ICD Code
Principal Diagnosis	
SYNCOPAL EPISODES RULE OUT SEIZURE DISORDER	
Secondary Diagnoses	
Principal Procedure	
Secondary Procedures	

Discharge Instructions

Activity: ☐ Bed rest ☐ Light ☐ Usual ☐ Unlimited ☐ Other:

Diet: ☒ Regular ☐ Low Cholesterol ☐ Low Salt ☐ ADA ☐ ____Calorie

Follow-Up: ☒ Call for appointment ☐ Office appointment on ____ ☒ **Other:** Call neurologist's office on Tuesday, 09/24 for possible report on electroencephalogram

Special Instructions: No physical education. No smoking.

Attending Physician Authentication:	Reviewed and Approved: JOHN BLACK MD ATP-B-S:02:1001261385: JOHN BLACK MD (Signed: 09/18/YYYY 22:19:00 PM EST)

SHELTON, RENEE Admission: 09/18/YYYY
IPCase009 DOB: 03/31/YYYY
Dr. BLACK ROOM: 322

Consent to Admission

I, Renee Shelton hereby consent to admission to the Global Care Medical Center (GCMC), and I further consent to such routine hospital care, diagnostic procedures, and medical treatment that the medical and professional staff of GCMC may deem necessary or advisable. I authorize the use of medical information obtained about me as specified above and the disclosure of such information to my referring physician(s). This form has been fully explained to me, and I understand its contents. I further understand that no guarantees have been made to me as to the results of treatments or examinations done at the GCMC.

Reviewed and Approved: Renee Shelton
ATP-B-S:02:1001261385: Renee Shelton
(Signed: 09/18/YYYY 11:00:00 PM EST)

Signature of Patient

Signature of Parent/Legal Guardian for Minor

Relationship to Minor

Reviewed and Approved: Andrea Witteman
ATP-B-S:02:1001261385: Andrea Witteman
(Signed: 09/18/YYYY 11:00:00 PM EST)

WITNESS: Global Care Medical Center Staff Member

Consent To Release Information For Reimbursement Purposes

In order to permit reimbursement, upon request, the Global Care Medical Center (GCMC) may disclose such treatment information pertaining to my hospitalization to any corporation, organization, or agent thereof, which is, or may be liable under contract to the GCMC or to me, or to any of my family members or other person, for payment of all or part of the GCMC's charges for services rendered to me (e.g. the patient's health insurance carrier). I understand that the purpose of any release of information is to facilitate reimbursement for services rendered. In addition, in the event that my health insurance program includes utilization review of services provided during this admission. I authorize GCMC to release information as is necessary to permit the review. This authorization will expire once the reimbursement for services rendered is complete.

Reviewed and Approved: Renee Shelton
ATP-B-S:02:1001261385: Renee Shelton
(Signed: 09/18/YYYY 11:00:00 PM EST)

Signature of Patient

Signature of Parent/Legal Guardian for Minor

Relationship to Minor

Reviewed and Approved: Andrea Witteman
ATP-B-S:02:1001261385: Andrea Witteman
(Signed: 09/18/YYYY 11:00:00 PM EST)

WITNESS: Global Care Medical Center Staff Member

Global Care Medical Center ■ 100 Main St, Alfred NY 14802 ■ (607) 555-1234

SHELTON, RENEE	Admission: 09/18/YYYY	**Advance Directive**
IPCase009	DOB: 03/31/YYYY	
Dr. BLACK	ROOM: 322	

Your answers to the following questions will assist your Physician and the Hospital to respect your wishes regarding your medical care. This information will become a part of your medical record.

	Yes	No	Patient's Initials
1. Have you been provided with a copy of the information called "Patient Rights Regarding Health Care Decision"?	X		
2. Have you prepared a "Living Will"? If yes, please provide the Hospital with a copy for your medical record.		X	
3. Have you prepared a Durable Power of Attorney for Health Care? If yes, please provide the Hospital with a copy for your medical record.		X	
4. Have you provided this facility with an Advance Directive on a prior admission and is it still in effect? If yes, Admitting Office to contact Medical Records to obtain a copy for the medical record.		X	
5. Do you desire to execute a Living Will/Durable Power of Attorney? If yes, refer to in order: a. Physician b. Social Service c. Volunteer Service		X	

Hospital Staff Directions: Check when each step is completed.

1. ✓ Verify the above questions were answered and actions taken where required.
2. ✓ If the "Patient Rights" information was provided to someone other than the patient, state reason:

   ____

   Name of Individual Receiving Information **Relationship to Patient**

3. ✓ If information was provided in a language other than English, specify language and method.
4. ✓ Verify patient was advised on how to obtain additional information on Advance Directives.
5. ✓ Verify the Patient/Family Member/Legal Representative was asked to provide the Hospital with a copy of the Advanced Directive which will be retained in the medical record.

File this form in the medical record, and give a copy to the patient.

Name of Patient/Name of Individual giving information if different from Patient

Reviewed and Approved: Renee Shelton
ATP-B-S:02:1001261385: Renee Shelton
(Signed: 09/18/YYYY 11:05:00 PM EST)

Signature of Patient **Date**

Reviewed and Approved: Andrea Witteman
ATP-B-S:02:1001261385: Andrea Witteman
(Signed: 09/18/YYYY 11:05:00 PM EST)

Signature of Hospital Representative **Date**

Global Care Medical Center ■ 100 Main St, Alfred NY 14802 ■ (607) 555-1234

SHELTON, RENEE	Admission: 09/18/YYYY	**Discharge Summary**
IPCase009	DOB: 03/31/YYYY	
Dr. BLACK	ROOM: 322	

ADMISSION DATE: 09/18/YYYY DISCHARGE DATE: 09/21/YYYY

ADMISSION DIAGNOSIS: Syncopal episodes, rule out seizure disorder.

DISCHARGE DIAGNOSIS: Same

SUMMARY: The patient is a 17-year-old female in good health who on 09/15 while doing some canning at home suddenly collapsed onto the floor apparently losing consciousness. There was no seizure activity noted, and there was no postictal period. She was seen in the Emergency Room, evaluated and sent home. She had a similar episode on 09/16 and again on the day of admission. The episode on the day of admission occurred while she was walking with a friend, and she suddenly collapsed and fell backward. Her friend took her home, put her to bed, but then she had another episode and was brought to the Emergency Room. There was no documented seizure activity with any of the episodes. Past Medical History contained in the admission history and physical. Physical exam on admission-blood pressure 138/88, pulse 88, respirations 20. Head Ears Eyes Nose Throat exam was normal. The pupils equal and reactive to light; extraocular movements intact. Sclera and conjunctiva clear. There was no nystagmus. Neck was supple with no thyromegaly. Lungs were clear. Heart had a regular rhythm with no murmur. Abdomen was soft, nontender, no masses or organomegaly. Breasts normal.

Laboratory: A complete blood count on admission - the white count was 8,700 with 55 segmented cells, 34 lymphocytes, 10 monocytes and 1 eosinophil. Hemoglobin was 13. Urinalysis was essentially normal. SCG II on 09/20 was within normal limits. Calcium was 9.5, total protein 6.6, albumin 4, creatinine 0.9. An electrocardiogram was completely normal with no ectopic beats noted.

Hospital Course: The patient was admitted to observe for further seizure activity and to attempt to initiate a workup for possible seizure disorder. Because of inability to schedule an electroencephalogram, one was not performed during the hospitalization. During the period of time in the hospital, she had no evidence whatsoever of any syncope or seizure activity. Consultation was obtained with Dr. Bernard Knapp. He concurred with the evaluation as it was to be undertaken. The patient did develop some cold symptoms or rather a worsening of the cold symptoms she had on admission. Her exam was unremarkable, and no specific therapy was given other than Tylenol. Her electroencephalogram was scheduled as an outpatient for 09/23. Since she has had no further seizure activity, she is discharged today to go home and essentially rest. She is to keep her activity to a minimum and return for the electroencephalogram which will be sleep-deprived, hyperventilated electroencephalogram. She was advised not to take any over-the-counter cold remedies prior to the electroencephalogram. Was also advised that she stop smoking. A note was given for physical education through 09/25.

DD: 09/21/YYYY

Reviewed and Approved: John Black MD
ATP-B-S:02:1001261385: John Black MD
(Signed: 09/21/YYYY 02:00:00 PM EST)

DT: 09/22/YYYY

Physician Name

GLOBAL CARE MEDICAL CENTER ■ 100 MAIN ST, ALFRED NY 14802 ■ (607) 555-1234

SHELTON, RENEE Admission: 09/18/YYYY
IPCase009 DOB: 03/31/YYYY
Dr. BLACK ROOM: 322

History & Physical Exam

09/18/YYYY

CHIEF COMPLAINT: Passing out episode.

HISTORY PRESENT ILLNESS: Miss Shelton is a 17-year-old female who has been in fairly good health without major problem with heart, lungs, kidney or diabetic problem. She had one episode on 09/15, Saturday about 2:30 while she was canning at home; suddenly she fell on the floor and collapsed. She didn't say there was any eye movement or tonic-clonic movement, and witness did not notice those movements either. She didn't have any pre- or post-episodic symptoms. She was in the Emergency Room and evaluated by the Emergency Room physician and was sent home. She had a similar episode on 09/16 between 8 and 9 which lasted about a couple of minutes, and at that time also she didn't have any eye movements or tonic-clonic movement of hands and no mucus coming out from the mouth, but this time she felt there was some chest pain and after that she collapsed. 09/18 about 8:30 to 8:45 she was walking downtown with a friend and she suddenly collapsed and fell backward. Her friend carried her home and put her in bed, but shortly after that episode she had another episode of and was brought to the Emergency Room. Each time there was no documented witness that she had tonic-clonic movement or eye rolling backward or mucus coming out such as typical grand mal seizure. From description what this sounds like may be short period of petit mal seizure. Because of this recurrence, probably will have to admit to the hospital and watch for development and then might have to do electroencephalogram. Since we don't have a neurologist here after stabilizing the patient probably have to send the patient to neurologist for evaluation.

FAMILY HISTORY: She doesn't know about father. Mother living, alive and well. She has three sisters and three brothers alive and well.

SOCIAL HISTORY: Living with mother and stepfather. She is in school. Normally she is doing average work. Smokes half a pack a day and occasional drinking.

REVIEW OF SYSTEMS: Unremarkable.

PAST MEDICAL HISTORY: Allergies - no known allergies. No medications. Tonsillectomy.

GENERAL: Well nourished, well developed, white female. No acute distress.

EENT: Eyes: pupils equal and responding to light and accommodation, extraocular movements intact.

NECK: Supple, no organomegaly or thyromegaly.

HEART: Regular at 88 without murmur.

LUNGS: Clear to auscultation and percussion.

ABDOMEN: Soft and nontender. No organomegaly.

Page 1 of 2

DD: 09/18/YYYY

DT: 09/19/YYYY **Physician Name**

GLOBAL CARE MEDICAL CENTER ■ 100 MAIN ST, ALFRED NY 14802 ■ (607) 555-1234

SHELTON, RENEE Admission: 09/18/YYYY
IPCase009 DOB: 03/31/YYYY
Dr. BLACK ROOM: 322

History & Physical Exam

Page 2 continuation

BREASTS: No masses, no nipple retraction.

PELVIC: Not done.

RECTAL: Not done.

IMPRESSION: Probably petit mal seizure.

PLAN: Will admit; watch for development and seizure precaution. Probably after we stabilize the patient, we may refer her to neurologist. We will also do an electroencephalogram.

DD: 09/18/YYYY

Reviewed and Approved: John Black MD
ATP-B-S:02:1001261385: John Black MD
(Signed: 09/18/YYYY 08:00:00 PM EST)

DT: 09/19/YYYY

Physician Name

GLOBAL CARE MEDICAL CENTER ■ 100 MAIN ST, ALFRED NY 14802 ■ (607) 555-1234

SHELTON, RENEE Admission: 09/18/YYYY	**Consultation Report**
IPCase009 DOB: 03/31/YYYY	
Dr. BLACK ROOM: 322	

DATE OF CONSULT: 09/16/YYYY

CHIEF COMPLAINT: Rule out seizures with syncope.

SOURCE: Ms. Shelton is a 17-year-old white female who presents with a history of being in reasonably good health until the Sunday prior to admission when she noted that while she was canning corn she had a "fainting spell." She passed out, fell to the floor, and took several minutes to revive. She had another one of these spells on the subsequent Monday while she was on the phone. She apparently was sitting on a stool and again fell to the floor and awoke on the floor, and this was the next thing that she remembered. Apparently there was no tonoclonic activity and no prodrome for these episodes. The day of admission she was walking with a friend at approximately 8:30 PM along the side of a road when she "collapsed" with apparent loss of consciousness. This was for an undetermined length of time but surely less than several minutes and she was able, following this episode, to walk across the street. However, once arriving across the street, she collapsed again, falling to the ground and took several minutes to revive again. She was able to make it home with the help of her friend and had a third episode at home essentially in bed. These three episodes occurred over approximately a one hour period of time and as noted previously no tonoclonic activity was noted at any of the times. She has not been ill otherwise, and she has only noted that on one occasion she was slightly dizzy prior to passing out.

PAST MEDICAL HISTORY: Unremarkable. PAST SURGICAL HISTORY: Reveals a tonsillectomy and adenoidectomy as a child. ALLERGIES: None known. IMMUNIZATIONS: Up-to-date. MEDICATIONS: At present, includes birth control pills which she has been taking for approximately six months that are dispensed through Family Planning, in Hornell. She stopped taking them on a routine basis on the Sunday prior to her difficulties. This is as scheduled. Her periods otherwise have been normal without problem. FAMILY HISTORY: Noncontributory. SOCIAL HISTORY: She lives in Almond with her mother, stepfather and siblings. She attends Alfred-Almond Central School where she is a senior; she reports no particular problems either at home or in school.

On physical exam we find a well-developed, slightly overweight white female in no acute distress. VITALS: Temperature 98.6. Heart rate 100. Respiratory rate 18. Blood pressure 100/70 sitting and 120/70 lying down. SKIN: Clear. Head Ears Eyes Nose Throat: Essentially unremarkable. Pupils equal, round and reactive to light and accommodation. Extra-ocular muscles are intact. Discs are flat with normal vessels. Nose and throat exam are normal. NECK: Supple. Without masses. CHEST: Clear to auscultation and percussion. CARDIO-VASCULAR: Normal heart sounds without murmur. It should be noted that there's a normal rhythm for at least two minutes of auscultation. Good peripheral pulses are noted. ABDOMEN: Benign, without hepatosplenomegaly, no masses or tenderness elicited. Genitourinary: Normal female Tanner stage five external. EXTREMITIES: Clear without hip clicks. NEUROLOGIC: Alert, active, cooperative, oriented x three white female in no acute distress. Cranial nerves two through twelve are intact. Deep tendon reflexes are +2 and symmetrical bilaterally. No clonus. Toes are downgoing bilaterally. Cerebellar exam, muscle tone and strength are all normal.

Page 1 of 2

DD: 09/20/YYYY

DT: 09/23/YYYY **Physician Name**

GLOBAL CARE MEDICAL CENTER ■ 100 MAIN ST, ALFRED NY 14802 ■ (607) 555-1234

SHELTON, RENEE	Admission: 09/18/YYYY	**Consultation Report**
IPCase009	DOB: 03/31/YYYY	
Dr. BLACK	ROOM: 322	

Page 2 continuation

INITIAL IMPRESSION: Ms. Shelton is a 17-year-old white female who presents with what appears to be five episodes of "passing out." These syncopal episodes occurred at many different times, including while canning corn, while talking on the phone, twice while walking and once while in bed but not asleep. She has a normal physical exam and it is difficult to elicit any organic etiology at this status of the investigation at present. Syncopal episodes in children and young adults have multiple etiologies. Surely not the least of these is petit mal or absence seizures. The differential diagnosis however or problems can be quite lengthy. This would include psychomotor seizures, syncopal attacks such as with prolonged QT interval, hysteria or hysterical hyperventilation syndromes in addition to a number of metabolic conditions with regard to hypoglycemia, hypoparathyroidism, etc. Obviously the workup for this young lady could be quite lengthy, and one should resist the temptation to shotgun her initially. I feel that the most appropriate examination to do at the present time would be an electroencephalogram to rule out the possibility of some type of seizure disorder. Following obtaining this examination, and should it be normal, then, perhaps, looking more into the cardiovascular area with Holter monitoring and/or stress testing might be appropriate. One thought does come to mind is in regard to electroencephalogram; she could be sleep-deprived and then hyperventilated during that procedure to precipitate any underlying seizure difficulty. Following the above mentioned examinations, further exams surely could be carried out but these would need to be following these mentioned tests and not coincident with them. At present I would recommend withholding medication as we don't know exactly what we would be treating with the medication. I think that reassurance can be given to the young lady as well as to her patents as to the seriousness, or actually non-seriousness, of her condition in that she has what would be considered completely normal physical findings.

Thank you for consulting me on this most interesting young lady. I'll continue to follow along with you as needed.

DD: 09/20/YYYY

Reviewed and Approved: Bernard Knapp MD
ATP-B-S:02:1001261385: Bernard Knapp MD
(Signed: 09/20/YYYY 02:20:44 PM EST)

Physician Name

DT: 09/23/YYYY

GLOBAL CARE MEDICAL CENTER ■ 100 MAIN ST, ALFRED NY 14802 ■ (607) 555-1234

SHELTON, RENEE IPCase009 Dr. BLACK	Admission: 09/18/YYYY DOB: 03/31/YYYY ROOM: 322	**Progress Notes**
Date	**Time**	**Physician's signature required for each order. (Please skip one line between dates.)**
09/18/YYYY	2300	CHIEF COMPLAINT: Passing out episodes DIAGNOSIS: Possible petit mal type seizure PLAN OF TREATMENT: Will admit Observe Electroencephalogram DISCHARGE PLAN: Home. No services needed. Reviewed and Approved: Ben King MD ATP-B-S:02:1001261385: Ben King MD (Signed: 09/18/YYYY 11:00:00 PM EST)
09/18/YYYY		History and physical dictated. Passing out episodes. Diagnosis: possible petit mal seizure Plan: Will admit Observe Electroencephalogram Reviewed and Approved: Ben King MD ATP-B-S:02:1001261385: Ben King MD (Signed: 09/18/YYYY 11:50:00 PM EST)
09/19/YYYY	0700	No episodes of seizures observed during night. Reviewed and Approved: John Carter MD ATP-B-S:02:1001261385: John Carter MD (Signed: 09/19/YYYY 07:04:00 AM EST)
09/20/YYYY	0800	No further seizure activity or syncopal episodes. Does not feel as well today, has cold, symptoms, headache. Awoke coughing during night and felt a little dizzy. Physical exam: Lungs clear. Afebrile. Assessment: Syncopal episodes. Rule out seizure. Plan: Electroencephalogram cannot be scheduled for several days. Will increase activity see if any episodes occur. If no symptoms, will discontinue and do electroencephalogram as outpatient. Check electrocardiogram, SCG II. Reviewed and Approved: John Black MD ATP-B-S:02:1001261385: John Black MD (Signed: 09/20/YYYY 08:04:00 AM EST)

Global Care Medical Center ■ 100 Main St, Alfred NY 14802 ■ (607) 555-1234

SHELTON, RENEE   Admission: 09/18/YYYY
IPCase009   DOB: 03/31/YYYY
Dr. BLACK   ROOM: 322

Progress Notes

Date	Time	Physician's signature required for each order. (Please skip one line between dates.)
09/21/YYYY	0830	Doing well. Feels fine. No episodes of dizziness, or syncopal or seizure activity. LAB electrocardiogram normal limits no ectopics, SCG II normal limits, Calcium 9.5 Creatinine 0.9, Total Protein 6.6, Albumin 4.0 Assessment: Syncopal spells rule out seizure disorder Plan: Discharge today. Electroencephalogram scheduled for 09/23 at 9:15 AM. Further workup pending test results. Reviewed and Approved: John Black MD ATP-B-S:02:1001261385: John Black MD (Signed: 09/21/YYYY 08:34:00 AM EST)

GLOBAL CARE MEDICAL CENTER ■ 100 MAIN ST, ALFRED NY 14802 ■ (607) 555-1234

SHELTON, RENEE IPCase009 Dr. BLACK		Admission: 09/18/YYYY DOB: 03/31/YYYY ROOM: 322 **Doctors' Orders**
Date	**Time**	**Physician's signature required for each order. (Please skip one line between dates.)**
09/18/YYYY	2300	Admit Dr. King Regular diet Bathroom with bathroom privileges Side rails up - seizure precautions Complete Blood Count, electrolytes in Emergency Room Urinalysis Intravenous D5W; keep vein open Valium 5 milligrams intravenous every 10 minutes 4 times as need for seizure or agitation Electroencephalogram in morning. Reviewed and Approved: Ben King MD ATP-B-S:02:1001261385: Ben King MD (Signed: 09/18/YYYY 11:09:30 PM EST)
09/19/YYYY	0940	Discontinue intravenous and intravenous medicines. Consult to Dr. Knapp Re: possible petit mal seizure disorder Reviewed and Approved: John Clark MD ATP-B-S:02:1001261385: John Clark MD (Signed: 09/19/YYYY 09:51:17 AM EST)
09/19/YYYY	1200	May be up as desired. Reviewed and Approved: John Black MD ATP-B-S:02:1001261385: John Black MD (Signed: 09/19/YYYY 12:16:27 PM EST)
09/20/YYYY	0700	Electrocardiogram today. SCGII today. Schedule electroencephalogram for next week (09/23) as outpatient, sleep-deprived. Patient to be hyperventilated during electroencephalogram. Reviewed and Approved: John Black MD ATP-B-S:02:1001261385: John Black MD (Signed: 09/20/YYYY 07:09:30 AM EST)
09/21/YYYY	0820	Discharge today. Reviewed and Approved: John Black MD ATP-B-S:02:1001261385: John Black MD (Signed: 09/21/YYYY 08:29:30 AM EST)

GLOBAL CARE MEDICAL CENTER ■ 100 MAIN ST, ALFRED NY 14802 ■ (607) 555-1234

SHELTON, RENEE	Admission: 09/18/YYYY	**Laboratory Data**
IPCase009	DOB: 03/31/YYYY	
Dr. BLACK	ROOM: 322	

SPECIMEN COLLECTED: 09/19/YYYY SPECIMEN RECEIVED: 09/19/YYYY

TEST	RESULT	FLAG	REFERENCE
URINALYSIS			
DIPSTICK ONLY			
COLOR	yellow		
SP GRAVITY	1.012		≤ 1.030
GLUCOSE	negative		≤ 125 mg/dl
BILIRUBIN	negative		≤ 0.8 mg/dl
KETONE	negative		≤ 10 mg/dl
BLOOD	negative		0.06 mg/dl hgb
PH	5		5-8.0
PROTEIN			≤ 30 mg/dl
UROBILINOGEN			≤ -1 mg/dl
NITRITES			NEG
LEUKOCYTE			≤ 15 WBC/hpf
W.B.C.	0-4		≤ 5/hpf
R.B.C.	--		≤ 5/hpf
BACT.	few		1+(≤ 20/hpf)
URINE PREGNANCY TEST			

End of Report

GLOBAL CARE MEDICAL CENTER ■ 100 MAIN ST, ALFRED NY 14802 ■ (607) 555-1234

SHELTON, RENEE	Admission: 09/18/YYYY	**Laboratory Data**
IPCase009	DOB: 03/31/YYYY	
Dr. BLACK	ROOM: 322	

SPECIMEN COLLECTED:	09/20/YYYY	SPECIMEN RECEIVED:	09/20/YYYY
IN:	0839	OUT:	1230

BLOOD CHEMISTRY 1

TEST	REFERENCE		RESULT
ACID PHOSPHATASE	0.0-0.8 U/I		
ALKALINE PHOSPHATASE	50-136 U/I		75
AMYLASE	23-85 U/I		
LIPASE	4-24 U/I		
GLUCOSE FASTING	70-110 mg/dl		
GLUCOSE	Time collected		89
BUN	7-22 mg/dl		
SODIUM	136-147 mEq/l		
POTASSIUM	3.7-5.1 mEq/l		
CARBON DIOXIDE	24-32 mEq/l		27
CHLORIDE	98-108 mEq/l		
CHOLESTEROL	120-280 mg/dl		203
SERUM GLUTAMATE PYRUVATE TRANSAMINASE	3-36 U/I		
SERUM GLUTAMIC OXALOCETIC TRANSAMINASE	M-27-47 U/I	F-22-37 U/I	26
CREATININE KINASE	M-35-232 U/I	F-21-215 U/I	
LACTATE DEHYDROGENASE	100-190 U/I		99
CREATININE	M-0.8-1.3 mg/dl	F-0.6-1.0 mg/dl	0.9
CALCIUM	8.7-10.2 mg/dl		9.5
PHOSPHORUS	2.5-4.9 mg/dl		3.1
BILIRUBIN-DIRECT	0.0-0.4 mg/dl		
BILIRUBIN-TOTAL	Less than 1.5 mg/dl		0.5
TOTAL PROTEIN	6.4-8.2 g/dl		6.6
ALBUMIN	3.4-5.0 g/dl		4.0
URIC ACID	M-3.8-7.1 mg/dl	F-2.6-5.6 mg/dl	4.7
TRIGLYCERIDE	30-200 mg/dl		

U/I = International Units g/dl = grams per deciliter

mEq = milliequivalent per deciliter mg/dl = milligrams per deciliter

GLOBAL CARE MEDICAL CENTER ■ 100 MAIN ST, ALFRED NY 14802 ■ (607) 555-1234

SHELTON, RENEE	Admission: 09/18/YYYY	**Laboratory Data**
IPCase009	DOB: 03/31/YYYY	
Dr. BLACK	ROOM: 322	

SPECIMEN COLLECTED:	09/18/YYYY	SPECIMEN RECEIVED:	09/18/YYYY
IN:	2219	OUT:	2245

BLOOD CHEMISTRY 1

TEST	REFERENCE		RESULT
ACID PHOSPHATASE	0.0-0.8 U/I		
ALKALINE PHOSPHATASE	50-136 U/I		
AMYLASE	23-85 U/I		
LIPASE	4-24 U/I		
GLUCOSE FASTING	70-110 mg/dl		
GLUCOSE	Time collected		
BUN	7-22 mg/dl		
SODIUM	136-147 mEq/l		143
POTASSIUM	3.7-5.1 mEq/l		4.1
CARBON DIOXIDE	24-32 mEq/l		29
CHLORIDE	98-108 mEq/l		108
CHOLESTEROL	120-280 mg/dl		
SERUM GLUTAMATE PYRUVATE TRANSAMINASE	3-36 U/I		
SERUM GLUTAMIC OXALOCETIC TRANSAMINASE	M-27-47 U/I	F-22-37 U/I	
CREATININE KINASE	M-35-232 U/I	F-21-215 U/I	
LACTATE DEHYDROGENASE	100-190 U/I		
CREATININE	M-0.8-1.3 mg/dl	F-0.6-1.0 mg/dl	
CALCIUM	8.7-10.2 mg/dl		
PHOSPHORUS	2.5-4.9 mg/dl		
BILIRUBIN-DIRECT	0.0-0.4 mg/dl		
BILIRUBIN-TOTAL	Less than 1.5 mg/dl		
TOTAL PROTEIN	6.4-8.2 g/dl		
ALBUMIN	3.4-5.0 g/dl		
URIC ACID	M-3.8-7.1 mg/dl	F-2.6-5.6 mg/dl	
TRIGLYCERIDE	30-200 mg/dl		

U/I = International Units
g/dl = grams per deciliter
mEq = milliequivalent per deciliter
mg/dl = milligrams per deciliter

GLOBAL CARE MEDICAL CENTER ■ 100 MAIN ST, ALFRED NY 14802 ■ (607) 555-1234

SHELTON, RENEE	Admission: 09/18/YYYY	**Laboratory Data**
IPCase009	DOB: 03/31/YYYY	
Dr. BLACK	ROOM: 322	

TIME IN:	09/18/YYYY 2219	TIME OUT:	09/18/YYYY 2245

CBC S DIFF

TEST	RESULT	FLAG	REFERENCE
WBC	8.7		4.5-11.0 thous/UL
RBC	4.34		5.2-5.4 mill/UL
HGB	13.0		11.7-16.1 g/dl
HCT	37.3		35.0-47.0 %
MCV	85.9		85-99 fL.
MCH	30.0		
MCHC	34.9		33-37
RDW			11.4-14.5
PTL	279		130-400 thous/UL
SEGS %	55		
LYMPH %	34		20.5-51.1
MONO %	10		1.7-9.3
EOS %	1		
METAS %			
BAND %			
GRAN %			42.2-75.2
LYMPH × 10^3			1.2-3.4
MONO × 10^3			0.11-0.59
GRAN × 10^3			1.4-6.5
EOS × 10^3			0.0-0.7
BASO × 10^3			0.0-0.2
ANISO			

End of Report

GLOBAL CARE MEDICAL CENTER ■ 100 MAIN ST, ALFRED NY 14802 ■ (607) 555-1234

SHELTON, RENEE
IPCase009
Dr.BLACK

Admission: 09/18/YYYY
DOB: 03/31/YYYY
ROOM: 322

EKG Report

Date of Electrocardiogram 09/20/YYYY Time of Electrocardiogram

Rate	60
PR	.12
QRSD	.08
QT	.40
QTC	

-- Axis --

P
QRS
T

Sinus rhythm normal.

Reviewed and Approved: Dr. Steven J. Chambers, M.D.
ATP-B-S:02:1001261385: Dr. Steven J. Chambers, M.D. (Signed:09/20/YYYY 12:00:44 PM EST)

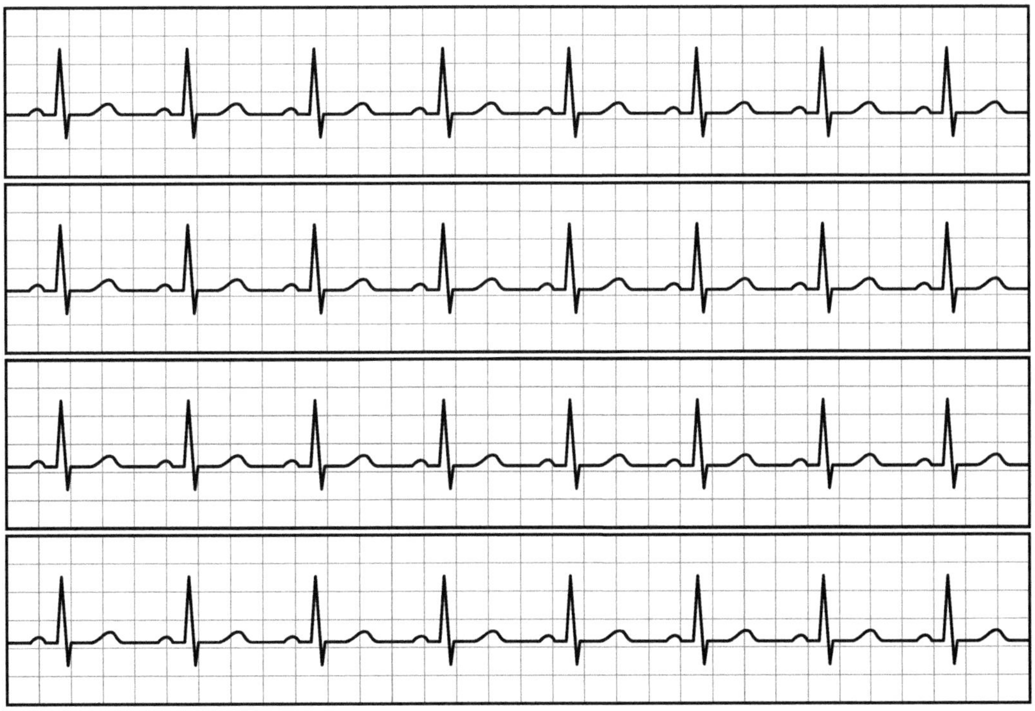

GLOBAL CARE MEDICAL CENTER ■ 100 MAIN ST, ALFRED NY 14802 ■ (607) 555-1234

SHELTON, RENEE	Admission: 09/18/YYYY	**Medication Administration Record**
IPCase009	DOB: 03/31/YYYY	
Dr. BLACK	ROOM: 322	

SPECIAL INSTRUCTIONS: Allergic to Penicillin

MEDICATION (dose and route)	DATE: 09/18 TIME	INITIALS	DATE: 00/00 TIME	INITIALS	DATE: 00/00 TIME	INITIALS	DATE: TIME	INITIALS
Single Orders & Pre-Ops								
PRN Medications:								
Valium 5 milligrams Intravenous every 10 minutes as needed for seizures or agitation								

INITIALS	SIGNATURE AND TITLE	INITIALS	SIGNATURE AND TITLE	INITIALS	SIGNATURE AND TITLE
VS	Vera South, RN	GPW	G.P. Well, RN		
OR	Ora Richards, RN	PS	P. Small, RN		
JD	Jane Dobbs, RN				
HF	H. Figgs, RN				

GLOBAL CARE MEDICAL CENTER ■ 100 MAIN ST, ALFRED NY 14802 ■ (607) 555-1234

SHELTON, RENEE IPCase009 Dr. BLACK	Admission: 09/18/YYYY DOB: 03/31/YYYY ROOM: 322	**Nurses' Notes**

DATE	TIME	TREATMENTS & MEDICATIONS	TIME	NURSES' NOTES
09/18/YYYY		No known allergies Airway and tongue blade at bedside	2235	Admitted to 322. Patient alert. See Admission sheet. Mom with. Ua out to lab. Resting quietly with complaint of "slight headache." Reviewed and Approved: J. Dobbs, RN ATP-B-S:02:1001261385: J. Dobbs, RN (Signed: 09/18/YYYY 10:35:44 PM EST)
09/19/YYYY		Thursday	2400	Sleeping. Intravenous infusing well. Reviewed and Approved: J. Dobbs, RN ATP-B-S:02:1001261385: J. Dobbs, RN (Signed: 09/19/YYYY 12:02:00 AM EST)
			0300	Continues to sleep. Reviewed and Approved: J. Dobbs, RN ATP-B-S:02:1001261385: J. Dobbs, RN (Signed: 09/19/YYYY 03:05:44 Am EST)
			0600	Sleeping. Reviewed and Approved: J. Dobbs, RN ATP-B-S:02:1001261385: J. Dobbs, RN (Signed: 09/19/YYYY 06:05:00 AM EST)
			0730	Resting quietly. No complaints. Denies any discomfort. Reviewed and Approved: V. South, RN ATP-B-S:02:1001261385: V. South, RN (Signed: 09/19/YYYY 07:30:00 AM EST)
			0800	Took diet well. Reviewed and Approved: V. South, RN ATP-B-S:02:1001261385: V. South, RN (Signed: 09/19/YYYY 08:00:00 AM EST)
			0900	Doctor Black in. Examined patient. Reviewed and Approved: V. South, RN ATP-B-S:02:1001261385: V. South, RN (Signed: 09/19/YYYY 09:00:00 AM EST)
			1100	Mother with. Denies complaints. Reviewed and Approved: V. South, RN ATP-B-S:02:1001261385: V. South, RN (Signed: 09/19/YYYY 11:00:00 AM EST)
			1200	Took diet well. Reviewed and Approved: V. South, RN ATP-B-S:02:1001261385: V. South, RN (Signed: 09/19/YYYY 12:00:00 PM EST)
			1400	Resting quietly without complaints. Reviewed and Approved: V. South, RN ATP-B-S:02;1001261385: V. South, RN (Signed: 09/19/YYYY 02:05:00 AM EST)

GLOBAL CARE MEDICAL CENTER ■ 100 MAIN ST, ALFRED NY 14802 ■ (607) 555-1234

SHELTON, RENEE	Admission: 09/18/YYYY	
IPCase009	DOB: 03/31/YYYY	**Nurses' Notes**
Dr. BLACK	ROOM: 322	

DATE	TIME	TREATMENTS & MEDICATIONS	TIME	NURSES' NOTES
09/19/YYYY			1530	Resting quietly. No complaints. Talking on phone. Denies any discomfort. Reviewed and Approved: O. Richards, RN ATP-B-S:02:1001261385: O. Richards, RN (Signed: 09/19/YYYY 03:34:00 PM EST)
			1645	Ate 100% for supper. Reviewed and Approved: O. Richards, RN ATP-B-S:02:1001261385: O. Richards, RN (Signed: 09/19/YYYY 04:45:00 PM EST)
			1830	Friend with. Patient out of bed. Instructed to stay in bed. Only bathroom privileges. Reviewed and Approved: O. Richards, RN ATP-B-S:02:1001261385: O. Richards, RN (Signed: 09/19/YYYY 06:30:00 PM EST)
			2000	Evening care. Shower taken. No complaints. Reviewed and Approved: J. Dobbs, RN ATP-B-S:02:1001261385: J. Dobbs, RN (Signed: 09/19/YYYY 08:33:16 PM EST)
			2130	Ice cream for snack. Watching television. Reviewed and Approved: J. Dobbs, RN ATP-B-S:02:1001261385: J. Dobbs, RN (Signed: 09/19/YYYY 09:47:41 PM EST)
			2200	Resting quietly. Watching television. No complaints. Reviewed and Approved: J. Dobbs, RN ATP-B-S:02:1001261385: J. Dobbs, RN (Signed: 09/19/YYYY 10:12:41 PM EST)
09/20/YYYY		Friday	0001	Sleeping with respiration easy and regular. Reviewed and Approved: J. Dobbs, RN ATP-B-S:02:1001261385: J. Dobbs, RN (Signed: 09/20/YYYY 12:02:00 AM EST)
			0100-0535	Sleeping with respiration easy and regular on hourly checks. Reviewed and Approved: J. Dobbs, RN ATP-B-S:02:1001261385: J. Dobbs, RN (Signed: 09/20/YYYY 05:37:00 AM EST)
			0600	Sleeping at present with respiration easy and regular. Reviewed and Approved: J. Dobbs, RN ATP-B-S:02:1001261385: J. Dobbs, RN (Signed: 09/20/YYYY 06:04:00 AM EST)

GLOBAL CARE MEDICAL CENTER ■ 100 MAIN ST, ALFRED NY 14802 ■ (607) 555-1234

SHELTON, RENEE   Admission: 09/18/YYYY
IPCase009   DOB: 03/31/YYYY
Dr. BLACK   ROOM: 322

Nurses' Notes

DATE	TIME	TREATMENTS & MEDICATIONS	TIME	NURSES' NOTES
09/20/YYYY			0730	Denies any complaints. Reviewed and Approved: V. South, RN ATP-B- S :02:1001261385: V. South, RN (Signed: 09/20/YYYY 07:32:03 AM EST)
			0800	Took diet well. Dr. Black in. Reviewed and Approved: V. South, RN ATP-B-S:02:1001261385: V. South, RN (Signed: 09/20/YYYY 08:05:41 AM EST)
			0930	Resting quietly. No complaints. Reviewed and Approved: V. South, RN ATP-B-S:02:1001261385: V. South, RN (Signed: 09/20/YYYY 09:45:28 AM EST)
			1100	Mother in. Reviewed and Approved: V. South, RN A T P -B- S :02:1001261385: V. South, RN (Signed: 09/20/YYYY 11:06:03 AM EST)
			1200	Took diet well. No complaints. Encouraged to ambulate in room. Reviewed and Approved: V. South, RN ATP-B-S:02:1001261385: V. South, RN (Signed: 09/20/YYYY 12:04:44 PM EST)
			1430	Resting quietly. Reviewed and Approved: V. South, RN A T P -B- S :02:1001261385: V. South, RN (Signed: 09/20/YYYY 02:34:00 PM EST)
			1530	Vital signs taken. Resting in bed. No complaints. Reviewed and Approved: O. Richards, RN ATP-B- S :02:1001261385: O. Richards, RN (Signed: 09/20/YYYY 03:32:.41 PM EST)
			1700	Appetite good for supper. Reviewed and Approved: O. Richards, RN A T P -B-S:02:1001261385: O. Richards, RN (Signed: 09/20/YYYY 05:04:10 P M EST)
			1800	Reading. Encouraged to ambulate. Reviewed and Approved: O. Richards, RN ATP-B-S:02:1001261385: O. Richards, RN (Signed: 09/20/YYYY 06:02:51 PM EST)
			1900	To tub room for shower. Reviewed and Approved: O. Richards, RN ATP-B-S:02:1001261385: O. Richards, RN (Signed: 09/20/YYYY 07:06:00 PM EST)
			2000	Friends in to visit. In good spirits. Reviewed and Approved: O . Richards, RN ATP-B-S:02:1001261385: O. Richards, RN (Signed: 09/20/YYYY 08:05:34 PM EST)

GLOBAL CARE MEDICAL CENTER ■ 100 MAIN ST, ALFRED NY 14802 ■ (607) 555-1234

SHELTON, RENEE Admission: 09/18/YYYY
IPCase009 DOB: 03/31/YYYY
Dr. BLACK ROOM: 322

Nurses' Notes

DATE	TIME	TREATMENTS & MEDICATIONS	TIME	NURSES' NOTES
09/20/YYYY			2200	Remain awake. No complaints. Reviewed and Approved: O. Richards, RN ATP-B-S:02:1001261385: O. Richards, RN (Signed: 09/20/YYYY 10:03:24 PM EST)
			2400	Sleeping - Respirations regular and even. Reviewed and Approved: J. Dobbs, RN ATP-B-S:02:1001261385: J. Dobbs, RN (Signed: 09/21/YYYY 12:05:44 AM EST)
09/21/YYYY		Saturday	0300	Continues to sleep. Reviewed and Approved: J. Dobbs, RN ATP-B-S:02:1001261385: J. Dobbs, RN (Signed: 09/21/YYYY 03:05:07 AM EST)
			0600	Sleeping. Reviewed and Approved: J. Dobbs, RN ATP-B-S:02:1001261385: J. Dobbs, RN (Signed: 09/21/YYYY 06:03:16 AM EST)
			0730	Vital signs taken. Resting in bed. Reviewed and Approved: V. South, RN ATP-B-S:02:1001261385: V. South, RN (Signed: 09/21/YYYY 07:37:41 AM EST)
			0830	100% diet taken. Dr. Black in. Patient to be discharged. Reviewed and Approved: V. South, RN ATP-B-S:02:1001261385: V. South, RN (Signed: 09/21/YYYY 08:32:21 AM EST)
			0945	Patient discharged. I walked to car. No services from us. Reviewed and Approved: V. South, RN ATP-B-S:02:1001261385: V. South, RN (Signed: 09/21/YYYY 09:47:20 AM EST)

GLOBAL CARE MEDICAL CENTER ■ 100 MAIN ST, ALFRED NY 14802 ■ (607) 555-1234

Global Care Medical Center
100 Main St, Alfred NY 14802
(607) 555-1234

Emergency Department Record

Patient Information:

Name:	SHELTON, RENEE	**Patient Number:**	IPCase009
Address:	9457 Park St,	**Admission Date & Time:**	09/18/YYYY
City:	Almond	**Discharge Date & Time:**	09/18/YYYY
State:	New York	**Condition on Discharge:**	
Zip Code:	14804	❒ Satisfactory	❒ AMA
Telephone:	(607)000-7176	❒ Home	❒ DOA
		☑ Inpatient Admission	❒ Code Blue
Gender:	F	❒ Transfer to: ___________	❒ Died
Date of Birth:	03/31/YYYY	❒ Instruction Sheet Given	

Nursing Documentation:

Allergies: ❒ No ☑ Yes **Explain:** Penicillin

Current Medications: ❒ No ☑ Yes Birth control pills

BP: 138/88 **P:** 88 **R:** 20 **T:** 99

CC: Dizziness

HPI: Patient states she was walking with a friend tonight when she suddenly collapsed. Her friend carried her home and she was put to bed. She then collapsed again. The patient states she remembers bits and parts of this experience. Denies any use of drugs or alcohol. Patient complains of some discomfort in her left arm and right leg. No redness, lacerations, abrasions, or swelling noted.

Condition: Possible fainting spell.

Assessment: Syncopal episode, rule out seizure disorder.

Signature of Primary Care Nurse: Reviewed and Approved: Cindy Stevens, RN
ATP-B-S:02:1001261385: Cindy Stevens, RN
(Signed: 09/18/YYYY 10:30:40 PM EST)

ICD Codes:					
CPT/HCPCS Level II Codes:					

Global Care Medical Center
100 Main St, Alfred NY 14802
(607) 555-1234

Emergency Department Physician Documentation

PATIENT NAME:	Shelton, Renee	**PATIENT NUMBER:**	IPCase009
LOCATION:	Emergency Room	**ED PHYSICIAN:**	Dr. Ben King
DATE OF SERVICE:	09/18/YYYY	**DATE OF BIRTH:**	03/31/YYYY

Physician Notes:

Symptoms: 17-year-old white female who was seen 3 days ago with a sudden syncopal episode and tonight while walking with a friend suddenly collapsed. She was somewhat groggy for a while, got up and walked and was light-headed and collapsed again and reportedly was unconscious and then got up and passed out twice more while lying down at home. There was another episode where she was talking on the telephone when she got chest pain across her chest and fell off the chair.

Objective: Patient is alert and awake at this time, fundi are benign, chest clear, heart regular rate and rhythm, reflexes normal, no carotid bruits.

Assessment: Syncopal episode, rule out seizure disorder.

Plan: Patient will be admitted.

Physician Orders:

SIGNATURE OF ED PHYSICIAN

Reviewed and Approved: Ben King MD
ATP-B-S:02:1001261385: Ben King MD
(Signed: 09/18/YYYY 11:59:52 PM EST)

SHELTON, RENEE   Admission: 09/18/YYYY
IPCase009   DOB: 03/31/YYYY
Dr. BLACK   ROOM: 322

Patient Property Record

I understand that while the facility will be responsible for items deposited in the safe. I must be responsible for all items retained by me at the bedside. (Dentures kept at the bedside will be labeled, but the facility cannot assure responsibility for them.) I also recognize that the hospital cannot be held responsible for items brought in to me after this form has been completed and signed.

Reviewed and Approved: Renee Shelton   09/18/YYYY
ATP-B-S:02:1001261385: Renee Shelton
(Signed: 09/18/YYYY 11:24:44 PM EST)

Signature of Patient   **Date**

Reviewed and Approved: Karla Brown
ATP-B-S:02:1001261385: Karla Brown
(Signed: 09/18/YYYY 11:24:44 PM EST)   09/18/YYYY

Signature of Witness   **Date**

I have no money or valuables that I wish to deposit for safekeeping. I do not hold the facility responsible for any other money or valuables that I am retaining or will have brought in to me.

I have been advised that it is recommended that I retain no more than $5.00 at the bedside.

Reviewed and Approved: Renee Shelton   09/18/YYYY
ATP-B-S:02:1001261385: Renee Shelton
(Signed: 09/18/YYYY 11:27:44 PM EST)

Signature of Patient   **Date**

Reviewed and Approved: Karla Brown   09/18/YYYY
ATP-B-S:02:1001261385: Karla Brown
(Signed: 09/18/YYYY 11:28:44 PM EST)

Signature of Witness   **Date**

I have deposited valuables in the facility safe. The envelope number is_______________.

Signature of Patient   **Date**

Signature of Person Accepting Property   **Date**

I understand that medications I have brought to the facility will be handled as recommended by my physician. This may include storage, disposal, or administration.

Signature of Patient   **Date**

Signature of Witness   **Date**

GLOBAL CARE MEDICAL CENTER ■ 100 MAIN ST, ALFRED NY 14802 ■ (607) 555-1234

IPCase010

Global Care Medical Center
100 Main St, Alfred NY 14802
(607) 555-1234
Hospital No. 999

Inpatient Face Sheet

Patient Name and Address	Gender	Race	Marital Status	Patient No.
WEST, KEITH	M	W	S	IPCase010
417 RUSH ROAD	**Date of Birth**	**Age**	**Maiden Name**	**Occupation**
ALMOND, NY 14804	05/23/YYYY	8 mo	N/A	N/A

Admission Date	Time	Discharge Date	Time	Length of Stay	Telephone Number
02-09-YYYY	15:55	02-11-YYYY	1300	02 DAYS	(607) 000-8107

Guarantor Name and Address	Next of Kin Name and Address
WEST, KEN 417 RUSH ROAD ALMOND, NY 14804	WEST, KELLY 417 RUSH ROAD ALMOND, NY 14804

Guarantor Telephone No.	Relationship to Patient	Next of Kin Telephone Number	Relationship to Patient
(607) 000-8107	Father	(607) 000-8107	Mother
Admitting Physician	**Service**	**Admit Type**	**Room Number/Bed**
Fred Moore, MD	N/A	N/A	331
Attending Physician	**Admitting Diagnosis**		
John Black, MD	BRONCHIOLITIS / CROUP		
Primary Insurer	**Policy and Group Number**	**Secondary Insurer**	**Policy and Group Number**
Blue Cross of WNY	76894567-900	N/A	N/A

Diagnoses and Procedures	ICD Code
Principal Diagnosis	
Bronchiolitis with fever	
Secondary Diagnoses	
Principal Procedure	
Secondary Procedures	

Discharge Instructions

Activity:	☐ Bed rest ☒ Light ☐ Usual ☐ Unlimited ☐ Other:
Diet:	☒ Regular ☐ Low Cholesterol ☐ Low Salt ☐ ADA ☐ Soft
Follow-Up:	☐ Call for appointment ☐ Office appointment on Recheck in one week.
Special Instructions:	
Attending Physician Authentication:	Reviewed and Approved: John Black MD ATP-B-S:02:1001261385: John Black MD (Signed: 02/09/YYYY 04:20:44 PM EST)

WEST, KEITH	Admission: 02/09/YYYY	**Consent to Admission**
IPCase010	DOB: 05/23/YYYY	
Dr. BLACK	ROOM: 331	

I, Keith West hereby consent to admission to the Global Care Medical Center (GCMC), and I further consent to such routine hospital care, diagnostic procedures, and medical treatment that the medical and professional staff of GCMC may deem necessary or advisable. I authorize the use of medical information obtained about me as specified above and the disclosure of such information to my referring physician(s). This form has been fully explained to me, and I understand its contents. I further understand that no guarantees have been made to me as to the results of treatments or examinations done at the GCMC.

Signature of Patient

Reviewed and Approved: Kelly West
ATP-B-S:02:1001261385: Kelly West
(Signed: 02/09/YYYY 04:32:05 PM EST)

Signature of Parent/Legal Guardian for Minor

Relationship to Minor

Reviewed and Approved: Andrea Witteman
ATP-B-S:02:1001261385: Andrea Witteman
(Signed: 02/09/YYYY 04:32:05 PM EST)

WITNESS: Global Care Medical Center Staff Member

Consent To Release Information For Reimbursement Purposes

In order to permit reimbursement, upon request, the Global Care Medical Center (GCMC) may disclose such treatment information pertaining to my hospitalization to any corporation, organization, or agent thereof, which is, or may be liable under contract to the GCMC or to me, or to any of my family members or other person, for payment of all or part of the GCMC's charges for services rendered to me (e.g. the patient's health insurance carrier). I understand that the purpose of any release of information is to facilitate reimbursement for services rendered. In addition, in the event that my health insurance program includes utilization review of services provided during this admission. I authorize GCMC to release information as is necessary to permit the review. This authorization will expire once the reimbursement for services rendered is complete.

Signature of Patient

Reviewed and Approved: Kelly West
ATP-B-S:02:1001261385: Kelly West
(Signed: 02/09/YYYY 04:36:17 PM EST)

Signature of Parent/Legal Guardian for Minor

Relationship to Minor

Reviewed and Approved: Andrea Witteman
ATP-B-S:02:1001261385: Andrea Witteman
(Signed: 02/09/YYYY 04:36:24 PM EST)

WITNESS: Global Care Medical Center Staff Member

Global Care Medical Center ■ 100 Main St, Alfred NY 14802 ■ (607) 555-1234

WEST, KEITH	Admission: 02/09/YYYY	**Advance Directive**
IPCase010	DOB: 05/23/YYYY	
Dr. BLACK	ROOM: 331	

Your answers to the following questions will assist your Physician and the Hospital to respect your wishes regarding your medical care. This information will become a part of your medical record.

	Yes	No	Patient's Initials
1. Have you been provided with a copy of the information called "Patient Rights Regarding Health Care Decision"?	X		
2. Have you prepared a "Living Will"? If yes, please provide the Hospital with a copy for your medical record.		X	
3. Have you prepared a Durable Power of Attorney for Health Care? If yes, please provide the Hospital with a copy for your medical record.		X	
4. Have you provided this facility with an Advance Directive on a prior admission and is it still in effect? If yes, Admitting Office to contact Medical Records to obtain a copy for the medical record.		X	
5. Do you desire to execute a Living Will/Durable Power of Attorney? If yes, refer to in order: a. Physician b. Social Service c. Volunteer Service		X	

Hospital Staff Directions: Check when each step is completed.

1. ✓ Verify the above questions were answered and actions taken where required.
2. ✓ If the "Patient Rights" information was provided to someone other than the patient, state reason:

Name of Individual Receiving Information **Relationship to Patient**

3. ✓ If information was provided in a language other than English, specify language and method.
4. ✓ Verify patient was advised on how to obtain additional information on Advance Directives.
5. ✓ Verify the Patient/Family Member/Legal Representative was asked to provide the Hospital with a copy of the Advanced Directive which will be retained in the medical record.

File this form in the medical record, and give a copy to the patient.

Name of Patient/Name of Individual giving information if different from Patient

Reviewed and Approved: Kelly West
ATP-B-S:02:1001261385: Kelly West
(Signed: 02/09/YYYY 04:35:05 PM EST)

Signature of Parent/Legal Guardian for Minor **Date**

Reviewed and Approved: Andrea Witteman
ATP-B-S:02:1001261385: Andrea Witteman
(Signed: 02/09/YYYY 04:35:47 PM EST)

Signature of Hospital Representative **Date**

Global Care Medical Center ■ 100 Main St, Alfred NY 14802 ■ (607) 555-1234

WEST, KEITH Admission: 02/09/YYYY
IPCase010 DOB: 05/23/YYYY
Dr. BLACK ROOM: 331

Discharge Summary

ADMISSION DATE: 02/09/YYYY DISCHARGE DATE: 02/11/YYYY

ADMISSION DIAGNOSIS: Bronchiolitis with hyperpyrexia; history of premature delivery with one hospitalization for lung immaturity at time of birth.

DISCHARGE DIAGNOSIS: Bronchiolitis with fever and poor fluid intake.

SUMMARY: This is an 8-month-old white male seen by Dr. White at the Lofty Pines Health Center for a viral-type syndrome. The mother states that the baby had a temperature over the weekend, going up to 104 and 103 the night prior to admission. The baby has progressively gotten more worked up, more short of breath and has had respiratory disease. The patient was hospitalized for his respiratory distress and lower respiratory disease.

Positive physical exam on admission included both lung fields filled with rhonchi and occasional rales. There were no signs of consolidation. The patient was put in a croup tent during his hospital stay and was placed on ampicillin four times a day for his two-day course. He tolerated the croup tent well and the antibiotics. His lungs progressively cleared, and the patient was discharged on 02-11-YYYY. He was discharged on the instructions to force fluids, saline nose drops and bulb suction as needed, amoxicillin 125 milligrams three times a day, and to return to the clinic in one week to see Dr. Swisher.

Lab data - white count was 10.7, hemoglobin was 12.2, hematocrit was 37.7, 13 segmented cells, 77 lymphocytes, 10 monocytes. Chest x-ray was within normal limits.

DD:02/11/YYYY

Reviewed and Approved: Fred Moore MD
ATP-B-S:02:1001261385: Fred Moore MD
(Signed: 02/11/YYYY 04:14:44 PM EST)

DT:02/20/YYYY

Physician Authentication

GLOBAL CARE MEDICAL CENTER ■ 100 MAIN ST, ALFRED NY 14802 ■ (607) 555-1234

WEST, KEITH Admission: 02/09/YYYY
IPCase010 DOB: 05/23/YYYY
Dr. BLACK ROOM: 331

History & Physical Exam

CHIEF COMPLAINT: Difficulty breathing and hyperpyrexia

HISTORY OF PRESENT ILLNESS: This is an 8-month-old white male seen by Dr. White at the Lofty Pines Health Center for a viral-type syndrome. The mother states that the baby had a temperature over the weekend with it being 104 on Saturday night and 103 last night. The baby has progressively gotten more worked up, more short of breath and has had more problems with congestion. The baby was admitted for observation and evaluation of his upper respiratory and lower respiratory disease.

PAST MEDICAL HISTORY: This baby only has one other hospitalization besides that of birth and that was for admission to the hospital for respiratory distress syndrome and was taken care of by Dr. Smith in the neonatal intensive care unit. He only stayed less than a week and did quite well and there was no need for follow-up. The mother states that the patient was born three weeks early and the doctors felt that this was secondary to her having a kidney stone. The child had a normal, spontaneous, vaginal birth. He was 19 inches at birth and weighed 6 pounds 15 ounces.

FAMILY HISTORY: There is a family history of diabetes, paternal great grandmother; heart disease, grandfather. One brother has congenital heart disease, and an uncle has congenital heart disease. There are 2 maternal aunts who died of myocardial infarction. There is no tuberculosis, hypertension, or cancer in the family. There also is a family history of paternal grandfather with allergies and desensitizations. Mother and father do not have allergies.

REVIEW OF SYSTEMS: Growth and development is within normal limits. Patient is a good eater, nonfussy. Still takes occasional ProSobee but is not on a strict formula diet at this time.

GENERAL: This is an 8-month-old looking his stated age with respiratory problems with a rapid rate and rather annoyed with a stuffed-up nose.

TEMPERATURE: 101.3 PULSE: 158 RESPIRATIONS: 62

DD: 02/09/YYYY
DT: 02/10/YYYY

Continued on next page

Physician Authentication

GLOBAL CARE MEDICAL CENTER ■ 100 MAIN ST, ALFRED NY 14802 ■ (607) 555-1234

WEST, KEITH	Admission: 02/09/YYYY	**History & Physical Exam**
IPCase010	DOB: 05/23/YYYY	
Dr. BLACK	ROOM: 331	

Page 2 continued

EENT: Extraocular movements are full. Pupils are equal, round, and reactive to light and accommodation - red reflexes within normal limits. Nose - stuffed up with clear rhinorrhea. Mouth - within normal limits.

CHEST: Both lung fields are filled with rhonchi and occasional rales. There were no signs of consolidation.

HEART: Regular rhythm. Without murmur, rub, or gallop that I can detect, but the patient indeed had a tachycardia at the time of examination.

ABDOMEN: Within normal limits.

GENITALIA: Circumcised male with testes descended. Good femoral pulses bilaterally. No hip clicks.

RECTUM: Anus patent.

EXTREMITIES: Within normal limits.

LAB DATA: Complete Blood Count revealed: White count was 10.7, hemoglobin was 12.2, hematocrit was 37.7, 13 segmented cells, 77 lymphocytes, 10 monocytes. Urinalysis was within normal limits except for trace blood on dipstick; doubt whether that is significant. Chest x-ray was within normal limits.

IMPRESSION: 1. Bronchiolitis with hyperpyrexia. 2. History of premature delivery with one hospitalization for lung immaturity at time of birth.

Patient will need forced fluids and close observation.

DD: 02/09/YYYY

Reviewed and Approved: Fred Moore MD
ATP-B-S:02:1001261385: Fred Moore MD
(Signed: 02/09/YYYY 04:14:44 PM EST)

DT: 02/10/YYYY

Physician Authentication

GLOBAL CARE MEDICAL CENTER ■ 100 MAIN ST, ALFRED NY 14802 ■ (607) 555-1234

WEST, KEITH	Admission: 02/09/YYYY	**Progress Notes**
IPCase010	DOB: 05/23/YYYY	
Dr. BLACK	ROOM: 331	

Date	Time	Physician's signature required for each order. (Please skip one line between dates.)
02/09/YYYY	1600	Chief complaint: Fever and coughing. Diagnosis: Bronchiolitis with fever Plan of Treatment: Croup tent. Fluids DISCHARGE PLAN: Home. No services needed Reviewed and Approved: Fred Moore MD ATP-B-S:02:1001261385: Fred Moore MD (Signed: 02/09/YYYY 04:10:55 PM EST)
02/10/YYYY	0800	Bronchiolitis / Respiratory distress Lungs - Rhonchi throughout - much looser Temperature lower Breathing easier - Respiratory rate 30 a minute. Reviewed and Approved: Fred Moore MD ATP-B-S:02:1001261385: Fred Moore MD (Signed: 02/10/YYYY 08:04:07 AM EST)
02/11/YYYY	0800	Bronchiolitis / Respiratory distress Lungs - Rhonchi throughout - much looser Temperature lower Intake good. Reviewed and Approved: Fred Moore MD ATP-B-S:02:1001261385: Fred Moore MD (Signed: 02/11/YYYY 08:10:32 AM EST)

GLOBAL CARE MEDICAL CENTER ■ 100 MAIN ST, ALFRED NY 14802 ■ (607) 555-1234

WEST, KEITH	Admission: 02/09/YYYY	**Doctors' Orders**
IPCase010	DOB: 05/23/YYYY	
Dr. BLACK	ROOM: 331	

Date	Time	Physician's signature required for each order. (Please skip one line between dates.)
02/09/YYYY	1650	Admit to service Dr. Black Admitting diagnosis: Bronchiolitis Vitals every shift Croup tent with oxygen continuous and while sleeping Daily weight Complete Blood Count Urinalysis Chest x-ray to rule out pneumonia Milk-free diet. Encourage fluids, Gatorade. Sudafed 2.5 centimeters 4 times a day as needed for congestion Amoxicillin 125/5 centimeters 4 times a day Nasopharynx and throat cultures Please call Dr. Moore when blood work and x-ray are done. Reviewed and Approved: Mary Stanley RN ATP-B-S:02:1001261385: Mary Stanley RN (Signed: 02/09/YYYY 04:54:07 PM EST)
02/09/YYYY	1700	I grain aspirin or 1 grain Tylenol by mouth or suppository every 4 hours as needed. Reviewed and Approved: Mary Stanley RN ATP-B-S:02:1001261385: Mary Stanley RN (Signed: 02/09/YYYY 05:04:07 PM EST)
02/09/YYYY	2315	Please do nose irrigation with normal saline 2-3 drops in each nostril - then suction with bulb syringe as needed. Reviewed and Approved: Mary Stanley RN ATP-B-S:02:1001261385: Mary Stanley RN (Signed: 02/09/YYYY 05:04:07 PM EST)

GLOBAL CARE MEDICAL CENTER ■ 100 MAIN ST, ALFRED NY 14802 ■ (607) 555-1234

WEST, KEITH	Admission: 02/09/YYYY	**Doctors' Orders**
IPCase010	DOB: 05/23/YYYY	
Dr. BLACK	ROOM: 331	

Date	Time	Physician's signature required for each order. (Please skip one line between dates.)
02/11/YYYY	1300	Discharge. Force fluids Saline nose drops and suction Amoxicillin 125/5 centimeters three times a day Return to clinic one week Summary dictated. Reviewed and Approved: Fred Moore MD ATP-B-S:02:1001261385: Fred Moore MD (Signed: 02/11/YYYY 01:05:52 PM EST)

GLOBAL CARE MEDICAL CENTER ■ 100 MAIN ST, ALFRED NY 14802 ■ (607) 555-1234

WEST, KEITH Admission: 02/09/YYYY
IPCase010 DOB: 05/23/YYYY
Dr. BLACK ROOM: 331

Laboratory Data

SPECIMEN COLLECTED: 02/09/YYYY 1630 SPECIMEN RECEIVED: 02/09/YYYY 1634

TEST	RESULT			
BACTERIOLOGY	OTHER ROUTINE CULTURES			
SOURCE:	Throat			
SMEAR ONLY:				
CULTURE	Normal flora			
1st PRELIMINARY				
2nd PRELIMINARY				
FINAL REPORT	Normal flora			
SENSITIVITIES	1.	AMIKACIN	1.	NITROFURANTOIN
R = Resistant	1.	AMPICILLIN		PENICILLIN G
S = Sensitive	1.	CARBENICILLIN		POLYMYXIN B
> = greater than	1.	CEFAMANDOLE	1.	SULFISOXAZOLE
	1.	CEFOXITIN	1.	TETRACYCLINE
	1.	CEPHALOTHIN	1.	TRIMETHOPRIM
	1.	CHLORAMPHENICOL		VANCOMYCIN
		CLINDAMYCIN		
		ERYTHROMYCIN		
	1.	GENTAMICIN		
		KANAMYCIN		
		METHICILLIN		
		NALIDIXIC ACID		

GLOBAL CARE MEDICAL CENTER ■ 100 MAIN ST, ALFRED NY 14802 ■ (607) 555-1234

WEST, KEITH	Admission: 02/09/YYYY	**Laboratory Data**
IPCase010	DOB: 05/23/YYYY	
Dr. BLACK	ROOM: 331	

SPECIMEN COLLECTED: 02/10/YYYY SPECIMEN RECEIVED: 02/10/YYYY

TEST	RESULT	FLAG	REFERENCE
URINALYSIS			
DIPSTICK ONLY			
COLOR	Yellow		
SP GRAVITY	1.020		≤ 1.030
ALBUMIN	Negative		≤ 125 mg/dl
BILIRUBIN	Negative		≤ 0.8 mg/dl
ACETONE	Small		≤ 10 mg/dl
BLOOD	Trace		0.06 mg/dl hgb
PH	6		5-8.0
PROTEIN			≤ 30 mg/dl
SUGAR			NEG
NITRITES			NEG
LEUKOCYTE			≤ 15 WBC/hpf
W.B.C.	0		≤ 5/hpf
R.B.C.	No intact RBC		≤ 5/hpf
BACT.	few		1 + (≤ 20/hpf)
URINE PREGNANCY TEST			

End of Report

GLOBAL CARE MEDICAL CENTER ■ 100 MAIN ST, ALFRED NY 14802 ■ (607) 555-1234

WEST, KEITH Admission: 02/09/YYYY
IPCase010 DOB: 05/23/YYYY
Dr. BLACK ROOM: 331

Laboratory Data

TIME IN: 02/09/YYYY 1634 TIME OUT: 02/09/YYYY 1815

COMPLETE BLOOD COUNTS DIFFERENTIAL

TEST	RESULT	FLAG	REFERENCE
WHITE BLOOD CELL	10.7		4.5-11.0 thou/ul
RED BLOOD CELL	5.17		5.2-5.4 milliliter/ upper limit
HEMOGLOBIN	12.2		11.7-16.1 grams per deciliter
HEMATOCRIT	37.7		35.0-47.0 %
MEAN CORPUSCULAR VOLUME	73.0		85-99 factor level
MEAN CORPUSCULAR HEMOGLOBIN	23.7		
MEAN CORPUSCULAR HEMOGLOBIN CONCENTRATION	32.4		33-37
RED CELL DISTRIBUTION WIDTH			11.4-14.5
PLATELETS	387		130-400 thou/ul
SEGMENTED CELLS %	13		
LYMPHOCYTES %	77		20.5-51.1
MONOCYTES %	10		1.7-9.3
EOSINOPHILS %			
BAND CELLS %			
ATYPICAL LYMPH			

Thou/ul = thousand upper limit

COMMENTS: N/A

End of Report

GLOBAL CARE MEDICAL CENTER ■ 100 MAIN ST, ALFRED NY 14802 ■ (607) 555-1234

WEST, KEITH	Admission: 02/09/YYYY	**Radiology Report**
IPCase010	DOB: 05/23/YYYY	
Dr. BLACK	ROOM: 331	

Date of X-ray: 02/09/YYYY

REASON: Rule out pneumonia.

TECHNICAL DATA: Anterior-posterior and lateral elevated 72 inches Pigg-O-Stat pediatric immobilizer.

REPORT

02/09/YYYY CHEST Anterior-posterior and lateral views show that the lungs are clear. The heart and pulmonary vascularity are normal.

DD:02/10/YYYY Reviewed and Approved: Randall Cunningham MD
ATP-B-S:02:1001261385: Randall Cunningham MD
(Signed: 02/10/YYYY 2:24:44 PM EST)

DT:02/10/YYYY **Physician Authentication**

GLOBAL CARE MEDICAL CENTER ■ 100 MAIN ST, ALFRED NY 14802 ■ (607) 555-1234

WEST, KEITH Admission: 02/09/YYYY
IPCase010 DOB: 05/23/YYYY
Dr. BLACK ROOM: 331

Medication Administration Record

SPECIAL INSTRUCTIONS: N/A

MEDICATION (dose and route)	DATE: 02/09 TIME	INITIALS	DATE: 02/10 TIME	INITIALS	DATE: 02/11 TIME	INITIALS	DATE: TIME	INITIALS
Amoxicillin 125/5 centimeters four times a day	12:00	----	12:00	VS	12:00	VS		
	18:00	----	18:00	OR	18:00	OR		
	24:00	----	24:00	JD	24:00	JD		
	06:00	JD	06:00	JD	06:00	----		
Single Orders								
PRN Medications								
Pseudofed 2.5 centimeters 4 times a day as needed for congestion	1650	OR	1215	VS				
Tylenol or Aspirin 1 grain by mouth or suppository every 4 hours as needed	1720	OR						

INITIALS	SIGNATURE AND TITLE	INITIALS	SIGNATURE AND TITLE	INITIALS	SIGNATURE AND TITLE
VS	Vera South, RN	GPW	G. P. Well, RN		
OR	Ora Richards, RN	PS	P. Small, RN		
JD	Jane Dobbs, RN				
HF	H. Figgs, RN				

GLOBAL CARE MEDICAL CENTER ■ 100 MAIN ST, ALFRED NY 14802 ■ (607) 555-1234

WEST, KEITH	Admission: 02/09/YYYY	**Nurses' Notes**
IPCase010	DOB: 05/23/YYYY	
Dr. BLACK	ROOM: 331	

DATE	TIME	TREATMENTS & MEDICATIONS	TIME	NURSES' NOTES
02/09/YYYY			1615	8-month-old white male admitted to room 331 in tent for possible pneumonia. Under services of Dr. Black. Throat and nasopharynx culture done. Blood work and chest x-ray done. Parents in. Patient's face flushed. Hot to touch. Taped for urinalysis. Reviewed and Approved: O. Richards, RN ATP-B-S:02:1001261385: O. Richards, RN (Signed: 02/09/YYYY 04:20:32 PM EST)
	1700	Temperature 101.3 Tylenol 60 milligrams by mouth	1630	Given bottle Gatorade. In tent sleeping. Reviewed and Approved: O. Richards, RN ATP-B-S:02:1001261385: O. Richards, RN (Signed: 02/09/YYYY 04:32:09 PM EST)
			1830	Sleeping. Respirations even/regular. Slightly rapid. Occasional congestive cough. Took small amount of Gatorade. Reviewed and Approved: O. Richards, RN ATP-B-S:02:1001261385: O. Richards, RN (Signed: 02/09/YYYY 06:32:19 PM EST)
	2000	Temperature 99.3 Dr. Moore is in.	2000	Evening care given. In tent. Patient is a little fussy. Mother with patient. Reviewed and Approved: O. Richards, RN ATP-B-S:02:1001261385: O. Richards, RN (Signed: 02/09/YYYY 08:07:33 PM EST)
			2230	Sleeping quietly. Respirations even and regular. Reviewed and Approved: O. Richards, RN ATP-B-S:02:1001261385: O. Richards, RN (Signed: 02/09/YYYY 10:34:33 PM EST)
02/10/YYYY		Tuesday Temperature 97	2400	Sleeping in croupette. Awakened for vital signs and medicine. Respirations congested, rate 36. Occasional congested cough. Nose irrigated and suctioned as ordered. Had yellow nasal drainage. Mother with patient. Reviewed and Approved: J. Dobbs, RN ATP-B-S:02:1001261385: J. Dobbs, RN (Signed: 02/10/YYYY 12:03:28 AM EST)
	0015	Sudafed 2.5 centimeters	0015	Given for congestion. Back in tent. Reviewed and Approved: J. Dobbs, RN ATP-B-S:02:1001261385: J. Dobbs, RN (Signed: 02/10/YYYY 12:17:28 AM EST)
			0100	Sleeping. Respirations remain slightly congested. Reviewed and Approved: J. Dobbs, RN ATP-B-S:02:1001261385: J. Dobbs, RN (Signed: 02/10/YYYY 01:03:28 AM EST)

GLOBAL CARE MEDICAL CENTER ■ 100 MAIN ST, ALFRED NY 14802 ■ (607) 555-1234

WEST, KEITH	Admission: 02/09/YYYY	**Nurses' Notes**
IPCase010	DOB: 05/23/YYYY	
Dr. BLACK	ROOM: 331	

DATE	TIME	TREATMENTS & MEDICATIONS	TIME	NURSES' NOTES
02/10/YYYY			0300	Sleeping. Aspirations slightly congested with snoring respirations. No cough presently. Skin cool and dry. Reviewed and Approved: J. Dobbs, RN ATP-B-S:02:1001261385: J. Dobbs, RN (Signed: 02/10/YYYY 03:04:16 AM EST)
		97.4 - 124 - 40	0600	Sleeping. Awakened for vital signs and medicine. Respirations slightly congested. Occasional congested cough. Reviewed and Approved: J. Dobbs, RN ATP-B-S:02:1001261385: J. Dobbs, RN (Signed: 02/10/YYYY 06:02:56 AM EST)
02/10/YYYY	0800	Regular diet without milk	0800	Mother with patient. Ate fair at breakfast. Bath given by mother. Respirations slightly congested. No cough. Reviewed and Approved: V. South, RN ATP-B-S:02:1001261385: V. South, RN (Signed: 02/10/YYYY 08:01:28 AM EST)
			1000	Sleeping in croupette. Respirations regular and even. Reviewed and Approved: V. South, RN ATP-B-S:02:1001261385: V. South, RN (Signed: 02/10/YYYY 10:11:22 AM EST)
	1200	Regular diet without milk	1200	Ate well at lunch. Good color - cheerful - smiling. Visitors with Dr. Moore. Reviewed and Approved: V. South, RN ATP-B-S:02:1001261385: V. South, RN (Signed: 02/10/YYYY 12:06:18 PM EST)
			1400	In croupette sleeping. Respirations regular. No cough. Reviewed and Approved: V. South, RN ATP-B-S:02:1001261385: V. South, RN (Signed: 02/10/YYYY 02:03:56 PM EST)
02/10/YYYY			1530	In tent. Mother in. Congestive, loose cough. Clear nasal discharge. Fussy at times. Reviewed and Approved: O. Richards, RN ATP-B-S:02:1001261385: O. Richards, RN (Signed: 02/10/YYYY 03:32:11 PM EST)
			1700	Took diet fair for supper. Fed by mother. Reviewed and Approved: O. Richards, RN ATP-B-S:02:1001261385: O. Richards, RN (Signed: 02/10/YYYY 05:05:55 PM EST)

GLOBAL CARE MEDICAL CENTER ■ 100 MAIN ST, ALFRED NY 14802 ■ (607) 555-1234

WEST, KEITH	Admission: 02/09/YYYY	**Nurses' Notes**
IPCase010	DOB: 05/23/YYYY	
Dr. BLACK	ROOM: 331	

DATE	TIME	TREATMENTS & MEDICATIONS	TIME	NURSES' NOTES
02/10/YYYY			1830	In tent. Little fussy. Reviewed and Approved: O. Richards, RN ATP-B-S:02:1001261385: O. Richards, RN (Signed: 02/10/YYYY 06:31:29 PM EST)
			2000	Evening care given. Took Gatorade. In tent sleeping. Reviewed and Approved: O. Richards, RN ATP-B-S:02:1001261385: O. Richards, RN (Signed: 02/10/YYYY 08:04:19 PM EST)
			2230	Sleeping quietly. Respirations even and regular. Loose congestive cough. Reviewed and Approved: O. Richards, RN ATP-B-S:02:1001261385: O. Richards, RN (Signed: 02/10/YYYY 10:33:33 PM EST)
02/11/YYYY		Wednesday	2400	Sleeping in croup tent. Respirations easy and regular. Reviewed and Approved: J. Dobbs, RN ATP-B-S:02:1001261385: J. Dobbs, RN (Signed: 02/11/YYYY 12:02:16 AM EST)
			0100-0500	Sleeping. Reviewed and Approved: J. Dobbs, RN ATP-B-S:02:1001261385: J. Dobbs, RN (Signed: 02/11/YYYY 05:00:46 AM EST)
		97.9 - 152 - 36	0600	Sleeping in croup tent. Respirations easy and regular. Had moderate amount of brown, hard constipated stool. Reviewed and Approved: J. Dobbs, RN ATP-B-S:02:1001261385: J. Dobbs, RN (Signed: 02/11/YYYY 06:02:36 AM EST)
02/11/YYYY	0800	97.9 - 152 - 36 Regular diet without milk	0800	Awake. 1 soft stool. Ate well at breakfast. Bath given. Dr. Moore in to examine. Out of tent. Reviewed and Approved: V. South, RN ATP-B-S:02:1001261385: V. South, RN (Signed: 02/11/YYYY 08:03:00 AM EST)
			1000	Content in crib. Tolerates out of tent well. Clear nasal drainage. Reviewed and Approved: V. South, RN ATP-B-S:02:1001261385: V. South, RN (Signed: 02/11/YYYY 10:11:48 AM EST)
			1200	Ate well at lunch. Parents here. Dr. Moore in to examine child and talked with parents. Patient to go home. Reviewed and Approved: V. South, RN ATP-B-S:02:1001261385: V. South, RN (Signed: 02/11/YYYY 12:06:09 PM EST)
			1300	Discharge. Refer to discharge summary sheet. Reviewed and Approved: V. South, RN ATP-B-S:02:1001261385: V. South, RN (Signed: 02/11/YYYY 01:01:01 PM EST)

GLOBAL CARE MEDICAL CENTER ■ 100 MAIN ST, ALFRED NY 14802 ■ (607) 555-1234

WEST, KEITH Admission: 02/09/YYYY
IPCase010 DOB: 05/23/YYYY
Dr. BLACK ROOM: 331

Nursing Discharge Status Summary

1.	AFEBRILE:	X	Yes		No				
2.	WOUND:		Clean/Dry		Reddened	Infected	X	NA	
3.	PAIN FREE:	X	Yes		No	If "No," describe:			
4.	POST-HOSPITAL INSTRUCTION SHEET GIVEN TO PATIENT/FAMILY:						Yes	X	No
	If NO, complete lines 5-8 below.								
5.	DIET:	X	Regular	X	Other (Describe): Increase fluid intake				
6.	ACTIVITY:	X	Normal		Light		Limited		Bed rest
7.	MEDICATIONS:								
8.	INSTRUCTIONS GIVEN TO PATIENT/FAMILY:								
9.	PATIENT/FAMILY verbalize understanding of instructions:						Yes		No
10.	DISCHARGED at	1300	Via:		Wheelchair		Stretcher		Ambulance Co.
	Accompanied by:	Reviewed and Approved: V. South, RN ATP-B-S:02:1001261385: V. South, RN (Signed: 02/11/YYYY 01:07:03 PM EST)				to	Front desk		
	COMMENTS:								

GLOBAL CARE MEDICAL CENTER ■ 100 MAIN ST, ALFRED NY 14802 ■ (607) 555-1234

WEST, KEITH Admission: 02/09/YYYY
IPCase010 DOB: 05/23/YYYY
Dr. BLACK ROOM: 331

Patient Property Record

I understand that while the facility will be responsible for items deposited in the safe. I must be responsible for all items retained by me at the bedside. (Dentures kept at the bedside will be labeled, but the facility cannot assure responsibility for them.) I also recognize that the hospital cannot be held responsible for items brought in to me after this form has been completed and signed.

Reviewed and Approved: Kelly West
ATP-B-S:02:1001261385: Kelly West
(Signed: 02/09/YYYY 04:36:44 PM EST)

Signature of Parent or Guardian of Patient

Reviewed and Approved: Andrea Witteman
ATP-B-S:02:1001261385: Andrea Witteman
(Signed: 02/09/YYYY 04:37:00 PM EST)

Signature of Witness

I have no money or valuables that I wish to deposit for safekeeping. I do not hold the facility responsible for any other money or valuables that I am retaining or will have brought in to me. I have been advised that it is recommended that I retain no more than $5.00 at the bedside.

Reviewed and Approved: Kelly West
ATP-B-S:02:1001261385: Kelly West
(Signed: 02/09/YYYY 04:36:59 PM EST)

Signature of Parent or Guardian of Patient

Reviewed and Approved: Andrea Witteman
ATP-B-S:02:1001261385: Andrea Witteman
(Signed: 02/09/YYYY 04:38:28 PM EST)

Signature of Witness

I have deposited valuables in the facility safe. The envelope number is__________.

Signature of Patient

Signature of Person Accepting Property

I understand that medications I have brought to the facility will be handled as recommended by my physician. This may include storage, disposal, or administration.

Signature of Patient

Signature of Witness

GLOBAL CARE MEDICAL CENTER ■ 100 MAIN ST, ALFRED NY 14802 ■ (607) 555-1234

APPENDIX

E

Mock Certified Professional Coder (CPC) Certification Examination

The Certified Professional Coder (CPC) examination is offered by the American Academy of Professional Coders (AAPC), and it is designed to evaluation a physician practice coder's knowledge of medical terminology, human anatomy, and coding concepts in CPT, HCPCS level II, and ICD-10-CM, including the use of modifiers. The examination is organized in three sections, and it contains 150 questions. Students are allowed five hours to complete the exam, and the use of CPT, ICD-10-CM, and HCPCS level II coding manuals is permitted.

INTERNET LINK: Go to www.aapc.com to locate information about CPC certification.

MOCK CPC EXAM

Circle the most appropriate response.

Section 1: Medical Concepts

Medical Terminology

1. A slow heart rate of less than 60 beats per minute is known as:
   a. bradycardia.
   b. fibrillation.
   c. heart flutter.
   d. tachycardia.
2. A disorder in which the heart is unable to pump out all of the blood returned to it, resulting in edema of body tissue, is called:
   a. arrhythmia.
   b. congestive heart failure.
   c. heart attack.
   d. myocardial infarction.
3. The death of a portion of the heart muscle due to an obstruction of a coronary artery is called:
   a. arrhythmia.
   b. congestive heart failure.
   c. myocardial infarction.
   d. pericarditis.
4. The ballooning of a portion of an artery because of a weak spot in its wall is called a(n):
   a. aneurysm.
   b. arteriosclerosis.
   c. atherosclerosis.
   d. phlebitis.
5. Elephantiasis is caused by a:
   a. flatworm.
   b. fungus.
   c. protozoan.
   d. roundworm.
6. Which refers to the permanent damage remaining after a disease has run its course?
   a. Complication
   b. Pathogenesis
   c. Prognosis
   d. Sequela
7. A deviation of the tip of the great toe toward the outer or lateral side of the foot is called:
   a. hallux flexus.
   b. hallux malleus.
   c. hallux valgus.
   d. hallux varus.

8. The loss of production of urine is called:
   a. anuria.
   b. oliguria.
   c. polyuria.
   d. uremia.
9. The life-threatening imbalance produced in the bloodstream by renal failure is called:
   a. alkalosis.
   b. anuria.
   c. hematuria.
   d. hyperkalemia.
10. Blood from the upper part of the digestive tract gives stools a dark, tarry appearance, which is called:
   a. achlorhydria.
   b. hematemesis.
   c. melena.
   d. peritonitis.

Human Anatomy

11. Which is included in hemoglobin?
   a. Cobalt
   b. Copper
   c. Iodine
   d. Iron
12. Which includes the correct sequence of anatomy of the renal tubule, from beginning to end?
   a. Descending limb of loop of Henle, ascending limb of loop of Henle, proximal convoluted tubule, distal convoluted tubule
   b. Distal convoluted tubule, ascending limb of loop of Henle, descending loop of Henle, proximal convoluted tubule
   c. Proximal convoluted tubule, ascending limb of loop of Henle, descending limb of loop of Henle, distal convoluted tubule
   d. Proximal convoluted tubule, descending limb of loop of Henle, ascending loop of Henle, distal convoluted tubule
13. Which tissue forms a loose-fitting sac around the heart?
   a. Endocardium
   b. Epicardium
   c. Myocardium
   d. Pericardium
14. Lymphocytes are responsible for:
   a. antibody-mediated immunity.
   b. cell-mediated immunity.
   c. producing antibodies.
   d. programming macrophages.
15. When excessively low arterial blood pressure occurs, glomerular hydrostatic pressure:
   a. drops and filtration decreases.
   b. drops and filtration increases.
   c. rises and filtration decreases.
   d. rises and filtration increases.
16. Which type of immunoglobulin is found in secretions of exocrine glands?
   a. IgA
   b. IgD
   c. IgE
   d. IgG
17. A major function of the large intestine is to:
   a. break down hemoglobin.
   b. reabsorb water from chyme.
   c. regulate the release of bile.
   d. secrete digestive enzymes.
18. The layers within the wall of the alimentary canal, from inside to outside, include the:
   a. mucous membrane, muscular layer, serous layer, submucosa.
   b. mucous membrane, submucosa, muscular layer, serous layer.
   c. serous layer, muscular layer, mucous membrane, submucosa.
   d. submucosa, mucous membrane, serous layer, muscular layer.
19. Which primarily regulates the movement of water and electrolytes between fluid compartments?
   a. Active and passive transport
   b. Diffusion and osmosis
   c. Hydrostatic pressure and osmotic pressure
   d. Pinocytosis and phagocytosis

20. Cerebrospinal fluid occupies the _______________ space within the meninges.
    a. cranial
    b. dura mater
    c. epidural
    d. subarachnoid

ICD-10-CM

21. CD-10-CM code A00.0 is an example of a:
    a. category.
    b. chapter.
    c. section.
    d. subcategory.
22. Select the residual condition for the diagnosis "nonunion of fracture of femur with osteoporosis and pain."
    a. Fracture of femur
    b. Nonunion
    c. Osteoporosis
    d. Pain
23. The diagnostic statement "rule out diabetes mellitus" as documented in the physician's office record is:
    a. assigned a health status code.
    b. coded as a confirmed condition.
    c. coded only if the condition has been ruled out.
    d. not coded because the sign or symptom is coded instead.
24. For the diagnosis "carcinoma of axillary lymph nodes," the lymph nodes are coded as a(n) _______________ condition.
    a. benign
    b. malignant primary
    c. malignant secondary
    d. unspecified
25. The phrase *status post cardiac pacemaker* means the:
    a. pacemaker needs to be adjusted.
    b. patient has a functioning pacemaker in place.
    c. patient is admitted for a pacemaker change.
    d. patient's pacemaker is malfunctioning.
26. In ICD-10-CM, main terms in the index are organized according to:
    a. anatomical site.
    b. disease condition.
    c. modifier description.
    d. surgical procedure.
27. To locate a code for "recurrent maxillary sinus polyp," refer to main term _______________ in the ICD-10-CM Index to Diseases and Injuries.
    a. Maxillary
    b. Polyp
    c. Recurrent
    d. Sinus
28. ICD-10-CM category I15 describes secondary hypertension. Which diagnostic statement is assigned a code from ICD-10-CM category I15?
    a. Benign essential hypertension
    b. Congestive heart failure due to hypertension
    c. Hypertension due to Cushing's disease
    d. Hypertensive cardiovascular disease
29. Which symbol is used in the ICD-10-CM index to enclose italicized codes that signify the use of more than one code to describe a diagnosis?
    a. Parentheses
    b. Quotation marks
    c. Section marks
    d. Slanted square brackets (or brackets)
30. Which is coded as a mechanical complication?
    a. Infected arteriovenous shunt
    b. Painful hip prosthesis
    c. Prosthetic joint implant failure
    d. Repair of ureterostomy stoma stricture

HCPCS Level II

31. HCPCS level II codes are used to:
    a. bill supplies, materials, and injectable medications.
    b. code diagnosis codes.
    c. report physician E/M services.
    d. track positive patient outcomes.

32. Which statement correctly describes modifiers?
    a. Modifiers are added to the beginning of a code.
    b. Modifiers are found in CPT and HCPCS level II.
    c. Modifiers are universally accepted by third-party payers.
    d. Modifiers can be two digits or four digits.

33. The HCPCS coding system was developed by the:
    a. American Medical Association.
    b. BlueCross/BlueShield Association.
    c. Centers for Medicare & Medicaid Services.
    d. Health Insurance Association of America.

34. The L group of codes represents:
    a. drugs and enterals products.
    b. orthotics and prosthetics procedures/products.
    c. pathology and laboratory services.
    d. speech and language services.

35. If a patient has trigger thumb release performed on the right, which modifier is reported to identify the anatomical location?
    a. -F4
    b. -F5
    c. -F9
    d. -FA

Coding Guidelines

36. The *ICD-10-CM Official Guidelines for Coding and Reporting* is developed by the ______________ to accompany and complement the official conventions and instructions provided within ICD-10-CM.
    a. American Health Information Management Association
    b. American Medical Association
    c. Cooperating Parties for the ICD-10-CM
    d. National Institutes of Health

37. Coding guidelines use the term *encounter* to describe ______________ regardless of health care setting. (Select two answers.)
    a. inpatient admissions
    b. office visits
    c. physicians
    d. qualified health care practitioners

38. The word "Includes" appears immediately under certain ICD-10-CM categories (or codes) to ______________.
    a. further define, clarify, or give examples of the content of a code category (or a code).
    b. indicate mutually exclusive codes and conditions that cannot be reported together.
    c. instruct the coder to go to a different main term or subterm to provide additional information.
    d. permit reporting of the code and an excluded code if supported by the documentation.

39. Upon verification of codes in the ICD-10-CM tabular list, when ICD-10-CM fifth through seventh characters are provided, they:
    a. apply to inpatient encounters only.
    b. are added to the residual code.
    c. are optional.
    d. must be assigned.

40. ICD-10-CM codes that classify factors influencing health status and contact with health services codes are:
    a. associated only with inpatient and nursing facility level of care.
    b. never reported as a first-listed code for inpatient or outpatient care.
    c. reported as a first-listed code for outpatient care when appropriate.
    d. used to track positive or negative patient outcomes for skilled care.

41. Codes that describe symptoms and signs for an outpatient case are reported:
    a. in addition to qualified and established diagnoses.
    b. instead of established diagnoses.
    c. when a qualified diagnosis is documented.
    d. with established diagnoses.

42. Etiology/manifestation conditions often require ______________ code(s) to be reported to completely describe a single condition that affects multiple body systems.
    a. one
    b. two
    c. three
    d. four

43. When the same condition is described as acute (or subacute) *and* chronic, usually:
    a. a code for each condition is assigned.
    b. etiology and manifestation codes are assigned.
    c. one combination code is assigned.
    d. residual and late effect codes are assigned.

44. One code assigned as a single code to classify two different conditions is called a(n) ______________ code.
    a. combination
    b. etiology
    c. multiple
    d. residual

45. A late effect (or sequela) is:
    a. assigned multiple codes for the etiology and manifestation.
    b. coded only if it occurs at least one year after the previous condition has resolved.
    c. considered an "impending" or "threatened" condition.
    d. the condition produced after the acute phase of an illness or injury has ended.

Section 2: Surgery and Modifiers

CPT Surgery 10000 (10)

46. Excision with simple closure of 2.0-cm diameter lesion, upper back, and 2.0-cm diameter lesion, left thigh. Pathology report reveals both were cystic lesions. Which CPT code(s) are assigned?
    a. 11402
    b. 11402, 11402-59
    c. 11404
    d. 11602, 11602

47. Per CPT surgery notes, when coding a biopsy of a lesion followed by excision of that same lesion, the coder should assign:
    a. a "destruction of lesion" code.
    b. one code for the excision only.
    c. the code that results in higher reimbursement.
    d. two codes, one for biopsy and a separate code for the excision.

48. Per CPT guidelines, a separate procedure is:
    a. always coded along with the code for the larger, more complex procedure.
    b. coded when it is performed as a part of another larger procedure.
    c. considered an integral part of another larger procedure.
    d. never coded under any circumstances.

49. Repair with layered sutures, 7-cm and 9-cm lacerations, left arm. Which CPT code(s) are assigned?
    a. 12002, 12004
    b. 12004
    c. 12035
    d. 12045

50. Excision, three lesions, back. The first lesion is 0.5 cm and is located on the upper right back, the second lesion is 1.3 cm and is located on the midback, and the third lesion is 5.0 cm and is located on the lower left back. Pathology report indicated squamous cell carcinoma. Which CPT code(s) are assigned?
    a. 11406
    b. 11406, 11400-51, 11402-51
    c. 11606
    d. 11606, 11602-51, 11600-51

51. TRAM flap single pedicle breast reconstruction. Which CPT code is assigned?
    a. 19364
    b. 19366
    c. 19367
    d. 19369

52. Electrosurgery of three flat warts, left side of neck. Which CPT code(s) are assigned?
    a. 11420
    b. 17000, 17003 × 2
    c. 17106
    d. 17110

53. Excision including wide margin, 3.5-cm skin lesion, right forearm. The total amount of tissue removed measured 6.5 cm in diameter, per the physician's report. The lesion was sent in total to pathology for analysis. Skin defect was closed in layers, including deeper layers of subcutaneous tissue, with 2.0 Vicryl and 1.0 nylon. Pathologist reported that the lesion is malignant.
    a. 11406, 12032-51
    b. 11604, 11606-51, 12032-51
    c. 11606, 12002-51
    d. 11606, 12032-51

54. Which type of repair includes layered closure of skin and single-layer closure of heavily contaminated wounds?
    a. Complex
    b. Fascia
    c. Intermediate
    d. Simple

55. CPT classifies Z-plasty, W-plasty, and V-Y-plasty as:
    a. adjacent tissue transfer or rearrangement.
    b. allografts.
    c. complex repairs.
    d. skin replacement surgery.

CPT Surgery 20000 (10)

56. Malunion of right radius and ulna treated with autograft. Short-arm cast applied at conclusion of procedure. Which CPT code(s) are assigned?
    a. 25420-RT
    b. 25420-RT, 29075-RT
    c. 25560-RT
    d. 25560-RT, 29075-RT

57. Akin procedure, left foot. Which CPT code is assigned?
    a. 28291-LT
    b. 28292-LT
    c. 28298-LT
    d. 28299-LT

58. Open reduction and external fixation, Monteggia fracture dislocation, left elbow. Large contaminated open wound was also noted, requiring extensive subcutaneous fracture site debridement. Posterior splint was applied. Which CPT codes are assigned?
    a. 24635-LT, 11010-51-LT
    b. 24635-LT, 20692-LT, 29105-51-LT
    c. 24650-LT, 11010-51-LT, 20692-51-LT
    d. 24685-LT, 11010-51-LT, 29105-51-LT

59. Which is the correct description of CPT code 28192?
    a. Removal of foreign body, foot; subcutaneous deep
    b. Deep
    c. Removal of foreign body, foot; deep
    d. Removal of foreign body, foot; deep, complicated

60. Open treatment of fractured big toe, left foot. Application of ambulatory-type short-leg cast. Which CPT code(s) are assigned?
a. 28515-TA
b. 28525-TA
c. 28505-TA
d. 28505-TA, 29425-TA

61. Arthroscopic knee meniscectomy, medial, including meniscal shaving. Which CPT code is assigned?
a. 29880
b. 29881
c. 29882
d. 29883

62. Open treatment of two fractures of two ribs with internal fixation, one on the right side and one on the left. Which CPT code(s) are assigned?
a. 21811
b. 21811-50
c. 21811, 21811-51
d. 21811-50

63. Surgical treatment is performed for a patient who has sustained a right humeral shaft fracture. The orthopedic surgeon performs open treatment of the fracture using an intramedullary implant and locking screws. Following the surgical procedure, a cast is applied. Which CPT code(s) are assigned?
a. 24516-RT
b. 24516-RT, 24516-RT
c. 24516-RT, 29065-RT
d. 29065-RT

64. Closed reduction and manipulation of right tibial shaft fracture with application of plaster cast. Which CPT code is assigned?
a. 27750-RT
b. 27752-RT
c. 27756-RT
d. 27759-RT

65. Incision and drainage infected bursa, left wrist. Which CPT code is assigned?
a. 25028-LT
b. 25031-LT
c. 25035-LT
d. 25075-LT

CPT Surgery 30000 (10)

66. Repair of mitral valve with patient under bypass. Which CPT code is assigned?
a. 33420
b. 33422
c. 33425
d. 33430

67. Insertion of a nontunneled central venous catheter. Patient is 4 years old. Which CPT code is assigned?
a. 36555
b. 36556
c. 36557
d. 36560

68. At 9 AM, patient underwent posterior control of epistaxis with cauterization. The patient returned at 4 PM for repeat posterior control of epistaxis with cauterization. Which code is assigned for the second procedure?
a. 30901
b. 30903
c. 30905
d. 30906

69. After administration of topical anesthesia, a piece of latex balloon was removed from a 10-year-old male's trachea using biopsy forceps through a flexible fiberoptic laryngoscope. The piece of latex balloon was found just past the larynx. It had threatened to obstruct the patient's breathing. Which CPT code is assigned?
a. 30300
b. 31511
c. 31530
d. 31577

70. Bronchoscopy performed due to patient's complaint of severe pain that began last night at dinner when the patient coughed up a mass of food. Bronchoscope was inserted, and a food bolus was noted in the patient's trachea. The bolus was removed. Which CPT code(s) are assigned?
a. 31622
b. 31622, 31635
c. 31635
d. 32151

71. Diagnostic bronchoscopy with transbronchial biopsy of the lung. Which CPT code(s) are assigned?
   a. 31622, 31628
   b. 31622, 76000
   c. 31628
   d. 31628, 76000

72. Insertion, Hickman catheter (cutdown) (age 70). Which CPT code is assigned?
   a. 36558
   b. 36561
   c. 36569
   d. 36571

73. Four-vessel coronary artery bypass graft (CABG) involving three saphenous vein grafts and a left internal mammary arterial graft. Which CPT code(s) are reported by the assistant surgeon?
   a. 33513-80
   b. 33519-80, 33533-80
   c. 33521-80
   d. 33536-80

74. Repair of thoracoabdominal aortic aneurysm with graft. Which CPT code is assigned?
   a. 33852
   b. 33875
   c. 33877
   d. 33880

75. Repair of diaphragm laceration. Which CPT code is assigned?
   a. 39501
   b. 39540
   c. 39560
   d. 39599

CPT Surgery 40000 (10)

76. Proctosigmoidoscopy with removal of two polyps by snare technique. Which CPT code(s) are assigned?
   a. 45300-59
   b. 45300-59, 45135
   c. 45315
   d. 45315, 45315

77. Proctosigmoidoscopy with ablation of one polyp. Removal of another lesion via snare technique. Which CPT code(s) are assigned?
   a. 45309
   b. 45320
   c. 45320, 45309-59
   d. 45320, 45309-51

78. A 37-year-old patient underwent colonoscopy with control of bleeding by laser treatment as well as blood transfusion. Diagnosis was angiodysplasia with hemorrhage, transverse colon. Which ICD-10-CM and CPT codes are assigned?
   a. K55.20, K92.2, 45382
   b. K55.21, 45382, 36430
   c. K55.20, K92.2, 45382, 36430
   d. K92.2, K55.20, 45382, 36430

79. Surgical care of total gastrectomy with bypass, esophagus to intestine. Which CPT code is assigned?
   a. 43632-55
   b. 43620-54
   c. 43632-54
   d. 43620-26

80. Diagnostic colonoscopy for evaluation of complaints of rectal bleeding. Patient was unable to tolerate the office procedure, and it was terminated. Patient successfully underwent procedure one week later in the hospital's ambulatory surgery unit, under sedation. Which CPT code(s) are reported for the terminated office procedure?
   a. 45378
   b. 45378-53
   c. 45378-53, 45378
   d. 45378-73

81. Colonoscopy with removal of polyps. Ascending colon polyps were removed via hot biopsy forceps. Transverse colon polyps were removed via snare technique. Which ICD-10-CM and CPT codes are assigned?
   a. D12.2, D12.3, 45399
   b. D12.2, D12.3, 45385, 45384-59
   c. D12.2, D12.3, 44392, 44394-59
   d. D12.2, D12.3, 45399, 45388-59

82. Laparoscopic esophagogastric fundoplasty. Which CPT code is assigned?
   a. 43280
   b. 43325
   c. 43327
   d. 49320

83. Colonoscopy performed to rule out carcinoma. During colonoscopy, severe diverticulosis was noted and identified as the cause of GI bleeding. A polyp at the splenic flexure and another polyp in the transverse colon were also noted. Splenic flexure polypectomy performed via hot biopsy, and transverse colon polypectomy was done via snare technique. Which CPT code(s) are assigned?
   a. 45388, 45384-59
   b. 45384
   c. 45385
   d. 45385, 45384-59

84. Patient received follow-up care by his primary care physician after having undergone surgery performed by a different physician to repair a sliding inguinal hernia. Which CPT code is assigned by the primary care physician?
   a. 49525-24
   b. 49525-25
   c. 49525-55
   d. 49525-77

85. EGD with biopsy of esophagus and stomach. Which CPT code(s) are assigned?
   a. 43235-59
   b. 43235-59, 43239
   c. 43239
   d. 43239, 43239

CPT Surgery 50000 (10)

86. Transurethral electrosurgical resection of prostate with diagnostic cystoscopy, urethral dilation, and internal urethrotomy was performed for benign prostatic hyperplasia. A urinary catheter was placed at the conclusion of the procedure. Twenty-four hours postoperatively, excessive bleeding from the catheter was noted and the catheter was removed. The surgeon inserted a larger catheter to control the bleeding. Which CPT code(s) are assigned?
   a. 52601
   b. 52601, 51702
   c. 52601, 52601
   d. 52601, 53010, 53600, 52344

87. Cystourethroscopy with bilateral ureteral meatotomy. Which CPT code(s) are assigned?
   a. 52204
   b. 52204, 52290
   c. 52204, 52290-51
   d. 52290

88. Total abdominal hysterectomy with bilateral salpingo-oophorectomy. Which CPT code is assigned?
   a. 58150
   b. 58150-50
   c. 58152
   d. 58200

89. Exploratory laparotomy with bilateral salpingo-oophorectomy. Which CPT code(s) are assigned?
   a. 58720
   b. 58720-50
   c. 58720, 47015
   d. 58720-50, 49000

90. Endoscopic laser surgery of 0.85-cm benign bladder tumor. Which CPT code is assigned?
   a. 52214
   b. 52224
   c. 52234
   d. 51530

91. A female patient presented with placenta previa and underwent emergency cesarean section, which was performed by Dr. Jones, obstetrician. Antepartum and postpartum care were provided by Dr. Garfield, general practitioner. (Dr. Jones and Dr. Garfield do not belong to the same group practice.) Which CPT code is reported for the procedure performed by Dr. Jones?
   a. 59400
   b. 59618
   c. 59514
   d. 59510

92. Male patient diagnosed with benign prostatic hypertrophy underwent transurethral destruction of the prostate via radiofrequency thermotherapy. Which CPT code is assigned?
   a. 52601
   b. 52648
   c. 53850
   d. 53852

93. A 35-year-old male previously diagnosed with renal calculus via x-ray underwent endoscopy for the purpose of passing an electrohydraulic lithotriptor probe through the ureter to pulverize the stone. An indwelling double-J stent was then placed to facilitate passing of any residual stones. Which ICD-10-CM and CPT codes are assigned?
   a. N20.0, 53256
   b. N20.0, 52353
   c. N20.1, 52352, 52332-51
   d. N20.1, 52353, 52332-51
94. A 29-year-old patient underwent evacuation of uterus for blighted ovum. She was in her second month. Which ICD-10-CM and CPT codes are assigned?
   a. O02.0, 59820
   b. O02.0, 59821
   c. O02.1, 59820
   d. O02.1, 59821
95. Chorionic villus sampling via ultrasound guidance. Which CPT code(s) are assigned?
   a. 59015
   b. 59015, 76945
   c. 59015, 84702
   d. 59015, 84703

CPT Surgery 60000 (10)

96. Bilateral laminotomy of C4–C5 interspace with posterior arthrodesis. Decompression of nerve roots and excision of herniated disc was also performed. Which CPT code(s) are assigned?
   a. 22600
   b. 63020, 63020-51
   c. 63020-50
   d. 63020-50, 22600-51
97. Right S2–S3 paravertebral facet joint anesthetic nerve block with image guidance, sacral level, for right sacroiliac joint dysfunction. Which CPT code is assigned?
   a. 62322-RT
   b. 64490-RT
   c. 64493-RT
   d. 64520-RT
98. Injection and continuous infusion of opioid, C3. Which CPT code is assigned?
   a. 62290
   b. 62292
   c. 62320
   d. 62324
99. Repair of perforating sclera laceration with resection of uveal tissue. Which CPT code is assigned?
   a. 65280
   b. 65285
   c. 65286
   d. 65290
100. Reduction of protruding ears. Which CPT code is assigned?
   a. 69300
   b. 69300-50
   c. 69310
   d. 69320
101. Excision of neuroma, digital nerve of left foot. Which CPT code is assigned?
   a. 28080-LT
   b. 28086-LT
   c. 64776-LT
   d. 64782-LT
102. Needle biopsy of thyroid. Which CPT code is assigned?
   a. 60100
   b. 60200
   c. 60210
   d. 60212
103. Injection of anesthetic agent into vagus nerve. Which CPT code is assigned?
   a. 64408
   b. 64447
   c. 64450
   d. 64746
104. Removal of impacted cerumen, requiring instrumentation, left ear. Which CPT code is assigned?
   a. 69200
   b. 69200-LT
   c. 69210
   d. 69210-LT

105. Iridectomy with extracapsular removal of cataract via phacoemulsification technique and insertion of intraocular lens, left eye. Which CPT code(s) are assigned?
   a. 66983-LT
   b. 66983-LT, 66635-LT
   c. 66984-LT
   d. 66984-LT, 66761-LT

Section 3: Additional Areas for CPC Exam

CPT E/M

106. Mr. Silver was seen by Dr. Gold today for a complaint of diarrhea. Mr. Silver is routinely seen by Dr. Gold every six months for recheck of the patient's hypertension and type 2 diabetes mellitus. During today's visit, Dr. Gold documented a problem-focused history and an expanded problem-focused exam. Medical decision making was of low complexity. Which CPT code is assigned?
   a. 99212
   b. 99213
   c. 99203
   d. 99204

107. Dr. Wilson treated new patient Mary Greene in his office. Ms. Greene's chief complaint was abdominal pain. Dr. Wilson performed a detailed history and comprehensive examination. Medical decision making was of moderate complexity. Which CPT code is assigned?
   a. 99203
   b. 99204
   c. 99211
   d. 99213

108. The documentation of a patient's maternal history, status of parents and siblings, would be considered part of the _______________.
   a. family history
   b. history of present illness
   c. past history
   d. social history

109. A 49-year-old female was evaluated by a specialist during an office consultation for possible hysterectomy. The patient's primary care physician arranged for the consultation services, which were required by the patient's third-party payer. The consulting physician performed a comprehensive history and exam, and medical decision making was of moderate complexity. Which CPT code is assigned?
   a. 99244
   b. 99244-32
   c. 99245
   d. 99245-32

110. Critical care services were provided to an adult who required constant physician attendance for 110 minutes. Which CPT code(s) are assigned?
   a. 99291-21
   b. 99291, 99292
   c. 99291, 99291-21
   d. 99291, 99292, 99292

111. Assign an E/M code based on documentation in the following office note for established patient Morris Smith.

   CHIEF COMPLAINT: Upper respiratory infection.

   SUBJECTIVE: This 69-year-old patient exhibits symptoms of an upper respiratory infection, which include a dry tickling cough for the past five days' duration. The patient is due to see Dr. Blane next week for follow-up about his prostate cancer.

   OBJECTIVE: Blood pressure 124/82, left arm sitting. Blood pressure 122/75, right arm supine. Oropharynx benign. Nose is not particularly congested. Lungs sound clear.

   ASSESSMENT: Upper respiratory infection. Hypertension. Prostate cancer.

   PLAN: Symptomatic care. Continue present medications for hypertension.

   Run PSA test next week in preparation for visit to Dr. Blane. Return in three months.

   a. 99202
   b. 99203
   c. 99212
   d. 99213

112. Liza Jones was seen by Dr. Adams for her first office visit. She has complaints of off-and-on epigastric abdominal pain with nausea. Dr. Adams documented a comprehensive history and a detailed examination. Medical decision making was of moderate complexity. He ordered an abdominal x-ray series and prescribed medication for the patient. Which CPT code is assigned?
   a. 99202
   b. 99203
   c. 99204
   d. 99213

113. A 54-year-old patient underwent an annual physical examination, which was performed by his primary care physician.
   a. 99213
   b. 99386
   c. 99396
   d. 99412

114. Dr. Smith provided critical care services to his 92-year-old male patient in the hospital on June 10 from 6:30 AM until 7:20 AM. He again provided critical care to the patient on June 11 from 7:00 AM until 7:30 AM. Which CPT code(s) are assigned?
   a. 99291
   b. 99291, 99291
   c. 99291, 99292
   d. 99291, 99292, 99292

115. A full-term baby boy was born at a local community hospital on August 9, at which time the infant's Apgar scores were 10 and 10 and the normal infant was examined prior to his admission to the nursery. On the morning of the second day of admission (August 10), the normal newborn was discharged home with his mother. Which CPT code(s) are assigned?
   a. 99460
   b. 99460, 99462
   c. 99461
   d. 99463

CPT Anesthesia

116. General anesthesia administered to a patient who underwent breast reconstruction with TRAM flap. Which CPT code is assigned?
   a. 00404
   b. 00406
   c. 00402
   d. 00400

117. General anesthesia administered to a patient who underwent transvenous insertion of a pacemaker. Which CPT code is assigned?
   a. 00560
   b. 00534
   c. 00530
   d. 00563

118. Regional anesthesia administered to a patient who underwent a C-section. Which CPT code is assigned?
   a. 01961
   b. 01963
   c. 01968
   d. 01969

119. General anesthesia administered to a 6-month-old patient who underwent repair of a cleft palate. Which CPT codes are assigned?
   a. 00172, 99100
   b. 00176, 99100
   c. 00190, 99100
   d. 00210, 99100

120. Regional anesthesia administered to a 50-year-old female patient with a recent history of fainting who underwent an interventional radiologic procedure, left carotid artery. Which CPT code is assigned?
   a. 00216
   b. 00350
   c. 01925
   d. 01933

CPT Radiology

121. Patient is a 45-year-old female who presents for her first mammography. The patient has no family history of cancer, and personal medical history includes only hypertension. The screening mammography is negative for the presence of any carcinoma and shows only mild fibrocystic disease in the left breast. Which CPT code is assigned?
 a. 77066
 b. 77067
 c. 77063
 d. 77065

122. Dr. Gusman provided the interpretation and report for a patient's lateral and AP views of right hand. This x-ray was done at another facility. Which CPT code is assigned?
 a. 73120
 b. 73120-26
 c. 73130
 d. 73130-26

123. Which term is used to describe applying a radioactive material inside a patient or in close proximity to the patient to generate local regions of high-intensity radiation?
 a. Brachytherapy
 b. Hyperthermia
 c. Interventional radiology
 d. Nuclear medicine

124. To report the administration of contrast material used during an outpatient radiologic procedure _______________.
 a. add the correct CPT modifier to the radiology code
 b. add the correct HCPCS level II modifier to the radiology code
 c. report an HCPCS code
 d. report an ICD-10-PCS procedure code

125. Which involves the administration of radioisotopes for the purpose of diagnosis?
 a. Clinical brachytherapy
 b. Nuclear medicine
 c. Radiation oncology
 d. Ultrasound

126. Which radiology technique uses high-frequency inaudible sound waves that bounce off body tissues and are then recorded?
 a. CT scan
 b. Ipsilateral
 c. Mammography
 d. Ultrasound

127. Complete pelvic ultrasound on a 20-year-old patient who is not pregnant. Which CPT code is assigned?
 a. 76856
 b. 76857
 c. 76970
 d. 76998

128. Whole body bone scan. Which CPT code is assigned?
 a. 78305
 b. 78306
 c. 78315
 d. 78350

129. CT scan of brain without contrast medium followed by contrast medium and further sections. Which CPT code(s) are assigned?
 a. 70450
 b. 70450, 70460
 c. 70460
 d. 70470

130. Unilateral digital breast tomosynthesis. Which CPT code is assigned?
 a. 77053
 b. 77054
 c. 77061
 d. 77062

CPT Pathology and Laboratory

131. Physician office laboratories are regulated by:
 a. CMS.
 b. CLIA.
 c. OIG.
 d. third-party payers.

132. Groups of codes in the CPT Pathology and Laboratory section that describe blood lab tests commonly performed together for a given reason are called _______________ codes.
 a. panel
 b. qualitative
 c. quantitative
 d. screening

133. Patient underwent basic metabolic blood panel, which included quantitative glucose, triglycerides, and CBC with WBC differential. Which CPT code(s) are assigned?
 a. 80048
 b. 82947, 84478, 85025
 c. 82947, 84478, 85027
 d. 80048, 82747, 84478, 85025

134. Gross examination of tonsils. Which CPT code is assigned?
 a. 88300
 b. 88302
 c. 88305
 d. 88309

135. Specimen from the peripheral nerve of the patient's left ankle submitted for morphometric analysis. Which CPT code is assigned?
 a. 88300
 b. 88309
 c. 88321
 d. 88356

136. Surgical pathology, gross and microscopic examination of biopsy of pancreas. Which CPT code is assigned?
 a. 88305
 b. 88304
 c. 88307
 d. 88309

137. Pathology frozen section analysis of breast tissue (one block) during surgery. Which CPT code is assigned?
 a. 88329
 b. 88331
 c. 88332
 d. 88333

138. Electrolyte panel, which tested for carbon dioxide, chloride, potassium, and sodium. Which CPT code(s) are assigned?
 a. 80051
 b. 80051, 82374, 82435, 84132, 84295
 c. 80051, 82374-51, 82435-51, 84132-51, 84295-51
 d. 82374, 82435, 84132, 84295

139. Cryopreservation of sperm. Which CPT code is assigned?
 a. 89258
 b. 89259
 c. 89260
 d. 89264

140. Testing for antibodies to rubella. Which CPT code is assigned?
 a. 86759
 b. 86762
 c. 86765
 d. 90710

CPT Medicine

141. Hepatitis A vaccine administered IM to a 30-year-old female. Which CPT code(s) are assigned?
 a. 90632
 b. 90632, 90471
 c. 90633
 d. 90633, 90471

142. Respiratory syncytial virus immune globulin administered via intramuscular injection. Which CPT code(s) are assigned?
 a. 90378
 b. 90378, 96372
 c. 86756
 d. 86756, 96365

143. Needle electromyography testing of the legs and both eyes was conducted. Which CPT codes are assigned?
 a. 92265-50, 95861
 b. 95861, 92265
 c. 95868-59, 95861
 d. 95870, 95861, 99201

144. Administration of rabies immune globulin. Which CPT codes are assigned?
   a. 90375, 96372
   b. 90376, 96372
   c. 90675, 90471
   d. 90676, 90471

145. IV infusion of chemotherapy for three hours. Which CPT code(s) are assigned?
   a. 96413, 96413, 96413
   b. 96413, 96415, 96415
   c. 96413, 96416
   d. 96416

146. Established patient received individual insight-oriented psychotherapy for 25 minutes. The physician also provided a problem-focused history and examination and straightforward level of medical decision making. Which CPT code(s) are assigned?
   a. 99212, 90833
   b. 90833
   c. 99212, 90785
   d. 90785

147. A 54-year-old patient with end-stage renal disease (ESRD) received ESRD services twice a week during the month of August, totaling nine encounters. Which CPT code(s) are assigned?
   a. 90960
   b. 90960 × 9
   c. 90961 × 9
   d. 90999

148. Suzie Matthews is a 22-year-old nursing student who received a Hep A and a Hep B vaccine via IM route prior to starting her clinical rotations. Which CPT codes are assigned?
   a. 90471, 90634-51
   b. 90471, 90636
   c. 96372, 90634
   d. 96372, 90633

149. Hearing aid examination and selection, binaural. Which CPT code is assigned?
   a. 92590
   b. 92591
   c. 92592
   d. 92293

150. Wet-to-moist dressing nonselective debridement for treatment of burn, right foot. Which CPT code is assigned?
   a. 97597-RT
   b. 97598-RT
   c. 97602-RT
   d. 97605-RT

APPENDIX

F

Mock Certified Coding Specialist—Physician-based (CCS-P) Certification Examination

PART I: CERTIFIED CODING SPECIALIST—PHYSICIAN-BASED (CCS-P) MOCK EXAM

The CCS-P certification exam is offered by the American Health Information Management Association (AHIMA). Detailed information on the exam including content, question format, testing sites, etc., can be found at the AHIMA site (www.ahima.org). Information about this certification exam is also provided in the *Candidate Handbook*, which can be downloaded from the AHIMA site. The first portion of the CCS-P exam consists of 60 questions in multiple-choice format. Provided in this appendix is a mock exam for coding practice.

NOTE:

The CCS-P certification exam also requires the assignment of ICD-10-CM, CPT, and HCPCS level II codes to actual patient records. Appendices A–C of the *Workbook to Accompany 3-2-1 Code It!* contain ambulatory surgery center, emergency department, and physician office records, all of which can be used to practice assigning ICD-10-CM, CPT, and HCPCS level II codes.

1. Andres Mink underwent a colonoscopy, performed by Dr. Hershey, in the ambulatory surgery unit of a local hospital. When submitting the claim for this service, which coding manual(s) would be used to assign diagnosis and procedure codes?
   a. HCPCS
   b. ICD-10-CM and CPT
   c. ICD-10-CM
   d. ICD-O-3

2. The coding supervisor at a local hospital reviews a report that contains information about codes assigned by a new coder. The new coder is responsible for assigning codes to emergency department and ambulatory surgery unit charts. The coding supervisor was particularly concerned about information presented in the table below. Based on information in this table, which statement below is valid? The new coder:

Patient Name	Patient #	Date of Surgery	First-Listed Diagnosis	First-Listed Procedure
M. Richards	23420	07/08/YYYY	E04.1	60240
C. Johnson	43940	07/08/YYYY	R63.0	0DJD8ZZ
J. Landing	56654	07/09/YYYY	N64.4	99214
S. Kelly	63565	07/09/YYYY	R22.2	0HB7XZX

   a. assigned first-listed diagnosis codes incorrectly from the ICD-10-CM coding manual.
   b. entered incorrect discharge dates and medical record numbers for the patients.
   c. incorrectly assigned codes for the first-listed diagnosis instead of the principal diagnoses.
   d. should have used the CPT coding manual to assign all first-listed procedure codes.

3. Which publication is released quarterly by the American Hospital Association and identifies issues and/or questions regarding ICD-10-CM coding guidelines?
   a. *Coding Clinic*
   b. *CPT Assistant*
   c. *JAHIMA*
   d. *The Coding Edge*
4. During the review of 10 records, it was noted that the following data were documented: (1) living arrangements prior to admission to home health care, (2) integumentary status, (3) activities of daily living (ADL) status, and (4) pain status. Which data set is used to capture this type of information?
   a. HEDIS
   b. OASIS
   c. ORYX
   d. UHDDS
5. The following information about patient John R. Wakefield was abstracted from his record and entered into a database. Which data set is used to capture this type of information?

Date of Birth:	10/17/68
Date of Admission:	08/09/2008
Time of Admission:	11:55 PM
Method of Arrival:	Personal Car
Patient Number:	456987
Facility NPI:	4567890120
Provider NPI:	8997678980
Admitting Dx Code:	R10.13
ED Procedures:	74019, 76770, 80050
Discharge Dx Code:	K29.00
Discharge Date:	08/10/2008
Discharge Time:	3:35 AM
Disposition:	Home

   a. DEEDS
   b. MDS
   c. UACDS
   d. UHDDS
6. Which is a function of physician orders?
   a. They document the provider's instructions for follow-up care and are given to the patient.
   b. They document a chronological summary of the patient's illness and treatment.
   c. They document the patient's current and past health status.
   d. They document the physician's instructions to other parties involved in providing care to a patient.
7. Which document would be excluded from the patient record for an elective inpatient surgery admission?
   a. Allergies and ROS report
   b. Anesthesia record
   c. Discharge summary
   d. EMT care sheet
8. Based on the information provided in the note (below), documented in John Cali's patient record, in what type of health care facility is Mr. Cali being treated?

   Medication History: Tylenol for headaches, Claritin for allergies, and Atenolol 50 mg for hypertension. 05/06/YYYY Mr. Cali was given 2 Tylenol capsules for complaint of headache. He was given water to take with this over-the-counter medication. Patient was observed while taking medication. Patient was then escorted back to the common area for planned group activity.
   Reviewed and Approved: R Karey RN ATP-B-S:02:1001261385: R Karey RN (Signed: 7/15/YYYY 2:20:44 PM EST)

   a. Acute care facility
   b. Correctional facility
   c. Home health agency
   d. Hospice agency

9. Codes in the ICD-10-CM tabular list with "unspecified" in the title are for use when the ______________.
   a. codes should not be reported as first-listed diagnoses
   b. description defines, clarifies, or provides examples of codes
   c. documentation is not sufficient to assign a more specific code
   d. documentation provides detail for which a specific code does not exist
10. A patient received scheduled chemotherapy treatment for right lung cancer in the hospital outpatient department. The patient underwent removal of a malignant right lung nodule four weeks ago. Which of the following ICD-10-CM diagnosis codes would be reported on the insurance claim?

    C34.91 Malignant neoplasm of bronchus and lung, unspecified
    Z51.11 Encounter for antineoplastic chemotherapy and immunotherapy
    Z85.118 Personal history of malignant neoplasm bronchus and lung

   a. All of the diagnosis codes would be reported, in the order listed, on the claim.
   b. Code C34.91 would be reported as the only diagnosis code on the insurance claim.
   c. Code Z85.118 would be reported as the first-listed diagnosis code on the insurance claim.
   d. Code Z51.11 would be reported as the first-listed diagnosis code on the claim, followed by code C34.91.
11. For a patient with a documented fracture and dislocation at the same anatomical site, which is coded?
   a. Dislocation only
   b. Fracture and dislocation
   c. Fracture only
   d. Query the physician as to which is clinically significant.
12. A 45-year-old female patient presents to the physician with a rash, right lower leg. The patient reports that she has had the rash for over six months, with no change upon application of over-the-counter topical medications. The physician examines the patient and determines that the patient has a fungal rash. Due to the history of this rash, the physician prescribes an antifungal medication to be taken by mouth. The patient takes the medication for three days, as prescribed, and returns to the office complaining of severe dizziness. She is found to be hypotensive upon examination during this visit. She is instructed to stop taking the oral antifungal medication, and she is given a prescription for an antifungal topical cream. The diagnosis of hypotension would be coded as a(n):
   a. adverse effect.
   b. overdose.
   c. poisoning.
   d. toxic effect.
13. When coding burns, assign ______________.
   a. nonhealing burns as sequelae of the original burn
   b. necrosis of burned skin and other tissue as nonhealed burn codes
   c. one single combination code, regardless of the number of burn sites
   d. separate and distinct codes for each burn site, based on physician documentation
14. A patient presents for treatment of a bullet wound, upper leg, through the femoral shaft. The bullet passed through the skin of the leg and is lodged in bone, resulting in a fracture. This type of fracture is classified as a(n):
   a. compound closed fracture.
   b. missile closed fracture.
   c. missile open fracture.
   d. open greenstick fracture.

15. Five-year-old patient Michael Walker underwent a reduction of a tarsal dislocation that included manipulation without anesthesia. After reduction, the physician applied a short-leg cast. CPT codes 28540 and 29405-51 were reported on the insurance claim for this encounter. Based upon review of the CPT codes and description below, which statement is correct?

28540	Closed treatment of tarsal bone dislocation without anesthesia
29405-51	Application of short leg cast

a. Code 29405-51 is included in code 28540 and should not be reported separately.
b. Code 29405-51 should be reported as the first-listed procedure.
c. Codes 28540 and 29405-51 should be reported on the claim, in that order.
d. Modifier -51 should not be reported with code 28540 or code 29405.

16. A 25-year-old patient is seen in the emergency department (ED) with a complaint of RUQ abdominal pain. The patient underwent a cholecystectomy eight weeks ago. The patient states that the current location of her pain is the same as precholecystectomy surgery. The ED final diagnosis is status postcholecystectomy due to chronic cholelithiasis. The coder should:
a. assign a code for chronic cholelithiasis as an active condition.
b. code the patient's reported symptom of RUQ abdominal pain.
c. query the physician to ask if the patient has postcholecystectomy syndrome.
d. report a V code as the first-listed diagnosis code.

17. Intrathecal drugs are administered into the:
a. brain.
b. CSF.
c. nerve(s).
d. PNS.

18. Lipomas, fibromas, and adenomas are classified as:
a. benign.
b. cancer *in situ*.
c. malignant.
d. uncertain behavior.

19. To determine a comprehensive exam level for an evaluation and management service under the 1995 E/M coding guidelines, review the patient record to locate documentation of:
a. 5 organ systems, 3 body areas, and a complete ROS.
b. 8 body areas.
c. 8 organ systems.
d. 8 organ systems and body areas.

20. The classification of a patient into a Home Health Resource Group (HHRG) is based on information collected from the _______________ data collection tool.
a. HCPCS
b. OASIS
c. RAVEN
d. RBRVS

21. In the ICD-10-CM coding system, an esophageal stricture due to a burn sustained from a house fire two years ago would be classified as a(n):
a. abnormal reaction.
b. current injury.
c. late effect or sequela.
d. mechanical complication.

22. Which of the following data sets is used by ambulatory care facilities?
a. MDS
b. OASIS
c. UACDS
d. UHDDS

23. During the incision and drainage of a deep abscess, the physician documented that the incision penetrated the fascia. To report the appropriate code, review the CPT Surgery _______________ subsection.
a. general
b. integumentary
c. musculoskeletal
d. operating microscope

24. What is the difference between the DEEDS data set and the EMDS data set?
  a. The DEEDS data set focuses on data collection for a specific emergency department encounter, whereas the EMDS data set is collected to build a health history.
  b. The DEEDS data set focuses on the collection of data to build a health history, whereas the EMDS data set is collected for a specific emergency department encounter.
  c. The DEEDS data set is collected for emergency department visits, whereas the EMDS data set is collected for physician office visits.
  d. The EMDS data set is used to collect data on ambulatory encounters (e.g., outpatient surgery), whereas the DEEDS data set is used to collect data about emergency department visits.

25. A local safety council has requested statistics about the number of head injuries that occurred as a result of motorcycle accidents during the past year. Which coding system would be used to collect that data?
  a. HCPCS level I
  b. HCPCS level II
  c. ICD-10-CM
  d. ICD-10-PCS

26. The placement of radioactive sources into a tumor-bearing area to generate high-intensity radiation is called:
  a. brachytherapy.
  b. external beam radiation.
  c. proton beam treatment.
  d. stereotactic radiation treatment.

27. A patient underwent bypass surgery for life-threatening coronary artery disease. With the aid of extracorporeal circulation, the right internal mammary artery was grafted onto the left anterior descending artery. Saphenous vein grafts were grafted from the aorta to the diagonal, right coronary artery and the posterior descending artery. ICD-10-PCS procedure codes would be reported for aortocoronary bypass of ______________ coronary arteries.
  a. one
  b. two
  c. three
  d. four

28. A condition is documented as both acute and chronic in the patient record, and upon review of the ICD-10-CM index, the coder notices two separate subterms. In this situation, the coder should assign:
  a. a code for the acute condition only.
  b. a code for the chronic condition only.
  c. codes for both the acute and chronic conditions, and sequence the acute condition first.
  d. codes for both the acute and chronic conditions, and sequence the chronic condition first.

29. Which ICD-10-CM code listed below could be reported as a first-listed diagnosis code?
  a. T59.891A (Accidental poisoning by gas distributed by pipeline)
  b. M9010/0 (Fibroadenoma NOS)
  c. Z37.2 (Outcome of delivery, twins, both liveborn)
  d. Z38.00 (Single liveborn, born in hospital)

30. A patient admitted to a local hospital for outpatient hernia repair surgery also has a low potassium level. Intravenous potassium was ordered by the attending physician and was administered to the patient. The attending physician did not include hypokalemia as a discharge diagnosis on the face sheet. Which action should the coder take?
  a. Assign a diagnosis code for hernia only.
  b. Code the hypokalemia as confirmed.
  c. Query the physician about the documented low potassium level.
  d. Report the low potassium level as an abnormal blood chemistry test.

31. ICD-10-CM code category I11 is reported for the diagnosis of:
  a. cardiomegaly with hypertension.
  b. congestive heart failure; hypertension.
  c. hypertensive heart disease.
  d. left heart failure with benign hypertension.

32. Which data set was designed to gather data about Medicare beneficiaries who receive home health services?
    a. HEDIS
    b. OASIS
    c. ORYX
    d. UHDDS

33. A patient presents to the emergency department after having been in a three-car motor vehicle accident (MVA) on a local expressway. The patient is in and out of consciousness and has an open femoral fracture with a possible arterial injury. The attending physician, who is also the head of the trauma service, examines the patient and documents the progress note below. Based on documentation in the progress note and the 1995 coding guidelines of E/M service, which level of evaluation and management services would be reported?

    Patient is a 42-year-old male involved in a motor vehicle accident, who sustained an open femoral fracture. There is severe bleeding and possible femoral artery injury. Patient is scheduled for immediate surgical repair. Patient is not able to provide any medical history since he is in and out of consciousness. Once he is stable for transport, he will be taken to operating room. No family members are present in the hospital at this time. Patient identification was retrieved from his wallet. Patient was alone in his vehicle.

    a. Level 1
    b. Level 3
    c. Level 4
    d. Level 5

34. The following progress note is documented for an established patient's office visit. Based on 1995 E/M coding guidelines, what is the level of exam that is documented for this visit?

    Mary Reynolds was seen complaining of painful and swollen right elbow. Patient reports no recent injury. Mary was shoveling snow over the weekend for herself and four of her elderly neighbors. She also reports low back pain. The patient took Tylenol and Motrin in an attempt to relieve the pain. These medications did not seem to help.

    S Right elbow and low back pain

    O Slightly limited ROM in right elbow. Left elbow ROM normal.

    A small amount of swelling posterior elbow, back with limited ROM. Neurological reflexes are normal 3 4. There is no bruising or redness of the skin noted for the areas of the arms or lower back. The entire trunk was examined for skin lesions. No bruising or lesions of the skin were found.

    A Strain lower back and right elbow.

    P Muscle relaxants for strains of back and elbow and x-ray of right elbow to rule out effusion or soft tissue damage.

    a. Comprehensive
    b. Detailed
    c. Expanded Problem Focused
    d. Problem Focused

35. The use of a transverse incision or horizontal slicing to remove epidermal and dermal lesions is called:
    a. debridement.
    b. excision.
    c. laser removal.
    d. shaving.

36. A patient swallowed part of a toy and is having difficulty breathing. The toy is found to be lodged in the patient's bronchus. The patient is scheduled for outpatient endoscopy to remove the foreign object. Which procedure would be used to retrieve this object?
    a. Flexible bronchoscopy
    b. Laryngoscopy
    c. Open tube bronchoscopy
    d. Thoracoscopy

37. Which is *excluded* from CPT's definition of a surgical package?
    a. Digital block anesthesia
    b. E/M visit to surgeon the day before surgery
    c. Incision and drainage of wound abscess in office during global period
    d. Patient evaluation in recovery room

38. In which section of the CPT coding manual is the lightning bolt symbol used?
    a. Anesthesia
    b. Surgery
    c. Medicine
    d. Pathology and Laboratory

39. A surgeon performed an intranasal lesion excision using a laser on the right and left nares of a patient, and a lesion from each nares was removed. Code 30117, Excision or destruction (e.g., laser), intranasal lesion, internal approach, is reported. Which modifier should be added to code 30117?
    a. None
    b. -50
    c. -51
    d. -59

40. Which are the contributory components associated with evaluation and management system CPT codes?
    a. Counseling, Coordination of Care, and the Nature of the Presenting Problem
    b. Critical Care Time and Nature of the Presenting Problem
    c. History, Examination, and Medical Decision Making
    d. Time and Nature of the Presenting Problem

41. Which is the format of a HCPCS level II modifier?
    a. 2-digit alphabetic or 2-digit alphanumeric
    b. 2-digit numeric
    c. 3-digit alphabetic or 3-digit alphanumeric
    d. 3-digit numeric

42. Regarding qualifying circumstance CPT codes, which statement is true? Qualifying circumstance codes are reported:
    a. as a stand-alone code for anesthesia services.
    b. for all anesthesia services provided.
    c. for all surgical procedures, inpatient and outpatient.
    d. only when they apply to that patient or situation.

43. Which code below is a CPT Category II code?
    a. 0085T
    b. 1035F
    c. 20555
    d. 99100

44. In which subsection of the CPT evaluation and management section is time *not* a descriptive component?
    a. Consultation, hospital, initial
    b. Custodial Care Services
    c. Emergency Department Services
    d. Office Visits, new patient

45. A 66-year-old patient underwent coronary artery bypass graft (CABG) surgery for which a pump oxygenator was used. During the procedure, an anesthesiologist placed a Swan-Ganz catheter. Per CPT anesthesia guidelines, a code for the placement of the Swan-Ganz catheter is:
    a. not reported because the CABG procedure was performed under conscious sedation, for which no anesthesia code is required.
    b. reported as a qualifying circumstance based on the patient's age.
    c. reported separately because placement of a Swan-Ganz catheter is not included in the anesthesia code.
    d. unnecessary because placement of a Swan-Ganz catheter is included in the anesthesia code.

46. Which is administered to a patient after exposure to a disease to help prevent the patient from becoming infected?
    a. Antigen
    b. Immune globulin
    c. Toxoid
    d. Vaccine

47. In order for a physician office to submit a claim for reimbursement of clinical lab testing, a ______________ waiver is required.
    a. CLIA
    b. CMS
    c. OIG
    d. state

48. Which abbreviation or acronym below is used when discussing Medicare's latest initiative to ensure provider compliance and to combat overpayment and underpayment of claims?
    a. CoP
    b. NCCI
    c. POA
    d. RAC
49. Which is used to analyze coding quality?
    a. Chargemaster review
    b. Chart audits
    c. Evaluation and management
    d. Review of systems
50. Which CPT term is used to describe lab tests that are commonly performed together?
    a. Allergy codes
    b. CLIA codes
    c. Panel codes
    d. Quantitative codes
51. Which type of drug testing determines how much of a specific substance is present in the sample?
    a. Qualitative
    b. Quantitative
    c. Suppression
    d. Toxoid
52. To correctly report a skin lesion removal, which information is reviewed in the patient record?
    a. Layer of lesion depth and size of lesion
    b. Lesion morphology, anesthesia used, and location of lesion
    c. Location and method of removal
    d. Location, size of lesion, method of removal, and lesion morphology
53. Wound repair that requires debridement and extensive undermining would be classified as:
    a. complex repair.
    b. destruction with debridement.
    c. intermediate repair.
    d. simple repair.
54. Which lesion would warrant Mohs micrographic surgery?
    a. Basal cell carcinoma
    b. Fibroadenoma
    c. Lipoma
    d. Seborrheic keratosis
55. A surgical service that is considered an integral part of one or more other surgical events would be classified as a(n):
    a. add-on code.
    b. global package.
    c. separate procedure.
    d. unlisted procedure.
56. When discussing CPT category III codes, which statement below is *false*?
    a. Category III codes are temporary codes.
    b. Category III codes are used if applicable instead of an unlisted Category I code.
    c. Category III codes are used to collect data on performance measurement.
    d. Category III may not conform to the requirements for Category I codes.
57. Which modifier is not approved for use in ambulatory surgery units (ASU)?
    a. -25
    b. -50
    c. -51
    d. -59
58. Which CPT appendix could be useful when updating a physician office's superbill?
    a. Appendix A
    b. Appendix B
    c. Appendix C
    d. Appendix D

59. A patient presents to a physician office with a complaint of a rash and a sore finger. The patient is examined with documentation of constitutional, integumentary, musculoskeletal, and lymphatic systems. After the patient is examined, the physician performs drainage of his subungual hematoma. The patient is provided a prescription for medication for his rash. Per CPT coding guidelines, a code from:
    a. both the evaluation and management (E/M) and integumentary subsections would be reported, with modifier -25 added to the E/M code.
    b. the evaluation and management and integumentary subsections would be reported, with modifier -25 added to the integumentary code.
    c. the evaluation and management subsection would be the only code reported.
    d. the integumentary subsection would be the only code reported.

60. Clinical examples are located in ______________ of the CPT coding manual.
    a. Appendix A
    b. Appendix C
    c. the Medicine Section
    d. the Pathology and Laboratory Section

PART II: CODING PATIENT CASES

Instructions

Assign ICD-10-CM and CPT codes to the following types of outpatient cases:

a. Hospital (e.g., outpatient treatment)
b. Emergency department
c. Operating room (e.g., operative report)
d. Physician office/clinic setting

NOTE:

- Assign diagnosis codes in accordance with ICD-10-CM coding conventions and instructional notations and the "Basic Coding Guidelines for Outpatient Services." Do not assign ICD-10-CM external cause of injuries and diseases codes or ICD-O-3 morphology codes. Do *not* assign ICD-10-PCS procedure codes.
- Assign procedure and service codes in accordance with CPT coding guidelines and notes. Do *not* assign CPT Category II or Category III codes. Do *not* assign modifiers.
- Evaluation and management (E/M) levels are included in each case that requires assignment of CPT E/M codes. It is not necessary to determine the level of history, examination, or medical decision making.

Hospital

1. HOSPITAL OUTPATIENT PATHOLOGY REPORT

   SPECIMEN RECEIVED: Right ear cholesteatoma.

   CLINICAL HISTORY: Congenital cholesteatoma, right middle ear.

   GROSS DESCRIPTION: Received in formalin labeled "right ear cholesteatoma" are multiple fragments of pink-tan material. The specimen is filtered and forms an aggregate 0.8 3 0.5 3 0.2 cm. The specimen is entirely submitted.

   FINAL PATHOLOGICAL DIAGNOSIS: Right ear cholesteatoma. Laminated keratinized debris and detached strips of keratinizing squamous epithelium consistent with cholesteatoma.

   ICD-10-CM: ______________________________

   CPT: ______________________________

2. HOSPITAL OUTPATIENT RESPIRATORY THERAPY VISIT

   REASON: Chronic emphysema.

   PROCEDURE: Patient received total vital capacity procedure for measurement of the largest volume of air he could expire from his lungs. Measurement of the amount of air inhaled and exhaled was calculated according to the patient's body size to determine lung capacity. Results indicated 5 liters, which is an excellent result for this patient.

   ICD-10-CM: ______________________________

   CPT: ______________________________

3. HOSPITAL OUTPATIENT DIALYSIS CENTER VISIT

   REASON: Chronic kidney disease, stage I.

   PROCEDURE: Hemoperfusion was performed to remove toxins from the patient's blood and to maintain fluid and electrolyte balance due to kidneys' dysfunction. Venipuncture was performed to draw the patient's blood, and hemoperfusion was performed through activated charcoal. As part of the hemoperfusion procedure, blood was transfused back into the patient using a needle and catheter.

   ICD-10-CM: ______________________________

   CPT: ______________________________

4. HOSPITAL OUTPATIENT AUDIOLOGY DEPARTMENT VISIT

   REASON: Failed hearing screening at patient's elementary school as part of annual screening.

   Patient underwent hearing test, pure tone, air only. Earphones were placed on the patient, who was asked to respond to tones of different pitches and intensities. This limited study resulted in appropriate responses from the patient. No further testing is needed. Patient's hearing is normal.

   ICD-10-CM: ______________________________

   CPT: ______________________________

Emergency Department

5. EMERGENCY DEPARTMENT VISIT

NOTE:

Patient received level 1 evaluation and management service.

HISTORY: This 64-year-old female presents to the emergency department stating that for the past few days she has had a fever and chills, has been extremely nauseous, and has had a poor appetite. Today, the patient became very tired and weak, ached all over, and had one episode of vomiting. The patient complains of no abdominal pains. Patient did say her last solid bowel movement was approximately 3–4 days ago.

PHYSICAL EXAMINATION: This 64-year-old female is alert, appears acutely ill. HEENT: Patient's mucous membranes are very dry. Neck is supple. Lungs are clear. Heart regular rate and rhythm with a 3 out of 6 high-pitched murmur heard over the entire chest. Abdomen is soft, nontender. Bowel sounds are somewhat remarkable. There is no evidence of any ankle edema.

LABORATORY DATA: All within normal limits.

DIAGNOSIS: Acute infectious viral gastroenteritis and dehydration.

ICD-10-CM: ______________________________

CPT: ______________________________

6. EMERGENCY DEPARTMENT VISIT

NOTE:

Patient received level 2 evaluation and management service.

CHIEF COMPLAINT: Fourteen-year-old male presents to the emergency department stating, "I cut my head."

HISTORY OF PRESENT ILLNESS: This 14-year-old male fell off his bike, injuring his head and sustaining a laceration that measures 4 cm and extends through the scalp to the skull. No step-off point was palpated.

REVIEW OF SYSTEMS: Patient denies dizziness, blurred vision, or headache. Bleeding from the laceration has ceased. Patient is experiencing pain at the laceration site and of the right elbow. Slight swelling of the laceration site is noted. Patient denies loss of consciousness.

PHYSICAL EXAMINATION: Exam of HEENT revealed the ears to be clear bilaterally. EYES: Pupils were equal and reactive. Funduscopic exam was normal. THROAT: The posterior pharynx was clear. NECK: Supple. Exam of the shoulders, chest, abdomen, hips, and lower and upper extremities was unremarkable with the exception of a small abrasion of the right elbow.

PROCEDURE: Under sterile technique, five simple 4-0 Prolene sutures were inserted in the scalp after the area was anesthetized with local anesthetic. The area was then dressed with a topical spray dressing and the patient was discharged after a skull x-ray revealed no apparent evidence of fracture.

However, the formal report is pending. Patient was given a head injury patient education form and advised to take aspirin or Tylenol only for pain. He is scheduled to be seen by the family physician on Tuesday for suture removal.

DIAGNOSES: Scalp laceration, 4 cm. Abrasion, of right upper arm.

ICD-10-CM: ______________________________

CPT: ______________________________

7. EMERGENCY DEPARTMENT VISIT

NOTE:

Patient received level 3 evaluation and management service.

HISTORY: This 37-year-old white female was seen in the emergency department today with a chief complaint of abdominal pain, nausea, vomiting, chills, and fever. The patient had started with pain in her abdomen on Saturday afternoon and this has not subsided much. She had fever of 103 at home, and at the present time her temperature is 104.

REVIEW OF SYSTEMS: She has had abdominal pain on both sides. It hurts her sometimes to walk. She has had a lot of frequency and urgency of urination, but she states that it does not hurt her to urinate.

LABORATORY DATA: Her white blood count was 17,000 with a preponderance of polys. Her urine shows a lot of white cells, too numerous to count, albuminuria, and some blood.

PHYSICAL EXAMINATION: Blood pressure 118/66, pulse 136, respirations 20, and temperature 104. The chest is clear to auscultation and percussion. Breath sounds are normal. No rales are heard. Heart reveals that the apex beats in the fifth interspace. A sinus tachycardia is present. No murmurs are heard. The abdomen is soft, but it is tender throughout both sides, a little more so on the right side. However, it is as bad in the right upper quadrant as it is in the right lower quadrant and quite a bit suprapubically. There was no rebound, no referred tenderness. Rectal examination revealed quite a bit of tenderness when the bladder was palpated but otherwise no particular tenderness in the pelvis. The perineum is quite excoriated, probably due to infected and very concentrated urine.

PLAN: The patient was hydrated and started on antibiotics, administered medication for the temperature elevation, and a culture and sensitivity of the urine was ordered. She is scheduled to return for recheck tomorrow at 9 AM.

IMPRESSION: Urinary tract infection.

ICD-10-CM: ______________________________

CPT: ______________________________

8. EMERGENCY DEPARTMENT VISIT

NOTE:

Patient received level 3 evaluation and management service.

This patient is a 20-year-old male who presents to the emergency department (ED) with a history of depression and apparently is under the care of his psychiatrist, Dr. Drake. Patient threatened to shoot himself in the abdomen twice on Sunday and, in fact, he carried out that suicidal ideation by having a loaded gun that was cocked and ready to fire. Since that time, he has continued to be depressed and was brought here, to the Crosby Medical Center ED, today by police. Apparently, the patient cried all the way over to the ED and then became very quiet here. When questioned he was tearful, claimed he had no intention of harming himself today, but he wanted to see Dr. Drake. This patient is an alert but depressed-appearing white male who is tearful and sullen and answers mostly by shaking his head "yes" or "no" or not at all. Dr. Drake was called, and he will be admitting the patient to the Karr Valley Psychiatric Hospital.

ASSESSMENT: Recurrent depression. Suicidal ideation.

PLAN: Transfer to Karr Valley Psychiatric Hospital for inpatient admission.

ICD-10-CM: ______________________________

CPT: ______________________________

Operating Room

9. OPERATIVE REPORT

PREOPERATIVE DIAGNOSIS: Basal cell carcinoma, skin of left jaw line, 12 mm.

POSTOPERATIVE DIAGNOSIS: Basal cell carcinoma, skin of left jaw line, 12 mm.

OPERATION: Excision of 1.2-cm lesion, skin of left jaw line, and closure with rhomboid flap.

ANESTHESIA: Local 1% lidocaine with 1:100,000 epinephrine.

INDICATIONS FOR PROCEDURE: This patient is a pleasant gentleman who was seen in my office with a lesion on his jaw line. This was felt to be a basal cell carcinoma. We discussed removal and he wished to pursue it. He was made aware of the risks of bleeding, infection, scarring, and recurrence and wished to proceed.

PROCEDURE: The area of planned incision was outlined with a marking pen, infiltrated with local anesthetic, prepped with Betadine solution, and sterile drapes applied. An incision was made around the lesion in a rhomboid pattern, carried through skin and subcutaneous tissue and the lesion was removed. It was tagged with a suture at the 12 o'clock position. A rhomboid flap was planned, elevated, and transposed into the defect. It was inset with interrupted buried 6-0 PDS sutures in simple interrupted running 6-0 Prolene sutures. It was dressed with Bacitracin. The patient tolerated it well.

ICD-10-CM: ______________________________

CPT: ______________________________

10. OPERATIVE REPORT

PREOPERATIVE DIAGNOSIS: Cervical dysplasia via Papanicolaou smears and colposcopy.

POSTOPERATIVE DIAGNOSIS: Moderate cervical dysplasia via Papanicolaou smears and colposcopy.

OPERATION: Cold cone biopsy of cervix. Fractional dilatation and curettage of uterus.

ANESTHESIA: General

CLINICAL POINTS AND DIAGNOSIS: The patient is a 48-year-old, white female who has had cervical dysplasia on Papanicolaou smears approximately 4–5 times in the last year. She had colposcopy done 6/12/02 which showed mild atypia. The recent Papanicolaou smears, however, have also shown dysplasia. The patient is currently taking no medications.

PROCEDURE: The patient was taken to the operating room and after preoperative medication she was prepped and draped in the dorsolithotomy position. Pelvic examination revealed the uterus essentially normal size, shape, symmetry, anterior in position and movable, with a mild amount of descensus present. The adnexal regions felt clear. A weighted speculum was placed in the posterior vagina. The anterior lip of the cervix was grasped with a single-tooth tenaculum and the endometrial cavity sounded to a depth of approximately 4½ inches. Cold cone biopsy of the cervix was then performed using a #11 blade. A specimen was sent in 2–3 pieces to Pathology for examination. The endocervix was then dilated with Hegar dilators and the endocervix was curetted and the specimen sent separately to Pathology for examination. The endometrial cavity was separately curetted and the specimen sent separately to Pathology for examination. The uterine cavity seemed essentially normal in size, shape, and symmetry at the time of dilatation and curettage. Bleeding points on the exocervix and endocervix were then cauterized with the Bovie unit and the cervix was bilaterally ligated with #0 chromic catgut.

Blood loss was approximately 100 cc. The tenaculum marks on the exocervix were also cauterized with the Bovie unit. The patient tolerated the procedure well and was sent to the recovery room in good condition.

ICD-10-CM: ______________________________

CPT: ______________________________

11. OPERATIVE REPORT

PREOPERATIVE DIAGNOSIS: Bicompartmental osteoarthritis, left knee. Rule out meniscal tear. Baker's cyst.

POSTOPERATIVE DIAGNOSIS: Bicompartmental osteoarthritis, left knee, with meniscal tear. Baker's cyst.

OPERATION: Arthroscopy, left knee with chondroplasty of bicompartmental osteoarthritis. Arthroscopic partial left posterior horn medial meniscectomy.

INDICATIONS: The patient is a 38-year-old man with bilateral knee arthritis. Both knees are equally symptomatic. The left has been evaluated with an MRI identifying a 4.7 3 1.3 3 1.3 Baker's cyst with osteoarthritic changes and possible meniscal pathology. It was suggested that he undergo the above operative procedure to decrease knee pain, as he continued with pain despite anti-inflammatories, isometric exercises, and knee braces. Risks associated with the procedure including infection, phlebitis, neurovascular or tendon injury, anesthetic complications, and failure of the procedure, among other risks, were discussed and accepted.

PROCEDURE: The patient was brought to the operating room and given a general anesthetic. He was given prophylactic Ancef 1 g push. A 34-inch tourniquet was placed proximally and the extremity was exsanguinated and the tourniquet elevated to 350 mm Hg. An Acufex knee holder was used. The knee was scrubbed, prepped, and draped in routine sterile fashion.

Prints were taken of the intra-articular anatomy, one set of which was provided to the family. The scope was passed through the anterolateral portal to the patellofemoral joint. There was a definite synovial effusion. There was no purulence to it.

The patellofemoral joint showed evidence of osteoarthritis. This was characterized by outer bridge 3, nearly grade 4, changes, particularly on the fovea of the femur. The patella tracked normally, but there was a near full-thickness loss. There was an irregular crevice in the fovea. The scope was then passed into the medial compartment where osteoarthritis was noted as well. This was characterized by outer bridge 3 changes over most of the medial femoral condyle. It was associated with the complex medial meniscal tear, including a radial tear, horizontal cleavage, and structurally mucoid tissue. Anterior cruciate ligament was normal and the lateral compartment was normal. It was felt the procedure of choice would be partial medial meniscectomy and chondroplasty.

Chondroplasty was performed with a 3.5 aggressive razor cut power tool. Any structurally loose articular cartilage on the patellofemoral and medial compartment was addressed. This was not an abrasion chondroplasty procedure. The partial meniscectomy was performed by morselizing the degenerative torn posterior mid-third junction site. It was taken back to a firm red-white level and further smoothed with the use of a power tool. There was a near complete meniscectomy, particularly at the junction of the posterior mid-third. Satisfied with the procedure, the wound was closed.

Closure was done repairing the skin portals with 4-0 Monocryl. It was felt that by addressing the intra-articular pathology, the synovial fluid would be hopefully alleviated, and the Baker's cyst would return back to a normal configuration and not require a separate operative procedure. He was told this would be expected 80 percent plus of the time. A pressure dressing was applied. There was normal capillary refill, so the patient was transferred to the recovery room in stable condition.

ICD -10-CM: ______________________________

CPT: ______________________________

12. OPERATIVE REPORT

PREOPERATIVE DIAGNOSIS: Sebaceous cyst, superior natal cleft.

POSTOPERATIVE DIAGNOSIS: Sebaceous cyst, superior natal cleft.

OPERATION: Excision of sebaceous cyst, superior natal cleft.

ANESTHESIA: IV Versed and 1% lidocaine.

COMPLICATIONS: None.

SPECIMENS: Clustered sebaceous cyst of superior natal cleft.

DRAINS: None.

INDICATIONS: The patient is a 74-year-old white female with a clustered group of approximately 5-6 sebaceous cysts of the superior and left side of her natal cleft causing disability and pain when the patient attempted to sit. The excised diameter measured 4 centimeters.

PROCEDURE: After placement of all appropriate monitoring devices, the patient was in prone position. The natal cleft was prepped and draped in the usual sterile fashion. IV Versed was administered.

One percent lidocaine field block was accomplished in, over, and around the natal cleft area of the sebaceous cysts, which were then excised through a longitudinal elliptical incision measuring approximately 4 3 3 cm. The skin and subcutaneous tissue and cyst was then excised using sharp dissection. Electrocautery for hemostasis until the area was circumferentially excised in its entirety.

The specimen was handed off for pathologic examination. The wound was then closed using interrupted sutures of 3-0 nylon. Sterile dressing was then placed. The patient tolerated the procedure well and was taken to the recovery room in satisfactory condition. All sponge and instrument counts reported correct at the end of the case.

ICD-10-CM: ____________________

CPT: ____________________

Physician Office Clinic

13. PHYSICIAN OFFICE SURGERY

Patient returns to the office for scheduled office surgery to remove an irritated 0.6-cm nevus, face, which is located on the right side of her nose.

Previous history reveals this 59-year-old woman has enlarging nevus of her face, which is chronically irritated by her glasses. It does not bleed. No personal or family history of skin cancer. Past medical history reveals high cholesterol, mitral valve prolapse. She does not smoke. She is unemployed. Current medications include Atenolol, Lipitor, multivitamins, cranberry juice, calcium, and low-dose aspirin. She has no known allergies. Physical examination reveals patient has fair skin. There is a 0.6-cm pale, fleshy nevus on the right side of the nose where the glasses ride.

PREOPERATIVE DIAGNOSIS: Irritated 0.6-cm nevus, face.

POSTOPERATIVE DIAGNOSIS: Irritated 0.6-cm nevus, face.

PROCEDURE: Excision of one lesion, face (right side of nose), 0.6 cm, with simple closure.

The patient's face was prepped and draped in the usual sterile fashion. One percent lidocaine field block was accomplished in, over, and around the right side of the patient's nose. The 0.6-cm nevus was then excised without incident. The specimen was prepared off transportation to the hospital for pathologic examination. The wound was closed using interrupted sutures of 3-0 nylon. Sterile dressing was placed. The patient tolerated the procedure well.

The patient was told to leave the bandage in place and avoid getting water or soap on that area. Patient will return to the office in one week for recheck, at which time bandage will be replaced.

ICD-10-CM: ____________________

CPT: ____________________

14. PHYSICIAN OFFICE VISIT

NOTE:

Patient received level 3 evaluation and management service.

CHIEF COMPLAINT: Patient presents to the office today with diagnosis of hyperparathyroidism.

HISTORY OF PRESENT ILLNESS: This is an established patient who has had multiple episodes of kidney stones. Workup of this problem revealed hypercalcemia with increased PTH level. The patient had a recent sestamibi scan performed, which showed a parathyroid adenoma in the right lower pole area. The patient was sent for evaluation for a possible parathyroidectomy.

PAST MEDICAL HISTORY: No known allergies. Negative history of alcohol or tobacco use. Current medications include Fosamax once per week. No past surgical history. Past illnesses include kidney stones, automobile trauma, and cardiac arrhythmia (occasional PVCs).

PHYSICAL EXAMINATION: Height 5 feet 10 inches. Weight 209 pounds. Blood pressure 130/74. A well-developed, well-nourished male in no apparent distress. Alert and oriented. HEENT: Unremarkable. RESPIRATORY: Respiratory effort normal. CARDIOVASCULAR: S1, S2 within normal limits. No S3, S4. No murmur. Pulses 21 and equal bilaterally. No bruits.

LABORATORY DATA: I reviewed the sestamibi films with the patient in my office and showed him that there is a clearly evident abnormal parathyroid gland in the right lower pole area of the neck.

ASSESMENT: Hyperparathyroidism secondary to a single parathyroid adenoma.

PLAN: We plan to do a neck exploration with parathyroidectomy. Prescription for Darvocet-N 100 q4h prn with 1 refill (for post-op pain) given to patient. Risks, benefits, alternatives, and potential complications have been discussed with patient and/or family and informed consent obtained for procedure/sedation. Patient's medical risk for this procedure at this time is acceptable.

ICD-10-CM: ______________________________

CPT: ______________________________

15. PHYSICIAN OFFICE CARDIOLOGY CONSULTATION

NOTE:

Patient received level 3 evaluation and management service.

A pleasant 69-year-old female presents to the cardiologist's office with past medical history of coronary artery disease requiring coronary artery bypass graft surgery in 1998, hypertension, and who was previously admitted to the hospital with symptoms of chest pain and diaphoresis, suggestive of angina.

PAST MEDICAL HISTORY: Significant for coronary artery disease treated with coronary artery bypass graft surgery in 1998 and hypertension. SOCIAL HISTORY: She is an ex-smoker. FAMILY HISTORY: Positive for coronary artery disease. ALLERGIES: Codeine and Procardia.

REVIEW OF SYSTEMS: Negative for syncope or presyncope. No orthopnea or paroxysmal nocturnal dyspnea. History is negative for cerebrovascular accident. Cardiac history, as mentioned previously. No history suggestive of claudication. No nausea, vomiting, diarrhea, or frequency. All systems were reviewed, and pertinent findings are as noted.

PHYSICAL EXAMINATION: Demonstrates a blood pressure of 147/76 mm Hg, pulse rate of 69, respiratory rate of 16. Afebrile. There is no jugular venous distension. Normal carotid upstrokes. No audible bruits. Examination of the heart revealed S1, S2. No S3. S4 is heard. Lungs are clear. Abdomen is soft. Bowel sounds present. Extremities demonstrate no pedal edema. Three plus distal pulses are noted, which are symmetric and equal in volume bilaterally. Twelve-lead EKG demonstrated sinus rhythm with T-wave inversions in the anterolateral leads. Compared to prior EKGs, these are not new changes.

LABORATORY DATA: Troponin is normal. Potassium is 3.6. BUN is 11, and creatinine is 0.8.

IMPRESSION: Chest pain. Possible angina. Hypertension. Status post-coronary artery bypass graft surgery. Family history of coronary artery disease.

PLAN: Serial troponins are recommended to exclude myocardial infarction. We will add nitroglycerine patch to current regimen at 0.2 mg/hr. Will discharge to home. There is no evidence of myocardial infarction based on cardiac enzymes.

Thank you for allowing us to participate in the care of this patient, and we will follow her with you.

ICD-10-CM: ____________________

CPT: ____________________

16. URGENT CARE CENTER VISIT

NOTE:

Patient received level 2 evaluation and management service.

HISTORY: This 65-year-old man was seen today for his first visit at the urgent care center because of his complaint of pain in the left foot. This has been present since about May. He was in Alabama and went to the clinic there, where he was diagnosed as having congestive heart failure, which caused swelling of his left lower extremity. This may also be compounded by the fact that he previously had a vein removed for a coronary artery bypass. He describes the pain as being primarily in his heel rather than in his ankle or lower leg. He was also previously seen by the ambulatory care clinic at the local hospital, where it was thought that he has vascular insufficiency of the left leg and foot.

PHYSICAL EXAMINATION: Lower extremities are normal, as far as weight-bearing is concerned. Both legs are warm. There are no skin changes. He has 11 pulses in both feet, both dorsalis pedis and posterior tibial.

ASSESSMENT: X-rays were reviewed. He has a calcaneal spur on his left heel, which is likely the cause of his pain. He is being referred to the Podiatry Service and has a scheduled appointment on September 4 for evaluation. As he was leaving the clinic, he complained of pain in his knees, particularly at night, and x-rays of his knees were ordered. He likely has degenerative joint disease in his knees as a cause of his pain.

PLAN: He will be seen in two weeks for evaluation of his knee x-rays.

IMPRESSION: Calcaneal spur, left heel.

ICD-10-CM: ____________________

CPT: ____________________

APPENDIX

G

Mock Certified Coding Specialist (CCS) Certification Examination

PART I: CERTIFIED CODING SPECIALIST (CCS) MOCK EXAM

The CCS certification exam is offered by the American Health Information Management Association (AHIMA). Detailed information on the exam including content, question format, testing sites, and more can be found at the AHIMA site (www.ahima.org) in the *Candidate Handbook,* which can be downloaded from the website. The first portion of the CCS exam consists of 60 questions in multiple-choice format, which is provided in this appendix as a mock exam for coding practice.

NOTE:

The CCS certification exam also requires assignment of ICD-10-CM and ICD-10-PCS codes. Appendix D of the *Workbook to Accompany 3–2-1 Code It!* contains inpatient records, which can be used to practice assigning ICD-10-CM and ICD-10-PCS codes.

Health Information Documentation

1. Which type of signature is a generic term that refers to the various methods by which an electronic document can be authenticated?
   a. Electronic
   b. Fax
   c. Handwritten
   d. Initials
2. Which is an accreditation organization that states that only authorized individuals may make entries in the medical record?
   a. County code
   b. Federal OIG
   c. Health department
   d. Joint Commission
3. Which serves as the business record for a patient encounter, contains documentation of all health care services provided to a patient, and is a repository of information that includes demographic data, as well as documentation to support diagnoses, justify treatment, and record treatment results?
   a. Hospital incident report
   b. Insurance claim
   c. Patient record
   d. Physician credentials
4. This department is responsible for allowing appropriate access to patient information in support of clinical practice, health services, and medical research, while at the same time maintaining confidentiality of patient and provider data.
   a. Billing and revenue
   b. Health information
   c. Hospital administration
   d. Legal and compliance
5. Which of the following statements is accurate?
   a. The medical record is the property of both provider and patient.
   b. The medical record is the property of the provider.
   c. The patient owns the documents in the medical record.
   d. The provider owns the information in the medical record.

6. Health care services rendered must be documented to prove that care was provided and that good medical care is supported by patient record documentation. Thus, inadequate patient record documentation may indicate:
   a. an illegible entry should be rewritten by the author.
   b. enhanced continuity of care.
   c. poor health care delivery.
   d. the need to adopt an authentication policy.
7. SOAP is the abbreviation for:
   a. Subjective, Objective, Analysis, Plan.
   b. Subjective, Objective, Analysis, Problem.
   c. Subjective, Objective, Assessment, Plan.
   d. Subjective, Objective, Assessment, Problem.
8. HIPAA requires Medicare fee-for-service claims to be retained for a period of no less than how many years?
   a. 6
   b. 7
   c. 8
   d. 10
9. Which would be performed as part of quantitative analysis?
   a. Abstracting information from the patient record into a computer software program
   b. Review of the face sheet and patient record to locate a diagnosis missing from the face sheet
   c. Review of the patient record for inconsistent documentation
   d. Review of the record to ensure that each document is present and authenticated
10. Qualitative analysis involves the review of the patient record for:
    a. inaccurate documentation.
    b. patient identification on each report.
    c. presence of authentication by providers.
    d. reports that are missing.

Diagnosis Coding

11. ICD-10-CM codes in square brackets are ______________ of other conditions.
    a. eponyms
    b. manifestations
    c. modifiers
    d. subterms
12. A 45-year-old patient presents with polyuria and polydipsia. The physician documents "suspected diabetes mellitus." Which is reported by the physician's office on the CMS-1500 claim?
    a. Diabetes mellitus
    b. Polydipsia
    c. Polyuria
    d. Polyuria and polydipsia
13. ICD-10-CM uses the format of indenting terms (below the main term) that are related to diagnostic information documented by the provider. When the diagnosis includes an indented term, that term is called a(n) ______________.
    a. eponym
    b. essential modifier
    c. general note
    d. nonessential modifier
14. The condition "Lyme disease" is an example of a(n) ______________.
    a. category
    b. eponym
    c. manifestation
    d. modifier
15. Which is an example of an outpatient setting?
    a. Acute care
    b. Emergency department
    c. Nursing home
    d. Residential care facility
16. When coding a *late effect*, the ______________ is sequenced first.
    a. acute disease
    b. main symptom
    c. original cause
    d. residual condition
17. The first step in coding is to locate the ______________ in the index, which is usually expressed as a noun.
    a. carryover term
    b. main term
    c. more specific subterm
    d. subterm

18. Which term is used to describe the required assignment of two codes to provide information about both a manifestation and the associated underlying disease?
    a. Combination coding
    b. Dual classification
    c. Essential modifiers
    d. Nonessential modifiers

19. The use of a single code to classify two diagnoses, a diagnosis with an associated secondary condition, or a diagnosis with an associated complication is called ______________.
    a. combination coding
    b. dual classification
    c. mandatory multiple coding
    d. qualified coding

20. Which of the following diagnoses are sequenced properly according to the official coding guidelines when the same condition is described as both acute and chronic conditions?
    a. Acute tonsillitis, chronic tonsillitis
    b. Chronic bronchitis, subacute bronchitis
    c. Chronic tonsillitis, acute tonsillitis
    d. Chronic pancreatitis, acute pancreatitis

Procedure Coding

21. The term *HCPCS* often refers to ______________.
    a. CPT level I and HCPCS level II
    b. CPT level I and HCPCS level III
    c. CPT level I and ICD-10-PCS
    d. HCPCS level II

22. Which was created in 1983 to describe common medical services and supplies not classified in CPT?
    a. HCPCS level I
    b. HCPCS level II
    c. ICD-10-CM
    d. ICD-10-PCS

23. Which professional association is responsible for the annual update of the CPT coding system and its two-digit modifiers?
    a. AHA
    b. AMA
    c. CDC
    d. CMS

24. Which includes five-digit CPT codes developed and published by the American Medical Association and classifies codes and descriptive terms used to report medical services and procedures?
    a. HCPCS level I
    b. HCPCS level II
    c. HCPCS level III
    d. ICD-10-CM

25. Which organization is responsible for annual updates to HCPCS level II codes and two-character alphanumeric modifiers?
    a. AHA
    b. AMA
    c. CDC
    d. CMS

26. Which codes contain *emerging technology* temporary codes assigned for data collection purposes, are assigned an alphanumeric identifier with a letter in the last field (e.g., 0001T), and are archived after five years?
    a. Category I
    b. Category II
    c. Category III
    d. HCPCS level II

27. Which type of patient is one who has not received any professional services from the physician, or from another physician of the same specialty who belongs to the same group practice, within the past three years?
    a. Established
    b. New
    c. Nonqualified
    d. Qualified

28. Which type of patient is one who has received professional services from the physician, or from another physician of the same specialty who belongs to the same group practice, within the past three years?
    a. Established
    b. New
    c. Nonqualified
    d. Qualified

29. CPT evaluation and management code selection is based on three key components, which include ______________.
    a. coordination of care, exam, time
    b. counseling, exam, medical decision making
    c. history, exam, counseling
    d. history, exam, medical decision making
30. Evaluation and management (E/M) documentation guidelines explain how E/M codes are assigned according to elements associated with comprehensive multisystem and single-system examinations. The first set of guidelines were created by CMS in ______________.
    a. 1992
    b. 1995
    c. 1997
    d. 1999

Regulatory Guidelines and Reporting Requirements for Acute Care (Inpatient) Service

31. Joint Commission standards specify that a history and physical must be completed within the first ______________ hours of patient admission to the hospital.
    a. 24
    b. 48
    c. 72
    d. 96
32. The condition established after study to be chiefly responsible for occasioning the admission of the patient to the hospital for care is the UHDDS definition of the ______________ diagnosis.
    a. first-listed
    b. primary
    c. principal
    d. principle
33. Inpatient progress notes are documented ______________.
    a. according to state government mandates
    b. as the patient's condition warrants
    c. at least once daily
    d. more than once a day
34. If a physician documents a complete history and physical examination in the office, it is acceptable to place a durable/legible copy on the inpatient record *if it was documented within ______________ days prior to admission.*
    a. 30
    b. 48
    c. 60
    d. 90
35. A discharge summary is required for all ______________.
    a. ambulatory surgery cases
    b. inpatient hospitalizations greater than 48 hours for uncomplicated cases
    c. inpatient hospitalizations regardless of length of stay
    d. normal newborn cases

Regulatory Guidelines and Reporting Requirements for Outpatient Services

36. An operative report should contain ______________.
    a. a description of the procedure
    b. a history of anesthesia reactions
    c. a postanesthesia status
    d. vital signs
37. Operative reports are to be documented within which of the following time frames after surgery?
    a. Immediately
    b. Next day
    c. 24 hours
    d. 48 hours
38. Laboratory tests are ordered by the ______________.
    a. laboratory technician
    b. medical technician
    c. pathologist
    d. responsible physician
39. Which statement would be documented in the physical examination?
    a. Admitted because of abdominal pain
    b. Had cesarean section two years ago
    c. HEAD: occasional migraine headache
    d. Negative bowel sounds, soft and tender

40. The tissue report is the written report of findings on surgical specimens and is documented by the _______________.
    a. attending physician
    b. pathologist
    c. radiologist
    d. surgeon

Data Quality and Management

41. Vital statistics are compiled for events, which include births, deaths, fetal deaths, marriages, and divorces. Which federal agency is responsible for maintaining official vital statistics?
    a. Census Bureau
    b. Department of Health and Human Services
    c. National Center for Health Statistics
    d. National Committee on Vital and Health Statistics

42. Which technique utilizes software to search for patterns and trends and is used to produce data content relationships?
    a. Data analysis
    b. Data collection
    c. Data mining
    d. Data warehousing

43. If more than one person with the same surname and first name has been admitted to the hospital, the master patient index is arranged alphabetically by _______________.
    a. date of birth
    b. discharge date
    c. middle name
    d. patient number

44. The master patient index (MPI) is filed _______________.
    a. alphabetically
    b. chronologically
    c. numerically
    d. reverse numerically

45. This accurate, complete, consistent, up-to-date, and the same no matter where the data are recorded is called _______________.
    a. data integrity
    b. data mining
    c. data quality
    d. data reliability

Information and Communication Technologies

46. Joint Commission standards require inpatient hospital records to be completed within _______________ days after discharge.
    a. 10
    b. 15
    c. 20
    d. 30

47. Which is an impact of the American Recovery Reinvestment Act (ARRA) on health care technology?
    a. Advancement of health information exchange
    b. Elimination of incentives for electronic health record adoption
    c. Establishment of new privacy regulations
    d. Increased HIM workforce opportunities

48. Which will result from utilization of electronic health records?
    a. Greater health care costs
    b. Improved health care quality
    c. Increased lengths of stay
    d. Proliferation of medical errors

49. The electronic or paper-based medical record that is maintained and updated by an individual for personal use is called a _______________.
    a. patient health record
    b. patient medical record
    c. personal health record
    d. personal medical record

50. Electronic health record standards are created by the _______________ under the direction of the U.S. Department of Health and Human Services.
    a. AHA
    b. AMA
    c. CMS
    d. HL7

Privacy, Confidentiality, Legal, and Ethical Issues

51. The physiological complexity that comprises the extent and interactions of a patient's disease as presented to medical personnel is called _______________.
    a. case mix index
    b. electronic data interchange
    c. overpayment recovery
    d. severity of illness
52. Interdisciplinary guidelines developed by hospitals to facilitate management and delivery of quality clinical care in a time of constrained resources are called _______________, and they allow for the planning of provision of clinical services that have expected time frames and resources targeted to specific diagnoses and procedures.
    a. case mix adjustments
    b. case mix indexes
    c. chargemasters
    d. critical pathways
53. Which unique identifier is used to file electronic claims with public and private insurance programs?
    a. Federal tax identification number (EIN)
    b. National health plan identifier (PlanID)
    c. National provider identifier (NPI)
    d. Social Security number (SSN)
54. Which methodology is utilized to reimburse physician services covered by Medicare Part B?
    a. Ambulatory surgical center (ASC)
    b. Inpatient Prospective Payment Services (IPPS)
    c. Outpatient Prospective Payment Services (OPPS)
    d. Resource based relative value scale (RBRVS)
55. Which is an inpatient prospective payment system (IPPS) that reimburses short-term hospitals predetermined rates for Medicare inpatient services?
    a. Ambulatory payment classifications (APCs)
    b. Diagnosis-related groups (DRGs)
    c. Home health resource groups (HHRGs)
    d. Resource utilization groups (RUGs)

Compliance

56. An attorney calls the physician's office and requests that a copy of his client's patient record be faxed immediately to the attorney's office. The insurance specialist should _______________.
    a. call the HIPAA hotline number to report a breach of confidentiality
    b. explain to the attorney that the office does not fax or copy patient records
    c. instruct the attorney to obtain the patient's signed authorization
    d. retrieve the patient's medical record and fax it to the attorney
57. A patient's spouse comes to the office and requests diagnostic and treatment information about his wife. The spouse is the primary policyholder on which his wife is named on the policy as a dependent. The insurance specialist should _______________.
    a. allow the patient's spouse to review the actual record in the office, but not release a copy
    b. inform the patient's spouse that he must request the information from his insurance company
    c. obtain a signed patient authorization from the wife before releasing patient information
    d. release a copy of the information to the patient's spouse, because he is the primary policyholder
58. Which is a civil case document that contains a list of questions that must be answered in writing?
    a. Deposition
    b. Interrogatory
    c. Precedent
    d. Regulation
59. Which Department of Health and Human Services agency is responsible for investigating a Medicare provider who is suspected of committing fraud?
    a. CDC
    b. CMS
    c. OIG
    d. SSA
60. Assigning passwords to users who are authorized to access patient records is a form of _______________.
    a. confidentiality
    b. privacy
    c. privilege
    d. security